POWER & CHOICE

POWER & CHOICE

AN INTRODUCTION TO POLITICAL SCIENCE

EIGHTH EDITION

W. Phillips Shively

University of Minnesota

Boston   Burr Ridge, IL   Dubuque, IA   Madison, WI   New York
San Francisco   St. Louis   Bangkok   Bogotá   Caracas   Kuala Lumpur
Lisbon   London   Madrid   Mexico City   Milan   Montreal   New Delhi
Santiago   Seoul   Singapore   Sydney   Taipei   Toronto

McGraw-Hill Higher Education

*A Division of The **McGraw-Hill** Companies*

POWER & CHOICE: AN INTRODUCTION TO POLITICAL SCIENCE
EIGHTH EDITION

2 3 4 5 6 7 8 9 0 DOC/DOC 0 9 8 7 6 5 4 3 2

ISBN   0–07–247666–4

Vice president and editor-in-chief: *Thalia Dorwick*
Publisher: *Lyn Uhl*
Sponsoring editor: *Monica Eckman*
Editorial coordinator: *Angela W. Kao*
Marketing manager: *Janise A. Fry*
Project manager: *Mary Lee Harms*
Production supervisor: *Enboge Chong*
Cover/interior designer: *Matthew Baldwin*
Lead photo research coordinator: *Carrie K. Burger*
Senior supplement producer: *David A. Welsh*
Media technology producer: *Lance Gerhart*
Compositor: *Carlisle Communications, Ltd.*
Typeface: *10/12 Times Roman*
Printer: *R. R. Donnelley & Sons Company/Crawfordsville, IN*

Library of Congress Cataloging-in-Publication Data

Shively, W. Phillips, 1942–
    Power & choice: an introduction to political science / W. Phillips Shively.—8th ed.
    p. cm.
    Includes bibliographical references and index.
    ISBN 0–07–247666–4 (acid-free paper)
        1. Political science. I. Title: Power and choice. II. Title.

JA66 .S47 2003
320–dc21

                                        2002016628
                                        CIP

www.mhhe.com

ABOUT THE AUTHOR

W. PHILLIPS SHIVELY is Professor of Political Science at the University of Minnesota, where he moved in 1971 after teaching at the University of Oregon and Yale University. He has also served as Visiting Professor at the University of Oslo in Norway. His research, which has appeared in numerous articles, deals with the comparative study of elections, and he has written *The Craft of Political Research,* an introduction to research techniques. He has also had practical political experience as a lobbyist in Minnesota. His true love is bird-watching.

To Ruth Phillips Shively
and
Arthur W. Shively

CONTENTS

PREFACE

This book provides a general, comparative introduction to the major concepts and themes of political science. For a number of years, I had taught a course that attempted to accomplish this aim, and that experience had shown me how badly we need a text that is conceptually alive and that engages students with concrete examples of analysis without losing them in a clutter of definitional minutiae. That is what I aimed for when I first wrote this book, and I've been most pleased at the response it has elicited.

The title of the book, *Power and Choice,* indicates a subsidiary theme that recurs at intervals. Politics may be seen as (1) the use of power or (2) the production of a public choice. Often one or the other is heavily emphasized in approaching the subject. Marxism emphasizes politics as the use of power, while pluralism and much formal modeling work emphasize the emergence of public choices. For our present purpose, I have defined politics as the use of power to make common decisions for a group of people, a definition that obviously demands that one hold both perspectives simultaneously. At various stages of my presentation, I note instances in which an emphasis on just one of the two halves of the definition may yield a distorted interpretation.

Behind this subsidiary theme lies a broader theme that remains largely implicit—that political analysis is best conducted eclectically, rather than being straitjacketed into a single approach. My own research is squarely in the "behavioral" realm, for instance, but I found as I was working on this book that necessities of exposition and understanding pulled me toward a greater emphasis on policy and institutions than I had originally intended. Similarly, the state as an organizer of politics thrust itself more to the fore than I had anticipated. Distinctions that provide useful boundaries for research proved unhelpful in my efforts to build an understanding of politics among students; I think this is a healthy sign.

Material in the book is presented topically rather than on a country-by-country basis; but in order to add the sort of detailed contextual grounding that students gain from a country presentation, I have included within each substantive chapter a couple of extended examples from countries that particularly display the conceptual material of that chapter. For instance, Chapter 3, which deals with the state, concludes with detailed sections on the European Union and on the establishment and maintenance of the Nigerian state. Similarly, Chapter 16 "Bureaucracy and the Public Sector," gives detailed treatment to France, Saudi Arabia, and Brazil.

NEW TO THE EIGHTH EDITION

Over the couple of decades since I first wrote this book, the world has proved to be a strange and wonderful place—even more than I realized at that time. The book has seen the joy and light of the young people who pulled down the Berlin Wall in 1989 and the darkness of the suicide attackers who destroyed the World Trade Center in 2001. As it has evolved across several editions during this time, very little that it started out with has remained unchanged. Its mood has also varied from time to time, but one thing that has been constant is a faith in people's capacity to shape their futures through politics.

In this eighth edition there is, of course, a great deal of general updating. When a book deals with all states of the world, a lot changes over even a couple of years. As regards more substantive change, while no one chapter has gotten a full re-make, I have tried to improve my presentation or have added substance in a number of places:

- I have expanded my treatment of nationalism and the state in several small ways.
- The chapter on ideology gives more respect to inchoate American ideologies.
- I have introduced the distinction between procedural and substantive justice and eliminated the rather idiosyncratic distinction between fairness and justice that I used in previous editions.
- I have expanded my consideration of the role of political culture in theories of politics and have noted the differences in political culture in western and eastern Germany as evidence that governments can, to some extent, shape culture.
- I have added a new box on presidential leadership.
- I have added treatment of the political strategy of courts in framing decisions that expand the range of their powers, using the European Court of Justice as the example.
- I have introduced the concept of neoliberalism and explore its relationship to globalization.
- And I have brought in the development of new international criminal law that transcends states, as exemplified in the Pinochet and Milosevic cases.

In addition to my changes in the book, with each copy of the text, McGraw-Hill provides access to PowerWeb for Political Science, a reservoir of course-specific articles and current events as well as a semester of access to the Northern Lights Research Engine. All of the articles and web links on PowerWeb have been recommended by a panel of political science reviewers, which means that it only includes clear and concise learning tools that are continuously updated. PowerWeb also includes quizzes, interactive exercises, study tips, research tips, a career guide and more. PowerWeb includes resources for instructors as well. Contact your McGraw-Hill representative for password access to these materials. In addition to PowerWeb, McGraw-Hill provides a book specific Online Learning Center at *www.mhhe.com/shively*. Interactive quizzing, research links and news sources are available for students. Instructors can access the online instructor's manual along with a template and software to generate their own course related webpages. Again, instructor access to passwords can be obtained through your McGraw-Hill representative.

I have been very pleased by the response to this book. It is a wonderful experience to run into people who have used it and feel that it has helped them. I am grateful to the following reviewers, who will notice many of their suggestions incorporated:

Dr. Jessica Adolino, James Madison University, VA
Dr. Maryjane Osa, University of South Carolina at Columbia, SC
Dr. William Kelly, Auburn University, AL
Dr. A. P. Simonds, University of Massachusetts, MA
Dr. Manwoo Lee, Millersville University, PN
Dr. Jose Garcia, New Mexico State University, NM
Dr. James Wallihan, Indiana University–Purdue University at Indianapolis, IN

W. Phillips Shively

PART ONE

INTRODUCTION

1

POLITICS:
SETTING THE STAGE

Everyone knows something about politics, and many people know a great deal about it. It is an interesting, amusing, and moving spectacle that ranks not too far behind professional sports in the eyes of many. Political scientists, however, *study* politics and *analyze* it. This involves doing pretty much the same sorts of things that other people do who follow politics: we read the newspapers and listen to press conferences, take part in political campaigns, and so on. However, we also do some things differently. We usually try to see both sides of any question and to keep our emotions in low key, because emotions can cloud judgment. We borrow deliberately from other disciplines—such as economics, history, sociology, psychology, and philosophy—to help us understand what is going on politically. Above all, as you will see later in this chapter, we try to be precise about the meanings of the words we use. Many words having to do with politics—such as *liberal, represent,* and even *politics*—are quite complex, but most people use them unthinkingly. Political scientists are careful to analyze the varied meanings of such words and to use them precisely, partly because it is important to know exactly what we mean by the words we use and partly because careful examination of a richly complex word may teach us a lot about the things it describes.

What do political scientists study? Over the years, we have seen work in which political scientists:

- Measured just how much it actually costs a country to lose a war
- Devised a new system of voting in primaries that might have led to a different set of candidates for most presidential elections
- Analyzed and explained the various styles that members of the U.S. Congress adopt in dealing with their constituents
- Studied the spread of welfare reforms across the states
- Showed that the roots of successful government may go back to social institutions several centuries ago

- Showed why most nations will ignore warnings about surprise military action by hostile nations
- Studied why democracies almost never wage war on other democracies

These are the sorts of things political scientists do. In this book you will be introduced to the broad principles of what we have learned about politics, especially about the politics of democracies like the United States. I hope the study will sharpen and enrich the more general understanding of politics that you already have.

This first chapter, in particular, involves the precise definition of several words with which you are already somewhat familiar. We must examine these definitions because you should start your study with some basic terms in place. You may also find it intriguing to see complexity in words, such as *politics,* that have probably not struck you before as being particularly complicated.

POLITICS

What is politics? What is it that makes an act political? Consider the following questions, all of which involve political circumstances. What do these have in common?

- How was Hitler able to take power through a series of supposedly democratic elections?
- Why does the U.S. Congress so often disagree with the president in framing energy policies?
- Why should workers sort letters the way their boss directs if they know a more efficient way?
- Why were southern blacks denied the vote and placed in segregated schools throughout the 1950s while at the same time their housing was not as segregated as that in the North?
- Should communists be barred from teaching in the schools?
- Should fascists be barred from teaching in the schools?
- Why does the United States have only two major political parties when most democracies have more?
- Should state and local governments have the right to force landholders to sell them land that is needed for public purposes?
- Was Harry Truman right to bomb Hiroshima and Nagasaki?
- Why do people so often feel guilty about not doing what their parents want them to do?

These questions deal with politics. The questions about bosses and parents may not have looked to you as if they belonged in this group, but their connection with politics should become clearer by the end of this chapter.

What is it that these questions have in common? There are two main things, and both have often been used as the defining characteristics of politics. First, all the questions involve the *making of a common decision for a group of people,* that is, a uniform decision applying in the same way to all members of the group. Second, all involve *the use of power* by one person or a group of people to affect the behavior of another person or group of people. Let us look at both of these in more detail.

POLITICS AS THE MAKING OF COMMON DECISIONS

Any group of people must often make decisions that will apply to all of them in common, as a group. A family must decide where to live, what sorts of rules to set for children, how to balance a budget, and so on. A class in a college or university (including the instructor as part of the "class") must decide what reading material to require, how students are to be graded by the instructor, how bright the light should be in the classrooms. A country must decide where to locate parks, what allies to seek out in war, how to raise revenue by taxing its citizens, how to care for the helpless, and many other things. Each of these requires the setting of common policy for the group, a single decision that affects all members of the group.

Not all human actions, of course, involve the making of a common policy for a group. When one brother teases another, he is not making a family policy, nor is a family member who decides to write the great American novel. A student who decides to read extra material on one section of the course (or, perhaps, to skip a bit of the reading) is not making a policy of the class. A person's decision to build a new house is not part of any common national policy, although the country may have policies—on interest rates, the regulation of building, land use, zoning, and so on—that affect this person's decision. Ford Motor Company's decisions on new-car styling are not part of a common national policy.

Those actions that contribute to the making of a common policy for a group of people constitute politics, and questions about those policies and the making of those policies are political questions. The political/nonpolitical distinction is not always easy to draw. The example of the Ford Motor Company, above, is tricky because Ford is so large that its decisions verge on being common policy for the whole United States, even though the company has no formal role in the nation's government. In other words, one might argue that because the U.S. government tolerates the concentration of our automobile industry among three giant corporations and because (as a result of this) the decisions of any one of the three bulk so large in American life, those decisions have a quasi-public character and are "sort of" political. In 1980, the quasi-public nature of large corporations was underlined when the government found that it had to become intimately involved in Chrysler Corporation's financing to prevent Chrysler from going out of business. Chrysler was so large that the economic health of the country was unavoidably bound to its economic decisions; therefore, the government decided it had no choice but to support Chrysler's loans. In this sense, decisions made by the management of Chrysler were to a degree binding on the country as a whole and became, to some extent, U.S. political decisions.

Another tricky aspect of the political/nonpolitical distinction is that it is partly a matter of perspective. Ford's design decisions are not (except via Ford's quasi-public nature) political decisions for the *United States*; but they *are* political decisions for Ford's stockholders, managers, and workers, because they set a common policy for the company. A family's decision to build a house is not a political decision for the *country,* but it is a political decision for the *family* as a group inasmuch as it involves a common policy for the family. "Company politics" is involved in Ford's decision, and "family politics" is involved in the family's decision. Neither, however, is a national political decision. Society consists of groups within groups within groups. Ford Motor Company is a group within the United States, and a family may be a group within the larger group of those dependent on Ford. Politics exists within any of these groups whenever a decision that will apply to all the members of the group is made. Depending on which group you are thinking of, a given decision—the decision of the Clauski family to build a house—may be treated as either political or nonpolitical. The Clauski decision is political for the family as a group but not political for the nation.

POLITICS AS THE EXERCISE OF POWER

A second characteristic of politics, one that runs through the questions at the start of this chapter, is that politics always involves the exercise of *power* by one person or persons over another person or persons. Power is the ability of one person to cause another to do what the first wishes, *by whatever means.* Politics always involves this: one person causing others to do what that person wants either by forcing or convincing them to do so. Looking back at the questions, we note that Hitler rose to high office by convincing many Germans to vote for him; the U.S. Congress disagrees with the president so often about energy policy because the president does not have much power either to force or to convince Congress to go along with his wishes in that area; and so on. In such ways, each of these questions involves the power of one person or persons over another or others.

The two defining characteristics of politics, then, are that (1) politics always involves the making of common decisions for groups of people *and* (2) those decisions are made by some members of the group exercising power over other members of the group. Power can consist of a wide variety of tools that help one person affect the actions of another. Power may be stark, as when a police officer stops a demonstrator from marching up the street; or it may be subtle, as when a group of poor people, by their very misery, elicit positive governmental action on their behalf.

Power may be exercised as *coercion* when we force a person to do something he or she did not want to do, as *persuasion* when we convince someone that that is what she or he really wishes to do, or as the *construction of incentives* when we make the alternative so unattractive that only one reasonable option remains. The ability to exercise any of these forms of power may be based on all sorts of things—money, affection, physical strength, legal status (the power of a police officer to direct traffic, for instance), the possession of important information, a winning smile, strong allies, determination, desperation (which helped North Vietnam to defeat the United States in the 1970s), and many more. Any of these can help some people get other people to act as they wish.

It is not necessary to learn the specific bases of power listed. They are meant to provide a sense of the variety and complexity of power, not as an exhaustive list of its important sources. The point is that all politics involves the use of power, and such power may take varied forms.

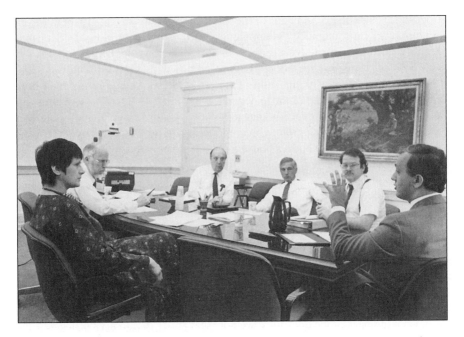

A business planning session. These people are conducting politics—using power to reach collective decisions.

(Beringer/Dratch/The Image Works)

IMPLICIT AND MANIFEST POWER

Power need not consist of any observable link at all between the people or groups involved. Scholars distinguish between *manifest* power and *implicit* power. Manifest power is based on an observable action by A that leads B to do what A wants. A police officer's signal that causes a driver to stop and wait is an example of manifest power. In the case of implicit power, B does what A desires not because of anything A says or does but because (1) B senses that A wants something done and (2) for any of a variety of reasons B wishes to do what A wants done. Many examples of implicit power are found in families, whose members are so attuned to one another that there is often no observable communication between members of the family who yet manage to "read" and comply with one another's wishes. A father may toss the car keys to his daughter on Saturday morning completely unprompted except by his knowledge of her habits and his desire to comply with her wishes. As she drives, the daughter may obey the 55-miles-per-hour speed limit because she knows that her parents feel strongly about it. In neither case is there any overt signal from one family member to the other.

A famous example of implicit power in a broader sphere of politics comes from the reign of King Henry II of England. The king had been involved in a series of disputes with Thomas à Becket, the Archbishop of Canterbury. Henry exclaimed one day, "Will no one rid me of this man?" Four of his knights overheard what the king said and proceeded to murder Becket. Historians still dispute whether the king really wished to have Becket killed.

What is most important and interesting about implicit power is that an observer would have a hard time deciding whether or not such power has been exercised in any particular instance. The source of implicit power may lie far away from its exercise. To understand why the daughter drives 55 miles per hour, for instance, we might have to look back to her early childhood, to observe the hugs and admonitions she received years before. Power can be analyzed easily in the case of one country telling another, "Cede the province Anemone to us or we'll invade you." It cannot be so easily analyzed if the resources on which it is based are varied and complex, as in the power of a defeated Germany to draw economic aid from the United States after World War II; or if it is in whole or in part implicit, as in the king's muttered remark in the presence of his soldiers.

An Example of the Difficulty of Analyzing Power

Both because power is important to politics and because it is difficult to measure precisely how and when power is exercised, there are recurrent disputes within political science about how much power various groups have. A famous dispute of the 1950s and 1960s centered on American cities, about which the following question was asked: "Is there a small group of people [the "downtown people," the political bosses, or what have you] who run things in American cities?" This might seem to be a simple question, but it was difficult for political scientists to answer, and we still do not have a clear answer to it. In a broader form, the dispute has continued to this day.

The dispute started when, in a study of Atlanta, Georgia, Floyd Hunter attempted to answer the question by asking journalists, officials, business leaders, and others who the most important people in the city were.[1] When his varied sources named roughly the same set of leaders, he concluded that Atlanta was run by a small group of "insiders."

In response, however, Robert Dahl observed that Hunter's respondents might all be mistaken, but in the same way; they might *think* that the downtown corporate elite ran Atlanta because that idea was part of the conventional wisdom about the city, but they might be wrong. That the downtown people had a reputation for power did not prove to Dahl's satisfaction that they really *had* power; rather, he said, we must actually see power being used. As a response to the earlier Atlanta study, he performed a new study of his own based on New Haven, Connecticut.[2] He chose a set of major issues that faced the community—education, urban renewal, and so on—and recorded who participated in making decisions on each type of issue. He was restricting himself to observable power; therefore, he had to ignore the possibility of implicit power. Other than that, his procedure was straightforward. He found that quite different groups of people were active on the different issues. Parents and "society people" were especially involved in education, for example, while downtown people were especially involved in urban renewal. He concluded that New Haven was not run by a single group of insiders but

---

[1]Floyd Hunter, *Community Power Structure* (Chapel Hill: University of North Carolina Press, 1953). Note that the politics of Atlanta today is very different from that which Hunter described in 1953. The most obvious difference is that Atlanta has now had a black mayor for a number of years. The power structure Hunter described was all white.

[2]Robert Dahl, *Who Governs?* (New Haven: Yale University Press, 1961).

that all sorts of groups were involved, moving in and out of participation depending on what issue was up for decision.

Still a third position was then staked out in the dispute. Two scholars criticizing Dahl's study of New Haven noted that it is not enough just to see who was active in various kinds of decisions but that we must also investigate why particular issues get raised in the first place.[3] Perhaps the most important decision is the one that governs which issues will be brought before the public. For instance, during the period Dahl studied, New Haven did not consider any policies for taking over utilities and running them publicly, for breaking up the residential racial segregation of the city, or for cutting property taxes sharply. At this level, decisions may or may not be controlled by a small "power elite"; we simply cannot tell from a study such as Dahl's.

Peter Digeser has added what he calls a "third face of power," drawing on the work of Steven Lukes and (implicitly) Antonio Gramsci. Taking Bachrach and Baratz beyond the notion of an elite controlling the agenda of discussion about different groups' needs and wants, he points out that the process they describe might consist of an elite controlling ideas and public opinion such that it does not even occur to some groups to want the things they should want: "Lukes contended that power could be exerted even if B consciously wants to do what A desires. Lukes claimed that if B acts contrary to her objective, real interests then power is being exercised."[4] In other words, the elite might exercise power not just by preventing discussion of proposals they do not want to see on the table, but by influencing what people want so that inconvenient proposals never occur to them in the first place. The test for Digeser (based on Lukes) is not whether people have proposals that never reach the table, but whether the things people want are contrary to their real interests. Such a disjunction between people's wants and their real interests, for Digeser, is the footprint of elite power. That is to say, the way the elite maintains its power is to maintain control over communications and ideas (Gramsci calls this control "hegemony"), such that people do not want (do not realize they need) things that threaten the elite. Of course, this becomes remarkably difficult to analyze, because it requires us to identify what people really need as distinct from what they merely think they need. Academics, who have very distinctive values themselves, are not always in a good position to judge other people's "true" needs.

Notice how complex the question of power in American cities has become. Hunter gave us a very straightforward assessment of Atlanta. Dahl complicated the issue by pointing out that in New Haven different types of people had dominant power with respect to different kinds of issues. Bachrach and Baratz reminded us that we must also consider who controls which issues will even come up for discussion. And Lukes added

[3]Peter Bachrach and Morton S. Baratz, "The Two Faces of Power," *American Political Science Review* 56 (1962): 947–53.

[4]Peter Digeser "The Fourth Face of Power," *Journal of Politics* 54 (November 1992): 980. Digeser goes on to describe still another approach to power (this is his "fourth face")—that of Michel Foucault, who develops a rich but elusive concept in which our definition of ourselves and of our very interests results from others' exercise of power over us. That is, the elite can maintain hegemony not only over what people want but also over how they define themselves. At this point, analysis becomes difficult—some would say it collapses—because nothing is anchored. References to Lukes and Gramsci are: Steven Lukes, *Power: A Radical View* (London: Macmillan, 1974); Antonio Gramsci, *Letters from Prison* (New York: Columbia University Press, 1994).

the consideration that this control might operate at an unconscious level, in elite control of how people form their very desires. In the end, it is difficult to say anything general and conclusive about the concentration of power in our cities because it is difficult to study what might have been—what issues might have entered public discussion but did not. This series of studies clearly illustrates the inherent complexity of power.

Although these studies certainly show that there are few blanket truths about power, one should not therefore conclude that power is impossible to study. Rather, an understanding of the complexity of power and the difficulty of measuring it can lead us to detailed examinations of very specific instances of power. In response to the Bachrach and Baratz article, for instance, several interesting studies appeared on the setting of agendas in American politics. These were a direct result of the argument that the most important power is that which decides what issues will be up for debate.

POLITICS AND POWER

Despite the complexity and elusiveness of power, we *can* say that all politics is based on some form of power and that its sources may be highly varied. For most questions about politics, however, it is not necessary to specify in detail exactly what sort of power is involved. For all political analysis, it is helpful to bear in mind that you are dealing with power of one sort or another; but that realization may often serve rather as a background or setting for your analysis. For instance, most of the questions posed at the opening of this chapter can be addressed without conducting precise analyses of the power relationships that form contexts for the questions.

Before we leave our consideration of power in politics, we might draw attention to the surprising universality of the use of power to determine common decisions for groups of people. People around the world vary remarkably little in physical strength and intelligence; they are also more or less equal in their basic talents. Yet millions of them will fear and obey another person whose intrinsic capacities are little superior to theirs.

It is understandable that this should be so within families because of the weakness and inexperience of children. The adult members of a family are stronger than the children, and it is perhaps natural that they should be able to control them. However, it is astounding that large numbers of adults will grant this sort of control over their own actions to a military officer, a member of Congress, a dictator, or a religious leader. How is it that political power is so universal and often so concentrated in small numbers of people?[5]

Simply posing the question in this way demonstrates once again that the bases of power must be varied and complex. Physical compulsion alone would not be sufficient to ensure the obedience that people all over the world give to their political leaders.

POWER AND CHOICE

Politics, then, consists of the making of common decisions for a group through the use of power. Though the concept involves some complexity, it will usually be clear to everyone concerned whether a given action is or is not political in this sense. From the

[5]R. M. MacIver, *The Web of Government* (New York: Macmillan, 1967), chap. 1.

Congratulations, keep moving, please. Congratulations, keep moving please.
Congratulations . . ."

two parts of our definition there stem two very basic ways of looking at the making of such common policies, and people often emphasize one or the other of these in evaluating any particular political action. In so doing, they may fail to consider how their viewpoint colors their conclusions. The two alternative viewpoints are as follows:

1.   Political action may be interpreted as a way to work out rationally the best common solution to a common problem—or at least a way to work out a reasonable common solution. That is, politics consists of *public choice*. (Even though this perspective emphasizes the cooperative aspect of decisions, power will still be involved in the making of choices; if nothing else, the power to persuade will be involved.)

2.   Political action may be interpreted as a way to accomplish the domination of some people by other people. That is, politics consists simply of the use of *power.* Here power is often thought of as power through coercion.

   In other words, two people who observe the same political action from these opposing viewpoints might have very different ideas of what is going on. For instance, a person operating from the "public choice" viewpoint might look at the large number of people who fail to vote in American presidential elections and conclude that this is a reasonably healthy situation, because if such a large number of people have chosen not to bother voting, they must be tolerably satisfied with things as they are. Someone else, operating from the "power" viewpoint, might look at that same large number of non-voters and conclude that American elections are a sham, that they are meant to give the appearance of popular choice without providing the voter with significantly different options (i.e., many voters do not bother to vote because their choices have been restricted).

Most often, *both* viewpoints are partly accurate. Politics generally involves considering at least the broad needs of the group for whom policy is being made: Pure tyranny is rare and is difficult to maintain. At the same time, the making of common policy generally means that one part of a group will be dominating another part to at least some extent. In the previous presidential voting example, both characterizations probably have some truth to them.

It is good to bear these two perspectives in mind, because we may then be able to avoid misjudging a particular political situation as being all one or the other. For example, a college or university class is a group for which common policies must be made and in which a single person (the instructor) is formally charged with responsibility. Thus, the group's politics will largely consist of domination of the students by the instructor. However, it is not solely or simply a system of domination because there are a number of informal mechanisms by which students participate in decision making, and these should not be overlooked. In short, the politics of a classroom also includes aspects of a rational working out of solutions to common problems. Such questions as the timing of tests, whether or not doors should be closed or the lights on, or the nature of special projects and examinations are often decided by the instructor in consultation with the students. In less direct ways, students—by their expressions of interest—often influence the content of a class. Thus, although the politics of a classroom consists primarily of domination, there is also some element of a common search for solutions to common problems. This might be overlooked if one were not alert to the two sides of politics.

It is especially important to bear in mind these two points of view when we consider political actions about which we have strong feelings and about which we may expect to be prejudiced. Until the opening up of democratic elections in the Soviet Union, for instance, Americans tended to dismiss elections in communist countries as simple fraud, since voters were given a single candidate to vote for, with no electoral competition for their votes. However, as you will see in Chapter 11, there was evident in the elections of most such countries a surprising element of broad participation in a search for common solutions. For instance, even during the period of noncompetitive elections, when only a single candidate appeared on the ballot, 28 percent of Soviet citizens reported that they had at one time or another attempted to persuade others to vote as they did; 19 percent had even contacted a state or national government official about some problem.[6] "The weeks preceding the election see the formation of countless study circles, discussion groups, campaign meetings, door-to-door canvassing, rallies, demonstrations and speeches."[7] There

---

[6]Richard D. Little, "Mass Political Participation in the U.S. and the U.S.S.R.," *Comparative Political Studies* 8 (January 1976), p. 439.
[7]Ibid.

appears to have been more to the Soviet Union's uncontested elections than we had commonly been able to see. Bearing in mind that it is rare, if not impossible, for a political choice to consist solely of the use of power can help us to remain alert to such possibilities even when we know we are strongly prejudiced about a subject.

To sum up this section of the chapter: Politics consists of the making of a common decision for a group of people through the use of power. Any act of politics may be viewed from either of two perspectives, either as a cooperative search for an answer to common problems or as an act by which some members of a group impose their will on other members of the group. It is important to remember that generally both viewpoints are valid. It is especially important to remember this when we might be prejudiced about the subject at hand, because keeping both viewpoints in mind can help us to avoid thinking about the subject in narrow, prejudiced ways. Power and choice, the two major themes by which we organize our views of politics, have provided the title of this book. They will recur in succeeding chapters as we examine various aspects of politics.

POLITICS OF THE STATE

One thing that has probably seemed odd to you in this chapter, right from the set of questions on page 3, is that things we do not always think of as "politics" have been described under this heading. There is some variation in common usage of the word. Family, workplace, church, and so on are not often thought of as political places, though they are *sometimes* thought of in that way. When we refer to "office politics," "campus politics," and "church politics," we mean activities that fit under the definition of politics presented in this chapter: the use of power to make common decisions for groups or people. When Kate Millett wrote a book about the relations between men and women, she titled it *Sexual Politics* explicitly to underscore her claim that men use various sorts of power to dominate the making of common decisions involving women:

> . . . a disinterested examination of our system of sexual relationships must point out that the situation between the sexes now, and throughout history, is a case of that phenomenon Max Weber defined as herrschaft, a relationship of dominance and subordinance. What goes largely unexamined, often even unacknowledged (yet is institutionalized nonetheless) in our social order, is the birthright priority whereby males rule females. . . . The fact is evident at once if one recalls that the military, industry, technology, universities, science, political office, and finance—in short, every avenue of power within the society, including the coercive force of the police, is entirely in male hands. As the essence of politics is power, such realization cannot fail to carry impact.[8]

This broad use of the word *politics* fits the general definition presented in this chapter, but a much more common use of the word is slightly narrower. If we say, "Frank went into politics," or "I'm fascinated by politics," we are not thinking of the family or corporation or church. In this sense of the word we are referring only to the kind of politics that has to do with government of the state.

---

[8]Kate Millett, *Sexual Politics* (Garden City, N.Y.: Doubleday, 1970), pp. 24, 25. Millett approaches politics almost exclusively from the standpoint of power, not choice.

State has a special meaning in political science. It is not the same thing as the states of the United States; instead, it is what we commonly call a country. The United States is a state in this sense, as are France, Russia, Algeria, Mexico, and so on.

In Chapter 3, we will look at the state in more detail, but for now it is enough to note that the state is a particular kind of social group. Over the last few centuries, people have focused increasingly on the state of which they are citizens, and the state has determined more of what goes on in their lives. Several centuries ago, most people were almost unaware of the state in which they lived; they noticed it only if the king's soldiers marched through their fields. At that time, many large geographic areas could hardly be said to have been organized as states at all. Gradually states have become more thoroughly organized and have demanded more from us. First, states became the prime focus of peace and war, maintaining peace within their borders and waging war with other states. Then, states became the organizers of commerce and industry within their borders, regulating prices and the quality of products, constructing roads and canals, and so on. Only for the last several decades has the state generally been expected by its citizens to maintain stability in the economy, guarantee employment, and keep the value of currency stable. A century or so ago, events in the economy were treated as "acts of God," and the state was not involved in them, but today the state is generally held responsible for economic conditions. The responsibilities of the state continue to grow. In the future might the weather, now treated as an "act of God," become part of the responsibility of the state?

For better or worse, the state has become critically important to us, and its politics has taken on great importance. When we say "politics," we usually mean "politics of the state." Political science shares this general preoccupation with politics of the state. Though we will occasionally look at other sorts of politics in this book, most of our attention will be directed to the politics of the state. Remember the more general meaning of *politics,* however, and remember that in dealing with the state we will be looking at politics only in one of its forms, albeit its most important and most complex form.

POLITICAL SCIENCE

Political science is the academic field that takes as its sole and general task the analysis of politics, especially the politics of the state. There has been continuing debate over how "scientific" political science should be. Some political scientists think that politics is so complex and involves such basic personal values that we should not try to pin it down to exact regularities. Rather, we should interpret each political event and idea more or less in and of itself, in a personal, subjective way. Such political scientists would model themselves upon historians, who interpret a particular sequence of events more or less in and of itself, seeking to retain the richness of its detail while making a general patterned interpretation of what process unfolded through the events.

Other political scientists think that their discipline should be more scientific than this, seeking out the basic essence of regularities across a whole set of events, even though this means sacrificing some of the rich detail with which each single event is laden. They think that the only way we will be able to explain and predict what happens in politics is to emphasize the underlying processes that a number of disparate events may have in common.

These political scientists would model themselves on other social scientists such as economists, who analyze events simply as instances of general processes, which they treat in the abstract. Economists, for instance, prefer to deal abstractly with supply-and-demand theories rather than analyze specifically what happens in a given used car lot.

The first type of political scientists are sometimes called "interpretivists," (or often "qualitative"), the latter "behavioralists" (or "quantitative"). Interpretive political scientists are most likely to deal in historical and philosophical aspects of politics and to seek detailed, nonnumerical information on a few cases. Behavioralists lean more to abstract, mechanical theories of politics and to statistical analyses of numerical information. They find numerical information especially attractive because it distills a set of complex details down into something very simple and basic—a number. Therefore, because behavioralists are looking for simple descriptions of basic processes, they see it as more useful to summarize party competition in many congressional districts with a single index number for each district than to try to digest masses of biography, newspaper accounts, and so on from a few congressional races.

This picture should not be seen as black and white. Political science does not consist of two warring camps, and most political scientists combine some element of "interpretivism" with some element of "behavioralism." However, there are different *degrees* of these among political scientists, which adds greatly to the variety of materials available in the field.

Whatever their preferred way of gathering information about the political world, political scientists tend, in their *thinking* about politics, to emphasize broad generalization and abstraction. Political scientists pursue generalization through *theory*.

A theory is a statement linking specific instances to broader principles. *Empirical theories* are theories describing how things work in the world we observe. They are usually explanatory; that is, they have to do with why things happen as they do. This means they consist of causal statements of the form "X causes Y." (For more on causation, see the discussion in the appendix, pp. 403–405.) An example of an empirical theory addressing one of the questions from page 3—why does the United States have only two major political parties—would be: "Single-member-district-plurality (SMDP) electoral systems, by disadvantaging small parties, tend to reduce the number of political parties to two." You will meet the single-member-district-plurality electoral system in Chapter 11. For now, the point is that this is a *causal* statement (SMDP causes two-party systems) and it links the specific case (United States parties) to a general principle.

Normative theories involve making a judgment about the world, not describing how it works. They address the question: "What should X be or do?" Again, these theories link specific cases to general principles. An example would be, "What sort of public health care plan should the United States have?" Normative theories would answer this question by applying general principles, such as "governments should intervene as little as possible in people's lives" or "societies are good to the extent that everyone has equal chances in life," to the specific policy question.

The important thing to note here is that both of our major kinds of theory—normative and empirical—are statements that deal with specific instances by linking them to general principles. Our relatively strong reliance on theory is what sets political scientists apart from others, especially historians, who also deal with politics as a subject.

Theories are the building blocks of political science, and you will find them throughout this book. A good example of normative and empirical theories is found in the box on page 135.

For practical purposes of curriculum and organization, the field of political science in the United States is divided into subfields according to the subjects in which political scientists specialize. The major subfields are:

- *American political behavior:* The study of individuals and nongovernmental organizations involved in politics and of why they do what they do. Studies of public opinion, elections, interest groups, and political parties would fall under this heading.
- *American political institutions:* The study of national governmental bodies, the Congress, the presidency, the bureaucracy, and—in part—the courts.
- *American public law:* The study of legal reasoning and of why courts hand down the decisions they do.
- *American public policy:* The analysis of the product of politics, the kinds of policies that are laid down.
- *American state and local politics:* The study of all of these, but at the level of "states" (such as California or Minnesota) and localities rather than the nation as a whole.
- *Comparative politics:* The study of all of these in any place but the United States. To lump together all aspects of politics outside of the United States is parochial, but that is what is usually done. Political scientists in other countries are as bad; Swedish political scientists have many subdivisions of the study of Sweden, as do the French for France, the Japanese for Japan, and so on.
- *International politics:* The study of politics between states—the making of common decisions for a group of states through wars, diplomacy, and so on. "International politics" is the only subfield that does this; all of the other subfields listed previously deal with politics *within* states, not between them.
- *Political theory:* The history of ideas about politics, and critical discussion of political values.

This book reviews the general findings of political science but blends U.S. politics and "comparative politics," treating the politics of all parts of the world (including the United States) comparatively.

THE PLEASURES OF POLITICS

I have led you through some rather dry material in this chapter because it was necessary to start you off with clarity on a number of concepts. Frequently throughout this book you will find that we are working toward greater precision than is found in everyday language; this usually requires abstraction and may also seem a bit dry. I hope, however, that as we do this, you will remember—and I can communicate—what a fascinating and dramatic thing we are studying.

"The use of power to reach collective choices"—think what this phrase means. We are talking about struggles for the souls of nations. The "use of power" has meant Thoreau going to prison to protest the United States' invasion of Mexico; underground resistance by the Catholic Church and the Communist Party against Nazi occupation troops in the Second World War; students braving police dogs and murderous assaults to integrate American businesses and public facilities in the 1960s; Mikhail Gorbachev and Boris Yeltsin juggling political coalitions to create democracy in the Soviet Union, where it had never been seen before. "Collective choices" have included the invention of democracy as a way to accomplish government by the people; the development of public education, park systems, public health; and also such horrors as the Nazis' murder of millions of Jews and other "undesirables."

I try in this book to write dispassionately about politics, because it is easier to keep a clear head that way, but a love of politics lies behind all of it. I switched from another undergraduate major to political science in the early 1960s because I was excited by John Kennedy's call for public service. I have remained a news "junkie" and sometime participant in politics ever since. The things we will be analyzing in the pages that follow involve real people devoting their energies to things they want and things they believe in. While you learn how to analyze what is happening in these events and to deal with the events dispassionately, I hope you will not forget the humanity that is moving through them.

FURTHER READING

Politics and Power

Dahl, Robert. *Modern Political Analysis.* 5th ed. New York: Prentice-Hall, 1990, chaps. 3 and 4.

Digeser, Peter. "The Fourth Face of Power." *Journal of Politics* 54 (November 1992): 977–1007.

Lasswell, Harold D., and Kaplan, Abraham. *Power and Society.* Yale Law School Studies, vol. 2. New Haven: Yale University Press, 1950.

MacIver, R. M. *The Web of Government,* rev. ed. New York: Free Press, 1965.

Maier, Charles S., ed. *Changing Boundaries of the Political.* New York: Cambridge University Press, 1987.

Nagel, Jack H. *The Descriptive Analysis of Power.* New Haven: Yale University Press, 1975.

"Power." In *The International Encyclopedia of the Social Sciences.* David L. Sills, editor. New York: Macmillan, 1968.

Wrong, Dennis. *Power.* New York: Harper & Row, 1979.

Political Science

Almond, Gabriel A. *A Discipline Divided: Schools and Sects in Political Science.* Newbury Park, Calif.: Sage, 1990.

Dogan, Mattei, ed. *Comparing Nations: Concepts, Strategies and Substance.* Cambridge, Mass.: Blackwell, 1994.

Easton, David; Gunnell, John G.; and Graziano, Luigi, eds. *The Development of Political Science: A Comparative Survey.* New York: Routledge, 1991.

Fenno, Richard. *Home Style: House Members in Their Districts.* Boston: Little, Brown, 1978. (The appendix to this book provides a good argument for qualitative social science.)

Goodin, Robert E., and Klingemann, Hans-Dieter, eds. *A New Handbook of Political Science.* New York: Oxford University Press, 1997.

King, Gary; Keohane, Robert; and Verba, Sidney. *Designing Social Inquiry: Scientific Inference in Qualitative Research.* Princeton, N.J.: Princeton University Press, 1994.
Lave, Charles A., and March, James G. *An Introduction to Models in the Social Sciences.* New York: Harper & Row, 1975. (Chapters 1–3 provide a good nontechnical argument for quantitative social science.)
Lichbach, Mark Irving, and Zuckerman, Alan S., eds. *Comparative Politics: Rationality, Culture, and Structure.* New York: Cambridge University Press, 1997.
"Political Science." In *The International Encyclopedia of the Social Sciences.*
Wahlke, John C. "Liberal Learning and the Political Science Major." *PS* 24 (March 1991): 48–60.
Wiarda, Howard, ed. *New Directions in Comparative Politics,* rev. ed. Boulder, Colo.: Westview Press, 1991.

BROAD WEBSITES OF GENERAL USE IN POLITICAL SCIENCE

American Political Science Association website, with many links:
http://www.apsanet.org/

University of Michigan library—probably the best one-stop shopping for links on government and politics:
http://www.lib.umich.edu

The CIA's *World Factbook,* with assessments and data on every country of the world:
http://www.odci.gov/cia/publications/factbook/index.html

The Library of Congress country studies:
http://lcweb2.loc.gov/frd/cs/cshome.html

The Center for the American Woman and Politics:
http://www.rci.rutgers.edu/~cawp/

Journalist Ron Gunzberger's grab bag of news, candidate biographies, and web links:
http://www.politics1.com

BBC online news:
http://www.bbc.co.uk

The International Herald Tribune (an excellent newspaper):
http://www.iht.com

International Political Science Association (similar to the American Political Science Association, but international and with many links to other countries):
http://www.ucd.ie/~ipsa/

A good page on political resources, based in Britain:
http://www.psr.keele.ac.uk/

Political Index, an index of thousands of links:
http://www.politicalindex.com/

2

MODERN IDEOLOGIES AND
POLITICAL PHILOSOPHY

Most people approach politics through an *ideology*—a set of related ideas that modify one another, an organized set of ideas. For instance, one person may believe that everyone is basically selfish, that politicians are all crooks, that a citizen owes nothing to the state, that it is all right to cheat on one's taxes, that gun control is a bad thing because it keeps us from protecting ourselves, and so on. This is an ideology—a set of ideas about politics, all of which are related to one another and that modify and support each other. The belief that everyone is basically selfish helps provide a justification for the need to carry a gun, the wish to cheat on taxes helps make one comfortable in the belief that the citizen owes nothing to the state, and so on. Another person may believe that individual freedom is terribly important, that government should regulate people as little as possible, that the United States should try to protect any people whose government is oppressing them, and that the U.S. government should not tell people whether they may carry guns. This is also ideology, an organized set of ideas that modify and support each other. In this second example, the high value placed on individual freedom supports both a wish to protect human rights around the world and a reluctance to have the government regulate the ownership of guns.

Ideologies are useful to people, both for their own personal ease and satisfaction and for their public political activities. From the *personal* point of view, an ideology helps us to make sense reasonably easily and quickly of the varied political questions that come to our attention. In any given week, the newspaper will raise questions about the control or deregulation of oil prices, the busing of schoolchildren to improve racial balance, the level of support for retired people in the Social Security system, the size of the military budget, federal acquisition of land for parks and wildlife refuges, and so forth. If we had to consider each of these issues anew, we would have an awesome task. However, if we approach each from the standpoint of a general ideology that we have developed over time, the job is much simpler. Most issues will turn out to be instances of more general principles that can quickly be settled by applying the principles.

The new issues may also modify our ideology, because an ideology is not graven in stone. For instance, devout Catholics who believe that the government should regulate people as little as possible may find themselves torn over the issue of legalized abortion and may modify some of their more general ideas about politics in light of the new issue. An ideology, then, is a continually developing, organized set of ideas about politics that helps us to make sense of the myriad of political questions that face us.[1]

An ideology also has *public* uses. In politics, we are typically concerned to convince others that a policy we favor is the right one. We usually have personal reasons for favoring the policy (we may want taxes to be cut because we are wealthy, oppose gun control because we like to collect guns, or favor national health insurance because we are poor), but these personal reasons are not usually good *public* reasons. People distrust a self-interested argument. Also, arguing for a policy by giving one's personal reasons for it would not win many allies; only those who are also rich could be convinced by the argument "I'm wealthy, therefore I want to see taxes cut." In political argument, we usually try to attract as many allies as possible to our position, and so personal reasons will not make good arguments. *Ideologies,* however, can serve this purpose very well. The wealthy person who argues, "Government spending and taxation hamper individual initiative," may appeal to a great many people who for various reasons favor individual initiative.

Ideologies are developed and maintained because of their usefulness to individuals in responding to events and their utility in public political argument. This is not a conscious, cynical process in which we deliberately frame an ideology so as to enlist allies in some cause or another. Rather, we are all comfortable with ideology and generally, over time, work out ideologies that fit our particular needs. Too, ideologies are not simply the creation of those who hold them; they tend to take on a life of their own and guide their holders' political views in unanticipated ways. A business leader who feels that government should regulate as little as possible (for what we may think are obvious reasons) may find that this ideology also leads to positions—not particularly connected to self-interest—on the censorship of books in public libraries or the regulation of handguns.

An ideology is an organized set of ideas that helps us make sense out of politics for ourselves and present arguments effectively in public. We develop our ideologies in such a way that they fit our needs and predispositions, reflecting what we want; but they also take on a life of their own and *guide* our decisions.

AMERICAN IDEOLOGIES

All of us have some sort of ideology, in the sense that our various ideas about politics bear some sort of relationship one to another. However, not every ideology is equally neat and tidy, nor is every ideology worked out in equally full detail. Americans' ideologies

---

[1]See Pamela Johnston Conover and Stanley Feldman, "Belief System Organization in the American Electorate," in *The Electorate Reconsidered,* ed. John Pierce and John L. Sullivan (Beverly Hills, Calif.: Sage, 1980); Michael Billig, Susan Condor, Derek Edwards, Mike Gane, Daniel Middleton, and Alan Radley, *Ideological Dilemmas: A Social Psychology of Everyday Thinking* (Beverly Hills, Calif.: Sage, 1988); Teun A. Van Dijk, *Ideology: A Multi-Disciplinary Approach* (Beverly Hills, Calif.: Sage, 1998).

tend to be more loosely organized than those of other peoples. In fact, Americans tend to admit exceptions and inconsistencies into their ideologies rather cheerfully.

Two main ideologies are found among Americans: "American liberalism" and "American conservatism." The former is characterized in the following ways. Compared with American conservatism, it is:

- More concerned about inequality (between the poor and the well-off, between blacks and whites, between women and men).
- More inclined to use the power of the government to make conditions for people more equal. Therefore, American liberals are more willing than American conservatives to see a larger government, supplied by higher taxes. They are more willing to see the government intervene through such devices as forced integration of schools and a graduated income tax to alleviate inequalities.
- More inclined generally to use the power of the government to achieve a diverse set of things they view as good ends. More inclined, therefore, to use government regulation to protect the environment, to ensure safe prescription drugs, or for other similar purposes.
- Less concerned about the maintenance of public values and less supportive of using governmental power to ban such things as prostitution, drug use, and gambling.
- Opposed to restrictions on abortion. This issue could really have gone either way historically, since in this case, liberals are opposing governmental intervention in an issue of health and safety. Indeed, in the early years of the abortion debate— before abortion had crystallized into an issue dividing liberals and conservatives— advocates and opponents of freedom of choice were found in both camps. Over time, things sorted themselves out, partly on the basis of people's gender and religious beliefs. Some of the "sorting out" involved pro-choice conservatives becoming more liberal and pro-life liberals becoming more conservative.
- More reluctant, at least in recent decades, to maintain a large military force and use military power abroad, although historically, American liberals and conservatives have gone back and forth on this issue.

American conservatism represents the other side of these comparisons.

American liberalism and American conservatism are not neat ideologies. It is hard to see, for instance, what logical connections exist among the various attitudes detailed. It frequently happens that an American political figure is "liberal" on some of these issues and "conservative" on others. American labor unions, for example, have generally been quite concerned about issues of equality but have not been equally concerned about an issue such as abortion rights. There are many other complexities as well. As one more example, American conservatives generally favor free trade but are also concerned about the repression of religion in China. This leaves them to grapple with the question of what sort of trade relations the United States should maintain with China.

As we shall see, American liberalism and American conservatism are variants of a more general and well worked out ideology known simply as *liberalism.* "American liberalism" and "American conservatism" are simply differing versions that have sprung up in a predominantly liberal society, to unite under the loose term "liberal" (American version) the weaker parts of society (the poor, those who were discriminated against, those whose moral values went against the dominant grain, those with unpopular ideas) against the stronger and more dominant parts, whose interests were represented by "conservatism" (American version). Both ideologies are therefore hodgepodges, representing marriages of political convenience, and it is difficult to find internal coherence among the various parts of either one.

However, even though the American ideologies are untidy, they have still had real influence. American labor leaders have probably been more concerned than they might otherwise have been with freedom of expression because of this issue's association with the redistribution of income in American liberalism. Americans concerned about high taxes have probably picked up more concern than they might otherwise have had for questions of public values because of the juxtaposition of these positions in American conservatism.

Over the last few decades, the intensity of ideological debate has strengthened markedly in the United States. I have described American ideologies as "hodgepodges," but they are still ideologies people care a lot about. The intensity of ideology today can be seen in the very strong reactions (positive and negative) to President William Clinton in the 1990s; it can be seen in the contemporary sharp contestation over judicial appointments in the Senate, which in the 1960s and 1970s would have been almost pro forma; and it can be seen in the proliferation of ideologically based interest groups and think tanks.

It is not obvious why we should have come to feel so much more strongly about our "hodgepodge" ideologies in the 1980s and 1990s than we did in earlier decades. In part, it may be because of new techniques and technology (direct mailings, focus groups, polling, e-mail) that have made it easier for ideologues to raise money and fire up their troops. In part, it may be because of the involvement of the newly active religious right, who have brought some of the emotion of religious belief into the political sphere. In part, it may be the addition to the political realm since 1973 of a new issue, abortion, which excites deep emotion and on which compromise is at best exceedingly difficult. In part, it may be the partisan realignment of the 1960s and 1970s in which the conservative South moved to the Republican Party, leaving the two parties more clearly divided along ideological lines than they had been and thus adding the emotion of partisanship to conflicts over ideology. But in the end, it is also because these ideologies do articulate real conflicts between real groups in the population. They may be hodgepodges intellectually—less neat systems of ideas than the more general liberalism, conservatism, and socialism that I describe in the next sections. But as systems of conflict, they are just as real as those more tightly knit intellectual systems.

LIBERALISM

The two American ideologies are actually variants of *liberalism,* one of the three great ideologies that developed in Europe in the eighteenth and nineteenth centuries. These ideologies—liberalism, conservatism, and socialism—have provided the framework for most political debate throughout the world since then.

To understand their development, we must remember that the medieval social order in Europe was one in which people were bound together in patterns of rather strict domination, with mutual responsibilities between those who were dominated and those who dominated them, between "top dogs" and "bottom dogs." Farmers often lived in a condition of near-slavery, subject to a local church official or a member of the nobility. A farmer paid heavy taxes to his local patron and had to provide him with specified periods of labor for road building, war, and so on. In many parts of Europe, the farmer was not allowed to leave his land and move elsewhere without the permission of his patron. Furthermore, farmers were required to offer the patron formal social respect and deference. In return, the patron was supposed to provide his farmers with protection and with help in times of illness or want. Such industry as existed was organized in guilds, which laid down strict rules as to how an item was to be manufactured, how many such items were to be produced, and what was to be charged for them. Trade in many items was subject to ancient rules: The king might have a monopoly on trade in a commodity such as salt, for instance, or a particular town might have the enduring right to receive all imports of some specific item. Jews were a pariah group, banned from many occupations and generally forbidden to own land. The Roman Catholic Church maintained a stern control over proper belief (a striking example of this occurred when, in 1616, the church forced the great astronomer Galileo to state, contrary to his true convictions, that he did not believe the earth orbited around the sun). To transport goods from one end of a country to another could be a complex affair in which the carrier of the goods was required to pay taxes, fees, and tributes to various local personages at all stages of the journey. Politics was the province of the king, the nobility, and the church.

For our present purposes, two things are important about these arrangements: (1) people were bound to each other in complex and cumbersome systems of domination; and (2) the arrangements were static, difficult to change. Ownership of the land, feudal privileges, the rights of the church, the political role of the king and nobility, the power of the guilds—all were granted in perpetuity and could only evolve slowly.

Onto this setting—faintly in the fifteenth and sixteenth centuries, in crescendo through the seventeenth and eighteenth centuries, and with a deafening crash in the nineteenth century—came modern large-scale commerce and industry. The new commercial and industrial leaders chafed under the static restrictions of medieval society. To carry on large-scale trade and manufacture, it was often necessary to move commodities over great distances; laborers had to be gathered at large factories, which often involved moving people from one end of the country to another; canals and roads had to be built, which would run through many different patrons' domains; prices and the nature of goods often had to be adjusted to reflect changing needs and technology; and science and invention had to be free to pursue truth wherever they found it, regardless of orthodoxy. These requirements collided with the organization of preindustrial medieval society. The new and increasingly powerful commercial and industrial elite cast about for ways to make society more fluid and manageable. One helpful solution, as we shall see in Chapter 3, was the invention of the modern state as a way to organize politics and government. Another was the appearance of liberalism.

Liberalism was not introduced by the commercial and industrial leaders themselves. Rather, it was invented by intellectuals who were moved by the general artistic and scientific restlessness of the age. However, it suited the new economic leaders, and they warmed to it. It gave them a view of politics that could make sense to them in light of their needs, and it allowed them to argue for their causes in ways that were less crass than simply saying, "We wish to limit the power of the nobility, the guilds, and the church because we want to make money."

Liberalism posits as the highest good of society *the ability of the members of that society to develop their individual capacities to the fullest extent.* That is, in a good society, all individuals should be able to develop their minds, musical talents, athletic abilities, or any other gift as much as possible. This requires, according to liberalism, that people be maximally responsible for their own actions, rather than having someone else do things for them or tell them what to do. It is only by acting and feeling the consequences of such action that we can develop our capacity to act.

This is the central assumption of liberalism, from which a number of consequences flow. For instance, in his essay *On Representative Government,* John Stuart Mill based his argument in favor of democratic government on liberal premises, as follows: The chief end of politics is to allow people to become responsible and mature. They can do this only if they take part in decisions affecting their own lives. Therefore, even though a wise and benevolent despot or monarch might make better decisions on behalf of the people than they could make for themselves, democracy would be better, because under it the people make their own decisions, mistakes and all. Therefore, some form of democracy is the best kind of government.

By the same sorts of argument, the following elements follow from the basic liberal premise; together, they constitute the liberal ideology:

- Democracy of some sort is the proper form of government.
- People should have full intellectual freedom, including freedom of speech, freedom of religion, and freedom of the press. (They should have responsibility for their own values, so that they will develop the ability to judge values.)
- Government should remain minimal and should regulate people's lives very little. (As few decisions as possible should be made *for* people, so that they learn to make decisions for themselves.)
- In particular, people should be free to regulate their own economic activity.
- Power of one person over another is a bad thing; hence, government should be organized to guard against abuses of power. (Again, one person should not make decisions for another.)

John Stuart Mill and Liberalism

John Stuart Mill (1806–1873) was a major figure in liberal thought. His father, James Mill, an important figure in the history of British philosophy, educated young John himself, following an incredible regimen: John was reading Greek at age three, and by the time he reached maturity he probably knew more of science and literature than anyone else in Britain. He spent his adult years in a sinecure with the British East India Company, which allowed him plenty of time to write. His main contribution to liberal thought was to reconcile, in a fairly tight logical system, individual freedom with the general good of society. Unusually for his time, John Stuart Mill was a strong feminist and advocated women's suffrage. Some have ascribed this to the influence of his wife, Harriet Taylor Mill, while others simply believe the logic of liberalism pushed him to this conclusion.

Liberalism flourished especially in Great Britain and its colonies, perhaps because Britain was the first country to industrialize. In Britain, liberal forces first gained control of the House of Commons and the cabinet in 1832; through the nineteenth century, political control of the country seesawed between liberals and conservatives. (See the section on "The Conservative Reaction" for a discussion of conservatism.) In the United States, the new Constitution of 1789, with its precautions against a concentration of power in any one part of the government and its guarantees of various individual freedoms, clearly signified the ascendance of liberalism. On the continent of Europe, liberalism was a potent force throughout the nineteenth century, but it was nowhere as strong as in Britain and its former colonies. Most Western European countries had liberal constitutions by the end of World War I, but by that time liberalism was fading quickly.

With regard to the distinction between the "choice" and "power" perspectives, liberals will strongly favor a view of politics as choice. To liberals, power is a bad thing that should be limited as much as possible. Power allows some people to force choices on others, which flies directly in the face of liberal principles. To a liberal, politics should properly consist of public choices, in the making of which each person shares equally. As many choices as possible should be kept private. That is, the sphere of politics itself should be limited.

THE CONSERVATIVE REACTION

When liberalism arose to challenge the existing social arrangements, the defenders of those arrangements needed an ideology to counteract the persuasive power of liberalism. Conservatism developed in response to this need.

Conservatism in the European sense is unfamiliar to Americans, because it is quite different from American conservatism. Defenders of existing arrangements in Europe pointed out quite properly that liberalism is an individualistic doctrine; that is, liberalism looks on society as consisting of the individuals constituting it. To liberals, the whole of society equals the sum of its component parts, so that a society is happiest when the total of individuals' happiness is greatest. This is implied in the basic premise of liberalism, that the goodness of a society is to be judged by the extent to which its members individually are able to develop their capacities.

In opposition to this, conservatism holds that societies and other groups of people are *more* than just the sums of their parts, that a group of people creates greater happiness through its existence and maintenance as a group than its members could individually produce for themselves. Liberalism, conservatives say, is a lonely and selfish philosophy whose ultimate result would be a group of people resolved to better themselves with no regard for the people around them.

Conservatives regard it as important that their society should have order and structure and that this structure should be stable enough to let people know where they stand with regard to each other. Most important, an ordered group develops and maintains religion and standards of morality. People gain greater happiness as members of a family, members of a church, and members of society than they could possibly gain individually. This is what conservatives see as the highest good of society: *the maintenance of ordered community and of common values.*

In such a society, it is silly to try to keep one person from doing things for another or to keep one individual from exercising power over another. The whole point of "community" is that people are important as members, not as individuals. What matters is how they fit into the web of mutual responsibilities.

The structure of the community should be relatively stable and predictable so that all may easily fit into their place in it; therefore, there is nothing wrong with assigning power to people by even such arbitrary devices as heredity if those people can be expected to use their power wisely. Patterns of domination that have evolved gradually should not be changed casually, because what has grown slowly is at least familiar to us and must have had some virtue to have lasted so long. Conservatism is an ideology that accepts and welcomes power; conservatives believe that appropriate arrangements for power will ensure good treatment for everyone.

It is obvious why this philosophy based on ordered community was useful to the aristocracy, the established church, and others who were trying to maintain their positions against the liberal challenge. However, ideologies take on a life of their own, and conservatism stresses another theme that might not otherwise have come so naturally to the defenders of the status quo: the responsibilities of power. Where liberalism is suspicious of power and seeks to limit it, conservatism sees power as binding and shaping its holder in good ways. Conservatives do not see a powerful monarch or president as one who is in a position to treat people capriciously. Rather, they see such an official as one who is in a position of awesome responsibility, with generally little choice as to courses of action. Conservatism stresses the responsibility of the powerful in a community to help the weak, a position opposed to the view of liberals that the weak should be given responsibility for their own affairs. European conservatives, because of this side of conservatism, have not been especially reluctant to help the poor or to develop the welfare state. In the late eighteenth century in Britain, under the conservative regime, there was already a system of guaranteed minimum income for anyone in Britain—a floor below which no one was to be allowed to fall. *Abolishing* this system was one of the first tasks of the liberals when they took power in 1832. To take another example, when Otto von Bismarck, the conservative chancellor of Germany from 1871 to 1890, introduced the world's first systems of unemployment insurance, workers' compensation, and social security, he had no apparent sense that he was doing something out of character.

Conservatism is unfamiliar to Americans. This is because, to the extent that the early immigrants had any ideas about politics at all, America was founded by liberals and

---

Edmund Burke and Conservatism

Edmund Burke (1729–1797) is perhaps the most important figure in the development of conservative thought, at least in Britain. He was born and educated in Dublin, Ireland, the son of a lawyer. Although he was a professional politician and a great orator in the House of Commons, he was too intellectual and independent to rise to a major position in his party. As a philosopher, he was not abstract and did not deal in logical systems. Rather, he drew pragmatically from experience. What was already a well-developed conservative ideology was sharpened for him by what he saw as the excesses of the French Revolution.

populated largely by liberals. Most of the early settlers were trying to escape the rigidities of the old order in Europe. Also, our more fluid society has had few ordered systems of domination; conservatism, a defense of such systems, has therefore been largely irrelevant.[2]

In recent years, however, one of our few ordered systems of domination has come under liberal attack and something rather like conservatism has arisen as a defense. The feminist attack on men's domination of women has often been framed as a classic statement of liberal argument. Women should be free to take on all sorts of responsibility, according to feminists, so that they can develop their capacities to the fullest. Protective laws (limiting the hours women may work, barring them from certain dangerous jobs, protecting them from combat in the armed forces, and so on) are wrong because in being protected from unpleasantness people are made weak and dependent. Feminists do not want women put "on a pedestal."

Opponents of feminism have often responded in ways that are akin to conservatism. The traditional family is a good thing in its own right, they say, especially if children are involved. It is the family we should be thinking of, not the individuals who make it up. Families work better, children are raised better, everyone is in the end happier, if there is a clear structure of authority in the family rather than a situation in which each member is striving individually.

Conservatism was a strong force throughout Europe in the nineteenth and early twentieth centuries. With the massive changes brought by World War II and its aftermath, European conservatism changed. The nobility were generally destroyed or discredited, the church was in ferment, and most countries had introduced a sweeping expansion of taxation and social services, the "welfare state," to make people more equal. After the huge destruction of the war, it was not always clear that there was a social order for conservatism to defend.

However, conservatism adapted fairly rapidly to these changed circumstances. Their traditional emphasis on the responsibility of the powerful to help the poor and weak, together with a willingness (in contrast to the position of liberals) to see power concentrated, made it fairly easy for conservatives to accept the welfare state. Also, conservatism welcomes active encouragement of religion by the state, whereas liberalism is suspicious of it; large numbers of Europeans after the war apparently felt a need for a stability of values offered by religion, although among the youngest recent generations religious practice has now dropped off sharply. While liberalism declined in Europe throughout the twentieth century, conservatism has lived on healthily. Its adherents have accepted the welfare state but urged that it be built in ways that are consistent with traditional moral values and that it should not lead to a leveling of society. In other words, conservatives feel that some structure should remain by which one part of society can lead the rest. In Britain, the Liberal Party declined during the 1920s and 1930s, but the Conservative Party remained as the chief opponent of the new Labour Party. When Labour introduced the welfare state in 1945, the Conservatives accepted it within a few years and went on to dominate British politics until the 1990s. In Europe, after the war, Christian Democratic parties arose in many countries; these adhere to an established

[2]Louis Hartz, *The Liberal Tradition in America* (New York: Harcourt Brace, 1955).

church but are flexible and pragmatic with regard to taxes and social programs. They have been especially strong in Italy and Germany, while a somewhat similar movement, the Gaullist movement, dominated French politics from 1958 to 1981. One can safely characterize the politics of most west European states since World War II as having consisted of a conflict between socialism (described in the section on "The Socialist Alternative") and a modified conservatism.

In the "South" (the poor states of the world), liberalism outside of Europe and North America, has generally been weak (countries that are trying to develop their economies apparently find that they cannot afford to limit and restrain concentrations of power) and conservatism is rather strong. Traditional religious leaders and the aristocracy, as in Saudi Arabia and Iran, or new elites of business leaders, as in Japan or Brazil, can often maintain a strong political movement to keep the political leadership of the state in their hands. And frequently, the two groups join forces.

There is often a strong element of direction from the military in such movements as well, as in the series of conservative regimes in South Korea from 1952 to 1987. While not all military governments are conservative, there is often an affinity between military leaders and conservative political parties. Military organization requires an ordered structure of command in which certain members of the military direct the activities of other members. This is rather similar to the conservative view of society as a whole and may help to make military leaders comfortable with conservatism.[3]

A major exception to the general weakness of liberalism in the South has appeared in recent years, as part of the worldwide rise of "neoliberalism" (see p. 33). This has involved reduced regulation by governments, privatization of government-run industries, and a general reliance on open markets for economic decisions. This picks up on the *economic* aspects of liberalism but not necessarily on any others. Under this impetus, a number of states of the South (the poor states of the world) have reduced governmental involvement in the economy.

THE SOCIALIST ALTERNATIVE

When liberalism first arose to challenge the established order, it drew considerable support from the "working class," the workers and their families who were beginning to congregate in the growing cities. Workers especially liked the assumption that all people were equal and should have an equal opportunity to develop their talents. They liked the liberal doctrine of democracy, which would recognize them as having full and equal citizenship rights. In 1848, a wave of attempted revolutions by liberals swept across the continent of Europe; in most of these, skilled workers played a leading part, along with shopkeepers and other small businessmen. In Britain, the leaders of most labor unions were active in the Liberal Party as late as 1900.

However, through the latter part of the nineteenth century, the enthusiasm of the working class for liberalism weakened. Liberalism implied not only that people should be politically equal but that they should be regulated and helped by the government as little as possible. Workers were in a weak position socially and economically, and they

---

[3]However, see the more detailed discussion of military governments in Chapter 9.

often found that they would like help from the government in ways that were inconsistent with liberalism. Governmental protection against unemployment and sickness, governmental regulation of working hours and of safety in the factories, governmental prohibition of child labor—these and similar wishes of labor were inconsistent with liberal principles. Naturally, compromises and accommodations could be reached within the movement, and labor was not left totally out in the cold, but the fact remained that labor often found that it had to buck the basic philosophy of the movement of which it was a part. When a new ideology appeared that was more congenial to labor, workers moved to it fairly readily. This ideology was socialism.

Socialism retained the assumption of liberalism that all persons deserve equal treatment by the state and should have equal opportunities to develop themselves; but unlike liberalism, it did not posit that people could develop individually, and it was not as suspicious as liberalism of the concentration of power and of positive action by the state. Karl Marx (1818–1883) was the greatest socialist writer, and socialism since Marx has been heavily influenced by his views. Marx thought that society consisted not of individuals but of _classes._ A class is a group of people who share the same relationship to the means of production and who therefore develop a distinctive view of themselves and of the world. Marx thought that the most important thing about us is our work, that this is what creates for us most of our view of the world; people who share similar work (a similar "relationship to the means of production") form the natural basis for a class. The aristocracy had been such a class, intellectuals were such a class, the industrialists were such a class, and now a new class—the working class—was appearing in Europe. To Marx, people did not develop themselves individually—in a vacuum, as it were—but of and through the class to which they belonged. According to this view, individuals do not form their own values, their own ideas about politics, their own sense of their needs; rather, they and the people they associate with form these things communally in ways that are difficult to specify. A person may contribute to these values and ideas, but so do the other members of his or her class. Each member draws much more from the class than any single member contributes to it.

For Marx, then, the basic unit of concern was the class. As he saw it, the working class was oppressed; it was made to give up its members' labor to feed the rich capitalist class. This was wrong, he said, because the working class were numerically much larger than the capitalist class and their oppression bred great misery. Therefore, the working class

---

Karl Marx and Socialism

Karl Marx (1818–1895) was raised at first in Bonn, Germany, and later in Berlin. After graduating from the university, Marx and his close friend Friedrich Engels (1820–1895) worked as journalists. In 1848 they wrote the _Communist Manifesto_ and, in the aftermath of unsuccessful revolutions in Germany in that year, were forced to flee Germany. They settled in London, where Engels's family had connections and Engels could take care of Marx. Marx did not return to Germany until shortly before his death. In London he worked as a correspondent for the _New York Tribune_ and wrote his massive, major work, _Das Kapital._ Marx combined a sweeping view of history with an astonishing appetite for the minutiae of economics. At its most basic level, his theory of politics, as of all other human activity, was that it is determined solely by economic processes and can be understood by economic analysis.

should take over control of the government and the government should take over industry, so that the workers, through their government, would control the industries in which they worked. This would ensure fair treatment for everyone.

The writings of Marx and other socialists derived their energy and moral force from the writers' awareness of the truly miserable conditions under which workers lived in the nineteenth century. Marx's friend and collaborator Friedrich Engels, in his study of the living conditions of English workers, quoted an Anglican priest's account in 1844 of conditions in his parish:

> It contains 1,400 houses, inhabited by 2,795 families, comprising a population of 12,000. The space within which this large amount of population are living is less than 400 yards square, and it is no uncommon thing for a man and his wife, with four or five children, and sometimes the grandfather and grandmother, to be found living in a room from ten to twelve feet square, and which serves them for eating and working in. . . . There is not one father of a family in ten throughout the entire district that possesses any clothes but his working dress, and that too commonly in the worst tattered condition; and with many this wretched clothing form their only covering at night, with nothing better than a bag of straw or shavings to lie upon.[4]

Engels goes on to describe his own investigation of the living conditions of the working class in the city of Manchester:

> One walks along a very rough path on the river bank, in between clothesposts and washing lines to reach a chaotic group of little, one-storied, one-roomed cabins. Most of them have earth floors, and working, living and sleeping all take place in the one room. In such a hole, barely six feet long and five feet wide, I saw two beds—and what beds and bedding!—which filled the room, except for the fireplace and the doorstep. Several of these huts, as far as I could see, were completely empty, although the door was open and the inhabitants were leaning against the door posts. In front of the doors filth and garbage abounded. I could not see the pavement, but from time to time, I felt it was there because my feet scraped it.[5]

Marx developed a theory of history arguing that a revolution of the working class was not only appropriate but inevitable. According to Marx's *dialectical* theory, all history has consisted of a successive unfolding of domination by one group, leading to revolution against that group, followed by domination by a new group (the group that had led the successful revolution), leading to yet another revolution, and so on. Thus, Europe in the Middle Ages was dominated by the nobility, but there was an internal contradiction in their rule: They needed the services of bankers and traders but were barred by their social codes from undertaking this work themselves. Therefore, they created a new class, the capitalist class, which (as we saw previously) eventually overthrew them in the Industrial Revolution and with the coming of liberalism. The capitalist class now dominated Europe, said Marx, but there was an internal contradiction in their rule as well, which would eventually lead to their overthrow. The capitalists had had to create a new class, the working class, to serve their needs. However, because capitalists are forced by their code to seek ever-greater profits, they would have to grind

---

[4]Friedrich Engels, *The Condition of the Working Class in England,* tr. by W. O. Henderson and W. H. Chaloner (Oxford, England: Basil Blackwell, 1958), pp. 35 and 36.
[5]Ibid., p. 61.

Karl Marx, architect of socialist ideology.
(UPI/Bettmann/Corbis)

the working class ever nearer to starvation, until at last the situation would be intolerable and there would be a revolution. Note that this theory of politics is based almost solely on the use of power.

Marx thought that the process of history would have worked itself out with the victory of the working class, because for the first time the dominant class would not be a minority but would include almost the whole population. His theory of history and revolution was powerfully attractive to workers. It told them that their unhappy plight was not their own fault as individuals but rather a condition imposed on them as a class by the working out of a broad historical process. Furthermore, it prophesied that they must, in the end, prevail over the capitalists because that is the way history works. Finally, it assured them that once they had prevailed, a brave new world would be created in which the cycle of revolutions was no longer necessary. In the words of a favorite British working class hymn:

> I will not cease from mental fight,
> Nor shall my sword sleep in my hand,
> Till we have built Jerusalem
> In England's green and pleasant land.
> (originally from William Blake's *Milton*)

Socialism burst explosively on Europe. In 1850, there were only a few socialists on the continent. By the early 1900s, the Social Democratic Party was the largest party in Germany and was growing fast; socialism was growing just as rapidly in other Western European countries.

COMMUNISM AND SOCIALISM

In 1917, a key event occurred in the development of socialism when Lenin's Bolsheviks succeeded in seizing control of the Russian Empire and transformed it into a socialist state renamed the Union of Soviet Socialist Republics (U.S.S.R.). Marx and Engels had never fully settled whether they thought the working class should take control of the state peacefully through electoral victory or violently through revolution. Many socialists thought revolution was the only answer, while others believed deeply in democracy. Lenin's successful revolution galvanized those who wanted to take the route of revolution, and over the years after 1917 they tried to dominate the socialist movement. They argued that the one state that had now successfully become socialist, the U.S.S.R., should lead all socialists in the world. The attempt to commit socialism to a revolutionary strategy led to a split in the socialist movement in the 1920s. The revolutionists set themselves up as Communist parties, while the democratic socialists continued to call themselves Socialist or sometimes Democratic Socialist parties.

The split has endured, so that there are two branches of socialism, although outside of a few places such as Cuba, communism has been in broad retreat for the last few years. Communists have generally held to a revolutionary strategy, although with the passage of time they have grown a good deal less emphatic about it. Socialists have been much more willing to settle for a portion of power within an only partially socialist system, and they have generally worked within a democratic framework. Socialists have also been more willing than communists to settle for partial improvements for workers, rather than holding out for a total change.

In the period after World War II, most of Eastern Europe was governed by communists, with military help from the U.S.S.R. By 1989, communism in Eastern Europe and the Soviet Union had become more a bureaucratic sink than a shining ideology, and over the next two years these communist regimes collapsed. The Eastern European states tend to look to democratic socialism, combined with free markets, as a model; the remnants of the Soviet Union have made stabs at economic change, but most have become preoccupied with working out ethnic and nationalistic conflicts. In Western Europe, Socialists have participated strongly in government for many years, and Socialists took the lead in bringing the modern welfare state to Europe. Communism and socialism have been strong forces in the Third World. China, Cuba, and Vietnam have more or less communist governments, while scores of Third World states have socialist governments.

FASCISM

In the 1920s and 1930s, there arose a political movement, fascism, that did not hang together well as ideology (the twentieth century, unlike the nineteenth century, did not emphasize the intellectual completeness of theories) but was rather more a style of politics and a popular movement. Adolf Hitler in Germany, Benito Mussolini in Italy, and Francisco Franco in Spain established fascist regimes at this time. Fascists did not generally write elaborations of their theory, because among other things, they despised intellectualism and ideology. Accordingly, most analysts of fascism as an ideology have looked mainly at what fascists did. The essence of fascism seems to have been a rejection of most institutions of modern life, combined with a national rebirth focused on a charismatic, dictatorial leader. Fascists were antisocialist, generally anticapitalist, and (at least in Hitler's and Mussolini's cases) hostile to the church. They tended to glorify instead a mythical war-based society of the past—for Mussolini the ancient Roman Empire, for Hitler the Teutonic knights of the Middle Ages and Wagner's dreamy stories about the old Germanic gods.

Their political style was opportunist. All used violence and terror to advance their movements. Somewhat paradoxically—remember, they despised modern institutions—they were also "up to date" and presented themselves as forward-looking. Hitler was the first German politician to campaign from an airplane, for instance, and the design of fascist propaganda and rallies was often done in the modern-looking art deco style.

Fascism appealed particularly to those who felt left out in the modern age. In Spain and Italy, these were mostly the traditional elites, who felt threatened by modern industrial managers and by socialist workers. In Germany, the "left out" appear to have been mainly the middle class, small farmers, and shopkeepers. The uprooting of European civilization in the First World War helped prepare the ground as well, adding to the sense of loss among the disinherited of modern life.

The details of fascism actually varied a good deal from one place to another. The Nazi party of Germany attacked the existing social system, including the churches, more actively than most. It had a strong element of anti-Semitic racism that was not present in Italian or Spanish fascism and that ultimately led to the murder of millions of Jews. Spanish fascism identified with conservative church leadership and supported the church. Italian fascism was marked by an attempt to reorganize the economy into "corporations"—guilds of employers and workers in each industry. Such variations in fascist policy again underscore that fascism was, and is, rather more a political style than a system of ideas.

The defeat of the fascist powers in World War II ended most organized fascism; but since then, when established sets of people have felt their positions threatened by modern change—especially by new racial or ethnic claims, or by immigration of new groups into the country—echoes of fascism have often been heard. The American Nazi party, anti-immigrant movements in Europe, and so on, often involve a dramatic leader, violence, and a denial of modern change in ways that show kinship with the old fascist movements.

THE GREAT IDEOLOGIES IN THE LATE TWENTIETH CENTURY

With the long period of general peace in Europe and among other industrialized states since World War II, some of the edge has worn off the conflict among the great modern ideologies. As modern society has become more firmly established, the old grievances do not seem to move people as strongly as they once did. With the decline of religion (outside of Islamic regions) and with the poor economic performance of socialist states, there has been a resurgence of liberalism—but a liberalism modified by considerable governmental support for the weak.

Many leaders of parties, especially those that hold responsibility for the government of a state, have begun to modify their ideologies in light of practical experience. The most dramatic example of this is provided by the collapse of the communist regimes of Eastern Europe and Russia. Many states of this region have become liberal democracies, and all have abandoned their old, ideologically based communist systems.

Other leaders, too, show a more compromised blend of ideologies. Britain's Margaret Thatcher was for fifteen years the leader of the Conservative Party, which among other things emphasizes ties to the Anglican Church and the monarchy. However, her personal ideology combined these conservative elements with a set of very liberal economic policies calling for a great shrinkage of the state's role in the economy, marked by the privatization (sale to private owners) of many government enterprises. On the other side of the spectrum, some socialists such as Felipe Gonzalez, leader of Spain's Socialist Party, or Tony Blair, the Labour Party prime minister of Britain, have so blended their socialism with concerns for efficiency and stable economic growth that it is scarcely recognizable as a doctrine of conflict between classes. Italy's former Communist Party, with even the word *Communist* now removed from its name, emerged in the mid-1990s as the Democratic Party of the Left, a left-of-center, democratic party—and is one of the leading parties of post–Cold War Italy.

However, ideological conflict was not dead in the late twentieth century. In Europe, new "green" parties raised a set of issues that established leaders, accustomed to the old ideologies, found hard to absorb into their debates. These issues, labeled "postindustrial issues" by Ronald Inglehart, included feminism, protection of the environment, and open and spontaneous styles of life.[6] In part, they were represented by totally new parties (among others, the Greens); in part, they found their way into established Socialist parties where they often represented a minority voice. In Socialist parties, the new mood especially produced interest in direct participation by workers in the management of their industries.[7] At the other end of the spectrum, anti-immigrant parties, such as France's National Front, raised issues of race and nationalism that had been thought dead since the Second World War. Outside of Europe, militant Islam, with its claims for a religious state, raised the political temperature in many states of North Africa, the Mideast, and South Asia.

History, and the development of ideologies, does not stop. The great modern ideologies were a product of the tension between Europe's industrialization and the static institutions Europe had inherited from its feudal past. As that tension recedes, other sources of ideological development have come to the fore, in a sometimes confusing mix of forces and tensions: the practical economic experiences of the Soviet Union and the United States; the increasing problem of degradation of the environment; the resurgence of militant Islam; the discovery of youth and women as classes, even though Marxist socialism saw classes as based solely on economic position; and the division of interests between rich states and poor states—the North and the South.

Perhaps most notably, in a new mood of "neoliberalism," many states have cut back on governmental regulation of the economy, privatized state-run businesses, made their central banks more independent of direction from the government, and opened business in their state to international competition by lowering trade barriers. In effect, these governments adopted the economic part of liberalism, though not necessarily the full ideology. (Many of these states established democracy at the same time, but some carried out "neoliberal" reforms without any of the other parts of liberalism; a good example is

---

[6]Ronald Inglehart, *Culture Shift in Advanced Industrial Society* (Princeton, N.J.: Princeton University Press, 1990).

[7]See, for example, W. Rand Smith, "Toward 'Autogestion' in Socialist France? The Impact of Industrial Relations Reform," *West European Politics* 10 (January 1987): 46–62.

China, whose communist government maintains tight control over politics and speech but has hugely opened up the economy.)

The impetus for this neoliberal tide seems to be less ideology than a practical desire to operate economies more efficiently. It was heightened, for example, by the economic success of the United States in the 1990s, which was taken by many states as a model to be imitated. The tide was also encouraged by the International Monetary Fund and U.S. foreign policy, which generally tied economic help in times of crisis to reforms along neoliberal lines.

Neoliberalism has also been connected with the growth of "globalization," in which states can no longer control the flow of ideas or goods across their borders as well as they once could. Since it is increasingly difficult for a state to control its affairs by itself, it must be able to connect with the states around it. And the openness that this requires fosters "neoliberal" competition with businesses beyond the state's borders.

As you will see in other parts of this book, many of the main sources of political conflict and ideological ferment in the world today involve questions of national, ethnic, or religious identity, gender, and what to do about the increasingly shared international problems of economic development and the environment.

POLITICAL PHILOSOPHY IN OTHER HISTORICAL ERAS

In this chapter, we have followed the development of modern ideologies, starting at approximately the eighteenth century. However, great minds throughout the ages have been concerned with the question of how politics should rightly be conducted. Different questions have engaged political philosophy at different times, depending on the problems and opportunities presented by historical circumstances. The ideologies we have looked at in this chapter, for instance, were all responses to the coming of modern industry and commerce. These posed challenges for society that political philosophy had to address; they also produced a broadening of economic and intellectual power beyond traditional elites, which offered new opportunities for the conduct of politics.

At earlier periods in history, political philosophers have faced different sets of challenges and opportunities. The scope of this book does not allow space enough to deal with this rich tradition of thought; I will just sketch some of the major strands for you here in order to place the presentations of this chapter in their broader context. I also hope this may whet your appetite to dig more deeply. Political philosophy of earlier eras is worth reading partly for its own sake, to see how intelligent people dealt with the problems they faced. But it also often applies, by analogy, to problems we face today. Thomas Hobbes, for example, struggled in the sixteenth century with the problem of what obligation and obedience he owed to the king of England. Today, we have kings only in a few countries, but we do have governments, and what obedience we owe to governments, whether deliberate disobedience of a government's laws is legitimate, and so on are live political questions.

The Greeks were the first great political philosophers, especially the Greeks of Athens a few centuries before the birth of Christ. They were especially concerned with the nature of justice and with the question of what sort of constitution would produce the best political community. Plato (428–347 B.C.) was the greatest of the Athenian philosophers. In *The Republic,* he describes a utopian political community in which good, gifted people are selected as infants to be the leaders ("guardians") and are carefully trained (their reading censored, their minds honed by the study of mathematics) so that they will be able to rule wisely and autocratically. His was an ideal world, not likely to be accomplished in fact. It is reminiscent of modern conservatism.

While Plato sought for the ideal, Aristotle (384–322 B.C.), another great Athenian, restricted himself more to observations of the world around him. Aristotle thought that if people could be trusted to rule unselfishly, the best constitution was one in which a single person ruled; the next best was aristocracy, the rule of the few; and the least good was rule by a large number of people. In practice, however, people were selfish, and Aristotle argued that—because the perversion of the best leads to the worst—selfish rule by a single person was worse than selfish rule by a large number. Therefore, in the end he argued for something like democracy.

With their concerns about the proper role of citizens, about the nature of justice, and about what sort of constitution produces a good community and good people, the Greeks laid the foundation for Western political philosophy that followed. During the Roman Empire, relatively little was done in this area, the Romans tending simply to rely on what the Greeks had already done. With the coming of the Christian church in the first centuries after Christ, however, a new period of activity began. The development of a church that claimed allegiance from people all over Europe raised to the forefront the question of just what obligation people bore to their *earthly* rulers. If they were ruled by God in Christ, why should they do what their king told them to do? What should they do, for instance, if ordered by their king to do something that was a sin?

Much of the development of political philosophy for a thousand years or so centered on this question, and the answers shifted as the relative power of the church and of secular rulers waxed and waned. Early Christian writers, perhaps reflecting the weakness of the young church, claimed a rather modest role for the church in the affairs of this world. The greatest of these writers was Saint Augustine (354–430), who argued that government was made necessary by humanity's sinfulness and that only once we were without sin could we be ruled by God. To Augustine, government was a necessary evil (*made* necessary by evil), which at least produced internal order for sinful humanity.

As the church grew in power, popes sought to assert more authority over secular rulers. By the Middle Ages, Saint Thomas Aquinas (1225–1274) was asserting that the church was responsible for people's spiritual well-being and rulers were responsible for their physical well-being; since the spiritual was more important than the physical, however, rulers must be guided by the church whenever the church held that spiritual needs were involved.

The church was not without opposition in this thrust, of course, especially as it weakened in later centuries. A curious and famous response to it was that of Niccoló Machiavelli (1469–1527), who wished to help kings resist the church and wrote *The Prince,* a primer of how to be a successful king, to help them. In it he argued that a king should be ruthless and pragmatic, not swayed by sentiment or morality.

Toward the end of the Middle Ages, and as Europe entered the modern period, kings grew stronger and the church weakened. This became particularly clear during the Reformation, when the historic Catholic Church was replaced in much of northern Europe by local Protestant churches established by local kings. The pendulum of political philosophy swung back against the church, as in the writings of Martin Luther

---

Analytic Political Philosophy

Much work in the study of political philosophy is of the sort presented in this chapter—a history of the development of political ideas, with critical commentary on them. An alternative way of approaching the study draws its inspiration from the modern school of "analytic philosophy," which concerns itself especially with the meaning of words.

This approach, called "analytic political philosophy," does not primarily concern itself with the history of political ideas or with critical argument about them at a general level. Rather, its practitioners feel that they can contribute most to our understanding of politics by clarifying the language we use when we talk about politics. Certainly, a problem of muddled language lies behind many political arguments. The United States calls itself a "democracy," and so did the Soviet Union throughout the post–World War II period until its dissolution. The two meant quite different things by the word, but this was often forgot-

ten in red-faced arguments along the lines of "We're a democracy!" "Are not!" "Are!" "Aren't!"

Some questions commonly dealt with by analytic political philosophers are, What is the state? (you will have a taste of the complexities of this question in Chapter 3) and, more important, What are our *obligations* to the state? What is the "public interest"? What should be considered "rights," as in "human rights"? What should be meant by "equality"? And so on.

One excellent example of work in the mode of analytic political philosophy is Hannah Pitkin's study, *The Concept of Representation,* in which the author examines the varied ways in which, over the last several centuries, the word *representation* has been used to make clear what general, central meaning it has.[1] A useful collection of analytic works is *Political Philosophy,* edited by Anthony Quinton.[2]

[1]Hannah Pitkin, *The Concept of Representation* (Berkeley: University of California Press, 1967).
[2]Anthony Quinton, ed., *Political Philosophy* (Oxford, England: Oxford University Press, 1967).

(1483–1546), who returned to Saint Augustine's doctrine that government is a necessity to which even faithful Christians should submit.

As kings became more powerful, questions of political philosophy shifted to what obligations people in general bore to *them.* This question was brought to a head in the English Civil War (1647–1649), in which a diverse group of opponents to the king succeeded in deposing him and set up a republic that lasted for a bit over a decade. This successful challenge to royal authority focused attention on the question of the duties owed to kings and eventually led to the development of liberalism, discussed previously.

One particularly important writer who participated in this debate was Thomas Hobbes (1588–1679), author of *Leviathan,* a strangely modern defense of authority. (Hobbes does not specify whether that authority must be vested in a king.) His argument is as follows: All people are selfish; in the absence of authority they will turn on each other, and life will be "solitary, poor, nasty, brutish, and short." To avoid this, people voluntarily band together into states and contract to give their rights to a sovereign, who will rule autocratically to provide peace and order for all. Hobbes's theory was intended primarily to justify the rule of kings, but it could be used to justify any sort of dictatorship. Of their free wills, by a cooperative decision, the people set up a power to dominate them for the common good.

With the questioning of royal authority at this time, the stage was set for the development of liberalism and of the other modern ideologies responding to liberalism; the bulk of this chapter has dealt with these ideologies. But while these ideologies have dominated political discourse in this century, they do not represent some kind of final stage of philosophical development. Ideologies are always rooted in the social challenges of their time, and at the end of the twentieth century numerous new questions of political philosophy arose that may go on to dominate political discourse in the twenty-first. Chief among these are a number of issues having to do with identity: feminist political theory, theories of politics based on a religion such as Islam, and theories of multiethnic politics. Emerging problems in the environment also stimulate philosophical discussion, especially regarding the question of what one generation owes the next.

The one sure thing is that as the new discourse develops, it will build on and absorb the old, just as liberalism, conservatism, and socialism did over the past couple of centuries.

FURTHER READING

Arendt, Hannah. *The Origins of Totalitarianism.* New York: Harcourt Brace, 1951.

Berlin, Isaiah. "Does Political Theory Still Exist?" In *Philosophy, Politics, and Society,* 2d series. Ed. P. Laslett and W. G. Runciman. Oxford, England: Basil Blackwell, 1962.

Bronowski, Jacob, and Mazlish, Bruce. *The Western Intellectual Tradition.* New York: Harper & Row, 1960.

Cassels, Alan. *Fascism.* Arlington Heights, Ill.: Harlan Davidson, 1985.

Conover, Pamela Johnston, and Feldman, Stanley. "Belief System Organization in the American Electorate: An Alternate Approach." In *The Electorate Reconsidered,* edited by John C. Pierce and John L. Sullivan. Beverly Hills, Calif.: Sage, 1980.

Dahl, Robert. *A Preface to Democratic Theory.* Chicago: University of Chicago Press, 1956.

———. *On Democracy.* New Haven: Yale University Press, 1998.

Ebenstein, Alan; Ebenstein, William; and Fogelman, Edwin. *Today's Isms,* 11th ed. Upper Saddle River, N.J.: Prentice-Hall, 2001.

Laqueur, Walter, ed. *Fascism: A Reader's Guide.* Berkeley: University of California Press, 1976.

Plamenatz, J. "The Uses of Political Theory." *Political Studies* 8 (1960): 37–47.

Rawls, John. *Political Liberalism.* New York: Columbia University Press, 1993.

———. *A Theory of Justice.* Cambridge, Mass.: Belknap, 1971.

Riker, William. *Liberalism Against Populism.* San Francisco: Freeman, 1982.

Sibley, Mulford Q. *Political Ideas and Ideologies.* New York: Harper & Row, 1970.

Strauss, Leo. "What Is Political Philosophy?" *Journal of Politics* 19 (August 1957): 343–68.

Voegelin, Eric. *Order and History.* Baton Rouge: Louisiana State University Press, 1956.

Wolin, Sheldon S. *Politics and Vision.* Boston: Little, Brown, 1960.

 WEBSITES OF INTEREST

Turn Left (American liberalism):
http://www.turnleft.com/liberal.html

Right Side (American conservatism):
http://www.rtside.com/

American political thought:
http://www.geocities.com/Heartland/Fields/9206/welcome.html

General resources in political philosophy:
http://www.ucd.ie/~politics/polphil.html

PART TWO

THE STATE AND
PUBLIC POLICY

3

THE MODERN STATE

In this book, I will focus on the politics of the *state*—rather than on "office politics," politics in the family, and so on—simply because the state has come to play such a central role in modern politics.[1]

The extent to which the state has come to dominate our attention is evident even in the way we treat individuals. When we think about a person who comes from a different country, we are likely to think of him or her primarily in terms of this—to the exclusion of other characteristics that may actually have more to do with what the person is like. If you knew a Danish engineer named Ole, for instance, and were asked to say quickly, in one word, what Ole is, you would be likely to say "a Dane." The other likely answer would be "a man"; gender has not given way even to the state in the amount of attention we give it. Ole is an engineer, and that should say a lot about him; but not many people would choose that over his nationality as a label for him. He may be a Lutheran or a Jew, pious or apathetic, tall or short, a charmer or a clod; still, most people who know him would characterize him first as a Dane. This does not make much sense, because almost all the other things mentioned would have told you more about Ole's personality or person than does the fact that he is a Dane. It is a result not of logic but of our modern fixation on nationality and the state.

If you have ever lived abroad, you will have noticed this phenomenon in a particularly striking way. Most of us do not ordinarily think of ourselves in terms of the state to which we belong. However, let us reside in a different state, and suddenly our native state becomes a most important aspect of our identity. Canadians living in the United States or Europe begin to think of themselves much more as Canadians than they ever have before, Nigerians studying or working in the United States suddenly begin to think of themselves as Nigerians, Americans living in Europe or Asia suddenly feel themselves to be vividly American, and so on. When everyone you meet responds to you as a Nigerian or an American, it is hard not to start feeling that way about yourself.

---

[1]As noted in Chapter 1, the word *state* as used here does not refer to a place such as California or Pennsylvania. Rather, it means approximately what is often called a "country," such as Canada, Nigeria, or the United States of America.

Our fixation on the state goes almost beyond what reason would dictate. We have seen that we could say more about Ole if we characterized him as tall or university educated than merely as a Dane. Another paradoxical result of our fixation on the state is that most people pay a good deal more attention to the national government, which is remote and inaccessible to them, than they do to their relatively more accessible local governments. In America, politics and attention to politics reach a peak every four years at the election of a new president. This national event so seizes our attention that enrollment in political science courses at American universities generally follows a four-year cycle, rising 10 percent or so in a presidential election year! Americans turn out to vote in considerably larger numbers at presidential than at local elections.

The paradox in such attention to national politics is that in a country as large as the United States, an individual voter has almost no chance of affecting the outcome of a national election. As a character in Skinner's *Walden Two* remarks to his friend,

> "How is the people's will ascertained? In an election. But what a travesty! In a small committee meeting, or even a town hall, I can see some point in voting, especially on a yes-or-no question. But fifty million voters choosing a president—that's quite another thing."
>
> "I can't see that the number of voters changes the principle," said Castle.

"The chance that one man's vote will decide the issue in a national election," said Frazier, speaking very deliberately, "is less than the chance that he will be killed on his way to the polls."[2]

By contrast, an individual voter in a modest-sized city has a small but significant chance of casting the deciding vote in a local election, where perhaps ten or twenty thousand other people will vote in the same election. One can also reasonably argue that the policies of local government are just as important as the policies of the national government. It is true that foreign policy and issues of war or peace, the state of the national economy, and the broad issues of social policy—all the purview of the national government—are extremely important to people's lives. However, the policies of local government are also important. The public schools, the condition of the street in front of your house, the purity and taste of your drinking water, how you are treated by police officers—all these and more are decided by your local government.

How odd, then, that most people pay so much more attention to their national than to their local government. This is just further evidence that our focus on the state and its operations goes beyond the demands of reason.

The people of the world have not always been so thoroughly organized into states. In the remainder of this chapter, we shall look at the history of how the modern system of states arose; we shall then consider the relationship between the modern state and "nationalism"; finally, we shall look at contemporary challenges to the state and emerging political forms that might serve as alternatives to the state.

THE DEVELOPMENT OF THE MODERN STATE

The invention of this thing to which we pay so much attention, the state, is fairly recent. Six or seven hundred years ago, people did not think of themselves as belonging to a state or nation as we know it. Most people lived on subsistence farms, intimately concerned with the village in which they lived but not caring much about the world beyond. Armies sometimes raided the village, but it did not make much difference to the villagers whether the army was hired by the king of France, by the pope, or by the Inca king. Barbara Tuchman's picture of today's "France" as it existed in the fourteenth century depicts a geographic region carved into various political divisions that might be controlled by the English king or by the French and whose populations did not seem to care much which of these was their ruler.[3]

In the fourteenth and fifteenth centuries, as European kings began to claim greater powers and to tighten their control over large territories, these shifting political divisions began to coalesce into states. Even in Europe, however, it was not until the early nineteenth century that states were well established in the form we know.

Throughout the early period of state building in Europe, populations continued to be largely indifferent about the state to which they belonged. During the early stages of its formation, for example, the state of Prussia was spread in little smears and droplets all over the map of northern Europe (see Figure 3–1), and this did not especially concern the Prussians. Some of these regions had been acquired for the crown by royal marriages,

---

[2]B. F. Skinner, *Walden Two* (New York: Macmillan, 1948), pp. 220–21.
[3]Barbara W. Tuchman, *A Distant Mirror: The Calamitous Fourteenth Century* (New York: Knopf, 1978).

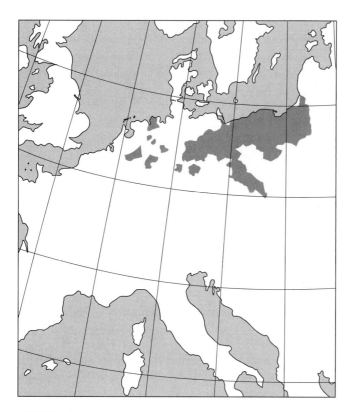

FIGURE 3–1
Prussia in 1789.

others by settlements of war or debt, and the people living in them were transferred like property from one ruler to another.

If ordinary people did not care much about the state, the leaders and the educated elite also saw it more as a convenience than as something special. This was particularly true early in its formation, but to some extent it remained true even as late as the eighteenth century. At the beginning of the period of state building, most members of the elite, if they could write, wrote in Latin rather than in their local tongue. Although daring writers such as Dante were breaking out in their local languages by the fourteenth century, most writers still tended to think of themselves well into the seventeenth century as belonging primarily to a cosmopolitan, European literary world rather than to a local English, French, or Spanish community.

The kings who were creating these new states often had family ties or other interests that took priority over their state. As late as 1714, a German line of kings whose members could not even speak English for the first generation came to power in England. Later, during World War I (after Britain and Germany had evolved into modern states), it would prove an embarrassment to the British royal house that the kaiser of Germany was their cousin—so much so that they changed their name from Hanover to Windsor.

Even military affairs were not as clearly divided by state through much of this period as they were at the end. Foreign mercenaries were an important part of most wars: Bands of English soldiers could be hired by the French king to fight the English, and vice versa. In the American Revolution, the king of England hired German troops (the Hessian soldiers) to do some of the fighting in America.

It was not until the early nineteenth century that the state as we know it could be seen—a relatively large territory with stable boundaries, whose people were bound together by intricate political ties and who thought of themselves distinctively in terms of the state to which they belonged.

The invention of modern states in Europe may be said to have been completed by Napoleon from 1800 to 1815. In France, he created one of the first recognizably modern states by joining the excitement and the passions of the French Revolution to an active and efficient bureaucracy and army. The resulting state was nearly invincible and succeeded in conquering most of Europe. Its power rested partly on the first European army whose members fought not only for what they themselves might gain but for their nation—*France*. The modern state had finally emerged. Even after Napoleon eventually overreached himself and was defeated, things could never be the same. He had demonstrated what could be accomplished by a full-fledged state, and the new or remaining states that emerged after 1815 tried, some eagerly and some with more hesitation, to emulate his method of organization.

Although the modern state had finally been invented in Europe and North America by the early nineteenth century, most other peoples of the world still lived under a variety of other arrangements. However, a great surge of European colonial expansion during the eighteenth and nineteenth centuries had divided the rest of the world into colonies organized somewhat as subsidiary states. When, in the twentieth century, European power waned as a result of two disastrous world wars, these colonies were able to break away and establish themselves as independent. Then their new leaders, almost all of whom had been educated in Europe, adopted the state as their own form of political organization. The modern state became the universal form of political organization.

You should not underestimate how novel this new way of organizing people's lives and efforts was. As Joel Migdal puts it (somewhat slyly):

> Unlike most premodern political structures, the state has aimed to impose uniform and ultimate conformity on social life within far-reaching (but still circumscribed) boundaries: Its leaders have sought obedience in even the most personal realms of social interaction, from whom one might sleep with to how one must bury the dead. Compliance to these sorts of social norms was not new, but the claims of a single centralized organization to enforce such norms over huge territorial expanses were novel almost everywhere they were made. And, indeed, one can point to real cases in which this kind of microregulation has been successfully achieved. Astonishingly, some states have been able to garner from people's yearly earnings a share equivalent to all their work performed through April or May or, sometimes, even June of that year and to sequester their children for 30 or so hours a week in a state institution. Premodern political leaders could not have imagined such audacious goals.[4]

---

[4]Joel Migdal, "Studying the State," *Comparative Politics: Rationality, Culture, and Structure,* ed. Mark Irving Lichbach and Alan S. Zuckerman (Cambridge, England: Cambridge University Press, 1997), p. 209.

THE ORIGIN OF STATES

What was it that led to the invention of the state over the last several centuries? Perhaps an exploration of this question will help us to better understand the nature of the state. There has long been a vigorous debate among scholars as to why states developed in Europe.[5] However, one thing is clear: The modern state developed there along with the coming of industry and of complicated commercial arrangements. Large-scale industry and commerce could be carried on most easily among large populations whose members could be held together with minimal difficulty and who were willing to have their economic activities coordinated. If most economic activity consisted of subsistence farming, cottage weaving, coastal fishing from small boats, and so on, almost any form of political organization would do. However, as larger-scale, more complicated economic operations developed, something like the state offered important advantages.

With the development of the state, merchants and industrialists could draw on a large, uniformly treated population as their pool of laborers, and they could sell their products across a large market subject to a single set of laws. Goods could be transported readily, without being subject to special taxes or duties as they passed from one part of the state to another. On the greater scale made possible by the modern state, large factories and ships could be built, and these could be involved in complex nets of transactions. Industry and commerce thus benefited from the development of the state.

In this sense, then, modern industry and commerce *needed* something like the state, and this partly explains why it developed when it did. However, modern industry and commerce also made the state *possible* by providing the hardware, the technology, and above all the ease of communication by which a large, widespread population could be readily controlled by an army. Before the coming of modern communications, it was difficult for the government of a state of even moderate size to control the population with any exactness. As late as the early nineteenth century, it took a stagecoach three days to cross southern England. Under those circumstances, the government's control was necessarily loose. With the coming of the railroad and the telegraph in the nineteenth century, however, governments could keep an instantaneous check on what was happening throughout their realm and could move troops rapidly to any trouble spot.

We can see that the relationship between the modern state and modern commerce and industry can be interpreted in two ways. On the one hand, commerce and industry needed something like the state, and so the state was invented. It emerged because it was an appropriate choice. On the other hand, modern commerce and industry made it easier to control people and seize taxes from them, and so the state was able to develop. Governments were able to spread their power more widely. Probably both explanations carry part of the truth. These interpretations embody "choice," and

---

[5]This theme and the theme of the next paragraph are well developed in Tilly (1992). In general, recent studies of the establishment of states in early modern Europe have emphasized the new possibilities for coercion in the 1500s much more than the new needs of society, so I am something of an outlier in my interpretation above. Two other good examples are Anderson (1974) and Ertman (1997).

The Marxist Theory of the State

In this chapter, the state has been interpreted partly as being made possible by modern military technology and communications and partly as required by modern commerce and industry. Another way of interpreting the rise of the state is offered by Marxist socialism. (See the fuller treatment of Marx and socialism offered in Chapter 2.)

Marx thought that modern society consisted of one class (the capitalists) dominating another (the workers). The workers had to be controlled because of the tensions caused by this domination, and for this the state was needed. The state keeps the workers under control partly by repression (the police) and partly by integrating them into the prevailing system by convincing them, in school and by other means, that their current situation is good.

Marx thought that eventually the workers would revolt and set up a socialist system in which one class would no longer dominate another. Then the state would have become unnecessary and would wither away through disuse.

This theory sees the state solely as an instrument of power and it does not analyze public choice. As you saw in Chapter 2, this is generally true of Marxist theory, which interprets politics solely as a matter of power.

Further readings in the Marxist theory of the state are Ernest Mandel, *Late Capitalism* (London: NLB, 1975), chap. 15; and V. I. Lenin, "State and Revolution," in *Sources in Twentieth-Century Political Thought,* ed. Henry Kariel (New York: Free Press, 1964).

"power," the two sides of politics introduced in Chapter 1. To the extent one believes that the state emerged because it was made necessary by the modern economy, its invention represents politics as choice. To the extent one believes that it developed because people could now be controlled more easily, it represents politics as power. Different scholars will lean more to one or another of these points of view. In extreme cases, such as that noted in the box headed "The Marxist Theory of the State," some may hold that one of the viewpoints explains everything; but to go wholly one way or another is probably a distortion.

"STATE," "NATION," AND THE "NATION-STATE"

Up to this point the word *state* has not been defined precisely, although we have considered the modern state, its development, and its characteristics at some length.

We will now distinguish between *nation* and *state*. We often use these terms loosely as synonyms, along with the more common word *country,* and they are clearly related. As one example of the relationship between the two, we will later in this chapter label as "nationalism" a passionate identification with the state. In fact, in ordinary conversation, most people use the words *state, nation,* and *country* interchangeably.

However, *nation* and *state* have more precise meanings for political scientists. A nation is *a large group of people who are bound together, and recognize a similarity among themselves, because of a common culture; in particular, a common language seems important in creating nationhood.* A state, on the other hand, is *a political unit that has ultimate sovereignty—that is, a political unit that has ultimate responsibility for the conduct of its own affairs.* France is a state, Brazil is a state, the United States of America is a state. The Jewish people do not make up a state, since they are not a political unit, but Israel is a state. General Motors and Exxon are not states, though they are large organizations. Chicago is not a state, although it is a political unit. It lacks sovereignty (the ultimate responsibility for the conduct of its own affairs) because another government, represented by the Supreme Court and the U.S. Army, has the right to intervene and force decisions on Chicago should that be necessary. A nation is a *cultural* and especially a linguistic grouping of people who feel that they belong together; a state is a *political* unit with sovereignty. Though we have this straight for our purposes, I must admit that the mixing of the terms in everyday use does cause confusion. Some of that confusion will be unavoidable in the rest of this book. The United Nations is an organization of states, for example, not of nations. We will still call it the United Nations, however, because that is what it calls itself!

One reason *state* and *nation* tend to commingle in common use is that leaders of states have almost universally tried to link the two to harness the emotional attachment of people to their nation and use that attachment to build support for the more abstract, legal entity—the state. If a state can coincide with a nation, then the state's leaders can more easily obtain acquiescence in the laws of the state and can build positive support in willingness to serve in the armed forces, pay taxes, and so on. It is striking and somewhat disturbing to see how much the modern state has been able in this way to enlist its people to its cause.

Figure 3–2 shows a linguistic map of Europe. Some apparent nations spread across the boundaries of states. For instance, the German language and culture spread well beyond the boundaries of Germany. Austria, a large part of Switzerland, and a small part of Italy are German, and there are pockets of German population across Eastern Europe. The Basques are spread across northwest Spain and southwest France. Switzerland encompasses a variety of linguistic groups that might qualify as nations.

Correspondence between nation and state is particularly loose in Africa and Asia. The boundaries of many African and Asian states are left over from the older colonial era, when they were drawn by the colonizing powers to suit their own convenience.[6] Thus, a crazy quilt of boundaries was superimposed on the land, with little regard for the culturally coherent groups of people living there. Once they regained their independence, of course, those people inherited these peculiar boundaries. The map of Nigeria in Figure 3–3 illustrates the loose correspondence between nation and state that exists in much of Africa today. In the Mideast, Turkey, Iraq, and Iran are home to parts of the Kurdish people, who are a minority in each of these countries and have made attempts to break away and form their own unified state. India includes fifteen official linguistic groups. Many other former colonies exhibit similar mixtures of state and nation.

With the modern importance of nationalism, we have come to think it a right of people, if they feel that they have a common nationality, to have a state to match that nationality. This "right" has become a constant source of political tension and conflict for two reasons. First, as just pointed out, many state boundaries do not coincide with the geographic

---

[6]The correspondence between state and nation is reasonably close in South and Central America, for an unhappy reason: Here the native population was either exterminated, to be replaced by a reasonably coherent population of settlers from Europe, or over a period of centuries, absorbed culturally in a *mestizo* blend of natives and Europeans.

FIGURE 3–2
Linguistic map of Europe: Note that languages tend to coincide with states' borders, but matchup is by no means perfect.

Source: From Kingsbury, *An Atlas of European Affairs.* Copyright © 1964 by Praeger Publishers. Reproduced by permission of Greenwood Publishing Group, Inc., Westport, CT.

distribution of nations. And second, the sense of nationhood is a subjective thing. A "feeling" on the part of a group of people may be stimulated or laid to rest by persuasive leaders and is therefore liable to change. Even if state boundaries could ever at any one time be brought into a perfect fit with the distribution of nations, this benign situation could not last, because new nations would gradually be invented and some old ones would fade and be forgotten. The small black nationalist movement in the United States is just one example of an attempt to arouse a "nation" (the nation of blacks) among a people who had not generally thought of themselves as belonging to a separate nation.

Main Ethnic Groups
Ibo
Hausa–Fulani
Yoruba
Minor Ethnic Groups
Kanuri
Nupe
Tiv
Ijaw, Ibibio, Efik
Edo
Other
Federal Capital Territory ✱

FIGURE 3–3

Ethnic map of Nigeria.

Source: From the *Wilson Quarterly,* Winter 1980. Copyright © 1980 by the Woodrow Wilson Institutional Center for Scholars. Reprinted with permission.

Another good example is Belgium, where the French- and Dutch-speaking regions of the state coexisted without much notice for a long time but then became agitated about their separate nationalities in the 1970s. Today they operate with such autonomy that they have almost become separate states within the state of Belgium.

At any given time, then, the system of states will not coincide with the system of nations. Points at which state and nation fail to coincide are likely to be hot spots politi-cally; indeed, many of the most intense political struggles in the present era have resulted from such situations. The movement to separate Quebec from the rest of Canada; the war between East and West Pakistan, which resulted in the formation of a new state, Bangladesh; the Basque nationalist movement in Spain; the conflict between French- and Dutch-speaking Belgians; the civil war in Nigeria in 1967; the activities of the Palestine Liberation Organization, which embodies the desire of Palestinians for a state of their own; the chronic unrest among Kurds in Iraq, Iran, and Turkey; the attempt by the region of Chechnya to secede from Russia; above all, the bloody ethnic wars of the 1990s in Bosnia, Croatia, and Kosovo—these are only a few examples of hot political conflicts occasioned by a disparity between state boundaries and people's sense of nationhood.

One striking, and sometimes disturbing, reality about the modern state is the way it has been able to enlist its people in its cause. Citizens of a state generally identify themselves strongly with it and will defend it with passion. This passionate identification with a nation, or with a state riding on the coattails of nation, is called "nationalism," and like any passion, it can make people either noble or base. Some have performed great acts of courage and self-sacrifice under the influence of this sentiment, and others have carried out cowardly assassinations and brutal massacres under the same influence. Whether it makes people noble or ignoble, nationalism is undeniably convenient for governments. It predisposes a large and varied population to obey the single government of the state; and if the state is attacked from outside, nationalist passion makes the defending soldiers a more formidable force than they would otherwise be. Therefore, all governments try to encourage nationalism—not necessarily a hate of others, but at least a national pride—by holding parades, using national symbols such as the flag, presenting the state's history to schoolchildren, and so on.[7]

Benedict Anderson points out that nationalism (even though it is an "ism") is more akin in many ways to a religious identity than to an ideology like conservatism or socialism.[8] It obviously reaches deeply into people's psyches, because men and women have often been willing to die for their nation. Anderson argues that ideologies, which mostly address the distribution of power and rewards among different groups of people, leave out an important part of people's lives—the deep, cyclical mysteries of death, procreation, birth and a continuity that extends beyond our own lives. For many centuries, religion met these needs, and when religion began to decline in the latter part of the eighteenth century in Europe, nationalism arose (or was created) to take its place. Like religion, nationalism offers an identity that takes us beyond ourselves and builds something that lasts across generations.

We have always been ambivalent about nationalism. Consider the two sides presented in the following quotations. The first is Sir Walter Scott's celebration of patriotism in his *Lay of the Last Minstrel:*

Breathes there the man, with soul so dead,
Who never to himself hath said,
This is my own, my native land!
Whose heart hath ne'er within him burned,
As home his footsteps he hath turned,
From wandering on a foreign strand!
[Such a man] concentered all in self,
Living, shall forfeit fair renown,
And, doubly dying, shall go down
To the vile dust, from whence he sprung,
Unwept, unhonoured, and unsung.[9]

---

[7]There is a large literature on what causes nationalism and how nationalist sentiments are maintained. See, for instance, Hugh Seton-Watson, *Nations and States: An Enquiry into the Origins of Nations and the Politics of Nationalism* (Boulder, Colo.: Westview Press, 1977); Tom Nairn, *The Break-up of Britain* (London: Verso, 1977); E. J. Hobsbawm, *Nations and Nationalism Since 1780* (Cambridge, England: Cambridge University Press, 1990); Benedict Anderson, *Imagined Communities,* 2d ed. (London: Verso, 1991); and David Laitin, *Identity in Formation: The Russian-Speaking Populations in the Near Abroad* (Ithaca, N.Y.: Cornell University Press, 1998).

[8]Benedict Anderson, *Imagined Communities,* 2d ed. (London: Verso, 1991).

[9]Walter Scott, *The Lay of the Last Minstrel,* canto 6, 1807.

The second gives the view of a cynical spy, portrayed in a novel by Eric Ambler:

> Love of country! There's a curious phrase. Love of a particular patch of earth? Scarcely. Put a German down in a field in Northern France, tell him that it is Hannover, and he cannot contradict you. Love of fellow-countrymen? Surely not. A man will like some of them and dislike others. Love of the country's culture? The men who know most of their countries' cultures are usually the most intelligent and the least patriotic. Love of the country's government? But governments are usually disliked by the people they govern. Love of the country, we see, is merely a sloppy mysticism based on ignorance and fear. It has its uses, of course. When a ruling class wishes a people to do something which that people does not want to do, it appeals to patriotism. And, of course, one of the things that people dislike most is allowing themselves to be killed.[10]

The idea of "nation" has been so adapted to modern states for their own use, especially to tap into the emotion of nationalism that is associated with it, that we often refer today simply to *nation-states.* This use recognizes that every state in the world tries to promote feelings of common nationhood among the people living within its boundaries. There is not a state in the world that is not to some degree a nation-state, and political scientists simply recognize that the basic units we deal with are a combination of state and nation. At the same time, it is good to keep the concepts "state" and "nation" clear because competing claims of nationhood continue to provide one of the strongest challenges to states.

While state leaders would like to enforce a one-to-one correspondence of state and nation, and while this is close enough to being the usual case that we generally use the term *nation-state* to describe the basic political unit, nations do not always or necessarily coincide with the political boundaries of states.

GOVERNMENT AND THE STATE

Who is the state? In the section on " 'State,' 'Nation,' and the 'Nation-State,' " I referred to "the state" acting in various ways; for example, I wrote, "One striking, and sometimes disturbing, reality about the modern state is the way it has been able to enlist its people in its cause." Who is acting here? If the people are the state, what does it mean to say that they enlist themselves to their cause? We defined the state above as a geographical unit of people who have the legal right to make and enforce rules within their boundaries. This definition implies that the state can be thought of in two ways:

- as everyone living in a given territory (the idea of the nation-state, for instance, emphasizes this usage), or
- the governing apparatus that makes and enforces rules.

In the latter vein, when we say "Egypt called for new peace talks in the Mideast," we do not mean that all 68 million Egyptians issued this call; it was the government of Egypt that did so. When we are referring to the *actions* of a state, it is the government we are talking about, because it is the government that acts for a state. This legal right to make

---

[10]Eric Ambler, *Journey into Fear* (New York: Knopf, 1943; rpt. Bantam), p. 166.

and enforce rules is such a central part of our basic definition of "state" that for many purposes, we simply equate the repository of that right (the government) with the state itself;
when we use the word in this way, by "state" we mean the government and bureaucracy.

Thus, the *government* is a key part of the state. The government of a state is a group
of people who have the ultimate authority to act on behalf of the state. (See Chapter 7
for a definition of *authority;* essentially, authority means that the government is regarded
by the people of the state as the appropriate group of people to make decisions for the
state and act on its behalf.) The government are a unique group in the state; only they
have the right to make decisions that everyone in the state has a duty to accept and obey.
When we speak of a state acting—as in the previous example, or as in "South Korea
asked the International Monetary Fund for help in its current crisis"—it is the government to which we refer.

An influential current of thought in political science has sought to sensitize us to the fact
that governments and their bureaucracies are often self-starters in questions of policy—that
they actively develop problems and seek solutions to them, rather than waiting for the
population to come to them with problems. To understand politics properly, according
to this current of thought, we must think of the government and bureaucracy itself as a
participant and claimant in politics, rather than as a passive adjudicator over a political
process that comes from outside it; this is often referred to as the theory of the
"autonomous state."[11] The idea is that the state may participate autonomously in political conflict and decision making.

There is a creative ambiguity here, because this theory requires us to speak of the government and the bureaucracy as the "state," while treating them as autonomous of the
rest of what we also call "state." In effect, we use *state* to mean both a territory and its
people as well as the government that acts on behalf of those people. This should not be
too difficult. In other circumstances, for instance, we are used to saying "the White
House" to signify both a building and the presidency that is headquartered in that building. Recognizing the creative ambiguity of our usage helps us address an inherent vague-
ness in our notion that the "state" acts—that it does things. In the example of the state
"enlisting its people to its cause," for example, the actions of the state in fostering nationalism come largely from government and bureaucracy (in outlawing burning of the flag,
for instance) but also to some extent from a broader group including television announc-
ers, religious leaders, teachers, and writers (as in the quotation from Sir Walter Scott).
The theory of the autonomous state helps sensitize us to this problem, but it cannot
answer it finally, because there is an inherent ambiguity in whom we mean when we
refer to the state as acting.

Another good thing about the theory of the autonomous state is that it emphasizes for
us that the government and bureaucracy may often participate in politics directly, as
claimants on their own behalf.[12] Especially in new states where diverse populations have
been thrown together into a state and where there is little consensus about proper directions to take, the state apparatus may be forced to (or find itself free to) govern in an

---

[11]P. B. Evans, D. Rueschmayer, and Theda Skocpol, eds., *Bringing the State Back In* (Cambridge, England: Cambridge University Press, 1985).

[12]This is especially relevant to the discussion of "pluralism" in Chapter 13.

authoritarian way.[13] Under these circumstances, free from the constraint of shared traditions and norms, governments sometimes pursue policies benefiting their own personal or class interests in a fairly direct way, which adds to the problems of the new state. This is part of what is going on in the example of Nigeria at the end of this chapter. Another example would be the Philippine government's charge that Ferdinand Marcos stole several billion dollars from the government during the period of his rule or the protected business interests of the family of President Suharto that came to light in the financial crisis of Indonesia in 1997. Some governments have even savaged the people of their state to further their own ends. Between 1975 and 1979, the government of Cambodia killed about 3 million people (out of a population of 9 million) in its effort to establish a new socialist society. From 1991 to 1994, Haiti's military government encouraged systematic terrorizing of the democratic opposition by troops and thugs.

Thinking of the government (and associated bureaucracy, media, public institutions, etc.) as "the state" is also useful because it allows us to draw a distinction between "state" and "society." As we have seen, the state is a set of legal arrangements involving sovereignty and embodied in a government. However, the people of the state have a *society* of personal, social, and economic interactions that is partially independent of the people's organization into a state. For instance, from 1989 to 1993, Czechoslovakia was organized as a single state. In 1993, it split into two states: the Slovak Republic and the Czech Republic. Before and after the split, the people of Czechoslovakia were involved in families, friendships, clubs, and economic arrangements (jobs, investments, etc.) that were only indirectly affected by the nature of state organization. A family that was spread across the new border did not cease to function as a family, for instance, merely because of the new state arrangements.

There is usually some tension between society and state. It is often thought that if "society" is too strong—that is, if pressure groups and special interests can easily force their views on the government—the state will be ineffective and will not be able to make clear policies. This is often cited as the reason the United States has difficulty setting clear economic policies and energy policies, for example. A reverse problem is that totalitarian states sometimes seek total control of society (this is why they are called "totalitarian"). Hitler's Germany abolished many private clubs and all labor unions, setting up instead its own organizations; it tried to undermine the family by drawing children away from their parents and into the Hitler Youth organizations.

This subtle distinction between state and society is a central concern in many theories of democratization and of economic policy making. We will see it again in Chapter 5, for instance, in our analysis of the economic progress of China and South Korea. The distinction is hard to express other than through the theory of the autonomous state.

---

[13]Here is another nice contrasting example of alternative "choice" and "power" interpretations of a political situation. In this sentence, I was uncertain whether to characterize the government as "forced" to govern in an authoritarian way (which would suggest that they were seeking the best public outcome and that circumstances forced them into authoritarian rule: a choice perspective) or to characterize them as "free" to govern in an authoritarian way (which would suggest that they were self-seeking and took advantage of the chance that was available to them to initiate authoritarian rule: a power perspective).

Opening Olympics ceremonies, Los Angeles, California.
(Douglas Kirkland/Corbis/Sygma)

CHALLENGES TO THE STATE

The state may have evolved over the last few centuries to be the dominant form of political organization, but today it is under strong challenge from above and below.

Above the state, world leaders are groping for structures that would replace many
functions of states and operate over a wider geographic range than the state. This has
developed especially in economic matters. In Europe, a European union established by
fifteen states (with another dozen or more trying to get into it) is in the process of taking over much of its member states' control of their own economies (discussed later). In
North America, the United States, Canada, and Mexico have established a free trade
zone within which trade will not be regulated by the governments. Worldwide, the International Monetary Fund (IMF) puts restrictions on its members' policies (Russia and
other parts of the former Soviet Union joined in 1993, expanding the influence of the
IMF). In the area of environmental regulation, many cross-state bodies have been
formed through which states give up their individual control of migratory species of
wildlife, the production of pollutants, and so on. The challenge from above is not only
in economic areas of policy. Across North Africa, the Middle East, and southern Asia,
militant Islam—the most dynamic religion in the world—seeks to replace the secular
states of the postwar period with religious political structures in which the state plays a
relatively minor role, state boundaries would (ideally) fade, and the Islamic community
would be ruled throughout by its religious leaders.

The state is also under attack from below. Far from fading away with the development of modern economies, as most scholars of all stripes thought they would do, ethnic and regional separatist movements have grown explosively. From the Walloons in

Belgium to Tamil separatists in Sri Lanka, to French Canadians in Quebec, to the Croatians and Slovenians in former Yugoslavia, to the Eritreans in Ethiopia, to the Baltic republics in the former Soviet Union—the list could include dozens of other examples—regional or ethnic aspirations, which many years ago were quiet, built up over the 1980s and 1990s into serious political movements capable at the least of paralyzing their states.

What has been happening? Why the challenges to the state? One way to look at it is to note ways in which the state may have become less valuable in meeting societies' needs. This could help explain the challenge from "above" and the challenge from "below." From above, a series of environmental problems have appeared that are clearly going to become even more pressing in future years and are not readily dealt with by individual states. Swedish trees are dying because of pollution from industry in Britain, Germany, and other states; the chimney swift, which breeds in Canada and the United States but winters in eastern Peru, may cross the boundaries of eleven states in its annual migration; "greenhouse" gases warm every state in the world, regardless of whether they helped to produce them. These are problems that need broader, more overarching political structures.

Economically, the appropriate scale of industry increased in the twentieth century. Few small states were ever able to develop an automobile industry, for instance. There is no Norwegian auto company or Dutch auto company; auto companies developed mostly in such large states as the United States, Britain, France, Italy, and Japan. Such dynamic industries as nuclear technology, the aircraft industry, and space technology require an even larger scale to work economically. Is it any wonder that states are banding together?

From the other end, the experience of the latter half of the twentieth century was that centralized states were rather clumsy structures for fine-tuning responses to varying local needs in housing, education, health care, and so on. This helped to fuel pressures for local and regional autonomy. Perhaps, too, with a waning of the symbols of nationalism in a world in which most states cannot control their own destinies militarily, ancient local symbolic attachments or religious symbolic attachments have risen more to the fore and have come to satisfy people's yearning for symbolic identity. Thus, from "above"—problems too big for states to deal with—and from "below" at the local level, states find themselves challenged.

The previous paragraphs give rather a "choice"-oriented explanation of challenges to the state: Other structures can meet some of the people's needs better than the state, I have argued, and so they have begun to rival the state. One could also develop a "power"-based explanation: The state really evolved as a military structure; the one thing that defined a state—that still defines *sovereignty*—was that the state wielded a military force that could protect its people against invasion from outside its boundaries and could put down any internal challenge to the government's authority as well. Two developments in the latter half of the twentieth century, both born in the Second World War, have weakened this claim by the state to a monopoly of military power. First, nuclear weapons were invented. In the nuclear age, no government can protect its people against destruction from abroad; it may be able to reply in kind, but it cannot prevent its own destruction. Nuclear weapons are too devastating for that. From the other end, guerrilla warfare came into its own in the Second World War; techniques for local, sustained military effort against superior central forces were developed that are being used today by insurgent local forces in dozens of places around the world. Militarily, the ability of states to control their destinies against other states and against internal insurgency has diminished.

Whether we can better understand this from a "choice" or a "power" perspective, it is clear that the state is seriously challenged.

ARE STATES LOSING THEIR ABILITY TO MAKE ECONOMIC POLICY?

In challenges to the state such as those discussed already, whole functions are taken away from the state (a supranational organization may take over the making of agricultural policy, for instance, as in the example of the European Union discussed later), or the state's sovereignty may be challenged (as in secession movements by regions of the state). But states may also see themselves diminished in another way—not by a formal reallocation of their powers but by the growth of actors and processes they cannot control. In this case, whole areas of policy in which the state might want to act may prove impossible for it to control. The state remains a state; it is just that the range of things the state has the capacity to control may have shrunk. In effect, the state is not challenged in its formal capacity but is hollowed out by a shrinkage in the range of things it can actually do.

It has always been the case that there are limits on states' capacities to control things. No state has ever been able to control the weather, for instance. Before the development of modern theories of contagion, states could not do much about epidemic illnesses. Small states have always had to take into account the wishes of powerful neighboring states, and that has constrained their range of possible actions. The capacity of states to exercise control over things within their boundaries is always shifting, affected greatly by changes in technology. Earlier, for instance, I suggested that it was partly the development of the telegraph, the railroad, and good systems of highways that made possible the expansion of the state's role in the seventeenth and eighteenth centuries.

Today, a number of developments in communications and in the world economy appear to be shrinking the range of state action. In the area of communications, the development of e-mail, the World Wide Web, satellite-transmitted television, and similarly cheap, easy means of communication have cut down on the capacity of states to regulate exchanges of information. Law enforcement agencies in the United States are trying in vain to limit the production and export of encryption software (programs that allow correspondents to write in almost unbreakable code), because they are afraid that once criminals are able to use sophisticated encryption, it will be difficult for police to track their transactions. Many autocratic regimes around the world have tried to limit their people's access to information by jamming television broadcasts, outlawing web access on computers, or even outlawing the use of copy machines. When the communist dictatorship fell in Romania in 1989, for instance, even the nuclear power plant did not have a copy machine! All such efforts are probably futile, however; it is almost impossible to put the genie of technology back in the bottle once it is out.

If the state has seen its power to regulate the exchange of information shrink, however, it is in the area of economic policy that the hollowing out of the modern state has been most pronounced. Regulating the economy is one of the most important functions of states. In fact, Chapter 5 is devoted wholly to the state and the economy. It is generally assumed that the state should set conditions for the operations of the economy within its borders. Who gets the blame if unemployment rises? The government. Who gets the blame if prices rise too high? The government. However, it is rapidly becoming less true that the state controls the operations of its economy. With the development of a large and fluid world economy, the world's investors and capital markets probably determine the state's economic development so strongly that the state—its government, its central bank—actually has only a rather narrow range of choice in economic policies.[14]

As late as 1970, trade (exports plus imports) was only about 8 percent of the U.S. gross national product, but by 1999, it had grown to be about 19 percent. For smaller countries, trade usually bulks even larger; for Denmark in the same year, the sum of exports and imports was 53 percent of the gross national product, and for Belgium, it was 136 percent. The international currency markets *each day* move more than a trillion dollars around the world—far more than any state's government or central bank can command. Most large corporations spread their operations over many states and, as a result, are not under strict control by any one state. In 1973, for instance, the U.S. government tried to order Exxon (an American company) to deliver oil to the United States despite an Arab oil embargo; Exxon replied that it could not do so, because it was subject not only to the laws of the United States but of the other states in which it operated.

Under these circumstances, states have begun to find that if their economic policies are too unlike those of their neighbors or look too suspicious to international investors, then capital flees their country and the economy turns down. As a result, all states have found themselves forced into the same relatively narrow range of economic policy alternatives.

The classic example of this is the socialist regime of Francois Mitterrand in France. In 1981, France elected Mitterrand to be its first socialist president since 1958. He immediately began a fairly radical expansionist and redistributive program. *Family allowances* (cash payments to families with children) were raised by 81 percent over two years. Housing allocations for the poor were raised 25 percent. All workers were given a fifth week of paid vacation. Pensions were increased. As a result of these efforts, unemployment dropped and the economy grew more rapidly than other European economies. Incomes became more equal.

However, the rapid expansion of people's purchasing power led to a surge of imports from other countries. France was soon importing far more than it exported, and the value of its currency dropped. Inflation climbed because this made all imported goods more expensive (each import had to be paid for with more francs). Inflation was also pushed up by the increase in domestic demand.

International investors, fearful that the francs they were holding would lose value because of the inflation, exchanged their francs for dollars, marks, and yen. No one wanted francs, so their value went even lower. Mitterrand's government was faced with a crisis,

[14]This theme is developed especially in Jeffrey A. Frieden, *Debt, Development and Democracy* (Princeton, N.J.: Princeton University Press, 1991); Sven Steinmo, *Taxation and Democracy* (New Haven: Yale University Press, 1993); and Peter Hall, "The Political Economy of Europe in an Era or Interdependence," in *Continuity and Change in Contemporary Capitalism,* ed. Herbert Kitschelt, et al. (New York: Cambridge University Press, 1999).

and within a year of having taken over as president, he abandoned his program to increase jobs and make incomes more equal. Never again in the twelve additional years that Mitterrand served as president would he move far from the middle of the road in economic policy.

A more recent example of international constraints on governmental policy was seen in 1998, when international investors suddenly became concerned about the financial reliability of several Southeast Asian states, such as Thailand, Indonesia, South Korea, and Malaysia, that had been growing rapidly. The investment community pulled out its money, and the economies of these countries went into abrupt recession. It was only after the governments of these states made changes in their financial regulation—especially of banks—that capital returned and a modest economic recovery ensued.

A further constraint on many of the world's poorest states—which might otherwise be expected to be rather experimental and innovative with their economic policies, because their current circumstances are so bad—is that they are by now heavily in debt to richer countries and to international banks. The International Monetary Fund (IMF) monitors these states and sets conditions under which the holders of the debt will be willing to stretch out countries' repayments. The IMF's conditions usually involve cautious economic policies: restraining government spending (especially reducing transfers within the population through subsidies) and raising interest rates to fight inflation. Even though many of these policies will be unpopular, debtor states' governments often feel they must abide by them. The only alternative is to refuse to pay their debts at all, which means no one would lend them anything in the future. That is a dead end because they all need capital if they are to develop their economies.

The overall result of all this has been that the states of the world—from rich, industrial states such as France to poor states such as Côte d'Ivoire—are constrained to follow a more or less uniform set of economic policies, regardless of what their governments might otherwise have wished to do.

This is only the most dramatic instance of a general phenomenon of global politics. As world communications improve and as the world's states come to depend more on each other economically, if we are to understand what happens "within" a state's politics, we must look at least in part to the state's international environment. To paraphrase the British cleric, John Donne: No state is an island, entire of itself. (Even if it *is* an island, a country such as Britain, with total trade equal to 41 percent of its gross national product, can no more ignore the world economy than could Mitterrand's France.)

SOME POSSIBLE ALTERNATIVES

The world is still groping for alternatives to the state. However, the state still has a lot of life left in it; by no means is it clear that it will go away! Four possible alternatives of varying sorts are presented in the following sections:

1. Regional Integration

Many regions in the world have attempted to establish regional organizations that would have at least limited power to overrule and coordinate the actions of their member states. The Organization of American States in North and South America, the African Union, occasional attempts at economic union in Central America, and several abortive attempts to form a united Arab republic all attest to this wish, though none of these has succeeded very well. The European Union, which includes most of Western Europe, has had considerable success at integrating the politics of its member states, so much so that one can at least conceive of a time at which one might ask whether its members were still sovereign states. (The European Union is discussed in greater detail later in this chapter.)

At its best, regional integration would only represent a consolidation of the system of states into a smaller number of larger states. However, this might represent progress in its own right, and the process by which states were brought to yield up portions of their sovereignty voluntarily to a higher organization might teach us much about how the world system as a whole could begin to coordinate its members' activities.

2. The United Nations

There does exist an organization of almost all states of the world that is supposed to stand above them and lead them into peaceful coordination of their activities. The United Nations has little power to force states to cooperate, but it does have considerable persuasive power and has helped at least modestly to defuse several crises that could have led to war. With the decline of Soviet-American rivalry in the 1990s, it has seemed at least conceivable that the United Nations could emerge as a major structuring force in international relations. The United Nations is discussed in more detail in Chapter 18.

3. Communications and a "World Culture"

As electronic communication makes it possible to send messages easily from one end of the world to another, as people travel more widely and observe cultures that are new to them, the world is beginning to develop a more common set of attitudes. Different nations are becoming slightly less distinctive in their points of view. Blue jeans have become almost an international uniform of young people, and English has become an almost universal second language in which business is conducted among strangers. Much cultural richness may be lost in this homogenization, but it may become easier for populations of different states to understand each other's point of view. Too much faith should not be placed in this, however, because conflicts may as easily arise from understanding as from misunderstanding; remember, most murders occur within families. Still, it may be a hopeful sign.

4. An Emerging International Law?

As we will see (p. 378), in the late 1990s, a body of law began to develop that might impose enforceable law on the leaders of states and thus on the states themselves. That is, an international community of law might supplant, or at least take its place alongside, the state as the maker of laws.

A key precedent was set when former Chilean President Augusto Pinochet, leader of a brutal military government, was arrested in Britain for Chile's violation under his presidency of the International Torture Convention; Pinochet was sent back to now-democratic Chile on Chile's promise to try him for the crime. This was the first time that any head of state, except the loser in a war, had been held responsible by the community of states for crimes committed in an official capacity. The Pinochet case was followed in 2001 by the trial in the Netherlands of former president Slobodan Milosevic of Serbia for the forcible deportation or murder of hundreds of thousands of ethnic Albanians in the Serbian province of Kosovo. These cases may be a straw in the wind, but it is still a huge step to consider circumstances in which the sitting leader of a state (as opposed to disgraced former leaders like Pinochet or Milosevic) could be tried for the actions of the state in international tribunals.

THE WEST, THE EAST, AND THE SOUTH

The states of the world have generally been grouped into three broad regions: the West, the East, and the South, the three regions indicated on the map in Figure 3–4. This is a set of categories that originally was based on the now-vanished Cold War between the Soviet Union and the United States. While the categories still make general sense, they are certainly not ideal. In particular, as you will see, the term *South* covers a diverse set of states.

The West comprises the industrialized states of North America and Western Europe, plus Australia, New Zealand, and (probably) Japan. These are economically prosperous states, with a moderate degree of governmental direction in their economies, linked in fairly similar foreign and military policies, often in partnership with the United States.

The East comprises the erstwhile Soviet Union and its former Eastern European satellites. A number of these states are also modestly prosperous, though not so well off as the West. Some others, such as Russia, have struggled to adapt to the shock to their economic systems since the fall of communism. All are involved in a massive effort to democratize their governments and reorient their economies from heavy governmental direction to more open systems like those of the West. Eventually, the East may look a lot like the West, but for now its states bear the mark of seventy years of a very different history.

These two regions make a good deal of sense, in that the states in each have much in common with each other and are different in important ways from the world's other states. The remaining region, the South, is something of a catchall region. During the Cold War, the region was often called the Third World, since the thing that distinguished its members was that they were neither of the West nor of the East. At that time, when the United States and the Soviet Union were trying to enlist other states to join their "side," this distinction may have been important enough in itself; but beyond that, the states had little uniquely in common. In effect, the term *Third World* just meant "none of the above."

South is not a perfect term, either. As you see in Figure 3–4, the states of the South are generally south of those in the West and East, but Australia and New Zealand are great exceptions. *South* also refers to what is often called North–South conflict: a set of economic conflicts over trade and natural resources that generally divide less industrialized states of the South and the industrialized states of the West.

Whatever term one picks, however—*Third World, South,* or something else—this is a region of quite varied states. Over two-thirds of the world's population lives in the South. Politically, the region ranges from still-communist states such as Cuba to conservative monarchies such as Saudi Arabia. Western culture is relatively new to most of the region, but many Latin American states have made active cultural contributions for

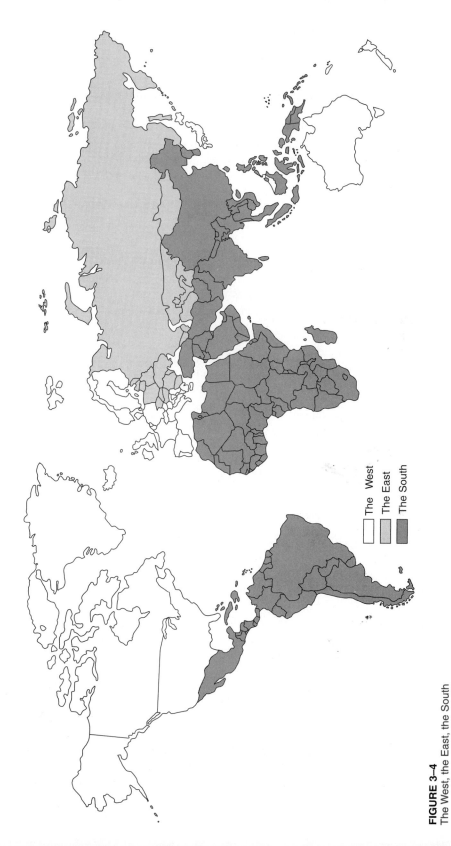

FIGURE 3–4
The West, the East, the South

- The West
- The East
- The South

centuries. Most states of the South are poor, but a number of them have great mineral wealth (such as Saudi Arabia and other oil-producing countries, for example), and some others, such as Argentina, Brazil, Singapore, Malaysia, Thailand, and South Korea have become rather heavily industrialized. Many less developed states of the South depend heavily on exports of raw materials or agricultural products—often on a single product, such as Honduras's bananas or Bolivia's tin—which makes them subject to jolts when commodity prices swing. Most states of the South have rather new political structures, and their populations are often not broadly involved in politics.

Example: State Building in Nigeria

No state's experience has been "typical," but it is useful to look at some examples to flesh out the concepts and analyses you have read so far in this chapter. In this section, we will take a brief look at how the Nigerian state was established; in the next section, we will consider the European Union and how it is drawing a number of Western European states into something new, which is a bit like a much broader "state."

Nigeria is a populous state on the west coast of Africa, with a population of 123 million. One out of five Africans lives in Nigeria, and its gross national product is second on the continent only to that of South Africa. The country is rich in oil, but it has so many people to feed that the average Nigerian is not especially well-off; in 1999, the average annual income was $260 per person.

Until 1960, Nigeria was a British colony; like most colonies, it was not constructed for internal coherence but rather for the administrative convenience of the British. Over 250 different languages and dialects are spoken within its borders, and there is also an important religious split, as the north is primarily Muslim and the south is primarily Christian. After World War II, Britain experimented with various ways of handling this diversity. The plan eventually adopted was a decentralized system under which Nigeria was divided into three regions, each centered on one of the three main ethnic groups (see Figure 3–3): (1) the northern region, based on the Hausa-Fulani, (2) the western region, based on the Yorubas, and (3) the eastern region, based on the Ibos. These regions were administratively distinct, each having its own budget.

This arrangement continued in the initial democratic structure set up in 1960. The central government of the new state left many functions under the control of regional governments, in what is called a "federal" system. The situation was unstable, however, because tensions soon developed among the regions. The democratic procedures that were written into Nigeria's constitution favored the north, because it was the most populous region, and the north quickly established political control under the first prime minister, a northern Muslim named Abubakar Balewa.

However, the Ibos in the eastern region—a restless, economically active, and well-educated minority—felt stifled by the political domination of the north. Ibos all over Nigeria were disproportionately urban and held many technical and administrative positions. Three-quarters of Nigeria's diplomats were from the eastern region, as were about half the students who graduated from Nigerian universities in 1966.[15]

In 1966, a coup by Ibo officers toppled the democratic government and put an Ibo general at the head of the state. Six months later, Muslim soldiers struck back, and a new government under Yakubu Gowon, a northerner but a Christian, was installed. At this point the eastern region seceded from Nigeria and proclaimed itself the state of Biafra. The federal government refused to accept Biafra's right to secede, and there followed a bloody civil war lasting two and a half years in which over a million people died. Eventually, the Ibos were starved out and had to give up on secession. Gowon wisely followed a generous, conciliatory policy toward the defeated province and its leaders, one calculated to make it easy for them to rejoin the rest of the country.

Gowon had promised an eventual return to democracy, but he proved slow to deliver and was ousted in yet another military coup in 1975. He was replaced by General Olusegun Obasanjo, a Yoruba Christian who proceeded carefully to build the basis for a return to democracy. Elected local governments were established, and a new constitution was designed under which regional diversity would be respected in local affairs and no one region could dominate the central government. The state was divided into nineteen federal districts that, to some extent, broke down the old Hausa-Fulani, Yoruba, and Ibo regions. To be elected president, one had to receive not only at least one-third of the total popular vote but also at least one-fourth of the vote in two-thirds of the nineteen regions. Finally, power was divided between the president and a congress, so that regions that had not supported the president had a chance to defend themselves in the congress.

The first presidential election was held in 1979, and a northerner, Sheliu Shagari, was elected. He ruled for four years and was reelected in 1983, but his administration was marked by corruption and economic decay. Many Nigerians—most critically, the military—were dismayed by the greed of the new political class and their inability to overcome the regional/tribal/religious divisions of the country. Shagari's government was overthrown shortly after his reelection in 1983.

From 1983 to 1999, the country was ruled almost continuously by the military. Generally, the military teased the public with promises of democracy while continually delaying its implementation. General Ibrahim Babangida, for instance, who ruled from 1985 to 1993, spent years setting up a structure for elections (including banning all existing politicians from participation and setting up two new, statewide parties—a bizarre way to establish democracy). When the elections were finally held, however, they were promptly annulled by the defense minister, General Sani Abacha, who took power himself. He promised democracy "in the future" but instead established an authoritarian regime. It took his death (of natural causes) in 1998 to allow a new

---

[15]Pauline H. Baker, "Nigeria: Lurching Toward Unity," *Wilson Quarterly* 4 (Winter 1980): 76.

opening in Nigerian politics. Elections were held in 1999, which resulted in the election of Olusegun Obasanjo, a former general but one who had not been implicated in the recent, corrupt regimes. Although Obasanjo is seen as "clean" politically, the election was dominated in all parties by the "big men" who had made money in the corrupt old regimes. Since his election, Obasanjo has moved cautiously to weed out a number of the most corrupt generals and officials.

The generals left things in bad shape for the new democracy. They had proved adept at corruption and holding onto power but little else. General Babangida became a very wealthy man during his eight years in power, but today the Nigerian economy is in deep distress. Oil revenues have declined because the government failed for years to invest in developing the oil and gas fields. The country owes vast debts to foreign lenders, and even as the election was proceeding, the military took many last grabs out of the public pot.

Democratic government is hampered by the religious, ethnic, and regional divisions between the north and the south. Southerners believe that the Muslim north will never allow them to gain power. (Babangida and Abacha were northerners; Chief Moshood K. O. Abiola, the winner of the annulled 1993 election who died in jail during the military regime, was from the south. The new president, Olusegun Obasanjo, is from the south but was attacked as a turncoat supporter of the north during the election and got few votes in the south.) Northerners fear that since the south has the oil and most of the economic activity of the state, they will be left with nothing if they give up political power to the south.

Example: State Building in the European Union[16]

The European Union (E.U.) is an association of fifteen states in Western Europe that have agreed to coordinate much of their economic policy and some other policy areas; toward this end, they have set up a weak governmental structure that has some limited power over the governments of the member states. The Union is of particular interest to political scientists because it represents the most serious experiment to date in getting states to give up some of their sovereignty voluntarily.

There had been mutterings about the need to unify Europe throughout the nineteenth and early twentieth centuries, but the first real push to do so came after World War II. Many people thought that France and Germany, which had twice in the century fought disastrously against one another, should be bound together in such a way that war between them would be inconceivable. Also, the advantages of operating as a large economic unit, with a single free market open to all, were obvious to those who were trying to rebuild Europe after the war.

With encouragement and some pressure from the American side, what would grow into the European Union was established in 1956. A French administrator, Jean Mon-

---

[16]Until 1993, this was called the "European Community."

net, was a key figure in this. He had led several European states through earlier cooperative efforts in coordinating their policies on coal, steel, and nuclear power to a
point at which they were willing to merge much of their economic policy making. Initially, only six states were members—West Germany, France, Italy, the Netherlands,
Belgium, and Luxembourg. To Monnet's great disappointment, Great Britain refused
at that time to join.

The main economic agreement among the initial members was that all trade would
flow freely within their borders. That is, no member could place a tariff on imports
of a product from another member to discourage local people from buying it. All the
combined populations of the six member states were freely available as customers to
any producer in any member state. Also, the member states soon coordinated their
agricultural policy, giving up control of most agricultural policy within their borders
to the governmental structure of the Union. It is the Union government that decides
how high price supports will be for a given commodity, what will be charged for that
commodity abroad, and so on. The Common Agricultural Policy was a breakthrough
in regional integration, although it has proved in practice to be cumbersome and
expensive, leading to large production surpluses and to high prices for consumers.

For about thirty years, the Union largely treaded water, gradually building somewhat greater institutional power but remaining held in check by strong nationalist
sentiments on the part of some member states, especially France. During this relatively stagnant time, the entrance of Britain, Ireland, Denmark, Portugal, Greece and
Spain was probably the biggest change to occur in the Union. Starting in 1985,
however, the Union entered a fifteen-year period of intense reform and institution-
building. Many internal barriers to trade were eliminated; the powers of the European
Parliament were increased (see below); decision-making rules that had protected the
special interests of member states were relaxed; and finally in 1999, the member
states adopted a single common currency to replace the separate currencies of twelve
of the fifteen member states. (Britain, Denmark and Sweden decided to opt out.)
These changes were significant, and difficult to achieve; the new treaties barely survived a referendum in France, and it took two tries to pass them in a referendum in
Denmark. But pass they did, and the end result is that much of Europe will soon have
something like a single economy; and politically, it will be approaching something
like a state.

Another huge change in the Union is the prospect of a great deal of further expansion of membership in the near future. Ten mostly poor states from Eastern Europe have
applied to join the Union and have been promised eventual admission by the Union.
These states will increase the population of the E.U. by about 30 percent but will only
increase gross domestic product (GDP) by about 4 percent. They will need a lot of help
in developing to the economic level of older members, and their disparate political and
economic interests are also likely to complicate decision making in the Union.

Though it will need to be changed substantially once these additional ten states
join, the current government structure of the Union has stood almost unchanged
since the original six countries set up the Common Market in 1956. The two most
important parts of the Union government are the Commission and the European
Council, which make most of the rules and carry out executive functions. Two

other parts are the Parliament and the Court of Justice. These have lesser powers but are still important.

The European Commission consists of twenty appointed commissioners who head a bureaucracy of about fourteen thousand people. Commissioners are appointed by their home governments for a term of four years, but they must swear an oath to act on a European basis rather than in the interests of their home country. In practice, the commission has been the focal point of broad European interests, as opposed to national interests. In this it has been cheered on by its thousands of bureaucrats, whose lives and careers are bound up in the Union. The commission has consistently pushed for a blending of states in the Union and has frequently been opposed in this by one or more member states fearful of giving up too much sovereignty.

The Commission has a great deal of power. It dominates the setting of most of the Union budget ($100 billion in 2000) and makes many rules. As the only permanent part of the executive branch of the Union's government, it also takes the lead in initiating new proposals for policy.

The other part of the executive is the European Council, in which national interests are represented. It consists of the foreign ministers of the member states; these meet together several times a year to consider proposals from the Commission.[17]

Any major policy proposal must be approved by the Council before it can go into effect. The Council votes on proposals, with large states getting extra votes. For many years, there was an unwritten rule that any state could veto a proposal if the proposal affected what the state considered to be a "vital national interest." This practice was canceled, however, as part of the 1993 package of political reforms to achieve closer political union. Over the years, the European Council, with its emphasis on states' governments and their needs, has tended to retard the blending of the Union, but it has probably also made possible such blending as has occurred. Without this haven for the individual interests of member states, the Union might have fallen apart long ago.

The Union also has a parliament, but until recently it did not have much legislative power. Policies of the Commission and Council are debated and criticized in the parliament, but the parliament does not have the final say over most decisions. For instance, it has final authority over only about 40 percent of the Union's budget. A change made in 1979, however, began a process of increasing the power of the European Parliament that continues today. Before 1979, members of the European Parliament were chosen by the parliaments of their home countries, but since then, the members have been directly elected by voters in their countries. While this was not a change that directly gave the European Parliament any new powers, it indirectly did a great deal. The members of the European Parliament are now the only officials of the Union who are elected, who are there because some ordinary people wanted them to be there. This gives them an advantage in prestige and standing, and has attracted more able, vigorous members. (In the earlier period, membership in the European Parliament was sometimes a way for a country's parties to kick their more tired members upstairs.) Since 1979, the European

---

[17]In addition, four times a year the Council consists of the prime ministers of the fifteen states. Important questions are saved for these "summit" meetings.

Parliament has used this new vigor to push for a greater role in the Union's decisions, and recent years have been marked by considerable squabbling between this body and the Council and Commission.

The European Parliament gained greater powers after 1993, and it appears to be slowly developing into a powerful body. The expanded power of the Union vis-à-vis member states, brought about by the expansion of its powers in economic and monetary policy, has led to a concern for the "democratic deficit"—the fact that national parliaments have less control now over their states' economies and that the E.U. itself, with its strong bureaucracy, has little democratic accountability. Expanding the power of the European Parliament, the only E.U. institution that is elected, would be a natural way to address this problem. The Parliament took a big step toward exercising greater power when in 1999 it forced the resignation of all twenty members of the commission over charges of corruption in one office. However, the Parliament is still limited by the power of the member states and by the fact that over half of the budget is outside its control. It walks a tightrope but has been steadily increasing its power.

Finally, the European Court of Justice is a court of twelve justices serving six-year terms. It rules on disputes over the treaties the states signed on joining the Union. Most cases that come before the Court involve trade problems, but it also decides disputes among the governing institutions of the Union and about the individual rights of citizens in the member states. Over the years, the Court has pretty well established itself as dominant over the states' governments, although it has had to tread cautiously to avoid stepping on any government's toes. While the Court has been careful in approaching difficult cases, some of the cases it has decided have demonstrated an astonishing willingness on the part of member states to subordinate themselves to the Union's laws. Court decisions have included such questions as whether British teachers could legally whip their students, how soldiers could be disciplined in the Netherlands, and the conditions under which people could be put in prison to await trial in West Germany. (For a more detailed discussion of the European Court of Justice, see Chapter 17.)

The original six members of the Union prospered economically after 1956, and gradually other states joined, until the Union reached its present size of fifteen states. Together, the members of the European Union have great strength. As seen in Table 3–1, the members of the Union combined have a population greater than that of the United States; they have more people under arms, and their combined gross domestic products are only slightly smaller. If they could pursue a unified foreign policy and develop a full-scale strategic nuclear force, they would be a superpower similar to the United States.

TABLE 3–1   EUROPEAN UNION COMPARED WITH THE UNITED STATES

	Total population	Total armed forces	Total gross domestic product (billions of dollars)	Defense expenditures (billions of dollars)
U.S.A.	275,636,000	1,365,800	$9152	$275.5
E.U.	375,751,000	1,693,609	$8493	155.0

Sources: International Institute for Strategic Studies, *The Military Balance 2000-2001* (Oxford: Oxford University Press, 2001); World Bank, *World Development Indicators 2001* (Washington: World Bank, 2001.)

How close is the European Union to being something like a state? Clearly, the member states have given up a good deal of their sovereignty to the Union. The Union has independent taxing powers, collecting a sales tax of just over 1 percent to finance its operation. It sets its members' tariff and trade policies and their policies on agricultural price supports, and it regulates many other areas of daily life. For twelve of the fifteen members, the Union sets financial policy and maintains a unified currency. The European Court of Justice has successfully imposed surprisingly political judgments on member states. On the other hand, military control is the real core of statehood; in that area, the Union has not developed any control over its members. Most—but not all—members of the Union are also members of the NATO alliance. However, even NATO has not been very successful at coordinating its members' military policies. (It has been difficult for NATO even to establish a standard caliber for rifle bullets, so its members could exchange ammunition in time of war.) With the end of the Cold War, however, the United States has become more detached from European defense; in 1991, it started a gradual reduction of 50 percent of its troops stationed in Europe. With the United States lessening its commitment, there might emerge more real military coordination among the Union members, and indeed, by 2003, the Union will have established its first common military force, a small mobile unit of 60,000 soldiers. Just what the E.U. will become is still open to the tides and chance of time. Today it illustrates nicely the gray area in which it may become difficult to distinguish clearly when a state is a state.

FURTHER READING

Anderson, Benedict. *Imagined Communities: Reflections on the Origin and Spread of Nationalism,* rev. ed. New York: Verso, 1991.

Cederman, Lars-Erik. *Emergent Actors in World Politics: How States and Nations Develop and Dissolve.* Princeton, N.J.: Princeton University Press, 1997.

Deutsch, Karl. *Nationalism and Social Communication.* Cambridge, Mass.: MIT Press, 1953.

Dinan, Desmond. *Ever Closer Union: An Introduction to European Integration.* Boulder, Colo.: Lynn Rienner Publishers, 1999.

Ertman, Thomas. *Birth of the Leviathan.* New York: Cambridge University Press, 1997.

Evans, P. B.; Reuschmayer, D.; and Skocpol, Theda, eds. *Bringing the State Back In.* New York: Cambridge University Press, 1990.

Gellner, Ernest. *Nations and Nationalism.* Ithaca, N.Y.: Cornell University Press, 1983.

Herz, John H. *The Nation-State and the Crisis of World Politics.* New York: David McKay, 1976.

Hobsbawm, E. J. *Nations and Nationalism Since 1780: Programme, Myth, Reality.* New York: Cambridge University Press, 1990.

Jackman, Robert W. *Power Without Force: The Political Capacity of Nation-States.* Ann Arbor: University of Michigan Press, 1993.

Krasner, Stephen D. "Approaches to the State: Alternative Conceptions and Historical Dynamics." *Comparative Politics* 17 (1984): 223–46.

Mandel, Ernest. *Late Capitalism.* London: NLB, 1975, chap. 15.

Migdal, Joel. *Strong Societies and Weak States: State-Society Relations and State Capabilities in the Third World.* Princeton, N.J.: Princeton University Press, 1988.

————. "Studying the State." In *Comparative Politics: Rationality, Culture, and Structure,* edited by Mark Lichbach and Alan Zuckerman. New York: Cambridge University Press, 1997.

Motyl, Alexander J., ed. *Encyclopedia of Nationalism.* San Diego, Calif.: Academic Press, 2000.

Nettl, J. P. "The State as a Conceptual Variable." *World Politics* 20 (July 1968): 559–92.

Scott, James C. *The Moral Economy of the Peasant.* New Haven: Yale University Press, 1976.

Skocpol, Theda. *States and Social Revolutions.* New York: Cambridge University Press, 1979.

Skowronek, Stephen. *Building a New American State: The Expansion of National Administrative Capacities, 1877-1920.* New York: Cambridge University Press, 1982.

Tilly, Charles. *Coercion, Capital, and European States, A.D. 990-1992.* Cambridge, Mass.: Blackwell, 1992.

Van Creveld, Martin. *The Rise and Decline of the State.* New York: Cambridge University Press, 1999.

Wallerstein, Immanuel. *The Capitalist World Economy.* New York: Cambridge University Press, 1979.

WEBSITES FOR THE EUROPEAN UNION AND NIGERIA

A guide to governmental and nongovernmental websites on Nigerian politics: *http://www.agora.stm.it /politic/nigeria.htm*

A well-organized guide to the multifarious websites of different parts of the European Union governance structure: *http://www.europa.eu.int/*

4

POLICIES OF THE STATE

In Chapter 3, we saw that the modern state is a relatively recent invention. It developed gradually over the last several centuries and is still developing as people come to expect the state to take care of more aspects of their lives and as military operations—the special purview of the state—become more complex and expensive. In this chapter, we shall survey some of the most important policies of modern states to consider the variety of things the state does today.

Figure 4–1 charts the growth of state activity since the nineteenth century for Great Britain, Sweden, and the United States.

The most interesting thing about the figure is that these three countries have developed in much the same way, though they have had quite different types of governments and their experiences during the twentieth century varied a great deal. Britain had a socialist government from 1945 to 1951 and intermittently after that. Sweden was ruled uninterruptedly by a socialist party from 1932 to 1976 and intermittently thereafter, and is well known for its wide-ranging welfare state. The United States, on the other hand, has never had a socialist government, though the New Deal after 1932 was strongly oriented toward reform and the expansion of social programs. Britain and the United States participated in both world wars, while Sweden was neutral in both. Despite these political and historical differences, the three countries show a rather similar expansion of state activity. During the latter part of the nineteenth century and into the early twentieth, all three devoted a stable and relatively small percentage of their wealth to the government: approximately 8 to 10 percent of all economic activity. Beginning about the time of World War I, however, governmental spending began to take up more and more of the economy, until by the 1990s, it accounted for 40 percent (U.S.A.) to 61 percent (Sweden) of all economic activity.

The two world wars appear to have contributed to this growth. Britain showed great jumps in the government's role in the economy at both wars, while the United States surged at the Second World War. (The United States entered World War I only near the end of the war.) When the governments' roles subsided again after the wars, they generally did not return to the same levels as before. This pattern is more pronounced in the

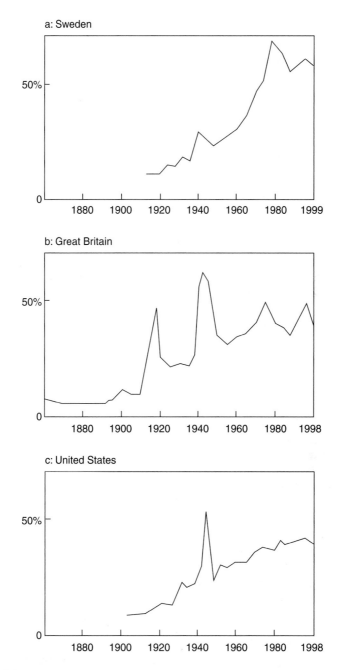

FIGURE 4–1

Government expenditures as a percentage of gross domestic product.

Source: U.S. Department of Commerce, *Historical Statistics of the United States;* Peter Flora ed., *State, Economy, and Society in Western Europe, 1815–1975* (London: MacMillan, 1983); International Monetary Fund, *Government Finance Statistics Yearbook 2000.*

British case, but it is evident in both. The lasting expansion of government as a result of these wars is probably due not only to the actual expenditures in the wars but also to the fact that in the "total warfare" of the twentieth century, governments became accustomed to controlling the lives of their people rather directly—rationing the goods they could buy, telling them what jobs they could work at, and so on. After the wars, the governments continued to intervene actively in people's lives and extended this intervention to a range of other policies as well.

Sweden was neutral during both wars, and so the conflicts did not have the same effect on Sweden as they had on Britain and the United States. However, Sweden, too, left behind the stable, low level of expenditure that had characterized its public sector in the earlier part of the period and, with a socialist government, began in the 1930s a steady increase in the government's share of the economy. By the 1960s, this had brought Sweden up to the same levels as the other two countries, and during the 1970s, Sweden surpassed both.

A strong governmental role in society appeared to be typical of industrialized democracies late in the twentieth century. When we note that 40 percent of the U.S. gross national product consisted of governmental expenditures, this means that well over one-third of all purchasing of goods and services was done by the government. There seems to be a strong pressure in industrialized democracies to expand the role of the state. This was well illustrated by Sweden in the late 1970s. In 1976, a nonsocialist government replaced the Socialists, who had been in power almost continuously since 1932. This new government had pledged to avoid expanding the role of government, but as Sweden entered a period of economic difficulty and businesses looked as though they might fail, the government felt it had to take over some of them and keep them going to prevent unemployment. Thus, the *non*socialist government ended up nationalizing a number of industries, including the country's largest shipbuilding firm.

As a result of such pressures, to which all industrialized democracies seem to be subject, the industrialized democracies do not vary a great deal with regard to the degree of governmental involvement in society and the economy. In all of them, the governmental role expanded greatly during the twentieth century and is now very large. We do see some reaction to the great expansion in a modest downward movement in the charts for Britain under Margaret Thatcher in the 1980s and for Sweden after 1978, a point at which governmental expenditures had risen to two-thirds of the gross domestic product (GDP). Obviously, the government's share of the economy cannot rise indefinitely, and resistance does build up. Still, the norm does seem to be substantial governmental involvement; by about 1999, the three countries for which we have information in Figure 4–1 ranged from 36 percent of GDP (U.S.A.) to 58 percent (Sweden). These figures actually represent a small pullback due to reductions in military spending in the aftermath of the Cold War's end and perhaps due also to the thrust of neoliberalism, with its attendant welfare reforms in the United States, and shrinkage of the welfare state in Sweden; in 1996, the similar figures had been 40 percent (U.S.A.) and 61 percent (Sweden).

In addition to this expansion of the government's role in the industrialized democracies, an even more marked expansion of this kind occurred with the establishment of communist governments in sixteen countries during the twentieth century. Most of these systems, however—at least, those in Europe—have now been engaged for the last decade in a massive move in the opposite direction, privatizing firms that had been owned and run by the state. This effort has dwarfed the rather small privatization movement that also occurred in many Western democracies. Conservative British Prime Minister Margaret Thatcher, for instance, privatized two dozen firms over a twelve-year period; Poland privatized over three thousand in just a couple of years.

I cannot present figures to measure the role the state had in communist societies, as I did for industrialized democracies in Figure 4–1, because the state was so closely enmeshed in a communist economy that one could not clearly delineate where state spending ended and private spending began. It is enough for our purposes here to realize that in communist systems, the state played a dominant role. However, it is also worth remembering that even in the communist systems, the state did not control everything that happened, either in the economy or in other affairs. In all the communist systems, there was some private economic activity. For instance, about 25 percent of agricultural production in the Soviet Union came from small plots (accounting for only 2 percent of the arable land!) that peasants were allowed to farm for profit. In Poland, almost all farms were privately owned. Apart from such exceptions, however, the coming of communism inevitably meant a massive expansion of the role of government.

If the industrialized democracies are similar with regard to the extent of governmental activity, the picture is different among states of the South. Here, there is a wider range of governmental activity, and governmental involvement is generally lower than it is in the industrialized democracies. Table 4–1 gives a few examples.

As we have seen, the South is a bit of a catchall category, and the politics of the countries grouped in this category varies greatly. The extent of governmental activity in the economy varies just as greatly, and it is hard to come up with explanations for this. It is perhaps no surprise that the Democratic Republic of Congo, which has been governed by primitive military dictatorships, does not have an especially active government; but then why does democratic India have a governmental profile that is not all that much higher than Congo's?

TABLE 4–1   CENTRAL GOVERNMENT'S REVENUES AS A PERCENTAGE OF THE GROSS DOMESTIC PRODUCT IN SELECTED STATES OF THE SOUTH, LATE 1990s

Country	Government's percent of economic activity	Location	Democratic/non since 1975
Democratic Republic of Congo	10%	Africa	nondemocratic
Thailand	16	Asia	mixed
Egypt	26	Middle East	nondemocratic
Israel	42	Middle East	democratic
Dominican Republic	17	South America	democratic
Argentina	14	South America	mixed
India	12	Asia	democratic

Source: World Bank. *World Development Indicators, 2001;* "Democratic/non since 1975," adapted from Adam Przeworski, et al., *Democracy and Development* (New York: Cambridge University Press, 2000), appendix 1.2.

Whereas the politics of industrialized democracies involves a rather standard set of pressures from business, interest groups, and the international community—which result in a similar level of governmental activity from one such country to the next—politics in the South is more variable, less developed, and more fluid. Thus, it is more difficult to generalize about politics of the South than about the politics of either industrialized democracies or the old communist systems.

WHAT DO GOVERNMENTS DO?

We have seen that governments became much larger in the twentieth century. What is it that these governments do? In general, their activities fall under four main headings, in order of the degree of governmental intervention: transfer of resources, subsidies with strings attached, regulation, and development and administration.

1. Transfer of Resources

A government often takes resources from some people and gives them to others without offering much direction as to what the transferred resources are to be used for. An American example of this is the Social Security system, which taxes employers and their workers, and gives the proceeds of the tax to retired people, the disabled, and the survivors of wage earners who have died young.

2. Subsidies with Strings Attached

As a somewhat more active form of intervention, the government may provide money to some of the people, but with the requirement that it be used in certain ways. The U.S. government provided a series of subsidies to Chrysler Corporation in the early 1980s, for instance, but with the requirement that Chrysler cut its costs, hold down wage increases, and so on. With its liberal tradition, the United States has been a bit reluctant to impose such state guidance, but in many other countries, the practice is quite pervasive. In the Scandinavian countries, for example, complex sets of purposive subsidies direct most aspects of the economy. As one example, the Norwegian government—as part of a general campaign over the postwar period to keep the population from concentrating in the southeast, in the vicinity of Oslo—has provided a state subsidy on all milk produced in the western part of the country. This has had the two desired effects: (1) Milk prices have stayed low for the consumer; and (2) the dairy industry in the east was destroyed, helping to keep the population more evenly distributed. Such governmental intervention is not free; tax money is used to pay the subsidy, and many dairy farmers in the east suffered from the change.

Frequently, government subsidies occur not as direct payments but as *tax expenditures,* reductions in taxes for people who use their money in certain approved ways. In the United States, taxpayers have been encouraged by targeted reductions in their taxes to do such things as buy municipal bonds, invest in oil companies, and make their homes energy efficient.

'HOW D'YA LIKE THAT? MOSCOW SAYS TO FORGET ABOUT COMMUNISM — THEY WERE JUST KIDDING.'

(Auth © 1976 *Philadelphia Inquirer.* Reprinted with permission of Universal Press Syndicate. All rights reserved.)

3. Regulation

The government may also directly lay down rules telling people how to conduct their affairs. Traditional areas of regulation prohibit crimes such as murder, theft, or extortion. The twentieth century saw an explosion of regulatory activity beyond this traditional sphere everywhere; many countries now regulate the way in which foods may be prepared or packaged, what sorts of things may be printed in books or newspapers, what type of access the handicapped must have to business premises, how many pollutants may be emitted into the air, and so on.

Regulations have rectified many abuses. In many countries, the air is cleaner, children are safer, food is more accurately labeled, workers are less vulnerable to injury—all because of government regulation. However, regulation, too, is not free. It does not cost the government a great deal to set and administer regulations, but critics charge that the complicated mass of regulations that exists in many countries channels too much of the people's effort into keeping records, paying for lawyers and courts, and so on.

A rough measure of the growth of regulatory activity in the United States is the number of pages in the annual *Federal Register.* This is a publication of the General Services Administration, which updates rules and regulations set by the federal government. Table 4–2 presents the number of pages published in the *Federal Register* during selected years. Note especially the huge growth in regulatory activity from 1966 to 1975 and the slight reduction under the Reagan and Bush administrations in the 1980s.

TABLE 4–2   PAGES CONTAINED IN SELECTED
YEARS OF THE *FEDERAL REGISTER*

1936	2,355
1946	14,528
1956	10,528
1966	16,850
1975	60,221
1984	50,997
1990	53,618
1998	72,356

Source: Morris P. Florina, *Congress: Keystone of the Wash-ington Establishment,* p. 93. Copyright © 1977 Yale University Press. Adapted with permission.

4. Development and Administration

Finally, the government is not restricted merely to supervising how other people conduct their affairs but may step in and do the job itself. Defense and diplomacy are obvious areas where the government must do this, and education is another activity in which governments have felt that they must be active. (In the latter case, however, they have not felt the need to have a monopoly. In the United States, for instance, significant numbers of children are educated in private or parochial schools.)

There are other, more controversial areas in which some governments have chosen to develop and administer programs themselves. Especially notable is nationalization, by which a government takes over one or another industry—the trains, the steel industry, auto manufacturing—and runs it. The intent is that the industry should then be operated for the public good rather than for private gain, but nationalized industries have not performed well. Critics charge, on the one hand, that nationalization makes the management of the industry cumbersome and inefficient and, on the other hand, that the civil servants who run the nationalized industries do not do things very differently than the old "selfish" managers did. Following a flurry of nationalization after socialist parties came to power (after World War II in Europe or on the establishment of national independence in the states of the South), nationalization has gone rather out of vogue. In the late 1970s and early 1980s, however, many European countries felt that they had to nationalize numerous industries to keep them from going bankrupt and putting their employees out of work. This is a shortsighted policy, because it means that inefficient businesses are kept in operation with the public absorbing their losses; but it is understandable that governments would not want to see large numbers of workers lose their jobs all at once.

Most countries, in both the South and Europe, have traditionally had more of their industry nationalized than the United States does. In France, for example, until the 1990s, the following industries were operated wholly or largely by the state: insurance, banking, automobile manufacturing, air transport, the railroads, natural gas, electricity, and coal. During the 1990s, a few of these were partially privatized. But France still retains a much greater range of publicly operated industries than the United States, with

---

Why are the World's States Expanding?

Almost all states in the world are expanding in the degree to which they intervene in their people's lives. Why this is so is a challenging puzzle for political scientists. David Cameron ("The Expansion of the Public Economy: A Comparative Analysis," *American Political Science Review* 72 [December 1978]: 1243–61) reviews five main explanations that have been advanced:

1. As people become more prosperous, they may want more done for them and are willing to pay for it. Therefore, as industrialization makes people more prosperous, the state naturally grows.
2. As governments have become more clever at using "hidden taxes" such as excise taxes and payroll withholding of income taxes, they can get away with taxing people more heavily, and the state grows.
3. Electoral democracy results in a "bidding up" of the state's operations as parties compete to see which can promise more services to the voters.
4. Once governmental bureaucracies are established, they develop internal

pressures for expansion. Inevitably, they succeed in slowly ratcheting upward the scope of their operations.
5. As world trade grows and states' economies become more subject to disruption by events in the international economy, their governments are less able to control what is happening in the state. The governments must then grow to compensate for the greater difficulty they find in functioning.

The jury is out, and will stay out for a long time, as to which among these explanations are valid. For examinations of evidence on the subject, see Cameron's article and also David Lowery and William D. Berry, "The Growth of Government in the United States," *American Journal of Political Science* 27 (November 1983): 665–94.

Of the five proposed explanations, note that numbers 1 and 5 are based on the perspective of politics as choice, numbers 2 and 4 are based on the perspective of politics as power, and number 3 is ambiguous.

Ironically, this expansion has coincided with growing challenges to the state (see pp. 54–58).

---

majority ownership of fifteen hundred companies and a minority stake in thirteen hundred others.[1]

These, then, are the four main forms of governmental activity: transfer of resources, subsidies with strings attached, regulation, and the development and administration of programs. In Chapter 5, we shall look more closely at whether one or another of these forms of activity is preferable. For the remainder of this chapter, let us look a bit more closely at some selected areas of policy to see what sort of attention various governments have paid to them. One broad and important area of policies, economic policy, will be addressed in Chapter 5, "Political Economy of the State."

DEFENSE POLICY

Defense is the one area of policy in which governments have almost without exception proceeded by developing and administering programs themselves and have insisted on holding a monopoly with regard to the policy. Private schools, private hospitals, and so on are sometimes tolerated by governments, but this is practically never true of private armies!

[1]"France's Public Sector: They Love It," *The Economist,* 26 May 2001, p. 50.

As Table 4–3 shows, states vary a great deal in the effort they expend on defense. The industrialized democracies spend a few percent of their GNP on defense. Canada, the United States, and Britain have volunteer armies, and none of the industrialized democracies in Table 4–3 spent more on defense than the United States (3.0 percent of the gross national product in 1999).

Countries of the South vary tremendously in their military expenditures. Paraguay and Madagascar show up as fairly low in Table 4–3, but Israel, Saudi Arabia, North Korea, and Myanmar are quite high. Some parts of the South have been the scene of continuing tensions, with frequent threats of war, and countries in those regions may spend shocking sums on defense. North Korea, in particular, has ruined its economy by its massive military expenditures. In the late 1990s, the country experienced mass starvation while spending as much as a third of its total gross domestic product on defense! In international "hot spots" of East Africa and the Middle East, many countries spend as much as 10 percent of their gross domestic product on defense. Even in calm parts of the world, military dictatorships such as that of Myanmar often support their military constituency with bloated

TABLE 4–3   DEFENSE PREPARATIONS FOR SELECTED STATES, LATE 1990s

	Democratic/non since 1975	Military service	Percent of population in active military	Percent of GDP spent on defense
Russia	mixed	18–24 months	0.7	5.1
Canada	democratic	voluntary	0.2	1.1
France	democratic	10 months	0.5	2.6
Germany	democratic	10 months	0.4	1.6
Great Britain	democratic	voluntary	0.4	2.6
United States	democratic	voluntary	0.5	3.0
Israel*	democratic	men: 3 years	2.8	9.0
		women: 21 months		
Egypt*	nondemocratic	18–36 months	0.7	3.4
Saudi Arabia*	nondemocratic	voluntary	0.6	15.6
Algeria*	nondemocratic	18 months	0.4	6.6
Colombia*	democratic	12–18 months	0.4	2.9
Paraguay*	mixed	12 months	0.4	1.4
South Korea*	mixed	26 months	1.4	2.9
North Korea*	nondemocratic	3–10 years	5.0	14.3
Tanzania*	nondemocratic	2 years (including civil duties)	0.1	1.7
Madagascar*	nondemocratic	18 months (including civil duties)	0.1	0.8
Myanmar*	nondemocratic	voluntary	0.9	6.9

*States of the South.
   Source: International Institute for Strategic Studies, *The Military Balance, 2000–2001* (Oxford University Press, 2001); "Democratic/non since 1975," adapted from Adam Przeworski, et al., *Democracy and Development* (New York: Cambridge University Press, 2000), appendix 1.2.

defense spending. Large defense budgets in poor countries are tragic, because defense spending neither feeds people nor furthers economic development.

The actual use to which this investment in the military is put varies a great deal from one country to another. The two superpowers, the United States and Russia, invested substantially in nuclear weapons and missiles during the Cold War, although they are now cutting back. Beyond this, Russia has always emphasized the development of a large land army, since it had long borders with potential enemies in China and Europe. The United States, with its peaceful borders, has emphasized more the development of its navy, so that it can keep in touch with its allies around the world and support them.

EDUCATION

The most basic service that most governments are expected to offer their people is education. This is a prerequisite of economic development for the country as a whole, and it greatly expands the world of the individuals who are educated. Many nations of the South, whose populations were largely illiterate at the time independence was acquired, have had an uphill fight in bringing education to their peoples.

As Table 4–4 shows, most countries invest a substantial effort in this area of policy and most countries of the South have already accomplished a good deal along these lines.

TABLE 4–4   EDUCATIONAL EFFORT FOR SELECTED STATES, LATE 1990s

	Percent of GDP spent on education	Percent of eligible girls/boys enrolled in primary school*	Percent of eligible girls/boys enrolled in high school*	Adult illiteracy rate (percent)	Democratic/non since 1975
Sweden	8.3	107/106	153/128	—	democratic
Canada	6.9	101/103	105/105	—	democratic
France	6.0	104/106	111/112	—	democratic
Great Britain	5.3	116/115	139/120	—	democratic
United States	5.4	101/102	97/98	—	democratic
Turkey**	3.2	104/111	48/68	15	mixed
Egypt**	4.8	94/107	70/80	45	nondemocratic
South Africa**	8.0	131/135	103/88	15	mixed
Nicaragua**	3.9	102/100	62/52	36	mixed
Indonesia**	1.4	111/116	48/55	13	nondemocratic
Mozambique**	4.1	50/70	5/9	56	nondemocratic
Botswana**	8.6	108/107	68/61	23	democratic
Chile**	3.6	100/103	78/72	4	mixed

*May exceed 100 percent because it is the "gross" percent: total enrollment in a grade (of whatever ages) divided by the population of the age at which one would normally attend that grade. Percents greater than 100 generally mean that the state is attempting to catch up with older students (including adults) who missed out on education at their "proper" age.

**States of the South.

Source: UNESCO, Statistical Yearbook, 1999; "Democratic/non since 1975," adapted from Adam Przeworski, et al., Democracy and Development (New York: Cambridge University Press, 2000), appendix 1.2.

Others have had to overcome great difficulties. One of these, Botswana, clearly exemplifies the problems faced by a poor state in attempting to educate its people. It takes almost 9 percent of Botswana's gross domestic product to provide sufficient education. Even at that, not many frills are possible; only 61 percent of boys between the ages of fourteen and seventeen were enrolled in school. However, 77 percent of adults can read, a dramatic improvement over the illiteracy rate at the time the country attained independence. A state such as Nicaragua shows a different face. Though it is a richer country than Botswana, only 3.9 percent of Nicaragua's gross domestic product is spent on education. Only half of its young people are enrolled in high school, and one-third of its adults are illiterate.

The effectiveness of states' education policies are dealt with in detail in an example at the end of this chapter.

RESEARCH AND DEVELOPMENT

If states of the South must concentrate on spreading basic education throughout their populations, the more highly developed economies of the industrialized democracies

---

Planning for Environmental Sustainability in Costa Rica[1]

Since the early 1980s Costa Rica has been working hard to transform its consumption patterns to rationalize human uses of natural resources and the environment.

In 1996 the country outlawed leaded petrol and has since cut its lead levels by two-thirds. All vehicles must now pass an annual emissions inspection, new imported cars must have catalytic converters, and industries are required to have systems to treat the contaminants that they produce. Last year the government, responding to citizens' protests, closed the Placer Dome Company's open-pit gold mine because of harm caused to the environment and local inhabitants.

Negative incentives are also used, such as higher import taxes on used imported vehicles without catalytic converters and fines for loggers who cut timber illegally. The hundred cleanest companies in Costa Rica are named annually, and a green seal of quality is given to gas stations with the best records in preventing air and water pollution and in treating waste water. A red stamp is for those with the worst records.

The government and civil society also apply moral suasion by using ad campaigns to convince people that a healthy environment is good in itself, contributes to human well-being and is good for tourism. Civil society, responding to a governmental programme, has organized 36 natural resource vigilance committees nationwide. These groups provide more than 3,000 citizens to serve as voluntary inspectors of natural resource use and compliance with environmental statues.

In the late 1980s, in one year alone, Costa Rica felled 10 million cubic metres of forest, with an estimated timber value of $422 million. In 1988 the Netherlands purchased part of Costa Rica's external debt at a cost of $5 million and then wrote it off on the condition that Costa Rica spend an equivalent amount in local currency on forestry redevelopment. In 1989 Sweden purchased a further $5.5 million of Costa Rica's debt for a similar purpose. Such debt-for-nature swaps are helpful but need to be pursued on a much broader scale.

Home to about 5% of the world's species of flora and fauna, Costa Rica has been a global leader in environmental sustainability, setting aside about 25% of the country as conservation or protected areas and arranging debt-for-nature swaps.

[1]United Nations Development Programme, *Human Development Report, 1998* Copyright © 1999 by Oxford University Press. p. 99. Used by permission of Oxford University Press, Inc.
Source: Crocker, Camacho and Romero 1997.

Peruvian schoolchildren.
(Paul Conklin)

depend on continuing technological development to give them a competitive edge in making high-tech goods (computers, electrical machinery, aircraft, etc.) for export. In most of these developed economies, labor costs are too high to allow basic industries such as the manufacture of clothing or of simple plastic goods to be competitive internationally. States of the South can produce such goods much more cheaply. The special province of the developed economies is in the production of high-tech goods and services, where their scientific and technological capacities allow them to outperform everyone else.

Table 4–5 shows how dependent the industrialized democracies, in particular, are on high-tech industry for their trade with other states. Over a third of the United States' manufactured exports were high-tech goods in 1999. And in addition, American firms netted over $23 billion through selling licenses for technical processes. This shows up in the fourth column of Table 4–5, "Net gain (over expenditure) in license fees, 1997." Brazil's companies, in contrast, paid out $1,252 million more than they earned in license fees.

A fascinating example, however, of a Southern state that has successfully established an embryonic high-tech industry is Costa Rica.[2] In the mid-1980s, the country cut its tariffs on computers from 133 percent to 10 percent in a successful effort to encourage computer use and literacy. The government assigns every Costa Rican an e-mail address that

[2]"Who Says the Chips Are Down?" *BusinessWeek,* 10 September 2001, p. 68E2.

TABLE 4–5 INVOLVEMENT OF SELECTED STATES IN RESEARCH AND DEVELOPMENT, LATE 1990s

	Percent of manufactured exports high technology	Scientists and engineers per million population	Government spending on research and development as a percent of GNP	Net gain (over expenditure) in license fees, 1997 (millions of $)	Democratic/non since 1975
Canada	15	2,719	1.7	−$1,424	democratic
France	23	2,659	2.3	−214	democratic
Great Britain	30	2,448	2.0	+1,641	democratic
United States	35	3,676	2.6	+23,192	democratic
Japan	27	4,909	2.8	−1,665	democratic
Egypt*	0	459	0.2	−165	nondemocratic
Madagascar*	3	12	0.2	−9	nondemocratic
Israel*	19	NA	2.4	+5	democratic
Brazil*	13	168	0.8	−1,252	mixed
South Korea*	32	2,193	2.8	−2,206	mixed
India*	6	149	0.7	−292	democratic

*States of the South.
Source: World Bank, *World Development Indicators, 2001;* "Democratic/non since 1975," adapted from Adam Przeworski, et al., *Democracy and Development* (New York: Cambridge University Press, 2000), appendix 1.2.

can be accessed at terminals in all post offices. And, by law, expenditures on education must equal at least 6 percent of the gross domestic product (compare this with other states of the South in Table 4–4). As a result of these and other efforts, technological products have become the largest category of Costa Rica's exports, topping coffee and bananas. Partly this is the result of a large Intel Corporation chip-manufacturing plant that was established in 1997, but partly it is also a result of over 140 locally owned software-development companies.

In all countries, the technology that makes this sort of industry possible is provided partly by government-sponsored research, partly by research carried on directly by the industries involved, and partly by basic research conducted in universities and other institutions of higher education. A good idea of the general level of such activity in a country may be gained by observing the number of scientists and engineers in the population. This figure is displayed for several states in the second column of Table 4–5, which gives the number of scientists and engineers engaged in research and development.

HEALTH AND SOCIAL WELFARE

Most modern states have accepted some responsibility for maintaining their people in reasonable health, in adequate housing, with financial security in their old age, and with some security against disability or disaster. Developed economies devote considerable

TABLE 4–6 SOCIAL WELFARE ACTIVITY BY SELECTED GOVERNMENTS, LATE 1990s

	Percent of governmental expenditures devoted to social security and welfare	Percent of governmental expenditures devoted to housing and community amenities	Democratic/non since 1975
Canada	28.0	2.2	democratic
Germany	37.9	3.7	democratic
Great Britain	35.6	2.9	democratic
United States	21.4	2.1	democratic
South Korea*	10.8	2.3	mixed
Bolivia*	19.0	4.9	mixed
Israel*	22.6	5.6	democratic
Tunisia*	18.8	4.6	nondemocratic
Philippines*	4.2	0.5	mixed
Madagascar*	0.9	0.0	nondemocratic
Syria*	5.4	1.7	nondemocratic

*States of the South.
Source: International Monetary Fund, *Government Finance Statistics Yearbook, 2000* (includes all levels of government); "Democratic/non since 1975," adapted from Adam Przeworski, et al., *Democracy and Development* (New York: Cambridge University Press, 2000), appendix 1.2.

resources to these purposes, while states of the South do not do as much. For the people of many poor states, daily life is a series of catastrophes, and it is all they can do to deal with those, much less prepare for future ones. Governments of the South must often use any surplus funds they have to develop systems of basic education or to build industrial plants for future economic growth. Finally, as we have already seen, many states of the South are burdened with large military budgets. All these circumstances put such strains on the economies of states of the South that social programs are usually put on a back burner.

This pattern is evident in the first column of Table 4–6, which lists the proportion of national budgets devoted to such items as health, recreation, unemployment insurance, pension systems, housing, and so on. The broad pattern is clear: The governments of developed economic systems make a considerable effort to ensure social welfare, whereas the governments of the South do less.

What sorts of things do governments do to promote social welfare? A vast number of programs have been used in one country or another for this purpose. To name a few: Governments may provide child care centers for working parents; psychiatric counseling for emotionally troubled people; medical care for their citizens—as the British government does and as the United States does for poor people and for all people over age sixty-five; governments may build residential housing and offer it at inexpensive rates; governments may give grants of money to all families with children to help them with the costs of child rearing (most European governments do this); governments may provide some sort of minimal national pension for people too old to work; and so on. There is a bewildering array of programs, and countries vary widely in the extent to which they give one or another type of aid. The second column of

TABLE 4–7   HEALTH EXPENDITURES AND OUTCOMES FOR SELECTED STATES

	Government spending on health care, % of GDP 1990–98	Private spending on health care, % of GDP 1990–98	Total spending on health care, % of GDP 1990–98	Life expectancy 1999	Infant mortality (per 1,000 live births) 1999	Democratic/ non since 1975	Per capita income 1999
Japan	5.9	1.6	7.6	81	4	democratic	$32,030
United States	5.8	7.2	13.0	77	7	democratic	31,910
Sweden	6.7	1.3	8.0	79	4	democratic	26,750
Great Britain	5.6	1.1	6.7	77	6	democratic	23,590
Canada	6.4	2.8	9.2	79	5	democratic	20,140
South Korea*	2.3	2.8	5.1	73	8	mixed	8,490
Tunisia*	2.2	2.9	5.1	73	24	nondemocratic	2,090
Philippines*	1.7	2.0	3.7	69	31	mixed	1,050
Bolivia*	4.1	2.4	6.4	62	59	mixed	990
India*	.8	4.2	5.4	63	71	democratic	440
Nigeria*	.8	2.0	2.8	47	83	mixed	260

*States of the South.
  Source: World Bank, *World Development Indicators, 2001;* "Democratic/non since 1975," adapted from Adam Przeworski, et al., *Democracy and Development* (New York: Cambridge University Press, 2000), appendix 1.2.

Table 4–6 illustrates this diversity in one area of social welfare policy, the provision of residential housing. The activity of governments listed in the table varies from Israel, where the government spends over 5 percent of its budget on housing, to Madagascar, where housing receives nothing in the budget.   •

A more detailed look at one area of social policy—the provision of health care—is presented in Table 4–7. The table displays the choice governments make of whether to provide a service directly or allow it to be dealt with privately. Outcomes of health care are also compared here, with life expectancy and infant mortality shown for each country.

In line with what we have seen in other policy areas, general expenditure on health is higher in the richer countries. And we see from the outcomes that this higher expenditure appears to work. Life expectancies are lower at the bottom of the table, and infant mortality rates are higher. The differences in life expectancies and rates of infant mortality between poor countries and rich countries are startling.

On the other hand, there are fairly large variations in expenditure among the rich countries, and among these countries, greater expenditure does *not* necessarily translate into better outcomes. The United States spends far more on health care than any of the other four rich, industrialized countries without achieving any better health outcomes. In a ranking of overall performance put together by the World Health Organization (WHO), the United States ranks thirty-seventh, compared with Japan's rank of tenth, Britain's rank of eighteenth, and Sweden's rank of twenty-third.[3] Of the five rich countries in the table, Japan, which spends the next to lowest percentage of its GDP on health, actually gets the best result: life expectancy of eighty-one, only four deaths in infancy for every thousand children born, and tenth place in the WHO rankings.

In fact, Japan spends only a bit more relative to its GDP than Bolivia does—but with dramatically different results. It may be that the main determinants of the health outcomes are not private or governmental expenditures on health per se, but other things associated with overall poverty: nutrition, education, and public sanitation.

DEMOCRACY AND PUBLIC POLICY

In Tables 4–1, 4–3, 4–4, 4–5, 4–6, and 4–7, I have indicated per capita income and whether the governmental system of the state has been consistently democratic over the past twenty-five years, consistently nondemocratic, or some mix of the two. It is looking ahead a bit to deal with democracy here, since it will be presented more fully in Chapter 8. However, although a number of more isolated factors also enter in, it is clear that a country's overall wealth and whether it has a democratic system of government are the two big factors that predominate in determining what governments do in various areas of public policy.

In some policy areas, such as research and development or defense spending, the distinction between democracies and nondemocracies is more muted. Even here, though, we saw in Table 4–3 that the military government of Myanmar spends 6.9 percent of the country's meager GDP on defense, even though it has no active potential enemies in the region.

The effect of democracy appears to be strongest in policy areas having to do with meeting broad needs in the population—education, housing, health. This makes sense, since democracy is a governmental system by which rulers are periodically made accountable to the broad population. Adam Przeworski and his collaborators demonstrate in a study using all states of the world that after we have taken into account how wealthy the states are, life expectancies tend to be lower in dictatorships than in democracies, and infant mortality is higher.[4] Population growth is higher in dictatorships, because contraception is less available. And school enrollments are higher in democracies than in dictatorships, for both boys and girls.

THE PLACE OF POWER IN POLICY ANALYSIS

It is easy to lapse into an almost pure "choice" perspective in this chapter, because we have been looking at policies, the product of the state. We are thus looking at a variety of choices that states have made, and it is easy to forget the interchanges of power that

---

[3]World Health Organization. *World Health Report 2000.*

[4]Adam Przeworski, Mike Alvarez, José Antonio Cheibub, and Fernando Limongi, *Democracy and Development: Political Institutions and Material Well-being in the World, 1950–1990* (New York: Cambridge University Press, 2000), chap. 5.

lie behind the states' decisions. The difference that democracy makes in policy, however, offers a good reminder that how power is organized in the state will have a lot to do with what kind of collective choice is made.

Good policy analysis will not only assess the objective merits of a policy but also take into account the political constraints under which the policy must work. For instance, any reasonable assessment of U.S. policy in banning the use of marijuana should take into account the difficulty of enforcing that law, the connivance of local governments with marijuana farmers, and so on. Once again, we see that even when our subject matter pulls us rather strongly toward one of the poles of power and choice, good analysis requires that we retain both perspectives to some extent.

Example: Norway's Program to Encourage Norwegian-Language Publications

As an example of how a state may address a problem through governmental policy, consider the plight of writers and publishers in Norway. Norway has a population of only about 4 million, roughly that of the state of Iowa. Few people outside of Norway can read Norwegian, and so an author who publishes a book written in Norwegian is limited to a relatively small potential market. By contrast, the potential worldwide market of an author writing in English is over 500 million, that of a Spanish author about 250 million, and that of a Japanese author over 100 million. How can a publishing house whose potential market is limited to just 4 million do enough business to survive? Left to its own devices, it would be forced to charge such high prices that no one could afford to buy its books. The Norwegian government—which, like most Scandinavian governments, is not shy about interposing itself in social choices to accomplish what it sees as worthy goals—has developed a complex set of policies to help publishers of materials written in Norwegian.

First, in Norway, the normal sales tax of 20 percent is not charged on books, which lowers their cost substantially (and artificially) compared with other things consumers may choose to spend their money on. In addition, the government buys the first thousand copies of every new Norwegian-language book of fiction, drama, or poetry and then donates them to public libraries. As a result, a publisher can be certain that sales on such books will never be less than one thousand copies.

To lower the price of books further, the government also helps with the publisher's payment of royalties to authors. Norwegian authors receive a royalty of 20 percent of the sales price on each copy of their book, but the government contributes half of that to the publisher on the first three thousand books sold and one-fourth of the royalty for the next two thousand books. This means that the cost to the publishers is lower and that they can charge their customers lower prices.

There are additional special subsidies for types of books the government especially wishes to see published: classic Norwegian works, illustrated children's books, and books written in minority dialects.

Finally, all booksellers are required by law to keep any new Norwegian title in stock for three years after it appears, whether people wish to buy it or not, in order to give it a fair chance.

The state intervenes directly and in precise detail to encourage publication in the Norwegian language. In this way, it can help to keep the language alive and protect it from being displaced by neighboring languages such as German or English.

Example: Economic Development Compared with "Human Development"

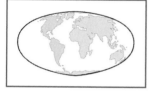

Economic growth is vital to people's well-being, but other things should also be taken into account—how equally the economic benefits are distributed, the state of the environment, the state of people's health, and so on. It is not enough to ask whether the people of a state are prospering; rather, we must ask, how well are they living?

This is hard to assess, because it involves so many diverse things, but a rough first stab has been taken in the "human development index" developed by the United Nations Development Programme (see Table 4–8).[5] The index combines indicators of gross domestic product per capita, life expectancy, and education into a single index; presumably, this measures broad well-being better than gross domestic product alone, and it is interesting to examine how states compare with each other on the two measures.

Luxembourg, whose people have the world's highest incomes, ranks lower when life expectancy and education are added into the equation. Champions at providing a good life given their level of prosperity are Sweden, whose people are only the twentieth richest but rank sixth on the human development index, and Great Britain (twenty-third in incomes, tenth in the index). A number of other industrialized Western states also do well, including Spain, Finland, Canada, New Zealand, and Denmark. The United States does well with its number three rank, considering that it is statistically impossible for it to go much higher than the number two it gets based on economics alone. States that have high income based on a restricted product or service, such as most Arab states (oil) or Singapore (commerce), tend to do the worst in these comparisons. In particular, many Arab oil producers such as Kuwait, Qatar, and the United Arab Emirates have accomplished little with great resources.

[5]United Nations Development Programme, *Human Development Report, 2000* (New York: Oxford University Press, 2000).

TABLE 4–8   THE WORLD'S MOST PROSPEROUS STATES, RANKED ON GROSS
DOMESTIC PRODUCT PER CAPITA AND ON THE HUMAN DEVELOPMENT INDEX

State	Gross domestic product per capita, worldwide rank	Human development index, worldwide rank	Difference in rankings
Luxembourg	1	17	−16
United States	2	3	−1
Norway	3	2	+1
Switzerland	4	13	−9
Australia	5	13	−8
Kuwait	6	36	−30
Iceland	7	5	+2
Singapore	8	24	−16
Canada	9	1	+8
Japan	10	9	+1
Belgium	11	7	+4
Austria	12	16	−4
Netherlands	13	8	+5
Germany	14	14	0
Ireland	15	18	−3
France	16	12	+4
Qatar	17	42	−25
Finland	18	11	+7
Hong Kong, China	19	26	−7
Sweden	20	6	+14
Italy	21	19	+2
Denmark	22	15	+7
Great Britain	23	10	+13
United Arab Emirates	24	45	−21
Cyprus	25	22	+3
Israel	26	23	+3
New Zealand	27	20	+7
Brunei Darussalem	28	32	−4
Malta	29	27	+2
Spain	30	21	+9

Source: United Nations Development Programme, *Human Development Report, 2000* (New York: Oxford University Press, 2000).

Example: Effectiveness of Educational Policies[6]

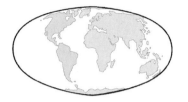

A class has 28 students and the ratio of girls to boys is 4:3. How many girls are there? Which of the following is made using bacteria: yogurt, cream, soap or cooking oil? Simple enough questions in any language (the answers, by the way, are 16 and yogurt). But when half a million pupils from around the world were set questions like these, some countries, just like some pupils, did very well and some very badly.

The tests were set for the largest-ever piece of international education research, the Third International Maths and Science Study (TIMSS). Of the 41 nations participating in this first phase, Singapore was teacher's pet: the average scores of its pupils were almost twice those of South Africa, bottom of the class (see Table 4–9).

East Asian countries have overtaken nations such as America and Britain which have had universal schooling for much longer. America came 17th in science and 28th in mathematics. England came 25th in maths and Scotland (whose pupils were tested separately) came 29th. The four richest East Asian economies took the first four places in maths.

Some former communist countries, notably the Czech Republic, Slovakia, Slovenia, and Bulgaria, also did significantly better than their richer western neighbors, even though they spend much less on education. Six of the top 15 places in both maths and science went to East Europeans. It seems that how much a country can afford to spend has less than you might think to do with how well educated its children are. American children have three times as much money spent on their schooling as young South Koreans, who nevertheless beat them hands down in tests.

These tests do not provide a sure-fire formula of exactly how much should be spent on schools, how schools should be managed and precisely how each subject should be taught.

All the same, the tests are already proving useful, especially for exposing myths. A popularly held view has it that "opportunity to learn" is the key to educational success— i.e., the more time children spend on a subject, the better they do at it. Alas, the evidence so far is not encouraging for the proponents of this theory. Taking the twelve countries which both took part in TIMSS and also had their average teaching hours measured in the OECD's recent study of school management, there seems little correlation between time spent on a subject and performance of pupils in tests. Young Austrians spend exceptionally long hours on maths and science lessons; for them, it pays off in higher test scores. But so do New Zealand's teenagers—and they do not do any better than, say, Norwegians, who spend an unusually short time on lessons in both subjects.

Next—and of particular interest to cash-strapped governments—there appears to be little evidence to support the argument, often heard from teachers' unions, that the main cause of educational under-achievement is under-funding. Low-spending countries

[6]Reprinted and abridged from *The Economist*, 29 March 1997, pp. 21–23.

TABLE 4–9   2+2=? 13-YEAR-OLDS' AVERAGE SCORE IN TIMSS* (INT AVERAGE = 500)

	Maths		Science	
1	Singapore	643	Singapore	607
2	South Korea	607	Czech Republic	574
3	Japan	605	Japan	571
4	Hong Kong	588	South Korea	565
5	Belgium (F†)	565	Bulgaria	565
6	Czech Republic	564	Netherlands	560
7	Slovakia	547	Slovenia	560
8	Switzerland	545	Austria	558
9	Netherlands	541	Hungary	554
10	Slovenia	541	England	552
11	Bulgaria	540	Belgium (F†)	550
12	Austria	539	Australia	545
13	France	538	Slovakia	544
14	Hungary	537	Russia	538
15	Russia	535	Ireland	538
16	Australia	530	Sweden	535
17	Ireland	527	United States	534
18	Canada	527	Canada	531
19	Belgium (W‡)	526	Germany	531
20	Thailand	522	Norway	527
21	Israel	522	Thailand	525
22	Sweden	519	New Zealand	525
23	Germany	509	Israel	524
24	New Zealand	508	Hong Kong	522
25	England	506	Switzerland	522
26	Norway	503	Scotland	517
27	Denmark	502	Spain	517
28	United States	500	France	498
29	Scotland	498	Greece	497
30	Latvia	493	Iceland	494
31	Spain	487	Romania	486
32	Iceland	487	Latvia	485
33	Greece	484	Portugal	480
34	Romania	482	Denmark	478
35	Lithuania	477	Lithuania	476
36	Cyprus	474	Belgium (W‡)	471
37	Portugal	454	Iran	470
38	Iran	428	Cyprus	463
39	Kuwait	392	Kuwait	430
40	Colombia	385	Colombia	411
41	South Africa	354	South Africa	326

*Third International Maths and Science Study †Flanders ‡Wallonia
Source: TIMSS

such as South Korea and the Czech Republic are at the top of the TIMSS league table. High-spenders such as America and Denmark do much worse (see chart 3). Obviously, there are dozens of reasons other than spending why one country does well, another badly, but the success of the low-spending Czechs and Koreans does show that spending more on schools is not a prerequisite for improving standards.

Another article of faith among the teaching profession—that children are bound to do better in small classes—is also being undermined by educational research. As with other studies, TIMSS found that France, America, and Britain, where children are usually taught in classes of twenty-odd, do significantly worse than East Asian countries where almost twice as many pupils are crammed into each class. Again, there may be social reasons why some countries can cope better with large classes than others. All the same, the comparison refutes the argument that larger is necessarily worse.

Further, the tests even cast some doubt over the cultural explanation for the greater success of East Asia: that there is some hard-to-define Asian culture, connected with parental authority and a strong social value on education, which makes children more eager to learn and easier to teach. Those who make this argument say it would of course be impossible to replicate such oriental magic in the West.

Yet the results of TIMSS suggest that this is, to put it mildly, exaggerated. If "culture" makes English children so poor at maths, then why have they done so well at science (not far behind the Japanese and South Koreans)? And why do English pupils do well at science and badly at maths, while in France it is the other way around? A less mystical, more mundane explanation suggests itself: English schools teach science well and maths badly; French schools teach maths better than science; East Asian schools teach both subjects well.

Apart from casting doubt on some widely-held beliefs, do international comparisons have anything constructive to say? So far, the conclusions are tentative, but some answers are emerging.

Teaching the teachers

As well as getting pupils to sit tests, the TIMSS researchers monitored the way lessons were taught in each country. Eventually this should point to which teaching method tends to be most successful, though the data are still being worked on. Meanwhile, other researchers have been searching for common factors among those countries whose schools seem to turn out well-educated pupils.

Julia Whitburn of Britain's National Institute of Economic and Social Research has studied the way maths is taught in Japan and Switzerland, two countries which are different in many ways but whose pupils seem to do consistently well at in the subject. She noted a number of common factors:

- Much more time is spent on the basics of arithmetic than on more general mathematical topics such as handling data;
- Pupils learn to do sums in their heads before they are taught to do them on paper; calculators are usually banned;
- Standardized teaching manuals, which are tested extensively in schools before being published, are used widely;

- A method known as "whole-class interactive teaching" is used widely. The teacher addresses the whole class at once, posing questions to pupils in turn, to ensure they are following the lesson. American and British schools have been criticized for letting pupils spend much of their time working in small groups, with the teacher rushing from one group to the next to see how they are doing. Ms. Whitburn notes that in Japan and Switzerland this method is only used in teaching arts and crafts;
- Finally, great efforts are made to ensure that pupils do not fall behind. Those that do are given extra coaching.

Learning, though, is not a one-way street. Just as western countries are busy seeking to emulate Japanese schools, schools and universities in Japan are coming under pressure from employers to turn out workers with the sort of creativity and individuality that the Japanese associate with western education. And just as American and British politicians are demanding that schools copy their more successful oriental counterparts and set their pupils more homework, the South Korean government is telling schools to give pupils regular homework-free days, so they can spend more time with their families—just like western children. Perhaps in education there is such a thing as a happy medium.

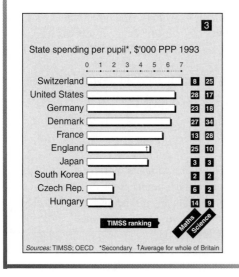

State spending per pupil*, $'000 PPP 1993

	TIMSS ranking	Maths	Science
Switzerland		8	25
United States		28	17
Germany		23	18
Denmark		27	34
France		13	28
England		25	10
Japan		3	3
South Korea		2	2
Czech Rep.		6	2
Hungary		14	9

Sources: TIMSS; OECD   *Secondary   †Average for whole of Britain

FURTHER READING

Chubb, John E., and Moe, Terry M. *Politics, Markets, and America's Schools.* Washington, D.C.: Brookings Institution, 1990.

Coulter, Philip B. *Measuring Inequality.* Boulder, Colo.: Westview Press, 1989.

Heidenheimer, Arnold J.; Heclo, Hugh; and Adams, Carolyn. *Comparative Public Policy.* 3d ed. New York: St. Martin's, 1990.

Human Rights Watch World Report 2001. New York: Human Rights Watch, 2000.

Jacobs, Lawrence R. *The Health of Nations: Public Opinion and the Making of American and British Health Policy.* Ithaca, N.Y.: Cornell University Press, 1993.

Page, Benjamin I. *Who Gets What from Government.* Berkeley: University of California Press, 1983.

Levi, Margaret. *Of Rule and Revenue.* Berkeley: University of California Press, 1988.

Moe, Terry M. *Schools, Vouchers, and the American Public.* Washington, D.C.: Brookings Institution, 2001.

Peterson, Paul. *City Limits.* Chicago: University of Chicago Press, 1981.

Phillips, Kevin R. *The Politics of Rich and Poor: Wealth and the American Electorate in the Reagan Aftermath.* New York: Random House, 1990.

Piven, Frances Fox, and Cloward, Richard A. *Regulating the Poor.* New York: Pantheon, 1971.

Reischauer, Robert D., and Aaron, Henry J., eds. *Setting National Priorities: 1999.* Washington, D.C.: Brookings Institution, 1999.

Schick, Allen. *The Federal Budget: Politics, Policy, Process,* rev. ed. Washington, D.C.: Brookings Institution, 2000.

Steinmo, Sven, and Watts, Jon. "It's the Institutions, Stupid! Why Comprehensive National Health Insurance Always Fails in America." *Journal of Health Politics Policy and Law* 20 (1995): 329–72.

Tinker, Irene, ed. *Persistent Inequalities: Women and World Development.* Oxford: Oxford University Press, 1990.

World Bank. *World Development Report 2000/2001.* New York: Oxford University Press, 2001.

World Health Organization. *World Health Report 2000.*

WEBSITES OF INTEREST

Brookings Institution, a nonpartisan, centrist policy research center:
www.brookings.org

American Enterprise Institute, a conservative research center:
www.aei.org

Economic Policy Institute, a research center with close ties to the labor movement:
www.epinet.org

Heritage Foundation, along with the American Enterprise Institute, one of the major conservative research centers in Washington, D.C.:
www.heritage.org

5

POLITICAL ECONOMY
OF THE STATE[1]

In chapter 4, we looked at the range of states' policies, but I left one especially important set of policies for separate treatment in this chapter. Economic policy is such a large
part of a government's responsibilities and the questions involved in economic policy
are sufficiently varied that it seemed to deserve treatment on its own. Also, the study of
economic policy is intertwined with the broad subfield of *political economy* in political
science. This is a part of political science with which you should become familiar, and
it seemed easiest to present economic policy and political economy together in their own
chapter.

Certainly, the state of the economy bulks large in our evaluation of a government. Bill
Clinton is famous for displaying a sign prominently in his campaign headquarters during his campaign for president in 1992 that said, "It's the economy, Stupid!" Governments fall into disfavor with their people when the economy is going badly—when
prices are high and jobs are scarce. Conversely, when the economy is performing well,
governments can count on good support from their people. Bill Clinton's moral and legal
problems in his second term as president never seemed to evoke as strong a response
from the electorate as they evoked from the media—at least partly, one might think,
because unemployment and the rate of inflation reached their lowest points in decades
at that time.

If nothing else, the centrality of economic policy in a government's responsibilities
should be obvious to us from the fact that all of the policies we looked at in chapter 4
require revenue. For everything else it wants to accomplish—developing military
power, educating youth, providing good housing to its people—a government relies on
a strong economy to give it the revenues it needs for the policies. Both in its own right
as well as instrumentally for the other policies it makes possible, a healthy economy is
important to the state.

---

[1]Portions of this chapter are adapted from W. Phillips Shively, ed., *Comparative Governance* (New York:
McGraw-Hill, 1996).

POLITICAL ECONOMY

Most of this chapter will focus on economic policy. However, it is also worth looking briefly at what political economy means in its broader sense. The subfield of "political economy" within political science focuses on how the state and the economy interact. A large part of this subfield involves analysis of economic policy in which we look at how the state's government influences the economy. That is the part of political economy on which we will spend most of our time in this chapter. But the economy also influences the state, and that is another important part of what is studied in political economy.

As one example of this, an important set of questions addressed by political economy is, "Why do states exist?" You will recall that in Chapter 3, I raised the question of why states arose in Europe in the sixteenth, seventeenth, and eighteenth centuries. Though I did not label the discussion as such, this came right out of political economy; the question was whether the driving force was the new economic activity of the time that created a *need for* the state to be invented or whether it was the new technology of weapons and communication that *made it possible* for the state to be invented. In other words, we were looking at how economic developments influenced the development of states.[2]

Another way in which political economy functions in political science is to bring the methods of economics to bear on political science questions. Economists have developed a distinctive style of analysis, which centers on a set of shared assumptions—especially the assumption of "rationality": the assumption that *individuals make their decisions in order to maximize specific goals.* Note that this is a specialized definition of *rational.* By *rational,* we do not mean "sensible" or "wise" but merely that actions are directed to achieving a goal or a set of goals and that they can be analyzed as strategies to meet those goals. Based on the assumption of rationality, plus (usually) other assumptions designed to address a particular theoretic question, economists then derive mathematically what the consequences of those assumptions should be. A good example is supply and demand analysis in economics. Based on an assumption that the seller and buyer are trying to maximize the amount of money they retain after a transaction (i.e., that they act "rationally"), plus some assumptions about the information they share, economists predict what price they will agree on under varying circumstances. Conclusions such as these can then be tested by observation, to see whether in the real world people act as one would assume they do based on the assumptions one has used.

This sort of analysis, which was brought into the field of political science by its political economy subfield, has now become so common throughout the field that it is often not labeled explicitly as "political economy." You will see numerous examples of it in the chapters to come. Two examples, which you will recognize when you hit them, are the question of whether it is rational for people to vote, given the small chance that their single vote will change the outcome of a national election (pages 234–236); and the question of under what circumstances rational actors will form an organization for common action (i.e., an "interest group"; box on p. 275).

---

[2]In a related argument, some political economists argue that for a market economy to operate, the one basic requirement is that property rights be defined and upheld. Since only the state can do this, they argue, that is the reason states should exist. See Douglas North, *Institutions, Institutional Change and Economic Performance* (New York: Cambridge University Press, 1990).

Let me hasten to add that while the "political economy" perspective is widely shared in political science, it does not have hegemony over the field. One of the good things about political science is that a number of perspectives are able to compete in the field. Not all political scientists would take rationality as a good base assumption for analysis. For instance, another important subfield of political science is *political psychology,* which looks at the roles of cognition, emotion, the framing of questions, and so forth in people's political decisions. These processes may go well beyond the rationality assumption of political economy.

Also, the questions we ask include normative questions that go behind the question of rationality to ask not "Are people making decisions in order to further specific goals" (our definition of rationality) but rather, "Which goals should people be furthering?" So, political economy is an important subfield and probably comes closer than any other to providing the dominant approach in the field of political science—but no subfield rules political science entirely.

In this chapter, we will concentrate on those aspects of political economy that deal with states' economic policies. First, we will look in the next three sections at some of the most important questions states deal with in making their economic policy. After that, we will look at some of the conditions that help or hinder them in doing so.

People's concerns about the economy generally boil down to two broad ones: (1) prosperity and economic growth, that is, the *performance* of the economy; and (2) the *distribution* of economic benefits (how evenly benefits are spread). Of course, these two are not independent of each other; each can affect the other. Many people argue, for instance, that if entrepreneurs' incomes are limited in order to increase income equality, then the entrepreneurs will not be moved to invest in risky growth opportunities (because they are not allowed to draw large profits from the venture if it defies the odds and is successful), and so economic growth will be reduced. Therefore, distribution might affect prosperity and growth. It also appears, though, that prosperity can affect distribution; the more prosperous states of the world tend to have more equal distributions of income than poorer states, though social scientists disagree as to why this happens.

The two basic concerns of performance and distribution are thus interrelated. Nonetheless, we shall separate them for analytic purposes and look at each in turn.

ECONOMIC POLICY I: ECONOMIC GROWTH

Probably the single thing by which governments are most judged is whether the economy of the state grows steadily and rapidly. That is, does the average income of individuals rise after one has taken into account the effects of inflation. This is called an increase in real *per capita income.* Alternatively, a measure based on gross domestic product (GDP, or the total amount of all economic transactions in the state) is called increase in real *per capita GDP.* This is calculated by dividing the gross domestic product by the number of people in the state and then adjusting for the effects of inflation.

States certainly vary in how well they provide prosperity and economic growth for their citizens. The map in Figure 5–1 shows the average per capita gross national product (roughly the same thing as per capita GDP) for the world's states in 1999.

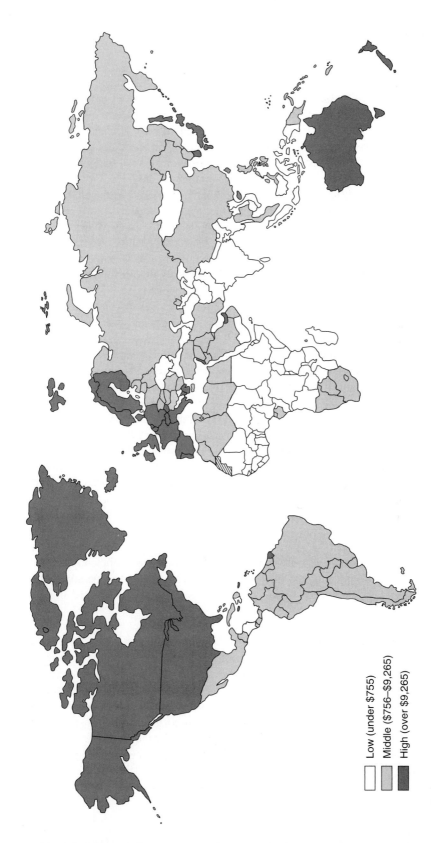

FIGURE 5–1

Per capita gross domestic product of the world's states, 1999.

Adapted from: World Bank, *World Development Indicators, 2001.* Used with permission.

Low (under $755)

Middle ($756–$9,265)

High (over $9,265)

There are tremendous variations here from one state to another. The average citizen of Switzerland enjoys $38,380 per year compared with the average citizen of Ethiopia, with $100 per year. The states of North America and Western Europe are quite prosperous, along with a few East Asian states: Japan, Australia, New Zealand, and South Korea. With a few exceptions, the states of Africa and central and East Asia are poor. Latin American states, the states of the former Soviet Union, and the states of the Middle East fall in between.

Some of these differences are due to differences in natural resources (Saudi Arabians, who enjoy $6,900 per capita annually, are lucky enough to sit on a lake of oil) or to long and peaceful development as in the case of Canada or the United States. States and their governments, though, do make a difference. In 1972, Ghana and South Korea had roughly the same per capita GNP ($310 and $300, respectively), but by 1999, the per capita GNP of Ghana was only $400, while South Korea's had risen to $8,490. Beyond the numbers, what this means is that Ghanaians are still mired in terrible poverty, while South Koreans have raised themselves to a level of reasonable comfort—in other words, these numbers really do mean something. However, South Korea is not especially well endowed with natural resources. What happened? The difference between the experiences of the two countries must lie in how they organized themselves and their economies.[3]

One obvious first crack at why countries vary in their growth is that some governments make big mistakes in guiding investment in the economy. Ghana, for instance, like most African states in their first few decades of independence, taxed farmers highly to subsidize food prices for the cities and to pay for ambitious, showy industrial projects. When the industrial projects flopped and at the same time farmers decided not to invest in improving operations on their farms because the government took most of their earnings, the economy was badly hurt.

A lesson that is often drawn from this type of experience is that governments should not try to make fine-tuned economic decisions. Economic decisions, it is said, require a nimbleness and capacity for handling detailed information that are simply beyond governments. Such decisions are better left to be made separately by individuals in thousands of specific investment decisions. An individual deciding whether to invest money in his or her farm, or perhaps in a nearby factory, can operate more efficiently and will more often choose rightly than the more cumbersome governmental operation. (The question of government's proper role in economic policy will be addressed in more detail, pro and con, in chapter 6.)

Rents and Rent Seeking

Another reason often advanced for governments to leave economic decisions to free markets is that governments are political arenas and those who are dominant within the government will use their control to extract what economists call *rents*. In this use, *rent*

---

[3]Another possibility would be that United States aid to South Korea after the Korean War helped that country to develop. But Ghana also attracted a good deal of aid, and South Korea was further handicapped by high military expenditures necessitated by its aggressive neighbor to the north. Probably all of these factors are roughly a wash.

does not mean the fee one pays to live in an apartment. Rather, rents are transfers of money that do not relate to production. If a government uses tax money to build a road or educate children, that is a *productive* transfer of money because the investment (in transportation or in an educated work force) allows the society to produce more. However, if the government uses the general tax money to give its supporters a break on their own taxes, that transfer does not increase society's productivity. It is a *rent*. Other examples of rents would be farm price subsidies, pork-barrel projects, and the creation of unnecessary public jobs for patronage. Governments are in the business of maintaining public support, so if they engage actively in managing the economy, there is certainly a danger that they will gravitate to the economic tool that most easily allows them to buy support—rents.

In the case of Ghana, it was because the government's supporters were mostly from the cities that the government taxed the farmers to subsidize cheap food for city dwellers. That is, the government used its power to provide its urban supporters with a rent.

The reason rent seeking hurts the economy is that it channels transfers of money into the pockets of the dominant coalition's supporters, rather than into what would be the most efficient economic use of the money. Some degree of rent seeking occurs in every state. In the United States, for instance, the politically dominant middle class has seen to it that the government subsidizes the owners of houses by allowing them to deduct mortgage interest payments on their federal income tax. As a result, there is probably more money spent on housing in the United States (and, therefore, less invested in farms and factories) than makes economic sense. While some degree of rent seeking occurs everywhere, the extent varies from one state to another. And like Ghana, most of the new states of Africa in the 1960s, 1970s, and 1980s were weak states, which could not easily force consideration of the interests of the unrepresented parts of society. The better organized parts of their societies—urban populations, the military, corrupt officials—made sure they were taken care of, as these states distributed rents with a vengeance.

Import-Substitution Industrialization

Another policy of the Ghanaian government that probably hurt the economy was the policy of *import-substitution industrialization.* This was a common practice for new, underdeveloped economies in the 1950s, 1960s, and 1970s. To transform their economies to advanced industrial economies, many governments in Latin America, Africa, and Asia set high tariffs to discourage imports of manufactured goods. They then encouraged the establishment of factories within their own states; without competition from producers in other countries, it was thought that these new factories would be able to prosper and thus transform the economy. Often, however, the owners of the factories (or their managers, if the factories were owned by the state) simply took advantage of the lack of competition to charge high prices for shoddy goods.

The argument so far would seem to be for keeping governments out of economic decisions. Governments, one might argue, are not well suited to the rapid, finely detailed decisions that are required. When they involve themselves in the economy, they are prone to distribute rents unproductively to their supporters.

The South Korean Experience

However, the South Korean side of the South Korea-Ghana comparison suggests another consideration, one on which political scientists are divided. It is not because the government left it alone that the South Korean economy grew at a wonderful rate. The South Korean state has long intervened directly in business's investment decisions. For many years, for instance, the government controlled which corporations were allowed to borrow money and expand. In addition, in many areas of the economy that it wished to control, the government created large corporate monopolies, which then allowed themselves to be guided by the government in many respects. Finally, the government closed off much international competition by laying down prohibitive tariffs to protect domestic industries. However, instead of aiming at import-substitution industrialization, the government pushed the protected industries to become exporters to other countries. This meant that at least in their export markets, they were still exposed to the discipline of competition with other manufacturers.

If government intervention hurts economic growth, as so many economists say it does, how can it be that South Korea's economy grew rapidly under these conditions? Apparently, the difference between Ghana and South Korea is that South Korea's government was somehow able to intervene in ways that helped the economy rather than hurt it.

First, South Korea had an unusually autonomous state.[4] The population of South Korea is remarkably homogeneous, so there were relatively few societal divisions for the government to balance off. More important, perhaps, the country was faced throughout the period with a strong security threat from North Korea, which had invaded the South once in the 1950s and threatened to do so intermittently thereafter. This threat tended to unite South Koreans and so dominated politics that few other conflicts could emerge. All of this gave South Korea's military government a relatively free hand with policy, so much so that *the government did not have to deal much with rent seeking.* Its supporters were mostly concerned with national security, and in the name of national security the government could pursue economically rational policies if it chose to do so, rather than diverting resources into subsidies to placate the farmers or pork-barrel projects to placate particular towns or regions. The government left many areas of the economy free to respond flexibly to market forces of supply and demand, even as the government controlled certain other strategic parts of the economy tightly.

Some political scientists also credit South Korea's long-established Confucian political culture for the fact that the government did not abuse its power to enrich its followers. The Confucian culture was one that envisioned leaders and followers as being in a natural harmony of mutual obligations, and in this culture leaders were supposed to be modest in their personal demands and fair and farsighted in making policy.

Finally, South Korea's authoritarian government organized itself in ways that apparently made it more nimble and flexible in economic decisions than is often the case. A good example is the government's response to the oil crisis of 1973, when Mideast oil producers first founded the OPEC cartel of oil producers and oil prices shot up around the world. It took the South Korean government just five months to produce a sophisti-

---

[4]For a discussion of the *autonomous state,* see pp. 52–53.

Southeast Asian stock markets, like this one in the Philippines, were swamped during the currency crisis of 1997.

(Enverga/Sipa Press)

cated plan to deal with oil prices.[5] By contrast, U.S. President Jimmy Carter proposed a comprehensive energy policy to Congress at about the same time but could not get anything passed. The United States never has adopted a comprehensive energy policy.

This rosy picture of South Korean development could easily leave a misleading impression of perfection. The regime through this period was, after all, an authoritarian military regime. Also, while it is true that the government did a number of things right and while it is true that it did not have to apply large areas of policy to create rents, still a number of bad investment decisions were made, and individual government officers often were corrupt. In other words, this picture is not perfect, though it was good enough to bring substantial economic growth to the country. In an analysis based on surveys of businesspeople who were asked how often they had to bribe government officials to do business in various countries, the Transparency International organization ranked South Korea forty-third out of eighty-five countries in its 1998 Corruption Perception Index— better than most countries of the South, which tend to be plagued with governmental corruption, but behind almost all countries of the West. In addition to the drain of

[5]Dilip K. Das, *Korean Economic Dynamism* (New York: St. Martin's Press, 1992), p. 149.

governmental corruption on the economy, the close relationships between governmental officials and the directors of state-sponsored monopolies often led to unwise investments, in which a failing business would be propped up by loans engineered from friendly banks by government officials. These are warts on the system, albeit important warts. This remains a system that lifted South Korea from deep poverty to become the eleventh largest economy in the world. A point was reached in 1997, however, at which the cumulative effects of such inefficiencies caught up with the Korean economy. Several banks either went into bankruptcy or proved to be on the verge of bankruptcy, and the South Korean state was forced, in what was a terrible blow to national pride, to seek financial help from the International Monetary Fund. This money came with strings attached and led to a large-scale reform of South Korea's banking systems. In 1999, South Korea emerged from the general Asian depression more quickly and more strongly than any of its neighbors.

It is not clear what we should conclude from these two cases about governmental intervention and economic growth. There are a large number of states around the world—not just Ghana, but most African states, the former Soviet Union, and many others—in which governmental intervention has been associated with economic stagnation or even collapse. There are a smaller number where interventionist governments have been associated with strong growth—Japan and smaller Asian countries such as South Korea and Taiwan, but also a country such as France, which has long been noted for its state's strong intervention in the economy. There are several other states, among them Hong Kong and the United States, where noninterventionist governments have presided over prosperity. Finally, many other countries, especially in Latin America, have seen their economies improve markedly when their governments became less interventionist.

Let me offer a speculation, based on these cases: The South Korean case suggests that a crucial factor may be the autonomy of the state apparatus. It is possible that all noninterventionist governments, whether or not their state apparatus is autonomous, offer a good possibility for reliable growth.[6] But for interventionist governments, autonomy may be the thing that distinguishes success from failure. According to this thesis, a relatively autonomous, interventionist government would be able to guide successful growth (witness the Korean and French governments). But less autonomous governments would be subject to so many rent-seeking claims that the money they would wish to guide into constructive investment is diverted instead to pay off supporters and cronies with wasteful projects or subsidies. I do not want to make too much of this argument—free market systems like that of the United States often have their own sorts of waste—but state autonomy, interacting with interventionist or noninterventionist strategies, may be part of the explanation.

ECONOMIC POLICY II: CONTROLLING INFLATION AND UNEMPLOYMENT

Another important question about the state and the economy is whether and how the state can control the twin problems of inflation and unemployment.

---

[6]However, both the United States and Great Britain, with relatively noninterventionist governments, went through several years of stagnation in the 1970s.

Inflation

Inflation is a general rise in prices, which means that the currency is worth less than it used to be. Prices of one or another thing will always go up or down, of course, but if prices of most things are rising, that is inflation; a dollar can then no longer buy as much as it could the year before. If everyone could simply adjust to such changes each year, inflation would be no problem. However, inflation hits different people differently. A person on a fixed income, such as an old person living on a pension, is badly hurt by inflation. Other people may make a great deal of money from it.

Inflation occurs when consumers and governments have a large amount of money to spend, relative to the supply of things they want to buy. This condition, often called "excess demand," means that potential purchasers bid against each other for scarce goods; this then drives up the price of the goods. It is important to note that this is a relative relationship: a large amount of money, *relative* to the supply of things. As such, many different factors can shift this relative balance in the direction of inflation:

- A frequent cause is deficit spending by governments. If a government spends more than it takes in taxes, this puts extra money to work without taking a corresponding amount out of private consumption through taxes. In this way, the "money to spend" side of the inflationary balance is raised.
- Another possible cause is a shortage in important goods. Bad storms, resulting in a low harvest of grain, can cause inflation by reducing the "supply of things" side of the inflationary balance. A prolonged strike in a major industry such as steel or automobiles can have much the same effect. Similarly, in the 1970s, the major oil producers of the Mideast cut their production of oil in order to force prices up, and this kicked off serious inflation in all other countries of the world.
- Monopolies, which allow one company or a group of companies to raise prices without having to worry that their customers will shift to another provider, also contribute to inflation.
- Similarly, trade restrictions between countries can give monopolies to local providers (since people cannot easily buy from producers in another country) and drive prices up.

With so many factors at work simultaneously, you can see that controlling inflation would be a complicated business—more an art form than a science.

Modern economies usually have some inflation, and societies are not badly disturbed by low, regular inflation of less than 5 percent or so a year. When inflation gets higher than that, it has two bad effects: (1) it churns the society up, accelerating the rise and fall of people's circumstances; social change accelerates, and there are winners and losers in the process. And (2) it diverts a good deal of people's energy into figuring out how to circumvent the effects of inflation, rather than how to invest productively.

In many states, at various times inflation has run at high levels. In 1994, for instance, China's inflation rate was 21 percent, Venezuela's was 69 percent, Turkey's was 108 percent, Russia's was 150 percent, and Brazil's was 3,173 percent. That is, prices in Brazil were thirty-one times what they had been the year before! A popular joke in Brazil at the time was that it was cheaper to take a taxi than to ride a bus, because with a bus you paid when you got on, while with a taxi you paid at the end of the trip, when the money you gave the driver was worth less than at the beginning of the trip. Levels of inflation like this can cause terrible hardship; this type of inflation destroys everyone's savings as effectively as if every bank in the country had failed. If the money you had saved was worth one thirty-first at the end of the year what it was worth at the beginning of the year, you have effectively lost all of it. One of many stories of personal tragedy in the hyperinflation that struck Germany in the early 1920s (and that many historians think contributed to the rise of Adolph Hitler, because of the misery it caused) is of a retired conductor of the Berlin Philharmonic Orchestra who withdrew his life savings from the bank, bought a subway ticket with it, rode once around his beloved city, went home and shot himself.

A remarkable worldwide development in the late 1990s was that in most countries of the world, inflation dropped a great deal. There were a variety of causes for this. A number of countries reduced their government's budget deficits, which helped to cut inflation. Also, commodities such as oil remained reasonably cheap. Perhaps the most important reason was that with the end of the Cold War and with various initiatives to make world trade more free and open, companies faced worldwide competition, making it difficult for them to raise prices. Whatever the cause, inflation in the United States was down to 3.2 percent in mid-2001, a relatively low level compared with recent years. Of the countries previously mentioned, many had reduced inflation a good deal: China's inflation rate was down to 1.7 percent, Brazil's to 7.7 percent, and Venezuela's to 12.6 percent. Turkey, however, was still at 52.4 percent and Russia at 25.0 percent.

Unemployment

Unemployment is a situation in which not enough jobs are available for everyone who wants to work. There is always some amount of unemployment present in any economy as people move from one occupation to another and are temporarily without jobs. Often, however—in fact, most of the time—economies have more unemployment than this minimum base. If a factory closes in a town and unemployed workers do not move away immediately, 20 or 30 percent of available workers in that town may be unemployed. Or throughout a state, economic activity may lessen so that large numbers of people cannot find jobs even if they are prepared to move.

Unemployment hurts society in two ways. First, those who are without work are devastated, because supporting oneself is a basic requirement for social respect in most societies. Being unable to find a productive use of one's time robs one of most claims to social standing, so a society with high unemployment is a society with many wasted souls. Second, unemployment is dreadfully inefficient. The economy would benefit if everyone who wanted to work productively could do so. There would be more manufactured goods, more food, more available medical care, more of everything.

To some extent, at least in the short run, controlling unemployment involves a trade-off with controlling inflation. As noted in the preceding section, inflation occurs when goods are in short supply and money is readily available, so that many buyers chase few goods and drive prices up by bidding against each other. Governments' main tool to counteract this is to raise the interest rates that people must pay for loans.

(A form of government intervention that even economists like!) As interest rates go up, fewer people borrow money, and the amount of money in play declines. Therefore, governments can fairly readily lower inflation by reducing the amount of money available to chase goods.

The problem is that when interest rates go up like this, economic activity declines and, at least in the short term, unemployment rises. Stable, low rates of inflation will eventually allow interest rates to come back down and allow unemployment to drop again—in fact, it will usually drop to a lower level than it had been at before. In the short term, however, fighting inflation by raising interest rates usually cuts back on employment. This temporary trade-off, and the fact that governments themselves like to borrow money and are inconvenienced by high interest rates, helps to explain why inflation is not always kept at low levels.

Unfortunately, we do not have as clear and simple tools to combat unemployment as we have for inflation. One might think that states could turn interest rates around and lower them to combat unemployment. Just as the effect of higher interest rates on unemployment was short-term and temporary, however, so is the effect of lower interest rates. Lowering rates heats up the economy as people borrow more money and spend it, and initially this does produce jobs. Governments often try this, and that is one reason that inflation is no lower around the world than it is. However, this is a temporary effect. The inflation that results from deliberately holding interest rates down in this way causes such economic dislocation after a short while that unemployment shoots back up anyway. Now you have managed to create inflation *and* unemployment.

Other state measures to combat unemployment have included creation of jobs through government projects. If governments could be quick at doing this, it would be an effective tool. Surplus labor that would otherwise be wasted could be used for needed investment in roads, schools, and so on. The United States did this to a modest extent during the Great Depression under Franklin Roosevelt. However, it is the rare government that can discipline itself to turn job programs on and off quickly as needed. Once a set of jobs has been established, a constituency has been created that will now use whatever political power it has in rent seeking to preserve the jobs as a government subsidy even after the unemployment problem has passed. And, the reverse is true: Governments are not only slow to turn off job programs when they are no longer needed, they are also often unable to get a job program started before the emergency for which it was created is almost over.

One useful tool for governments is to reduce the "natural" unemployment, which is always present as workers move between jobs or look for new work after local factories have closed, by retraining displaced workers and encouraging them to relocate quickly. Sweden has been particularly successful at this, with large retraining programs and support for workers who relocate to find a job. However, while making the labor market operate better in ways like this is useful, it cannot prevent all unemployment.

Evidence that governments find it difficult to reduce unemployment is offered by numerous Western European states whose governments are strong and skillful and have tried hard to reduce unemployment but continue to have unemployment levels of 10 percent or more.

In mid-2001, for instance, even though their economies were on the upswing, unemployment levels in some Western European countries were:

Germany	9.3 percent
France	8.7 percent
Italy	9.9 percent
Belgium	10.0 percent
Spain	13.1 percent

These numbers mean, for instance, that of all people in Spain, who were ready and willing to work, one out of every eight did not have a job.[7]

The key to governments' efforts to minimize both unemployment and inflation, as well as sustain economic growth, is to maintain a balance. Low inflation, low unemployment, and high rates of growth are all good things, but each of them is caused by numerous factors. As we noted in looking at inflation, this makes governmental intervention more an art than a science. Things get even worse when we look at all three together, because as we saw in the case of lowering or raising interest rates, tools that improve one of these three often make one or both of the others worse. (Raising interest rates to cool down inflation, for instance, will usually slow economic growth and raise unemployment.)

Some factors, however, improve all three simultaneously. Education, for instance, gives workers more flexible skills so that they are able to adapt more readily as jobs shift; it reduces inflation, by making work forces more efficient so that products can be priced more cheaply; and it feeds economic growth. Technological innovation also has a benign effect on all three. It lowers the cost of making things, which lowers inflation; and companies make strong profits because of their lowered costs, so they are able to expand their work forces. This means that unemployment stays low. Some think that the long period of strong growth in the United States in the 1990s, combined with low inflation and low unemployment, was the result of technological innovation in the computer industry and the World Wide Web.

ECONOMIC POLICY III: MANAGING DISTRIBUTION TO ADDRESS INEQUALITY

At the outset of this chapter, I noted that not only was the overall performance of the economy important but also the distribution of goods within the economy. We care not just about how much wealth is generated in the economy but how that wealth is shared among the people of the state.[8]

Governments play a role not only in the overall level of economic activity but also in *distribution* within the economy. They have two options if they want to create greater

---

[7]By way of comparison, unemployment at the time in the United States was 4.4 percent and in Japan, 4.8 percent.

[8]In the present chapter, we will look primarily at economic policies and distribution; in Chapter 6 we will look at the normative question of how much the government *should* try to reduce inequalities and of which sorts.

equality: (1) special subsidies and aids for the poor and (2) systems of *progressive taxation*. A progressive tax is one that takes a greater percentage of income from a person who is relatively well off and a smaller percentage from one who is not doing so well. Graduated income taxes are designed to be progressive, though they are often filled with loopholes that benefit the better off (which makes the tax less progressive). For instance, if an income tax is set up so that a person earning $10,000 a year pays no tax, while a person earning $20,000 a year pays $2,000 (10 percent of that income) and a person earning $50,000 pays $10,000 (20 percent of that income), then the tax is progressive.

Not all taxes are progressive. Many are *regressive* in that they take a higher percentage of poor people's income than they do of the income of those who are better off. The Social Security tax in the United States is an example. In 2001, workers in the United States had to pay 6.2 percent of their income to Social Security, up to a maximum income of $80,400. Any income over this amount was untaxed; thus, a person earning $30,000 a year paid 6.2 percent of that in Social Security, while a person earning $120,000 a year paid $4,984.80 (that is, 6.2 percent of $80,400) in tax, which was only 4.1 percent of the $120,000 income.

In the United States over recent years, taking all sorts of levies into account, the progressive and regressive taxes have just about canceled one another out, so that people's relative incomes have been about the same before and after taxes.

Table 5–1 displays income inequalities in a number of countries. In the table, the percentage of all income that goes to the poorest 20 percent is compared with the percentage of all income that goes to the richest 20 percent of the population. The greater this difference is, the more unequally are incomes distributed.

TABLE 5–1   INCOME INEQUALITY IN SELECTED STATES, LATE 1990s

	Per capita GNP, in $	Democratic/non since 1975	Percent of income earned by poorest 20% of population	Percent of income earned by richest 20% of population	Difference
United States	$30,600	democratic	5.2	46.4	41.2
Sweden	25,090	democratic	9.6	34.5	24.9
Great Britain	22,640	democratic	6.6	43.0	36.4
Canada	19,320	democratic	7.5	39.3	31.8
Portugal	10,600	mixed	7.3	43.4	36.1
Slovenia	9,890	mixed	8.4	35.4	27.0
Brazil	4,420	mixed	2.5	63.8	61.3
Belarus	2,630	nondemocratic	11.4	33.3	21.9
Russia	2,270	mixed	4.4	53.7	49.3
Philippines	1,020	mixed	5.4	52.3	46.9
Cote d'Ivoire	710	mixed	7.1	44.3	37.2
Zimbabwe	540	mixed	4.0	62.3	58.3
India	450	democratic	8.1	46.1	38.0

Source: World Bank, *World Development Report, 2000/2001;* "Democratic/non since 1975," adapted from Adam Przeworski, et al., *Democracy and Development* (New York: Cambridge University Press, 2000), appendix 1.2.

Several things are apparent in this table. First, poorer states are often burdened with considerably greater inequality of incomes than developed economies. It is paradoxical that in the midst of poverty, especially in Asian and Latin American states, there may be found a small group of people who are quite rich. Modern development—with its widespread education, mobility of populations, trade unions, and so on—alleviates inequality compared to countries with backward economies, where deep inequalities may be present. As seen from the first column (per capita GNP), the states are arrayed in the table from richest (top) to poorest (bottom). Although there are plenty of exceptions, in general as we move lower in the table, disparities between rich and poor become larger. The average difference between the poor and the rich (fifth column) is 32.9 for the six richest countries, 44.7 for the remaining seven.

Second, we also see that democracy makes a difference, as was the case with regard to social welfare policies, as discussed in Chapter 4. Where government is accountable to the broad population, it is more likely to make an effort to ease the situation of the large numbers who are not well off. This shows up in Table 5–1, where it is likely to account for India's unusual performance.

The table also shows that when governments make a special effort to do so, they can redistribute incomes somewhat. Belarus, which was part of the Soviet Union, still has a rather unreconstructed communist-led government, and it continues the communist tradition of trying to promote equality. Among industrialized democracies, Sweden, with its string of socialist governments and a strongly communal culture, has made special efforts to redistribute income, through large and steeply progressive income taxes. India, the poorest state in Table 5–1, has made real efforts at redistribution. We can see in the table that these states' efforts have made a difference.

The clearest message of the table, however, is that incomes are unequal in *all* systems. On any absolute scale, variations among these governments have made rather little difference. The truth is, those who have high incomes usually also have a good deal of political clout and are able to defend their interests vigorously. Whether it is the landowners of Brazil or the privileged bureaucrats of Belarus, those who are well off in society generally make sure that governmental redistribution does not bite very deeply.

INDEPENDENT CENTRAL BANKS

In the first four sections of this chapter, we have looked at three general areas in which governments take responsibility for the proper functioning of the economy: growth, inflation and unemployment, and inequality. In doing so, we have looked at a number of the things governments can do to accomplish these things, and we have looked at some of the things that stand in their way. We will conclude the chapter by looking at one major tool: independent central banks, discussed in this section; and at one major impediment: corruption, discussed in the next section.

One institutional tool that many think can help governments make economic policy effectively is a fairly independent central bank. A central bank is a bank that is set up by a government to help handle its transactions; to coordinate the policies of private banks;

and above all, to control interest rates either by lending its reserves freely (to lower interest charges by increasing the amount of money in circulation) or by increasing its reserves (to pull money out of circulation and thus raise interest rates). Every modern state has such a bank. In the United States, it is called the Federal Reserve Bank; in Britain, it is the Bank of England; in Germany, the Bundesbank.

Though each of these banks is set up by the state and is thus a public agency, central banks vary from one state to another in how autonomous they are of the state's political leaders. Some central banks operate independently, while some are controlled by political leaders. What constitutes "autonomy" may be fairly subtle since the political leaders do after all appoint the directors of the bank. Britain, for instance, extended greater autonomy to the Bank of England in 1994 by starting to publish the minutes of the monthly meeting of the governor of the bank and the chancellor of the Exchequer (similar to the Treasury secretary in the United States). Publishing the minutes made it more difficult for the chancellor to direct the bank to take actions that the bank's governor deemed unwise. This may not look like much, but in the stately world of high finance, it was seen as a major step toward bank independence.[9]

Why might it be important for the central bank to be independent of the government's political leaders? Using interest rates to control inflation requires unpopular decisions. In particular, raising interest rates to cut back on economic growth when jobs are expanding rapidly is not a good way to make friends! One chair of the Federal Reserve Bank once said that its job was "to take away the punch bowl when it looks as though people are beginning to enjoy the party." For this reason, political scientists and economists have long thought that a central bank that was closely controlled by political leaders would not work very hard to reduce inflation and that if a state wanted to keep inflation low, it should make its central bank fairly autonomous.

Indeed, as seen in Figure 5–2, states with relatively independent central banks tend to have stronger records on inflation than those whose central banks are more directly run by the government. Switzerland and Germany, with the most independent central banks, averaged about 3 percent inflation from 1955 to 1988, while New Zealand, with the least independent bank, had inflation of almost 8 percent. Also, when Britain extended more independence to the Bank of England in 1994, that change was indeed followed by an unusually bold increase in interest rates. Thus, there would seem to be something to this.

However, it often happens in political science that although two things coincide, it is not clear which causes which. It might appear obvious from the figure that independent central banks bring lower inflation, but it is at least possible that things are the other way around. It might be that in states where inflation is reasonably low, so that central banks do not have to do the unpopular thing too often, the state's leaders are willing to tolerate a good deal of autonomy in their central bank. If the bank has to make people angry fairly often, however, the leaders may act to take control of it and stop it from raising rates so frequently. In other words, it could be that low inflation creates

---

[9]In 1997, the newly elected Labour government went even further and gave the Bank of England full, formal independence from the cabinet.

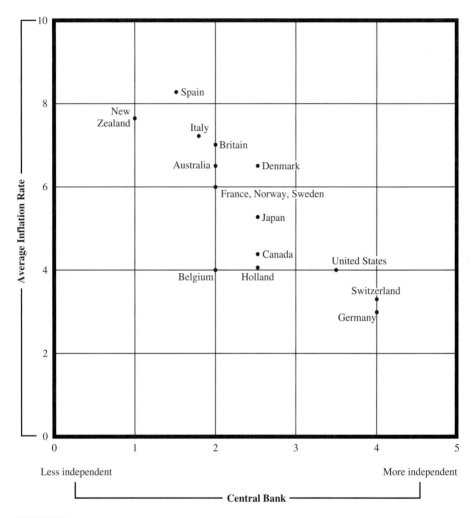

FIGURE 5–2
Inflation and central-bank independence. Annual average inflation rate (percent), 1955–1988.

Source: A. Alesina and L. Summers, "Inflation and Central-Bank Independence," The Economist, November 20, 1993, p. 94. Copyright © 1993 The Economist Newspaper Group, Inc. Reprinted with permission. Further reproduction prohibited. www.economist.com

the conditions for independent central banks, rather than the other way around. There is some evidence for this. Javier Ortiz Batalla shows that many Latin American states had established rather autonomous central banks by the late 1920s but that under the pressures of the high inflation of the mid-1930s, most took away that autonomy.[10] In

[10]Javier Ortiz Batalla, *Essays on the Early History of Latin American Central Banking.* Ph.D. dissertation in economics, University of California-Los Angeles, 1993.

these cases, it looks as though high inflation may have produced central banks that were closely directed by their governments, rather than vice versa.

Thus, there are two possible stories to tell about the picture in Figure 5–2 and some evidence for each. This is often the case in political science because we do not have the experimenter's luxury of controlling which things will vary and under what conditions. We have to take our coincidences where we find them and interpret them to the best of our ability. This does not mean we must throw up our hands, however. In this example, for instance, while both possibilities are plausible, the first is probably more compelling. There is strong reason to believe that political leaders, if they controlled banks, would allow higher inflation than independent bankers would otherwise have allowed, and thus most people would find it hard to reject that explanation.

On the other hand, the presence of a second potential explanation, with some attendant evidence, makes us keep our eyes open and seek further evidence to help us choose between the two. This is actually a rather typical example of how political science develops its ideas in all areas.

These two explanations also illustrate nicely the twin concerns of political economists: how state policies affect the economy and how the economy in turn affects the development of the state. The mainstream interpretation of Figure 5–2 sees the state's central bank policies as affecting the economy; the interpretation suggested by Batalla's finding is one in which the condition of the economy affects the structure of the state's institutions.

CORRUPTION

Another political-economic condition that affects the functioning of economies is the degree of corruption in the society. In the most general sense, *corruption* means that something has been changed so that it no longer meets its proper purpose. (Therefore, when meat spoils, we say that corruption has set in.) Specifically regarding politics, our concern is with officials performing their public tasks improperly to receive personal benefits: elected officials selling their votes, police overlooking crimes in return for a bribe, a housing inspector ignoring an unsafe building in return for a favor, and so on.

Frankly, I have never been quite sure where to deal with corruption in this book. It is not a factor only in economic policy, which is the main focus of this chapter; certainly, corruption relates to politics and policy well beyond economics. If a voter accepts a payoff in exchange for voting a certain way, that is corruption, for instance, even though it is not part of economic policy. On the other hand, corruption usually does involve an exchange of cash or of something with cash value. In that sense, it represents a meeting ground of sorts for politics and the economy. And, as we will note in this section, the level of corruption in government influences powerfully how the economy functions. So, this chapter seems as reasonable a location as any for the discussion of corruption.

(© 2002 by Sidney Harris. Reprinted with permission.)

One might first ask, why bother about corruption? It has always been present in human exchange, and there does not seem to be much we can do about it. It may even be the case that corruption occasionally serves good purposes by greasing the skids for commerce. The answer to this is twofold. First, the effects of corruption are horrid, and it is not something society should tolerate. Second, while it does surely exist everywhere, it is worse in some places than in others, so there are clearly things we can do about it.

What does corruption do to the community? Its worst effect may be to produce cynicism, lack of faith, and disregard for the rule of law. This can also contribute to broader political instability; from the earlier description of Nigerian state building (p. 63), you will recall that the Nigerian military overthrew the democratic government over charges of corruption—and it was largely because of the corruption of the civilian government that the military takeover was widely accepted.

Corruption also has direct economic costs. Some of these are obvious and dramatic, such as the billions of dollars the dictator Ferdinand Marcos apparently extracted from the impoverished Philippine economy for himself and his family. More generally, the cost of government services not properly provided and the inflated cost of government programs due to corruption reduce economic growth and the benefits we receive from governmental services. According to Hong Kong's Independent Commission Against Corruption, bribes to Chinese government officials add 3 to 5 percent to operating costs for businesses investing in China.[11] It is estimated that corruption has added as much as 15 percent, or $200 billion, to Italy's national debt.[12] A new Internet-based procurement system that Mexico introduced in the late 1990s reduced the Mexican government's purchasing costs by 15 percent, largely by eliminating the personal dealings that breed corruption.[13] Corruption does not always involve bribes. "Personal gain" may result from cozy relationships between vendors and government purchasing agents in the form of job prospects for the purchasing agents when they leave the government or from the connection between moneyed interests and candidates to whom they made large contributions. These may be part of the background on the recurrent miniscandals in government purchasing in the United States ($100+ toilet seats) and some of the spectacularly failed savings and loan associations in the late 1980s. They also had much to do with the rash of bank failures across East Asia in 1997.

What can be done about corruption? First, corruption is not equally pervasive everywhere, and that should give us some hope. If it varies, there must be reasons that cause it to be greater in one place than another. Unfortunately, a number of these reasons do not offer much leverage. Societies undergoing rapid change often appear susceptible to corruption, partly because norms of behavior are in flux so people do not have stable moral guides for behavior and partly because there are so many opportunities for corruption in a situation of rapid economic change. Two good examples of this today are China and Russia, where corruption has exploded in the shift away from planned economies. This doesn't help us much, though—should we tell societies not to undergo rapid change?

The presence of foreign businesses has also been noted as a catalyst for corruption, because they may seem like easy marks and are often better situated financially than local officials, so that what may be a huge bribe to the official may look like a normal expense to the foreign business.

It is also generally the rule that industrialized states have less corruption than nonindustrialized Southern states—though Italy is a glaring exception, and there is certainly enough corruption to go around even in industrialized states.

None of these is something we can do much about, but Robert Klitgaard does offer a number of practical suggestions to reduce corruption.[14] Based on several case studies, including the anticorruption programs of Justice Effren Plana of the Philippines

---

[11]"The Destructive Cost of Greasing Palms," *Business Week,* 6 December 1993, p. 136.
[12]Ibid., p. 138.
[13]"Stopping the Rot in Public Life," *The Economist,* 16 September 2000, p. 41.
[14]Robert Klitgaard, *Controlling Corruption* (Berkeley: University of California Press, 1988).

Corruption, on a Scale of 0 to 10

Transparency International, an international organization dedicated to documenting and tracing levels of governmental corruption, has ranked countries for 2001 by their level of corruption. The ranking was done by combining several polls of businesspeople rating agencies and the general public as to how much corruption there is in governments they've worked with. A score of 10 means politics is totally clean; 0 means that it is totally corrupt. Here are the scores of the ninety-one countries for which measures were developed:

Finland	9.9	Brazil	4.0
Denmark	9.5	Bulgaria	3.9
New Zealand	9.4	Croatia	3.9
Iceland	9.2	Czech Republic	3.9
Singapore	9.2	Colombia	3.8
Sweden	9.0	Mexico	3.7
Canada	8.9	Panama	3.7
Netherlands	8.8	Slovak Republic	3.7
Luxembourg	8.7	Egypt	3.6
Norway	8.6	El Salvador	3.6
Australia	8.5	Turkey	3.6
Switzerland	8.4	Argentina	3.5
United Kingdom	8.3	China	3.5
Hong Kong	7.9	Ghana	3.4
Austria	7.8	Latvia	3.4
Israel	7.6	Malawi	3.2
United States	7.6	Thailand	3.2
Chile	7.5	Dominican Republic	3.1
Ireland	7.5	Moldova	3.1
Germany	7.4	Guatemala	2.9
Japan	7.1	Philippines	2.9
Spain	7.0	Senegal	2.9
France	6.7	Zimbabwe	2.9
Belgium	6.6	Romania	2.8
Portugal	6.3	Venezuela	2.8
Botswana	6.0	Honduras	2.7
Taiwan	5.9	India	2.7
Estonia	5.6	Kazakhstan	2.7
Italy	5.5	Uzbekistan	2.7
Namibia	5.4	Vietnam	2.6
Hungary	5.3	Zambia	2.6
Trinidad and Tobago	5.3	Cote d'Ivoire	2.4
Tunisia	5.3	Nicaragua	2.4
Slovenia	5.2	Ecuador	2.3
Uruguay	5.1	Pakistan	2.3
Malaysia	5.0	Russia	2.3
Jordan	4.9	Tanzania	2.2
Lithuania	4.8	Ukraine	2.1
South Africa	4.8	Azerbaijan	2.0
Costa Rica	4.5	Bolivia	2.0
Mauritius	4.5	Cameroon	2.0
Greece	4.2	Kenya	2.0
South Korea	4.2	Indonesia	1.9
Peru	4.1	Uganda	1.9
Poland	4.1	Nigeria	1.0
		Bangladesh	.4

Industrialized states tend to have the cleanest politics, though Singapore (9.2), Hong Kong (7.9), Israel (7.6), Chile (7.5), and Botswana (6.0) show that states of the South are not necessarily corrupt; and Italy (5.5) shows that the industrialized states are not necessarily clean. The United States, tied for sixteenth of the ninety-one states, does not show up especially well with its score of 7.6.

and Hong Kong's Independent Commission Against Corruption, his recommendations include public education programs (if stable behavioral norms are part of the problem, perhaps these can be reinforced); acting as watchdogs; making examples of some high officials; changing incentive programs; and professionalizing the bureaucracy (these appear to be part of the explanation for the better performance of industrialized states). International pressure can also help. The 1977 Foreign Corrupt Practices Act, which bans U.S. multinational corporations from including bribes as part of their operating budgets, has probably helped to reduce corruption in other countries.

CONCLUSION

A number of policies are available to governments to pursue their general goals of encouraging growth, controlling inflation and unemployment, and shaping the distribution of wealth. We have looked here in some detail at two such policies: maintenance of independent central banks and combating corruption. Others include:

- Measures to increase the rate at which people in the society save, which thus makes more money available for investment. The main tools for this are various tax breaks to benefit saving and investment.
- Measures to maintain competition among companies, which forces them to keep their prices down or risk losing their customers. The main tools for this are regulation to prevent a single company or a couple of companies establishing a monopoly in a particular product.
- Measures to increase education, which makes everyone in the society more productive.
- Measures to make it easier for workers to move from one job to another, which reduces unemployment. The main tools for this are retraining programs and unemployment compensation.
- Research and development to develop new technology that will build new businesses or make older ones more productive.
- Measures such as the graduated income tax or social welfare programs to redistribute the fruits of the economy.

In a sense, we have come full circle. I said at the beginning of Chapter 4 that we would set aside political economy and economic policy for separate treatment in this chapter. In looking back at the policies I have bulleted above, however, you should see that many of the policies a state can follow to direct its economy are policies we looked at in their own right in Chapter 4. The truth is that the economy is so bound together with society as a whole that all policies are economic policies and economic policy affects everything else in society as well. For all that, the economy is a particularly critical part of the society. We have only been able to scratch the surface of the concern for political economy in political science or of the variety of questions revolving around economic policy. These concerns will arise repeatedly in succeeding chapters.

Example: Political Economy of Germany

From the ruins of World War II, West Germany rose to be one of the world's major economies by the 1970s and 1980s. With its merger with formerly communist East Germany in 1990, united Germany clearly will be an economic giant, even though the East German economy will require a long time before it is a match for its western counterpart. Germany currently has the third-largest gross domestic product in the world, topped only by the United States and Japan.

German political economy is characterized by three special things: (1) labor relations and the training of workers are set up to enhance cooperation and emphasize quality; (2) the economy is highly organized through a series of regulations and special government-corporation arrangements known as *Ordnungspolitik* (roughly "policy of structured arrangements" but difficult to translate); and (3) policy has focused strongly on controlling inflation. We shall look here more specifically at each of these and then look also at two new challenges: merging the two very different economies of East and West Germany and maintaining German productivity so that a high-wage, high-benefit labor system can continue in the face of growing international competition.

Labor policy. Relations between labor and management are set up to emphasize cooperation and the peaceful resolution of conflicts. A German innovation after the war, and an institution that typifies German economic relationships, is the system of *codetermination.* For companies with over two thousand employees, by law half of the members of the board of directors must be representatives of the workers. Therefore, workers are involved, along with shareholders, in the management of each company. In practice, this has led to better pay and benefits, better worker training programs, and increased satisfaction among workers.[15] It may also have contributed to Germany's admirable strike record: In 1995, on any given day a German worker was only one-seventh as likely as an American worker to be out on strike. Other things that have also probably contributed to this are Germany's pattern of industry-wide, rather than company-specific, negotiations between management and labor; and the pattern, seen throughout German politics, of a reliance on cooperation and negotiation more than on confrontation.

Germany also has an unusual system for worker training, which has helped the country build a highly skilled work force. About 30 percent of young Germans go on to the university after high school, but almost all of the remaining 70 percent enter an elaborate system of apprenticeships run by industry. Over five hundred thousand companies offer apprenticeship training programs in everything from hairdressing to computerized manufacture of optical equipment. High school graduates enroll in

---

[15]Jutta Helm, "Codetermination in West Germany: What Difference Has It Made?" *West European Politics* 9 (1986): 637–58.

these programs for a period of three to three and a half years, receiving one or two days a week of formal academic training in school, with the other days spent at the plant. As of 1992, German firms spent more than $17 billion a year to train apprentices.[16]

Ordnungspolitik. The German economy is highly regulated. The proper content for manufactured goods is stipulated in law and regulation, as are such things as the working condition of machinery or the hours stores may be open (no stores are allowed to be open on Sundays, for instance, and permissible hours on the other days are set by law). These regulations are often fine-tuned to a degree that seems strange to Americans. Under the original rules, for instance, an exception was allowed in the store-closing law, so travelers at train stations, airports, and gas stations could buy shaving supplies, magazines, and so forth. In 1992, a Hamburg court ruled that the gas station stores had to classify their goods as either essential or nonessential and sell only the essential ones on the weekends. Thus, one could buy handkerchiefs at Hamburg gas stations on Sunday but not T-shirts![17]

As a result of the net of regulation of *Ordnungspolitik,* combined with a population of knowledgeable consumers who are not tolerant of defects, German industry has come to be known for consumer products that are finely engineered and of excellent quality but that are not inexpensive. Germany is not a throwaway society.

Anti-inflation policy. In fiscal policy (whether the government's budget operates in surplus or in deficit) and in monetary policy (regulation of the supply of money, which helps determine the value of the currency), the German government has emphasized as its chief goal controlling inflation. This may result partly from the historic experience of ruinous hyperinflation in the 1920s. It probably also results in part from so much decision making in Germany being by consensus, with a heavy involvement of the bureaucracy and a resultant lessening of the impact of elected officials. Elected officials have a weakness for inflation. If one spends money this year without raising the necessary funds to pay for what is purchased—that is, if one runs a deficit—the resulting inflation doesn't kick in until a year or two later. People can then feel artificially good for awhile, and if an election is coming up soon, elected officials have plenty of reason to make people feel artificially good. Therefore, democracies tend to run in deficit and to produce inflation. While the German system certainly is a democratic one, its officials are hemmed in more than in most countries by a bureaucratic consensus that constrains them against indulging in this way.

Problems. Labor peace, a passion for quality, and institutional structures that have provided low inflation—these have helped to give Germany enviable economic strength as a state and have given its people a high standard of living. Two large clouds are on the horizon, however: the costly reunification of Germany and international challenges to Germany's competitiveness. (A third challenge, adjusting to the common currency of the European Union, is less peculiarly a German problem, so in the interest of brevity, I will not deal with it in this section. It is a complex issue, but it certainly adds further strains to the system.)

---

[16]Gail E. Schares, "Experts in Overalls." *Business Week,* 23 October 1992, p. 90.
[17]Philip Glouchevitch, *Juggernaut: The German Way of Business* (New York: Simon & Schuster, 1992), p. 48.

When East and West Germany were reunited in a burst of enthusiasm in 1990, severe economic problems quickly developed from both sides. East German industry turned out to be even less efficient than had been thought, and much of it simply had to be scrapped. To sort out productive facilities and get people back to work, Germany set up a huge holding company, the *Treuhandanstalt,* to dispose of state properties in East Germany. Over a three-year period from 1991 to 1994, the Treuhandanstalt took inventory of the properties, closing many and selling the rest to investors with some sort of negotiated guarantees about how much added investment the new owners would make and how many of the old workers would be retained. At some points in this process, unemployment in the eastern parts of Germany rose as high as one worker out of three, and it was still 17 percent by 2001.

The cost to the overall German economy of this effort has been great. Just in direct supports to ease the transition in the East and repair infrastructure there, the government spent about $640 billion in the decade following unification. But indirectly, there were also major costs.

The initial high valuation of East Germany currency proved inflationary, as the West Germany currency was diluted by the added currency from the East. Inflation, which had been 1.1 percent in West Germany in 1988 and 2.9 percent in 1989, rose in reunited Germany to 3.6 percent in 1991 and 4.0 percent in 1992. To fight this inflation, the central bank had to cut down the amount of consumer spending and corporate investment by pushing interest rates up to 8.8 percent in 1991 and 9.6 percent in 1992. By curtailing spending, these higher interest rates also helped to send Germany into a deep recession in 1992 and 1993. All this brought inflation back down to 2.6 percent by 2001, but at the cost of 9.3 percent unemployment (West and East combined).

Though the economic strains of reunification have been real, they will at least diminish over time, and Germany should eventually begin to reap some economic rewards for the effort. A more serious, less easily solved, and probably more enduring problem has also arisen in the 1990s, however: Germany's increasing difficulty remaining competitive internationally in the 1990s. Germany's economy is hugely dependent on selling goods to the rest of the world. The very traits that I described approvingly with the terms *labor peace* and *Ordnungspolitik*—the extensive regulatory structures that ensure broad security and benefits for workers and quality of products—may prove a drawback in the more competitive world that is emerging.

German labor input costs (the cost of wages and benefits per year) are far higher than its competitors', as is seen in Table 5–2. This means that for German goods to be sold at competitive prices, each German worker must produce almost twice as much per hour as, say, a worker in the United States—and must produce about fifty times as much as a worker in nearby Poland. In other words, German productivity must be much higher than its competitors'.

However, in a study in 1993 of nine industries in the United States, Germany, and Japan, Germany did not have the highest productivity in any of the industries. Japan led in five and the United States in four.[18] The trend in productivity was in the wrong

---

[18]"Europe Has a Novel Idea: Cut Costs," *New York Times,* 17 July 1994, section 3, p. 1.

TABLE 5–2   LABOR COST PER WORKER
IN MANUFACTURING, 1995–1999

Germany	$63,956
Japan	40,104
France	38,900
USA	32,013
Britain	26,045
Hungary	2,777
Poland	1,257

Source: World Bank, *World Development Indicators 1999.*

direction as well. Throughout the late 1980s and early 1990s, while productivity in Germany improved at a rate of about half a percent a year, productivity increased more than twice as fast in Japan and the United States. Faced with such high costs and finding it difficult to reduce them in Germany's highly regulated economy, many large German firms are moving part of their production abroad to lower-cost labor markets such as the United States (for skilled workers) or Eastern Europe (for less-skilled jobs). This has been a major contributory factor to Germany's 10.5 percent unemployment. Note that the problem here is *not* high pay. If manufacturers can use highly educated workers with technological equipment to produce fifty times as much per hour as their competitors in Poland, then there is no problem paying them fifty times as much. The problem only occurs if they are producing thirty times as much but being paid fifty times as much.

In general throughout the postwar period, Germany and its workers have prospered precisely because they have been highly productive. And therefore German workers' high pay has been a good thing and not a problem at all. To continue in this way, however, they will need to continually improve their productivity if they are not to fall behind rival industrial states. How can they do this? They will have to become flexible, with workers willing to move to new jobs and management innovating to reduce procedures and paperwork. This creates a tension, however, with the regulatory state that has served Germany well in the past. It may be that the real question is whether a highly regulated state can prosper under the competitive pressure of a globalized economy. Germans have begun to talk about the challenge and how to handle it, but so far not much has happened.

Example: Political Economy of Indonesia

 Indonesia is a vast state in Southeast Asia with 193 million people inhabiting several thousand islands. Since the state became free of the Netherlands at the end of World War II, it has been ruled by military governments, especially the government of General Suharto, which took power in 1967. Suharto was a clever and capable ruler who under most conditions was able to guarantee that his main real opposition was his own eventual mortality rather than any political force. He was brought down only by the regionwide economic crisis that swept over Southeast Asia in 1997.

The state Suharto took over in 1967 was poor and economically underdeveloped, but it had huge natural resources in oil, metal, and forests. Suharto pursued a policy of development hinging on education of the population, market-centered financial policies, and the use of revenue from the exploitation of natural resources to build economic infrastructure for the future. At the same time, he used the economy for his own political support and the support of his family and cronies, in ways that kept it from developing as well as it could have done.

By standards of the South, Indonesia by the mid-1990s had done reasonably well—per capita GNP was $1,100 in 1997. This was accomplished through economic growth that was usually in the range of 5 to 7 percent annually. By the 1990s, Indonesia had clearly turned the corner from a subsistence economy to one that was active and diversified. Early in that decade, for the first time, manufacturing accounted for a greater percentage of the gross national product than did agriculture. In 1997, however, Indonesia was caught up in the general economic tailspin of Southeast Asia as currencies crashed in value and foreign investors pulled their money out of the country. It is just now, in a very tentative way, recovering from that shock.

Though it is certainly ironic at this point to talk about Indonesia's progress under Suharto in light of the economic collapse of 1997 and his removal from the presidency, it is still useful to look back at how Indonesia moved from a very primitive country to one on the verge of an industrial economy. The base for Indonesia's economic development under the Suharto regime was laid down, first, by educating the population. In 1973, just 60 percent of Indonesian children attended primary school, but attendance is almost universal today. The illiteracy rate has dropped from 43 percent of the adult population in the 1970s to 16 percent. In addition to emphasizing education, Suharto relied on a largely American-trained group of economists for his basic economic policies. These were led by Widjojo Nitisastro (Berkeley Ph.D.), who shaped the policies of the 1970s and 1980s, and was then brought back out of retirement in 1997 to deal with the currency crisis of Southeast Asian banks.

Nitisastro lifted the tight controls that Indonesia had maintained on transfers of capital before 1967, which made it possible for trade to operate much more freely and for foreign corporations to invest in Indonesia. Instead of trying vainly to hold the value of the currency at a fixed point, Indonesia allowed it to move several percent a year in its ratio to the dollar, so that pressures for revaluation did not build up. The government did not operate with too great a deficit, and therefore, its debt to foreigners did not get out of hand.

Along with these free-market oriented financial policies, the government intervened on a huge scale in development of the country, with mixed results. "Mixed" in this case is not code for "terrible," however. The results were truly mixed. There were some successes in a program for rice production and marketing and in the state's family planning program. Suharto also used such programs, however, to conduct a massive personal pork-barrel program of infrastructure projects in villages labeled "Presidential Instruction" programs. The resulting roads, wells, sewage disposal facilities, and so on undoubtedly helped cement Suharto's personal rule at the same time as they laid the basis for further economic development.

More questionable than these projects is what is reputed to have been a large "under the table" economy in which favors were done for businesses by the government and unreported personal donations were made by the businesses. Many of these business leaders were ethnic Chinese, a minority of about 4 percent of the population who have often been subject to racial violence in the past and find themselves in a vulnerable position vis-à-vis the government leaders who ask them for cash. You will recall that in the box on page 114, Indonesia ranked eighty-eighth out of ninety-one countries in the overall level of business leaders' perception of the depth of political corruption. All of this sets back normal economic operations. Rizal Ramli, an economist with Econit, a consultancy, was quoted by *The Economist* in 1997 as estimating that bribes and arbitrary fees made up 10 percent to 15 percent of the capital cost of setting up a new small business.[19] Much of this traffic in cash was reputed under Suharto to be formally organized in the government, especially through Pertamina (the state oil company) and the Logistics Affairs Agency (a state company that monopolized the importation of agricultural products and that controlled the domestic trade in rice).[20] Aside from economic inefficiencies like this, government and military officials' close collusion with businesses surely contributed to a sorry record of environmental spoilage in Indonesia. In the fall of 1997, for instance, all of Southeast Asia suffered under a huge cloud of smoke from the burning of Indonesia's rich hardwood forests.

Large-scale business operations conducted by members of Suharto's family, especially his daughter Tutut and his son Tommy, also complicated the situation. One of Tommy's companies, for instance, was granted an exclusive import arrangement in 1996 to establish a national automobile manufacturing industry. In addition to allowing him free imports (while other automobile importers had to pay a 125 percent tariff), the government forced a consortium of banks to lend him $690 million for the enterprise.

When the currency crisis hit Southeast Asia in 1997, at first most observers expected Indonesia to escape any pain. Its financial balances were in fairly good shape, and its currency should have weathered the storm. Indonesia did in the end get caught up in the crisis, however—partly because of the general panic in the region and partly because the government and the banks turned out to have colluded to make the country's debts seem artificially low (so that in fact, it was not in as good shape as people had thought—though it was still not in terrible shape).

Since 1997, Indonesia has gone through rapid changes. Suharto's government collapsed in the face of popular demonstrations in 1998; in the ensuing election after democracy had been established, an enigmatic politician, Abdurrahman Wahid, was elected president. Wahid was the leader of a major Islamic party and had a strong base of support in that movement. However, he frittered away his power in inconsistent decisions, glib jokes where serious statements were required, a revolving door in his

---

[19]"Indonesia Survey," *The Economist*, 26 July 1997, p. 14.
[20]William Liddle, "Indonesia," in *Comparative Governance*, Primis database.

cabinet, and general incapacity to lead. He was impeached in July 2001, nominally for corruption but in reality for incompetence, and was replaced by his vice president (from a rival party), Megawati Sukarnoputri.

The economy of Indonesia had actually recovered fairly well—though slowly and tentatively—under Wahid, but economic progress was retarded by spectacular political and social crises that sapped the energy of the country. With regard to the economy, the government moved rapidly in 1998 to seize the failed banks' assets. Today, the government owns industrial assets worth about one-quarter of Indonesia's GDP, which it will eventually sell to achieve a new beginning in the economy. There have been some reforms. The Suharto family were ousted from their privileged positions in the economy, for instance, and the power of the National Logistics Board was trimmed. While growth in the economy was less than 1 percent in 1999, the year 2000 saw over 4.5 percent growth. As of this writing, of course, a worldwide economic slowdown is underway, and all countries of Southeast Asia are caught in it. But Indonesia appears to be faring about as well as its neighbors and should be able to move forward once the business cycle shifts.

However, the political system over the last few years has done nothing to help the economy. Indonesia *should* be doing at least as well as its neighbors—if nothing else, it sits on a big lake of oil. Indonesia suffered both from the very long damming up of conflict under Suharto, which burst out more sharply than in most countries with democratization in 1998, and from its deep ethnic divisions. In the aftermath of the economic collapse of 1997, vast anti-Chinese riots drove much of the entrepreneurial and middle-class Chinese population from the country—a loss Indonesia could not easily afford when rebuilding was needed. And immediately once democracy was established, the province of East Timor pushed for independence from the rest of the country; it won this, but only after military massacres and destruction that ruined its economy. Regional violence in another part of Indonesia, the Aceh province, caused Exxon in March 2001 to close its giant natural gas plant there, which alone produced about 3 percent of Indonesia's total GDP. The basic problems of Indonesia's economic collapse and recovery have all along been more political and social than economic. Now everything will depend on the new president, Megawati Sukarnoputri, and here at least the initial signs are good. The Indonesian rupiah gained 10 percent in value against the dollar on the day she was named president and has stayed at that higher valuation. And the International Monetary Fund freed up a $5 billion aid package once she was named. Megawati appears to be a more able political leader than her predecessor, but the social and political problems of Indonesia remain deep and difficult.

FURTHER READING

Alesina, Alberto. "Elections, Party Structure and the Economy." In *Modern Political Economy,* edited by Jeffrey Banks and Eric Hanushek. New York: Cambridge University Press, 1995.

Alt, James, and Alesina, Alberto. "Political Economy: An Overview." In *A New Handbook of Political Science,* edited by Robert Goodin and Hans-Dieter Klingemann. New York: Oxford University Press, pp. 645–74.

Bates, Robert. *Markets and States in Tropical Africa: The Political Basis of Agricultural Policies.* Berkeley: University of California Press, 1981.

Evans, Peter. *Embedded Autonomy: States and Industrial Transformation.* Princeton, N.J.: Princeton University Press, 1995.

Frieden, Jeffry. *Debt, Development, and Democracy.* Princeton, N.J.: Princeton University Press, 1991.

——. "Invested Interests: The Politics of National Economic Policies in a World of Global Finance." *International Organization* 45 (1991): 425–51.

Gourevitch, Peter. *Politics in Hard Times: Comparative Responses to International Economic Crises.* Ithaca, N.Y.: Cornell University Press, 1986.

Haggard, Stephan. *Pathways from the Periphery: The Politics of Growth in the Newly Industrializing Countries.* Ithaca, N.Y.: Cornell University Press, 1990.

Hall, Peter. *Governing the Economy: The Politics of State Intervention in Britain and France.* New York: Oxford University Press, 1986.

Landes, David S. *The Wealth and Poverty of Nations: Why Some Are So Rich and Some So Poor.* New York: W.W. Norton, 1999.

North, Douglas. *Institutions, Institutional Change and Economic Performance.* New York: Cambridge University Press, 1990.

Olson, Mancur. *The Rise and Decline of Nations.* New Haven: Yale University Press, 1982.

Rose-Ackerman, Susan. *Corruption and Government: Causes, Consequences, and Reform.* New York: Cambridge University Press, 1999.

Sen, Amartya. *Development as Freedom.* New York: Knopf, 1999.

Shirk, Susan. *The Political Logic of Economic Reform in China.* Berkeley: University of California Press, 1993.

Steinmo, Sven. "Political Institutions and Tax Policy in the United States, Sweden, and Britain." *World Politics* 61 (1989): 500–35.

"Survey: The World Economy." *The Economist,* 25 September 1999, p. 64 ff.

Teague, Paul. "Lean Production and the German Model." *German Politics* 6 (1997): 76–94.

Vogel, Steven. *Freer Markets More Rules: Regulatory Reform in Advanced Industrial Countries.* Ithaca, N.Y.: Cornell University Press, 1996.

World Bank. *World Development Report 1998/99.* New York: Oxford University Press, 1998.

 WEBSITES OF INTEREST

Organization for Economic Cooperation and Development (OECD):
www.oecd.org

International Monetary Fund:
www.imf.org/

World Bank:
www.worldbank.org

Transparency International's website on corruption:
www.gwdg.de/~uwvw/icr.htm

Federal Reserve Bank of Chicago (with links to all of the other Federal Reserve banks):
www.chicagofed.org/

Country Reports on Economic Policy and Trade, maintained by the U.S. State Department:
www.state.gov/r/pa/bgn/

6

POLITICAL CHOICES: THE PROBLEMS OF JUSTICE AND EFFICIENCY[1]

In Chapters 4 and 5, we reviewed the varying things that governments do (or do not do) on behalf of their people. In this chapter, we will shift from the "is" to the "ought," as we review the ethical and moral basis of policy making. What are the considerations that lie behind these policies? What things must the leaders and their people think about in considering what the state should do? If you were the leader of a state, what sorts of policies would you opt for?

There seem to be two broad characteristics that almost everyone wants to see in state policies: (1) the policies should be "just"—that is, people in the state should be treated in the way they deserve; and (2) the policies should be "efficient," producing the greatest good at the least cost. As you might expect, the problem with these criteria is that both are multifaceted and hard to pin down. In addition, even these two broad criteria sometimes come into conflict, because what is most "just" may not be most "efficient," and vice versa. Sorting out the various factors that make one policy "good" and another "bad" is more an art than a science, and people of goodwill may frequently come up with differing conclusions regarding a policy. In this chapter, we shall look at some of the things that make a policy "just" or "efficient" and also, perhaps, come to see how complex the final evaluation of a policy must be.

THE PROBLEM OF JUSTICE[2]

What do we mean by "justice," by the notion that people should be treated "as they deserve"? Does justice consist of treating everyone equally? Surely not, because we can

[1]Any author of an introductory book owes debts to many people, but in this chapter, a special debt is owed to Charles Anderson, whose splendid book *Statecraft* (New York: Wiley, 1977) pursued similar themes in more detail and with greater elegance than I have done here.

[2]Those who have used earlier editions of this book may notice that I have departed in this edition from my practice of treating justice as a component of a broader concept I called "fairness." That practice was always idiosyncratic, and I have concluded that the confusion it caused far outweighed any benefits. I want to thank A. P. Simonds for finally convincing me to change this section.

think of many instances in which treating everyone equally would seem quite unjust. If you had worked especially hard on a paper but your instructor decided to give everyone in the class the same grade, this would seem unjust. You had worked hard while others sloughed off, yet all got the same reward. *Different members of the class had contributed different amounts, and justice would seem to require that they be rewarded accordingly.* A rather different consideration appears in the following example: Suppose six people were waiting on a corner on a cold, rainy day, and one of the six was suffering from asthma. Suppose further that a car came along that could take only one additional passenger. Equal treatment would require that the six draw lots to see who should get to go in the car. However, would not justice require that the other five defer to the asthma victim, who was suffering more from the rain than they were? In this case, justice would seem to require that the person whose *needs* were greatest should get special treatment.

Should justice, then, be based solely on the weight of contributions or solely on need? Neither of these can provide a sufficient basis for justice, though obviously both are part of the picture.

There are many problems with the "weight of contributions." People's contributions are frequently as much a matter of luck as of virtue, and we are often a bit queasy when rewards are based solely on such "lucky" contributions. To continue with the example of grades, what if you worked very hard on your paper but a friend, who happened to have been born very intelligent, dashed off a brilliant piece in one evening while drinking beer and got a better grade than you did? You would probably have mixed feelings about the justice of the grades. To follow the same line of thought, is it just that a ballplayer such as Sammy Sosa should be paid a very high salary because his shoulders and back are so constructed as to help him hit the long ball? Is it just that a worker living in West Virginia should have so few opportunities to find a job as compared with a worker living in Connecticut? Contribution alone, then, cannot provide a sufficient criterion for determining justice. Contribution may often involve elements of luck, so that we are uncertain how much it should be rewarded. Looking only at contributions would cause us to ignore questions of need; even if four of the six people on the rainy corner had managed to stop a cab (thus contributing more than the other two), we might think it "just" if one of them were excluded to make a place for the asthma victim.

Similar problems arise if need alone is used as a criterion for justice. Like "contribution," "need" is a tricky thing, and we are not always sure that it should be rewarded. If some members of an office staff are having a hard time economically because of bad luck (or bad judgment) in the houses they bought and the debts they've run up, should they get bigger raises than members of the staff who are not in trouble economically? Should parents get better pay because they have children to support? Would this be unjust to single people who are doing the same work as the parents are doing? Again, if need alone were used as a criterion, this would mean that contribution would have to be ignored. To return finally to the example of grades, how would you feel if the papers were graded solely on the instructor's assessment of each student's need for a "positive self-image"?

Justice, then, is a complex issue. It involves a number of things that are often in conflict and need to be balanced—the contributions people have made, their varying needs, and even some further sense that people should not be treated *too* unequally. Not only

Justice? On June 7, 1976, officials in a small town in Pennsylvania notified a Mr. Selby that he would have to tear down a backyard tree house because he had not obtained a permit and the house exceeded the 40-foot height restriction. Mr. Selby ignored the notice, and the following month two police cars, a dump truck, and a powerline truck with a cherry picker returned to the tree house and demolished it.

do these things have to be balanced, but each of them is itself ambiguous and hard to pin down.

This does not mean that justice is an unworkable concept but simply that it is a difficult one. We all have a strong sense for the justice or injustice of certain things, and there is a good deal of agreement among us about these. If this were not so, the examples used previously could not have been expected to mean roughly the same thing to each reader. It is when we judge a question of justice differently, though, that we must tackle the problem of working out our disagreement. Different people will weigh contribution, need, and the necessity of equality differently; and they will also disagree on precisely what sort of need or what sort of contribution exists, or on what sorts of things need to be equal. Many would see no injustice in Sammy Sosa's salary. One could argue that the amount of pleasure he has given millions of people merited this pay, or one could see justice in a black being well paid, or one could note the limited period during which Sosa can play baseball, since he likely will need to retire in his thirties.

Justice is a complex question, but one on which we can talk productively. By bringing out and examining the differing ways people evaluate contribution, need, and the necessity for equality and by examining the differing weights people place on each, we may at least *clarify* disagreements about the justice of a policy.

OTHER ASPECTS OF JUSTICE: PROCEDURAL JUSTICE

The tack I have taken in the section on "The Problem of Justice" falls under the general rubric of "substantive justice"—any conception of justice that emphasizes people receiving what they need and deserve. This is in fact, to me, the central concept of justice. But the question of justice is sufficiently complex that it goes well beyond the already rich tension between need and contributions that I laid out in that section. Justice is a highly contested concept, a central philosophical problem in all of our consideration of life and humanity. Another conception of justice, less concerned with the fairness of distribution that I emphasized in the "Problem of Justice" section, emphasizes justice as embodied in the *procedures* by which decisions are reached about people. Though this idea of "procedural justice" is complex and philosophers' approaches to it are quite varied, I will raise in this section some of the sorts of issues that are involved in procedural justice: *(1) whether governmental action is "arbitrary," (2) whether special basic rights are violated, and (3) whether special overriding social needs are present.*

Arbitrary Policies and Due Process

Governmental action is *arbitrary* if decisions are made and communicated capriciously, that is, if the people affected by a decision do not know what to expect before the decision is made and do not learn on what grounds it was made. Decisions that single out particular individuals for punishment or reward are arbitrary. For instance, highway patrols sometimes appear to be especially strict in enforcing speed limits and other regulations on drivers of brightly colored sports cars just because of the cars' appearance. (And "racial profiling" is of course an especially abhorrent example of the same problem.) This is arbitrary action. Librarians are acting arbitrarily when they allow people owing fines to escape without paying provided that they are "properly sorry about having been late." In some dictatorships such as Nazi Germany or Idi Amin's Uganda, a person could be killed because someone in the government bore a grudge against him or her. This was the worst sort of arbitrary terror.

The question of arbitrariness is not the same as a question of substantive justice. A policy we regard as substantively unjust might be reached by means we admit are not arbitrary. (A prohibitive tax on chocolate to reduce consumption might be regarded by many people as wrong; but if it were passed constitutionally and applied equally to everyone, it would not be arbitrary.) Arbitrary means could also produce results we considered substantively just.[3] Regardless of the substantive justice of the result, however, arbitrariness lessens the justice of a policy.

The notion of *due process* has evolved to help control arbitrary decision making. This is the idea that certain standard procedures must always be followed in making some

---

[3]This often produces uneasiness about legal processes in the United States and other countries with protections against arbitrary criminal investigation. If the police had stopped a sports car and found a bloody ax in the back seat, justice would appear to require that the driver be investigated for murder. However, the initial search was arbitrary, and a court might dismiss the evidence on the grounds that it had been obtained unfairly. Citizens frequently find it difficult to appreciate these distinctions!

policies and that if those procedures were not followed in making a given policy, then the policy should be void. This prevents policy makers from acting arbitrarily, since they want to see their policies stick. To keep from having their policies voided, they stay within the standard set of procedures in making policy.

This sort of standardization involves some costs in that it lessens governmental flexibility. It is not set up for all areas of policy making. Britain, the United States, and Canada especially emphasize due process in criminal trials, because historically those countries have been especially concerned with protecting their citizens from unfair prosecution by the government. In criminal trials in English-speaking countries, due process consists of the following:

1. People may not be accused of crimes unless they could have learned of the existence and meaning of the law before they committed their acts.
2. When people are accused of crimes, they are entitled to know what crimes are charged, they are entitled to know on what evidence the charges are based, and they are entitled to gather and present their own evidence to rebut the charges.
3. Judges must be disinterested, unbiased, and attentive.
4. Once a judgment has been made, some means for later reconsideration must be available.
5. If any of these conditions has been violated in an American, Canadian, or British court except under certain special circumstances, the trial is ruled invalid.[4]

In other areas of policy, such as the setting of regulations, assignment of people to schools, levying of taxes, and so on, the general spirit of due process is still supposed to be followed—that is, policy making is not to be arbitrary—but there are usually not such precise and strict rules to safeguard due process.

Special Basic Rights

Another added factor that enters into considerations of procedural justice is the existence of certain basic rights whose violation is thought to be unjust in and of itself. Such rights have a special status in that only extraordinary circumstances would make it appropriate for policy makers to violate them for anyone. Although almost everyone would think that some such rights exist, it is not always possible to get people to agree on exactly which rights have this status. Three rights that have frequently been held to have the special status are:

1. *The Right to Survive.* It can be argued that because death negates all other rights, the right not to be killed should be kept almost absolute. Opposition to capital punishment is often based on this idea, as is opposition to abortion.

---

[4]To some extent, this is an idealization of what happens. In fact, American courts, at least, are badly overworked and many shortcuts are tolerated to move the business through. For instance, in plea bargaining, a deal is struck between the accused, the prosecutor, and the judge by which the accused pleads guilty to a lesser charge, the prosecutor's original charge is withdrawn, and the trial ends. Therefore, many of the theoretical protections listed are avoided.

2.   ***The Right of Free Speech.*** It can be argued that because politics depends on the exchange of ideas, policy makers should be especially reluctant to regulate the expression of ideas. Decreasing the flow of ideas decreases politics itself.

3.   ***The Right to Privacy.*** It can be argued that if one's very personality is to exist, there must be some space that can be called one's own, where no one else may peek in, and that governments must if at all possible respect those boundaries. It is for this reason that in British, Canadian, and American law, people may not be compelled to speak about themselves in court and wives or husbands may not be compelled to testify against their spouses.

Few people would hold any of these special rights to be *absolute*. Most people would agree that it would have been good if Hitler had been assassinated in 1942, even those who believe strongly in the right to survive. Almost everyone recognizes that the special right of free speech must have some restrictions, as well; the classic example is that no one should have the right to yell "Fire!" in a crowded theater. Similarly, there must also be some ultimate limits to the right to privacy.

Thus, "special rights" are not absolute. However, to the extent that the idea of special rights is accepted, a society sets aside those rights as having a top priority, so that it would take something unusual for us to compromise them. Under these circumstances, substantive justice, or even due process, might have to be tempered in the interests of one or another special right. As one example of this, many people have opposed the establishment of a central, computerized data file of information about Americans because they are concerned about the potential abuses of people's right to privacy that could result if all official information about a person—military record, tax returns, criminal record, health information, record in school, and so on—were brought together and made easily accessible. Those opposing the file grant that justice would be better served if such a file existed, because tax fraud and other crimes would be easier to detect, but they think that the right to privacy is more important than these other needs of justice.

Overriding Social Needs

Finally, justice in a broad sense may require that to be just to most of the people, the state must be less just to some people. That is, there may be overriding social needs that enter into considerations of justice. The best example is the military draft. In many countries, young men (and at least in Israel, women) are required to serve a fixed period of time in the military, whether they wish to do so or not. The reasoning behind this is that the people of the state need to have a strong army, but it is difficult to get people to serve in an army of their own free will. Therefore, some people must be compelled to do so for the greater general good. Similarly, affirmative action programs for employment in the United States often require that minorities and women should be given a slightly better than even break in hiring decisions (even though an even break would be the "just" decision) to help overcome historic patterns of unjust decisions going the opposite way. The argument is that society will benefit from an integrated work force and that at least modest levels of individual injustice during the transition period are not too great a price to pay.

Another example of this sort of consideration is seen during wars. When they are at war, most countries subordinate almost everything else to winning the war. Among the subordinated things is a concern for individual justice, due process, and special individual rights. Governments are often given extraordinary powers during wars, and they are not expected to be primarily concerned with justice to individuals. Sometimes governments do things during war that they later regret. The internment of hundreds of thousands of Japanese Americans in prison camps during World War II, because of their national origin, is a shameful piece of America's past that occurred under the stress of war.

Revolutionary governments often justify suspensions of due process and justice because of the great good that will eventually result from the revolution. Thousands of British sympathizers were driven into Canada at the end of the American Revolution, aristocrats and many others were beheaded during the French Revolution, and millions of farmers were executed or deported to forced-labor camps in the Soviet Union in the 1930s.

Each of the examples given here—the draft, affirmative action, wartime civil liberties, the needs of a revolution—in fact, any claim to an overriding social need is based on an assumption that ends can justify means. This assumption should not be too easily accepted *or* too readily rejected. It would be wrong to read into the assumption an exaggerated claim that means can be ignored. Clearly, there are many means that cannot be justified by many ends. The internment of Japanese Americans by the U.S. government during World War II did nothing to help the American war effort; even if it had helped in small ways, the enormity of the injustice would not have been worth it. That internment was unjustified. Similarly, even if many Soviet citizens had benefited from the Russian Revolution, the immense human suffering during that revolution and the limitation of free speech throughout the existence of the Soviet Union were horribly unjustified.

However, if we should not accept too easily the notion that ends can justify means, neither should we reject it totally. Some social ends, such as secure national borders, may be worth modest degrees of individual injustice. *Some* ends can clearly justify *some* means—as anyone must agree who has ever told a "little white lie."

In the end, then, we see that justice may be a mix of several things: substantive justice (which is itself a mixture: of concerns for contribution, need, and equality); governmental action that is not arbitrary; consideration of special rights; and the possibility of overriding social needs. It is because so many things are involved that people can honestly disagree on whether a policy is just. At the same time, being aware of what goes into justice can help us to understand and work out such disagreements.

EFFICIENCY

We have seen that one question for the policy maker is whether a policy is *just,* both to individuals and to society more broadly. The other basic question is whether the policy is *efficient.* An efficient policy is *one that gives the state and the people of the state the greatest benefits at the least cost.* The trick in dealing with efficiency is that often neither the benefits nor the costs of a policy are easy to calculate.

First, many of the effects of a policy are difficult to measure and compare. They bring up the old problem of "apples and oranges" in its severest form. How can we compare the amount of recreational value gained by building a dam and the value of the protection against flooding that is gained by building it against the cost of pain and inconvenience of those who have to leave their homes to make way for it, the economic loss of farm production on the flooded lands, and the government's cost in constructing it? There is no common unit by which to measure recreational value, protection against flooding, pain and inconvenience, and agricultural loss, and so it is difficult to say whether in this case the gains are greater than the costs.

A second reason the costs and benefits of a policy are not always clear is that policies always have a variety of effects, many of which one cannot anticipate when the policy is set up. These are often referred to as the *unanticipated consequences* of a policy.

As one example of such an unanticipated consequence, consider the following: A study of phosphate pollution of Lake Erie—which had at one time killed off almost all life in the lake—yielded the surprising finding that in the 1960s, the level of phosphates in the lake had jumped sharply and remained at that high level thereafter. It appeared that some massive new source of pollution had appeared on the scene at the time of the jump in phosphate levels, but no such new source could be found. On investigation, it turned out that at the time of the jump, the state of Michigan had ordered Michigan steel mills to stop dumping waste acid into the lake. The acid had been combining with phosphates in the water to form a solid, which then dropped to the bottom of the lake. In other words, the acid had been cleaning phosphates out of the lake water; and when, in the name of pollution control the source of acid was shut off, phosphate levels in the water shot up!

This is only one of the numerous incidental costs and benefits of stopping the dumping of acid into Lake Erie, many of which may not have been anticipated. As another example of unanticipated (and in this case, directly perverse) consequences of a policy, Douglas S. Massey and Kristin E. Espinosa have shown that a series of "get tough" policies against illegal immigration on the United States-Mexican border actually had an effect opposite of what was intended. In the late 1980s and early 1990s, the U.S. Immigration and Naturalization Service added extra guards and imposed punishments on employers found to be employing illegal immigrants, with one thousand extra Border Patrol officers added each year through 2001. Massey and Espinosa found that since the border crossing has been made tougher, illegal immigrants who originally would have come to the United States and stayed only for a few months of seasonal labor now stay year-round because they know that it will be hard to get back if they go home. The end result is that the number of illegal immigrants present at any given time is increased, not decreased, by the stepped-up enforcement.[5]

As a third example of the varied effects that a policy may have, consider the Social Security program of the United States. This is a fairly simple program. As of 2001, all employed workers except government employees paid a tax of 6.2 percent of their salary (up to a maximum salary of $80,400), and their employers paid a matching tax of the

---

[5]Douglas S. Massey and Kristin E. Espinosa, "What's Driving Mexico-U.S. Migration? A Theoretical, Empirical, and Policy Analysis," *American Journal of Sociology* 102 (January 1997): 939–99.

same amount.[6] From the proceeds of this tax, pensions are paid to people age sixty-five and older who have retired; also, support payments are paid to disabled workers and to children of workers who have died young. The direct purpose of the program is to provide a national system of pensions and catastrophe insurance. Among the many *side* effects of the program, some good and some bad, are the following:

1. People with low salaries are taxed relatively more heavily than people with high salaries (see Chapter 5). Therefore, the distribution of incomes in the state is made less equal.

2. Retired people have been made less dependent economically on their families. This has surely been a good thing for them, but it may also have helped to lessen the ties of the extended family, which are already weak in our highly mobile society.

3. The age of retirement has been made more or less standard nationally.

4. The overall production of goods and services has been reduced for the country and all the people are economically somewhat less well-off than they would otherwise be because people are encouraged to retire at age sixty-five rather than at a later age.

5. Conversely, the policy has allowed many who wish to stop working at age sixty-five to do so without being forced by economic need to work beyond that age.

6. The payroll tax on employers takes a higher percentage of the payroll for low-pay employees than for high-pay employees. For example, the employer pays a tax of 6.2 percent of the salary of an employee who earns $30,000 a year but only 4.15 percent of the salary of an employee who earns $120,000 a year ($0.062 \times$ $80,400 is $4,985, which is just 4.15 percent of $120,000). Therefore, the policy encourages industries such as the electronics and computer industries, which have highly paid work forces, while it discriminates against industries such as steel and automobile manufacturing, which employ large numbers of workers at lower pay. This encourages the development of clean industries with a great deal of potential for export sales, but it also hurts economically weak areas of traditional industry.

As this example shows, even a fairly simple program like Social Security has many effects beyond those for which it was originally designed. Some of these were not anticipated by the designers, and some have probably not yet even been noticed by scholars. Certainly the previous list does not exhaust all the consequences of the Social Security plan.

As a final example of the unintended consequences of policy, some studies have suggested that stiffer penalties for those caught driving while intoxicated may have led to an increase in hit-and-run accidents, as drunk drivers flee the scene of accidents to avoid the tougher punishment for driving while intoxicated.

Any judgment of the *efficiency* of a policy must take into account *all* its costs and benefits—so far as we can guess what these are—not just the *intended* costs and benefits. It is often hard to put a price tag on these, as we have seen in the example of Social

---

[6]An additional 1.45 percent tax on *all* wages, also matched by employers, supports medical care for people over sixty-five years of age.

Security; we are usually comparing apples, oranges, bananas, and grapefruit. Many of the consequences may be difficult to foresee. As a result, it is just as much an art to judge the efficiency of a policy as to judge its justice. There is nothing terrible in recognizing that policy making is not an exact science; it is simply a good thing to realize that policy choices are neither simple nor direct.

MODES OF DECISION: INCREMENTAL VERSUS RADICAL

How do policy makers react to the complex and difficult decisions they must make? One important way in which they may differ is in style. A decision maker may, to varying degrees, take an *incremental* or a *radical* approach to the making of policy.

A decision maker who operates more *incrementally* will make only a small change in policy at any one time, wait to see what the results of that change are, then make another small change, and so on. A person who is worried about the uncertainty in devising policies—and about the possibility of making big, costly mistakes—will tend to be an incrementalist. As we have seen, it is often very difficult to assess all the costs and benefits of a policy; therefore, an incrementalist stance is certainly not unreasonable.

A *radical* decision maker, on the other hand, is more concerned about lost opportunities than about the possibility of costly errors. A radical is likely to feel that while the incrementalist is creeping up on a decision, a chance for a decisive breakthrough may be lost. Sometimes, says the radical, bold action may accomplish something that could never be done in small steps. A decision maker of relatively radical mood might hasten to buy up land for a state park all at once, before land prices rise to prohibitive heights, rather than announce a ten-year plan for gradual land acquisition.

Neither of these styles is necessarily preferable. Partly, the choice is a matter of individual personality, as some people are more averse to risk than others. The incrementalist's caution in the face of uncertainty and complexity makes a lot of sense, and so does the radical's worry that opportunities may be lost through slow, cautious movement.

Some types of policy seem to lend themselves better to one style of decision making than to the other. Anything based on age and generational change is probably best handled incrementally, for instance, because we know well in advance what is coming and all change is rather slow. Closing schools or expanding school systems in response to changes in the number of school-age children can be managed incrementally. We know years in advance what we can expect by watching local birthrates.

Military policies, on the other hand, often require boldness because even the difference of an hour can change a situation, as armies change position, attacks are launched, and so on. History's great generals—Napoleon, Robert E. Lee, and others—have been gamblers.

One would not wish to say that one or the other of these stances is *the* right one. Which mix of the two is best depends on circumstances and on the character of the decision maker. What *is* true, though, is that modern politics tilts things heavily in favor of incrementalism. In fact, other than in revolutions, radical policy changes are rare. Partly this is because in our complex and active societies, a group will arise to protest vociferously against almost any change; such groups can usually force a compromise that is, in effect, an incremental change. The other reason for the predominance of incremental

---

Incrementalism: Normative and Empirical Analysis

Analysis in political science may be of either the normative sort or the empirical. Normative analysis deals with values: What should be? Empirical analysis deals with observation: What is? Incrementalism offers an interesting example of how a given thing may be dealt with either normatively or empirically.

In an influential normative book in the mid-1960s, Charles Lindblom argued that central direction of policy could not work but that a variety of decision makers, each operating incrementally, could produce good policies (*The Intelligence of Democracy* [New York: Free Press, 1965]). In this sense, incrementalism can be held up as a normative guide to how policies should be made.

However, incrementalism has also functioned importantly as a descriptive category to help empirical students of politics understand how politics actually happens. In their pioneer study of how governments design budgets, Davis, Dempster, and Wildavsky concluded that the budgetary decisions of the president and Congress could be described as simple incremental decisions. Agencies were rarely created or disbanded; rather, each year each agency received a budgetary increase of some small percent—an incremental way of designing the budget ("A Theory of the Budgetary Process," *American Political Science Review* 60 [September 1966]: 529–47). Here, then, "incrementalism" is not a *value* to be debated but a descriptive category that is applied to U.S. budgetary politics.[1]

[1]This use of incrementalism is reviewed critically in William D. Berry, "The Confusing Case of Budgetary Incrementalism: Too Many Meanings for a Single Concept," *Journal of Politics* 52 (February, 1990): 167–96.

---

change is that officials and bureaucrats are rarely punished for a continuously unsatisfactory state of affairs, but they know that they *will* be punished for any dramatic failure. This makes for timid decisions.

MODES OF DECISION: AUTHORITY VERSUS THE MARKET

Another basic choice about policy is whether we want to rely more on *governmental authority* or on *market mechanisms* to carry it out. "Governmental authority" is just what it sounds like. Under governmental authority, policy is made by the government telling people what they may or may not do, how much they may spend on X, how much the country is to invest in Y, and so on. Many policies with which you are familiar are matters of governmental authority. The public school system, in which the government fixes a minimum number of years of education that each child must receive and sets up free public schools to provide that education, is an instance of policy provided by governmental authority. The system of highways and streets, in which the government decides where streets should run and then uses public money to build and maintain them, is another example. So is the nationalized coal industry of China, in which the government owns all coal mines and decides how much coal is to be mined, what sort of equipment is to be built, how much the miners are to be paid, and how much the coal will cost.

Under a "market mechanism," the government leaves the choice as to what people are to do, what goods they are to receive, and so on, up to the people to choose for themselves, through their exchanges of goods and services with each other. Through the operation of supply and demand, if large numbers of people want G.I. Joe dolls and are willing to pay high prices for them, producers will make more G.I. Joe dolls. If no one wants to pay people well to care for children during the day, there will not be many child care centers. Therefore, collective choices come to be made by millions of individual decisions about proper prices and what objects to purchase. The government depends on the *costs* of action, of goods and so on to restrain people in their choices so that they will end up choosing to do or buy only those things they most want (or can afford). In the coal industry of the United States, which is not nationalized, the choice as to how much coal is to be produced is a matter for a number of mine operators to decide on the basis of their operating costs; their decision is strongly affected by the choices of millions of customers as to how much coal they will buy at a given price. The policy decision—how much coal is to be produced—which in China is made directly by the government, is made in the United States by the interplay of a large number of individual decisions.

In a modification of the market mechanism, a government may leave a policy to be settled by the market but may intervene to structure the individual decisions that go to make up the market choice.[7] Almost every country, for instance, taxes liquor and tobacco products heavily to raise their prices and make it less likely that people will choose to consume such unhealthy substances rather than, say, meat and vegetables. The choice as to what to consume is still the customer's, but the government has taken steps to help determine what that choice will be. By contrast, in banning the consumption of heroin, the U.S. government is relying on governmental authority rather than on a market mechanism to determine the level of consumption of a dangerous substance.

Whether authority or a market mechanism is a better way of making policy is a continual subject of debate. Is it better for the government to nationalize railroads, airlines, and such, and run them in the public interest? Or is it better to leave decisions on scheduling, allocation of investment, salaries, and so on, to be worked out by management, workers, and customers through their individual choices? In an energy shortage, should gasoline be rationed (with a set number of gallons allocated per family), or should the price be allowed to shoot up, so that those who do not need gasoline as much as others or who cannot afford it as readily will reduce their driving? Either policy would reduce consumption to meet the short supply, but they would have different side effects. *Both* types of policy—authority and the market—have considerable disadvantages, as well as advantages.

Problems with Authority-Based Policy

The two main problems with authority as a means of policy are that (1) authority does not get things to the people who will value them most—that is, it does not *allocate optimally,* and (2) there is a lack of good incentives to encourage authority-based policy to use resources as efficiently as they might be used. (These are close variants of the twin problems of "justice" and "efficiency" with which I introduced this chapter.)

Regarding the first of these problems, it stands to reason that if government officials make a choice on behalf of all the people, it is difficult for them to take into account the infinitely varying needs of those people. They might write a thousand exceptions and special conditions into their decision, but it would still be a clumsy instrument for deciding

---

[7]See Chapter 4.

(© 2002 by Sidney Harris.
Reprinted with permission.)

who is to get how much of what. Consider the example of gasoline rationing. If the government states that each family may receive forty-two gallons of gasoline a month, should they not allow rural families more than that because of the long distances they must drive? Then what about an urban resident who must drive to a job twenty miles away? Perhaps the government should allow less gas to those living near a bus line. How about people with weak hearts—should they receive extra gasoline? How about people with small children? People who own a vacation house forty miles out of town? This can go on forever, and even if the government writes terribly complicated rules, there will still be many people who do not receive gasoline in proportion to their desire and need for gasoline. As Lindblom has put it, authority systems have "strong thumbs, no fingers."[8]

The second main problem with policy made by authority is that it often does not lead to a very efficient use of resources.[9] When the government decides how much is to be invested in what ways in schools, highways, coal mining, or whatever, the government officials responsible do not *personally* gain much of anything from a wise decision or

[8]Charles Lindblom, *Politics and Markets* (New York: Basic Books, 1977).
[9]This is not to say that private decision making does not involve any waste, however! Expensive wood-paneled executive conference rooms are just one of the possibilities. The point is that overall, the incentives of a market system push toward efficiency even if there are many lapses, while the incentives of an authority system do not.

lose much of anything from an unwise one. Under a market arrangement, however, the people making such decisions save money directly from wise decisions and lose money directly from unwise ones. Even with the best intentions in the world, it is natural that, in systems of authority, decision makers may be more careless with resources than they would be under a market system. As a fairly extreme example of the sort of inefficiency that can result, the Soviet Union at one time allowed its farmers to manage small plots themselves and to sell their produce in competitive markets, though most Soviet agricultural products came from large government-managed collective farms. On the private plots, on the average, it took four pounds of feed grain to produce a pound of meat; on the collective farms, it took up to *thirteen* pounds of feed grain to produce a pound of meat.[10]

Problems with the Market

Given these two serious problems, why would anyone ever use authority? Why don't governments leave the decisions to market mechanisms? The reason is that market mechanisms themselves suffer from several serious defects; we shall consider three of them here.[11]

First, as we saw in Chapter 5, wealth and income are distributed unequally in all societies, with some people poor and others better off. When decisions are left to the market, goods and opportunities flow to those who can afford them, and these will not necessarily be the people who need them most. In the section on "Problems with Authority-Based Policy," I wrote that authority systems could not easily sort out varying levels of need in making allocations; market systems are terrific at doing this for two people who have the same amount of money. But when incomes vary, ability to pay enters along with need in determining what individuals choose, so the allocations will still probably not be the ideal ones. If medical care is allocated by letting the price rise, for instance, poor people who need surgery to avoid being crippled might have to do without, while richer people might be able to afford casual cosmetic surgery. Where a need is especially important, the government may step in to make certain that justice is done in a way that cannot be guaranteed by a market mechanism. This is part of the motivation behind systems of free public education, socialized medicine (such as the national medical care programs that serve people of all ages in Britain, Canada, and many European states, or Medicare, which serves those over age sixty-five in the United States), and the rationing of food during shortages.

A second problem with market mechanisms is that they are not very effective in producing *collective goods*. A "collective good" is something that benefits all members of the community and that no one can be prevented from using; every member of the community can enjoy the benefits of it whether that person has helped pay for it or not. Some examples of collective goods are national defense, medical research, weather forecasting, and public health programs to control the spread of disease. All members of the community benefit from such programs, whether or not they have helped pay for them.

---

[10]*The Economist,* 7 February 1981, p. 14.
[11]For a more thorough discussion, see Lindblom, *Politics and Markets,* chap. 6, n. 6.

An army, for instance, cannot defend just those people who have helped pay for it; it defends a territory and unavoidably defends everyone in that territory. Left to the market, such collective goods would be terribly difficult to finance. Each individual could quite sensibly think, "If I don't pay my share, the army will still be there, and I'll get all the benefits of it; why should I pay? I'll let someone else do it!" As a result, no one would pay to finance the army, there would be no army, and all would lose out. Rather than let such paradoxical failures occur, governments often decide not to rely on the voluntary choices of a market mechanism. Instead, they force the people to pay taxes, and they use those taxes to provide the collective good that all (or most) desire.

A good example of the painful dilemma of producing collective goods through individual choices is familiar to anyone who watches public television in the United States. Every few months, everyone watching public television has to sit through excruciating sessions in which the station's staff run on in a staccato patter to try to encourage viewers to help pay the costs of running the station by becoming members. They appeal to guilt: "Only one in ten of you who watch this station is a member." They appeal to greed: "For the basic $35 membership, we offer this lovely ceramic mug, embossed with the logo of the station." Perhaps the most effective pitch was made a few years ago in Minnesota, when the Twin Cities station staff promised that if they reached their goal early, they would cut off the fund drive before its scheduled conclusion. Contributions flooded in.

Public television stations are caught in the classic bind of those who produce collective goods. They cannot restrict watching their shows only to those who have contributed (as pay-per-view television providers can), and so they can offer no incentive to force anyone to contribute. As a result, only about one in ten viewers sends in a contribution. This is actually a fairly generous response—but it still makes life difficult for the station.[12]

A third problem with market mechanisms is that they do not take into account *externalities* of individual transactions. An "externality" exists when there are social costs or benefits beyond the individual costs and benefits between two individuals. For example, let us say that a couple contract with a trash company to dump refuse on their land. The trash company presumably has greater benefits than costs from the deal. For the landowners, the benefit is the money paid by the trash company; the cost is the odor, the sight of the trash, and the portion of their land that is occupied by the trash. Presumably, the landowners are satisfied with the deal (the benefit outweighs the costs), or there would have been no deal. So, the trash company and the landowners are happy, and according to market practices, the deal will be struck. However, there is an externality. All the landowners' neighbors, including a nursing home and a day care center, must also suffer the sight and smell of the trash. They receive no benefits, and so there is a large *social cost* that should be taken into account but does not enter into market calculations. This is the problem of externalities, a problem in which governmental authority is often brought to bear to make certain that the broader social costs and benefits are taken into account in transactions, along with the narrower individual costs and benefits of those

---

[12]Of course, about one-fourth of the operating costs of public television comes from government subsidies. But for the marginal dollar, which makes or breaks the station, public television relies on membership contributions.

Factories and their neighbors in South
Boston, Massachusetts. A strong example
of "externalities."

(Spencer Grant/Index Stock Imagery)

making the choices. The most obvious externalities are negative ones—pollution, the
setting up of ugly structures, and so on. However, there can also be *positive externalities,* in which there are positive social benefits that would not be taken into account in
individual transactions and that government may step in to guarantee. Two examples are
the preservation of historic buildings and the requirement that every member of society
acquire a basic education. (The notion in the latter case is that society as a whole benefits from literacy above and beyond the benefit any single individual gains from being
literate.)

Governmental authority and market mechanisms, then, are two modes for the making of policy. There are problems with each, and so it is hard to argue an absolute case
for one as opposed to the other; and personal preferences will play a role. Furthermore,
it is clear that certain areas of policy lend themselves better to one mode than to the
other. Defense is always provided by governmental authority, not by a market mechanism, probably because it is so difficult to provide collective goods through a market
mechanism. Art and science seem to flourish best when left to a "marketplace of
ideas" rather than being made to conform to decisions of governmental authority.
Many other policy areas—industrial production, health care, and others—seem susceptible to either mode of decision; and examples of both modes from numerous countries can be found.

CONCLUSION

At this point, you might think the message of this chapter is that policy making is awfully complicated. This is understandable. We have seen that the question of justice is complex and subjective, and that reckoning efficiency is similarly tricky—that it is difficult to count accurately the costs and benefits of a policy to choose the one that gives the greatest benefits at the least cost. The making of policy is an art, not a science.

Unfortunately, a description of the complexity of policy decisions could lead some people to give up in discouragement. If it is difficult to decide what policy is most just and most efficient, why bother to try? Carried too far, an appreciation of complexity can be paralyzing.

We must always carry on a difficult balancing act between recognizing that our decisions are fallible and therefore require continual reexamination, and being able to act decisively on our best judgment at any given time. The fact that analysis is complex does not mean that "anything goes" or that one opinion is always as good as another. These questions are important enough to justify hardheaded analysis. It is the duty of those who recognize the complexity of decisions to hold themselves always ready to act despite knowing that their choices might be wrong. Otherwise, the only people to act would be those who did not understand the complexity of policy choices, and the world would be ruled by simpletons.

Example: Political Choice

Here are four examples of policy questions that have concerned governmental decision makers. In each instance, the policy issue is stated; this is followed by some of the questions that those making a decision on the issue must consider:

1.   *The Problem of Need-Based Scholarships.* Most systems for providing college scholarships are based on some definition of financial need, with scholarships generally being given only to those students who most need financial help to attend school.

Is need, rather than academic ability, the best basis on which to choose those students who are to be encouraged to attend college?

- Which way of choosing who gets aid is the more just?
- Which is the more efficient? Is the overall educational level of society increased more by giving financial aid to bright students or to needy students? Presumably, the aid offers more leverage to needy students, because they all need the money to attend college, whereas many of the bright students would attend college in any case. However, is a smaller number of bright students the more important addition?

Assuming we wish to use need as a basis, how do we determine "need"?

- Is need a function of parents' income? What, then, do we do about children of wealthy parents who are living independently of them and get no aid from them? Should they be punished for their parents' wealth? If they are given aid, won't all students, to get aid, claim to be independent of their parents?

- Is need solely a matter of family income, or shouldn't we take a family's financial obligations into account? Doesn't it make more sense to give aid to someone whose parents must put eight children through school than to someone from a family of four with the same income? In a possibly parallel situation, should a family that carries big mortgages on two large homes get preference because they don't have much money left to spend on college? (Many scholarship systems do count mortgage payments as contributing to need.) Does doing this merely reward imprudence? Is there a difference between the case of the eight children and the case of the large mortgages?
- How should parents who are not married but are living together and supporting their children jointly be counted? Most systems allow just one of the parents to be counted as the "supporter," and if the one who earns less is so designated, the family will show up as more "needy" than most people would consider them to be. Is this fair to married couples? Does it discourage marriage? If it is not allowed, how can one address the problem of separated couples where one of the parents does not pay a fair share of support? In this case, the single responsible parent and children would appear as *less* needy than they really are. Whichever way you decide to define need in the case of unmarried parents, how can you police the system?

2.   *The Problem of Water Pollution.* Most states have laws to limit the pollutants that can be dumped into the water.

- How do we decide which pollutants to ban? Should we ban primarily those that are dangerous to human health? Those, such as phosphates or DDT, that have especially bad effects on fish, birds, and mammals? Those that discolor the water? Those that stink?
- Who is to bear the cost of cleaning up the water?
- Is it better to use a flat ban on pollution or to charge people and corporations a stiff fee for polluting? (This is an example of the choice between government authority and market mechanisms.) The main argument against the latter is that it puts the government in the position of saying that pollution is acceptable (or at least legal) as long as one can pay the fee. The main argument for it is that it adds flexibility to the law. Cleaning up pollution always carries costs and may lead to plant closings, higher prices for consumers, and other socially undesirable consequences. The fee system would allow some continued pollution where the cost of cleaning up would be prohibitive. Where the cost is not so high, people would choose to clean up rather than pay the fee. Therefore, the system would be made more efficient but at the expense of losing some of the moral and symbolic vigor of the law. Which is the better course?

3.   *Children as a Collective Good.* A society needs to raise children to replace its members who die, or the society would disappear over a couple of generations. One could, therefore, think of the production of children as a collective good. Those who do not have children benefit from the child-raising labors of those who do; they enjoy a society of varied ages in which to live as they grow older, and a labor force of younger people is available to support them in their retirement. Should all not then share in the economic costs of raising the children? In the United States, the cost of educating children is borne collectively through the system of public education, but most other costs of raising children are treated as private costs of the parents. In about half the world's states, however, the full society assumes some of the responsibility for all costs of child rearing by giving direct grants to families with children. These grants are often pegged to the median income of workers in the country: 10 percent of the country's median income might be given to any family raising two children, for example.

- Should such aid go to all families with children or only to poor families? Public education goes to all families, but should this be treated the same?
- How would it change society to define the raising of children as a collective effort, rather than a private effort of parents?
- Would this be a good way to address such problems as malnutrition, child abuse, and poor education?
- In a sense, this would mean the government was paying people to have children. Is this a wise policy in a period of massive worldwide population growth?

4.   *The Problem of Gender-Based Pension Payments.* Almost all insurance companies have varying insurance rates for low- and high-risk categories of people. Many companies give lower insurance rates to students who maintain a B average, for instance, on the assumption that those students drive better (or less often) than others and therefore will have fewer accidents. Similarly, young drivers carry higher rates for auto insurance, nonsmokers have lower rates for life insurance with many companies, almost all companies give lower life insurance rates to women because women live longer than men, and so on. In the same spirit, until recently most insurance-based pension plans have paid women who retired at age seventy a lower monthly pension than men who retired at that age because, since women have a longer life expectancy, the companies can reasonably expect to make payments to the women for a greater length of time.

- Is it just that a woman who has worked as hard as a man should not enjoy as comfortable a retirement as the man?
- On the other hand, if payments are made equal, a man who has worked just as hard as a woman can expect to draw out a smaller total amount of retirement income before he dies. Is this just?
- If the system is changed to give equal payments, will men reinvest their retirement savings in other ways that allow them to draw out their retirement income in whatever way they wish? This could result in an insurance-based scheme with only female clients, thus defeating the purpose of the change.
- Why should gender be singled out as a basis for this distinction? People who live in Iowa live longer, on the average, than people from Rhode Island. If we're to be consistent, shouldn't Iowans draw a smaller pension than Rhode Islanders? How about people who exercise regularly, people who don't smoke, slender people, and so on?

FURTHER READING

Anderson, Charles. *Statecraft.* New York: Wiley, 1977, especially chaps. 1–6.

Freeman, John R. *Politics and Markets: The Politics of Mixed Economies.* Ithaca, N.Y.: Cornell University Press, 1989.

Hardin, Garret. "The Tragedy of the Commons." *Science* 162 (13 December 1968): 1243–48 (the original statement on the problem of producing collective goods through voluntary contributions).

Hochschild, Jennifer. *What's Fair? American Beliefs About Distributive Justice.* Cambridge: Harvard University Press, 1981.

Levi, Margaret. *Of Rule and Revenue.* Berkeley: University of California Press, 1988.

Lindblom, Charles. *Politics and Markets.* New York: Basic Books, 1977.

Ostrom, Elinor. *Governing the Commons: The Evolution of Institutions for Collective Action.* Cambridge, England: Cambridge University Press, 1991.

Schulman, Paul R. "Nonincremental Policy Making: Notes Toward an Alternative Paradigm." *American Political Science Review* 69 (December 1975): 1354–70.

Scott, James C. *Seeing Like a State: How Certain Schemes to Improve the Human Condition Have Failed.* New Haven: Yale University Press, 1998.

Solomon, Robert C., and Murphy, Mark C., eds. *What Is Justice? Classic and Contemporary Readings.* Oxford: Oxford University Press, 1990.

Titmuss, Richard M. *The Gift Relationship: From Human Blood to Social Policy.* New York: Pantheon Books, 1971.

Wildavsky, Aaron B. *Speaking Truth to Power.* New Brunswick, N.J.: Transaction Books, 1987.

PART THREE

THE CITIZEN
AND THE REGIME

7

AUTHORITY AND LEGITIMACY: THE STATE AND THE CITIZEN

In Part Two, we looked at the state and at questions that go into the setting of state policies. Now we have reached a point in the text at which we should look inside the state. How does "the state"—which comprises many different people—choose a particular set of policies? What goes on within a state that determines the policies it will pursue? The state is not a simple decision-making mechanism, and its complex organizational structure strongly influences the processes of political choice. In the next two parts—Chapters 7 through 9 and 10 through 17—we will look at those internal structures.

In this chapter, we shall consider the relationship between the state and its citizens. Every state has some sort of government, which sets its policies. A "government," when you think about it, is an unusual body within the state. It is the only group of people entitled to make decisions that everyone in the state has a duty to accept and obey.[1] There are many groups of people who have power over others, in that they can force others to do what they wish; for example, General Motors may induce a local government to give it a special tax break in return for locating a plant in the town, or a union may force an employer to increase wages.[2] The government, however, has a different kind of power, which we call *authority*. (We used this term in the preceding chapter also, as an alternative to market mechanisms for making public choices.)

If General Motors tries to convince a family to sell their house and the family refuses, that is all there is to it. The family may have made a wise or an unwise decision; but whether they sold or not, the decision was theirs to make, and either decision is socially acceptable. If the school bully tells another child to eat dirt and the child runs away or fights the bully, no one faults the child for not doing what the bully commanded. General Motors does not have authority to make someone sell a house, and the bully does not have authority to make another child eat dirt.

[1]See Chapter 3, p. 52.
[2]See Chapter 1 for a fuller discussion of power.

Authority is power based on a general agreement (1) that a person or group has the right to issue certain sorts of commands and (2) that those commands should be obeyed. If a person fails to obey authority, that failure is socially unacceptable, because the authority itself is based on a general acceptance of its exercise.

Various individuals or groups in a society have limited sorts of authority that extend over specific ranges of behavior. A parent has authority to tell children of a certain age when they should go to bed, with whom they should play, and so on; but as children grow older, the range of activities over which a parent has authority dwindles until it disappears. A teacher in a classroom has the authority to tell students how they should prepare for classes, but the teacher cannot tell them whom they may date or what political candidate to support. A General Motors supervisor has the authority to tell an assembly-line worker which bolts to tighten, but he or she cannot tell the worker how to spend coffee breaks; and when the worker resigns, the supervisor has no authority at all.

A *government* is unique in society in that all of its power involves authority, and at least potentially, there is no limit to the range of activities over which it may exercise authority. Most governments themselves impose some limits on their authority; for instance, the U.S. government, in its Constitution, rules out the exercise of authority over what religion people are to follow, what people are to say to each other, and so on. However, these limitations are self-imposed and not necessarily "natural" to governments. Many governments around the world, at one time or another, have claimed authority to tell people what religion they should follow, what they should or should not say to one another, what sort of sexual activity they were permitted, what they might eat or drink, or what sorts of sports and recreation they could take part in. It is safe to say that there is no area of human activity over which some government or another has not at some time exercised authority. Government, then, is set apart from all other groups in society because all of its power is based on authority and, at least potentially, there is no limit to the range of activities over which it may exercise authority.

Authority is a particularly efficient kind of power. It may be backed up ultimately by the threat of coercion (the police will haul you off and punish you physically if you do not do what those in authority tell you to do), or it may be backed up ultimately by persuasion (if you keep your well clean, as the government tells you to do, you will be sick less often). However, if people do what the government tells them to do, without having to be coerced or persuaded, everything goes more smoothly and—at least from the government's point of view—more satisfactorily. In general, authority does not require the actual use of coercion or persuasion to any great extent. No one has to stand at street corners to *force* cars to stop at red lights, and no one has to stand there to *persuade* them to do so. One of the things that makes the modern state such an efficient form of political organization is the very fact that the state has *authority* and therefore can ensure that people will comply with its commands with a minimum of expensive and time-consuming coercion or persuasion.

People do obey the authority of the state. Actions against authority are by definition "outlaw" behavior and therefore extraordinary, so we can think of many vivid examples of refusals to obey authority—burglary, speeding on the highways, tax evasion, and so on. The startling thing, however, is that few people steal things even when it would be safe to do so, most people drive at or near speed limit even though only a sprinkling of police are available to monitor what they are doing, and most people pay the taxes they owe. It is authority that makes this system of commands and obedience work as smoothly as it does, and this makes the modern state appear to us to be the most natural form of political organization.

Authority is not a simple thing that is either present or absent. Rather, it is a matter of degree. Remember that authority exists because it is "generally agreed on"; that is, most people believe it exists. There will probably never be a state in which every person agrees on the existence and range of the state's authority. Often, when a state issues certain commands, a portion of the people do not accept its authority to do so. If enough people deny the authority of the state, the state has a problem. In the early twentieth century, the government of the United States attempted to command people not to drink alcohol. So many people denied the authority of the state in this area that enforcement proved impossible and the law was eventually abandoned. More seriously, in the 1860s, the whole southern region of the United States denied that the national government had any authority over it at all. The states in that region set up their own new government instead, and it took a long and bloody Civil War to reestablish the authority of the U.S. government over them.

LEGITIMACY AND AUTHORITY

The crux of the state then, and of its ability to function effectively, is the government's wide-ranging authority to organize the lives of its people. Paradoxically, this authority exists only because the people believe it to exist and that it is appropriate. If authority were to fail, it might still be possible for a government to organize its people by coercion and persuasion but at such great cost that this approach could probably not be sustained over the long haul. A pure tyranny, existing without the benefit of at least some degree of authority, probably could not last long.

It is crucial to a government that large numbers of its people should believe that it has authority and that it properly *should* have that authority. We call the existence of this sort of feeling, to the extent that it does exist, the *legitimacy* of the government. Legitimacy, like authority itself, is a matter of degree. Not everyone in a state will necessarily always agree that its government is legitimate or that a given type of governmental act is legitimate. Much of the violence of politics in Cambodia in the 1990s, for instance, resulted from a failure to agree on what sort of government could be legitimate.

SOURCES OF LEGITIMACY

How does a government achieve a reasonable degree of legitimacy? There are many ways by which the people's allegiance may be bound to a government so that it is considered legitimate.

1. Legitimacy by Results

First and foremost, a government may gain and retain legitimacy from its people by providing for them the things they most want: security against physical assault, security of their country's borders against invasion, pride in their nation, and economic security. If the government can provide these things, its legitimacy will be greatly strengthened. If it cannot, its legitimacy is likely to be called into question.

A good example of "legitimacy by results" is the rule of Adolf Hitler in Germany in the 1930s. In 1933, Hitler took power legally but through dubious maneuvers and with at most a bare majority of support. The most votes the Nazi party had received in a fully free election was 37 percent—enough to make it the largest party in the country but hardly a mandate for dictatorship. Once in power, Hitler could initially count on the free support of only about one-third of the Germans, and powerful forces were arrayed against him—the labor unions, the Catholic Church, much of the army's general staff. What solidified Hitler's hold on Germany and gave him a degree of legitimacy by the end of the 1930s were the *results* of his early policies. He reduced unemployment by large-scale deficit spending; by some audacious bluffs, he outmaneuvered France and England and reestablished Germany as a great power; he built the autobahn system of superhighways; he even pioneered the Volkswagen "bug" automobile. In spite of his suppression of free speech, his oppression of Jews, and the vulgar behavior of his party comrades, these accomplishments brought him widespread and deep support from the German people. By the late 1930s, it probably would have been impossible for anyone to seek to overthrow his rule. It was not until 1944, when he had obviously lost World War II, that a group of generals were able to muster sufficient strength to try to depose him; even then, the attempt failed.

Adolf Hitler dedicating his latest project, the Volkswagen; Fallersleben, Germany, 1938.

(The Bettmann/Corbis)

2. Legitimacy by Habit

Once a government has been around for a while, people become accustomed to obeying its laws. People expect to operate under some government or other, and so whatever government is in place and has been obeyed in the past is likely to be regarded as legitimate—unless a particular crisis arises or some force (another state, perhaps) intervenes from outside. In other words, once a particular government has been in place for a while, so that the people have developed the habit of obeying it, it no longer has to perpetually justify its existence. Rather, the burden of proof lies with whoever would propose an alternative government. The existing government remains legitimate unless and until a compelling alternative comes along. We should not underestimate the importance of habit in maintaining governments in power.[3]

3. Legitimacy by Historical, Religious, or Ethnic Identity

Many governments enhance their legitimacy by the ties that exist between themselves and the people because of the government leaders' past accomplishments (their historic role) or because of the religious and/or ethnic similarity between the government leaders and the people.

This may be especially important in a new state, in which the government has not yet been in place long enough for the people to have developed the *habit* of treating it as legitimate and in which the many economic and social problems that plague most new states make it difficult for the government to achieve legitimacy by *results*.

Many governments of new states are able to buy time by virtue of the status they acquired in leading the state into independence in the first place. George Washington was revered as the "father of his country" after his success as commander of the Revolutionary Army. He and his associates enjoyed a couple of decades in which the people of the United States regarded them as their natural government, and this time allowed them to get the Constitution into place and to establish among the people the habit of obeying it. Similarly, the Labor Party in Israel, the Congress Party in India, the party of Julius Nyerere in Tanzania, and the National Liberation Front in Algeria had a breathing space in which their governments were accepted, because they had led the independence movements that had established their states in the first place. Religious or ethnic ties may also be used by a government to enhance its legitimacy. In Iran, the regime of the Ayatollah Khomeini and his successors has used its ties to the dominant Shiite Muslim sect and has played on antagonisms between the Persian majority in the country and the Arab populations in the rest of the Mideast to strengthen its legitimacy. Similarly, the former, white-dominated government of South Africa long used whites' fears of blacks to strengthen its legitimacy among the white population.

---

[3]Also, a government that is in place is usually able to foster a supportive mythology. For some examples of this in the case of the United States, see Dan Nimmo and James Combs, *Subliminal Politics: Myths and Mythmakers in America* (Englewood Cliffs, N.J.: Prentice-Hall, 1980); and Barry Schwartz, *George Washington: The Making of an American Symbol* (New York: Free Press, 1982).

4. Legitimacy by Procedures

Finally, a state may strengthen the legitimacy of its government by following certain procedures in setting itself up—procedures in which many people have confidence, so that they will start off with a fund of trust for any government that has been established along these lines.

The best example of this is democracy—a state in which the citizens participate in selecting their leaders and perhaps also in determining the state's policies. Typically, democratic governments are chosen by competitive elections in which citizens vote to decide which of various alternative leadership teams are to govern. The resulting government has won broader support than any alternative; therefore, it gains a strong base of legitimacy. It is the government "of the people."

The *procedures* of democratic election are what give such a government a good part of its legitimacy. One may dislike particular leaders or think their policies unwise, but it is hard to argue with their right to govern as long as they have been selected by the proper procedures.

Democratic government is the preeminent example of legitimacy by procedures—so preeminent that democratic procedures are often imitated through staged elections in dictatorships. At other times, other procedures have served as the basis for legitimacy; all that is important is that the procedure be accepted as appropriate. Until a few centuries ago, for instance, it was accepted that political leadership was most properly passed on by inheritance. One king ruled; when he died, his heir became the new king. This procedure was so important as a basis of legitimacy that great care was taken to lay out precise rules of inheritance; if no clear heir was available, the result was sometimes civil war.

Authority, then, through the legitimacy on which it is based, depends on the relation between the state and its citizens. A particularly interesting problem in authority and legitimacy is posed by modern democracy. A democracy is a state in which fully qualified citizens vote at regular intervals to choose, among alternative candidates, the people who will be in charge of developing the state's policies. It is in one sense an odd sort of state, because the government has power over the citizens (it makes the laws), but the citizens also have power over the government (they can vote it out of office). What sort of relationship between state and citizens is best in a democracy?

THE "DEMOCRATIC CITIZEN"

The one most special thing about the relationship between a democratic state and its citizens is that democracy requires citizens who will do more than obey and follow the government. In our previous discussion, it was more or less sufficient, for authority to exist, that the people regard the actions of the government as legitimate. This would ensure obedience to the laws.

Some nondemocratic states go a step farther and try to generate *enthusiastic* support for the government. Hitler—through his pageantry, his rallies, and his network of youth organizations, sports clubs, and so on—tried to generate enthusiastic support for nazism that would help him to build a powerful German military force more rapidly. The Soviet

Union and other communist countries always tried to build enthusiastic support through rallies, discussion groups, parades, and strenuous campaigning, even when their elections were restricted to a single party.

Democracy goes yet a step further than this. In a democracy, it is hoped not only that people will obey the laws and be enthusiastic citizens but that they will also and at the same time be *critical* citizens. Democratic citizens are expected to walk a difficult line along which they support enthusiastically the authority of their government leaders but, at the same time, are critical enough of those leaders that they might readily vote them out of office at the next election. This requires a complex and sophisticated view of politics. It is not easy to be a citizen of a democracy.

What characteristics would we look for in a "democratic citizen"?

1. *Tolerance.* If varied groups are to support their opinions, it is necessary that the people have a reasonable tolerance for diversity. If people could be prevented from setting forth unpopular ideas, then the democracy would not function well. Therefore, citizens must be at least minimally tolerant of different races, different social behaviors, different religions, and political beliefs that may depart sharply from their own. At the very least, most citizens in a democracy must be willing to allow these various groups to present their cases freely. If they are not, then there is a danger that the voters will not be allowed a full range of options from which to choose.

2. *Active Participation.* Democracy requires that citizens do more than just obey the laws the government lays down. Authority in a democracy is a two-way street; therefore, the citizens must take concrete political actions to exercise their authority over the government. At the very least, they should vote in elections. Better yet, they should maintain frequent contact with the government by writing to their representatives, serving on citizen committees, and so on. If the citizens do not do this, a state simply cannot be a democracy. Its government will have authority over its citizens, *but not vice versa.*

3. *High Level of Interest and Information.* It is not enough that citizens participate actively. If they do not know what is going on, they can be as active as they wish but they will have little effect on what the government does. Action based on no interest or understanding would be aimless, and one person's act would tend to cancel the other's out. If the citizens' active participation is to be constructive, democracy requires also that those citizens be well informed.

4. *Support for the State.* Finally, while the three characteristics noted are required in order for the people to maintain authority over the government, democracy requires also that the government maintain authority over the people. This is difficult, since the people are required to remain skeptical about the holders of government positions and must stand ready to vote them out of office if that is necessary. What is necessary, if this balancing trick is to work, is that citizens retain an abstract support for the state—and for the democratic procedures that place certain individuals into positions in the government— even while they remain skeptical about the particular individuals currently holding those positions.

"...AND FINALLY, ALL THE POLLS SHOW THAT THE TYPICAL VOTER WILL NOT VOTE."

(© 2002 by Sidney Harris. Reprinted with permission.)

HOW WELL ARE THESE REQUIREMENTS MET?

As you see, it takes work to be a citizen in a democracy. How well do the citizens of modern democracies measure up? In particular, how do citizens of the United States measure up?

1. Tolerance

The citizens of most democracies will readily agree with abstract statements guaranteeing minorities the right to express their opinions freely. However, concrete applications of this principle may be another matter. First, there is often not much support for any kind of participation beyond "conventional" acts such as running for office and voting in elections. A survey of the Italian public in 1975 showed that only 75 percent approved of people participating in peaceful demonstrations and only 36 percent would be willing to take part in a demonstration; furthermore, only 49 percent approved of people signing petitions and only 27 percent would be willing to do so themselves.[4]

Second, people often think that even conventional political participation should be banned for those who they think are wrong or dangerous. In a 1987 study in the United

---

[4]Sartori and Marradi, cited by Giacomo Sani in Gabriel Almond and Sidney Verba, eds., *The Civic Culture Revisited* (Boston: Little, Brown, 1980), p. 312.

States, people were asked to name the political group they liked the least. (For instance, one might ask them to choose among skinheads, militant gays, born-again Christians, secular humanists, the American Civil Liberties Union, the Ku Klux Klan, etc.) They were then asked several questions about what rights that group should have to participate in politics. Only 27 percent thought that members of the group they disliked should be allowed to serve as president if elected, only 18 percent thought that members of that group should be allowed to teach in the public schools, and only 32 percent thought that the group should not be outlawed. A related study in Israel in 1985 showed Israelis to be even less tolerant in these ways than Americans.[5] A study of Moscow citizens in newly democratic Russia, while it yields the same disturbing levels of tolerance as the American and Israeli studies, is probably encouraging for the prognosis for democracy in Russia, in that the tolerance levels are not much lower than those in the well-established democracies of the other two countries. Twenty-four percent of Moscow citizens thought that a member of their least-liked group should be allowed to run for public office, and 28 percent thought the group should not be outlawed.[6]

2. Active Participation

At the very least, citizens in a democracy should vote regularly in elections. As we shall see in Chapter 11, even this cannot be taken for granted. However, it is also necessary, if the democracy is to function well, that good numbers of citizens go beyond voting to involve themselves in more demanding tasks such as writing or phoning officials, organizing neighborhood groups, working in political campaigns, and so on.

Table 7–1 presents the results of a survey of the American public in which people were asked whether they participated in a variety of ways. In looking at this table, you must bear in mind that people usually tell pollsters that they are more active than they truly are; actual turnout in the 1992 presidential election was 50.2 percent, for instance, although 70 percent of the people polled said that they had voted. Still, the figures give a rough idea of the relative frequency with which people participated in these various ways.

Do the people depicted here participate a lot or a little? Political science is often the science of the half-filled glass. (Is it half full, or is it half empty?) Against a standard of what a democracy *should* be, these citizens fall short. Only 17 percent of them (or fewer, if some were exaggerating) had worked with others to solve a local problem. On the other hand, against a standard of what we might feel we could realistically expect, these figures show considerable activity. To turn the earlier sentence around, fully 17 percent of the people polled had worked with others to solve a local problem in that year.

For comparison, Table 7–2 gives results from a similar survey of British citizens. (An asterisk denotes items that are more or less comparable in the two tables.) It is striking

[5]John L. Sullivan, Pat Walsh, Michal Shamir, David G. Barnum, and James L. Gibson, "Why Politicians Are More Tolerant: Selective Recruitment and Socialization Among Political Elites in Britain, Israel, New Zealand and the United States," *British Journal of Political Science* 23 (January 1993): 60.

[6]James L. Gibson and Raymond M. Duch, "Emerging Democratic Values in Soviet Political Culture," in A. H. Miller, W. M. Reisinger, and V. L. Hesli, eds., *Public Opinion and Regime Change* (Boulder, Colo.: Westview Press, 1993), p. 76.

TABLE 7–1   PERCENTAGE OF AMERICANS ENGAGING IN SEVEN DIFFERENT ACTS
OF POLITICAL PARTICIPATION

Type of political participation	Percent
*Voted in the most recent presidential election	70
*Worked in a campaign for the most recent election	8
Made a campaign contribution for the most recent election	24
*Contacted a government official within the past year	34
Attended a protest, march, or demonstration within the past two years	6
Worked informally with others in the community to deal with some community issue or problem within the past year	17
Served in a voluntary capacity on a local governing board or attended meetings of such a board on a regular basis within the past two years	3

*Comparable items in Table 7–2.
Credit: From "Percentage Engaging in Fourteen Acts of Participation, 1967 and 1987" in *Voice and Equality* by Sidney Verba, Kay Lehman Schlozman, Henry E. Brady, p. 72. Cambridge, Mass: Harvard University Press (1995). Source: 1967 data, Verba and Nie, Participation in America, data file. 1987 data, National Opinion Research Center Social Survey.

TABLE 7–2   PERCENTAGE OF BRITISH CITIZENS ENGAGING IN SEVERAL DIFFERENT
ACTS OF POLITICAL PARTICIPATION

Type of political participation	Percent
*Voted in last election	68
*Taken an active part in a political campaign in last two or three years	3
*Presented my views to a local councilor or member of Parliament in the last two or three years	13
Helped on fundraising drives in last two or three years	31

*Comparable items in Table 7–1.
Source: Adapted from Eric Jacobs and Robert Worcester, *We British: Britain Under the MORIscope* (London: Weidenfeld and Nicolson, 1990), p. 171.

that while reported voting in elections is about the same, participation in acts that demand more than simply going to the polling place appears to be lower in Britain than in the United States. Eight percent of Americans but only 3 percent of the British report having worked in a recent political campaign. And 34 percent of Americans report having contacted a government official within the last year, while only 13 percent of the British report having presented their views to a local councilor or member of Parliament in the past two or three years.

3. High Level of Interest and Information

Of course, people who regularly turn out and vote in elections might know little or nothing about the candidates among whom they were choosing; in that case, they would contribute little to the working of democracy. How interested are citizens of democracies in

TABLE 7–3   PERCENTAGE ACCURATELY STATING CANDIDATE'S POSITION

	Issue			
	Public works jobs	Defense spending	Welfare spending	Tax burden
Ford	35	57	43	22
Carter	54	29	22	40

Source: Adapted from *The Mass Media Election* by Thomas E. Patterson (New York: Praeger, 1980), p. 154. Reprinted by permission of the author.

what goes on politically, and how accurately informed are they? Voters in the United States are rather interested in politics, according to most studies. For instance, a poll of Americans in 2000 showed that 27 percent said they followed what was going on in government and public affairs most of the time, 37 percent said they followed it some of the time, 25 percent now and then, and 12 percent hardly at all.[7]

Of course, most people will exaggerate to a stranger how much they do something as virtuous as following public affairs. But in actuality, how well informed are these virtuous-sounding people? Not very. Only 29 percent of a national survey of American adults could name their representative in Congress, and only 30 percent could name both of the senators from their state.[8]

In a study of the 1976 presidential election in two U.S. cities, Thomas E. Patterson found that even by October, surprisingly few voters could accurately state the positions of the two candidates, Gerald Ford and Jimmy Carter. As seen in Table 7–3, in only two of eight instances could more than half of the voters accurately state a candidate's position on an issue.

4. Support for the State

You will recall that what is needed here is a general abstract support for the state and for its democratic form of government, which can coexist with skepticism about the qualities of individual officeholders. Many democracies seem to be fairly successful at commanding this type of respect from their people.

In a survey in 1959, Americans were asked, "Generally speaking, what are the things about this country that you are most proud of?" They could mention anything they wished to, including religious values, the wealth of the country, landscape, culture, and so on. Over 60 percent of the things mentioned were aspects of government and politics.[9] At about the same time, in a survey in 1958, 73 percent of those polled said that they trusted the government in Washington to do what was right either "most of the time"

[7]University of Michigan, Center for Political Studies, 2000 National Election Study. Data made available by the Inter-University Consortium for Political and Social Research.

[8]Michael X. Delli Carpini and Scott Keeter, *What Americans Know About Politics and Why It Matters* (New Haven: Yale University Press, 1995).

[9]Gabriel Almond and Sidney Verba, *The Civic Culture* (Boston: Little, Brown, 1965), p. 102.

or "just about always."[10] As we shall see later in this chapter, there has been a steady erosion since then of this sort of generalized confidence and support of their government by the American people. The point is, such support was maintained at a time when, in the same study, Americans felt considerable skepticism about the *people* running the government. In 1958, 24 percent thought that "quite a lot" of the people running the government were crooked, 37 percent said that the people running the government did not usually know what they were doing, and 85 percent said that the people in government wasted "some" or "a lot" of the money they paid in taxes. At about this time also, the American electorate repudiated their Republican President Dwight Eisenhower by giving the Democrats a landslide victory in the congressional election of 1958.

This balance between support for state institutions and skepticism about officials is hard to maintain, and many shaky democracies are rarely able to achieve it. As we shall see in examples later, one democracy, West Germany, had to build it up over a twenty-year period, while another, the United States, may have to some extent lost it.

SOCIAL CAPITAL

Robert Putnam and his co-authors, in a study of what makes democratic government effective in Italy, concluded that the necessary ingredient is what they called "social capital": intricate webs of voluntary involvement in organizations that bind people together and give them the political resources and mutual trust that are needed to make any cooperative form of government work. Democracy is the quintessentially cooperative government form. Examples of the interwoven organizations they addressed would be people's involvement in trade unions, community choirs, PTAs, bird-watching clubs, professional organizations, social service organizations to help the needy, the American Legion, churches, book clubs, and so on. In parts of Italy where people were involved in rich networks of such participation, democratic government worked well; in parts where people were not so involved, democratic government did not work well.

"Social capital" might seem slightly out of place in this chapter, because it is not an attitude or a set of attitudes. Rather, it is a pattern of community interaction that *produces* desirable attitudes of efficacy and trust, and that gives people practical experience in persuasion and collective action that helps them to function well in a democracy. It appears vital to an understanding of democratic citizenship, however, and that is why I have included it here.

The United States has long been considered a society with high voluntary participation in community organizations, although there is a debate whether that high level of participation is diminishing.[11] Putnam argues that Americans are turning inward and individualistic. He points out, for instance, that while bowling alley use is up in the

---

[10]University of Michigan, Center for Political Studies, 1958 National Election Study. Data made available by the Inter-University Consortium for Political and Social Research.

[11]For a pessimistic view, see Robert Putnam, "Bowling Alone: America's Declining Social Capital," *Journal of Democracy* (January 1995), "The Strange Disappearance of Civic America," *American Prospect* (Winter 1996): 34–48, and *Bowling Alone* (New York: Simon & Schuster, 2000). For an opposed view, see the June/July 1996 issue of *Public Perspective*. Everett C. Ladd, "The Data Just Don't Show Erosion of America's 'Social Capital,' " *Public Perspective* (7 June/July 1996): 1; and associated reports, pp. 7–47.

United States, bowling league membership is down; more Americans are "bowling alone." Whether or not voluntarism and participation in civic organizations have declined in the United States, though, they still appear to be relatively high compared with other countries. A set of surveys in the early 1990s found that 49 percent of Americans had done volunteer work in the preceding twelve months compared with 13 percent of Germans and 19 percent of French respondents.[12]

POLITICAL CULTURE

Political scientists have given the name *political culture* to the types of basic attitudes addressed in this chapter. The political culture of a society consists of all attitudes and beliefs held communally by a people, which form the basis for their political behavior. We have borrowed the term from anthropology, in which the term *culture* (a people's whole interrelated set of beliefs and ways of thinking) forms a central organizing concept.

It is clear that political culture varies a good deal from one state to another and that it is responsible for major differences in how politics is conducted. We can often detect differences in culture by looking at popular behaviors and sayings. For instance, we sense that the Japanese put a greater emphasis on consensus than do Americans and value conflict less than Americans, when we compare two popular sayings:

> The nail that sticks out will get pounded down. (Japan)

and

> The squeaking wheel gets the grease. (United States)

Basic differences such as those reflected in these sayings must surely have something to do with the fact that compared with the United States, political decisions in Japan are more likely to be made on the basis of unanimous consent rather than by a vote (with one side losing). Individualistic assertion and challenges are less highly valued in Japan than in the United States.

Political culture is important, but it is a difficult thing to evaluate concretely. It almost seems that such a big concept resists precision and invites fuzzy generalization. It is too easy to lapse into stereotyping of peoples: lockstep, obedient, efficient Germans; unflappable British; breezy, pragmatic Americans; hot-blooded Latins. While there is often a germ of truth in such stereotypes, it is usually only a germ, lost in a gross oversimplification. Even in the hands of careful scholars, the concept can lead away from precision. The best work on political culture in recent decades (Gabriel Almond and Sidney Verba, *The Civic Culture* [Boston: Little, Brown, 1965]) was criticized justly because it casually assumed that the ideal culture for democracy was one that, perhaps unsurprisingly, looked much like American culture.

However, even with these difficulties, political culture is too important to ignore. A work that demonstrates the potential importance of cultural analysis is *Culture Shift in Advanced Industrial Society* by Ronald Inglehart (see p. 33). Inglehart argues that pros-

---

[12]Helmut K. Anheier, Lester M. Salamon, and Edith Archambault, "Participating Citizens: U.S.-Europe Comparisons in Volunteer Action," *Public Perspective* 5 (March-April 1994): 17.

perous, industrial societies are undergoing a shift in culture in which concerns for security are being replaced by concerns for self-expression, and he uses this shift to account for broad generational changes occurring across Europe.

One striking characteristic of political cultures is that they usually change slowly. A good example of this is provided by Alexis de Tocqueville in *Democracy in America*.[13] De Tocqueville visited the United States in the early nineteenth century to examine the workings of U.S. democracy, but his description of the American approach to politics is still recognizable—the emphasis on individuality and freedom, reliance on local politics and voluntary organizations, the restlessness and desire for progress. This despite the fact that the America he saw was an almost totally agricultural society, without modern means of communication and without the quasi-imperial world role the United States has adopted since the Second World War, and despite the fact that since his study, American society has absorbed many waves of immigrants who initially came to America with very different cultures. Our state and society have changed immensely since he wrote his book, but the underlying culture has remained recognizably the same.

The role of political culture in political science theory is somewhat like the role of history. Essentially, political science theory is a search for levers that might at least potentially help us to change society. This is why almost all political science theory is causal (see the methodological appendix, pp. 403–405.) If we understand causal relationships, they allow us to predict that a change in A (something under our control) will cause a change in B (the thing we wish to change); in this way, they offer us at least a potential lever for change. Thus, we are interested in the sources of political parties' influence because that knowledge can at least potentially help us to make parties more influential or less influential. Similarly, we look at the roles of political institutions, the effects of regulating campaign finance, the impacts of different systems of organizing health care, because understanding these things can offer us tools that might help us to effect change.

History and political culture play a slightly different role in our theories; they do not themselves offer levers, because we cannot easily change them. History is beyond our manipulation, and a culture is very difficult to change. It is in this sense that Hernando de Soto, a community activist, once said:

Culture is interesting to read about, but what does one do with it?[14]

History and culture are important, however, as the *context* within which any levers will succeed or fail. They may not be things we can control, but the effects of all the things we *can* control will vary depending on the history and culture of the society within which we try to use them. Political parties, for instance, can be expected to operate differently and to have different effects in Japan than they do in the United States.

We must understand the effects of the historical and cultural context if we are to understand properly how any of our levers will work. A common mistake is to export an institution from Western democracies to a new democracy and assume it will work there as we expect it to. The tragedy of the Balkans in the 1990s was due in part to NATO leaders' failure to understand the political culture of that region and the burden of history there.

---

[13]Alexis de Tocqueville, *Democracy in America* (New York: Knopf, 1980).
[14]Matthew Miller, "The Poor Man's Capitalist," *New York Times Magazine,* 1 July 2001, p. 47.

POLITICAL SOCIALIZATION

The values and assumptions people hold about politics are acquired in a process called *political socialization,* which simply means the learning of political values and factual assumptions about politics.[15] In principle, this can occur at any age and under any circumstances, but it tends to be concentrated at certain points of our lives.

The importance of political socialization is evident, if nothing else, in the fact that without it, any political culture would disappear after one generation. All of the cultural underpinnings of politics, and many other more transient values, are learned by children and other new citizens through political socialization. It is political socialization that allowed the United States to absorb millions of Irish, Italians, Russians, Poles, Chinese, Vietnamese, and so many other peoples and yet maintain political continuity.

Like most learning, political socialization apparently comes most easily and fully in childhood, and diminishes as we grow older. However, explicit and detailed information about politics tends not to be picked up much before the teen years. Children learn in their families many basic social attitudes, such as trust in people and attitudes toward authority, that will be important in shaping their later response to politics. But most children acquire only rather primitive ideas about what government is and how politics works. These things are primarily learned in adolescence and early adulthood and continue to be learned throughout adult life. For example, Table 7–4 shows the percentage of Swedish youths of varying ages who were undecided as to which political party was the best. Among eleven- to twelve-year-olds, 73 percent did not have a preference among the parties. This indecision declined to 35 percent by early adulthood. I realize

TABLE 7–4   DEVELOPMENT OF POLITICAL ORIENTATIONS AMONG SWEDISH YOUTH

Age	Percent undecided as to best party
11–12	73
13–15	66
16–18	55
19–21	47
22–24	32
25–27	35

Source: Adapted with permission from The Free Press, a division of Simon & Schuster, Inc., from *Political Socialization: A Study in the Psychology of Political Behavior* by Herbert H. Hyman table 12, p. 82. Copyright © 1959, 1969 by The Free Press.

[15]A good general review of political socialization is Pamela Johnston Conover, "Political Socialization: Where's the Politics?" in William Crotty, ed., *Political Science: Looking to the Future,* vol. 3 (Evanston, Ill.: Northwestern University Press, 1991), pp. 125–52. See also Stanley W. Moore, et al., *The Child's Political World* (New York: Praeger, 1985); Orit Ichilov, *Political Socialization, Citizenship Education, and Democracy* (New York: Teachers College Press, 1990); and Roberta S. Sigel, *Political Learning in Adulthood* (Chicago: University of Chicago Press, 1989).

that these findings come from quite an old study, but I have not found a more recent study that gets at this; I believe most political scientists would expect that similar relationships are not much different today.

One of the concerns of political scientists studying socialization is to assess the varying roles of different *agents of socialization.* We must learn about politics *from* someone, and the various sources of learning are what we call the agents of socialization. Different agents operate in different ways and affect different areas of our values and assumptions about politics. We learn about politics from many different agents, but a few particularly important ones are our families, schools, and peer groups.

From our parents we acquire a number of social values that will apply to politics as they do to other aspects of our lives. It is also thought that we may gain expectations about how politics should occur in the state by extension from the way politics (the making of family decisions by the use of power) is conducted in the family; an authoritarian family may prepare one for an authoritarian state and a democratic family for a democratic state.[16] More specific political values and assumptions do not develop as much through the family as we might suppose, since they tend to be acquired during adolescence—a period when most children are trying to establish an independent identity.

Schools are of particular interest to students of political socialization because they are agents of socialization that the state controls and through which the leaders of the state can attempt to mold the citizenry. In all states, there is some degree of guided socialization through the schools. Schools in the United States try to develop informed, patriotic citizens directly through civics classes and salutes to the flag and indirectly through class materials in history, literature, and other courses. Some states such as Cuba, China, and Nazi Germany have used the schools vigorously and directly to attempt to remake their citizens. In general, however, governments have had relatively little success in doing this. The Nazis failed notably, for example, in their attempts to produce the "new German man."

Peer groups are extremely influential in developing adolescents' tastes and their view of the world, but they vary considerably in their political impact. In most friendship groups of adolescents, politics does not figure importantly in the attention of the group. The group will influence its members' choices in clothes or social behavior strongly but will leave their political identity to develop independently. However, youths who are already somewhat involved in politics may gravitate together as a friendship group, and when this happens, the group may have a profound impact on the political development of all its members.

From our discussion of schools as socializing agents, one would probably conclude that governments do not have much of an impact on political culture, even if they try. One instance, however, in which governments were able to affect political culture rather strongly is offered by the cultures of East and West Germany at the time they were united in 1991. After the Second World War, Germany was divided into two states, the Federal Republic of Germany (West) and the German Democratic Republic (East). The two

---

[16]This is a controversial position; many scholars think it oversimplifies a complex process of the development of values. A good presentation of the position is Harry Eckstein and Ted Robert Gurr, *Patterns of Authority* (New York: Wiley, 1975).

states were aligned with opposite sides in the Cold War, and though they shared a common history and culture leading up to the defeat in 1945, for the next forty-five years, they were separated by international events. Indeed, from 1960 on, any travel between the two was made impossible by the infamous Berlin Wall.

When scholars began to study the culture of newly united Germany after 1991, they found many sharp contrasts between the cultures of West Germans and of East Germans. For instance, 31 percent of West Germans but only 11 percent of those from the East prided themselves on the democratic institutions of Germany.[17] And 81 percent of Easterners but only 44 percent of Westerners agreed with the statement "Socialism is basically a good idea that was only badly carried out."[18]

Why was Germany an exception? One factor is probably just the long time that the two governments had at their disposal; they had from 1945 to 1991 to work on the cultures of their states. Also, at least after 1960, the two populations were forcibly isolated from each other; anthropologists have even found that villages a few miles apart but separated by the Wall developed over that period of time recognizably different accents and dialects of German. And finally, as described in the example on Germany in this chapter, the culture of defeated Germany was in many ways a shattered remnant and was probably easier than most cultures to reshape. Whatever the explanation, Germany provides an example demonstrating that major cultural shaping is not impossible—though it may take an unusual constellation of advantageous circumstances for it to occur.

---

[17]David P. Conradt, "Political Culture in Unified Germany: Will the Bonn Republic Survive and Thrive in Berlin?" *German Studies Review* 21 (1998), p. 92.
[18]David P. Conradt, *The German Polity*, 7th ed. (New York: Longman, 2001), p. 85.

Example: Building Authority and Legitimacy in West Germany After World War II[19]

After the defeat of Germany in 1945, the Germans as a people were demoralized politically. They had bought a dream of greatness from Adolf Hitler, but he had brought them defeat and international disgrace. They were hated throughout Europe, their country had been cut up on the map, and their industries and farms were in ruins. Germans who were fifty years old in 1945 could not be blamed if, having been dazzled by politics, they now withdrew from it. They had grown up under the kaiser's monarchy and had seen it overthrown in disgrace at the end of World War I, when they were in their early twenties. They had then lived through fifteen years of a chaotic attempt at democracy, which never really established its authority and legitimacy with the people and ended in Hitler's dictatorship. They were thirty-eight years old when Hitler came to power; in the next

---

[19]West Germany and East Germany were reunified as Germany in 1991.

twelve years, they saw Germany approach world conquest and then come close to total destruction. They could be pardoned if they were shy of politics after all of this.

In many ways, West Germany after 1945 gave political scientists much the same opportunity to observe an evolutionary development as a new volcanic island rising from the sea offers to biologists. When a new island is formed, biologists get a rare chance to observe which animals are the first to appear on it and see how long it takes a diverse flora and fauna to be established. Similarly, political scientists get few chances to see attitudes toward politics establish themselves among a people who initially have essentially no attitudes. West Germany after the war did provide such a case.

For many years, political observers asked themselves whether democratic behavior and attitudes could possibly develop among Germans. Some said that the people who had put Hitler into office could not develop into democrats. Others thought that if Germany was lucky enough to have a period of peace and economic stability, democracy would be able to establish itself. No one could hazard a guess as to how long the process would take.

As we can see in Tables 7–5, 7–6, and 7–7, the optimists were correct; in fact, the development of democratic support occurred steadily and fairly rapidly. As we see in

TABLE 7–5   ATTITUDES TOWARD THE "PAST," 1951–1970

Q.: When in this century do you think Germany has been best off?

	Year of survey			
	1951 (Percent)	1959 (Percent)	1963 (Percent)	1970 (Percent)
Federal Republic (present)	2	42	62	81
Under Hitler before the war (1933–1939)	42	18	10	5
Under the kaiser, before World War I	45	28	16	5

Source: Adapted from David Contradt, "Changing German Political Culture," *The Civic Culture Revisited,* edited by Gabriel Almond and Sidney Verba, p. 226. Copyright © 1980 Sage Publications Inc. Reprinted by permission of Sage Publications, Inc.

TABLE 7–6   TRUST AND HOSTILITY AMONG GERMANS, 1948–1976

a. Percent "trusting most people"

1948	1959	1967	1973	1976
9%	19%	26%	32%	39%

b. Percent thinking more people are evil minded than good minded

1949	1951	1953	1971	1976
46%	43%	34%	17%	16%

Source: Adapted from David Contradt, "Changing German Political Culture," *The Civic Culture Revisited,* edited by Gabriel Almond and Sidney Verba, p. 226. Copyright © 1980 Sage Publications Inc. Reprinted by permission of Sage Publications, Inc.

TABLE 7–7   FREQUENCY OF POLITICAL DISCUSSION, 1953–1972

	1953 (Percent)	1959 (Percent)	1961 (Percent)	1965 (Percent)	1969 (Percent)	1972 (Percent)
Daily	9	11	10	10	37	50
Occasionally	29	50	51	66	40	34
Never	63	39	39	25	23	16

Source: Reprinted by permission of the publisher from *Germany Transformed: Political Culture and the New Politics* by Kendall L. Baker, R.J. Dalton, and K. Kildebrandt, Cambridge, Mass: Harvard University Press. Copyright ©1981 by the President and Fellows of Harvard College.

Table 7–5, during the first twenty years, the democratic regime established itself as the best arrangement Germany had known—better than Hitler's dictatorship or the kaiser's monarchy.

It was not simply that the country was economically well off. The political institutions of democracy became more popular during this period. In 1959, in a survey similar to that mentioned earlier for the United States, Germans were asked what they were proud of about their country. Only 7 percent pointed to Germany's political institutions. In 1978, the question was repeated in a survey. By that time, 31 percent of the things mentioned were aspects of government and politics. By 1988, the figure had grown to 51 percent.[20]

Support for democracy in the abstract also grew across the first two decades. In 1953, only a bit over 55 percent of the Germans stated in the abstract that democracy was the best form of government.[21] By 1976, 90 percent answered yes to the same question.[22]

The sort of social relations among people that are required if a loose system of authority (such as democracy) is to work was also developing. In a society where people are hostile and suspicious of each other, democracy cannot work well. As we see in Table 7–6, trust grew steadily and social hostility decreased during this time.

Finally, it is necessary that the people begin to be active and interested citizens. As we see in Table 7–7, this also developed steadily.

West Germany did not necessarily become an ideal democracy, but it is interesting to see that there were established, over a couple of decades, patterns of behavior and support similar to those of such democracies as the United States or Great Britain. No one would have predicted this with any confidence in 1950, and it was an eye-opener for political scientists.

[20]David Conradt, *The German Polity,* 5th ed. (New York: Longmann, 1993), p. 55.
[21]Kendall Baker, Russell Dalton, and Kai Hildebrandt, *Germany Transformed* (Cambridge: Harvard University Press, 1981), p. 24.
[22]David Conradt, "Changing German Political Culture," in Gabriel Almond and Sidney Verba, eds., *The Civic Culture Revisited* (Boston: Little, Brown, 1980), p. 234.

Example: Declining Democratic Legitimacy in the United States

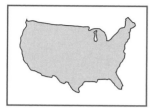

The story of the last few decades in the United States has been in some respects the opposite of what we have seen in Germany. Since about the mid-1960s, there has been a puzzling decline in people's confidence in officials and in the political system. It might not seem so strange that the political turmoil of the 1960s and the Watergate scandal of 1973 shook people's faith, but there appeared to be further erosion during the calmer period of the late 1970s and the 1980s.

Table 7–8 shows a downward trend in the percentage of Americans thinking that one can trust the government to do what is right most of the time or always and an upward trend in the percentage thinking that the government is run for the benefit of a few big interests and that quite a lot of people running the government are crooked. The steadiness of the trend across various events and various presidents makes it look as though it were not a response to particular disappointments, but political scientists are frankly at a loss to say just what *has* caused the decline.[23]

TABLE 7–8   DECLINE OF CONFIDENCE, 1958–1996

	1958	1964	1968	1972	1976	1980	1984	1988	1992	1996
Percent who trust the government to do what is right "most of the time" or "always"	73	76	61	53	33	25	44	40	29	33
Percent thinking the government is run for a few big interests	—	29	40	53	66	70	55	64	75	70
Percent thinking "quite a lot" of government people are crooked	24	29	25	36	42	47	32	40*	46*	44*

Source: University of Michigan, Center for Political Studies, National Elections Studies. Data made available by the Inter-University Consortium for Political and Social Research.
*Slightly different question wording after 1988: "quite a few" crooked.

[23]Arthur Miller and Jack Citrin present an interesting interchange concerning the possible causes of the decline in "Political Issues and Trust in Government: 1964–70," *American Political Science Review* 68 (September 1974): 951–1001; see also Arthur H. Miller and Stephen A. Borrelli, "Confidence in Government During the 1980s," *American Politics Quarterly* 19 (April 1991): 147–73; and Burns Roper, "Democracy in America: How Are We Doing?" *Public Perspective* 5 (March-April 1994): 3–5.

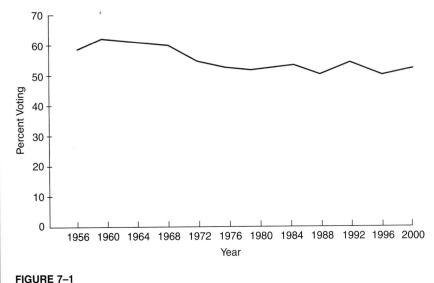

FIGURE 7–1
Percentage of voting-age population voting, United States

Source: U.S. Bureau of the Census, *Statistical Abstract of the United States.*

While this plunge in trust and legitimacy has been occurring, Americans have remained an attentive and reasonably active citizenry. As you can see in Figure 7–1, while turnout in elections has dropped somewhat, the decline is a fairly gentle one, from 59 percent of the electorate voting in the 1956 presidential election to 50 percent in 2000.

The number of people performing the more substantial act of writing to members of Congress has risen steadily, from 6 percent in 1958 to 36 percent in 1992.[24]

Finally, the percentage who state that they follow what is going on in government and public affairs some or most of the time has remained essentially unchanged: 63 percent said that they did so in 1960 and 64 percent in 1998.[25]

The combination of a still fairly attentive citizenry whose trust of the government has dropped off sharply is alarming and puzzling. It does not bode well for a continuation of stable, constructive democracy, and for this reason it is important that we find out the causes of the change. The person who does so will have made an important contribution to our understanding of democracy.[26]

---

[24]*Public Perspective* (June-July 1996): 12.

[25]University of Michigan, Center for Political Studies, National Election Studies. Data made available by the Inter-University Consortium for Political and Social Research.

[26]Part of the explanation may lie in the fact that something similar appears to have been happening in most of the world's mature democracies over the same period. See Susan J. Pharr and Robert Putnam, eds. *Disaffected Democracies: What's Troubling the Trilateral Countries?* (Princeton, N.J.: Princeton University Press, 2000).

FURTHER READING

Almond, Gabriel, and Verba, Sidney. *The Civic Culture*. Boston: Little Brown, 1965.

———, eds. *The Civic Culture Revisited*. Boston: Little, Brown, 1980.

"Authority." In *International Encyclopedia of the Social Sciences*.

Barber, Benjamin. *Strong Democracy*. Berkeley: University of California Press, 1984.

Conover, Pamela Johnston. "Political Socialization: Where's the Politics?" In *Political Science: Looking to the Future*, vol. 3, edited by William Crotty. Evanston, Ill.: Northwestern University Press, 1991, pp. 125–52.

Dahl, Robert. *Modern Political Analysis*. 4th ed. Englewood Cliffs, N.J.: Prentice-Hall, 1984.

Dalton, Russell J. "Communists and Democrats: Democratic Attitudes in the Two Germanies." *British Journal of Political Science* 24 (1994): 469–93.

Delli Carpini, Michael X., and Keeter, Scott. *What Americans Know About Politics and Why It Matters*. New Haven: Yale University Press, 1996.

Gellner, Ernest. *Culture, Identity, and Politics*. Cambridge, England: Cambridge University Press, 1987.

Graber, Doris. *Mass Media and American Politics*. Washington, D.C.: Congressional Quarterly Press, 1980.

Huntington, Samuel P. *The Clash of Civilizations and the Remaking of World Order*. New York: Simon & Schuster, 1996.

Inglehart, Ronald. *Culture Shift in Advanced Industrial Society*. Princeton, N.J.: Princeton University Press, 1990.

Iyengar, Shanto, and Kinder, Donald R. *News That Matters: Television and American Opinion*. Chicago: University of Chicago Press, 1987.

Laitin, David. *Hegemony and Culture*. Chicago: University of Chicago Press, 1986.

Lane, Robert E. *Political Ideology: Why the American Common Man Believes What He Does*. New York: Free Press, 1962.

"Legitimacy." In *International Encyclopedia of the Social Sciences*.

Marcus, George E.; Sullivan, John L.; Theiss-Morse, Elizabeth; and Wood, Sandra L. *With Malice Towards Some: How People Make Civil Liberties Judgments*. New York: Cambridge University Press, 1995.

Niemi, Richard G., and Junn, Jane. *Civic Education: What Makes Students Learn*. New Haven: Yale University Press, 1998.

Norris, Pippa. *Critical Citizens*. New York: Oxford University Press, 1999.

Nye, Joseph S., Jr.; Zelikow, Philip D.; and King, David C. *Why People Don't Trust Government*. Cambridge: Harvard University Press, 1997.

Patterson, Thomas E. *The Mass Media Election*. New York: Praeger, 1980.

———. *Out of Order: How the Decline of Political Parties and the Growing Power of the News Media Undermine the American Way of Electing Presidents*. New York: Knopf, 1994.

Pharr, Susan J., and Putnam, Robert D. *Disaffected Democracies: What's Troubling the Trilateral Countries?* Princeton, N.J.: Princeton University Press, 2000.

Putnam, Robert D. "Bowling Alone: America's Declining Social Capital." *Journal of Democracy* 6 (January 1995): 65–78.

———. *Making Democracy Work: Civic Traditions in Modern Italy*. Princeton, N.J.: Princeton University Press, 1994.

Rokeach, Milton. *The Open and Closed Mind: Investigations into the Nature of Belief Systems and Personality Systems.* New York: Basic Books, 1960.

Sapiro, Virginia. "Political Socialization During Adulthood: Clarifying the Political Time of Our Lives." In *New Directions in Political Psychology,* edited by Robert Y. Shapiro, Michael X. Delli Carpini, and Leonie Huddy. London: JAI Press, 1994.

Sniderman, Paul. *Personality and Democratic Politics.* Berkeley: University of California Press, 1975.

Sullivan, John L.; Shamir, Michal; Walsh, Patrick; and Roberts, Nigel S. *Political Tolerance in Context: Support for Civil Liberties in the United States, Israel, and New Zealand.* Boulder, Colo.: Westview Press, 1985.

Tarrow, Sidney. "Making Social Science Work Across Space and Time: A Critical Reflection on Robert Putnam's *Making Democracy Work.*" *American Political Science Review* 90 (1996): 389–98.

Verba, Sidney; Schlozman, Kay Lehman; and Brady, Henry E. *Voice and Equality: Civic Voluntarism in American Politics.* Cambridge: Harvard University Press, 1995.

Zaller, John R. *The Nature and Origins of Mass Opinion.* New York: Cambridge University Press, 1992.

 WEBSITES OF INTEREST

National Election Studies Guide to Public Opinion and Electoral Behavior:
www.umich.edu/~nes/nesguide/nesguide.htm

The Gallup Polls
www.gallup.com/

8

DEMOCRACY AND
ITS RECENT SURGE
IN THE WORLD

A democracy is a state in which all fully qualified citizens vote at regular intervals to choose, from among alternative candidates, the people who will be in charge of setting the state's policies. Democracy is "government of the people"; therefore, there is also a sense that the full population of citizens will be actively engaged between elections in debate over alternative policies and in the work of setting the policies; how fully engaged they are varies across democracies, and whether they are sufficiently engaged has long been a matter of debate.[1]

Most of you are familiar with democratic government from your own experience. Only a relatively small number of the world's states are stable democracies—though most of the world's states have been democracies at one time or another since the 1960s. Democracy requires an implicit agreement by the conflicting groups in a state to accept the possibility that they will lose out in the making of policy. In effect, it requires an agreement among labor unions, corporations, farm groups, environmentalists, vegetarians, motorcycle enthusiasts, and all other groups to take their chances on the outcome of a process of policy making in which the population as a whole gets the deciding voice. Each group accepts that it must abide by the end result and hopes that it will be able to get enough of what it wants out of the process. This is the "democratic bargain."

When we look at it in this way, it is easy to see why democracy might be fragile. All that is needed to make a democracy collapse is for one or more important groups to reject the results of the democratic bargain and to have access to enough power to overthrow the system. Many parts of the world are beset by problems of overpopulation, ethnic and religious conflict, poverty, and chancy positions in world trade—problems so fierce that it becomes difficult for powerful groups to face policy defeats philosophically; the

---

[1]Examples of this debate include proposals for referendums, workplace democracy, and citizen caucuses.

stakes are too high. And military forces or popular movements usually lie close at hand, willing and able to overthrow the system.

As one might suspect, under these circumstances only a small number of the world's states are stable democracies. Of the ninety-seven states that were independent for at least forty years in the year 2000, only twenty-four had an uninterrupted record of electoral democratic government during that time.[2] Most of these were prosperous industrialized states whose people can more easily afford to compromise on the "democratic bargain." However, poor, small states such as Jamaica, Malta, Botswana, and Costa Rica also had steady histories of democratic government.

THE WAVE OF DEMOCRATIZATION IN THE 1980S AND 1990S

The world's imagination was seized in 1989 when the Iron Curtain fell, and the Berlin Wall with it, and most of the communist states of Eastern Europe suddenly threw off their old systems and established democracies. The drama of the failed coup in the Soviet Union in 1991 and the victory of the pro-democratic forces there had people glued to their television sets. These dramatic changes were only part of a larger move toward democracy that has covered two decades and ranged across many parts of the world.

Southern Europe saw three shifts from right-wing dictatorships to democracy in the late 1970s: in Greece, Portugal, and Spain. A bit later, a wave of democratization swept Latin America, as several states reestablished democracies after periods of military (mostly right-wing) dictatorship: Ecuador and Peru in 1978, Bolivia in 1982, Argentina in 1983, Uruguay in 1984, Brazil in 1985, and Chile in 1989.

Finally in 1989 and 1990, along with the wave of democratization in the formerly communist states of Eastern Europe (East Germany, which has since merged with former West Germany; Poland; Czechoslovakia; Hungary; Bulgaria; Romania; and Yugoslavia), several states scattered around the world moved to democracy: Algeria over the period 1989–1991 (and at the same time Egypt, Jordan, and Tunisia moved closer to being democracies); Haiti in 1990; South Korea in 1987; Nepal in 1990; Nicaragua in 1990; Pakistan in 1988; the Philippines in 1986; and South Africa in 1994.

However, this was not a story of uniformly forward progress. After establishing democracy in Algeria, the military was afraid that the fundamentalist Islam party would be victorious, and it abruptly banned elections in 1992. In Haiti, the military ousted newly elected President Jean-Bertrand Aristide in a 1991 coup; he was only reinstated in 1994 after strong pressure from the United States and the temporary occupation of Haiti by U.S. troops. The military overthrew the democratically elected government in Pakistan in 1999 and installed their commanding general in power. Democracy is tenuous in most parts of the former Soviet Union. And the new elections in Africa include only a few in which a government has actually been replaced; more often, the old dictators have managed to prevail under the new democratic rules. Overall, however, there has been a clear movement toward more democracy.

[2]Adam Przeworski, et al., *Democracy and Development* (New York: Cambridge University Press, 2000), appendix 1.2.

The shifts of the 1980s occurred in regional waves, but they were all part of a larger wave of democratization, often called simply the "Third Wave." The first wave of democratization came in the wake of World War I, as Germany became a democracy in 1918 and new democracies were created in Eastern Europe; at about the same time, a number of Latin American states also established democratic regimes. Many of the democracies established at this time, however, failed either under the economic pressures of the Great Depression or in the violence of World War II. A second wave of democratization occurred after World War II, as democracy was reestablished in countries such as Germany and Italy and large numbers of former European colonies in the South achieved independence. Again, while many of those democracies survived, many also fell to military coups. The third wave is considered to have started in the late 1970s with the successful reintroduction of democracy to Spain and Portugal.

POSSIBLE EXPLANATIONS

How may we explain this Third Wave of shifts to democracy? Four possible reasons are: fatigue of some authoritarian regimes; international pressures; people's desire for security against arbitrary abuse; and people's desire for economic development.

In a few cases, authoritarian systems became "tired" and lost popular support. In Spain and Portugal, long-term dictators died, and their regimes lost steam long before their deaths. In Argentina, the military government lost a war with Britain. Most dramatically, the exhaustion of the Soviet Union at maintaining its control of Eastern Europe was a critical element in the wave of democratization in that region in 1989, and the corruption and senility of its Communist Party led to the victory of democracy in the Soviet Union. This was evident in the communists' botched countercoup in 1991; the old party could not muster enough imagination and organization to take advantage of a good opportunity to reestablish its rule.

Also, there has sometimes been international pressure on nondemocratic regimes to change. Spain, Portugal, and Greece came under pressure from their neighbors to become democratic, and the "carrot" of membership in the European Union was offered to them implicitly if they established democratic systems.[3] South Africans were under international trade and investment sanctions for several years to force them to give democratic rights to their black majority, and those sanctions led to democratic government in 1994. Though pressure for democracy in China has been repulsed since the Tiananmen Square massacre in 1989, concern for international reactions has slightly softened the suppression of democratic movements there. Nicaragua's government held free elections under quasi-military pressure from the United States, which promoted a civil war in the country to force a change in regime.

Probably more important than either international pressures or the weakness of the old regimes, however, are the remaining two factors: a desire for human rights and security against abuse and, especially in the communist states of Eastern Europe, economic failure. A desire for security and dignity must have been high among the reasons for democratization in South America, where many of the military regimes had been brutally oppressive. In Argentina and Chile, thousands of people disappeared during the dictatorships and are

---

[3]See Chapter 3, for a discussion of the European Union.

(© 2002 by Sidney Harris.
Reprinted with permission.)

presumed to have been tortured and killed. In the Philippines, the murder of Corazon
Aquino's husband sparked the move for democracy. In East Germany, after the overthrow
of the communist regime, it was learned that the secret police had maintained files on 6
million people, out of a total population of 16 million, and had employed hundreds of thousands of informants. In the formation of most democracies, a yearning for dignity and
security has always played a large part. This was true in the establishment of the first
democracies in Europe and North America in the nineteenth century, and it is true today.

The fourth factor in the surge to democracy was the economic stagnation of many
authoritarian states, which contrasted with the dynamic prosperity of democracies such
as Japan and (then West) Germany. This was particularly true of democratization in
Eastern Europe, where establishing democracy was intermingled with the dismantling
of inefficient socialist economies and the establishment of market economies. The connection between free markets, democracy, and prosperity is not all that clear, as we will
see; but in many democratizing states, part of the thrust for democracy came from a
sense that the state had stagnated economically, that it was not "modern" (not up-to-
date), and that democracy was part of being modern.

THE END OF HISTORY?

While these have been exceedingly important changes, there is also a danger that we
could read more into them than is there. One author, noting these events, declared that

capitalist democracy had won the great ideological debate of the nineteenth and twentieth centuries and that history, as we have known it, had ended because there was nothing left to fight about.[4] Well, the end of history has been declared several times over the past century, but history does not stop.

First, just as we have had a surge of democratization, there have been other periods during the twentieth century when the world saw surges in the other direction, toward dictatorship. The 1920s were such a period, as Germany, Italy, Spain, and various Eastern European states overthrew democracy; and in the 1950s and 1960s, a wave of dictatorship spread over South America and Africa. It is possible that basic circumstances have changed—especially the diminished superpower rivalry of the Soviet Union and United States in the 1990s, which makes it less important for both sides to maintain client dictators—so that the current set of changes will prove long-lived. It is also possible, though, that we have simply been watching one long wave in a slow surge back and forth between democracy and authoritarianism.

One thing that should give us pause is that while in many states such as Spain, Portugal, Greece, Argentina, Brazil, Poland, Czechoslovakia, and Hungary, there is a broad base of support for the new democracy and a full understanding of the "democratic bargain," in others, democracy has been adopted primarily as an alternative to a hated earlier regime; and neither its implications nor its requirements were fully prepared for. In Haiti, for instance, the despicable Duvalier dictatorship was ousted in a democratic movement in 1986; but the Duvaliers had destroyed most alternative leadership, and so a stable democratic regime has not developed. The years since have been marked by violence, strikes, military coups, and occasional chaos.

Romania is another country for which "democratization" may have been as much as anything else a banner under which to overthrow the oppressive Ceausescu dictatorship. Under the democratic government established after Ceausescu's fall, a cult of reverence developed for Ion Antonescu, the fascist dictator during Hitler's occupation who was executed in 1945 for having killed 250,000 Jews. In 1991, the Romanian parliament voted unanimously to honor Antonescu with a minute of silent tribute. Honors for Antonescu were supported by all major newspapers, and only President Ion Iliescu courageously opposed the Antonescu revival and its accompanying anti-Semitism.[5] One has to wonder about the depth of democratic commitment under these circumstances; and indeed, it should not surprise us if Romania, which has had only fleeting experiences of democracy in its past, failed to immediately settle into stable democratic habits after ousting Ceausescu in a spasm of popular uprising. At the least, the Romanian future is unclear.

Aside from the fact that a broad base of support for democracy may be lacking in a number of the new democracies, another aspect of democratization that we should bear in mind is that democracy's openness often unleashes regional nationalist pressures that had been held in check by more oppressive regimes. Unless the state is strong and lucky, it may be pulled apart. Alternatively, the danger to the state may then prompt an antidemocratic reaction from the military, and we may end up back at dictatorship.

---

[4]Francis Fukuyama, "The End of History?" *National Interest* 16 (Summer 1989): 3–19.
[5]"Rising Verbal Attacks Shake Romania's Jews." *New York Times,* 19 June 1991, section 1, p. 10.

The new democracy in Spain, for instance, was immediately challenged by a terrorist movement for separation of the Basque region, and it weathered that challenge only with difficulty. In 1990, the new democratic system of Yugoslavia was immediately faced with the secession of its two most prosperous provinces, Slovenia and Croatia, and a bloody war resulted. Finally, the Soviet Union, as it gradually became more democratic after 1986, saw violent national conflicts between Armenians and Azerbaidzhanis and between Uzbeks and Turks, and attempts by Georgia, Estonia, Latvia, Lithuania, and Ukraine to secede. The upshot of the triumph of democracy in the failed coup of 1991 was the disintegration of the union and its division into a number of new, independent states.

None of the cautions in this section is meant to make you discount the importance of what happened in the late twentieth century. We have seen great events. However, it is a common weakness for social scientists, as for people in general, to assume that what is happening now will continue into the future. Understanding some of the complexities of democratization may help to guard us against this.

WHAT HAVE WE LEARNED?

Theories of political science have had difficulty encompassing the wave of democratization, probably because what is grouped as "democratization" actually consists of many different sorts of processes, in different parts of the world, where the push for democracy came from many different causes and motives. (I have tried to give you some sense of the variety of these processes of "democratization.") Accordingly, political scientists have not been able to come up with a single theory of democratization that is at all general.

The challenge of explaining the Third Wave has led to a fairly substantial shift in the whole field of comparative politics. Explaining *distinct changes,* as compared with analyzing ongoing stable situations, leads us to emphasize individuals' choices and especially the choices of individual leaders. Stable situations are often appropriately analyzed by looking at the balance of groups' power, at broad economic structures, and at the historical background of a current situation. But an event that occurs at a particular point in time is usually not determined in any precise way by such factors, so to analyze it, we must look more specifically at the strategic situations of the actors involved and at their decisions.[6]

This is the way that comparative politics—the study of politics through comparisons of different states' politics—has moved in light of the challenge posed to us by the Third Wave. What have we learned?

1.   *The Importance of "Pacts."* An early work that formed the basis for most further analysis of the Third Wave was a broad review by O'Donnell and Schmitter (1986) of what were then the most recent cases of democratization, primarily in Latin America and southern Europe.[7] This study does not so much develop a theory as note and comment on similarities across cases.

---

[6]For an opposed view, see Nancy Bermeo, "Myths of Moderation: Confrontation and Conflict During Democratic Transitions," *Comparative Politics* 29 (April 1997): 305–22.

[7]Guillermo O'Donnell and Philippe C. Schmitter, *Transitions from Authoritarian Rule: Tentative Conclusions About Uncertain Democracies* (Baltimore: Johns Hopkins University Press, 1986).

Lenin's statue dumped near a cemetery after a failed August 1991 Soviet coup.
(Andy Hernandez/Sipa Press)

One important conclusion the authors reach is that it is important for successful democratization that the democratizers form "pacts" with those whom they are ousting to ensure a smooth transition and to lay a good base of support for the future democracy. Such pacts might include, for instance, amnesty from prosecution for crimes committed under the dictatorship; symbolic affirmation of the old regime, as in the maintenance of a powerless or weak monarch; or guarantees of funding for the army. "Pacts" figured importantly in the Spanish case, described in detail in an example in this chapter.

As always in looking at democratization, however, there are few universal truths. In the wave of democratization across Eastern Europe in 1989, which occurred after the study by O'Donnell and his coauthors, pacts were not nearly so important. Unlike Latin America, this was not a case of ousting a military associated with powerful domestic forces, which had to be dealt with gingerly. Rather, the force being ousted was primarily the Soviet army, and broad nationalist sentiment coincided with the democratic thrust. Therefore, the new democratic leaders did not need to bargain very much with their discredited predecessors.

2.   *Sudden Changes.* Many of the recent shifts to democracy have taken observers by surprise. No one predicted in 1988, for instance, that by the end of 1989, many Eastern European states would be democracies. One scholar

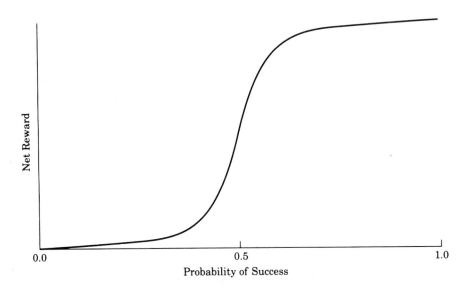

FIGURE 8–1
Probable reward for coming out in favor of democracy, as probability increases that democracy
will in fact be established.

has provided a good explanation for why these shifts might be sudden and difficult to predict.[8]

Under an authoritarian regime, there are few rewards and many punishments for anyone coming out in favor of democracy. However, this is a function of how likely it is that
democracy will be established; if democracy in the end is established, there will be many
rewards and no punishments for those who had come out in favor of it. The key factor
is that net rewards of coming out may tip suddenly as the probability of success shifts
over from less than even to greater than even. This is depicted graphically in Figure 8–1.
As the probability of success rises from zero to 0.2, 0.3, or 0.4, the net rewards for favoring democracy do not increase much. In fact, regimes may crack down more on opponents as their situation becomes slightly less secure than it had been. Suddenly, however,
at some point the danger in favoring democracy appears to decrease. People find that
when they demonstrate in the street, there are thousands of other people there, too many
for the government to take on. Almost overnight, favoring democracy may shift from
being a dangerous activity, restricted to the hard core, to an easy activity that may carry
future rewards.[9]

---

[8]Adam Przeworski, "Some Problems in the Study of Transition to Democracy," in Guillermo O'Donnell,
Philippe C. Schmitter, and Laurence Whitehead. eds., *Transitions from Authoritarian Rule: Comparative Perspectives* (Baltimore: Johns Hopkins University Press, 1986).

[9]I do not mean here that the process is automatic from this point on. China is an example of where this
point had been reached in 1989; thousands were flocking to the democratic banner, but the government
responded with the Tiananmen Square massacre, thus moving the probability of success back to a lower level.

3. ***Crisis or Noncrisis?*** Stephen Haggard and Robert Kaufman have pointed out that a transition to democracy occurs differently if it comes in response to an economic crisis in the state than if it occurs under good economic conditions.[10] Some examples of "crisis" transitions are the Eastern European transitions of 1989–1991 and most of the recent Latin American transitions. On the other hand, a number of East Asian transitions, such as those in Thailand and Korea, occurred in the presence of prosperity, as did transitions in Spain, Turkey, and Chile.

When a transition is spurred by economic crisis, the ruling authoritarian government often has little credibility and cannot influence the path of the transition much at all. Pacts are less important in such transitions, and the military are less likely to retain any influence in the new regime. In Turkey and Thailand, with their "noncrisis" transitions, the resulting democracies have had to constantly look over their shoulders to see how the military viewed any decisions. When a pro-Islamic cabinet was formed in Turkey in 1997, for instance, the military forced it to dissolve after several months because they thought it would weaken the secular, Western-oriented doctrines they supported.

Politics is also likely to be more open after crisis-driven transitions, with fewer restrictions on broad participation by a full range of parties and interest groups. As a result, the politics that follow are likely to be marked by greater representation of the political left, and to be more tumultuous, than the politics that follow a noncrisis transition.

4. ***Democracy and Freedom.*** Analyzing the thrusts for democracy has also *reminded* us of an old truth: Democracy and individual freedom are certainly related, but they are not identical; while moving toward one means moving toward the other, there is not an automatic or inevitable correspondence between them, and there may be occasional instances of marked disparity.

That democracy and individual freedom have some sort of connection should be apparent. Democracy and a variety of individual freedoms derived originally from the same basic principles of liberalism.[11] Also, for purely practical reasons, democracy requires at least minimal levels of freedom of speech and freedom of association if the public bargaining that is the essence of democracy is to proceed at all.

However, a variety of other freedoms—such as freedom of religion, free markets (see point 5 on "Democracy and Capitalism"), freedom to travel where you will, freedom to consume alcohol, and so on—are *not* necessarily companions of democracy, although we may find in practice that they usually go together.

A good example showing that freedom and democracy do not necessarily imply each other is Hong Kong, which as a British colony until 1997 never had democratic government but which had an open society with many liberal freedoms—a free press, freedom of religion, freedom of speech and association, and so on. The United States also furnishes examples from its history in which, although we are a democracy, we have seen the level of freedoms rise and fall. The internment of Japanese-Americans during the Second World War, the system of legal racial segregation in many parts of the country

---

[10]Stephen Haggard and Robert Kaufman. *The Political Economy of Democratic Transitions* (Princeton, N.J.: Princeton University Press, 1995).

[11]As we saw in Chapter 2.

through the first two-thirds of the twentieth century, the McCarthy period in which freedom of expression was limited—all help to demonstrate that there is not an automatic correspondence between democracy and freedom. Perhaps the most dramatic demonstration that freedom and democracy do not automatically coincide is that for the first half-century of its democratic history, the United States continued a brutal, institutionalized system of slavery.

The question of how and whether democracy and individual freedom are linked arises especially in the case of democratization because in a number of countries authoritarian systems have gradually become more liberal and open, often with no shift to democracy for some years. Democracy has then come—or not come—only as a last step. Thus, it has been necessary, in analyzing the process of democratization, to separate the two processes. It appears that democratization may work best where it has been preceded by slow liberalization, which has provided time for opposition leadership to form, for organizations of representation to be established, and for working relationships to be established between the old regime and the forces for change. For example, in Brazil a process of *abertura,* or "opening," was begun by the military regime in 1974, under which discussion became more open, local governments became more independent, and political parties could form. It was not until 1985 that democracy was established.[12]

5.   ***Democracy and Capitalism.*** The surge of democratization in Eastern Europe had much to do with the failure of the communist economic systems to provide prosperity and flexible production of goods and services. Especially in the Soviet Union, what came first seems to have been a realization that the Soviet economic system was not competitive with the market systems of the West; steps toward democratization were largely a part of the way Soviet leaders tried to adjust the overall system to improve their economic performance. Does a decision to adopt market mechanisms for the economy also imply a move to democracy?[13]

As in the case of freedom and democracy, we might expect that free markets and democracy would go together, because both are based on the aggregation of individual choices as a way to make collective decisions and both reflect the basic liberal value of making individuals responsible for their choices.[14] Therefore, it is no surprise that most democracies of the world have market-based economies.

However, there have been plenty of nondemocratic states in the past that used market mechanisms for their economy. Hong Kong, again, is a good example. It operates with an open market economy yet has never had fully democratic government, either under Britain or now as part of China. Many dictatorships and military governments in Africa rule states that essentially have market economies. China, even as it has brutally been putting down the movement for democracy since 1989, has allowed a rapid evolution of its economy away from communist planning and toward market mechanisms.

Therefore, there is no automatic connection between democracy and capitalism, and the Eastern European states could in principle have made a shift in their economies with-

---

[12]For a discussion of why military regimes might choose to yield up power in this way, see Chapter 9.
[13]See Chapter 6 for a discussion of "market mechanisms."
[14]See Charles Lindblom, *Politics and Markets* (New York: Basic Books, 1977), chap. 12.

out moving to democracy. Very likely, however, their rejection of the past and their desire for change and integration with the West were such that it seemed natural to become "Western" in politics as well as in economy. A radical change in the economy would have been very difficult without a thorough change of leaders; therefore, a basic governmental change of *some* sort was probably necessary, whether or not it was a move to democracy.

Example: Democratization in Spain

For a brief period in the 1930s, Spain had a democratic government; but the army, supported by Hitler and Mussolini, overthrew the government at the end of a long and bloody civil war in 1939 and established Francisco Franco as a fascist dictator. Franco ruled from 1939 until his death in 1975.

His dictatorship was ironfisted and authoritarian in the early years, but for the last decade or two of his rule, there was considerable liberalization in Spain. Labor unions, which were technically still illegal, were tolerated and bargained collectively for large numbers of workers. Public education, which had earlier been suppressed, blossomed: In 1957, there were only 120 high schools in Spain, one *fewer* than in the last year of the Republic, but in the next decade, the number of students attending high school went up 1,000 percent. The Spanish economy, organized as a free market in contrast with the political structure, grew rapidly and diversified; the large landowners who formed the core of Franco's support became less and less central to the economy.

Thus, when Franco died in 1975, the stage was set for change. However, everyone was apprehensive. Against the promise of a more modern society in 1975 were set the bloody memories of the civil war of the 1930s, characterized by shocking brutality and atrocities.

There seems agreement that the transition was eased by unwritten agreements ("pacts") between the army and the democratic forces. The army apparently acquiesced in establishment of a democracy on three conditions:

1. The monarchy (which Franco had set up to succeed to power after his death) was to be retained.
2. The political right, rather than the army's old enemies on the left, were to lead the change.
3. The country's regions should be given no self-determination.

In 1976, King Juan Carlos and his conservative prime minister, Adolfo Suarez, put a democratic constitution before the people of Spain in a referendum. The referendum was important because it added the legitimacy of popular approval to the new democracy. The constitution, reflecting the king's wishes, established more of a democracy than the army had probably envisioned, one with a constitutional, mainly symbolic monarch.

Over the next few years, the new democracy was plagued by disorganized party conflict in the parliament, together with a rising campaign of terrorism by Basque nationalists. The terrorists' targets were primarily officers of the police and the army, which added to the tension because those institutions were potentially dangerous if they became disenchanted with the new system. In 1981, there was a serious attempt to overthrow the regime. A group of soldiers seized the parliament when it was in session, with the entire cabinet present, and announced that they were taking over the state in the name of the king. However, they failed to cut off communications into and out of the palace; Juan Carlos telephoned the commanders of the army, some of whom were already preparing to set out for Madrid in support of the coup, and told them they would have to depose him if they wished to overthrow the democracy. The coup failed, and the political leaders were freed.

Afterward, Juan Carlos reportedly met with the parliamentary party leaders and told them they would have to work out better techniques of decision making and compromise, because he doubted he could thwart another coup if one were attempted. In the next several years, Spanish democracy was solidified in several ways:

- In 1982, a moderate socialist, Felipe Gonzalez, became prime minister. His long, not very radical rule helped to calm fears of the "reds" and lay the civil war to rest.
- Considerable power of self-government was devolved onto the regions.
- Spain became a member of the European Community in 1986, integrating it into a democratic organization of democratic states.

Spain appears to have successfully established a stable base for democracy, marked by a peaceful and straightforward replacement of Gonzalez's socialist government by a right-of-center cabinet following the 1996 election.

Example: Fragile Democratization in Peru

In contrast to the (relatively) smooth progress of democratization in Spain, Peru illustrates the uncertain and fragile process by which democracy is often established.

Peru is a poor country on the west coast of Latin America—a poor country, but one with a vibrant cultural life and a long history of intellectual contributions; three of its universities are over three hundred years old. The country has long been torn by ethnic, economic, and regional conflicts. Approximately half of its people are Amerindians, mostly living in the impoverished interior of the country. Economic disparities between the interior and the more prosperous coast are indicated by the fact that infant mortality in the coastal region is 46 per thousand births but 128 in the lower areas of the interior and 156 in the mountains.[15]

From the Second World War until 1978, except for a five-year interlude of democratic government from 1963 to 1968, Peru was ruled by various military groups, which replaced each other from time to time by seizing power in coups d'état (see "Military Government" in Chapter 9). In 1977, General Francisco Morales Bermúdez announced a plan to restore civilian rule. A constitution-writing assembly was elected, the new constitution emerged in 1979, and a new president and Congress were elected in 1980.

From 1980 to the present, there have been regular presidential and congressional elections every five years, so one might conclude that steady democracy had been established in the democratization of 1979. However, the experience of democracy since 1980 has not been that smooth, and the outlook remains uncertain. In this, Peru is probably more typical of newly established democracies than is Spain.

Not long after the first election of the new democracy, a left-wing terrorist movement appeared in the interior that called itself *Sendero Luminoso,* the "Shining Path." It developed broad-based strength in the region and drew down on itself an unprincipled retaliation from the military that was almost as destructive of society as *Sendero Luminoso* itself. At the height of the movement's activities in 1989, the government reported that 3,198 people had been killed in terrorist violence. At the same time, it was estimated that since 1982 approximately three thousand people had been executed by the military, and another three thousand had "disappeared" in military jails and were assumed dead.[16] The government appointed peace commissions to investigate human rights abuses by the military, but both commissions eventually resigned, stating that they could get no cooperation from the military.

The economy also did badly during the initial years of the democracy. Real incomes in the area around the capital city of Lima declined by 1990 to about one-third what they had been in 1980.[17] By 1990, inflation was running at 7,650 percent a year. (If inflation were to run at that rate in the United States, a shirt that cost $10 at the beginning of a year would cost $765 by the end of the year!) Governmental economic policy had been crippled by opposition from businesses and labor unions. The latter had launched several general strikes at various times, in which all unions went out on strike simultaneously, for maximum political impact.

In the 1990 election, a little-known agronomist of Japanese descent, Alberto Fujimori, won on a pledge to fight inflation and corruption. He initiated an austerity plan for the economy—abolishing subsidies, breaking up monoplies, simplifying the tax system, and privatizing a number of publicly owned industries. In November 1991, Fujimori convinced the Congress to give him 150 days of emergency dictatorial power to deal with economic problems; he used this power to deregulate most forms of transport and to open telecommunications, the postal services, the schools, and

---

[15]James D. Rudolph, *Peru: The Evolution of a Crisis* (Westport, Conn.: Praeger, 1992), p. 8.
[16]Europa Publications Ltd., *Europa Yearbook 1995* (London: Unwin Brothers Ltd.), p. 2360.
[17]Susan C. Stokes, *Cultures in Conflict: Social Movements and the State in Peru* (Berkeley: University of California Press, 1995), p. 46.

other services to private competition. He also gave the military added leeway in combating *Sendero Luminoso.*

His relations with Congress deteriorated as a result of these actions, and on April 5, 1992, Fujimori carried out what has been called an *autogolpe* ("self-coup"). He announced suspension of the 1979 constitution, had troops seize the Congress and all television and radio stations, and placed large numbers of labor leaders and leaders of Congress under house arrest. Tanks patrolled the streets of Lima.

A week later, when censorship was lifted, opposition leaders called on the people to take up arms against the president, a right that had been guaranteed in the 1979 constitution. However, the *autogolpe* had been fairly popular, and there was no response to the opposition's call to arms. Fujimori presented his revised version of the 1979 Constitution to the electorate in 1993, with new provisions allowing the president to run for reelection and setting a death sentence for terrorist activity. The revised Constitution was approved with 52 percent of the vote.

Over the next couple of years, Fujimori maintained good relations with the military. He and his courts protected military officers from charges of human rights abuse, transferring even well-documented cases of murder from civil courts to the military courts, for instance, where the officers received relatively mild sentences. The government gradually won the twin battles against inflation and *Sendero Luminoso,* capturing *Sendero*'s leader in 1994.

In the 1995 presidential election, Fujimori won in a landslide with 65 percent of the vote, and his party gained a majority in Congress. Over the next few years, he cemented his relationship with the military further, issuing an amnesty in 1995 for all military officers and police convicted of human rights violations since 1980 in connection with the counterinsurgency campaign. He also claimed credit as a tough leader when a guerrilla group (not part of *Sendero Luminoso*) occupied the Japanese embassy in 1996, taking everyone in the building hostage. After four months of highly publicized deadlock in negotiations with the guerrillas, Fujimori ordered a military assault in which the hostages were successfully freed. The guerrillas were killed—some of them reportedly after they had surrendered.

During Fujimori's second term, even though he had successfully put down rebellion and gotten the economy into reasonable order, Peru still had intense lines of political animosity. The military remained highly political and was a lightning rod for angry passions on both sides, and Peru remained a poor country with huge disparities of income and education. Fujimori undermined any infant sense of constitutionalism that might have emerged in the country, operating fast and loose with the rule of law. The constitution he wrote in 1993 limits presidents to two terms, but Fujimori manipulated rules furiously during his second term to evade this provision and run for a third term in 2000. When three Constitutional Court justices ruled that he could not do so under the constitution, he removed them from the court. And when a television station aggressively investigated abuses by the Peruvian intelligence service, its Israeli-born owner was stripped of his Peruvian citizenship; thereupon, his shares in the station were impounded under a law stating that foreign citizens may not own Peruvian television stations.

The election in which Fujimori ran for his unconstitutional third term, in April 2000, was marked by massive irregularities, especially in the voting rolls. A popular alternative candidate who had arisen in the campaign, Alejandro Toledo, an economist of Amerindian heritage, rejected the first-round results of the election when they showed Fujimori had just under 50 percent of the vote. Toledo refused to participate in the runoff election in May (the constitution required that the two leading vote-getters face each other in a runoff if no one received 50 percent of the vote on the first round). Citing widespread rigging of the first round and the election commission's refusal to institute reforms for the second round, Toledo urged his supporters to vote spoiled ballots in protest, and he did not campaign for election. The outcome of the runoff was that Fujimori got 51 percent, Toledo (whose name was still on the ballot) garnered 17 percent, and written-in "No to fraud" got 32 percent.

Despite the controversy, and despite condemnation of the election by the Organization of American States (most of whose members did not send official representatives to his inauguration in August), Fujimori took office with a defiantly anti-reform cabinet. However, the street protests against his election, which had never stopped, took on a new ferocity when a few months later, a video was leaked to the media showing Fujimori's secret police head, Vladimiro Montesinos, bribing a member of Congress. Montesinos was the "gray eminence" of Fujimori's regime, commanding an internal spy network of four hundred professional agents and sixteen thousand paid informants spread throughout the population. Under pressure of the pro-reform protests, the government's control of the country became ever more tenuous, and finally in November, Fujimori stepped down. A new election was called.

Three main candidates emerged in this election: Toledo again; Lourdes Flores, a woman representing the center-right; and Alan Garcia, a controversial populist former president (Fujimori's predecessor from 1985 to 1990) who had fled abroad in disgrace after a regime marked by hyperinflation and the rise of guerrilla violence. The campaign was remarkably dirty and personal, including charges of drug use and sexual scandals against Toledo. In the end, Flores—who had started out as a popular, fresh voice for reform—became too closely tied to Lima and the upper class, and finished third. In the runoff election, Toledo beat Garcia and was installed as president in June 2001. He symbolically held two inaugurations—one in Lima and another the next day at Cuzco, the ancient Inca capital in the Andes.

The first twenty-two years of democracy in Peru have certainly been difficult! What might explain the differing experiences of democratization in Spain and Peru? There is probably no one answer to this question. Some possible factors include:

- Income and educational disparities are much greater in Peru than in Spain.
- Ethnic divisions in Peru split the population about fifty-fifty, which is very hard to handle. In Spain, regional/linguistic splits distinguish smaller minorities of the population.
- The military in Spain look to role models in the rest of Europe who deliberately avoid involvement in politics. The NATO alliance structure draws the Spanish

military away from domestic political concerns and more toward broader European security issues.

- Spain is a member of the European Union, a rather tightly integrated regional association that could exercise strong sanctions if Spanish democracy were under attack. Peru is a member of the Organization of American States, a much weaker organization. During Fujimori's coup, the Organization of American States could never bring itself to go any further than passing resolutions.

FURTHER READING

Bermeo, Nancy. "Myths of Moderation: Confrontation and Conflict During Democratic Transitions." *Comparative Politics* 29: 305–22.

Bratton, Michael, and van de Walle, Nicholas. "Neopatrimonial Regimes and Political Transitions in Africa." *World Politics* 46 (1994): 453–89.

Casper, Gretchen. *Fragile Democracies: The Legacies of Authoritarian Rule.* Pittsburgh: University of Pittsburgh Press, 1995.

Centeno, Miguel. *Democracy Within Reason: Technocratic Revolution in Mexico.* University Park: Penn State University Press, 1994.

Comparative Politics 2 (April 1997). The entire issue is devoted to articles on democratization and democratic consolidation.

Diamond, Larry; Plattner, Marc F.; Chu, Yun-han; and Tien, Hung-mao, eds. *Consolidating the Third Wave Democracies.* Baltimore: Johns Hopkins University Press, 1997.

di Palma, Guiseppi. *To Craft Democracies: An Essay on Democratic Transitions.* Berkeley: University of California Press, 1990.

Drake, Paul, and McCubbins, Mathew, eds. *The Origins of Liberty: Political and Economic Liberalization in the Modern World.* Princeton, N.J.: Princeton University Press, 1998.

Fukuyama, Francis. "The End of History?" *National Interest* 16 (Summer 1989): 3–19.

Haggard, Stephan, and Kaufman, Robert R. *The Political Economy of Democratic Transitions.* Princeton, N.J.: Princeton University Press, 1995.

Huntington, Samuel P. *The Third Wave: Democratization in the Late Twentieth Century.* Norman: Oklahoma University Press, 1991.

Joseph, Richard. *State, Conflict, and Democracy in Africa.* Boulder, Colo.: Lynne Rienner Publishers, 1998.

Linz, Juan J., and Stepan, Alfred. *Problems of Democratic Transition and Consolidation.* Baltimore: Johns Hopkins University Press, 1996.

O'Donnell, Guillermo, and Schmitter, Philippe C. *Transitions from Authoritarian Rule: Tentative Conclusions About Uncertain Democracies.* Baltimore: Johns Hopkins University Press, 1986.

Opp, Karl Dieter; Voss, Peter; and Gern, Christiane. *Origins of a Spontaneous Revolution: East Germany 1989.* Ann Arbor: University of Michigan Press, 1995.

Pridham, Geoffrey, and Vanhanen, Tatu, eds. *Democratization in Eastern Europe.* London: Routledge, 1994.

Przeworski, Adam. *Democracy and the Market.* Cambridge: Cambridge University Press, 1991.

————. *Sustainable Democracy.* Cambridge: Cambridge University Press, 1995.

————; Alvarez, Mike; Cheibub, José Antonio; and Limongi, Fernando. *Democracy and Development: Political Institutions and Material Well-Being in the World, 1950–1990.* New York: Cambridge University Press, 2000.

Schmitter, Philippe, and Karl, Terry. "What Democracy Is . . . and Is Not." *Journal of Democracy* 2 (1991): 75–88.

Sisk, Timothy. *Democratization in South Africa: The Elusive Social Contract.* Princeton, N.J.: Princeton University Press, 1995.

Whitehead, Laurence. "Comparative Politics: Democratization Studies." In *A New Handbook of Political Science,* edited by Robert E. Goodin and Hans-Dieter Klingmann, pp. 353–71. New York: Oxford University Press, 1997.

WEBSITES OF INTEREST

Political Database of the Americas, maintained by Georgetown University:
www.georgetown.edu/pdba

National Endowment for Democracy:
www.ned.org/

The Carter Center's unit for oversight of elections in new democracies:
www.cartercenter.org/elections.html

9

AUTOCRATIC GOVERNMENT

I noted in Chapter 8 that in recent decades, the worldwide trend has been toward democracy, but I also noted that democracy is a fragile thing: of the ninety-seven states that were independent for at least forty years at the millennium, only twenty-four had had an uninterrupted record of electoral democratic government during that time. Autocratic government has its own fragilities, however. In this chapter, we will (1) look at some of the major forms of autocratic government and (2) explore the sources of their fragility and success.

What is autocracy like? The autocratic alternatives to democracy are by no means of one piece. Consider this sampling:

- **The Union of Soviet Socialist Republics (1917–1991)** From the Russian Revolution (1917) until a couple of years before the breakup of the union in 1991, power in the Soviet state was lodged clearly with the Communist Party. It was self-sustaining, recruiting new young members who could progress through it to build careers. Although Stalin's rise to power in the 1930s was bloody, after Stalin the party saw five peaceful, orderly transitions of leadership. As far as we know, decisions were made collectively within the party, with strong leadership by the party head and a great deal of influence from such groups as the army. Ordinary people did not have a great deal of personal freedom, but—compared with the bloody past—laws were at least predictable and dealings with the governmental apparatus were usually orderly.
- **Pakistan** Pakistan is a country of 150 million people in South Asia, adjoining India (on its east) and Iran (on its west). It achieved independence in 1947, along with India, and became the Moslem counterpart to Hindu India; the two have had tense relations ever since. Since attaining independence, Pakistan has alternated between democracy and military governments. The new country was a democracy until 1958, when a coup installed a military government. That government lasted until 1971, when democracy was restored. For the next six years, Pakistan once again

had democratic government, with Z. A. Bhutto serving as its prime minister. In 1977, General Muhammad Zia ul-Haq took over the government. His military government executed Bhutto in 1979, and for several years Zia headed a repressive military regime that sought to establish Pakistan as an Islamic state. In 1983, a coalition of opposition leaders, many of them in exile, began a campaign called the Movement for the Restoration of Democracy. In 1985, General Zia yielded some power in a partial return to democracy: all military officers were removed from government posts except Zia himself, who remained as an extremely powerful president and head of the armed forces. In 1988, Zia was killed in a suspicious plane crash, and democracy was restored. Benazir Bhutto, Z. A. Bhutto's daughter, became the prime minister, but the democratic government had a rocky career. It was difficult to form a clear majority in a country deeply divided ethnically and economically, and the legacy of the constitution Zia had written in 1985 made it difficult for government to function. In the 1997 election, Bhutto's party lost badly, and Nawaz Sharif became prime minister in the first peaceful, democratic transfer of power in Pakistan's history. In 1999, however, after Pakistan suffered a defeat in a border skirmish with India, General Pervez Musharraf took over the government in yet another military coup. As has often been the case, the military takeover in 1999 was at least initially quite popular. The performance of the democratic government had not inspired respect.

Pakistan's fifty-year history of sporadic, brief democratic rule punctuated by military takeovers has not been good for the country. Two-thirds of Pakistanis cannot read, and the economy is primitive. The strong military presence in government has ensured that the military are well taken care of: 6.1 percent of Pakistan's GDP is spent on the military, compared with 2.4 percent of democratic India's.

- **Saudi Arabia** Saudi Arabia was an absolute monarchy for most of the twentieth century, with power lodged in the Saud family. This is a large, extended family that provides not only the king but also most of the council of ministers and other high government officials. It appears that while the king figures importantly in the making of decisions, this is a genuinely collegial effort in which the council of ministers (including the king) discusses issues and decides on policies. The Saud family are conservative in religious matters and enforce strict Muslim standards of behavior, though they have been enthusiastic about economic modernization. Even the turmoil of the Gulf War left this system essentially unchanged.

- **Democratic Republic of the Congo (formerly known as Zaire)** Zaire became independent from Belgium in 1960 and immediately plunged into a civil war fomented by Belgian mining interests. After a chaotic period of civil war, coups, assassinations, and attempts to establish democracy, power was seized in 1965 by Colonel Joseph-Désiré Mobutu, with strong support from the United States. Mobutu established a one-party state and remained in power from then until 1997, as president and, at various times, chair of the single party and head of the armed forces. His rule was characterized by charges of massive corruption and of widespread abuses of human rights; but Mobutu proved adept at maintaining his rule despite unrest by giving ground at critical moments and retaking it when the opportunity arose. From about 1982, an organized opposition operated, based mainly abroad but sometimes openly, when circumstances permitted, in Zaire. In the 1990s, Mobutu fended off strong opposition pressure and student riots, while the country sank more deeply into social and economic disorganization. In 1997, a rebel group led by Laurent-Désiré Kabila, a long-time opponent of Mobutu from the eastern region of Zaire, finally defeated Mobutu's forces. Mobutu fled, and Kabila renamed the country and established himself as president. His regime was marked by the same sort of oppression as Mobutu's reign, but he was never able to establish full control of the country. He was assassinated in 2001 and succeeded by his son, Joseph Kabila. The country is a wreck; continuing civil wars, fomented by its neighbors, have almost broken it into a set of disparate regions.

These examples are roughly representative of autocratic systems. First, they are quite varied politically; they range from conservative Saudi Arabia to the bureaucratic Soviet Union to the personal dictatorship of Zaire. Second, many of the autocracies are not organized stably. Of these examples, Pakistan has alterated between democracy and military government. Most parts of what was once the Soviet Union are moving toward democracy or at least toward change. Mobutu did not ultimately retain power in Zaire, though his successor was as much an autocrat as he was. Saudi Arabia, on the other hand, appears to have a rather stable system.

MILITARY GOVERNMENT

The most dramatic alternative to democratic government is military government, in which a group of officers use their troops to take over the governmental apparatus and run it themselves. This is called a coup, from the French coup d'état (strike at the state). Less than a tenth of the world's states are under military government.

Why is military government not more common than that? The military in any state control more armed power than anyone else. If they choose, as a group, to oust the existing government—or even if only a part of the military choose to do so and the rest decide to sit it out—there is no one who can stop them. Civilian governments must depend for their safety on the military's satisfaction, on their disunity, or on their reluctance to take over the government. While each of these protective shields is evident in many military groups, it must not be so unusual that all three would from time to time fail and that the military would break out in a coup. This is particularly likely in a new state, where a tradition of civilian government has not had time to take hold. It is not surprising that military coups occur with some frequency around the world.

In a few states, coups have become so routine that they have almost been institutionalized as the normal method of governmental change. In such cases, other political forces have come to be involved informally, much as they would under other arrangements. Key groups such as labor unions may be sought out by one or another military faction as potential allies, and—even though they do not themselves bear arms—their weight is felt.[1]

---

[1]Martin C. Needler, "Political Development and Military Intervention in Latin America," American Political Science Review 60 (September 1966): 616–26.

Are Military Coups Contagious?

A number of observers have noticed that military coups cluster at certain times. Suddenly a rash of coups will break out in a region such as Latin American or southern Africa, and then coups will once again decrease. Statistical tests have shown that this is not coincidental. Coup makers apparently watch each other's success, and if they have seen a number of their neighbors succeed, they are likely to have fewer qualms about undertaking a coup themselves. Furthermore, if a number of coups have recently occurred in the neighborhood, this lessens the problems of legitimacy. If coups are a frequent thing in the region, initiating a coup will not seem as flagrantly illegitimate as if yours were the only army doing it.

Beyond considerations in any one state, then, coups appear to involve broad, wave-like regional processes. Statistical analysis to measure these processes has proven to be complex and challenging. A good example is Richard P.Y. Li and William R. Thompson, "The 'Coup Contagion' Hypothesis," *Journal of Conflict Resolution* 19 (March 1975): 63–88.

Actually, it is likely that regime changes of *any* sort operate in this way, at least in part. As we saw in Chapter 8, democratization occurred in waves at different times, in different parts of the world. Most Eastern European states shifted to democracy between 1989 and 1991, for instance. There is evidence that movements for democracy in one area are often influenced by movements in another.[1]

[1]See, for instance, Douglas Anglin, "Southern African Responses to Eastern European Developments," *Journal of Modern African Studies* 28 (no. 3, 1990): 431–56.

In Bolivia, for instance, factions of the armed forces in the past regularly depended on other political groups when they were attempting a coup.[2] In 1978, a right-wing government was overthrown by the army, who were aided by left-wing allies in the unions and political parties. After an attempt at an election in 1979, a right-wing coup was tried, but it failed because its leaders were not able to get the support of Congress. In 1982, yet another military group was forced out of office by a general strike led by the unions. In a bizarre way, coups under these circumstances become a system that draws a fairly wide range of people into the political process. Usually, however, they are more isolated events.

Military governments vary greatly in their political role. In Paraguay, General Alfredo Stroessner seized power in 1954 and secured his position with repression and torture until he was deposed by a military coup in 1989. It was estimated that in 1982, one-quarter of the Paraguayan people were in exile outside the country's borders.[3] In Nigeria, a series of military governments ruled from 1966 to 1978 and again from 1983 to 1999. During much of that time, except for the corrupt and vicious rule of General Sani Abacha from 1993 to 1998, there was considerable civilian support for the military regime. Greece was ruled by a right-wing group of officers from 1967 through 1973; this government maintained itself by harsh, repressive measures. It broke up in 1974, and democracy was reestablished. In Turkey, the military have taken over the

[2]Bolivia experienced military coups regularly—almost annually—until 1985. Since 1985, Bolivia has had a democratic regime.
[3]Europa Yearbook 1983. vol. 2, p. 1228.

government three times since World War II—in 1960, 1971, and 1980—each time when Turkey's democratic government was verging on chaos. The Turkish takeovers have been broadly supported and have been followed by a return to democracy after stability was restored.

Military governments vary widely in the one thing in which we might have expected that they would be similar: their political direction. They are not all of the political right or of any other direction, even though the usual stereotype is of the right-wing officers' coup. Some coups are clearly of the right or the left, but many are not identifiable as either. Which sort results depends on which group of officers leads the coup; there are many officers of the left in most countries, as well as of the right, especially if recruitment is not limited to the upper class. Studies that have compared fairly large numbers of military regimes with civilian regimes conclude, on the whole, that whether or not a state has a military regime has little effect on the state's rate of economic development. That is, as a group, military governments are neither especially good at guiding their states' economies nor especially poor at doing so.[4]

These two aspects of coups—that they sometimes become incorporated in the broader political process and that they have no clear political complexion, of the left or of the right—have made political scientists a bit cautious in assessing them. In a study of Venezuelans' views of democracy and military coups, David J. Myers and Robert E. O'Connor found that Venezuelans considered occasional coups part of the normal political process but distinguished sharply between coups and military dictatorships:

> . . . self-professed democratic Venezuelans perceive no incompatibility between endorsing democracy and supporting an occasional coup to rectify problem situations. Approving military intervention differs from favoring long-term military dictatorship. We find no evidence of the latter but widespread support of the former. Many respondents seemed to view coups as a device equivalent to a parliamentary vote of no confidence. It is indeed a serious action but is consistent with their understanding of democratic rules.[5]

And as Martin C. Needler noted some time ago:

> I would still affirm the general correctness of the position I took on this question ten years ago [that military coups are a repressive move backwards, thwarting necessary social change]. However, subsequent events have suggested that I underestimated the extent to which apparently democratic political processes could in fact be manipulated by elite economic interests to its advantage. This means that interruption of those processes by military seizures of power could, at least in some cases, be a force for promoting development instead of retarding it.[6]

[4]See Robert Jackman, "Politicians in Uniform," American Political Science Review 70 (December 1976): 1098–1109.

[5]David J. Myers and Robert E. O'Connor, "Support for Coups in Democratic Political Culture: A Venezuelan Exploration," Comparative Politics 30 (January 1998): 206.

[6]Martin C. Needler, "The Logic of Conspiracy: The Latin American Military Coup as a Problem in the Social Sciences," Studies in Comparative International Development 13 (Fall 1978): 31.

"Good news. The 'Times' has upgraded us from a 'junta' to a military government."

WHY AREN'T THERE MORE MILITARY GOVERNMENTS?

Good or bad, though, it is still surprising that more countries are not governed by the military. There are not as many coups as we might expect, and most military governments stay in power only a few years. This may be partly because most states take pains to imbue their military officers with inhibitions against political intervention. Adolf Hitler required officers to swear oaths of personal allegiance to him, for instance; and in the training of its officers, the U.S. government ensures in many ways that they will understand their proper role to be nonpolitical.

However, more important than such inhibitions are a series of significant problems faced by military governments—problems that make officers somewhat reluctant to take and hold power. A uniquely serious one for them is that of legitimacy, which was discussed as a general problem of all governments in Chapter 7. A military government takes power through no regular process but simply seizes it, so how can it claim that no other group should similarly displace it? A democratic government is legitimized by the electoral process that produced it; a monarchy is legitimized by the rules of succession on which it is based; a communist government is legitimized by Lenin's theory that the Communist Party must lead the revolution. No process of selection legitimizes the military government, though. Those who live by the sword shall die by the sword, they say, and a military government must always be concerned to justify its existence. To this end, many military governments add civilians to their governing apparatus or set future dates for a return to democracy. Others try to rally the people through wars and appeals to nationalism.

Another problem of most military governments is that while their leaders may be skilled politically, there is little in the profession for which they have been trained that makes this likely. Military organization is usually marked by a fairly orderly passage of commands from higher officers to lower officers, without a great deal of argument in between. This orderliness should not be exaggerated, but many military officers are clearly frustrated by the jabber of daily political requests and arguments with which they must deal once they have taken power.

Finally, many military governments are fairly shaky alliances, united primarily by their opposition to the regime they have displaced and likely to fall apart as new issues arise that may divide their members.

As a result of these problems, purely military governments are actually rather fragile. Unless they set up the institutions to transform themselves into one-party states, there is a good chance that they will eventually yield to the establishment of democracy. If a military regime is internally divided or has problems generally in governing and if enough of the key figures concerned feel that the uncertainty of the outcome of democratic choice is preferable to the certainty of any other particular group being in control, the stage is set to introduce democracy—or reintroduce it, as the case may be.[7] In the 1980s and 1990s, twenty-two states switched at least for a time from purely military government to democracy.[8]

ONE-PARTY STATES

Most autocracies are not straight military governments but one-party states. The one-party state is distinguished by the fact that the government is based on and supports a political party that is the only party allowed in the state. One-party arrangements have often had their origins in military coups. For example, in Libya, Colonel Muammar Khadaffi seized power in a coup in 1969 and established the Arab-Socialist Union as the sole political party; its general congress, chaired by Khadaffi, is in effect the chief governing body of the state. Other one-party arrangements originated in national independence movements, which were then institutionalized as the single party. In Tanzania, for example, Julius Nyerere led the movement for independence, and his independence movement, the Tanganyika Africa National Union, won seventy of the seventy-one seats in the first election to the National Assembly. Four years later, a constitution was written that established it as the state's sole party.[9] A number of one-party states originated

---

[7]For an expansion of this argument, see Adam Przeworski, "Some Problems in the Study of the Transition to Democracy," in Guillermo O'Donnell, Philippe C. Schmitter, and Laurence Whitchead, eds., Transitions from Authoritarian Rule: Prospects for Democracy (Baltimore: Johns Hopkins University Press, 1986), pp. 47–63.

[8]Argentina, Bangladesh, Bolivia, Brazil, Burkina Faso, Burundi, Chile, Ecuador, Fiji, Ghana, Honduras, Nigeria, Pakistan, Panama, Paraguay, Peru, the Philippines, Portugal, South Korea, Thailand, Turkey, and Uruguay.

[9]Although there is only one legal party, there are still many contests between individuals in elections. A majority of the seats in the National Assembly are filled by election, the rest being appointed. Defeats of individual incumbents in elections are common, though all candidates must come from the ruling party.

in socialist revolutions, either indigenous, as in the cases of Cuba, China, or the U.S.S.R., or imposed by the U.S.S.R., as in the cases of (pre-1989) East Germany, Czechoslovakia, and other Eastern European states.

What distinguishes these states from other autocratic systems, especially from straight-forward military governments, is the existence of a reasonably large national political party that bolsters the government and provides an institutional basis for it. Compared with military rule, the one-party state offers a more stable and responsive form of government. The military government is necessarily limited by the field of vision of the officers who hold power. There is little provision for dealing with broad factional conflict or for the intrusion of diverse opinions. The government itself came into being by irregular means; therefore, there exists no regular set of arrangements to provide for the replacement of old leaders by new. These are things that may be provided for by the single political party.

A national party is likely to embrace at least a reasonable range of the social groups in a state—labor leaders, industrialists, intellectuals, and military leaders. Not all of these may be equally happy with the party; however, they have little choice but to coop-erate with it if asked. The party, on its side, needs to involve them if only to keep tabs on potential troublemakers. As a result, the single party as an organization is usually able to have a better feel for opinion in the countryside than a group of officers will have. It provides institutional links between the government and the population.

Second, the party can provide an arena in which varied political positions can develop into factions. In this way, new conflicts may develop within an existing system rather than arising outside it and posing a threat to it.

Finally, the single party may provide a set of arrangements by which a transition of leadership can be accomplished. An example of this capacity was the fairly easy transi-tion from Konstantin Chernenko to Mikhail Gorbachev in the Soviet Union after Cher-nenko's death in 1985. During Chernenko's illness, there had been some process at work by which the Communist party leadership decided who would take over from him.

The one-party state must be distinguished from a democracy with a dominant-party system.[10] A few democracies have party systems in which a single party has dominated government over a long period. Italy is a good example: From 1945 to 1994, without a break, the Christian Democratic Party received the largest vote of any party at each elec-tion, and except for a couple of years, it dominated all coalition cabinets during that period. (It finally fell from grace in 1993 due to its leaders' involvement in massive scandals.) What distinguished Italy from the one-party states during this period is that other parties were able to organize and did so; it was also universally recognized that those other parties would gain office if enough people voted for them—and in fact, this did happen in 1994.

To sum up our treatment of one-party systems: This is the most frequently seen form of autocratic government. It may originate in all sorts of ways—military coups, move-ments for national independence, socialist revolutions, and many others. Distinctively, the one-party state has one (and only one) political party that is fostered by the govern-ment. This party adds to the government's capacities and helps to make these regimes more stable than straight military governments.

[10]See Chapter 12.

"COURT" POLITICS

A characteristic of many autocracies—especially of monarchies and of personal dictatorships like that which the Duvalier family exercised in Haiti from 1957 to 1986, but
also of many military governments and one-party states—is that a single person may
hold almost all power in the system and that politics revolves around that single person.
It must be emphasized that this is not true of all autocracies; many have plural institutionalized bodies for decision, as in the central committee of a communist state or the
officers' councils that guide some military governments. However, it is frequently the
case. Extreme examples are the great power held by Hitler in Nazi Germany, Stroessner
in Paraguay, Duvalier in Haiti, and the apparently undisputed preeminence of the Ayatollah Khomeini in Iran from 1977 to 1989.

Politics revolving heavily around one person in this way is called "court" politics, after
the royal courts of the great European monarchs. Court politics is usually marked by:

- Less emphasis on the rule of the law and more on the arbitrary whim of the ruler:
  In a more plural system, politics is based on competing forces, which may need to
  agree on the relatively neutral devices of laws and legality to settle their disputes
  rather than confront each other directly. In a system dominated by a single person,
  that person's wishes are likely to dominate over legal considerations.
- Heavy competition by other figures for access to the leader: Access to the leader's
  ear may be a major factor in political outcomes. Lower officials may not dare to
  take vacations, for instance, for fear of missing such a chance.

Muammar Khadaffi, leader of Libya.
(Reuters/Bettmann/Corbis)

- Unusual importance of even apparently nonpolitical figures who necessarily have access to the leader by virtue of their other roles in the leader's life: Doctors, hairdressers, and even childhood friends may turn up as important political figures. Martin Bormann, Hitler's personal secretary, was probably the second most important political figure in Germany toward the end of the Third Reich; doctors, astrologers, and others also had political influence.
- Flattery and attempts to shield the leader from unpleasant reality:[11] A graphic illustration of court politics is described in the second example at the end of this chapter, in the excerpt from Albert Speer's Inside the Third Reich.

"POWER AND CHOICE" AGAIN

To return to the theme of our text, these governments—especially the military governments—might appear to embody a rather pure strain of politics as power. After all, when political control depends on who has the guns, it is hard to deny that power is at work. On the other hand, it is a common mistake to think of autocratic governments simply as raw examples of power at work.

One-party governments often see themselves as pursuing communal objectives and develop organizational mechanisms for bringing a wide spectrum of opinion to bear on the government's decisions. Even military governments usually portray themselves as heeding the country's call, and there is often broad support among the people for a military coup. We shall deal with governments such as these more wisely if we remember that the picture is not black or white but that politics in these states—as in democracies—consists of power and choice.

CONCLUSION

To sum up, the autocratic alternative is quite a diverse thing and not necessarily stable. A number of autocratic states have set up institutions of politics, especially through a single party or a monarchy, that provide for politics to be conducted over the long haul; straight military governments, however, have not. There is a good deal of flux among regimes, with rather few stable democratic regimes, even fewer stable autocratic regimes, and a great many states that are likely to shift among regimes of different sorts. We who live in a stable democracy tend to think of democracy as something that a state either has permanently or does not have at all. It is probably better thought of as a mode of government that is used by many states some of the time but to which relatively few states are permanently committed. Even ancient Athens, the birthplace of democracy, moved in and out of democratic government and dictatorship from time to time. Such a perspective helps us not only to view democracy as less than a permanent attribute of states but also to see the autocratic alternatives to democracy in the same way.

---

[11]Actually, aspects of "court" politics (especially this and the preceding one) can be seen wherever great political power is held by a single person. The American presidency shows distinct signs of it. Reprinted with the permission by Orion Publishing Group, Ltd., from *Inside the Third Reich* by Albert Speer, translated by Richard and Clara Wilson. Copyright © 1969 by Verlag Ullstein GmbH, English translation copyright © 1970 by Macmillan Publishing Company.

Example: Civilian Participation in Nigeria's First Military Regime

Professor Henry Bienen has studied the nature of the military government that ruled Nigeria from 1966 to 1974.[12] Although this regime included some civilian politicians, the military leaders always had the ultimate last word, a not uncommon pattern for military governments. Professor Bienen studied this regime from the standpoint of the civilians by interviewing a large number of politicians from the Western Province of Nigeria.

About a year after the 1966 coup, the military government brought a number of civilian politicians into the cabinet. At that time, a civil war was raging in Nigeria, as the eastern provinces were trying to secede, and the military apparently thought they needed help to mobilize the population and to keep in touch with the grass roots. In the Western Province, General Adebayo, the governor, consulted with local party leaders before he appointed civilian commissioners to the provincial government. The military also set up advisory bodies called Leaders of Thought, in which military and civilian leaders met regularly on an informal basis.

The commissioners to whom Professor Bienen spoke disagreed as to how much real influence they had over the actions of the government, but they thought that while the military held ultimate control, the cabinet had considerable power over day-to-day decisions:

Adebayo said the cabinet was purely advisory. We told him we have an executive council. A Governor in Council. The Secretary Odumosu (civil service head in the state) told him we were right. The attorney general did the same thing. He ignored this often, particularly where the profit margin was involved. . . .

To some extent I would agree that commissioners did not have the old ministerial powers. Legally speaking we did, but not practically speaking. As a military regime [sic], the governor is the final authority. A commissioner is his advisor. In practice he of course cannot see to everything. He allows you to take decisions on consultation. He invariably approves. . . .

The cabinet was an executive body; that's a correct view. It was not just advisory. Only once or twice did Adebayo try to assert his position as military governor, and then he reconsidered and took the consensus advice. There were no votes.[13]

The bureaucracy apparently had greater leeway under the military regime than they had had under democracy, and there was a technical rather than political air to decision making. Of the political leaders who were interviewed, 60 percent thought that most of the bureaucracy would not welcome a return to democratic government, while only 10 percent thought that the bureaucracy would want such a return.[14]

---

[12]This presentation relies heavily on his study. Henry Bienen, "Military Rule and Political Process: Nigerian Examples," Comparative Politics 10 (January 1978): 205–25. See also Henry Bienen with Martin Fitton, "Soldiers, Politicians and Civil Servants," in K. Panter-Brick, ed., Soldiers and Oil (London: Cass, 1978), pp. 27–57.

[13]Bienen, "Military Rule," p. 213.

[14]Bienen and Fitton, "Soldiers, Politicians," p. 42.

If the governmental machinery operated somewhat more smoothly under military rule, this was offset by a lack of communication between the population and the government. It was to address exactly this problem that civilians were added to the government. In the Western Province, the government was severely pressed when widespread rioting by farmers broke out in 1968 and 1969. Farmers attacked the federal prison in daylight in September 1969, freeing all its occupants; many police were ambushed or disappeared; tax collections nearly ceased. The military were caught unprepared for the level of grass-roots discontent because they had not had enough contact with the villages to sense what was building up. The civilians in the cabinet gained somewhat in power during this period, as the military leaders depended on them to help assess the farmers' discontent and rebuild a coalition of support for the regime.

How did the civilian politicians rate the military rulers? Though they were predisposed to be critical of the military, they distinguished among the military government's strengths and weaknesses.

The greatest criticism of the military was that they failed to represent and take into account the various groups in the population.

Those cabinet members who felt that the [civilian] cabinet was politically strong, that its members had grass-roots support, did not see the military as having local links. Individual members mentioned many times how "little people" were afraid to go and see military officers, because to do so they had to pass a series of armed soldiers. Nigerian politicians were often outraged that although the officers and soldiers became rich they spent money only on themselves and their close relatives. The money did not trickle down.[15]

Of the politicians, 81 percent thought that the military had been less successful than civilians in representing the people.[16]

On the other hand, the politicians credited the military with creating national unity more successfully than the civilians (by a margin of about 3 to 1) and with bringing stability (by a margin of 2 to 1). They split on whether the military had been more successful in promoting economic development than the civilians, and by about a 2 to 1 margin, they thought the military had been less successful than civilian governments at developing health and educational services.

Example:"Court" Politics in Nazi Germany

Albert Speer was the relatively nonpolitical coordinator of industrial production for Adolf Hitler during the latter part of World War II. He offers the following accounts of politics in Hitler's inner circle. These provide good examples of the peculiarities of the "court" politics described previously.[17]

In the winter of 1942, during the Stalingrad crisis, Bormann, Keitel, and Lammers decided to close their own ring around Hitler more tightly. Henceforth, all orders to be signed by

[15]Bienen, "Military Rule," p. 219.
[16]Ibid., p. 220.
[17]Albert Speer, Inside the Third Reich (New York: Macmillan, 1970), pp. 300–306, 389–93.

the Chief of State had to be cleared through these three men. This would supposedly prevent the unconsidered signing of decrees and therefore put a stop to the command confusion caused by this practice. Hitler was content so long as he retained the final decision. Henceforth, the divergent views of various branches of government would be "sifted" by this Committee of Three. In accepting this arrangement Hitler counted on objective presentation and a nonpartisan method of working.

The three-man committee divided up its jurisdictions. Keitel, who was to be in charge of all orders relating to the armed forces, came to grief right from the start, since the commanders in chief of the air force and the navy utterly refused to accept his authority. All changes in the powers of the ministers, all constitutional affairs, and all administrative questions were supposed to go through Lammers. As it turned out, however, he had to leave these decisions more and more to Bormann, since he himself had little access to Hitler; Bormann had reserved the field of domestic policy for himself. But he not only lacked the intelligence for these matters; he also had insufficient knowledge of the outside world. For more than eight years he had been little more than Hitler's shadow. He had never dared go on any lengthy business trips, or even to allow himself a vacation, for fear that his influence might diminish. From his own days as Hess's deputy, Bormann knew the perils of ambitious deputies. For Hitler was all too ready to treat the second men in an organization, as soon as they were presented to him, as members of his staff and to make assignments directly to them. This quirk accorded with his tendency to divide power wherever he encountered it. Moreover, he loved to see new faces, to try out new persons. In order to avoid raising up such a rival in his own household, many a minister took care not to appoint an intelligent and vigorous deputy.

The plan of these three men to surround Hitler, to filter his information and thus control his power, might have led to an abridgement of Hitler's one-man rule—had the Committee of Three consisted of men possessing initiative, imagination, and a sense of responsibility. But since they had been trained always to act in Hitler's name, they slavishly depended on the expressions of his will. What is more, Hitler soon stopped abiding by this regulation. It became a nuisance to him, and was, moreover, contrary to his temperament. But it is understandable that those who stood outside this ring resented its stranglehold.

In fact Bormann was now assuming a role which could be dangerous to the top functionaries. He alone, with Hitler's compliance, drew up the appointments calendar, which meant that he decided which civilian members of the government or party could see, or more important, could not see, the Fuehrer. By now, hardly any of the ministers, Reichsleiters, or Gauleiters could penetrate to Hitler. They all had to ask Bormann to present their program to him. Bormann was very efficient. Usually the official in question received an answer in writing within a few days, whereas in the past he would have had to wait for months. I was one of the exceptions to this rule. Since my sphere was military in nature, I had access to Hitler whenever I wished. Hitler's military adjutants were the ones who set up my appointments.

After my conferences with Hitler, it sometimes happened that the adjutant would announce Bormann, who would then come into the room carrying his files. In a few sentences he would report on the memoranda sent to him. He spoke monotonously and with seeming objectivity and would then advance his own solution. Usually Hitler merely nodded and spoke his terse, "Agreed." On the basis of this one word, or even a vague comment by Hitler, which was hardly meant as a directive, Bormann would often draft lengthy instructions. In this way ten or more important decisions were sometimes made within half an hour. De facto, Bormann was conducting the internal affairs of the Reich. A few months afterward, on April 12, 1943, Bormann obtained Hitler's signature to a seemingly unimportant piece of paper. He became "Secretary to the Fuehrer." Whereas previously his powers, strictly speaking, should have been restricted to party affairs, this new position now authorized him to act officially in any field he wished.

[Speer developed an infected knee and was hospitalized.]

Dr. Gebhardt, SS Group leader and well known as a knee specialist in the European world of sports, ran the Red Cross's Hohenlychen Hospital. It was situated on a lakeside in wooded country about sixty miles north of Berlin. Without knowing it, I had put myself into the hands of a doctor who was one of Heinrich Himmler's very few intimate friends. For more than two months I lived in a simply furnished sickroom in the private section of the hospital. My secretaries were quartered in other rooms in the building, and a direct telephone line to my Ministry was set up, for I wanted to keep on working.

Sickness on the part of a minister of the Third Reich involved some special difficulties. Only too often Hitler had explained the elimination of a prominent figure in the government or the party on grounds of ill health. People in political circles therefore picked up their ears if any of Hitler's close associates was reported "sick." Since, however, I was really sick, it seemed advisable to remain as active as possible. Moreover, I could not let go of my apparatus, for like Hitler I had no suitable deputy at my disposal. Though friends and associates did their best to give me the opportunity to rest, the conferences, telephone calls, and dictation conducted from my bed often did not stop before midnight.

My absence unleashed certain elements, as the following incident will illustrate. Almost as soon as I arrived at the hospital, my newly appointed personnel chief, Erwin Bohr, telephoned me, quite excited. There was a locked filing case in his office, he said. Dorsch had ordered this case transported at once to the Todt Organization headquarters. I instantly countermanded this, saying that it was to stay where it was. A few days later representatives of the Berlin Gauleiter's headquarters appeared, accompanied by several moving men. They had orders, Bohr informed me, to take the filing case with them, for it was party property along with its contents. Bohr no longer knew what to do. I managed to postpone this action by telephoning one of Goebbels's closest associates, Naumann. The filing case was sealed by the party officials—but the seal was placed only on its door. I then had it opened by unscrewing the back. The next day Bohr came to the hospital with a bundle of photocopied documents. They contained dossiers on a number of my time-honored assistants—adverse reports almost without exception. Most of the men were charged with attitudes hostile to the party; in some cases it was recommended that they be watched by the Gestapo. I also discovered that the party had a liaison man in my Ministry: Xavier Dorsch. The fact surprised me less than the person.

Since the autumn I had been trying to have one of the officials in my Ministry promoted. But the clique which had recently taken shape in the Ministry did not like him. My then personnel chief had resorted to all sorts of evasions, until I finally forced him to nominate my man for promotion. Shortly before my illness I had received a sharp, unfriendly rejection from Bormann. Now we found a draft of that sharp note among the documents in this secret file, composed, as it turned out, by Dorsch and Personnel Chief Haasemann (whom I had replaced by Bohr). Bormann's text followed it word for word.

From my sickbed I telephoned Goebbels. As Gauleiter of Berlin he was head of all the party representatives in the Berlin ministers. Goebbels agreed at once that my old assistant Gerhard Fränk was the man for this post in my Ministry. "An impossible state of affairs! Every minister is a party member nowadays. Either we have confidence in him or he must go!" Goebbels said. But I could not find out who the Gestapo's agents in my Ministry were.

The effort to maintain my position during my illness proved almost too much for me. I had to ask Bormann's state secretary, Gerhard Klopfer, to instruct the party functionaries to stay within their bounds. Above all I asked him to look out for the industrialists working for me and to see no obstacles were placed in their way. For I had no sooner fallen sick than the district [Gau] economic adviser of the party had begun making inroads into my system. I asked Funk and his assistant Otto Ohlendorf, whom he had borrowed from Himmler, to take a more affirmative attitude toward my principle of industrial self-responsibility and to back me against Bormann's district economic advisers.

Sauckel, too, had already taken advantage of my absence to "make a general appeal to the men involved in armaments for an ultimate commitment." Faced with these effronteries from all sides, I turned to Hitler to tell him of my woes and ask his help. My letters—twenty-three typewritten pages that took me four days—were a sign of the funk I was in. I protested against Sauckel's arrogation of power and against the thrusts of Bormann's district economic advisers, and I asked Hitler for a statement of my unconditional authority in all questions that fell within my jurisdiction. Basically, I was asking for the very thing I had unsuccessfully demanded in such drastic language at the conference in Posen, to the indignation of the Gauleiters. I further wrote that our total production could be carried out rationally only if the "many offices which give directions, criticism, and advice to the plant managements" were concentrated in my hands.

Four days later I appealed to Hitler again, with a candor that really was no longer in keeping with our present relationship. I informed him about the camarilla in my Ministry which was undermining my program. I said there was treachery afoot; that a certain small clique of Todt's former assistants, led by Dorsch, had broken faith with me. I therefore considered myself forced, I wrote, to replace Dorsch by a man who had my confidence.

This last letter, with its news that I was dismissing one of Hitler's favorites without asking him beforehand, was particularly imprudent. For I was violating one of the rules of the regime: that personnel matters must be broached to Hitler at the right moment and by skillful insinuation. Instead, I had bluntly come at him with charges of disloyalty and questionable character in one of his men. That I also sent Bormann a copy of my letter was either foolish or challenging. In doing this I was running counter to all I knew about the nature of Hitler's intriguing entourage. I was probably acting out a certain attitude of defiance, forced upon me by my isolated position.

My illness had removed me too far from the true focus of power: Hitler. He reacted neither negatively nor positively to all my suggestions, demands, and complaints. I was addressing the empty air; he sent me no answer. I was no longer counted as Hitler's favorite minister and one of his possible successors—a few whispered words by Bormann and a few weeks of illness had put me out of the running. This was partly due to Hitler's peculiarity, often noted by everyone around him, of simply writing off anyone who vanished from his sight for a considerable time. If the person in question reappeared in his entourage after a while, the picture might or might not change. It disillusioned me and snapped some of my ties of personal feeling toward Hitler. But most of the time I was neither angry nor in despair over my new situation. Physically weakened as I was, I felt only weariness and resignation.

FURTHER READING

Collier, David, ed. The New Authoritarianism in Latin America. Princeton, N.J.: Princeton University Press, 1979.

Diamond, Larry; Kirk-Greene, Anthony; and Oyediran, Oyeleye, eds. Transition Without End: Nigerian Politics and Civil Society Under Babangida. Boulder, Colo.: Lynne Rienner Publishers, 1997.

Downing, Brian. The Military Revolution and Political Change. Princeton, N.J.: Princeton University Press, 1992.

Linz, Juan J., and Stepan, Alfred. The Breakdown of Democratic Regimes. Baltimore: Johns Hopkins University Press, 1978.

Maravall, José Maria. "The Myth of the Authoritarian Advantage." Journal of Democracy 5 (1994): 17–31.

Needler, Martin C. "The Logic of Conspiracy: The Latin American Military Coup as a Problem in the Social Sciences." Studies in Comparative International Development 13 (Fall 1978): 28–40.

Neumann, Franz. Behemoth: The Structure and Practice of National Socialism, 1933–1944. New York: Oxford University Press, 1944.

O'Donnell, Guillermo; Schmitter, Philippe; and Whitehead, Laurence. Transitions from Authoritarian Rule: Prospects for Democracy. Baltimore: Johns Hopkins University Press, 1986.

Reno, William. Warlord Politics and African States. Boulder, Colo.: Lynne Rienner Publishers, 1998.

Roeder, Philip G. Red Sunset: The Failure of Soviet Politics. Princeton, N.J.: Princeton University Press, 1993.

Rouiquie, Alain. The Military and the State in Latin America. Berkeley: University of California Press, 1987.

Sartori, Giovanni. Parties and Party Systems. Cambridge, England: Cambridge University Press, 1976, especially chap. 7.

Skidmore, Thomas E. The Politics of Military Rule in Brazil, 1964–1984. Oxford: Oxford University Press, 1988.

Stepan, Alfred. Rethinking Military Politics: Brazil and the Southern Cone. Princeton, N.J.: Princeton University Press, 1988.

Valenzuela, Arturo. "The Military in Power: The Consolidation of One-Man Rule." In The Struggle for Democracy in Chile, 1982–1990, edited by Paul Drake and Ivan Jaksic. Lincoln: University of Nebraska Press, 1991.

 WEBSITES OF INTEREST

Amnesty International, a global organization working to protect human rights, especially in autocratic systems:
www.amnesty.org/

Human Rights Web, with connections to a range of human rights sites:
www.hrweb.org/resource.html

PART FOUR

THE APPARATUS OF GOVERNANCE

10

CONSTITUTIONS AND THE DESIGN OF GOVERNMENT

Every state—in fact, every political organization, club, or other group—has a constitution, or set of rules by which power is distributed among the members. No group of people engaged in politics could exist without rules of this kind.

We speak of such an encompassing set of rules as a "constitution with a small *c*," meaning the understood rules, both formal and informal, by which power is distributed in any political group—rules that have come to be accepted over time. These rules may be either formally laid down in statutes and other documents or informally understood.

Most organizations and states have as a part of their constitution a formal set of central rules that outline the basic ways in which they conduct their affairs. The Constitution of the United States (note the *Capital C*) is such a document, as are Canada's Constitution Act of 1982, the Basic Law of Germany, and the Constitution of the Netherlands. Typically, such a document tells who is to carry out the major functions of politics (proposing, deciding on, and implementing laws); how the people holding those positions are to be chosen; who is to be in charge during an emergency; and by what procedures the constitution itself may be changed. Often there is also a section, such as the Bill of Rights in the U.S. Constitution, that sets out certain basic rights of the citizen or basic aims of the state. Thus, a constitution may state that citizens are guaranteed the right of freedom of speech (U.S.A.) or that the state guarantees full employment (France) or that the state is socialist (China).

Before the United States was ever founded as a state, the American Indian Iroquois Confederation had an elaborate constitution, maintained in an oral tradition. It takes several days for elders to recite the constitution, which specifies a veto right for each member nation but dominance for the Mohawk nation in making new initiatives; the establishment of a ruling council and procedures for selecting confederation leaders; special elevation for those who excelled at war; and provisions for relations with other nations not in the confederation.[1]

---

[1]Donald S. Lutz, "The Iroquois Confederation Constitution: An Analysis," *Publius* 28 (1998): 99–127.

No state can put *all* the rules governing the distribution of power into its formal constitution: Much must always be left to informal arrangements or to other documents. In the United States, the Constitution lays out a basic structure for politics. However, the "constitution with a small *c*" includes a great deal more than just the Constitution. It includes the understanding that the U.S. Supreme Court may overturn an act of Congress—a rule not written into the Constitution but only developed later under the strong Chief Justice John Marshall. Furthermore, it includes the tradition that presidents take a leading role in the making of foreign policy, and it includes much else besides. All these things are rules governing the distribution of power, which are not part of the Constitution but *are* part of our constitution.

There is often some disparity between the formal rules of the Constitution and actual political power. In the United States, a reading of the Constitution would lead one to think that the members of the electoral college had great power, because they are elected to meet and select a president; in fact, however, the practice and expectation have developed that the members of the electoral college ratify the vote of the citizens of their states, so that in practice, they have essentially no political power. As another example of the frequent disparity between formal political power and actual power, consider that no constitutions in Europe or North America mention the great political power of newspapers and television networks other than in passing.

VARIATIONS IN FORMALITY

Constitutions vary as to how much is set out formally in a central document and how much has gradually developed outside of it. Older constitutions put less into a central document; newer ones, more. Two of the oldest political bodies in the world, Great Britain and the Catholic Church, have no central written constitution. Rather, the rules of politics for each are embodied in a variety of documents, traditions, and accepted practices. Each has a constitution (with a small *c*); people are aware of it and cite it frequently in British or church politics, but they are not referring to a single document when they do.

The United States is a relatively old state, and the original U.S. Constitution was approximately forty-three hundred words long; approximately twenty-nine hundred words have been added in amendments. Germany is a new state, and its Basic Law, written in 1949, is approximately 19,700 words long; this includes numerous amendments. France's most recent constitution, published in 1958 and amended only slightly since, is about ninety-one hundred words long. Perhaps constitutions that have been written in more recent years are longer because their writers are aware of the greater size and importance of the state and have taken greater pains to protect the state's power from difficulties that might arise. A large part of Germany's Basic Law is devoted to who is to govern during emergencies, though this is unusual. The one thing that is true of recent constitutions is that they are *specific* and complicated.

THE VIRTUE OF VAGUENESS

Such specificity is by no means always an advantage. Napoleon once said that a constitution should be short and obscure. If rules are stated specifically, it becomes difficult to adapt a constitution to unforeseen or changing circumstances. Just as French generals in the period from 1919 to 1933 devised a marvelous fortification (the Maginot line) that would have served well for the trench warfare of World War I but was useless against the changed strategies of World War II, writers of constitutions often include in their design solutions to the problems with which *they* have become familiar. If these solutions are precise and inflexible, they are likely to produce new problems. Republican lawmakers in the United States were upset that Franklin Delano Roosevelt (a Democrat) had served more than the customary two terms as president. After his death, they wrote a stern amendment into the Constitution, limiting presidents to two terms of service. A few years later, they were faced with Dwight Eisenhower, a popular Republican candidate whom they would have loved to nominate for a third term but who was constitutionally barred from running again.

Similarly, the writers of the Basic Law of Germany were preoccupied, after the war, with the fact that Hitler had been able to take over the democratic government of Germany peacefully and more or less legally in 1933 and transform it into a dictatorship. In dozens of ways, they tried to make their new constitution "Hitlerproof." One of the many devices they added was a restriction on the ability of the parliament to unseat the chancellor and his cabinet. This power of parliament was hemmed about by numerous conditions, which led to an unpleasant comic opera when in 1972, the socialist-led government of Willy Brandt had lost so much support in the parliament that it could not even pass the national budget. Brandt and his cabinet wished to step down and call for a new election, since, under the circumstances, they could not govern effectively. But for six months, no one could think of a way by which this could be arranged under Germany's complicated constitutional provisions, without the embarrassment of the socialists formally voting themselves out of office (which they were not willing to do). The authors' precise and detailed constitutional tinkering with the Basic Law, designed to "win the last war," led to unforeseen difficulties in governing Germany.

Another example of misplaced specificity in writing constitutions comes from a regional political science association in the United States. This group publishes a scholarly journal, the editor of which is changed every three years. At one time, it was suggested that the term of the editor might be lengthened to four years, since it cost the association a few thousand dollars each time the editor was changed and the journal's operations had to be moved from one campus to another. This was not a big issue, but everyone agreed that the change would be a good idea because it would save some money and inconvenience. On looking at the association's Constitution, however, it was found that the change could not be made easily. This document, instead of sensibly stating that the editor should serve a term "to be determined by the association's council," plainly said that "the editor shall serve a term of three years. . . ." An amendment to the Constitution, tedious and difficult to arrange, would have been required to change the editor's term; therefore, the idea was dropped. One would think that the political scientists who wrote this document would have known better!

OTHER PRINCIPLES OF CONSTITUTIONAL DESIGN

Let us assume that you are in a position to help design or amend a state's constitution. Are there any additional principles that might help guide you? Beyond the general principle that you should not try to be too specific, a few additional rules of thumb you might consider are as follows: (1) The constitution should preferably not break drastically with long-standing traditions of government, (2) the constitution should be relatively easy to change, and (3) "incentive compatibility" should be built in as much as possible, so that the holders of power will find it personally advantageous to do what society as a whole needs from them. Let us consider each of these in some detail.

The Importance of Long-standing Traditions

If a set of rules is to work, it must not be too far out of line with what most people in the state wish to do. One famous instance of a rule that did not work because it deviated too far from the people's wishes was the prohibition of liquor in the United States in the 1920s. In 1919, a constitutional amendment forbidding the possession or consumption of alcoholic beverages in the United States was passed. While many people supported this amendment (else it would not have been passed), many opposed it. The law was openly disobeyed, and criminals such as Al Capone flourished from the illegal traffic in liquor. Eventually, the state gave up, and in 1933, the Constitution was amended to make alcoholic beverages legal again.

It is not enough, either, to set up rules that the people are willing to obey only reluctantly; something more is needed than bare acquiescence. As we saw in Chapter 7, it is important that a state have a reservoir of goodwill and positive support from its people to carry it over the occasional rough times. A good constitution will not only be one that people are *willing* to obey but also one that comes close enough to their preconceptions that they will be able to identify enthusiastically with the system. Many historians think it is unfortunate that when Germany lost World War I, the monarchy to which its people were accustomed was destroyed. The democratic constitution of 1919 did not provide for the sort of personal, emotional attachment that the monarch always had. Instead, the first president of the new system was a quiet man, the son of a lowly saddle maker, with no dash or glamour. Hitler was later able to exploit the people's hunger for an exciting focus of patriotic devotion. How much better if the constitution of 1919 could have made a less dramatic break with the past by including a powerless but handsomely dressed monarch. This of itself would not have solved all of Germany's problems, but it might have helped.

This is not to say that a constitution can never depart from what the people expect. Many revolutionary states—such as China, in 1949, for example—have imposed new systems of government and society that transformed their people's expectations. There has always been a great deal of tension associated with this, however, and such states have had to keep tight control of things, causing much human suffering, to ensure the state's stability. There is inevitably a price to be paid in instituting rules for which the people are not prepared; but in some instances, this price might be worth paying.

The Importance of Amendability

If a new constitution must come reasonably close to reflecting the people's expectations, it must also be open to revision or amendment in response to changing needs. It is always a temptation, when writing a formal document, to "protect" it by making it difficult to change.

The U.S. Constitution, for example, was designed to be difficult to change. As a result, in the more than two hundred years that it has been in force, only sixteen amendments beyond the original Bill of Rights have been added. Such inflexibility could have been dangerous, because the conditions of U.S. politics obviously must have changed immensely over two or more centuries. Fortunately, a new device for adaptation appeared when the Supreme Court took onto itself the power to interpret the Constitution with a certain amount of discretion. The Constitution was sufficiently "obscure," in Napoleon's sense, that the Court could adapt it with reasonable ease to changed circumstances. In 1954, for instance, the Court ruled that, in light of modern sociological theory, "separate but equal" schools for blacks and whites could not be taken to provide the equal protection under the laws that the Constitution guarantees. The Court ruled in this way despite that in earlier decisions, without the benefit of such theory, it had ruled that segregated school systems were constitutional.[2] Allowing nine judges who are appointed for life the discretion to adapt the Constitution may not be the best or the most democratic way to proceed, but it has at least provided a flexibility that the authors of the Constitution were not wise enough to build in.

In many states, provisions for adapting the constitution are much simpler. Often, a simple majority in the parliament is sufficient.

The Importance of Incentive Compatibility

In any political system, it is important that people in positions of power have personal incentives to do what society as a whole needs from them. That is, holders of power should find that they are personally rewarded when they do what society needs done and personally punished when they do not.

We may safely assume that when people find that what is good for them personally conflicts with what is good for the state, they will usually choose what is good for themselves. This is not to say that people are extremely selfish. It is easy for the individual to conclude that the damage to the state will be tiny compared with the benefit to him or her because the state and the individual are so different in size. As a result, people can usually make the "selfish" choice without feeling that they are doing much damage to the state. If a little cheating on my income tax can save me $300, what does that matter to a national budget of billions upon billions of dollars?

The problem, of course, is that if large numbers of people find themselves in a similar position, the result can be serious. Precisely this problem occurs in constitutions. The constitution—the set of rules determining who has what kinds of political power—places individuals in positions in which they will make certain choices that society needs to have made. Presidents and members of a congress or parliament are expected to make laws for the state, public health officials are expected to watch out for epidemics, judges are expected to settle legal disputes fairly, police officers are expected to keep order, members of town councils are expected to set rules within their towns, and so on.

It is not enough to *say* what a person is to do in one of these positions, however. If costs and benefits are not set up to encourage officials to act in the intended manner,

---

[2]Brown v. Board of Education, 347 U.S. 483 (1954).

"THE HECK WITH THE CONSTITUTION—
I'M GOING TO SHOUT 'FIRE'."

(© 2002 by Sidney Harris.
Reprinted with permission.)

there is a good chance that they will act in ways that suit their personal interests rather than those of society.

For instance, the U.S. Congress was set up to make rules for the country as a whole. However, members of Congress are rewarded or punished not by the country as a whole but by the voters of their districts. It is a well-known problem of American democracy that if the two conflict, members of Congress will frequently pursue the needs of their districts rather than those of the country as a whole. If the United States had stronger political parties, which could develop national programs and punish members of the Congress who did not support their party's program, then the personal incentives to members of the Congress would be different, and we might expect to see them support national interests even when these conflicted with their own districts' interests. As we will see in Chapter 12, many of the world's states do have political parties of this sort, and there we find that members of the parliament are less prone to place local needs over national ones.

As another example, consider the role of civil servants. Society needs to have civil servants develop programs creatively and administer them to the public efficiently, that is, at as low a cost as possible. However, in almost all countries, civil servants are personally rewarded most highly if they are cautious about innovation (in this way they will avoid ever making a dramatic mistake) and always spend all the money that had been allocated to them (if they show that they can do the job for less money, they're likely to be given less money the next year). These rewards have the effect of pushing civil servants toward uncreative, inefficient administration of programs.

Other examples could be drawn to show the importance of designing incentive structures to reward people for doing what the constitution intends them to do rather than for something else. It should be stressed that this is necessary *not* because holders of public office are especially greedy or cynical or selfish. Rather, like the income tax cheater, they are faced with differences in scale such that important things for them personally (security in their jobs, advancement) are balanced against almost trivial losses to the state (What does it really matter if I vote for an inefficient project for my district? It is tiny compared with the overall budget. Is it really that important to the United States that my office—the transcribing division of the Southwest Regional Advisory Branch of the Weedgit Marketing and Regulatory Board—function at top form?). As with the problem of tax evasion, the problem here is that from the point of view of the single official, little damage is done to the state; but because there are thousands of officials like this, their combined impact may be grave. We can expect most of these individuals to do what they are actually rewarded for doing, not necessarily what they are meant to do. Therefore, we must try to design our constitution so that rewards follow for what officials are meant to do.

THE GEOGRAPHIC CONCENTRATION OF POWER

In later chapters, we will look at a variety of questions on one aspect or another of constitutional design: how officials should be chosen, how laws should be passed, what is the best way of administering policies, and so on. However, one general question of constitutional design deserves treatment in this chapter.

That is the question of how much political power should be concentrated in the central government and how much should be distributed among the governments of cities, of "states" (as in the United "States"), or of regions. Some constitutions place almost all political power in the central government, with little independent decision making left to localities or regions. Others create a relatively weak central government, with many political decisions being made at lower levels. A variety of arrangements that fall between the two are possible.

What makes this a particularly important question is that all over the world, hot conflicts frequently rage between central governments and local groups. This is the single greatest cause of political conflict—a more incendiary one, for instance, than the perennial conflict between haves and have-nots or any of the newer conflicts such as those associated with feminism or protection of the environment. In Spain, separatists for several years waged an intermittent campaign of terror on behalf of their claims for a separate Basque state or at least for a greater degree of local independence in making political decisions. Since 1982, Canada has been involved in a divisive constitutional crisis over the relationship between Quebec and the rest of the country. In Britain, a Scottish nationalist party has from time to time been able to sweep most of the Scottish seats in the Parliament with its claim for greater independence for Scotland and has been rewarded by the establishment of a separate Scottish Parliament. India is divided into many districts speaking different languages; these districts operate fairly independently of the central government, and disputes over language policies and job preferences for those speaking different languages are always hot political items. Until 1991, the Soviet Union consisted of fifteen governmental units called "republics" (one of which was Russia); many of these had their own languages, and there were frequent conflicts among them. In the end, the union had to be dismantled, with each of the republics declaring independence. In another part of the world, many parts of Africa have had intense center-region conflicts; civil wars have been fought in Nigeria, Ethiopia, the Sudan, and Zaire between the central government and one or more regions that wished to break away. In the Mideast, Kurdish regions of Turkey, Syria, Iraq, and Iran have been a source of political tension for those countries for many years. As one last example, remember that the one time that politics in the United States heated up to the level of civil war was 1861, in a dispute between the central government and a region of the country.

"FEDERAL" AND "UNITARY" STATES

The question of central versus local control is thus a hot item of politics; how is it dealt with constitutionally? There is a formal distinction between states that are "unitary" and those that are "federal." We shall look first at the formal distinction (a characteristic of constitutions with a capital C) and then consider less formally (and more realistically) the division of power between central governments and their local or regional units.

A *unitary state* is one in which no other governmental body but the central government has any areas of policy that are exclusively under its control. In a unitary state, local and regional political bodies may potentially be overruled by the central government in any political decision they make. In a *federal state,* by contrast, local governmental authorities of some sort are set up by the constitution (usually for regions of the state, as in the "states" of the United States or the "republics" of the Soviet Union), and these authorities are given certain political decisions over which they have a legal monopoly of control.[3] In a *federation,* then—a federal state—two governments control the same group of people but with regard to different political questions.

Germany is an example of a federation. The regional governments, called *Länder,* have total control of education, television, and radio; the central government has total control of defense, diplomacy, currency and monetary policy, the postal service, railroads and air transport, and copyrights; the central government and *Länder* share responsibility for all other areas of policy.

A federal system has often been the result of a compromise by which reluctant members were induced to join in a state; this is how the United States was originally formed, for instance. Federal systems usually exist where there was some difficulty in uniting the state or where the state is so large or so culturally diverse that it is thought there may be problems holding it together. Small states are less likely to be federal systems than large ones because problems like these are more likely to have cropped up in large states with diverse populations.

As of 2001, a total of twenty states were federal systems while 173 were unitary. From this it might appear that the question of federalism is unimportant, because so few states are federal systems. However, the federal states tend to be the larger ones. Though these twenty states represent only 10 percent of the world's states, they contain 37 percent of the world's people and cover 49 percent of the world's land area. The twenty states are indicated in Figure 10–1.

---

[3]William Riker, *Federalism: Origin, Operation, Significance* (Boston: Little, Brown, 1964), chap. 1.

FIGURE 10-1
Federal systems (shaded areas) of the world.

THE DISTINCTION BETWEEN "UNITARY" AND "CENTRALIZED" STATES

A formal definition like that given in the " 'Federal and Unitary' States" section usually needs to be supplemented by an understanding of informal arrangements. I stated that in a federal system, separate governmental units coexist on the same territory, each with its own constitutionally set areas of policy. In a unitary system, by contrast, the central government is given the authority to make all policies, although it may deputize other governmental structures to act on its behalf. From this, we can see that in at least a *formal* sense, political power is more *centralized* (concentrated more on a central authority) in unitary systems than in federal ones.

However, politics is filled with surprises, and there are many informal arrangements that modify the centralizing tendency of the unitary state and the opposite tendency of the federal state. First, actual control of money counts at least as much in politics as the formal authority to make decisions. "Who pays the piper, calls the tune," as they say. Table 10–1 shows the percentage of governmental revenues collected and controlled by central, regional, or local governments in a variety of federal and unitary systems. While the central government usually controls more of the money in unitary systems than in federal systems, there is considerable variation within each category and some overlap across the two. Japan's central government draws only 64 percent of governmental revenues, well under the 85 percent drawn by Malaysia's central government, the most centralized of the federal systems displayed here. Clearly, if we look at the control of cash, there is considerable variation in degrees of government centralization that goes beyond the constitutional distinction between "federal" and "unitary."

In other ways, less easily measured than revenues, states vary in their degree of centralization. France and Britain, for example, look fairly similar on Table 10–1. Both are unitary states, and the central government of France draws 87 percent of revenues while the central government of Great Britain draws 92 percent. However, *how* authority and revenues are used is as important as *whether* they are used. In Britain, the central government has traditionally kept only a loose control over local governments' actions and expenditures. For instance, the choice of whether to shift to the modern "comprehensive" high school was left entirely to localities. As another example, consider that the British central government faced a serious difficulty several years ago in writing its budget: It had to provide money to local governments to pay their work force, but it did not know in advance how big the raises granted by local authorities to their civil servants would be. In effect, local authorities had control over the writing of a significant chunk of the national budget.

In France, on the other hand, power was for centuries lodged firmly in Paris. A minister of education in the late nineteenth century is said to have demonstrated this to a visitor, when, checking his watch, he looked up and said, "My friend, at this moment every third-grade pupil in France is reciting 'The Blue Bird.' " Power in France was quite centralized for many years; there was a time that for almost any major decision—whether to build a new town hall or school, for instance—cities had to gain the approval of the government in Paris. In 1981, however, President François Mitterrand instituted a number of

TABLE 10–1   PERCENTAGE OF REVENUE COLLECTED BY DIFFERENT LEVELS
OF GOVERNMENT

	Central government	"State," regional and/or local governments
Federal Systems		
Malaysia	85	15
Germany	69	31
Australia	67	33
India	67	33
Brazil	66	34
Switzerland	57	43
Argentina	58	42
United States	58	42
Canada	48	52
Unitary Systems		
Iran	100	0
Indonesia	97	3
Thailand	92	8
Chile	92	8
Great Britain	92	8
Israel	91	9
Romania	90	10
South Africa	90	10
France	87	13
Zimbabwe	86	14
Spain	81	19
Sweden	70	30
Japan	64	42

Source: International Monetary Fund, *Government Finance Statistics Yearbook 2000.*

decentralizing reforms, devolving many functions on new regional and departmental councils. But the system remains, on balance, centralized.[4]

To sum up, the degree of centralization in politics is greatly influenced by the formal constitutional choice between federalism and a unitary arrangement, but it is also strongly affected by all sorts of less formal arrangements.

[4]See Vivien A. Schmidt, *Democratizing France: The Political and Administrative History of Decentralization* (Cambridge, England: Cambridge University Press, 1991).

HOW MUCH CENTRALIZATION IS GOOD?

Any country has to strike some balance between centralized and decentralized politics. With totally decentralized politics, the state would cease to exist; it would be broken up into many small independent states. Even short of this, strong decentralization might lead to uncoordinated policies and confusion. Great centralization, on the other hand, especially in a state that is large or geographically varied, would make for inflexible and insensitive government.

How much centralization is good will vary from state to state and with the circumstances the state faces. Large and diverse states find it necessary to be less centralized than other states in order to meet varying local needs flexibly. If a given state is faced with an emergency, as in time of war, it may feel that all power must be pulled together centrally so that it will be able to concentrate its resources on the single goal of meeting the emergency. (Most decentralized systems do give their central governments extraordinary temporary power during war.) There is no single level of centralization of politics that one should necessarily prescribe for all states at all times.

The industrialized states of the world have shown signs of converging toward a fairly similar degree of centralization. Apparently, the circumstances in which these states find themselves are sufficiently similar that a common level of centralization has seemed appropriate to the leaders of each.

Therefore, a centralized state like France attempted over the latter half of the twentieth century to decrease the centralization of power. The Mitterrand reforms of 1981 sharply decreased the powers of the "prefects," civil servants who had used to be responsible for keeping Paris in control of what local governments were doing. On the other hand, in the decentralized United States, the last fifty years—despite recurrent attempts to reverse the trend—have been marked by an extension of power by the central government over the states and localities. This has often been accomplished by aid grants from the central government to the state or local government that carry with them some control over how the money is to be spent. As one example of this, the central government now has the power to order school districts to supply certain services to handicapped students. This would have been unthinkable fifty years ago.

We cannot give a simple answer to the question of how much centralization of government is good. However, around the world, complex industrialized states are indicating by their own choices that they are most comfortable with a considerable but limited degree of centralization. The main exceptions are states such as Belgium and Canada, where deep ethnic conflicts have boiled up to threaten the state, and a radical decentralization may be the best solution.

"CONSTITUTIONALISM"

A somewhat different question from the *nature* of constitutions is the question of "constitutionalism": Given that each state has a constitution, how faithful is a state to its constitution? That is, how fully do the leaders of the state honor the rules of politics in the state? "Constitutionalism" is the doctrine that states should be faithful to their constitutions because the rules so provided are all that can protect the citizens from arbitrary decisions by powerful people. There is also a notion in "constitutionalism" that constitutions should be designed fairly, rather than to give undue advantage to one particular group.

Constitutionalism is strong in Britain, the United States, Canada, Australia, and New Zealand. In the United States, for example, the Supreme Court, rather insulated from political pressure, has the power to overturn any act of government if it finds that the act is unconstitutional. The Court has been particularly active in guarding the Bill of Rights, a list of personal freedoms from governmental action that is written into the Constitution. Britain, Australia, Canada, and New Zealand do not have a supreme court to enforce the formal constitution, but in all of them, there is a long tradition of impartial obedience to the rules of politics and to the protection of individuals from arbitrary official action. Even in these five countries, however, constitutionalism is only *relatively* strong. It is not, and probably can never be, an absolute. Especially in times of national emergency, the governments of these countries have sometimes felt that it was necessary to temporarily suspend rights that they would ordinarily honor. Great Britain, for instance, held no elections for the duration of World War II, even though an election had been due in 1940; Churchill and the other party leaders thought that an election would be an unnecessary distraction during wartime, and they were critical of the United States for going ahead and holding its presidential election in 1944. Similarly, President Roosevelt ordered the internment of most Japanese-Americans during the war on the grounds that they were security risks. The president would never have had the power to do this in peacetime.

A country in which traditions of constitutionalism are a bit weaker is France. While individual rights are secure there, leaders' faithfulness to the rules of politics is a more fragile thing than in the United States, Canada, or Britain. Over the last century, France has had four constitutions, and it has had a total of nine systems for holding elections. Election laws, in particular, are manipulated to benefit the party in power. Also, it is understood that the party in power will manipulate news reports on public television and radio to enhance its election chances, and French embassies abroad have often tried to manipulate absentee voting to help the party in power. Finally, aside from these cynical manipulations of the rules of electoral politics, three times in the twentieth century French military leaders gave up on democratic rules altogether and tried to seize power; twice they were successful.

If France is a bit weak in its constitutionalism, though, many states are far weaker. Most of the world's people live in systems that give them only small protections against arbitrary power. In China from 1966 to 1976, over a million people were killed in the Cultural Revolution, which the state's leader, Mao Tse-tung, initiated to restore the Communist Party to its original revolutionary zeal. A similar disregard for individuals was shown in the 1989 suppression of the student movement at Tiananmen Square. In *The Gulag Archipelago,* Alexander Solzhenitsyn described the network of concentration camps in the Soviet Union under Stalin; in these, several million Soviet citizens were arbitrarily confined, often without trial.[5] In the late 1970s under a right-wing military regime, several thousand Argentinians "disappeared" when they were seized by the state police; they were never tried and were not seen again.

[5]Alexander Solzhenitsyn, *The Gulag Archipelago, 1918–1956* (New York: Harper & Row, 1974).

Example: Constitutional Government in Great Britain

Great Britain is an unusual example of constitutional government in that it has no written constitution—no single document that claims to set out the central principles of the organization of power.

What does the British constitution consist of? Some of it is made up of statute, or acts that Parliament has passed. For instance, Tony Blair's Labour government, elected in 1997, has been especially active in constitutional matters. In its first couple of years, it moved through the Parliament seventeen constitutional bills, including bills to establish quasi-federal autonomy for Scotland and Wales, a bill to incorporate the European Convention on Human Rights into English law, and a bill to remove most hereditary peers from the House of Lords. The Parliament has the power, by a simple majority vote, to change any aspect of the British constitution.

Much of the rest of the constitution consists of court precedent, decisions that have been made by judges in cases of constitutional significance. And some important parts consist of practice—behavior that has arisen in the day-to-day conduct of government and is not written down anywhere. In all of this, Parliament is ultimately supreme, because a new statute passed by it would override decisions by any court and would, of course, override any practices that had grown up. In the absence of contrary action by the Parliament, however, court decisions or practices stand. Much of the British constitution consists exactly of this: court precedent and practices that the Parliament has not chosen to change by statute.

The Magna Carta is one of the earliest parts of the British constitution. In 1215, an unpopular king (John) was forced by rebellious barons to sign this document limiting the king's authority over them in a number of ways. This document was later read into statute in 1295. Other important statutes have settled the system for determining who succeeds to the crown when a king or queen dies (Act of Settlement of 1701) and have laid out the powers of the two houses of Parliament (Parliament Acts of 1911 and 1949). Many smaller matters are also dealt with in statutes.

Court precedents have also contributed importantly to the constitution. For instance, the powers of the queen are largely determined by a long series of precedents from court cases over the centuries. The definitions of individual rights—which in the United States are written into the Constitution as the Bill of Rights—evolved over centuries of court decisions in Britain.

Finally, and this is probably the most puzzling thing to non-British readers, important parts of the constitution are not written in any document whatever but exist in practice. They are "what one does." For instance, the prime minister and cabinet are probably the most powerful single part of the process of government in Britain. All but a few of the bills considered by Parliament each year are initiated by the cabinet, and the cabinet controls closely what happens in the Parliament. (You will see more about this in Chapter 14.) But nowhere in any statute or in the decision of any court is the cabinet set up or its powers defined. The only law that mentions the cabinet even indirectly is one setting the salaries of cabinet ministers.[6] The rules governing the cabinet's behavior and defining its powers have arisen in practice and remain as unwritten understandings.

One might ask how a constitution like this gets enforced. How do we make sure that people play by the rules if not all of the rules are even written down? For instance, the prime minister is dominant within the cabinet and can ask members to resign or to exchange posts. This is a matter of practice. What would happen if a prime minister fired a cabinet minister, but the cabinet minister did not leave? As another example, an important aspect of the British constitution is that a British monarch will always sign into law a bill passed by the Parliament. Without the signature, the bill does not become a law, and in principle, the monarch has a right to veto acts of Parliament. In practice, however, this is not done. (What would happen if a monarch were to try to exercise the right? The answer, probably, is a constitutional crisis in which the monarchy would be eliminated.)

Queen Elizabeth II, the
ceremonial head of state of
the United Kingdom.

(Tim Graham/Corbis/Sygma)

[6]Ministers of the Crown Act 1937, from S. B. Chrines, *English Constitutional History* (London: Oxford University Press, 1947), p. 21.

"Ancient and unwritten," by the way, does not mean unchanging. At present, there is a great deal of constitutional ferment in Britain. The state's entry into the European Union was itself a major constitutional change, and it in turn stimulated a movement to develop an official British code of individual legal rights (like the United States' Bill of Rights) to allow British law to function more easily with the European Court. On another front, when Tony Blair became prime minister in 1997, he undertook several major constitutional revisions. Scotland and Wales have been given a significant degree of autonomy, almost to the point of transforming Britain into a federal system. And beyond that, Blair has pushed to change the electoral system and to alter radically the basis for membership in the House of Lords—the upper house of Parliament—which has consisted primarily of members of the hereditary aristocracy.

The British themselves puzzle over how an uncodified system like this can work. The authors of a British textbook write:

Why have countries found it necessary to draw up [formal constitutions]? Three reasons can be advanced. First, they are needed when nations make a fresh start with their institutions, as when India, Pakistan, Ceylon, etc. gained their independence after World War II. Secondly, the country may contain groups of people distinct from each other through race, religion or language. In order to incorporate all people within the nation, each group must be given some guarantee that its identity will be maintained. Thirdly, in large countries, people in different parts may have particular interests and needs which they feel cannot be adequately provided for by a government in a remote capital. Here some form of federalism is likely, the division of powers between federal and state authorities being laid down in a written constitution. None of these considerations applies to Britain.[7]

This does not ring true, however. Certainly, Britain has been subject to major stresses, especially the breaking away of Ireland in the early twentieth century and the continuing troubles in Northern Ireland. It is not plausible that the British have been so peaceful that they have not needed a set of rules to govern them. In the end, one must conclude that the system depends on the goodwill of those who are involved in it. They must *want* to have the system work and see this as in their interest; otherwise, it would not work. It may be that the existence of an unwritten constitution pushes people to behave cooperatively. Where there is a formal set of rules, clever people often feel challenged to find loopholes. Where there is only a set of practices based on certain commonsense principles, clever people will find it necessary always to cite those central commonsense principles and to tailor their arguments and their behavior to them.

For good or bad, however, an "unwritten" constitution is not something a state can decide to start at any time. It must be received from the past, and so it is unlikely that a state could deliberately imitate Britain and set up an unwritten constitution! However, we may draw the lesson from Britain that it is well to leave some aspects of our constitution to custom, if that is practical, rather than trying to write everything down.

---

[7]J. Harvey and L. Bather, *The British Constitution,* 3d ed. (London: Macmillan, 1974), p. 510.

Example: Constitutional Government in Russia

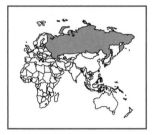

One of the many challenges facing the new Russian government after the breakup of the Soviet Union in 1991 and the subsequent collapse of the communist regime was establishing a new constitutional order for the state. Russia did not bring from the Soviet period much of a tradition of constitutionalism. Constitutions had never been seen in the Soviet Union as a solid foundation for government, which should regulate the government's actions. Rather, they were seen as ratifications of whatever power relationships were currently in place. From the Soviet revolution of 1917 until the breakup of the union in 1991, the Soviet Union had four different constitutions. These were seen more as descriptions of how the government operated than as guides to how government should operate; when power relations shifted, a new constitution was written to reflect the new situation.

Not only were constitutions seen as readily exchangeable, they also were seen as only minimally binding even while they were in place. Great disparities between the constitutional description and actual political reality were tolerated. For instance, the Constitution of 1977 gave each of the fifteen republics of the Soviet Union (units such as Russia; Ukraine; the three Baltic republics of Latvia, Lithuania, and Estonia) the right to secede from the union; in fact, the republics were kept under tight control through the army and party structures. Similarly, the Constitution assigned to the Soviet parliament the supreme power to pass laws. However, the parliament met only twice a year for a few days, during which time it heard long reports from the Central Committee of the Communist Party and ratified the reports unanimously with a show of hands. Constitutionalism was almost nil in the Soviet Union.

In truth, the Soviet constitution (with a small *c*—*not* the formal Constitution) could have been summarized very simply just by noting that the Communist Party was supreme in running the country. Regardless of the formal governmental structure, the party maintained its control in a practical sense by carefully placing party members in key positions in the armed forces, universities, bureaucracies, and the government.

With the collapse of communist rule, Russia's leaders needed to design a governmental structure to replace it. President Boris Yeltsin presented a draft constitution in November 1993, and the Constitution was ratified in a referendum a month later. This was a document clearly designed to benefit Yeltsin (it gives the president massive power), and it was never certain how long it would last beyond his presidency. The uncertainty was not helped by the fact that in the turbulent period of 1991 to 1993, when Yeltsin was locked in a conflict with the old parliament, *everyone* played fast and loose with the then-valid Constitution. This period of extraconstitutional jockeying culminated in Yeltsin sending tanks to destroy the Parliament Building. If the old Constitution could be violated so casually, what did that say about the new one?

Since the election in 2000 of President Vladimir Putin, however, the new heavily presidential Constitution seems to be working as it was intended to do. And in fact, it may fit well with Russian traditions—going back long before the Communist system—of strong, almost authoritarian, central rule. Under the new Constitution, citizens elect a president and a Federal Assembly that consists of two chambers. The president has direct and immediate control of all parts of the government that use weapons—the armed forces, the police, and what is left of the old secret police and intelligence networks. This is particularly important, given the extent of armed confrontation in politics in the past. Other operations of the state, such as economic policy, health policy, education, and so on, are administered under a prime minister who is appointed by the president but who must also work closely with the Federal Assembly and who can be voted out of office by the Federal Assembly.

The Federal Assembly has the sole power to pass laws for Russia, and unlike the old Soviet parliaments, this power is actually used and often brought the Federal Assembly into conflict with Yeltsin. After 1993, Yeltsin's opponents (mainly the remains of the old Communist Party, on one hand, and a new ultranationalist right-wing movement organized by Vladimir Zhirinovsky on the other) controlled both houses of the Federal Assembly. A dramatic example of their willingness to challenge Yeltsin was a law passed early in their first session to free the leaders of the 1991 coup attempt, all of whom were among Yeltsin's most bitter enemies. (The president has a number of constitutional devices to prevent bills passing without his approval, so for most legislation, unless the president and the National Assembly agree, nothing will be done. In this case, though, the National Assembly took advantage of a provision that gives it the sole power to give pardons for crimes.)

Russia, like the Soviet Union of which it used to be a part, is a federal system, with eighty-nine separate federal units.[8] The federal arrangements still leave a great deal of power to the central government. All legislation passed by the parliaments of the federal units, for instance, must be approved by a head of administration appointed by the president. The president may suspend any administrative act of a federal unit.

A Constitutional Court is included in the Constitution, with the power to decide on the constitutionality of laws and resolve jurisdictional disputes among various parts of the governmental structure. The Constitution also guarantees certain legal protections for citizens, such as a right to trial by jury and a guarantee that judges will be independent of the state. However, the general tradition of constitutionalism is so weak in Russia, and the political turmoil and disregard of rules from 1991 to 1993 is so fresh in people's experience, that it is still not clear how this part of the Constitution will work out. As of late 2001, for instance, it still was the case that many judges made $100 a month, less than half the pay of a secretary, and were dominated by the often politically powerful prosecutors. In 1995, Russia had only twenty thousand independent lawyers for a population of 148 million people. This compared with eight hundred thousand lawyers in the United States.[9]

---

[8]The basis for "federal units" varies a good deal. The cities of Moscow and St. Petersburg are federal units, for instance; other federal units are ethnically distinct regions such as the Tatar territory; and others are more general geographic divisions of Russia.

[9]"Russian Law: Groping Ahead," *The Economist,* 2 September 1995, pp. 42–48.

FURTHER READING

Bakvis, Herman, and Chandler, William M. *Federalism and the Role of the State.* Toronto: University of Toronto Press, 1987.

"Constitutions and Constitutionalism." In *International Encyclopedia of the Social Sciences.*

Duchacek, Ivo D. *The Territorial Dimensions of Politics Within, Among and Across Nations.* Boulder, Colo.: Westview Press, 1986.

Friedrich, Carl. *Limited Government: A Comparison.* Englewood Cliffs, N.J.: Prentice-Hall, 1974.

Goldwin, Robert A.; Kaufman, Art; and Schambra, William A., eds. *Forging Unity Out of Diversity: The Approaches of Eight Nations.* Washington, D.C.: American Enterprise Institute, 1989.

Harvey, Jack, and Bather, L. *The British Constitution.* 3d ed. London: Macmillan, 1974.

Horowitz, Donald G. *A Democratic South Africa? Constitutional Engineering in a Divided Society.* Berkeley: University of California Press, 1991.

Jennings, W. Ivor. *The British Constitution.* 3d ed. Cambridge, England: Cambridge University Press, 1950.

Lijphart, Arend. *Patterns of Democracy.* New Haven: Yale University Press, 1999.

Riker, William. *Federalism: Origin, Operation, Significance.* Boston: Little, Brown, 1964.

Schlesinger, Joseph. *Ambition and Politics: Political Careers in the United States.* Chicago: Rand McNally, 1966 (especially with regard to incentive compatibility).

Tribe, Lawrence H., and Dorf, Michael C. *On Reading the Constitution.* Cambridge: Harvard University Press, 1991.

Weiler, J. H. H. *The Constitution of Europe.* New York: Cambridge University Press, 1999.

Wheare, K. D. *Federal Government.* 4th ed. London: Oxford University Press, 1963.

   WEBSITES OF INTEREST

Constitution of the United States—Analysis and Interpretation, maintained by the Congressional Research Service:

http://www.access.gpo.gov/congress/senate/constitution/toc.html

International Constitutional Law Project, a site with the constitutions, amendments and recent constitutional commentaries for most states of the world:

http://www.uni-wuerzburg.de/law/index.html

11

ELECTIONS

In the long swing of history, elections with broad mass participation are rather new. Such elections originated with democratic government, which means that they came along at the end of the eighteenth century and the beginning of the nineteenth. Today elections are widespread around the world, even though a number of the world's states are not democracies. Many nondemocratic states, such as the pre-1989 Soviet Union, have held them regularly. Why are elections so in vogue?

Part of the answer, of course, is that *democracy* is a word that purrs with respectability. Even states that are not democratic wish to appear democratic, and holding elections is one of the easiest ways to follow some of the forms of democracy even if the state is not democratic.

A second reason is that elections can serve more purposes for the state than merely the democratic one of allowing the mass of people to help in the selection of leaders and policies. Elections were invented to make democracy possible; but once invented, they turned out to have further uses. This is an interesting aspect of political institutions that we shall encounter frequently in later chapters. Institutions may be devised to serve a particular purpose, but once they are in existence, they may be adaptable to a variety of purposes.

In this case, the thing that recommends elections to the leaders of autocratic states is that they can serve *two* main purposes: (1) *the purely democratic purpose of allowing the mass of people to have some direct say in the choice of leaders and policies, but also (2) the more or less universal purpose of allowing the state to mobilize its people and to build up their support for the state by acting out support and participating in the process of government.*

ELECTIONS AS A MEANS OF BUILDING SUPPORT

Let us consider the second of these first. One example of an autocratic state in which elections figured importantly is the Soviet Union before 1989. (Since 1989, most parts of what had been the Soviet Union, including Russia, have moved toward open electoral democracy.) One can make a good case that mass political participation among Soviet citizens was always as great as it was among citizens of the United States.

To quote a study from the 1970s:

> Campaign activities draw upon the efforts of millions of Soviet citizens, just as they do Americans. Soviet national election campaigns last about two months, and the campaigning is extremely intensive. The party leadership mobilizes millions of "agitators" and "propagandists," as well as ordinary citizens, to publicize the election, explain the issues and programs which the party considers important, and ensure that the entire population goes to the polls. The weeks preceding the election see the formation of countless study circles, discussion groups, campaign meetings, door-to-door canvassing, rallies, demonstrations and speeches.[1]

Similar comparisons could have been made in other areas of political activity, beyond elections per se. For example, about one person out of five in the United States has ever contacted a local government official about some issue or problem. Soviet citizens seem to have been about as active in this sphere as Americans, though directly comparable measures of activity are not available. One study noted at the time that "in the first four months of 1962 some 11,803 citizen demands poured into the offices of the Kirov raion of Moscow. In the first half of 1963 officials of a single raion in Leningrad received over fifteen thousand letters and visits from the populace involving demands of various sorts."[2] On another front, a study found that 8 percent of Americans belong to some sort of political organization. By way of comparison, about 10 percent of Soviet adults were members of the Communist Party through most of the postwar period.

In elections specifically, a similar comparison can be made. While only about 50 percent of Americans vote regularly in presidential elections, 99 percent of Soviet citizens voted in their national elections. There was great social pressure to vote in Soviet elections, and turnout was high:

> The network of agitators is fully activated during the ten days preceding the election. Agitators must visit each voter in the precinct, explaining the virtues and qualifications of the sole candidate. The mass media publicize the biography of each candidate to the larger soviets and urge a resounding vote of confidence for the regime. The candidate spends no money campaigning but holds meetings with voters. . . . Refusal to vote is regarded as an unpatriotic act. Even the sick are expected to vote and ballot boxes are brought to the bedsides of hospital patients. Voting occurs on ships that are at sea on election day if there are at least twenty-five voters aboard; the votes are added to those cast in the ship's home port. Passengers on long-distance trains vote in special precincts while in transit.[3]

The elections took up a great deal of time and cost a lot of money. Over 2 million candidates were elected each time—better than one out of every hundred adults—and they invested a great deal of time and energy in the campaign. Millions more were engaged in agitation, in serving on electoral commissions, and so on. It was an expensive business.

---

[1]Richard D. Little, "Mass Political Participation in the U.S. and the U.S.S.R.: A Conceptual Analysis," *Comparative Political Studies* 8 (January 1976): 439.

[2]James Oliver, "Citizen Demands in the Soviet System," *American Political Science Review* 63 (June 1969): 467. Cited in Little, "Mass Political Participation," n. 1.

[3]John S. Reshetar, Jr., *The Soviet Polity,* 2d ed. (New York: Harper & Row, 1978), p. 196.

Rene Preval, a candidate in the 1995 presidential election in Haiti, greets supporters.
AFP/Bettmann-Corbis

However, until the democratic reforms of 1989, there was never any suspense over the outcomes. Only a single candidate was nominated for each position. Voters could vote *against* that candidate by crossing out the name, and if a majority of those voting did this, the candidate was not elected. That happened only rarely. Of the 2.2 million candidates for election to local soviets in 1977, only 61 were dumped in this way, and almost all of these were from small villages.[4] Clearly, the purpose of all this electoral activity was not to choose who would govern the Soviet Union, but it must have had *some* purpose or else the authorities would not have invested so much in it.

The most reasonable guess is that the main purpose of elections in the Soviet Union was to renew the people's enthusiasm and support for the regime. Elections provided a recurring opportunity for the newspapers to pour out praise for the leaders of the state and for citizens, through their actions, to feel that they were a part of it. As behavioral therapists know, a good way to ingrain a particular point of view in a person's consciousness is to have the person act it out. This would be reason enough for the Soviet Union to have put its population "through their paces" at regular intervals.

The Soviet Union was not unusual among autocratic states in investing a great deal of time and energy in elections. Nazi Germany's election extravaganzas were famous, and approximately 99 percent of the German people regularly proclaimed their loyalty to Adolf Hitler in this way. In modern times, such states as Guatemala, Egypt, Romania, Algeria, Chile, North and South Korea, Paraguay, Hungary, Czechoslovakia, Cuba, the Ivory Coast, and many others have staged elaborate elections of which the outcome was

[4]Ibid., n. 3, p. 197.

TABLE 11–1   PERCENTAGE AGREEING THAT ORDINARY PEOPLE HAVE LITTLE SAY IN GOVERNMENT

	Voters	1968 Nonvoters	Total
Before the election	71	83	74
After the election	37	58	42
Change	−34	−25	−32
	Voters	1972 Nonvoters	Total
Before the election	34	58	40
After the election	29	54	36
Change	−5	−4	−4

Source: Recalculated from Benjamin Ginsberg, *The Consequences of Consent:Elections, Citizen Control, and Popular Acquiescence* (Reading, Mass.: Addison-Wesley, 1982), pp. 167 and 170.

never in doubt. The only plausible reason for such elections is to strengthen the people's attachment to the state.

While we do not normally think of elections in democracies as functioning to build support for the system, it can be shown that elections serve this purpose as much in democracies as in autocracies. A 1982 study of presidential elections in America highlighted this quite well. [5] At the 1968 and 1972 presidential elections, a sample of American adults were asked before and after the election whether they agreed or disagreed with the statement "People like me don't have any say about what the government does." Before the 1968 election, most people, whether or not they ended up voting in the election, agreed with the statement, as can be seen in Table 11–1. The electorate in 1968 was quite disillusioned and had lost a great deal of its faith in the nation's leaders. Conflict over civil rights and American involvement in the Vietnam War had soured people on politics, and the American public had seen the Democratic nominating convention in Chicago torn apart by demonstrations and by the reaction of the police to the demonstrations. Of those who voted in that election, 71 percent initially agreed that ordinary people do not have any say in government, as did 83 percent of those who ended up not voting. Over the campaign and the election, this outlook changed considerably. After the election, only 37 percent of those who had voted agreed with the cynical view of government, for a drop of 34 percentage points. Among those who did not vote but who experienced the period of campaigning and election, the figure also dropped, but by somewhat less—25 percentage points.

[5] Benjamin Ginsberg, *The Consequences of Consent: Elections, Citizen Control, and Popular Acquiescence* (Reading, Mass.: Addison-Wesley, 1982), pp. 166–70. See also Wendy M. Rahn, John Brehm, and Neil Carlson, "National Elections as Institutions for Generating Social Capital," in Theda Skocpol and Morris P. Fiorina, eds., *Civic Engagement in American Democracy* (Washington, D.C.: Brookings Institution, 1999), pp. 111–62.

The circumstances in 1972 were different, but there again the election apparently served to reassure the public about the political system. The pre-election public in 1972, in contrast to that of 1968, was not turned off to politics. The incumbent Nixon administration was popular (Nixon would get 61 percent of the vote), and the Vietnam trauma had passed. Only 34 percent of those who would eventually vote and 58 percent of those who would not initially agreed with the cynical view of government. The campaign was not one to inspire confidence in the system. It was marked by the forced withdrawal of Thomas Eagleton as the Democrats' vice-presidential nominee because it became known that he had a history of mental illness; by a great deal of personal vituperation between the candidates; and by rumors of corruption and "dirty tricks" that would later produce the painful Watergate scandal.

In spite of this, the campaign period and election of 1972 produced small moves toward greater support of the system, even among an electorate who were already rather supportive before the election. After the election, 5 percent fewer voters and 4 percent fewer nonvoters agreed with the cynical view.

In Chapter 7, we examined the state's need to maintain sufficient support among its citizens so that its authority would continue undiminished. For democracies and autocracies alike, elections apparently furnish a potent tool to help ensure this popular base of support. At regular intervals, people's acceptance of the system is reinforced as citizens act out their identification with the state and its leaders.

ELECTIONS AS A MEANS OF SELECTING LEADERS AND POLICIES

In many countries, however, elections are meant to do more than bolster support for the regime. They may also be the means by which leaders and (sometimes) actual policies are chosen by the people. For this to be the case, an election must involve a *choice between candidates* or a *choice whether a particular policy is to be followed.* In democratic states, elections are set up in this way. In some states that are not democratic at the level of national government, elections are allowed to function in this way at least at the local level.

In democracies, the choice of political leaders at all levels is made by competitive elections. In addition, some democracies provide for the *referendum,* a device by which the voters choose directly through their ballots whether a particular proposal will become law. Controlled referendums are also sometimes used in autocracies to exhibit and stimulate support in the same way as other elections. The referendum is discussed in the "Referendums" section of this chapter.

ELECTORAL SYSTEMS

If elections are to be used to choose political leaders, there must be some rule for translating people's votes into a particular selection of leaders. This is not as simple a matter as one might think. For instance, one might state simply that the candidate who gets the most votes will win the election and take office. What of the people who voted for a losing candidate: Should their votes count for nothing? What if there were a dozen candidates and the one who got the greatest number of votes had only about 20 percent of the vote: Would we want that person to take office? There is no single obvious way to translate the votes cast by the electorate into the people who will take office. States need to design rules determining which people win office as a result of any particular result in the voting; these rules are called the *electoral system* of the state.

Rulers of states could, if they wished, write many detailed differences into their electoral systems. At one or another time and place, for instance, a party has been required to win at least 5 percent of the vote to get a seat in the legislature, owners of businesses have been given double votes to increase their weight in the electoral choice, some seats in a legislature have been reserved for members of one or another race, and votes have been counted separately and weighed differently for rich people and poor people. The possibilities are limited only by the imagination of those in charge of the state.

However, two broad types of electoral system are used in almost all democracies: *single-member-district plurality systems* and *proportional representation systems.* For convenience, they will be referred to from this point on by their initials, SMDP and PR.

SMDP and PR Systems

In the SMDP system, the state is divided into a set of districts, usually having roughly equal populations. One representative is elected from each district to be a member of the legislative body of the state, and whoever gets a plurality of the votes wins the seat. (A *plurality* is the largest number of votes cast for any candidate; if there are many candidates running, the plurality may be less than a majority of votes cast.) Hence the name: A *single member* is elected from each *district* by a *plurality* of votes.

This arrangement is familiar to U.S. and Canadian students, because both countries use versions of the SMDP system. In Canada, the members of Parliament are elected by the SMDP system. In the United States, members of the House of Representatives are elected by an SMDP system and members of the Senate by a variant of SMDP. (There are two senators from each state of the United States, but they are elected in separate years by a plurality so that, in effect, the senatorial electoral system is SMDP.)

Britain is an SMDP system, and these systems tend to be limited, worldwide, to Britain and such of its former colonies as the United States, Canada, and India.

Most electoral democracies of the world use versions of proportional representation (PR). PR is simple. Though various formulas and methods are used to calculate the proportional result, the basic principle of PR is that political parties' representation in the legislative body is set roughly proportional to their strength in the electorate. That is, if the Fundamentalist Neopejorative Party got 18 percent of the votes cast in the election, it would get roughly 18 percent of the seats in the legislative body; if it got 30 percent of the votes, it would get roughly 30 percent of the seats.

This may not seem an unreasonable result, but PR was invented precisely because SMDP does *not* give such a proportional result. Instead, SMDP generally favors large parties and hurts small ones. This is because a small party, if its voters are spread evenly geographically, will have only a small number of voters in each district and may not have

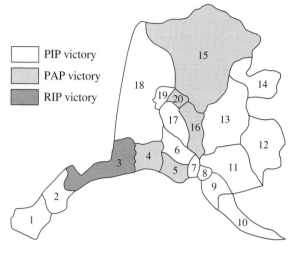

FIGURE 11–1
A hypothetical SMDP result.

enough in any one district to achieve a plurality and win there. This is illustrated in Figure 11–1. The hypothetical country of Aksala is divided into twenty districts, each having 50,000 voters. In its most recent election, the Prudential Improvidence Party (PIP) polled 450,000 votes, or 45 percent of the total; the Protection of Artifacts Party (PAP) polled 350,000 votes, or 35 percent of the total; and the Revolutionary Inaction Party (RIP) came in third with a still substantial poll of 200,000, or 20 percent of the votes. As you can see from the map, the PIP won fourteen seats with its 450,000 votes, the PAP won five seats with its 350,000 votes, and the poor RIP got only one seat for its 200,000 votes. That is, 45 percent of the vote got 70 percent of the seats, 35 percent of the vote got just 25 percent of the seats, and 20 percent of the vote got only 5 percent of the seats.

RIP received a lot of votes—20 percent of the total—but these votes were spread around so that RIP received 15 percent in one district, 25 percent in another, 30 percent in another, 8 percent in another, and so on. Only in district number 3 did RIP's share of the vote top the shares of PIP and PAP, so that it won.

This is a fairly typical result of SMDP. Although the example is made up, it was not deliberately constructed to produce this result beyond stating the initial condition that the three parties were of those sizes and had a more or less even distribution of their voters across the country. Most "real life" examples of SMDP fit the same pattern. In the British election of 2001, for instance, the Liberal Democrats polled 18 percent of the votes but won only 8 percent of the seats in the House of Commons.

In their early elections, most European states used electoral systems similar to SMDP. It was at the urging of small or new parties that felt unfairly discriminated against that most states changed to PR systems in the early part of the twentieth century. Why, you may ask, do any states retain SMDP as an electoral system when it is so unfair? The reason is that there is a practical benefit to the distortion in favor of large parties, which many observers think compensates for the unfairness to smaller parties. Small parties are disadvantaged by SMDP; therefore, there is a tendency for them to disappear or to merge over time. As a result, SMDP electoral systems tend to encourage the emergence of two large parties rather than a variety of smaller parties.[6] With only one major exception—Canada—SMDP systems have only two major parties, which makes it easier to govern the state. And with only occasional exceptions, all PR systems have more than two major parties. This may make it difficult to govern the state, but only if parties have difficulty cooperating; while in some notable cases multiparty government has been associated with instability, most PR/multiparty governments function smoothly. (We will discuss the relative merits of having two parties in Chapter 12.)

The trade-off between the two systems is one of fairness to minorities and small parties, on the one hand, versus simplifying the party system by weeding out small parties, on the other. Two other issues that may enter into a choice between the two electoral systems are:

- Electoral participation is likely to be higher under PR than under SMDP. Under SMDP, voters who are in the minority in their district (a Republican in Boston, a Conservative in Quebec City, a Democrat in suburban San Diego) may feel that there is no sense in voting, because their candidates cannot win.
- SMDP provides legislators with a tie to a particular locality, with a particular set of constituents, while most PR systems do not make this kind of connection.

Two Conditions for the SMDP Bias   The bias of SMDP in favor of large parties is a function of two conditions: *First, if a small party has most of its strength concentrated in just a few districts, it may not be hurt by the SMDP system,* because it may have enough strength in those few districts to win there. Consider if a Southwestern Autonomy Party had appeared in Aksala and had polled 60,000 votes in the four southwestern districts. Depending on how its votes were spread among the four districts, it might well have won in one or two of them. (It would have averaged 30 percent of the vote in the four districts, and the rest of the vote would have been spread among three parties.)

Again, there are plenty of "real life" examples of this exception to the rule of SMDP bias. One is the Plaid Cymru, a Welsh nationalist party, which in June 2001 polled only three-fourths of 1 percent of the vote nationally but, by concentrating that vote in Wales, won four of the 659 seats in the House of Commons. Another good example is Canada, which, as noted, is the major exception to the rule that SMDP electoral systems tend to limit a country to two major parties. Five major parties are active in Canadian politics, but each of them has a distinct regional identity, so that there is little selective pressure on them from the SMDP system.

Second, the smaller the number of districts, the more likely it is that small parties will be hurt by SMDP. If the state is divided into a small number of large districts, there is less chance that a small party will happen to have enough votes to win in a particular district.

---

[6]The standard statement on the effects of electoral systems is Maurice Duverger, *Political Parties* (New York: Wiley, 1954). See also Douglas Rae, *The Political Consequences of Electoral Laws,* rev. ed. (New Haven: Yale University Press, 1971); Rein Taagepera and Matthew S. Shugart, *Seats and Votes: The Effects and Determinants of Electoral Systems* (New Haven: Yale University Press, 1989).

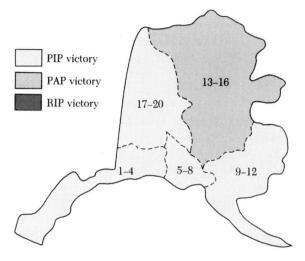

PIP victory

PAP victory

RIP victory

13–16

17–20

1–4   5–8   9–12

FIGURE 11–2
A hypothetical election by SMDP, with Aksala divided into only
five districts.

This is illustrated in Figure 11–2, in which the districts of Aksala from Figure 11–1 have been grouped by fours, so that there are five larger districts. Under this arrangement, the largest party (PIP) expands its share of the seats from 70 to 80 percent, the PAP drops from 25 to 20 percent, and the "small" RIP (with 20 percent of the vote) disappears.

To carry this to an extreme, if there were only one seat in the legislative body, the whole country would be one single-member district, with a plurality winning. In this case, the ultimate distortion would occur, with the candidate of the PIP winning 100 percent of the "seats" (i.e., the one seat), even though PIP had gained only 45 percent of the total vote.

This last extreme possibility is mentioned because it does occur in the real world. If a state has a president who is popularly elected by all the voters, the election functions, in effect, as a legislative election with one seat under SMDP. (Most democracies do not have a powerful president, but some do—the United States, France, Mexico, and others. Presidential government is discussed at length in Chapter 15.) Where there is a presidency, small parties are driven out of contention, and there is strong pressure for the system to evolve into one with two large parties. An example of this is France, which in 1962 shifted to a popularly elected presidency. Since that time, small parties have been gradually declining, until today there are four parties arranged by pairs in loose alliance into a bloc of the Left and a bloc of the Right, plus a fifth party off on its own dimension of opposition to immigrants. The conclusion is unavoidable that the institution of the presidency has forced France's quarrelsome parties to coalesce into something like two large parties.

To summarize the point of this section dealing with electoral systems: *The SMDP system tends to drive out small parties and ultimately to produce an arrangement consisting of two large parties. This effect is less strong if the parties have geographic concentration of voters and may disappear altogether, as in the case of Canada, if the parties' strengths are concentrated by region. The effect is heightened by reducing the number of districts and is especially strong when the state is a single district, as in presidential elections.*

REFERENDUMS

Many democracies restrict their citizens' involvement in the affairs of state to a vote that expresses their choice among potential political leaders. The state's policies are then set by the elected leaders, without any direct input from the voters. Some democracies, however, allow voters under some circumstances to choose directly, in an election, whether a given policy should be followed. Such an electoral choice is called a *referendum*. The United States does not have any provision for national referendums, but many localities and states do provide for them. California is particularly noted for their use, as in the famous Proposition 13 referendum in which the state's voters chose to limit property taxes to 1 percent of the value of the property. Outside the United States, a few democracies provide for the regular use of national referendums. France and Switzerland are two examples, the latter relying on them rather heavily.

Beyond these few instances, many democracies that would not accept the regular use of referendums *do* use them on rare occasions for decisions of great gravity, where it is felt that all the people should be involved in the decision. Spain, for instance, when it initiated its new democratic Constitution in 1978, held a referendum so that the Constitution could be ratified by the people. Similarly, when the powers of the European Union were to be expanded in the 1993 Maastricht Treaty, France, Ireland, and Denmark held referendums to allow their people to decide whether they should sign the treaty. (France and Ireland voted yes; the Danes voted no, but the treaty was rewritten to accommodate them, and on a second try they voted yes.)

Why are democracies so reluctant to give "power to the people" by using the referendum to make laws? The main objection is that a proposed law cannot get the sort of careful consideration and detailed examination in an election campaign that it would get in a legislature or parliament. Voters typically do not have the time or resources to inform themselves about the intricacies of a bill. In a sense, that is "what they hire politicians for." Especially when many bills are voted on in a single campaign—as in California, where twenty or more may appear on a single ballot— only one or two will have been widely discussed among the voters. The other bills will be decided by chance factors such as how enticingly they are worded or where they appear on the ballot, or by the small number of people who may stand to gain from them in special ways and therefore take a special interest in them.

ELECTORAL PARTICIPATION

Let us shift from elections and electoral systems to examine how voters act in elections. We shall confine our attention to voters in democratic elections.

It is evident that not all of those who are entitled to vote do vote. In the 2000 American presidential election, for instance, only 50 percent of those who were eligible to vote did so; in most elections for local office, the turnout is even less than this.

There is great variation from one place to another, and among different sorts of people in any one place, as to how active people are in elections. At roughly the same time
that 50 percent of eligible Americans voted in the 2000 presidential election, the following percentages of the eligible electorate voted in a variety of European elections:
Great Britain, 71 percent; Czech Republic, 76 percent; Germany, 82 percent; Sweden,
81 percent. European democracies usually exhibit higher levels of electoral participation
than the United States. Even within the United States, electoral turnout varies a good
deal by geography. In 2000, Hawaii had the lowest turnout among the fifty states, with
only 40 percent; the highest, 67 percent, was Minnesota's.

Beyond geographic variation, certain types of people seem especially likely to vote.
Table 11–2 lists various types of people who seem especially likely or especially unlikely
to vote.

What is it that leads some people to vote more regularly than others? Partly it seems
to be a matter of cultural traditions. The high electoral turnout in Minnesota, for instance,
seems likely to be a result of the tradition of constructive citizenship that was strong
among the Scandinavian immigrants who made up a large part of Minnesota's early
population.

Partly it is a function of practical, almost mundane questions—whether polling day
is on a working day (as in the United States), which is less convenient than a Sunday; or
whether registration to vote is a cumbersome procedure or an easy one. (In some countries, registration is automatically done by the local authorities and requires no specific
action by the person being registered.)

Partly it is a function of the difficulty of making political decisions. This may help
explain why well-educated people are more likely to vote than people with less education; those with less education presumably find politics more puzzling and confusing
than those who are better educated. This problem surely helps to explain why voting
turnout is low in referendums, which demand more from a voter than choosing a party
or a candidate.

Finally, it is partly a function of the political circumstances under which the election
is held. A close election stimulates greater turnout than one that promises to be a walk-
away for one side. National elections, because of the great stakes of war and peace that
are involved, get a higher turnout than they probably deserve as compared with local
elections. As noted, elections conducted under a PR electoral system get higher participation than those under SMDP, because under PR no one need worry about "wasting" a

TABLE 11–2   WHO IS LIKELY OR UNLIKELY TO VOTE?

Groups unusually high in participation	Groups unusually low in participation
Suburban residents	Young people
Well-educated people	Poor people
Well-off people	Women (except in Europe and North America)
Farmers (U.S.A.)	Racial minorities (U.S.A.)
Blue-collar workers (Europe)	Blue-collar workers (U.S.A.)

vote on a candidate who has no chance to win. Blue-collar workers in Europe participate more faithfully than those in the United States partly because unions in Europe are more active than American unions in mobilizing their voters. In most European states—unlike the United States—there are explicitly working-class socialist parties that draw blue-collar workers into political activity.

The fact that some social groups are more likely to vote than others makes a real difference in what views are brought to bear on the election—and therefore on what views elected officials will pay attention to. In the United States, young, poor, ethnic citizens are less likely to vote than older, better off, white citizens, and the impact on the views officials must consider is dramatic. In September 1998, the *New York Times* ran a poll in which it distinguished those citizens most likely to vote in the next election.[7] (Such citizens said they definitely expected to vote in the 1998 election, they were paying a lot of attention to the campaign, and they had voted in both 1994 and 1996.) The set of all registered voters polled (not just those most likely to vote) broke 44 percent to 39 percent in favor of the Democrats in the House election; 66 percent approved of President Bill Clinton's performance in office; and only 29 percent thought that hearings should be started to impeach Clinton. But many of these respondents would not, in fact, vote. Looking only at the "most likely to vote" group, we find they broke the other way, with 53 percent to 41 percent going for the Republicans; only 48 percent approved of Clinton's job performance; and 50 percent thought impeachment hearings should begin.

THE PARADOX OF PARTICIPATION

We might also flip the question of participation around, and instead of asking "Why doesn't everyone vote?" ask, "Why are all these people voting?" Looked at in one way, it appears irrational to take the trouble to vote. Seeing how unlikely it would be for a single vote to decide a U.S. presidential election, one might consider it hardly worthwhile to spend a half hour and 8 cents worth of gasoline to get to the polling place. (The odds must be less than one in a trillion that the other 80 million voters would split exactly evenly, so that one vote could decide the outcome.) We met the cynic of Skinner's *Walden Two* earlier:

> The chance that one man's vote will decide the issue in a national election is less than the chance that he will be killed on his way to the polls. We pay no attention to chances of that magnitude in our daily affairs. We should call a man a fool who bought a sweepstakes ticket with similar odds against him.[8]

This is what we call the "paradox of participation."[9] It is paradoxical because, if things are considered from this perspective, *no one who is sensible should vote.* If the result of the election is nearly certain to be the same whether you vote or not, why should you take the time and go to the expense? To put it in the concrete terms alluded to in the quotation from Skinner, over the years more people are hit by trucks and

---

[7]"Likeliest Voters Favor Republicans," *New York Times,* 25 September 1998, p. A18.

[8]B. F. Skinner, *Walden Two* (New York: Macmillan, 1948), p. 221.

[9]William H. Riker and Peter C. Ordeshook, *An Introduction to Positive Political Theory* (Englewood Cliffs, N.J.: Prentice-Hall, 1973), pp. 45–68, esp. pp. 57–58.

What Is the Best Level of Participation?

A major argument among political scientists in the 1960s and 1970s turned on this question: Is more participation always better, or is there some optimal level of participation that is lower than 100 percent? Among others suggesting that more was not always better, Gabriel Almond and Sidney Verba expressed the opinion, in *The Civic Culture* (Boston: Little, Brown, 1965), that the ideal citizen participated up to a point but then sat back and trusted government officials to take things from there. This guaranteed an attentive citizenry, but one that would also give its government trust and support. Seymour M. Lipset also fueled the distrust of excessive participation by his finding, in *Political Man* (Garden City, N.Y.: Doubleday, 1960), that the high turnout in the German elections of 1932 and 1933 had had a great deal to do with Adolf Hitler's victories.

Of the several responses, that of E. E. Schattschneider—*The Semisovereign People* (New York: Holt, Rinehart and Winston, 1960)—suggested that nonparticipants were like a time bomb waiting to disrupt the system. They were not building patterns of support for the existing system by participating; therefore, they could cause dangerous results, if they suddenly flooded in as the German voters for Hitler did. Schattschneider concluded that we should try to get everyone to participate as much as possible. Carole Pateman, in *Participation and Democratic Theory* (Cambridge: Cambridge University Press, 1970), drew an argument straight from classical liberal theory. A main purpose of participation was to help people improve themselves by exercising their judgment and by informing themselves of what was going on. Whether or not instability results, more participation is in and of itself a good thing; the more there is, the better.

The argument seems to have been resolved for now in favor of the defenders of participation. Today, one does not often hear arguments against full and extensive participation. But this argument has been going on sporadically since the time of the ancient Greeks. We may anticipate that it will come up again.

killed on the way to the polls than change the results of national elections by their single votes. On the average and over the long run, voting is apparently a dangerous and unproductive act.

Paradoxes have solutions, and we can try two possible solutions for this one. First, the paradox obviously holds only for voters taken one at a time. If a large group of voters chose to sit out an election, it is quite possible that their absence could change the outcome. In fact, most politicians spend more time and effort in their campaigns in trying to make sure that the right people get to the polls than in trying to change the minds of people who are planning to vote for their opponents.[10] Politicians certainly recognize the importance of turnout rates in determining elections. Therefore, the paradox of participation is a paradox only for voters taken individually. This might resolve the problem for us except that a voter's decision whether to vote is taken individually. That is, groups do not decide whether to vote, *voters* decide whether to vote. So the paradox remains.

A second way of addressing the paradox is to note that it looks at voting solely as an act to provide benefits or costs to the individual voting. The paradox arises only if we think that voters vote solely because of their wish to exercise their own power in

---

[10]However, see W. Phillips Shively, "From Differential Abstention to Conversion: A Change in Electoral Change, 1864–1988," *American Journal of Political Science* 36 (May 1992): 309–30,

making the government's policies. While it is true that this is the democratic justification for holding elections, we must realize that it casts voting as essentially a *selfish* act in which voters participate only to increase their own political power. However,
we saw at the beginning of this chapter that in many countries, high electoral turnout
occurs even though the voters have no choice of candidates. Clearly, voters in those
countries are voting for some reason other than to exercise their individual political
power, because *their* votes represent no individual political power whatever. They are
voting out of a desire to do their duty, out of a love of country, and often because of a
good deal of social pressure from those around them. In other words, voting for them
may be more of a communal act than an individual one.

There is no reason to think that these communal aspects of voting are absent in a
democracy. This would certainly help to explain what is otherwise unexplainable—that
millions of people vote in elections even though it can easily be demonstrated that voting is of no individual benefit to them. This seems an attractive resolution to the paradox partly because it elevates our discussion of voting above selfish calculations of
individual costs and benefits. Love of country is a noble sentiment, and if electoral participation is based partly on it, all the better for elections.

THE BASES OF INDIVIDUALS' ELECTORAL CHOICES

For whatever reason, then, a great many people vote in elections. How do they choose
which party or candidate to vote for? Any number of things may serve as the basis for
voting choice in one country or another.

We can distinguish usefully between short-term factors and long-term factors in voting choice. Short-term factors are things about a particular election that may lead a person to vote one way or another. The state of the economy usually operates in this way,
for instance. If times are bad, a number of people will vote against whoever is in office
as a way of showing their unhappiness. Edward Tufte once calculated that a 2 percent
increase in real disposable income, compared with a 2 percent loss, should make a difference of about 2.5 percent of the vote for the president's party in midterm congressional elections in the United States; this would generally mean that about twenty to
thirty more seats would go to the president's party in the good year.[11]

Other short-term factors may include the particular appeal (or lack of same) of a candidate. This appears to be particularly the case in the United States and Canada, where
the personalities of possible presidents and prime ministers sway a large number of voters. In most European countries, on the other hand, the voters seem to weigh primarily
the various political parties as whole organizations, with less emphasis on the personal
characteristics of a party's leading candidate. In 1979, for instance, polls in Britain
showed that Margaret Thatcher, the Conservative candidate for prime minister, was less
admired and respected personally than James Callaghan, the candidate of the Labour
Party. However, the British electorate did not hesitate to defeat Labour soundly and put
the Conservatives—and Thatcher—in power. As will be seen in Chapter 12, political

---

[11]Edward R. Tufte, *Political Control of the Economy* (Princeton, N.J.: Princeton University Press, 1978),
p. 112.

"HOW BINDING ARE CAMPAIGN PROMISES
MADE ONLY IN PRIMARIES?"

(© 2002 by Sidney Harris.
Reprinted with permission.)

parties in the United States and Canada are weak organizations compared with those in most countries; as a result, individual candidates in American or Canadian elections carry more personal weight. In countries with strong parties, the focus of the electorate is more on the parties, and individual candidates do not count for as much.

A particular candidacy, the state of the economy, and international crisis—such short-term factors can be potent in deciding an election. However, most elections most of the time are determined largely by things that do not change much or that change only gradually.

One such long-term factor is the identification of some people with a particular political party. We all know some older person who says he or she has been a Democrat (or a Republican or a Conservative or a Liberal or a Labour voter or whatever) "since I was a young child." To such a voter, a particular candidacy or the state of the economy makes less difference than to other voters. Most of the time this person is going to vote by party no matter what is going on. Political scientists call this sort of continuing tie *party identification*.[12] It adds a good deal of stability and predictability over time to election results. We will discuss party identification in more detail in Chapter 12.

---

[12]Angus Campbell, Philip Converse, Warren E. Miller, and Donald Stokes, *The American Voter* (New York: Wiley, 1960), chaps. 6 and 7.

TABLE 11–3   SOCIAL BASES OF SUPPORT FOR THE SOCIAL DEMOCRATIC PARTY
OF WEST GERMANY, 1953–1972

	1953	1957	1965	1969	1972
Percent voting socialist of:					
Working class	58	60	57	58	70
Middle class	28	23	31	46	53
Those who never attend church	63	64	64	77	74
Those who occasionally attend church	48	39	48	45	61
Those who frequently attend church	17	19	17	32	28

Source: Calculated from *Germany Transformed: Political Culture and the New Politics,* by Kendall Baker, Russell Dalton, and Kai Hildebrandt, Cambridge: Harvard University Press, Copyright © 1981, by the President and Fellows of Harvard College.

Another long-term factor that adds stability over time is the commitment of various social groups to one or another party. As we see in Table 11–3, the basic commitment of the working class and the less religious to the Social Democratic Party of West Germany was fairly stable from 1953 to 1972; the flip side of this is that the middle class and the religious were rather consistent in *not* supporting the Social Democratic Party.

I have noted that long-term factors are things that do not change or that *change slowly.* In Table 11–3, we see that the effect of religion did not change over the twenty years, since the difference between those who are religious and those who are not stayed about the same. However, notice the gradual change in the effect of social class. The difference between the two classes was considerably greater at the beginning of the twenty-year period than at the end. In 1953, there was a 30-percentage-point spread between the two classes, but this had narrowed to a 17-point spread by 1972.

The decline in class voting over this period apparently resulted from attempts by the Social Democratic Party to become less exclusively a representative of the working class. Over the next couple of decades, however, the Social Democratic Party became increasingly isolated and fell back on its working class base. By 1990, within the territory of what had been West Germany before the unification of East and West Germany, the percentage-point spread was back up to 28 percent—about what it had been in 1953.

In other countries and at other times, the following social differences have functioned importantly as bases for voting distinctions:

- Region (The "solid Democratic South" of the United States from the 1870s to the 1960s is an example, or the regional basis of all Canadian parties.)
- Language (The Swedish People's Party of Finland is an example.)
- Farming (Many countries have had Agrarian parties; Norway and Sweden are two examples.)

- Country of origin (Irish and Italian voters in the United States tend to be Democrats; German and Anglo-Saxon voters tend to be Republicans.)
- Race (Blacks tend strongly to vote Democratic in the United States; the politics of Guyana has been almost totally determined by conflicts between blacks and East Indians.)
- Gender (Women in many countries favor conservative parties, although this may be an indirect effect of religion rather than a direct effect of differences between men and women; by contrast, a "gender gap" has opened in the United States and several European countries, with *men* voting more conservatively than women.)
- Age (In 1994, for instance, 19 percent of Germans aged eighteen to twenty-five voted for the Green Party, while only 2 percent of those over sixty did so.)

Example: Proportional Representation Elections in Israel

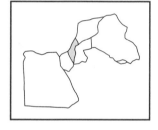

The Knesset (Israel's parliament, with 120 seats) is elected every four years by an unusually simple and direct form of proportional representation. Parties submit lists of candidates (in ranked order) to the electoral commission. Any party that receives 1.5 percent or more of the vote nationally gets at least one seat in the Knesset, and each party's number of seats is proportional to how large a proportion of the vote it received. Compared with most countries, this is a simple and straightforward PR system. The accounting is done across the state as a whole, rather than separately for different regions of the state. The threshold of 1.5 percent is low enough to be quite generous to small parties; in Germany, for instance, a party receives no representation unless it has received at least 5 percent of the vote.

To put a list on the ballot, the party must submit a petition containing a few thousand signatures and pay a fairly small deposit (usually a couple of thousand dollars). Usually twenty or more lists are on the ballot.

Voters then cast their vote for a list. Candidates on the list enter the Knesset according to their rank in the list; for instance, the Shas Party qualified for seventeen seats in the Knesset in 1999, so the first seventeen names on the list became Knesset members. If a seat is vacated before the next election, the next person on the list steps in.

Where candidates rank on their party's list is obviously important. Parties put their key leaders at the top of their lists, to make sure that they are elected, but beyond that, groups and factions compete to get their people placed high. Who does the placing varies by party. Of the two largest parties, Labour uses a primary election to determine the internal placement of its candidates on its list; in the Likud Party, the "center" (a gathering of one thousand to three thousand leaders of the party, broadly representative of its constituent parts) does the ordering.

Larger parties do get a slight advantage in the distribution of seats under Israel's system, because of the formulae for the distribution of "surplus" votes. "Surplus" votes occur when a party gets less than 1.5 percent of the vote so that its votes do not count toward any party's share, or when rounding off in assigning Knesset seats to parties leaves some votes unused. And as in almost all other proportional representation systems in the world, in Israel the formulae used to allocate the surplus votes among the various parties favor the larger parties slightly. In 1999, these leftover votes gave Labour and its allies (with 20.2 percent of the vote) 21.7 percent of the seats in the Knesset; Likud, with 14.1 percent of the vote, got 15.8 percent of the seats. This is only a minor advantage, however. The bottom line is that the Israeli system of PR is unusually straightforward and faithful to proportionality.

As a result, a lot of parties usually get into the Knesset. In 1999, the results were:

	Votes (%)	Seats
One Israel (Labour and its allies)	20.2	26
Likud	14.1	19
Shas (ultra-orthodox)	13.0	17
Meretz (left-liberal)	7.6	10
Yisrael B'Aliyah (Russian immigrants)	5.1	6
Shinui (anti-orthodox)	5.0	6
Center Party	5.0	6
National Religious Party	4.2	5
United Torah Front	3.7	5
Arab Democratic Party	3.4	5
National Union	3.0	4
Yisrael Beiteinu	2.6	4
Hadash (Arab-Jewish)	2.6	3
One Nation	1.9	2
National Democratic Alliance	1.9	2

Such a diverse party system could produce unstable government, as it might prove difficult to combine enough different parties to make up a working majority in the parliament (especially when, as in Israel, they are deeply divided on policies). This has not proved the case in Israel, possibly because the country's constant exposure to external danger has forced the parties to cooperate in spite of their inclinations. However, one major result of the dispersion of the parties is evident. It is almost impossible to form a governing majority without including at least one of the religious parties; this has given them a good deal of leverage, by which they have commanded patronage and policy concessions way out of proportion to their electoral strength.

Example: Elections in Nigeria

Nigeria has had elected democratic government for only ten of its more than forty years of independence— from 1960 to 1966, from 1979 to 1983, and again starting in 1999. Obviously, Nigeria's democracy is fragile; elections there illustrate well the difficulties of conducting an election in a large, new state whose diverse ethnic elements are still only weakly united.

Even aside from the military's propensity to throw out the results, electoral politics is difficult for any country like Nigeria. First, it tends to bring out sectarian conflicts between tribes and regions of different religions, which always threaten to tear the state apart. Nigeria fought a bloody regional civil war from 1966 to 1969, and thousands of people have died in Christian-Moslem riots. Violence between ethnic groups is also common.

Second, Nigeria is a large, spread-out country. The difficult logistics of an election, together with the passions of hostility that an election awakens, leave the process open to violence and fraud. At the time of the 1983 election, Nigeria was a country of 80 million or so people, spread over a large area with often primitive communications. The elections were held in five weekly installments. First, the president was elected; then, a week later, governors of the states; a week later, the senate was elected; then the house of representatives; and finally the state assemblies. The first task facing the government in setting up the election was to draw up a roll of eligible voters. Throughout the country, 158,000 voting stations were established, and men and women were asked to go to the stations to register themselves for the election. The problem of security that this involved is indicated by the fact that with ninety thousand police in Nigeria, there were nearly twice as many voting stations as there were law enforcement personnel.

The two main concerns of most observers were violence and the possibility of rigged results. Violence did break out; scores of people were killed, and the last three waves of elections had to be canceled in two states because of rioting. However, the violence did not reach levels that made it impossible to respect the elections. Fraud, or the suspicion of it, was a far greater problem. The published roll of registered voters was particularly suspect, because it listed 65 million people. In a country of approximately 80 million, there could not be that many adults, and it was thought that many fraudulent entries had been made. When the incumbent President Alhaji Shehu Shagari won more strongly than anyone had expected and his party succeeded surprisingly well in the further elections, the other parties cried foul. There were plenty of examples of fraud for them to point at. The village of Modakeke, for instance, cast 170,000 votes for Shagari, about five hundred votes per household.[13]

Shortly after that election, the military took over the country and ruled continuously until 1998. When democracy was reestablished in 1999, elections had to be set

---

[13]*The Economist,* 20 August 1983, p. 38.

up anew. The 1999 election was again held in stages, with local elections in December 1998, state elections in January, and elections for Parliament and president held two weeks apart in February. Hundreds of millions of dollars were spent on the campaigns. One particular problem arose when about 20 million of the 60 million registration cards were bought up by politicians. To prevent the use of these cards in fraudulent multiple voting, the polling stations required all voters in the district to register on the day of the election. Voters then were required to wait in the registration station until everyone had registered, at which point all voted together, so that no one could come back and vote more than once. Devices such as this were apparently successful; international observers declared the elections to be generally free and fair.

The parliamentary election had only about a 20 percent turnout, since the eviscerated Parliament of the period of military rule had inspired no respect. But the presidential election generated great excitement and a respectable turnout. The two final candidates, Olusegun Obasanjo and Olu Falae, were both members of the Yoruba ethnic group from the southwestern part of the country. This reflected the fact that issues other than ethnicity have begun to broaden politics in Nigeria; the Yoruba are probably the only ethnic group today whose members vote unitedly on a "one-issue" basis for their group. Obasanjo was in the end distrusted by his own group, partly because he had generated a good deal of support in the rest of the country. He won handily, with majorities in twenty-seven of the country's thirty-six states; but he lost heavily in the six home states of his Yoruba group. In the state of Lagos, the financial center of Nigeria, he got only 12 percent of the vote.

FURTHER READING

Barnes, Samuel H.; Kaase, Max; and Allerbeck, Klause. *Political Action: Mass Participation in Five Western Democracies.* Beverly Hills, Calif.: Sage, 1979.

Bowler, Shaun; Donovan, Todd; and Tolbert, Caroline J., eds. *Citizens as Legislators: Direct Democracy in the United States,* Columbus: Ohio State University Press, 1998.

Campbell, Angus; Converse, Philip; Miller, Warren; and Stokes, Donald. *The American Voter.* New York: Wiley, 1960.

Cox, Gary W. *Making Votes Count: Strategic Coordination in the World's Electoral Systems.* New York: Cambridge University Press, 1997.

Cronin, Thomas. *Direct Democracy: The Politics of Initiative, Referendum and Recall.* Cambridge: Harvard University Press, 1989.

Dalton, Russell J. *Citizen Politics in Western Democracies.* 2d ed. Chatham, N.J.: Chatham House, 1997.

Duverger, Maurice. *Political Parties.* New York: Wiley, 1954.

Flanigan, William H., and Zingale, Nancy H. *Political Behavior of the American Electorate.* 8th ed. Washington, D.C.: Congressional Quarterly Press, 1994.

Gaines, Brian. "Duverger's Law and the Meaning of Canadian Exceptionalism." *Comparative Political Studies* 32 (1999): 835–61.

Iyengar, Shanto, and Kinder, Donald R. *News That Matters: Television and American Opinion.* Chicago: University of Chicago Press, 1987.

Jones, Mark. *Electoral Laws and the Survival of Presidential Democracies.* Notre Dame, Ind.: University of Notre Dame Press, 1995.

Leduc, Lawrence; Niemi, Richard G.; and Norris, Pippa, eds. *Comparing Democracies: Elections and Voting in Global Perspective.* Beverly Hills, Calif.: Sage, 1996.

Lewis-Beck, Michael S. *Economics and Elections.* Ann Arbor: University of Michigan Press, 1988.

Lijphart, Arend. *Electoral Systems and Party Systems.* New York: Oxford University Press, 1994.

Patterson, Thomas E. *Out of Order: How the Decline of Political Parties and the Growing Power of the News Media Undermine the American Way of Electing Presidents.* New York: Knopf, 1994.

Pierce, John C., and Sullivan, John L., eds. *The Electorate Reconsidered.* Beverly Hills, Calif.: Sage, 1980.

Popkin, Samuel L. *The Reasoning Voter.* Chicago: University of Chicago Press, 1991.

Powell, G. Bingham, Jr. "American Voter Turnout in Comparative Perspective." *American Political Science Review* 80 (March 1986): 17–44.

———. *Elections as Instruments for Democracy.* New Haven: Yale University Press, 2000.

Rae, Douglas. *Political Consequences of Electoral Laws,* rev. ed. New Haven: Yale University Press, 1971.

Riker, William H., and Ordeshook, Peter C. *An Introduction to Positive Political Theory.* Englewood Cliffs, N.J.: Prentice-Hall, 1973.

Rosenstone, Steven J., and Hansen, John Mark. *Mobilization, Participation and Democracy in America.* New York: Macmillan, 1993.

Sorauf, Frank J. *Inside Campaign Finance.* New Haven: Yale University Press, 1992.

Taagepera, Rein, and Shugart, Matthew S. *Seats and Votes: The Effects and Determinants of Electoral Systems.* New Haven: Yale University Press, 1989.

Teixeira, Roy A. *The Disappearing American Voter.* Washington, D.C.: Brookings Institution, 1992.

WEBSITES OF INTEREST

Election Notes, with daily coverage of elections from around the world; a good source for the results of recent elections:
http://www.klipsan.com/elecnews.htm

Electoral websites, a source to survey the world's elections:
http://www.agora.stm.it/elections/election.htm

International Institute for Democracy and Electoral Assistance worldwide data on turnout in elections:
http://www.int-idea.se/voter_turnout/index.html

FECInfo, a source on campaign contributions and expenditures in U.S. elections:
http://www.tray.com/fecinfo/

12

PARTIES:
A LINKING AND LEADING
MECHANISM IN POLITICS

In preceding chapters, I have talked a good deal about political parties. The political party crops up in all aspects of politics. It is an invention that first developed in the nineteenth century in response to the appearance of elections involving large numbers of voters. Politicians developed the political party at that time as a device to help themselves and like-minded friends get elected, but the party proved to have many other uses as well and went on to become a ubiquitous feature of modern politics.

I shall explore this theme in later sections, but first, questions of definition.

THE POLITICAL PARTY

A political party is a group of officials or would-be officials who are linked with a sizable group of citizens into an organization; a chief object of this organization is to ensure that its officials attain power or are maintained in power.

The latter part of this definition distinguishes the political party from the "interest group," discussed in Chapter 13. In most countries, there are many interest groups—such as the American Medical Association, the American Dairy Farmers' Organization, the Natural Gas Supply Association, Friends of the Earth, and so on—groups of people with a common interest who band together to try by way of lobbying, campaign contributions, and other tactics to make sure that the government's policies will be in tune with their wishes. Interest groups are distinguished from political parties in that they try to influence which policies are chosen without actually taking power or setting policies; parties, on the other hand, have as their central purpose the acquisition of power and the direction of policy.

There is nothing about the definition that says political parties are restricted to democracies and to electoral activity. Revolutionary parties may be organized not to win elections but to seize control of the government by force. And totalitarian parties—such as the Nazi party of Germany in the 1930s—may oversee the machinery of a nondemocratic state.

Finally, a party joins people together in a formally organized structure. U.S. political parties surely fall at an extreme in the looseness of their organization, but in most countries, the parties are clearly delineated, with formal membership that sets those who are in the party apart from the rest. For instance, the Conservative party of Britain has about 330,000 dues-paying members. The Communist party of China has about 58 million members, who must pass a probationary and training period, generally taking more than a year and a half, before they are accepted for full membership.

The party's nature as a structure, tying together a large group of officials and citizens, provides an avenue by which one part may control or communicate with another. It is this that has made it such a versatile tool of modern politics. This will be explored in more detail.

ORIGINS OF THE MODERN PARTY

Although the party has turned out to be useful for a variety of tasks that require control or communication, it was first invented for more limited and self-serving purposes. Long before the coming of electoral democracy, the state had had a varied structure of public officials—mayors, members of parliament, ministers for defense, and so on. Before democracy arrived, people attained these offices in a variety of ways: by being born into them, by buying the office (much as we might today purchase a fried-chicken franchise), by bribery, by appointment.

Once democracy was introduced, however, many of these positions were filled by election. This was different from the old ways of choosing officials in one important respect: In the old ways, the person who wished to have the office dealt with a single king or perhaps with a few people who could be bribed; under democracy, the would-be official had to seek the votes of a thousand or more people.

It did not take long for politicians in the new democracies to see that some sort of club or organization that bound them together with large numbers of voters would help them to attain and hold office. Furthermore, large national clubs binding together a whole set of officials with voters throughout the country could function more effectively than a local club built around a single official. With a nationwide organization, voters were not "lost" to the club as they moved from one place to another; a popular official could go from place to place, helping to convince the voters to choose other candidates of the organization; and there would be enough money to hire professional staff who could help with the job of organizing thousands of voters. Thus, the political party was born.

The first modern electoral democracy was the United States of America, and it was here that the first parties developed. By the 1820s, there were well-organized parties, and the Democratic Party, which can trace its roots back to that time, is the oldest political party in the world.

In Britain, 1867 was the first year in which there was a reasonably widespread extension of the vote. As of that year, 10 percent of the population was entitled to vote. Directly as a result of this expansion of the electorate, the first modern party organization Britain had known was established in the city of Birmingham:

[In 1867] the Registration Societies, the Reform or Liberal Associations which had sprung up since 1832, were groups of subscribers, of amateurs, and were in the hands of traditional leaders incapable of getting at the masses who had just been brought on the political stage by the extension of the franchise. Birmingham received 30,000 new electors. The [Liberals] believed that to ensure the victory, the party organization ought to reach all these voters, to make them feel that they were about to fight *pro aris et focis,* that the Liberal party was their own party, the party of each one of them. To meet these views, one of the Radical leaders, Mr. W. Harris, architect, man of letters, and secretary of the Birmingham Liberal Association, proposed a plan of organization according to which all the Liberals of the locality were to meet in every ward, and elect representatives to manage the affairs of the party.[1]

The possibility that an expanded suffrage would lead to the development of political parties was one of the arguments raised by some members of Parliament against expanding the suffrage in 1867:

... with a widely enlarged suffrage the candidate would find himself less and less able to come face to face with his constituency, and would be compelled in consequence . . . to rely more and more on the aid of the election agent, and, as in America, of that of committees and canvassers whose mouthpiece and delegate he would have to make himself.[2]

In the United States, suffrage had been expanded earlier than in Britain, and it was in the United States, in the first decade of the nineteenth century, that the first modern parties had appeared. Similarly, all over Europe, whenever a reasonably large and varied electorate was established with the coming of democracy, the political party appeared.

Like elections themselves, political parties have been widely copied and are found in many countries that are not electoral democracies. The Communist parties of the Eastern European states were obvious examples of this, but many another autocratic state has had a political party that functioned importantly in its politics. Egypt, for instance, is governed by the National Democratic Party, Zimbabwe by the Zimbabwe African National Union–Patriotic Front, Kenya by the Kenyan African National Union, and Syria by the Ba'ath Party. Many more examples could be noted, for many regimes that do not require parties to win elections have found that the modern political party—with the links it creates between masses of people and a set of political leaders—is useful to them. One of the wonders of modern politics is that this invention, originally devised in order that some officeholders could keep their jobs, has proved adaptable to all sorts of other purposes. The political party has become a "miracle glue" of sorts for politics. Whenever one group of people is to be controlled by another group or even just kept in contact with them, the party has turned out to be a useful tool.

Let us look at some of the ways in which the political party has been used to do these things. Parties provide the following: a basis for the mobilization of masses of citizens; a means of recruiting and socializing political leaders; structured political identity at the mass and elite levels; and a method of control within a government structure. We shall look at each of these in turn.

POLITICAL PARTIES AND THE MOBILIZATION OF THE MASSES

I argued in Chapter 11 that one of the main effects of holding elections was to involve the masses of ordinary citizens in acting out their support for the state and, by so doing,

---

[1]M. Ostrogorski, *Democracy and the Organization of Political Parties,* vol.1 (Garden City, N.Y.: Doubleday, 1964), p. 80.
    [2]Ibid., p. 78.

Menaka Gandhi addressing a party rally in India.
(Baldev/Corbis/Sygma)

strengthening that support. For this to happen, millions of voters must be stimulated to go out and take the trouble to vote. Governments cannot easily get people out to the polls, so how to reap this particular advantage of elections poses a bit of a problem. The problem is particularly great where only one slate of candidates is allowed, so that there is no suspense whatever about the outcome of the election. How can the voters be mobilized to get out and vote under these circumstances? A political party is a handy instrument with which to stir up the electorate and get them to the polls. It is controlled by its leaders, who are at the same time the rulers of the state; and it may have a membership that extends down into every village, so it is strategically placed to turn out large numbers of people.

In the United States, political parties make great efforts to get out the vote. They do this not to bolster support for the regime, although that is a side effect, but to help themselves win elections. In the Soviet Union, the Communist party had no such motive for stirring up the electorate, but its leaders were anxious to generate a good show of support, and so the party did much the same things as American parties do at election time.

Aside from elections, political parties may serve to mobilize the people for special purposes or to meet crises. When President Anwar Sadat of Egypt was assassinated in 1981 and was succeeded by Vice President Hosni Mubarak, over a million people joined a demonstration in Cairo to show their support for Mubarak. The demonstration was partly organized by the government apparatus itself but also, in large part, by the ruling National Democratic Party. When the regime of Charles de Gaulle was threatened in France by a general strike in 1969, the turning point at which his opposition was defeated came when his Union of Democrats for the Republic Party organized a massive demonstration in Paris for which thousands of supporters were bused in from the countryside.

A party may also mobilize masses of people *against* a regime. Many of today's political parties in states of the South—the Congress Party in India, for example, or the National Front for Liberation in Algeria—were initially organized to carry out a campaign to overthrow a colonial ruler such as Britain or France. When German armies occupied much of Europe during World War II, it was the churches and the political parties that provided the basis for a resistance movement because these were the only structures binding together large and widespread groups of people in ways that made coordinated resistance possible. Today, the most important focus of opposition to many regimes lies with political parties.

POLITICAL PARTIES AND THE RECRUITMENT AND SOCIALIZATION OF LEADERS

Another use to which parties have lent themselves, beyond what they were originally designed for, is the recruitment and socialization of leaders. Somebody has to do this in any society, and where there are political parties, they are an obvious choice for the task. What other organization could better seek out promising young people, give them experience at relatively small jobs, and gradually move those who do well to more important jobs, while imbuing them with the values that the political leadership wishes to encourage?

In Britain, for instance, an ambitious young woman who was interested in entering politics might work for a while at lesser tasks for one of the major parties, such as the Conservative Party. Before too long, if she were interested in standing for Parliament, she might be nominated from a district. To get the nomination, she would have to convince the local selection committee of the Conservative Party in that district that she was their best nominee. As a beginner, she would probably be selected in a hopeless district, where no Conservative had much of a chance; but once she had proved that she could campaign well in one or two lost causes, she might get the nomination from a decent district, win, and enter the House. In the House, she would continue to be molded and guided by the party. If she were the sort that party leaders like—witty in debate, hard working, and above all a faithful party voter—she might advance into positions of real responsibility, such as party spokesperson on defense or on health. Eventually, she might aim so high as to be prime minister. To be selected for this position, she would have to win an internal election at which all the Conservative members of the House of Commons vote to narrow the choice of nominees to two of their members; the 330,000 enrolled members of the party then vote by mail ballot to choose which of the two will be party leader. Throughout this career, her advancement would have been primarily due to her support from her party organization, and she would have risen to the top only because she was the sort of person her party wanted and because, in each position she held, she had learned from the rest of the party how to behave in the ways they preferred. This is essentially the only way to make a political career in Great Britain.

In the United States, too, parties are important as devices for the recruitment and socialization of leaders. However, parties in the United States are weaker organizationally than those in Britain, and so they do not hold the same monopoly in this regard that British parties do. Most political leaders have worked their way into place through the apparatus of either the Democratic or Republican Party, starting at fairly lowly positions. However, primary elections at which a candidate can appeal directly to the voters for nomination, rather than relying on party leaders, can allow a popular celebrity such as the astronaut John Glenn or basketball star Bill Bradley to enter directly into politics at a high level. (The existence of primary elections, which take the selection of candidates out of the hands of party leaders, is often considered the single most important cause of American parties' organizational weakness.) Furthermore, people who have distinguished themselves at some other career are often appointed to a president's cabinet directly without any prior political career and thus without any screening by a party. When John Kennedy appointed his brother Robert as attorney general, when Richard Nixon appointed Harvard professor Henry Kissinger to be secretary of state, and when Bill Clinton appointed career civil servant Madeleine Albright to be secretary of state, no party experience was involved.

In a one-party state such as Yugoslavia was before 1990, the single party may serve as the major avenue to any sort of political or economic advancement. The Yugoslav Communist Party actually restricted its membership to keep out opportunists who would join to advance themselves. By strict entrance requirements and by purges, the party was limited to a membership comprising about 5 percent of Yugoslavia's population. Party leaders had good cause to be concerned about the problem of opportunism. There was ample reason for ambitious young people to seek membership no matter what their political beliefs because all factory directors, all important public officials, and most leaders of institutions such as universities were required to be Communists.

POLITICAL PARTIES AS A SOURCE OF POLITICAL IDENTITY

Another unforeseen effect of political parties was the extent to which parties, once one was associated with them, would become an important part of one's identity. Party is probably not the first thing a person would mention when asked "What are you?" A more likely reply would be "I am a Presbyterian," "I am a woman," "I am a student," "I am a Canadian," and so on. Along the way, if you keep prompting, you may well be given the name of the political party with which that person feels associated. As we saw in Chapter 11, this source of identity is called *party identification.*[3] For those who become quite active, the political party may become a vital and central personal concern. What would John Kennedy or Lyndon Johnson have been without the Democratic Party? What would Willy Brandt of West Germany have been without the Social Democratic Party and Yeltsin of Russia without the Communist Party (initially as a source of identity and later as a foil)?

[3]The concept of "party identification" was first developed fully in Angus Campbell, et al., *The American Voter* (New York: Wiley, 1960), chaps. 6 and 7. For a review, see W. Phillips Shively, "The Nature of Party Identification: A Review of Recent Developments," in John C. Pierce and John L. Sullivan, eds., *The Electorate Reconsidered* (Beverly Hills, Calif.: Sage, 1980).

"WHAT I DON'T UNDERSTAND IS HOW, IN A FEW YEARS, WE'LL BECOME CONSERVATIVE REPUBLICANS."

(© 2002 by Sidney Harris. Reprinted with permission.)

One important thing about party as a source of identity is that it can provide continuity in a political world that is otherwise quite fluid. Candidates come and go, wars start and end, political issues arise and fade and are replaced by others, but parties may go on and on. The two major parties of the United States are over a century old; the largest party of Mexico is about seventy years old, as was the Communist Party of the Soviet Union at the time of its collapse; Britain's Conservative Party is over a century old, and its Labour Party is over a half-century old.

By furnishing individuals and politically active people with a lasting political identity, the party can give them a source of political community throughout their lives. Parties may provide an even longer-range continuity in politics than that of a single lifetime if party connections are passed on from parents to children or if local party organizations continue their activity across generations. An ironic instance of the way in which parties can create this sort of continuity is provided by the state of Indiana.[4] Since the Civil War, there has been a political split between the southern part of the state and the northern part. There was a good deal of sympathy for the Confederacy in the 1860s in southern Indiana; this trans-

---

[4]This case was first presented by V. O. Key, Jr., and Frank Munger in Eugene Burdick and Arthur J. Brodbeck, eds., *American Voting Behavior* (Glencoe, Ill.: Free Press, 1959) chap. 15. Their analysis has been updated here.

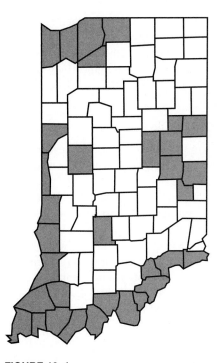

FIGURE 12–1
Indiana counties that voted 40 percent or
more Democratic, 2000.

FIGURE 12–2
Indiana counties with over 30 percent of the
labor force employed in manufacturing, 1990.

lated into support for the Democratic Party, which was more sympathetic to the Confed-eracy at that time. In northern Indiana, abolitionist and Union sentiment ran strong, and this led northern voters to support the Republican Party. One hundred thirty-five years later, this pattern still holds! As may be seen in Figure 12–1, most of the counties in which Democratic presidential candidate Al Gore received 40 percent or more of the vote in 2000 fell in the southern part of the state. In northern Indiana, Gore got as much as 40 percent of the vote in only a handful of counties, which is to say that Republican George W. Bush got over 60 percent of the vote almost everywhere in northern Indiana.

This distribution of support bears little relation to what we think of as the basis for Democratic and Republican voting. Figure 12–2 shows the counties in Indiana in which over 30 percent of the labor force consists of workers in manufacturing industries. Such workers are commonly thought to be the mainstay of the Democratic Party, yet a com-parison of the two maps show that whether a county is heavily industrial has little to do with whether it is strongly Democratic. Indeed, there is a slightly negative relationship between the two: While 40 percent of the counties that are "nonindustrial" in Figure 12–2 are unusually Democratic in Figure 12–1, only 18 percent of the "industrial" counties are unusually Democratic.

The basic north-south split in the state has been a political fact of life continually since the 1860s. The chief determinant of the geographic distribution of party support is not the economy and not the distribution of industry but events that occurred and were pretty well disposed of 135 years ago. The ability of parties—through their organizational structure and through their grip on people's consciousness—to establish stable lines of conflict is impressive. In this case, the results border on the ludicrous, because it must make little sense that Indiana elections in 2000 were determined by who took what position on slavery and secession in 1860.

POLITICAL PARTIES AS A CHANNEL OF CONTROL

A final unforeseen effect of political parties was to provide some political leaders with a new channel through which to exert control over other leaders. This has been an important factor in modern politics.

Remember that a party is an organization that binds a sizable group of political leaders together with a sizable number of ordinary citizens. It is the only sort of organization that regularly does this. It spreads so widely within the set of political leaders and out into the mass of people that it offers an excellent channel for power through which political leaders can control the actions either of other political leaders or of the citizens.

As a channel for controlling other political leaders, the party is important in all sorts of states. The leaders of a party have many punishments and rewards at their disposal— nomination for various offices, support in passing favored legislation, and so on. Perhaps the greatest carrot or stick most of the time is the chance to advance to more powerful positions within the party. Leaders use these inducements deliberately to force obedience on lesser party figures in legislative votes, campaign activity, and so on. Sam Rayburn, who was for many years the leader of the Democratic Party in the U.S. House of Representatives, used to caution new members, "To get ahead, get along." That is, to advance within the House hierarchy, obey orders. In the British House of Commons, the party organizations expect such pure obedience in voting that the life of ordinary members is in some ways rather dull, because they are following orders in how they vote.

As we shall see in Chapter 14, this channel of control is crucial in making the parliamentary governments of Western Europe and other parts of the world work. However, party functions as a channel for power in all sorts of other systems as well. In one-party states, the party may provide a means by which the apparatus of the state, especially in touchy areas such as the armed forces, is kept under the control of the party leaders. As much as possible, only party members were allowed to serve as high-ranking officers in the armies of the communist countries, for instance, and their advancement was strongly affected by their standing in the party.

Parties may also be used as a channel for power by which the leaders of the state control the mass of citizens. This is more common in authoritarian states than in democracies, where direct control of citizens is supposed to be the exception rather than the rule. For example, one particular problem for authoritarian systems is the control of intellectual activity, which might pose a threat to the leaders of the state if it proceeded freely. By placing party members in leadership positions in writers' organizations, universities, professional associations, and the media, the leaders of the state can help to ensure their control over what the citizenry thinks and says. This has particularly been the practice in communist systems, although military dictatorships, the fascist regimes of the 1930s, and other authoritarian regimes have attempted it as well.

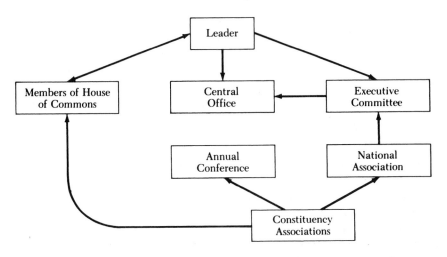

FIGURE 12–3
Organizational structure of Great Britain's Conservative Party.

PARTY ORGANIZATION

Political parties in the United States are unusual in their organizational structure because they are loose and informal. Any other organization in the country—a savings bank, a bird-watchers' club, a church—would have some sort of formal membership, for which one applies and in return receives a membership card of some sort. Political parties in the United States do not require this of their "members"; in fact, it is often difficult for people to be sure whether or not they are members of a party or indeed which party they are members of. Political scientists have some difficulty specifying just what group of people they are describing when they speak of the "Republican Party." Do they mean only the elected Republican officials in Congress and elsewhere? Do they mean the people who run the party's offices? Do they mean just the people who work for Republicans in election campaigns? Do they mean those who are "registered" as Republicans (even if they regularly vote Democratic)? Do they mean those who sympathize with the Republicans? There is no formal organization defining those who "belong" and those who do not, therefore anyone is free to define the set as desired.[5]

In other states, however, parties are set up in a more normal way as formal organizations; if one wishes to be a member of the party, one applies for membership, pays some sort of dues, and is formally enrolled with a membership card. As explicit, well-defined organizations, these parties have *organizational structure,* which may greatly affect their political role.

The Conservative Party of Great Britain offers a fairly typical example of organizational structure. As we see in Figure 12–3, the party consists of several parts. The key position is occupied by the leader of the party, who is a Conservative member of the

[5]For a more detailed analysis of this problem, see Paul A. Beck, *Party Politics in America,* 8th ed. (Reading, Mass.: Addison-Wesley, 1997), chap. 1.

House of Commons, elected by the other Conservative members of the House. If the Conservative Party is in power, the leader serves as prime minister for Britain.[6]

One-way arrows (indicating power) go out from the leader to all other units with which the leader interacts except the members of the House. With regard to the latter, power is a two-way street—the members may unseat the leader, and this occurred several times in the twentieth century; but the leader directs the business of the Conservative Party in the House.

Other parts of the party serve as a supporting structure for the leader and the party's members in the House. There are about 330,000 dues-paying party members organized into constituency associations. These determine local party policy—including the important question of who will be the party's candidate from that district—but they have little say otherwise in national party policies. Their only influence in this regard is to send delegates to the party's annual conference, from which, as seen in Figure 12-3, *no* arrows of power go anywhere. Issues are discussed at the conference and resolutions passed; these are not binding on anyone, although the party's leaders may treat them as important symptoms of discontent that must be taken seriously.

The National Association is not elected but consists of members of Parliament, prospective candidates, party officials, representatives of the constituency associations, and others: about three thousand in all. It meets annually and elects an executive committee of 150, which meets several times a year. These bodies consider the direction of the party, organizational questions, and so on, but the fact that they meet so infrequently indicates that what they do is not terribly important.

The Central Office is a large and well-financed party bureaucracy that hires regional and local party agents, conducts research on policy, and publishes propaganda. The Central Office is closely controlled by the leader, who directly appoints most of its top officials.

Thus, the Conservative Party has a complex structure, dominated by the members of the House of Commons through their leader. Other parts of the structure are important to the members of the House as a support group, but except for the important power over nominations held by local constituency associations, they have little power over the party's policies. This is not to say that the outside structure is unimportant; if nothing else, the dues paid by its members are the major source of party finance.

Most parties outside the United States have organizational structures more or less similar to this. They may vary in the degree of power given to the outside structure. (The Labour Party of Britain, for instance, gives more real power to its annual conference than does the Conservative Party.) Or, they may vary in how tightly control is exercised. In communist parties, "lower" units in power generally have to toe the line much more precisely than in noncommunist parties; this allows the leader to direct party policies more completely and more efficiently than leaders of other parties can.

PARTY FINANCE

Parties get the money with which to finance their activities from a variety of sources. In the United States, parties do not have a monopoly on political finance, since much of it

---

[6]This arrangement is discussed in more detail in Chapter 14.

is raised directly by candidates from individual contributors and organized interest groups. However, in recent years, "soft money" raised and allocated by the parties themselves has become quite important in campaigns, though it is legally restricted to organizational and "get out the vote" efforts.

Outside of the United States, parties generally raise the money and determine its use themselves.[7] The money may come from many kinds of sources:

- *Public finance:* Most states pay a portion of their parties' campaign expenses from public funds. It is always difficult to decide how much money to give to which parties, and established parties benefit disproportionately.
- *Individual memberships:* These may provide a good deal of income to a party, especially one with a large membership. Socialist and communist parties have been particularly successful in this; in some countries, members pay a percentage of their income as dues to the party.
- *Bribes and kickbacks:* Especially where a single party is associated with a dictatorship, the closeness of the party to government allows it to organize corruption on its own behalf. In 1993, the Liberal Democratic Party of Japan, which had ruled without interruption for so long that it closely approximated one-party government, became embroiled in a huge scandal involving kickbacks of millions of dollars from construction contractors.
- *Interest-group donations:* Business and labor groups, and a few others, may subsidize favored parties heavily.
- *Profits from business enterprise:* Many parties own their own newspapers, banks, and other service firms, which they operate for the benefit of their members. Usually these cost money rather than make it, but some may be profitable.
- *Subsidies from foreign countries:* The United States, the Soviet Union, Libya, China, Israel, France, Japan, and other states have, at times, subsidized parties in other countries to further their own policies.

POLITICAL PARTY SYSTEMS

So far I have addressed the questions of what a political party does, how it is structured, and so on. All these questions have involved a single political party, looked at by itself. Another important set of questions revolves around the *pattern* formed by the political parties in a state. We speak of a "party system" as the set of all parties. Political scientists distinguish such systems primarily by the number and relative size of the parties.[8]

A *one-party system* is one in which only a single political party is allowed to be active. The former communist states of Eastern Europe; Egypt, Tanzania, and many other new states of the South; and the right-wing dictatorships of Nazi Germany or Franco's

---

[7]A general review of party finance is Herbert Alexander and Rei Shiratori, *Comparative Political Finance Among the Democracies* (Boulder, Colo.: Westview Press, 1994).

[8]For good discussions of each of the party systems examined here, see Maurice Duverger, *Political Parties* (New York: Wiley, 1954); and Giovanni Sartori, *Party and Party Systems* (Cambridge, England: Cambridge University Press, 1964).

Michels' "Iron Law of Oligarchy"

In *Political Parties* (first published in 1915), Robert Michels argues that a political party can never be faithful to the program and constituency for which it was originally founded. For the party to vie successfully for power, he wrote, it is necessary that it be organized through a specialized division of labor in which certain people become full-time leaders. Once this has happened, however, the leadership group inevitably develops a set of values and perspectives that is different from the original aims of the party. The leaders deal daily with the enemy, sitting with them in parliament, bargaining with them; the party may develop its own stake in the status quo (many European parties, for instance, own banks, newspapers, and other business enterprises) that makes its leaders cautious about rocking the boat; and finally, it is in the leaders' interests for the party to grow as large as possible, and the easiest way to effect this is to moderate the party's positions so as to bring in new groups that had previously not been willing to support it. In short, a political party is caught in a dilemma: It may refuse to develop central leadership, in which case it will probably not attain power; or it may develop central leadership, but at the cost of losing its soul.

Political Parties is perhaps the most influential social scientific work of the twentieth century. Michels's theme has been picked up time and again to explain why parties disappoint their followers. It was popular among Eastern European critics of their communist regimes. It provided the theme of George Orwell's novel *Animal Farm*. The Green parties of several Western European states (radical environmental protection parties) have taken it to heart, with the West German Greens at times rotating their leadership at short intervals so that they will not develop a "leadership class."

Whether one regrets Michels's conclusion depends to some extent on whether one likes radical parties. However you feel about the question, though, two factors put it in a slightly different light:

1. All the factors that Michels sees at work (contact with the enemy, development of a stake in society, etc.) are things that occur over time. If a movement is successful quickly, we might expect to see Michels disproved. The Bolshevik seizure of power in Russia in 1917 and the Nazi seizure of power in Germany from 1930 to 1933 are two such cases, and both parties followed their original programs fairly closely. On the other hand, large communist parties have been attempting, since 1945, to gain power in France and Italy, but without success, and both have moderated their positions considerably; in fact, the Italian party dropped the title "communist" in 1991. This suggests that for the opponents of a radical movement, "buying time" is not a trivial strategy but can systematically help to change the movement.

2. Even if Michels is right, all is not lost from the radical standpoint. It may be true that every radical party gradually becomes more moderate, yet we might also see party systems in which, over long periods of time, there were always radical parties present, because new parties would replace older parties. This apparent paradox depends on whether we look at things from the viewpoint of the individual party or of the party system. A similar paradox exists with regard to our own lives. Everyone is constantly growing older and, à la Michels, "youth is impossible to maintain." This is true for each individual, but it is not true for society because new young persons are continually being born to replace their elders.

Spain are examples of the one-party system. In such systems, the government and the party are closely identified, because the government enforces the rule that other parties are not allowed to be active. The party may closely control the governmental apparatus, as was the case in communist states, or the party may simply have been created by those in charge of government. The party in a one-party system concentrates heavily on the tasks of mobilization, communication, and control. It cannot serve well as an alternative source of political ideas because it is so closely tied to those who are already running the state.

A *dominant-party system* is similar to the one-party system in that a single party holds power all the time, but it differs from the one-party system in that other political parties are allowed to function openly and with reasonable effectiveness.[9]

A good example of a dominant-party system is that of Mexico. This system broke down in 1997 and looks unlikely to reestablish itself, but it provides a good illustration of the system. For seventy years, a single party, the Party of the Institutionalized Revolution (PRI), won every presidential election, usually with 60 to 70 percent of the vote. It was well understood in Mexico that serious politics occured only within the PRI. Because of this party's long dominance of politics, the whole governmental structure from the civil service on up had intimate ties to it, and the party had an identification with the system (which it dominated) of the sort that we observe also in one-party states. Thus, the PRI was concerned about raising electoral turnout not because it thought it would be more likely to win a high-turnout election—it would win in any case—but because the system that it dominated needed high electoral participation to build citizen support for the regime. In many ways, then, a dominant-party system is like a one-party system. However, the tolerance of other parties in the system does lead to important differences. For one thing, the existence of alternative parties provides a base for criticism of the government and guarantees that there will be more open debate about politics than in a one-party system. Alternative points of view must inevitably be openly present in a dominant-party system. The largest opposition party in Mexico, for instance, was for many years the National Action Party, a party of the middle class that had been opposed to the PRI's emphasis on labor and the poor. In 1982, for the first time, a group of socialist parties to the left of the PRI also figured significantly in a presidential election, gaining about 10 percent of the vote. In the 1988 election, the candidate of the Left almost beat the PRI candidate—would have beaten him, most observers believe, but for fraudulent counting of the votes. The 1994 election was more genuinely competitive—and the PRI did not win automatically. Finally, in the 1997 election, the PRI lost control of the lower house of Congress and lost the powerful mayoralty of Mexico City. It appears that Mexico's party system will be an open one from now on.

This pattern of long-term dominance eventually giving way to true competition is typical of dominant party systems.

A frequent pattern associated with dominant-party systems in states of the South is for the independence movement and its leaders to form a political party once independence

---

[9]See Alan Arian and Samuel Barnes, "The Dominant Party System: A Neglected Model of Democratic Stability," *Journal of Politics* 36 (August 1974): 592–614. Also Ariel Levite and Sidney Tarrow, "Legitimation of Excluded Parties in Dominant Party Systems: A Comparison of Israel and Italy," *Comparative Politics* 15 (April 1983): 295–327.

has been achieved. They will have been united in the movement for independence, and so it is easy for them to come together in a single party. Furthermore, the problems facing a new state are so awesome that its leaders often agree that it would be better if the state were spared internal disagreement for some time. However, once the dominant party that results from this has ruled for a few decades, it may begin to lose its dominance. Corruption may set in with a group of entrenched officials; the state, now better established, can more easily afford internal disagreements; and the issues of independence fade while new issues that may divide the old ruling group arise. Indeed, this is part of what happened in Mexico; governmental corruption was one of the most important issues in the 1997 election.

In addition to Mexico, two other examples of this pattern are provided by India and Israel. For three decades after attaining independence in 1947, India was dominated by the Congress Party, which represented Mohandas K. Gandhi's independence movement. Elections during this period were sure to provide a Congress majority in Parliament, and important political maneuvers occurred solely within the Congress Party. In 1977, however, Congress slipped below 50 percent of the vote and a coalition of many small, opposed parties came into power. Since then, Congress has held power most of the time, but its dominance has not been ensured in the way it was in the decades after independence.

Israel provides another example. After the state of Israel was established in 1948, the Labour Party (formed by the mainly European leaders of the Zionist movement) held nearly unchallenged power until 1977. It was a great surprise to everyone when, in that year, a coalition of opposition parties called Likud, led by Menachem Begin, defeated Labour at the polls. In this case, the usual problems of a party that had been in power too long were magnified by demographic change. In the 1950s and 1960s, there had been massive immigration into Israel of Jews from other parts of the Mideast, and by 1977, the country was split about evenly between voters of European origin and those of non-European origin. The almost exclusively European-led Labour Party had drifted badly out of touch with about half of the electorate.

A new example of a dominant party system may now be developing in South Africa. South Africa ended *apartheid* in 1990, after a long struggle led by the African National Congress party. In the first two elections of the new democracy, the African National Congress received 63 percent of the vote in 1994 and 66 percent of the vote in 1999. Meanwhile, parties opposed to the African National Congress were quite fragmented, with none receiving more than 20 percent of the vote in either election.

The point of these examples is that, while a dominant-party system is similar in important ways to a one-party system, the availability of other active parties does guarantee that there will be fairly open discussion and debate, and it also provides for possible long-term flexibility and adjustment in the system.

A third variant is the *two-party system*. This is typified by the fact that no one party can count on always holding power but only two parties can normally expect to have a chance at doing so. In a two-party system, the two major parties will typically receive over 90 percent of the votes cast, but neither party will very often receive more than 55 or 60 percent of the vote. A prime example is the U.S. party system, in which only the Republican and Democratic parties are normally serious contenders for power. A two-party system does not necessarily *have* only two parties; a dozen or so parties run regularly in a U.S. presidential election, including the Vegetarians, the Prohibitionists, the Libertarians, and the Socialist Workers' Party. But only the two major parties usually have any expectation of winning. Other examples of two-party or nearly two-party systems are those of Great Britain and Austria.

In contrast to a dominant-party system, a two-party system offers somewhat more regular variety and choices in policies and candidates. At the same time, a single party usually wins an election cleanly and is able to govern by itself without forming a coalition with other parties. Thus, two-party systems are typified by a certain amount of choice combined with fairly stable and straightforward governance.

The final type of party system dealt with here is the *multiparty system*. This system consists of more than two major parties. A good example is Norway, whose Parliament, after the election of 1997, consisted of representatives from the following parties:

Labour Party	65 seats
Christian People's Party	25 seats
Progress (anti-tax) Party	25 seats
Conservative Party	23 seats
Centre (agrarian) Party	11 seats
Left Socialists	9 seats
Liberal Party	6 seats
Coast Party	1 seat

There are 165 seats; therefore, eighty-three are required to control a majority vote in the Parliament, and no one party had enough seats to rule by itself. In this case, no group of parties with eighty-three or more seats among them was willing to form a coalition. Instead, the Christian People's Party, the Centre Party, and the Liberal Party formed a coalition based on their forty-two seats; other parties agreed to support them on certain bills, while remaining out of the government. Such a cabinet is called a "minority government."

Most democratic systems are multiparty systems. The one factor that seems strongly to determine whether a given state will have a two-party or a multiparty system is its electoral system. If a state uses a form of single-member district plurality electoral system, it will almost surely have a two-party system. If it uses a proportional representation system, it will almost surely have a multiparty system. The reason for this should be clear from the discussion in Chapter 11. Under a plurality system, large parties have such an advantage that small parties are driven out, until only two major parties are left.

Compared with a two-party system, a multiparty system offers the voter a wider range of choice. Not only are there *more* choices, but the parties are able to be more distinctive than they could be in a two-party system. In a two-party system, because a party must command half or more of all votes cast in the election to succeed, there is great pressure on both parties to appeal simultaneously to many different groups. A party may not stake out a clear appeal to farmers, for instance, because it might alienate its supporters in the cities; it cannot appeal clearly to the East because it might lose votes in the West, and so on. Such parties are apt to present a pretty fuzzy picture to the electorate. Parties in a multiparty system do not have this problem. The formation of a coalition is likely in any case; therefore, a party does not *have* to be huge to get some share of the power. In the Norwegian example, the Labour Party represents the special interests of the labor unions, fishing crews, and various other groups; it is a bit bland. The Conservative Party represents especially the urban middle class, who want taxes kept down and do not want moralistic constraints imposed by the state. The Christian People's Party represents devout Lutheranism and favors prohibition of liquor, religious instruction in the schools, and a ban on abortion. The Centre Party has a special concern for farmers. The Left Socialists have a variety of programs but are most noted for their opposition to Norwegian membership in NATO. The Progress Party is a right-wing party sharply opposed to the welfare state and to immigration. What a "smorgasbord," compared with any existing two-party system! The voter simply has a greater range of choice in multiparty systems than in two-party systems.

However, there is a balancing advantage to the two-party system. Most of the time, multiparty systems require a coalition government to operate smoothly; therefore, a government cannot be set up unless two or more parties agree to cooperate by forming a coalition. Now this may be fine. Sweden, Norway, Finland, Germany, and other countries have been ruled by stable coalitions of one sort or another through most of their postwar history. If the need for a coalition coincides with a great deal of animosity among the political parties, however, there may be trouble. Under this combination of circumstances, it may be difficult to put together a coalition of parties; or if one is formed, it may be torn apart by mutual mistrust before it has lasted very long. A prime example of this problem is Italy, governed by fifty-nine different coalitions since 1945.[10]

CONCLUSION

The disjunction between politics as choice and politics as power has led to some distortion in our view of political parties in a democracy. We have viewed the party much as what Michels wishes it could be—an instrument that expresses politically the unified choice of its members. We have viewed parties as unitary actors and have thought of them, from the standpoint of their members, predominantly in terms of choice. We have not thought of a party as consisting of various groups that may be at odds with each other and that exercise power over one another.

More often than not, a chief function of a party is to serve as a conduit by which one part may exercise power over another. It is this that has made the party almost as important to nondemocracies as to democracies, and we have seen that it is also an important function of democratic parties.

Our emphasis on the party as a vehicle for expressing choice has often helped make us insensitive to its importance as a channel for the use of power. Once again, power and choice are necessary to a full understanding of politics.

---

[10]Italy recently changed its electoral system from proportional representation to a mostly single-member district electoral system, however, and the 2001 election produced, for the first time, a cabinet with what appears to be a stable majority of support in the Chamber of Deputies.

Example: The Communist Party of the Soviet Union (1917–1991)

The Soviet Communist Party originated in the revolutionary socialist movements of the late nineteenth century, which eventuated in the establishment of the Soviet Union in 1917. Though the Soviet Union collapsed in 1991, this party still stands as our best example of a bureaucratic authoritarian party leading a nondemocratic state.

In 1917, drained after three years of fighting World War I, the Russian monarchy collapsed; and in the ensuing confusion, the Communist Party seized power and established the Soviet system. This party was intimately tied into the state apparatus that it controlled. Until 1990, for instance, Article 6 of the Soviet Constitution stated, "The leading and guiding force of Soviet society and the nucleus of its political system, of all state organizations and public organizations, is the Communist Party of the Soviet Union."

By placing party officials in key positions in the army, the bureaucracy, universities and schools, factories, and so on, and by controlling the legislative and executive portions of the government, the party determined public choices in the Soviet Union.

This was the situation until the late 1980s. In the early 1990s, as part of the collapse of the Soviet system, the party lost its preeminent position and disbanded. However, a number of party leaders have regained a portion of their old power—ruling some of the new states of the former Soviet Union and leading the opposition in others, including Russia. Though it no longer holds power, indeed no longer exists, the Communist Party of the Soviet Union is still well worth studying as the most important example in this century of a party ruling a one-party state.

The Communist Party was a disciplined organization. One did not join it casually:

> To be eligible for party membership, an applicant must be eighteen or older, have a good personal record, and know the basics of Marxism-Leninism. Every applicant is required to secure written recommendations from several members who have belonged to the party for at least five years. The application is then considered at a meeting of the entire primary organization, with the applicant present and obliged to answer questions pertaining to his or her political beliefs, private life, personal ambitions, and familiarity with Marxism-Leninism. A favorable decision by the primary organization must be approved by the appropriate upper-level party office. During the first year, the new member, or "candidate," is on probation and may not vote. All members pay monthly dues, ranging from a token fee required from students and pensioners (ten cents per month), to 3 percent of the salary of high-ranking officials. Members are expected to attend periodic meetings of their primary organization, take an active part in various political campaigns, and set an example for nonmembers in work, study, and general conduct. Party members are also expected to do volunteer work in various community projects.[11]

As of about 1990, approximately 19 million Soviet citizens, or 10 percent of the adult population, were members of the party. In return for their service to the party, they received good jobs and various privileges, along with the possibility of being able to work their way

---

[11]Vadim Medish, *The Soviet Union,* 2d ed. (Englewood Cliffs, N.J.: Prentice-Hall, 1984), p. 87.

up to positions of power. Those who joined the party submitted to the discipline of what was called "democratic centralism." Under this rule, lower levels of the party were unconditionally subordinate to higher levels. Absolute obedience was required, and disobedience was punishable by expulsion. This once meant arrest and exile, and later meant that one was fired from his or her job and blacklisted for future employment. Such discipline was the "central" part of "democratic centralism." The "democratic" side required that as decisions were in the process of being made, there should be wide discussion of them at lower levels, with communication of the sense of these discussions all the way up to the central level. It was a participatory but tightly disciplined way of organizing the party.

At the national level of organization, the lowest of the important organs of power was the party's Central Committee. It consisted of two hundred to three hundred members plus perhaps half as many nonvoting probationary members. The Central Committee met a few times a year. It did not actively make major governmental decisions—it could hardly do so, meeting so infrequently—but as the "crème de la crème" of Soviet politics, it might function importantly in times of crisis. When a new leader of the Soviet Union had to be chosen, for instance, the Central Committee presumably played an important role. It elected members to the two highest levels of the party, the Politburo and the Secretariat; however, the Central Committee merely ratified the nominations it received from the previous members of the Politburo and Secretariat.

The Politburo was the party's most important body. It was small (fourteen members in 1981) and included all the chief leaders of the Soviet Union. It met frequently and dealt with the important decisions of the state. How it functioned varied with the power and personality of the party's general secretary, who presided over the Politburo. Stalin presumably was able to dictate to the rest of the Politburo. Later general secretaries, Yuri Andropov and Konstantin Chernenko, were not in as strong a position within the party, and Politburo proceedings were presumably more lively. Mikhail Gorbachev, the last general secretary of the party and a leader of reform, had greater power in the Politburo than his predecessors because he was able to appoint allies to several new positions in it.

The party Secretariat was nearly as important as the Politburo. Its membership overlapped with that of the Politburo, and the party's general secretary presided over it and over the Politburo. While the Politburo dealt with important decisions of the state and many specific party issues, the Secretariat was more specialized. It dealt with the internal affairs of the party—appointments, rules, relations with communist parties in other countries, and so on.

To sum up, the Communist Party of the Soviet Union was a large and demanding organization that intertwined itself with the apparatus of the state to a point at which it was difficult to distinguish the two. I could describe the formal organization of the party, but—because so much depended on informal political processes within the Politburo, Secretariat, and Central Committee—that still would leave us with large areas of ignorance about how decisions were made.

After seventy years of almost total domination of Soviet politics, the party found itself in the late 1980s under fire from reformers emboldened by Mikhail Gorbachev's program of *glasnost* ("opening"). It was fully and finally discredited when it attempted a coup d'état in 1991 to turn back Gorbachev's reforms, but the coup was more its last gasp than the cause of its fall. It had been decisively weakened a year before.

At the 28th Congress of the Communist Party in February 1990, Gorbachev had pushed through a reform program in which the party voted to abolish its monopoly of power as guaranteed in Article 6 of the Constitution. It was now possible for multiple parties to organize; and although initial efforts to do so were chaotic (150 separate parties formed in the small state of Georgia), the party could no longer count on election.

The party had also lost much of its old control over government operations. After the 28th Congress, the once-powerful Politburo was allowed to meet only once a month, and it was not allowed to discuss government policy. Boris Yeltsin, the president of Russia (at that time the Soviet Union's largest republic), had banned Communists from meeting and maintaining organizations in factories and government offices in Russia shortly before the 1991 coup. (Indeed, this may have precipitated the coup attempt.)

Finally, the party's popular base crumbled. From 1989 to 1991, more than 3 million members left the party, including such prominent figures as the president of Russia, the mayors of Leningrad and Moscow, and Eduard Shevardnaze, former foreign minister and Gorbachev's close ally; public opinion polls, which had in late 1989 showed 70 percent support for the Communist Party, by late 1990 showed only 20 percent support.[12] Essentially, the party had experienced meltdown.

After the break-up of the Soviet Union, the old Communist Party was able to revive itself in a number of the new states formed out of parts of the old union. The Communist Party could no longer be blamed for current conditions because it no longer held the autocratic power it had held before the coming of democracy. As the transition to democracy and free markets was usually painful in a variety of ways, the Communist Party was in a splendid position to say "we told you so" and play to popular discontent. Furthermore, though the remnants of the party were tattered, often they were the most organized force remaining in chaotic transitional societies. In Russia, for instance, which is by far the largest state of the former Soviet Union, the Communist Party received 23 percent of the vote in the parliamentary election of 1995 and has the largest delegation in the parliament.

Example: Mexico's Dominant Party System

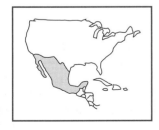

From 1929, when a decade of bloody violence was ended by its establishment in power, until the congressional elections of 1997, the PRI (Partido Revolucionario Institucional) had uninterrupted control of Mexican politics.[13] Mexico was in a formal sense a democracy, but with almost no real political competition. Until the 1988 election, no PRI presidential candidate had ever received less than 60 percent of the

---

[12]"Gorbachev Says Hard-Liners Risk Communist Demise," *New York Times,* 4 July 1991, p. 1; "Survey," *The Economist,* 20–25 October 1990, p. 19.

[13]Just how violent this period was can be seen in that about 1 million people, or one out of every fifteen Mexicans, died violently from about 1910 until order was established. The trauma of this violence may help to explain the staying power of the PRI afterward.

vote, only a handful of members of the Chamber of Deputies had other than PRI affil-
iation, and no candidate of another party had ever been elected as governor of a state.
The only well-organized opposition party before 1988 was the PAN, a right-of-center,
business-oriented party with its greatest strength in the northern provinces bordering
the United States; the PAN, however, could normally muster only 10 to 20 percent of
the vote.

The PRI maintained its ascendancy in a number of ways. It held to the symbols of
revolution, with a formal structure representing the three revolutionary "sectors":
organized labor, small farmers, and the civil service unions. Its leadership was largely
from the middle class, and it grew over the years to represent the interests of an inter-
locked structure of monopolies—trade unions, producers' associations, and so on—
in close cooperation with the government and bureaucracy. This gave the party a
genuinely broad base of support, although not necessarily as broad as the election
results showed; furthermore, because the PRI was the "only game in town," it
attracted much of the ambitious young talent for political leadership. The PRI also
benefited, from about 1940 to 1980, from forty years of strong economic growth.

However, over recent years, the increasingly well-educated Mexican population
became more disillusioned with the PRI and the system of monopoly power it represented. Although the PRI had enjoyed broad support, it had also used considerable
election fraud to maintain its lock on power. "Michel Basañez, a former senior PRI
official and now one of Mexico's best pollsters, had the most accurate pre-election
poll in 1988 because he corrected his data to include a 7% estimate of fraud"[14]
(i.e., he took what people told him as their voting intentions and added 7 percent as
his estimate of what the PRI would add fraudulently). Corruption was also a serious
problem; in 1982, it flared up when the outgoing administration was found to have
stolen as much as $3 billion from the treasury. A good indication of general alienation
from the PRI was the declining participation in its elections, from 77 percent in 1964
to 65 percent in 1970 and 62 percent in 1976. Participation turned upward in 1982
and 1988, when stirrings of reform made the elections more significant.

The 1988 election was a great watershed event. The PAN was joined in opposition
by a new left-wing party, the Party of Democratic Revolution (PRD), led by
Cuauhtenoc Cárdenas, a popular figure on the left wing of the PRI who broke with
the party. Amid financial depression, and with widespread dissatisfaction with the
PRI, the PRI presidential candidate Carlos Salinas won with only 50.4 percent of the
vote (and this almost surely included some fraudulent component), against 31 percent
for Cardenas and 17 percent for the PAN's candidate.[15] The PRI won only 260 of the
499 seats in the Chamber of Deputies.

The PRI had, however, responded to the temper of the times by nominating in Salinas a strong reform candidate. While Salinas concentrated on opening up the econ-

[14]Robert A. Pastor, "Post-Revolutionary Mexico: The Salinas Opening," *Journal of Interamerican
Studies and World Affairs* 32 (Fall 1990): 10.
[15]The PAN candidate had proved so effective on television that he was barred from appearances on the
government-run television station. See Howard Wiarda, "Mexico: The Unravelling of a Corporatist
Regime?" *Journal of Interamerican Studies and World Affairs* 30 (Winter 1988–89): 7.

omy, he also worked to make elections somewhat more open and democratic and to reform the organization of the PRI.

The end of Salinas' term in 1994 saw a flurry of reforms—audited lists of voters, the use of international observers at polling booths, changes in the way the PRI's candidates were nominated. This was a time of great unrest in Mexico. The PRI presidential candidate, Luis Donald Colosio, was assassinated in the midst of the campaign, probably at the direction of the PRI old guard. Leftist guerrillas seized the national imagination (pro and con) with a campaign in the impoverished state of Chiapas. In a fairly clean election, the new PRI candidate, Ernesto Zedillo, won convincingly with 50 percent of the vote against 27 percent for PAN and 17 percent for the PRD.

After taking office, even while coping with a tailspin in the nation's economy, Zedillo pressed forward with reforms. He appointed a member of PAN to be his attorney general, and he promised that he would break with the old tradition of naming his own successor. In state elections, the two other parties were allowed to take office.

Finally, in the second great watershed event of Mexican reform, the elections of 1997 brought a non-PRI candidate to the mayoralty of Mexico City—a hugely important political post. The PRI also lost control of the lower house of Congress, though it remained the largest party in that house and continued to control the Senate. President Zedillo proved adept at working cooperatively with the opposition, while playing off the inevitable differences among five opposed parties to get his major programs through. Still, to say that the position of PRI in Mexico changed greatly at that time is almost an understatement.

The process of breaking down the PRI's dominance was completed by the presidential election in 2000, which was open and reasonably fair. This election went so well for two reasons. First, and most important, Zedillo in 1996 made the National Election Commission independent, with the power to investigate charges of fraud. Electoral hanky-panky was difficult as voters were now required show a photo-ID card in order to vote. After they voted, a hole was punched in their card, and their thumb was painted with indelible ink. It was hard to vote twice!

Second, Zedillo established a national primary election as the way for the PRI to choose its presidential candidate. Before, the outgoing president had simply designated his choice as candidate. Zedillo's reform of the party did produce a modern and moderate candidate, but nonetheless, public reaction to the old PRI swept Vincente Fox of the PAN party into the presidency. After seventy years of uninterrupted rule, the PRI was cast into the role of chief opposition party.

Initially, at least, the party was devastated by the defeat and hardly knew what to do. It may, in fact, turn out that the party simply breaks up and disappears now that its central purpose of seventy years has disappeared. It may be, however, that the reforms Zedillo started will continue and that the PRI will become a modern, competitive party. Certainly, the system of primary elections has helped. The old party apparatus was widely scorned by Mexicans, yet in state elections between 1996 and 1999, whenever the state PRI used a primary election to choose its gubernatorial candidate, the figures who won in the party primaries also went on to win in the general election. In other states, the PRI nominated so-called "dinosaurs"—traditional party leaders—and usually lost.

Other reforms that should also help to ventilate the old party include the first-time-ever election by party members of the general secretary of the party in April 2001 and the November 2001 national conference, at which at least one-third of the delegates were required to be rank-and-file members, not party officials—and at which at least one-third of the delegates were required to be under age thirty. Whether all this will be too little, too late remains to be seen. The party is still reeling and needs to open up more and establish a new sense of purpose. But it will be a remarkable achievement if this corrupt old party, after seventy years in power, can reform and reconstitute itself.

FURTHER READING

Aldrich, John. *Why Parties? The Origin and Transformation of Party Politics in America.* Chicago: University of Chicago Press, 1995.

Beck, Paul Allen. *Party Politics in America.* 8th ed. New York: Addison-Wesley, 1997.

Burnham, Walter Dean. *Critical Elections and the Mainsprings of American Politics.* New York: Norton, 1970.

Dalton, Russell J., et al., eds. *Electoral Change in Advanced Industrial Democracies: Realignment or Dealignment?* Princeton, N.J.: Princeton University Press, 1984.

——— and Wattenberg, Martin P., eds. *Parties Without Partisans: Political Change in Advanced Industrial Democracies.* New York: Oxford University Press, 2000.

Downs, Anthony. *An Economic Theory of Democracy.* New York: Harper & Row, 1957.

Duverger, Maurice. *Political Parties.* London: Methuen, 1954.

Epstein, Leon. *Political Parties in the American Mold.* Madison: University of Wisconsin Press, 1986.

Hendel, Samuel. *The Soviet Crucible.* Boston: Duxbury, 1980.

Katz, Richard S., and Mair, Peter. *How Parties Organize: Change and Adaptation in Party Organizations in Western Democracies.* Thousand Oaks, Calif.: Sage, 1995.

———, eds. *Party Organizations: A Data Handbook.* Thousand Oaks, Calif.: Sage, 1992.

Kitschelt, Herbert. *The Transformation of European Social Democracy.* New York: Cambridge University Press, 1994.

Lipset, Seymour Martin, and Rokkan, Stein. *Party Systems and Voter Alignments.* New York: Free Press, 1967.

Loewenberg, Gerhard. "The Remaking of the German Party System." *Polity* 1 (Fall 1968): 86–113.

Mainwaring, Scott. "Party Systems in the Third Wave." *Journal of Democracy* 9 (1998): 67–71.

———, and Scully, Timothy, eds. *Building Democratic Institutions: Party Systems in Latin America.* Stanford, Calif.: Stanford University Press, 1995.

Maisel, L. Sandy, ed. *The Parties Respond: Changes in the American Party System,* 2d ed. Boulder, Colo.: Westview, 1997.

McCormick, Richard L., ed. *Political Parties and the Modern State.* New Brunswick, N.J.: Rutgers University Press, 1984.

Panebianco, Angelo. *Political Parties: Organization and Power.* New York: Cambridge University Press, 1988.

Party Politics is a specialized journal of political science research about parties.

Przeworski, Adam, and Sprague, John. *Paper Stones: A History of Electoral Socialism.* Chicago: University of Chicago Press, 1986.

Rogowski, Ronald. *Commerce and Coalitions: How Trade Affects Domestic Political Coalitions.* Princeton, N.J.: Princeton University Press, 1989.

Rose, Richard. *Do Parties Make a Difference?* Chatham, N.J.: Chatham House, 1980.

Sartori, Giovanni. *Parties and Party Systems.* Cambridge, England: Cambridge University Press, 1976.

Schlesinger, Joseph A. *Political Parties and the Winning of Office.* Ann Arbor: University of Michigan Press, 1991.

Stokes, Susan C. "Political Parties and Democracy." *Annual Review of Political Science* 2 (1999): 243–67.

Strøm, Kaare, and Svåsand, Lars, eds. *Challenges to Political Parties: The Case of Norway.* Ann Arbor: University of Michigan Press, 1996.

WEBSITES OF INTEREST

Democratic Party:
http://www.democrats.org

Republican Party:
http://www.rnc.org/

Labour Party:
http://www.labour.org.uk/

Conservative Party:
http://www.conservatives.com/

Liberal Democratic Party:
http://www.libdems.org.uk/

Scottish National Party:
http://www.snp.org.uk/

Reform Party of the United States:
http://www.reformparty.org/

College Republicans of America (check out activities on your campus):
http://www.crnconline.org

College Democrats of America (check out activities on your campus):
http://www.collegedems.com

Green Party of the United States:
http://www.greenpartyus.org/

13

STRUCTURED CONFLICT: INTEREST GROUPS AND POLITICS

In Chapter 12, we distinguished the political party from the interest group. The former is associated with the process of leadership selection and the organization of government, while the latter is concerned primarily with trying to affect what those in power do. *The interest group is an organized group of citizens one of whose goals is to ensure that the state follows certain policies.*

All sorts of organized groups may function as interest groups. Some are organized solely to lobby governmental officials on behalf of one or another cause. The Sierra Club, a U.S. organization that lobbies for the preservation of wilderness areas, is an example of such an organization. Other groups may be organized primarily for other purposes but take on lobbying and other ways of influencing policy as an important task. Examples of such groups are labor unions, primarily organized to bargain with an employer but also usually active politically. Still others focus on other goals but give some attention to politics. An example would be a university, whose first concern is to educate students and conduct research but is likely to maintain one or two people to lobby the government on bills that concern it.

There are a great many interest groups in a modern state, so many that it is hard to form a precise idea of their numbers. There is available a reasonably good census of interest groups in Germany in the mid-1990s; it is presented in Table 13–1. Note how many of these are economic interest groups (industrial organizations, trade unions, and professional organizations); this is fairly typical of industrialized countries. However, noneconomic groups have been growing relative to economic groups, which is also fairly typical, at least for Western European and North American countries. In a comparable census of interest groups in Germany twenty years earlier in 1974, 79 percent of all groups were economic groups; we can see from Table 13–1 that by 1994, this figure had dropped to 65 percent. The major gainers over the twenty years were cultural, recreational, and environmental groups.

TABLE 13–1   GERMAN INTEREST GROUPS, 1994, BY TYPE

Category	Number of organizations
Economic	65%
Corporate groups	41%
Unions	5%
Professions	15%
Other	3%
General	35%
Ideological	3%
Social help	16%
Cultural	11%
Recreation, sports	2%
Environmental	3%

Source: Martin Sebaldt, *Organisierter Pluralismus* (Opladen, Germany: Westdeutscher Verlag GmbH, 1997), pp. 79–82.

No one knows exactly how many different interest groups a large and diverse country such as the United States has, but there must be many thousands.[1] In 1997, it was estimated that thirty-five hundred to four thousand interest groups lobbied the German government in Bonn.[2] The 1991 directory of pressure groups lobbying the European community governmental structure counted 818 groups, about 80 percent of which were corporate or trade associations; the other 20 percent consisted of unions and humanitarian and religious groups.[3]

Interest groups are not confined to democracies or open societies. All states have interest groups. Some do not permit a wide diversity of formally organized, politically active groups to exist, since this would seem threatening to their governments. However, even in such states, organizations set up for other purposes—the army, universities, natural history clubs, scientific associations, sports clubs, factories—exert political influence to help mold government policies.

In the Soviet Union, for instance, before 1988 only six "social organizations" were officially sanctioned—inventors', athletes', lifesaving, and stamp-collecting clubs; the Red Cross; and an organization for the preservation of historical and cultural monuments—and these were closely monitored.[4] Other social or political organizations outside the Communist Party, such as certain religious groups and groups of intellectual dissidents, were harassed and were often either disbanded or forced underground. At the same time, it was

[1]The best estimate is that as of 1990, there were 11,600 interest groups active in Washington, D.C. Beyond this, there were many local interest groups that were not active in Washington. John R. Wright, *Interest Groups and Washington Representatives* (Boston: Allyn and Bacon, 1996), p. 10.
[2]Thomas Saalfeld, "Germany: From Dictatorship to Parliamentary Democracy," *Parliamentary Affairs* 50 (July 1997): 386.
[3]Alan Bult Philip, ed., *Directory of Pressure Groups in the European Community* (London: Longmann, 1991).
[4]John S. Reshetar Jr., *The Soviet Polity*, 2d ed. (New York: Harper & Row, 1978), p. 224.

understood that conflict among functionally important groups such as the army, the secret police, the collectivized farms, the scientific establishment, the industrial bureaucracy— each trying to defend its turf—was a main driving force of Soviet politics, right up to the highest national levels.

INTEREST GROUPS AND REPRESENTATION

Interest groups are probably the main vehicle in most states for representing public opinion and bringing it to bear in an organized (and therefore effective) way on the governmental authorities. Political parties cannot do this very well, because they are involved in trying to acquire governmental power for themselves. This quest for power forces parties to incorporate many compromises in their programs to appeal to the broadest spectrum of support. If the state is a democracy, this may take the form of an attempt to appeal to a wide range of voters; if the state is not a democracy, it may mean trying to have such a broad appeal that neither the army, the air force, the navy, urban workers, the church, nor any other major group will try to overthrow them. Whatever the case, a political party, by virtue of its most basic goal, cannot serve to articulate and represent people's wishes. It has a different task: to blend various wishes into a larger coalition. The party seeks to make differences fuzzy, but each interest group is free to present its group's wishes clearly and precisely. The task of repre-

TABLE 13–2 PERCENTAGE OF ELIGIBLE EMPLOYEES
WHO ARE ENROLLED IN LABOR ORGANIZATIONS,
BY INDUSTRY AND GENDER, UNITED STATES

Type of Industry	
Agriculture (wage and salary workers)	2
Mining	14
Construction	19
Manufacturing	16
Transportation and public utilities	26
Wholesale and retail trade	6
Finance, insurance, real estate	2
Services	5
Government	37
Gender	
Women	12
Men	16

Source: U.S. Bureau of the Census, *Statistical Abstract of the United States 2001*, p. 444.

senting the people's desires, then, falls on the interest group. How well do interest groups do this?

Interest groups usually accomplish this fairly well; otherwise, they would not be the workhorses of political advocacy that they are. However, there are three important barriers that keep interest groups from functioning as well in this area as we might wish:

1. *Not all interests are equally well organized.* Groups whose members have enough leisure to be active in politics are likely to enlist more of their potential clientele than other groups. Similarly, we will see high enrollment among interests whose members are concentrated in particular localities, rather than spread out; have a basic economic stake in the outcome of politics; are well educated; and so on. Table 13–2, for example, lists enrollment percentages for labor organizations in several different occupational groups.

Perhaps the most universal and significant break between groups that are readily organized and those that are difficult to organize is represented by "producer" interests and "consumer" interests. A producer interest is any group of people involved in producing something. For any product, there may be a few producer interests: a corporation, a trade union, one or more professional organizations. Examples of producer interests are Microsoft Corporation, the AFL-CIO, the American Medical Association, and the National Farmers' Union. A consumer interest is a group of people consuming a product. Examples would include the National Association of Homebuyers and the American Automobile Association; it is harder to come up with examples of consumer groups, however, because most groups of people who share in consuming a product are not formally organized.

Migrant farm workers, Imperial Valley, California. Moving frequently, working long hours, lacking education and political skills, such workers find it difficult to organize themselves for political action.

(Peter Menzel/Stock, Boston)

Producer interests are always easier to organize than consumer interests, because their interest is more concentrated. Consider the price of milk, for instance. For the hundreds of millions of milk consumers in the United States, an increase of 10 cents a gallon for milk would be a nuisance, but it is not something they would give up evenings and weekends to organize against. However, 10 cents a gallon produces a large total sum of money when it is accumulated over many million gallons sold; since that large sum of money is concentrated on perhaps a couple of thousand dairies and their workers nationwide, the small price increase might mean a difference of 10 or 20 percent in the profits of the companies and the earnings of their workers. This is something people *will* give up evenings and weekends for. You can bet that Washington would be saturated with letters, campaign contributions, and lobbying visits from the affected companies and their unions—but would hear very little from the people who are to pay the extra dime.

In every country of the world, producers are more fully organized than consumers, and the result is a general skewing of government policies in favor of producers. In Germany, for instance, as shown in Table 13–1, 61 percent of all German interest groups were corporate groups, unions, or professional associations. Only 3 percent were "other" economic groups (mostly consumer groups).

As a result of these and other disparities, some interest groups can speak strongly and confidently as representatives of their interest, and they are listened to with respect. Other interest groups, which formally represent only a small percentage of their potential clientele, must speak with a somewhat muted voice. The overall system of interest groups, as a result, does not represent all interests equally well. Those that are easy to organize bulk larger in the system, and their voices are heard more loudly than they should deserve on the basis of their numbers.

2.   *Also, some groups command a disproportionate voice in the interest-group system because they have special advantages.* Consider the following examples:

- In almost all Western countries, business groups have influence beyond what one would expect based on the size of their memberships. They gain added influence for several reasons: they have a great deal of money to spend on politics; they have a good deal of expertise in advertising and organization, which can be used to political benefit; and the well-being of the country is so closely tied to their own well-being that they must be listened to with respect.
- In many states whose governments are shaky, large landowners as a group gain exaggerated political influence because of their ties to the army, which may be expected to intervene politically on their behalf.
- In Israel over past decades, rather small groups of fundamentalist Jewish sects have wielded influence out of proportion to their numbers because the Labour and Likud parties have been so evenly matched in elections that the small religious parties have held the balance of power.
- In almost all countries with much coastline, the fishing industry has had disproportionate influence because its members are concentrated in what are often key locations politically and because they are willing to go to great lengths to protect their livelihood and their traditional way of life. (It is for this reason, for instance, that it has been so difficult for other countries to get Japan to stop the hunting of whales, even though only a few thousand members of Japan's huge labor force are involved in the whaling industry.)

Such examples are numerous. Partly because not all interests are equally well organized and because some have special advantages such as these, the sum total of interest-group representation may give quite a distorted picture of the interests in a country.

3.   *Finally, most interest groups are not organized democratically; their leaders are not closely responsive to the members' wishes.* The leaders of an interest group are usually able to build a base of support within the administrative structure of the group and among its members, which makes it difficult to unseat them. Even where the members of the group elect the leader periodically—as is true of most labor unions, for instance—an "inside" group usually dominates the election, so that the same person is elected year after year.[5] Many interest groups—such as universities, armies, and factories—are not even set up to allow periodic elections.

The internal structure of interest groups is not very democratic; therefore, there is a real danger that their leaders may gradually drift away from the ordinary members and

---

[5]Seymour Martin Lipset, Martin A. Trow, and James S. Coleman explored an exception to this rule in *Union Democracy* (Garden City, N.Y.: Doubleday, 1962). Another, more recent example was the running battle during the 1990s between the reform and the traditional factions in the Teamsters union.

TABLE 13–3   PERCENTAGE OF MEMBERS WHO WOULD
STAY IN THE ASSOCIATION IF IT DID NOT LOBBY AT ALL

Minnesota Farm Bureau	77
Minnesota Farmers' Union	63
Minnesota Retail Federation	57
Minnesota-Dakotas Hardware Association	70
Printing Industries of the Twin Cities	94

Source: From Terry M. Moe in *The Organization of Interests,* p. 210. Copyright © 1980 The University of Chicago Press. Reprinted with permission.

follow their own political line. Democratic accountability to the membership could prevent this, but in its absence, there is little to keep it from happening.

We might expect that the free market would provide a control over this. That is, if the
leaders drifted too far from the ordinary members, the latter would be able to "vote with
their feet" and join a competing group. For example, there are many different conservation societies, and so we might expect that if some members of, say, Friends of the Earth
did not like their leaders' positions, they would drop their membership and join some
other group, such as the National Wildlife Association.

The trouble with this solution is that the situation with regard to conservation groups
is rather atypical. Often, a group's political positions are *not* major factors determining
an individual's continued membership in the group; this is especially true of economic
interest groups. For most union members, the important thing is how skillful their union
is in negotiating a good contract with their employer. Another important consideration
is the package of extra benefits the union can provide—low-cost group insurance, educational and entertainment programs, low-cost package vacations, and so on. For most
members, the union's political activity is a weak runner-up among the things that matter to them.[6]

A survey of several business and agricultural associations asked members whether
they would stay in their association if it stopped its political activity altogether but
continued to offer them the other benefits they enjoyed. As seen in Table 13–3, a
majority of each group said that the association's other benefits were important
enough to them that they would continue their membership even if the group did nothing in politics.

These side benefits, which the leaders of groups may manipulate to maintain membership in the group, are called *selective incentives.* (They give members an *incentive*
for being in the group; they are *selective* in that they may be targeted selectively to members of the group.) If the selective incentives available through an organization are sufficiently attractive, they can provide the leaders of the organization with a great deal of
leeway in their choice of political positions. Leaders of labor unions have been able to
take political positions varying from rather conservative Republican (the Teamsters
union in the United States, at various times) to communist (many French and Italian

---

[6] Mancur Olson, *The Logic of Collective Action* (Cambridge: Harvard University Press, 1965).

The Logic of Collective Action

One of the more interesting works of abstract theory in the social sciences is Mancur Olson's *The Logic of Collective Action* (Cambridge: Harvard University Press, 1965), which is particularly applicable to the study of interest groups. Olson notes that organized groups will be plagued by the problem of collective goods. (You will recall from Chapter 6 that a collective good is one that no member of the group can be prevented from enjoying.) Even if a business owner does not join the local chamber of commerce, for example, he or she will still benefit from its lobbying activities with the state government.

To Olson, this means that the potential members of the group will be inclined to save their dues money and not join the group, because they can enjoy the benefits of the group's activity whether or not they join. What is rational for the individual may be tragic for the group, however, because if every potential member did what was rational, there would be no interest group at all and no benefits for anyone.

Olson notes four possibilities that help to explain how one might be able to organize groups in spite of the problem of collective goods:

1. If a group is *sufficiently small,* it may be easier to organize. Each member's contribution is then not trivially small, and so all potential members can see that there will be less of the collective good available if they withhold their contribution to the group.
2. The group may offer *selective incentives,* such as life insurance programs or travel packages, that can be withheld from those who do not enter the group.
3. The group may be able to *coerce* members to join whether they wish to or not. The closed shop is an example of this in labor relations. In "neocorporatist" systems (see pages 286–288), the government may require that the group be formed so that it can help to carry out the government's policies.
4. If one member of the group bulks large relative to the others, then that member may see that the collective good would be impossible to attain without its participation. Therefore, that member may join and carry things forward even though smaller members who do not join get a free ride. The largest department store in town, for instance, can hardly avoid joining the chamber of commerce. For a slightly different "group," this helps to explain why the United States figures so importantly in the NATO alliance and provides its smaller allies with a partially free ride.

unions), and their members have not objected strongly as long as their wage settlements and other benefits were good.[7]

Interest groups, then, are not on the whole democratically organized, and their leaders may depart considerably from the members' views. Add to this our two earlier points (that the groups themselves may be rather unrepresentative of the population as a whole, because some kinds of people participate more in groups than others; and that some groups, because of strategic advantage, are able to have more impact than they would deserve on the basis of their numbers), and we can see that the overall result of lobbying and other political activity on the part of interest-group leaders may be quite unrepresentative of the overall wishes of the population.

---

[7]An added factor that may hold members in groups and that certainly operates in the case of many labor unions is *coercion.* "Union shop" contracts often require that a worker must be a member of the union to hold a job.

As a few examples of how the interest-group system may distort public opinion, consider the following:

- In Israel, in deference to small orthodox groups, the national airline El Al does not fly on the Sabbath even though it is expensive to have the planes sit idle and most Israelis would prefer to have Sabbath flights.
- In the United States, a majority of those sampled in public opinion polls favor the regulation of handguns, but the National Rifle Association has effectively blocked such laws in most localities.
- In countries with state-run television networks, programming is almost always more "educational" (and dull) than the people would prefer. Leaders of cultural associations are in part responsible for this.

TYPES OF INTEREST GROUPS

Three major types of interest groups are "sectoral" interest groups, "institutional" interests groups, and "promotional" interest groups:

1. Sectoral Groups

Sectoral groups are those that represent a sector of the economy—a corporation, a union, an association of members of a profession, or, less frequently, a consumer group. Examples would include the National Manufacturers' Association, Ford Motor Company, the National Farmers' Union, the AFL-CIO, and the American Automobile Association. Since these are groups associated with the economy, they often combine great financial resources with fairly narrow concerns. An industrial organization might find, for instance, that the issue making the greatest difference to its members' earnings is an obscure and highly technical rule about depreciation rates, a rule that falls below most other groups' radar. And with its resources, the organization can vigorously pursue changing that rule. Needless to say, sectoral groups are usually effective. They also dominate most interest-group systems. We saw in Table 13–1 that 65 percent of Germany's interest groups are "economic" (sectoral).

2. Institutional Groups

Institutional groups are set up primarily for purposes other than political activity and would certainly exist even if they did not deal with politics; they become politically active only to defend their own interests in the state's policy decisions. Examples of this sort of group would include an army, set up to defend the state, that may become active—even dominant—in the politics of the state to help the defense budget and further the common interests of its members; a public university, set up to educate students and conduct research, that may hire lobbyists to procure a larger annual budget from the government; the Red Cross, set up to help people in emergencies, that may become actively engaged in lobbying for national emergency help grants; and so on.

3. Promotional Groups

Promotional groups organize around an idea or a point of view—to support an ethnic group (the National Association for the Advancement of Colored People), a foreign policy position (Women Against Military Madness), religious values (the Christian Coalition), a position on the environment (National Audubon Society), a recreational activity (National Rifle Association), or whatever.

Around the world, promotional interest groups have increased in recent decades. We noted in connection with Table 13–1 that the fastest growing categories of interest groups in Germany from 1974 to 1994 were the cultural, recreational, and environmental groups. In Britain, the Royal Society for the Protection of Birds has more members than the three major political parties combined and has increased in size by 1,300 percent since 1971. Amnesty International, an organization that campaigns against political oppression, has 115,000 members. The National Viewers' and Listeners' Association, which campaigns to ban sex on television, has 183,000 members.[8]

Promotional interest groups appear to be especially important in the politics of the United States, compared with most other states of the world. This is probably because: (1) our parties are weaker and less unified on policy than most other states' parties and thus are not well equipped to lead in a debate over ideas; and (2) our two-party system does not provide room for small, specialized parties such as Israel's religious parties, able to directly seek a portion of the governmental power through participation

[8]"A Nation of Groupies," *The Economist,* 13 August 1994, pp. 49–51.

in coalitions. Instead, those seeking to pursue an ideological goal in the United States must usually operate indirectly through an interest group to *influence* those who have attained power.

In contrast to the promotional groups, sectoral groups probably vary less in their role from one state to another. The economy is such a central part of society that sectoral interest groups have a natural entrée to government everywhere. Therefore, their presence and their activities are probably less variable than is true of promotional interest groups. Some states such as the United States and Sweden have active feminist groups, for instance—although in Sweden, this interest is channeled somewhat more through political parties—while in others such as Japan, there is almost no feminist presence. Nearly every state, however, has a politically active manufacturers' association.

TACTICS OF INTEREST GROUPS

The tactics an interest group will use are determined by the sources of its power and by the opportunities that the political system offers for the use of power. An interest group with many members but little money will concentrate on tactics that take advantage of numbers rather than money, while a group with few members but plenty of money will follow different tactics. Groups that have similar sources of power but find themselves faced with different sorts of political structures may also be expected to follow different tactics. In their political activity, U.S. labor unions, for instance, emphasize electoral activity and campaign contributions to public officials. For Solidarity, the labor union that transformed the politics of Poland in the 1970s and 1980s in spite of suppression by the communist government, these focuses of political activity were not available, and so it concentrated instead on sit-ins and mass demonstrations.

Let us look specifically at several tactics available to interest groups in a democracy. What leads a group to choose one or more of these?

1. Control of Information and Expertise

Sometimes the members of an interest group control specialized information that is important to the government—information that may even be required if the group is to be controlled by the government. Doctors, for example, are the only people with the necessary expertise to judge the quality of medical treatment. Scientists are the only ones sufficiently skilled technically to judge a variety of scientific questions. Oil corporations know more about the oil business than anyone else. In all these cases, a government that wishes to make policy relating to an interest group must depend on the members of the group for the necessary information and expertise. This gives the group a great deal of power, because the resulting interpretation of things is likely to be slanted a good deal toward the group's prejudices. It does not require that anyone operate dishonestly. Everyone always has a certain slant on things, and if the members of an interest group are the only ones giving the government analysis and interpretation, their slant is inevitably going to enter in.

This tactic requires that relevant information and technical skills be scarce. Labor unions, religious groups, or hobby organizations cannot make good use of the tactic, because the skills and information they have are widely available. A dramatic example of power based on the control of information appeared during the Arab states' oil embargo of the United States in 1977, when it turned out that the only source for information on how much oil was in transit to the United States was the oil companies. The government had no independent source for this information.

2. Electoral Activity

Electoral activity is especially suitable for groups with a large number of members who are at least moderately committed. Such a group may raise money from among its members to contribute to candidates, provide campaign workers to candidates, and deliver its own members' votes for candidates—all in an effort to ensure that people favorably disposed to the group end up in office. If the members of the group are not sufficiently committed to it to choose their vote on the basis of its recommendations, this tactic is of little use; an automobile club, for instance, would not be able to deliver its members' votes. Groups that have used this tactic successfully include labor unions, large religious organizations, and ethnic groups. Some other special organizations such as the National Rifle Association in the United States or the wine growers of France have also been successful in this way.

3. Use of Economic Power

An interest group of economic importance to the state may influence the state by threatening to disrupt its economic contribution. Strategically placed unions, such as those of railroad or postal workers, have often been able to enlist the government's help by threatening a strike that would be catastrophically disruptive to the state. At some times, as in France in 1968 or Germany in the 1920s, a *general strike* in which all unions stop working at the same time has been used to try to force an unpopular government out of office. Businesses often threaten communities by telling them that if they don't give them tax advantages or other considerations, they will move their operations elsewhere. Professional sports franchises have been particularly skillful at this kind of threat, forcing communities to provide them with subsidies and build stadiums to house them. The civil rights movement of the 1960s in the United States gained great impetus when an unknown preacher named Martin Luther King, Jr. organized a boycott of the city bus system of Montgomery, Alabama, to force the city to allow blacks to sit anywhere they wished on the buses. Similarly, economic boycotts of white businesses were an effective tool for blacks in South Africa in the late 1980s.

This tactic requires that a large economic stake be maneuverable. That is, the group must be able to turn on or turn off a large enough part of the economy to threaten dire results. This can be accomplished either by a single large corporation, for which it is usually fairly easy, or by a large number of people who, though they are not individually that important to the economy, are willing to coordinate economic disruption (a strike or boycott) so that their combined impact is important. Mass action like this is usually difficult to accomplish, because it requires a large number of people to make an economic sacrifice by stopping work, finding an alternative to riding buses, or whatever. It requires a large and unusually devoted membership.

Another way in which economic power can be used is in contributions to political candidates. Here the group's economic strength is not used to produce the threat of disruption but rather to buy access to political leaders. Ballooning expenditures on political campaigns in the United States have made political leaders more dependent on interests that can provide money. Around the world, states vary considerably with regard to the importance of interest groups' money for campaigns, depending on election laws and on custom. In most European states, campaign expenditures are regulated and do not bulk as large as they do in the United States. Japan, on the other hand, is a state where the appetite of parties for campaign finance is insatiable.

4. Public Information Campaigns

A group that does not necessarily have a large mass base but does have substantial access to the media may try to change policy by the most indirect of means—by changing the minds of the entire population in the hope that this will influence government policy. Institutional interest groups frequently use this tactic, because many other tactics are barred to them. The U.S. Air Force has at times helped to encourage comic strips such as *Steve Canyon,* which put the Air Force in a good light. Government agencies in all states use "public service advertisements"—giving health advice, moral admonition, and so on—to keep themselves in the public eye while they also accomplish indirectly a secondary goal of the advertisements: to build public support for the agency.

This tactic is also useful for an interest with enough money to buy advertising time, especially if other tactics do not look promising. In the 1970s, American corporations were faced with a new environmental movement that was difficult to combat. How could a group argue effectively for dirty air? An expensive and skillfully executed ad campaign on the theme "businesses don't cause pollution, people cause pollution" helped them to shift the terms of national debate.

In the United States in the 1990s, this technique was further refined as interest groups learned to target public opinion in the districts of members of Congress who were seen as swing votes on important bills. In 1997, for instance, labor unions targeted about thirty congressional districts with television ads against expanding free trade when Congress was considering legislation to give the president special negotiating powers to arrange lower trade barriers between the United States and other countries. In the same year, a consortium of businesses opposed to an international pact to limit the emission of greenhouse gases conducted a widespread television ad campaign against the proposed Global Warming Treaty.

5. Violence and Disruption

An interest group may also try to dramatize its case by violent or disruptive activity, or it may try by violence and disruption to convince the leaders of the state that they will pay a high price in turmoil by not yielding to the group's demands. Disruptive but non-violent protest may be an effective way for an interest group to bring attention to its cause, especially if it has few resources other than a dedicated mass following. However, violence is also sometimes used. It may occur spontaneously, as in the urban riots of

1968 in the United States. Or it may be organized, as in campaigns of assassination and kidnapping by terrorist organizations such as Italy's Red Brigade.

Terrorism is usually not an effective technique, as it is likely to cost the disruptive group what public sympathy it has and to call forth strenuous efforts at control by the authorities. A group with a decent chance of accomplishing its goals by other means is not likely to use violence as a tactic. However, there are two circumstances under which groups may resort to it:

- For a small group of extremely committed people, terrorism can be a useful tactic. One must remember that a small group (say, fifty to a hundred people) is not likely to be able to bring about major political changes in any case. If no other tactics would succeed anyway, terrorist violence offers them a long-shot possibility. Even a few people may attract a great deal of attention by way of bank robberies, murders, and kidnappings. They would have little chance of parlaying this attention into the accomplishment of their political goals, but if they were totally committed, they might try despite the odds.
- The second case in which terrorism might be an effective tactic appears when one region is united in its opposition to the rest of a state and wishes to separate from it or at least to change its legal relationship to the government. A separatist group under these conditions can launch violent attacks on the rest of the state without losing the sympathy of the only "public" that counts for them, the people in their part of the state. The violence is likely to bring down harsher regulation and police activity in their region, which will serve to further strengthen local support for the separatist cause. Many separatist movements—the Irish Republican Army in Britain, the Basque separatists in Spain, Moslem separatists in the Philippines—have used this tactic with success.

6. Litigation

In litigation an interest group attempts to affect policy by working within the court system. The historic reversal of segregated schooling in the United States was begun in this way when, in 1954, the National Association for the Advancement of Colored People (NAACP) sponsored a constitutional test of segregation in the courts. A black student, with the help of the NAACP, sued her school board to force it to admit her to the white school, and she won.

Through court cases, an interest group may hope to change the interpretation of a law or, in some countries, even get it thrown out as unconstitutional. Also, court procedures can be so slow and expensive that the mere threat of tying a governmental agency up in court may get the agency to compromise.

However, litigation is a strategy based on weakness. For a group to be successful at litigation, it must depend on the way the law was initially written—something over which it has little control if litigation is its main tactic. It must depend on finding a sympathetic court, which is also rather chancy. The great appeal of litigation is that it does not require large numbers (all one has to have is a lawyer) or enormous economic power. Therefore, it appeals particularly to small weak groups. Groups that have depended fairly heavily on litigation in the United States include environmentalists, the handicapped, and groups favoring abortion rights. These are relatively weak groups that have usually been on the defensive.[9]

The history of the civil rights movement in the United States provides varied examples of how circumstances determine strategy. In the 1940s and 1950s, the movement for civil rights for blacks was relatively weak. The majority of blacks were still barred from voting in the South; blacks were poor and did not have a great deal of money to contribute; and the movement did not have many white allies, either in public office or outside it. The chief civil rights organization at this time was the NAACP, and its chief tactic was litigation. It achieved several important successes in court, among other things overturning segregated schooling in the South and outlawing the exclusion of black voters from primary elections.

With the increase in support for civil rights in the 1960s and partly as a result of these successes, more money and resources became available to the movement. Blacks had become bolder politically; many more were willing to march in demonstrations to help draw attention to their cause, and they began to acquire significant white allies. At this time, new, rival organizations wishing to use different tactics appeared. The Congress on Racial Equality (CORE) and Martin Luther King, Jr.'s Southern Christian Leadership Conference (SLCLC) were two new organizations that emphasized, as ways of attracting sympathy and forcing segregationists to yield, the use of economic power and the provocation of segregationists into violence. (Note the clever twist on the use of violence as a tactic—here white officials were goaded into violence so that they would lose public sympathy.) Massive demonstrations were held, requiring large numbers of dedicated black and white participants. Violence of their own was never a part of these leaders' strategy; but the provocation of white violence was useful, and the black urban riots of 1965–68, which occurred spontaneously, were used by civil rights leaders as evidence for their claims that blacks had to be treated more fairly.

At this time, electoral activity was not especially emphasized because, first, during the 1960s many southern blacks could not vote or were just acquiring the vote and, second, demonstrations and disruption were proving to be such powerful tools. By the 1970s and 1980s, however, demonstrations began to be less effective. The public was more used to them and therefore less impressed by them, and police and public officials had learned not to respond in the picturesquely violent ways that demonstrators had once counted on. At the same time, the electoral importance of blacks had grown. The black percentage of the electorate in many northern cities had reached a point at which blacks could often determine the outcome of mayoral and other elections. In the South, thanks to the gains of the 1960s, most blacks were free to vote and could determine many elections. In the 1970s and 1980s, accordingly, the activity of black civil rights groups shifted to emphasize more their importance in elections.

---

[9]See, for example, Susan M. Olson, *Clients and Lawyers: Securing the Rights of Disabled Persons* (Westport, Conn.: Greenwood Press, 1984). In 1989, the abortion rights movement strengthened a good deal in a popular reaction to an unfavorable court decision, and with its increased strength, it began to shift its attention from litigation to electoral activity.

We can see in this evolution of the tactics of the civil rights movement a good illustration of our general principle that interest groups will pick those tactics that best fit the group's resources and the political opportunities offered by those resources.

SOCIAL MOVEMENTS

All of the preceding sections of this chapter have dealt with "interest groups"— organizations conducting politics within the decision-making structure of the state, but with a goal of influencing one or more policy outcomes rather than achieving overall governmental power. However, there is a related type of group, the *social movement,* that has become increasingly important over the last couple of decades and that, at least at times, has driven the politics of many states during this period.

A social movement is a group of people who ordinarily have little power—"ordinary people"—but challenge the state power in loosely organized ways, usually through disruption and sometimes violently. The object of a social movement is usually a highly emotional issue; after all, that is what it generally takes to mobilize "ordinary people" who are not usually much engaged in politics. As a result, social movement politics is usually dramatic. Sometimes it occurs around local, emotional issues such as a school curriculum or the construction of a highway through a residential neighborhood. But it may also address the very constitution or identity of the state. Social movements were a key factor, for instance, in the fall of the communist regimes of Eastern Europe.

Social movements have driven more and more of politics in the 1990s. In the Introduction of *Power in Movement,* Sidney Tarrow takes up a single issue of the *International Herald Tribune* (March 17, 1997) and notes that the lead story covers a riot in Albania that brought down the government. He goes on:

> The same issue of the *Trib* features seven other stories relating to social movements, protests, and rebellions from around the world. Also on page 1 are a report on the armed rebellion in eastern Zaire and another on the peaceful march of Belgian, French, and Spanish workers to protest the recent closure of an auto plant in Belgium. Page 4 covers both a peaceful protest march of twenty thousand poor people in Thailand against a government development project and a violent clash between rival ethnic groups in Indonesia. Page 8 features brief reports of a gunfight between Algerian troops and the Islamic militants who have been locked in a savage civil war with the regime for the past five years, and on the Salvadoran elections, which promise to bring the Farabundo Marti National Front—a former guerrilla movement—into the government. Even the business pages cannot avoid contention: a story on page 15 describes the previous week's protest of German coal miners threatened with layoffs. One ordinary day's newspaper coverage: ten stories coming from places as different as Belgium and Borneo, indicating the continuing power of contentious politics and social movements.[10]

Social movements are a critical part of politics, particularly at those moments in politics when great change occurs, but they can be difficult to get a handle on. More than is the case with most political phenomena, the particular circumstances of the dispute at hand and the cultural context in which it plays out shape strongly the social movement

[10]Sidney Tarrow, *Power in Movement: Social Movements and Contentious Politics,* 2d ed. (New York: Cambridge University Press, 1998), p. 1.

and its involvement. We saw this also in our discussion of democratization (which is often fueled by a social movement) on page 174.

One thing that is certainly important to the success of a social movement is its ability to communicate rapidly and easily across its group—how else can one mobilize the unmobilized? Technical advances in communication have therefore always gone hand in hand with social movement politics. The French Revolution could probably not have occurred without the invention of printing. And more recently, communist governments in the 1970s and 1980s drastically limited access to new tools of communication in a vain attempt to keep the lid on social change. In 1989, for instance, Romania's nuclear power plant had still not been allowed by the government to buy a photocopier!

With the advent of the Internet, new opportunities for the mobilization of social movements have arisen. We already see the effect of the Internet today in the mobilization of support for Amerindian rebels in the Mexican province of Chiapas and in the mobilization of racist, neo-Nazi groups in the United States.

PATTERNS OF ORGANIZED INTEREST-GROUP ACTIVITY

Let us return now to the "interest groups" we discussed in the earlier sections of this chapter. In all of our discussions of interest groups, we have talked about them primarily from the point of view of the individual group. However, we must also look at the pattern of all group activity in a state. In looking at political parties, we found that the overall pattern formed by the system of parties was important to the state's politics; similarly, we will see that the overall pattern of interest-group activity is also important. Interest-group systems vary in (at least) two important ways.

1. Degree of Organization

In some countries, people are heavily organized by groups; in others, they are not heavily organized at all. Most states of the South are only weakly organized. Institutional interest groups such as the church and the army bulk much larger in the politics of these states than they would otherwise, because interest groups of other sorts are weak.

Among industrialized states, there is also a good deal of variation. In authoritarian states such as the Soviet Union before 1991, the formation of groups is suppressed, and here again institutional interest groups gain in importance by default. Even among open societies, there is a good deal of variation. The Scandinavian countries are probably more thoroughly organized than any others in the world. For example, 88 percent of Swedish workers are members of trade unions, compared with 49 percent for Great Britain and 12 percent for the United States.[11] The percentage of people belonging to political organizations is about twice as high in Norway as in the United States.[12]

---

[11]Britain, 1995; Sweden, 1997; USA, 1997. Source: United Kingdom, Central Statistical Office, *Annual Abstract of Statistics 1997;* Sweden, Statistiska Centralbyrån, *Statistisk Årbok '97*; United States, U.S. Census Bureau, *Statistical Abstract of the United States 1998*.

[12]Robert B. Kvavik, *Interest Groups in Norwegian Politics* (Oslo: Universitetsforlaget, 1976), p. 46; a dated source, but the difference is probably about the same today.

2. Degree of Direct Involvement of Interest Groups in Government and Administration

We saw earlier in this chapter that government officials must often depend on interest groups for information and expertise. The way in which governments may tap into this varies from casual arrangements, in which officials occasionally call up interest-group representatives or look up a figure in the group's publication, to quite formal arrangements in which interest-group representatives may sit by right on administrative committees of the government. Under the latter arrangement, which is fairly common in northern Europe, it may be hard to draw the line between interest groups and government.

Two important types of interest-group systems can be identified by variations on these two dimensions. These are *pluralism* and *neocorporatism*. They are important concepts for understanding how interest groups operate in democratic systems.[13]

PLURALISM

Pluralism is a system in which all interests organize and compete freely and no one group is able to dominate. The government is open to pressure from the interest groups, and politics consists largely of the competition among these interest groups to see that the policies they favor are adopted by the government.[14] In terms of our two dimensions listed in the section on "Patterns of Organized Interest-Group Activity," pluralism is high on the scale of "organization" and low on "direct involvement of interest groups in government"; that is, interest groups are well organized but are quite distinct from the government. There is no state that is perfectly "pluralist"; the term is an abstraction. The United States approaches the type more closely than most and is often used as a chief example of pluralism at work.

Those who favor a pluralist system of politics point out that with numerous groups operating, there is a good deal of spontaneity. It is relatively easy for new ideas to appear from the grass roots, and there is a good deal of flexibility. Furthermore, because the government is simultaneously influenced by many competing groups, negotiation and compromise should be the order of the day. Politics should typically be pragmatic and nonradical.

Pluralist writers see pluralism as an ideal way to reach the common ground of society. The various interests in society pull in their varying directions, and the government responds to their pressure by ending up at a kind of equilibrium point where the pressures balance. With a minimum of distortion, the most desired mix of policy is reached.

Critics, however, point out that in any real state—as distinct from the idealized abstraction—the set of interest groups cannot represent the people of the state very well, because not all interests are equally able to "organize and compete freely." This was discussed at the beginning of this chapter in the section "Interest Groups and Representation." If the criticism is true, then a pluralist system might have the advantages cited by

---

[13]Here, as in our discussion of interest-group tactics in this chapter, we will focus attention on democracies.

[14]The chief source is David Truman, *The Governmental Process* (New York: Knopf, 1951). See also "Pluralism" in *The International Encyclopedia of the Social Sciences.*

those who favor it, yet we would still have to be suspicious of it because policies based on "pluralist" deliberations could be expected to slant systematically in favor of those groups that can operate effectively and against those that cannot.

NEOCORPORATISM

Neocorporatism is another abstraction.[15] It is a system in which all interests are organized and the government deals directly with all affected interests at all stages in the making and administration of policy. Unlike pluralism, under neocorporatism the government does not merely respond to the interest groups' pressure but actively involves the groups in the job of governing.[16] In terms of our two dimensions listed in the "Patterns of Organized Interest-Group Activity" section, neocorporatism is high on the scales of "organization" and "direct involvement of interest groups." And it is higher than pluralism on the "organization" scale; the practice of involving interest groups in government generally stimulates an especially high degree of participation in interest groups, just because the stakes of interest group activity become higher.

Not only does the government draw interest groups into the governmental process in neocorporatism, but parts of the government may also act rather like interest groups. This is not so much a matter of "institutional interest groups" lobbying for their own perquisites and budgets as it is active engagement in political debate on behalf of certain policies. Parts of the bureaucratic apparatus may take on a greater role of representing popular constituencies and initiating policy demands than is common under pluralism. They are in effect "self-starters" who try to mobilize popular support for their positions. An example is the founding of the European Common Market in 1956; the campaign for unification was spearheaded not by party leaders but by civil servants. From both sides, then, the boundary between government and interest groups becomes fuzzier in a neocorporatist system.

The Scandinavian states approach the neocorporatist model more closely than any others. For instance, in Sweden:

- The government is constitutionally required to send copies of any bill it is drafting to affected interest groups and to solicit their responses at all stages of the legislative process.

[15]Neocorporatism takes its name from a system called *corporatism,* in which instead of individuals being represented by right of being citizens, as in liberal democracy, *functions* of society were to be represented in governmental decisions. The basis of corporatism was the idea that the various functional parts of society (business, labor, agriculture, universities, etc.) were all vital and must be taken into account, much like the parts of the body (hence the word's root in *corpus,* Latin for *body*). And like the parts of the body, the various functional units should not be in conflict with each other (how can the heart fight the liver, for instance?). This notion of representation came up in various settings in the early twentieth century, including the left wing of the Labour Party in Britain, but was most noteworthy in its adoption by Mussolini's fascist dictatorship in Italy. The latter, of course, left it with a strong and unpleasant odor. Neocorporatism consists of corporatist-like practices that have appeared in a number of countries since the fall of Mussolini: they have often arisen more or less spontaneously in well-established democracies like Sweden, but in their nondemocratic form, they have also sometimes been imposed from above, as in Brazil's military dictatorship in the 1970s.

[16]A good presentation of the model is Martin O. Heisler and Robert B. Kvavik, "Patterns of European Politics: The 'European Polity' Model," in Martin O. Heisler, ed., *Politics in Europe* (New York: David McKay, 1974), pp. 27–90.

- The drafting of any important bill is shaped by discussions in a special royal commission set up to consider the bill. Civil servants and representatives of all affected interest groups sit on such a commission.
- Once the bill is passed, its administration will often be turned over to the affected group. For instance, governmental policies on the price of eggs are administered by the egg-growers' cooperative marketing board rather than by a governmental agency.
- Policies are set in a spirit of cooperation and compromise. There is a reluctance to push any affected group to the wall.

Those who admire neocorporatism point to the cooperative attitude brought forth by such a system. For such a system to work, there *must* be a cooperative spirit, and putting the system in place may therefore help to call forth the required cooperation.

Also, neocorporatism eases the problem of unequal organization of groups, which flaws pluralism. Groups must be well organized to take part in governing; therefore, it becomes more important that they organize their members, and they tend to do so. Indeed, the government sometimes writes a law in such a way that its administration requires the creation of a group that does not yet exist; when this situation has arisen, the government has organized the group![17]

On the other hand, the neocorporatist system is a fragile one, because it depends so much on cooperation and on everyone's willingness to avoid rocking the boat. Neocorporatism sets up an officially sanctioned set of actors in the system, each with rights to a piece of the pie; therefore, no group can go for the jugular of another without endangering the whole system.

This suggests a second important problem in neocorporatism. It defines a set of groups with claims on the state and routinizes the process by which the state consults with them. As a result, the neocorporatist system tends to petrify the existing line of conflict as of the time it was established. In effect, the government "licenses" an existing set of interest groups. We can expect that lines of conflict will change over time, as old conflicts fade and new ones arise. It is difficult for the neocorporatist system, with its intricate organizational structure of established and "entitled" interest groups, to adjust to such change. As an example of this problem, one of the more difficult challenges faced by Swedish politics in the 1970s and 1980s was to find a way of providing political expression to the new concern over the advisability of nuclear power and protection of the environment.

In this section, we have considered what one might call "cooperative" neocorporatism of the sort typified by politics in the Scandinavian states. Neocorporatism of this sort arises from the desires of the government and the interests to develop consensus and minimize conflict in policy making. Another form of neocorporatism, usually called "state neocorporatism," was found especially in Latin America (Brazil in the 1970s and Perón's Argentina). This system is imposed on the interests by the state to keep them under its

---

[17]This illustrates what is probably the most basic difference between the pluralist and neocorporatist models. Under pluralism, it is assumed that the state apparatus responds to the system of interest groups. Under neocorporatism, the state is taken to have a good deal of autonomy; to some extent, it creates the system of interest groups and determines how it operates.

control. Though both types of government are "corporatist" in that the government deals directly with groups, the nature of politics is very different in the two types.

POWER AND CHOICE

Of "power and choice," pluralist writers certainly emphasize a "choice" perspective. The public choice—policy—is seen as a balanced outcome of the different pressures of organized interests, almost like a physical equilibrium, and the government is treated rather as an unexamined "black box." Power relations within the government, and especially the difference in power of various interest groups, tend to be played down in this abstraction.

One might expect that the main alternative abstraction, neocorporatism, would take an opposed side of this great divide, but oddly it, too, embodies more of a "choice" than a "power" perspective—at least in the "cooperative" form we have looked at here. (Where corporatism is analyzed as a tool by which authoritarian governments construct their control of society, the emphasis is more on a "power" perspective.) In its "cooperative" form, neocorporatism is seen as a system in which, as in pluralism, the interests of society in a rather natural way come together to produce their most-preferred mix of policies. The main difference between the two abstractions is in the role accorded government in the process: Under pluralism, the government is a passive receiver of pressures from interests; under neocorporatism, it is seen as a stimulator and shaper of those pressures, and the government blends with the system of interest groups. In both abstractions, the production of policy is portrayed as the natural outcome of a process designed to produce public choices. An interesting exercise would be to design an alternative abstraction of interest-group activities in democracies that is based more on a "power" perspective.

Example: Interest Groups in France

France has a system that probably falls somewhere between the pluralist and neocorporatist models of politics. It also shows interesting peculiarities of its own, especially in a certain looseness and unpredictability of structure. French interest groups are rather fragmented, and compared with groups in other states, they are relatively more likely to engage in provocative violence.

French interest groups have fairly low enrollments from their potential members. Labor unions enroll only about 10 percent of their potential membership, and other sorts of groups have similarly low enrollments.

Furthermore, the organized groups are deeply divided. Frequently, several different organizations compete for the same membership, which in other countries would be united behind a single organization. Workers, for instance, are organized in four major, separate unions: the CGT (a communist union with 29 percent of the total union strength), the CFDT (an independent-minded, socialist union with 30 percent of the organized workers), Force Ouvrier (a reformist union independent of parties with 17 percent of the organized workers), and the Catholic Confederation (with 7 percent). Independent unions account for the rest.[18] Farmers' interests, which figure importantly in French politics, are divided among no fewer than five hundred rural defense organizations at the national level.[19]

French politics at all levels is punctuated by sporadic, intense activity against a background of cynical disengagement, and this holds as true of interest groups as it does of other aspects of politics. In fact, the line between interest groups and social movements is even harder to draw in France than in other countries. The weakly organized interest groups of France flare up from time to time into what really should be thought of as social movements. This is most notable in the periodic national crises that engulf France. One of these occurred in May 1968, when a dispute between the students and administration of a provincial university flared up into a national confrontation between students on the one hand and administrators and police on the other. It was marked by the occupation of campuses and pitched battles in the streets. Stimulated by the violence and seeing that the government was floundering in its response to the students, workers all over France went on strike to push their own demands for wage increases and greater control over working conditions. At its height, the strike probably involved half of all employees in France, and it effectively closed down the economy. It was not a tactical move by the union leaders, most of whom opposed the strike, but a spontaneous response by the workers. The combination of battles with the students and paralysis of the economy almost brought down the entire system of government.

It is not only in general crises that groups engage in confrontation. In the events of May 1968, violence and strikes were the result of spontaneous group activity, but the leaders of organized groups also use violent confrontation from time to time as a deliberate tactic. Farm groups occasionally attract considerable attention by barricading highways or overturning trucks carrying produce they do not wish to see marketed. There have been numerous violent incidents involving agricultural imports from Spain. Other groups from which we might not ordinarily expect violence also occasionally tap into it in France. French shopkeepers have engaged in confrontational politics under the leadership of several groups, organizing tax strikes, kidnapping officials, and battling with police.

The incidence of violence on the part of French interest groups should not be taken to suggest that this is the tactic most frequently used by French groups. It is of interest to us because it occurs more frequently in France than in other industrialized states, but most of the time French interest groups spend their energy in less spectacular pursuits—meeting with bureaucrats and elected officials, dealing with political parties, engaging in court actions, and so on.

In their relations with the government, French interest groups are in some instances bound to the government by formal ties of intimacy of the sort we associate with neocorporatism. More often, interest groups and government maintain the sort of distance we expect under pluralism. The agricultural sector comes closest to the

[18]Ministry of the Economy, INSEE, *Annuaire Statistiques de la France 1997,* p. 159.
[19]Henry Ehrmann, *Politics in France,* 4th ed. (Boston: Little, Brown, 1983), p. 187.

neocorporatist model. Not all agricultural interest groups are tied intimately to the government, but one group, the Federation Nationale des Syndicats d'Exploitants Agricoles (FNSEA), has become something like the "official" agricultural group for the government. The FNSEA claims to represent about 55 percent of the French farmers, low for a group that is to play a quasi-official role in the neocorporatist mode but quite respectable by French standards. During the 1970s, the government turned a number of administrative duties over to the FNSEA, including most of the educational and training tasks carried out in other countries by agricultural extension agents. In most areas, the government recognized the FNSEA as the coordinating representative of farming interests, and this influence continues.[20]

Usually, however, interest groups are not this close to the government. In a 1979 survey, 44 percent of the group leaders reported that they met with government officials only "sometimes," "rarely," or "never," and only 21 percent reported that they did so "almost daily."[21] When one considers that the *job* of the interest-group leader is to influence government policy, this suggests that considerable distance is maintained. Similarly, when asked what their most effective means of action was, only 18 percent named participation in government committees or contacts with civil servants. Table 13–4 lists the percentage of interest-group leaders who stated that their groups used specified tactics "often" or "from time to time." It gives a good overall profile of the activity of French interest groups.

TABLE 13–4   REPORTED FREQUENCY OF INTEREST-GROUP ACTIONS

	Often (Percent)	From time to time (Percent)	Rarely or never (Percent)
Parliamentary lobbying	32	59	8
Participation in government committees	55	31	14
Formal meetings with government officials	54	32	15
Public relations campaigns	33	44	23
Informal meetings with government officials	47	29	24
Action in the Economic and Social Council	26	26	48
Influencing parties and their leaders	10	37	53
Demonstrations, strikes, direct action	13	20	67
Blocking or sabotaging policy decisions	10	22	68
Legal action	8	20	72

Source: From Frank L. Wilson, "French Interest Groups: Pluralist or Neocorporatist?" in *American Political Science Review*, Vol. 77, December 1983, pp. 895–910. Reprinted with permission.

[20]Clive S. Thomas, *First World Interest Groups: A Comparative Perspective* (Westport, Conn.: Greenwood Press, 1993), pp. 117–18; John T. S. Keeler, "Agricultural Power in the European Community," *Comparative Politics* 28 (1996): 127–49. For a dissenting view, see Pepper D. Culpepper, "Organizational Competition and the Neo-Corporatist Fallacy in French Agriculture," *West European Politics* 16 (July 1993): 295–315.

[21]The following survey results are drawn from Frank L. Wilson, "French Interest Groups: Pluralist or Neocorporatist?" *American Political Science Review* 77 (December 1983): 895–910.

Example: Interest Groups in Japan: Attenuated Neocorporatism

The Japanese system of interest groups is a strongly neocorporatist system. However, it is one that is sharply attenuated, by European standards; labor does not play the important role in the system that we usually see in neocorporatism, and many noneconomic groups that we often see in Europe and North America are missing.

The bureaucracy is the key to the Japanese system. The higher civil service in Japan is an elite that is almost autonomous in making policy. It is a well-respected elite, drawing the best university graduates and trading on the general public scorn for politicians to maintain its independence. Until the early 1980s, the Japanese system was a three-way arrangement among the bureaucracy, big business interest groups, and the Liberal Democratic Party (LDP). Agricultural groups, critical to maintaining the LDP in power, played a supporting role in return for subsidies and agricultural trade protection. Business interests gave the LDP the huge amounts of money on which Japanese electoral politics was based ($2.6 billion in 1989), and the LDP cooperated as the bureaucracy and the business interests set up most public policies.[22]

The LDP was the dominant party in a "dominant party system" (see pages 257–258), and it remains clearly the leading party of Japan. Since the 1980s, however, its dominant position has been challenged. Public disgust with the system of corruption and "big-money politics" has led to the rise of reform movements, and voters have proved willing to consider alternatives to the LDP, so the party corner of the LDP-business-bureaucracy triangle is undergoing change. The role of the bureaucracy appears unchanged, however, and may be strengthened because no clear party leadership has yet emerged to take the place of the weakened LDP hegemony. Interest groups and the bureaucracy mingle closely. As is so often the case in neocorporatist systems, government advisory committees heavily weighted to the bureaucracy and interest groups are important in policy making. Bureaucrats often take high-level positions in the interest groups when they retire from the civil service.

One reason for the dominance of economic interest groups in Japan (at least business groups and agriculture) is that paradoxically, although Japanese society is oriented to social groups—one's family or factory or association demands intense loyalty and support—the Japanese are rather apathetic about politics and groups formed around political issues. There are few environmental or consumer-oriented groups in Japan, and there is essentially no feminist movement. There are rather important ideological groups on the right, which are anti-labor, honor the emperor, and refuse to apologize for Japan's role in World War II. As of late 1988,

---

[22]Ronald J. Hrebenar and Akira Nakamura, "Japan: Associational Politics in a Group-Oriented Society," in Clive S. Thomas, *First World Interest Groups: A Comparative Perspective* (Westport, Conn.: Greenwood Press, 1993), p. 212.

it was estimated that these groups had over 125,000 members.[23] The Left is not as well organized; it is represented primarily by the National Teacher's Union, which is aggressively of the Left.

So economic groups fill most of the political space: business groups, agricultural groups, and labor. Of these, only the first two figure importantly; in the past, labor has been almost excluded from the political process.

There are a large number of business groups in Japan, but one group, the Japanese Federation of Economic Organizations, is accepted as speaking on behalf of "business." It represents primarily large businesses; its members make up only 1 percent of Japanese firms but account for 40 percent of sales.[24] In addition, there are many trade organizations, often for quite specific activities, such as an association for manufacturers of tea services or an association of manufacturers of pens. Beyond these organizations, much business policy is made by a business leader directly approaching a bureaucrat.

Agriculture's peak organizations are based on the agricultural cooperatives. These are organizations of farmers that have the right to be the sole marketers of rice; they also distribute some services on behalf of the government. As a result, farmers have little choice but to be members of their cooperative; Japanese society is so group-oriented, however, that this does not appear to be viewed as an imposition. The cooperatives have about 8 million members, but their political power is greater even than this would suggest. The old electoral system, which was changed in 1994 as part of the present trend of reform, gave rural areas undue representation and for a long time allowed farmers to flex strong political muscles. The farmers have also proved to be politically flexible. In 1989, for instance, they shifted many of their members' votes to the Socialist Party to punish the LDP for being too open to free trade; this was a major reason for the LDP's loss of the upper house of parliament, and it demonstrated to everyone that the agricultural cooperatives could not be taken for granted. The power of the agricultural groups is one of the main reasons for Japanese-American tensions over trade; political leaders are reluctant to open up the Japanese market to American agriculture products.

T. J. Pempel has dubbed the Japanese system "corporatism without labor."[25] Most Japanese workers are organized in company unions, not industrywide unions, and these organizations tend to be less politically active and more compliant and to look to their companies' interests. The main exceptions are the public employees' unions, such as the National Teachers' Union. These unions have been marginalized in Japan's generally conservative society because they are quite far to the left on almost all issues. Labor is also split into two main organizations, one based on company unions and the other based on the public employees' unions. As a result, political leadership in Japan has been able to safely ignore labor on most issues.

Change is in the wind in Japan, however. Scandals have publicized the reliance of parties, especially the LDP, on large illegal contributions of cash. (One scandal involved a

---

[23]Ibid., p. 207.

[24]Ibid., p. 204.

[25]T. J. Pempel and Keiichi Tsunekawa, "Corporatism Without Labor? The Japanese Anomaly," in Philippe Schmitter and Gerhard Lehmbruch, eds., *Trends Toward Corporatist Intermediation* (Beverly Hills, Calif.: Sage, 1979).

bribe so large that the firm's secretary had to use a supermarket cart to carry the cash across a parking lot.) The electoral system has been changed, and reformers claim that they will change the system of campaign finance. The two labor organizations combined in a cooperative political movement in 1989, to some effect. And finally, the Finance Ministry—the most powerful of the powerful bureaucracies—lost a great deal of its prestige during the long-lasting economic crisis of the 1990s. So this may be a system in transition. On the other hand, the Japanese culture still reveres scholarly "nonpolitical" authority such as that of the bureaucrats. And Japan still sees much of its postwar prosperity as having been accomplished by an alliance between government and business.

In the clearest indication that there may indeed be a tide of reform after several years of economic and national disappointment, Junichiro Koizumi, a maverick politician, won the leadership of the LDP in 2001, which automatically also made him the prime minister. He was not really the old politicos' choice, but they were desperate. Shortly thereafter, the electorate gave him a mandate for change by giving the LDP a majority in the upper house, something that would never have happened without him. He vows reform of the economic structures of Japan, starting with the banks. Though he is immensely popular, it is still not entirely clear where things will end. Koizumi is something of an unknown quantity politically, and though he has been clear that he wants reform, he has been much less clear about precisely how he wants to accomplish it. He also has mixed his radical stance on reform with a strong nationalist stance that appeals to conservatives. Exactly what he will be and whether his popularity will last when tough decisions need to be made are as yet unanswered questions.

FURTHER READING

Alvarez, Sonia. *Engendering Democracy: Women's Movements in Transition Politics.* Princeton, N.J.: Princeton University Press, 1990.

Ball, A., and Millard, F. *Pressure Politics in Industrial Societies.* Atlantic Highlands, N.J.: Humanities Press International, 1987.

Bauer, Raymond A.; de Sola Pool, Ithiel; and Dexter, Lewis A. *American Business and Public Policy.* New York: Atherton, 1963.

Baumgartner, Frank, and Leech, Beth. *Basic Interests: The Importance of Groups in Politics and Political Science.* Princeton, N.J.: Princeton University Press, 1998.

Berry, Jeffrey M. *The Interest Group Society.* 3d ed. New York: Longmann, 1997.

Christiansen, Peter Mark, and Rommetvedt, Hilmar. "From Corporatism to Lobbyism? Parliaments, Executives, and Organized Interests in Denmark and Norway." *Scandinavian Political Studies* 22 (1999): 195–220.

Dalton, Russell, and Kuechler, Manfred, eds. *Challenging the Political Order: New Social Movements in Western Democracies.* New York: Oxford University Press, 1990.

Gerber, Elisabeth R. *The Populist Paradox: Interest Group Influence and the Promise of Direct Legislation.* Princeton, N.J.: Princeton University Press, 1999.

Haber, Paul Lawrence. "Identity and Political Process: Recent Trends in the Study of Latin American Social Movements." *Latin American Research Review* 31 (1996): 171–88.

Horowitz, Donald L. *Ethnic Groups in Conflict.* Berkeley: University of California Press, 1985.

Lehmbruch, Gerhard, and Schmitter, Philippe C., eds. *Patterns of Corporatist Policy-Making.* Beverly Hills, Calif.: Sage, 1982.

Loomis, Burdett A., and Cigler, Allan J., eds. *Interest Group Politics.* 5th ed. Washington, D.C.: Congressional Quarterly, 1998.

Mansbridge, Jane J. *Why We Lost the ERA.* Chicago: University of Chicago Press, 1986.

Marks, Gary, and McAdam, Doug. "Social Movements and the Changing Structure of Political Opportunity in the European Union." *West European Politics* 19 (1996): 249–79.

Meyer, David S., and Tarrow, Sidney, eds. *The Social Movement Society: Contentious Politics for a New Century.* Lanham, England: Rowman & Littlefield, 1998.

Moe, Terry. *The Organization of Interests.* Chicago: University of Chicago Press, 1980.

Nelson, Barbara, and Chowdhury, Najma, eds. *Women and Politics Worldwide.* New Haven: Yale University Press, 1994.

Olson, Mancur. *The Logic of Collective Action.* Cambridge: Harvard University Press, 1965.

―――. *The Rise and Decline of Nations: Economic Growth, Stagflation and Social Rigidities.* New Haven: Yale University Press, 1982.

Ramseyer, J. Mark, and Rosenbluth, Frances. *Japan's Political Marketplace.* Cambridge: Harvard University Press, 1993.

Schlozman, Kay Lehman, and Tierney, John T. *Organized Interests and American Democracy.* New York: Harper & Row, 1986.

Scott, James C. *Weapons of the Weak: Everyday Forms of Peasant Resistance.* New Haven: Yale University Press, 1985.

Siaroff, Alan. "Corporatism in 24 Industrial Democracies: Meaning and Measurement." *European Journal of Political Research* 36 (1999): 175–205.

Skilling, H. Gordon, and Griffiths, Franklyn, eds. *Interest Groups in Soviet Politics.* Princeton, N.J.: Princeton University Press, 1971.

Tarrow, Sidney. *Power in Movement: Social Movements and Contentious Politics.* 2d ed. New York: Cambridge University Press, 1998.

Thomas, Clive S. *First World Interest Groups: A Comparative Perspective.* Westport, Conn.: Greenwood Press, 1993.

Truman, David B. *The Governmental Process.* 2d ed. New York: Knopf, 1971.

Walker, Jack L., Jr. *Mobilizing Interest Groups in America.* Ann Arbor: University of Michigan Press, 1991.

Wilson, Frank L. "French Interest Groups: Pluralist or Neocorporatist?" *American Political Science Review* 77 (December 1983): 895–910.

Wilson, James Q. *Political Organizations.* New York: Basic Books, 1973.

 WEBSITES OF INTEREST

Emily's List (organization endorsing women candidates for office): *http://www.emilyslist.org*

National Right to Life: *http://www.nrlc.org*

Planned Parenthood: *http://www.plannedparenthood.org*

National Rifle Association:
http://www.mynra.org

Environmental Defense Fund:
http://www.edf.org

U.S. Chamber of Commerce, interest group for industry:
http://www.uschamber.org/

AFL-CIO, interest group for labor:
http://www.aflcio.org/home.htm

American Conservative Union:
http://www.conservative.org/

Americans for Democratic Action, a liberal interest group:
http://adaction.org/

Children's Defense Fund, an interest group for children's issue advocacy:
http://www.childrensdefense.org/

Christian Coalition:
http://www.cc.org/

U.S. Taxpayers, an anti-tax interest group:
http://www.USTaxpayers.org/

14

NATIONAL DECISION-MAKING INSTITUTIONS: PARLIAMENTARY GOVERNMENT

In this and Chapter 15, we will examine formal arrangements for governing democracies. This chapter will deal with "parliamentary" government, while Chapter 15 will deal with "presidential" government. Parliamentary government is conceptually the simpler of the two and is the form found in most democracies. It will seem unusual to many American readers, however, since the United States is one of the democracies that operates with a presidential system.

The basic principles of a pure parliamentary system are as follows:

1. A parliament of representatives is elected by the citizens of the state. It normally consists of from two hundred to several hundred representatives. The parliament is the only elected body in the state. Bills passed by the parliament are the law, and no one can overrule them.

2. The executive power of the state (managing the bureaucracy, conducting relations with other states, etc.) is lodged with a *cabinet* of women and men who are selected by the parliament to conduct the affairs of the state. Most or all members of the cabinet are usually members of the parliament who take on executive responsibilities in addition to their legislative chores.

3. The cabinet retains executive power only as long as it has the "confidence" of the parliament; that is, only as long as it can command a majority of the votes. At any time, a majority vote in the parliament may unseat a cabinet and cause a new set of people to be selected as a cabinet. This is referred to as the "government falling." If no vote is actually taken to unseat the cabinet but the cabinet finds that it is unable to put together majorities to pass its important bills, it is expected that the cabinet will resign.

4. Just as the parliament holds the cabinet in jeopardy, the leader of the cabinet (called variously "premier," "prime minister," "chancellor," etc.) usually has the right to have the parliament disbanded, forcing a new election that will lead to a new distribution of power.

This, in a nutshell, is parliamentary government. We will examine some finer points and some variations, but these four principles are basic. It is a simpler form than presidential government because, at least in its pure form, it does not allow for any separation of powers. The parliament and the cabinet that operates only by the support of the parliament hold all the state's governmental political power.

With this simple concentration of power, political decisions should in principle be made clearly and directly, with a minimum of delay. The cabinet and the parliament should always be in agreement on important issues—if they were not, presumably the cabinet would fall—and their will cannot be blocked by a court or any other body.

Such a system has two special advantages and disadvantages.

Advantages

1. The government can respond fairly directly to changed circumstances because power is unified. For example, parliamentary systems were more successful than fragmented systems such as the United States at developing national energy policies in response to the shortages of oil in the 1970s. In a parliamentary system, all it takes to make a law is a majority of the votes in the parliament, and so it is straightforward for the party or parties in power to develop a policy and write it into law. In more fragmented systems such as that of the United States, many barriers are raised that can slow down or halt the passage of a law. The president may veto the law, the Supreme Court may rule it unconstitutional, states may have proper jurisdiction over it, and so on.

2. A second advantage to a parliamentary system is that the lines of responsibility for policy making are clear. Elections should mean more, because voters can know exactly whom to blame for their current situation: the party or parties in power. Parties can be held pretty well to their election promises once they are in office, because there is nothing to prevent them from accomplishing in office what they had said they would do. In a more fragmented system such as that of the United States, this is not so. There are so many independent centers of power that an unhappy policy cannot be blamed on any one of them. The president can say that Congress did it, Congress can point to the Supreme Court, and so on. President Harry Truman was famous for his desk-top slogan, "The buck stops here"; but in 1948, he campaigned across the country on the theme that the "do-nothing" Congress, controlled by the Republican Party, was to blame for his not having accomplished his goals as president. Elections can mean more with regard to public policy in a parliamentary system than in a more fragmented system because once election results are in, the party or parties that have won control of the parliament have no excuse for not enacting the policies they had promised.

Disadvantages

1. In a parliamentary system, there are few protections for a minority that feels it is being wronged. In a presidential system, a minority may hope that even if it has lost its fight in the legislature, it may retrieve things with the president, or vice versa. As a result, the support of a bare majority is usually not enough to get a law enacted.

    This may be seen as either an advantage or a disadvantage. It is the flip side of the advantage noted previously, that in a parliamentary system policy making is straightforward. Though this is in general a good thing, it is clear that there must be some times when we would wish that the government had been slowed down and had been prevented from taking hasty action or action that did not have fairly broad support. A parliamentary system, because of its efficiency, does not do this.

2. A second disadvantage to the parliamentary system is that it *may* produce unstable government. I have spoken above of the "party or parties" that control a parliament. If no one party holds a majority of the seats, then two or more parties must form a *coalition* to control the parliament. In forming a coalition, they will divide up the positions of the cabinet among themselves (party A gets to name the premier, the minister of economics, the foreign minister, and the minister for agriculture; party B gets to name the minister for defense and the minister for industry, etc.). In the parliament, they agree that their combined parties' votes will always be cast on behalf of legislation proposed by the cabinet.

    This is fine if the partners of the coalition are in general agreement on most issues. But the coalition is strictly a marriage of convenience. If the parties in it disagree on enough things, it may be hard to keep them together and cooperating for very long. A socialist party may pull out because the coalition has not been able to agree on a program to stimulate employment, a Hindu party may pull out over a question of religious policy. At that point, the government "falls," and a new coalition must be negotiated.

    If this happens only occasionally, it is no problem. Political change must come from time to time. But in a parliamentary system, it sometimes happens that the numerical strength of the parties and their relationships with each other are such that it is always difficult to keep a coalition together. This may lead to a paralyzing succession of governmental breakups, in which governmental control is so unstable that people lose confidence in the whole process. Germany suffered from this problem from 1918 to 1933, when Hitler overthrew the weakened democracy. France suffered from it until 1958, when the military intervened and imposed a presidential system. Italy has suffered from it chronically since 1945; in fifty-six years (as of 2001), Italians have had fifty-nine different governments. On the other hand, most parliamentary systems have not had this problem. The Scandinavian countries, the Low Countries, Germany, and others have had long histories of stable government by coalitions.

CABINET CONTROL

If parliamentary government is to function smoothly, the cabinet must be able to control what goes on in the parliament. If a cabinet could be voted out casually because the mood of the parliament had changed, no one would find that a satisfactory situation; government would be far too unstable. Particularly if the cabinet is based on a coalition of parties, the basis for bargaining on the makeup of the cabinet is the number of votes each party can deliver. If the cabinet was not able to count regularly on the votes of one or another of the parties, the rest of the coalition would feel cheated and the coalition would not last long. As it happens, this was a large part of the problem for many years in Italy; the Christian Democratic Party was an important part of almost every coalition from 1945 to 1994, but it was a fragmented party and was never able to guarantee its parliamentary support very well.

On the basis of this reasoning, we might expect to see, in the many smoothly functioning parliamentary systems, that the cabinets dominate their parliaments. And this is indeed the case. The usual situation is that legislation is proposed by the cabinet and is *debated* in the parliament; after all, it is only there that the opposition parties have their innings. Aside from the addition of minor amendments, however, there is rarely any question but that the legislation will be passed by the parliament. In effect, the parliament is a rubber stamp for the cabinet.

It is ironic that a body that is elected by the parliament and can be brought down at any time by it—a body that is, in effect, created by the parliament—can turn around and control what the parliament does. It is readily understandable that this should be the case, however, if we recall that the members of the cabinet are top leaders of their parties. They are skillful politicians, and they have every reason to find ways to control what happens in the parliament to protect the power they enjoy as cabinet members.

In Chapter 12, we saw that a side effect of political parties was that, as organizations, they bind a number of people together and provide a channel by which some of those people can control others. It is by this channel that cabinets control their parliaments. The members of a cabinet participate in parliamentary debates; they vote in parliament; but most important, they are leaders or powerful members of their party organizations in the parliament. For the other members, the party provides the avenue for advancement in the parliament. Debate time, committee assignments, the chance of a cabinet post someday—these are controlled for members of parliament by their party. Those who do not cooperate with their party's leaders do not advance. It is by this source of discipline, in their capacity as the leaders of their party, that the cabinet members are able to impose their will on the parliament.

WHAT DOES A PARLIAMENT DO?

The governmental role of a parliament, because it is so controlled by the cabinet, is difficult for students from the United States to appreciate. With regard to the passage of legislation, most parliaments are rubber stamps. From 1945 to 1978, for instance, of bills that the British cabinet submitted to the House of Commons for consideration, 97 percent were approved by the House. Amendments to bills are also tightly controlled by the cabinet in Britain. From 1967 to 1971, the cabinet proposed 1,772 amendments to various bills; of these, 1,770 were approved. By contrast, other members of the House proposed 4,198 amendments during the same period, but only 210 of these passed.[1]

---

[1]Richard Rose, "Still the Era of Party Government," *Parliamentary Affairs* 36 (Summer 1983): 284–85.

"Delegate" and "Trustee" Models of Representation

An enduring debate in political science centers on what role representatives should assume vis-à-vis their constituents. In the "delegate" model, they should regard themselves as speaking for the constituents and should cast each vote as they think the constituents would wish it to be cast. In the "trustee" model, it is assumed that representatives learn more about an issue than any of their constituents could possibly know and have been chosen on the basis of their superior judgment; we would then expect that on at least a few occasions they would vote differently than their constituents would wish them to vote.

Edmund Burke put the case for the trustee model beautifully in a speech to the electors of Bristol on November 3, 1774, after they had chosen him to represent them:

> Certainly, gentlemen, it ought to be the happiness and glory of a representative, to live in the strictest union, the closest correspondence, and the most unreserved communication with his constituents. Their wishes ought to have great weight with him; their opinion high respect; their business unremitted attention. It is his duty to sacrifice his repose, his pleasures, his satisfactions, to theirs; and, above all, ever, and in all cases, to prefer their interest to his own. But, his unbiased opinion, his mature judgment, his enlightened conscience, he ought not to sacrifice to you, to any man, or to any set of men living. These he does not derive from your pleasure; no, nor from the law and the constitution. They are a trust from Providence, for the abuse of which he is deeply answerable. Your representative owes you, not his industry only, but his judgment; and he betrays, instead of serving you, if he sacrifices it to your opinion.
>
> My worthy colleague says, his will ought to be subservient to yours. If that be all, the thing is innocent. If government were a matter of will upon any side, yours, without question, ought to be superior. But government and legislation are matters of reason and judgment, and not of inclination; and, what sort of reason is that, in which the determination precedes the discussion; in which one set of men deliberate, and another decide; and where those who form the conclusion are perhaps three hundred miles distant from those who hear the arguments?
>
> To deliver an opinion, is the right of all men; that of constituents is a weighty and respectable opinion, which a representative ought always to rejoice to hear; and which he ought always most seriously to consider. But *authoritative* instructions; *mandates* issued, which the member is bound blindly and implicitly to obey, to vote and to argue for, though contrary to the clearest conviction of his judgment and conscience; these are things utterly unknown to the laws of this land, and which arise from a fundamental mistake of the whole order and tenor of our constitution.

Source: Works of Edmund Burke (Boston, 1839: Charles C. Little and James Brown), vol. 2, p. 12.

It is apparent that whatever things parliaments do, deciding what legislation is to become law is not chief among them. In the unified governmental arrangement of a parliamentary system, it is expected that the executive and legislative parts of government will work together to make legislation; and because over the years cabinets have learned to protect themselves by controlling their parliaments, it is generally accepted that cabinets call the tune in designing laws.

Is parliament then a useless appendage? No, because it still serves a number of purposes that are similar to those of the U.S. Congress, and one further purpose that is peculiar to parliamentary systems.

First, a parliament furnishes a forum for the public debate of bills. The opposition parties have a chance, before a bill is passed into law, to present their position on it and to stimulate public discussion.

Second, a parliament is a place where a bill that the cabinet wants to enact into law is submitted to detailed scrutiny both by the friends of the cabinet and by its enemies. It may be that a number of small problems may be uncovered in a complicated bill, problems that the cabinet is happy to have brought to its attention. In the British example, almost all of the 1,772 amendments introduced by the cabinet were amendments to its *own bills,* because almost no legislation is considered by the House of Commons except legislation submitted by the cabinet. Most of those amendments were cabinet responses to problems that were brought to members' attention in the course of parliamentary consideration of their bills.

Third, a parliament is one of the few parts of the governmental apparatus that has an interest in keeping a critical eye on how the cabinet is administering public policy. The opposition parties are especially eager participants in this, for obvious reasons, but there is also a tradition that the cabinet must report regularly to the parliament how it is managing the affairs of the state. This sort of accounting takes many forms. In most parliamentary systems, there is some sort of annual speech made to the parliament describing in broad outlines the state of things and the cabinet's plans for the coming year. In addition, many parliaments use a device called "question time," in which various cabinet members appear regularly to answer questions from other members of the parliament about the way their ministry is being run. The answers they give may spark lively debates.

This third function of parliaments—watching what the executive part of the government does—is not met as well in parliamentary as in presidential systems. The reason is that committees are not strong in parliaments, as will be seen. Committees in a legislature have the potential to provide a powerful site for overseeing the executive. They are groups of legislators who specialize in a particular area of policy and who may become expert in it over the years. If they have a good professional staff, they may be able to match the offices of the executive in expertise and in the ability to handle evidence. If the committee can hold hearings and subpoena witnesses, it can provide a strong investigative force. But committees in parliamentary systems are usually weak, and so the oversight function devolves primarily on individual members of the parliament, who are not much of a match for the experts of the executive office. In presidential systems like that of the United States, in contrast, congressional committees can at their best operate as tough and knowledgeable watchdogs. (At their worst, of course, they can be tough, cranky, and perverse watchdogs—to some extent, this depends on one's point of view.)

From the discussion up to this point, it might seem that a parliament is a poor fish. It has little control over legislation except inasmuch as the cabinet can be persuaded to amend its own bills, and it is not as powerful in oversight of the executive as legislatures elsewhere. The one thing we have noted that it does well is to conduct public debate of bills. All this looks meager as compared, say, with the Congress of the United States.

However, there is another function of parliaments that is peculiar to parliamentary systems. The fourth function of a parliament in a parliamentary system is to provide a pool of trained people for service in the executive and a setting in which they operate while serving in the executive; a legislature like the U.S. Congress does not do this. In most parliamentary systems, nearly all members of the cabinet and other political appointments in the executive are members of parliament. In Britain at any given time, about two hundred members of the House of Commons are serving in such positions as prime minister, minister for defense, first lord of the admiralty, other cabinet positions, or lesser executive positions such as parliamentary secretary to the minister for defense. These are members from the party that has a majority in the House, and so at the same time, something like another two hundred members of the opposition parties are hoping for electoral success that will give *their* parties control of parliament and put them into executive positions. At any given time, about two-thirds of the members of the House of Commons either hold executive positions or are waiting for them.

The members of the political executive in a parliamentary system are men and women who have been selected by the other members of their party for executive tasks, and that selection is based largely on how well they have performed in debate and other tasks in the House. They are selected after some years of service in the House, which, like any organization, imposes norms of behavior on its members and in many subtle ways changes their behavior and the manner in which they react to things. Once they are in executive positions, these people are still sitting members of the House and take part in its daily business of debate, voting on bills, and so on. Even while they hold executive office, they rub shoulders daily with their colleagues in the House.

Thus, an important task of parliament in a parliamentary system is to produce those who will hold executive office, train them in the ways of politics, select them, and then serve as the site from which they conduct the executive functions. In a presidential system, the legislative part of government exercises its strength in *opposing* the executive; but in a parliamentary system, it exercises its strength *through* the executive.

THE LIFE OF A MEMBER OF PARLIAMENT

What is it like to serve in such a body? Consider the situation of a young member of the British House of Commons:

> In the 1974 general election, Mr. Dorrell offered himself as the Conservatives' sacrificial lamb in the solidly Labor dockside district of East Hull. "They want you to make your first mistakes in an area where it doesn't matter," he remarks. "But you make them all over again where it does."
>
> Then in 1976, he was chosen out of 105 applicants for what he saw as the "reasonably winnable" seat in Loughborough, a pleasantly diversified manufacturing and farming district in the East Midlands, about 120 miles north of London. The local party organization didn't particularly care for his youth and bachelorhood—he will be married in September—but his energy and articulateness carried the day. Once nominated, he bought a house in the district.
>
> In a typical parliamentary week, Mr. Dorrell first reads the morning papers in his small apartment a few minutes' walk from Westminster. Most MPs have some quarters, from a shared apartment to an elegant town house, "within the sound of the bells"; when the bells ring for a Commons vote, as they may a dozen times a night, MPs have eight minutes to get to the voting "lobbies."

Routine Work

After breakfast he is off to the tiny, sparsely furnished office he shares with another Tory fresh-man, Timothy Eggar, a block from Parliament. His secretary is two floors away in a crowded office shared with other secretaries. Mornings usually go to correspondence and constituent work or research for a magazine or a speech to a private group (junior MPs don't get many chances to speak on the Commons floor). Or there may be a routine committee meeting, where Mr. Dorrell's main role is to vote periodically for government motions to speed a bill along.

Afternoons bring more tiresome committee work, and for the rest of the day he may sit around the House chamber, the tearoom or a dinner table discussing problems with other back-benchers. With the late-night sessions and frequent votes, MPs don't have much of a London social life.

Few members attend the unconsequential Friday sessions, so on most Fridays Mr. Dorrell drives 2 1/2 hours to Worcester, where the family business is, and later another hour and a half to Loughborough "to talk to any group that wants to hear me." After the Saturday "surgery," he stops by a local fair or other social gathering. Sunday he tries to keep free for family or friends.[2]

Why would anyone put up with such drudgery? The obvious reason must be that it is through good soldiering in the supporting role that one may advance to interesting and powerful positions in the executive.

PARLIAMENTARY COMMITTEES

Committees of the U.S. House of Representatives and Senate are well known as inde-pendent, bristly bodies that presidents, bureaucrats, and even other members of the Con-gress defy only at their own risk. The State Department quivered in the 1950s when the House UnAmerican Affairs Committee investigated some of its younger personnel. Most bills that are introduced in the U.S. Congress are killed by a committee that refuses to vote them out with a recommendation, or else they die through delay in committees. This may be as true of bills originating in the presidential office as it is of those that are projects of individual members of Congress.[3]

Such independent bodies within a parliament would greatly weaken the central unity of parliament with the executive, because as independent sources of power, the com-mittees would make it more difficult for the executive leaders to control what happened in the parliament. For a parliamentary system to work well, power must as much as pos-sible be lodged with the leaders of the parties and no one else.

For this reason, committees of a parliament are generally a good deal weaker and less assertive than those in the U.S. Congress. All parliaments must have committees, of course. If hundreds of bills are to be submitted to a parliament in a year, the work of scru-tinizing those bills carefully must be divided up among the membership in some way or

---

[2]*Wall Street Journal,* 5 August 1980, p. 25.

[3]A good example is the refusal in 1997 of Jesse Helms, chair of the Senate Committee on Foreign Rela-tions, to hold hearings on President Bill Clinton's nomination of William Weld for the position of ambassador to Mexico. Eventually, the president had to withdraw his nomination because he could not get the Senate to act on it as long as Helms'committee kept it bottled up.

Debate in the Canadian House of Commons.
(Canapress Photo Service)

other; there is simply not time for each member of the parliament to do a careful job on all bills that come down in a year. But care is taken that the committees do not operate too independently in doing their work.

As an extreme example of this, consider committees in the British House of Commons. Where the U.S. Congress uses "standing committees"—such as the Committee on Foreign Affairs, with a set group of members who serve for years and may become expert in the areas of policy that they cover—the British set up an ad hoc committee for each bill as it comes in. The members of this committee are not people who regularly work together; they have been put together to consider this bill. They have not had years of specialized experience in a particular area of policy. They cannot subpoena witnesses and do not hold open hearings on their bill. They have no permanent staff. As one might imagine, their ability to transform legislation and put their own stamp on it is quite limited. The cabinet need not fear that its bill will be stopped or mangled by a committee in the House of Commons.

Other parliamentary systems are not so extreme. It is more convenient to use standing committees, so that a new group does not have to be constituted for each bill. Even the British have set up limited standing committees for the House of Commons (to oversee the executive and bureaucracy, not to review proposed bills). In smoothly working systems, however, even standing committees still do not operate with the independence of the committees in the U.S. Congress.

EXCEPTIONS TO PARLIAMENTARY SUPREMACY

I have described a "pure case" of parliamentarism, which is probably not met with exactly in any country of the world, although Great Britain comes close. Most parliamentary systems have incorporated one or another institution that divides the political power of the state and thus compromises the principle of parliamentary supremacy. For instance, Germany, Canada, India, and some other parliamentary systems are federal states; this means that important areas of policy are taken out of the hands of the cabinet and parliament. Germany and some other parliamentary systems tolerate fairly strong and independent committees in parliament. A few parliamentary systems—Austria and Germany are two examples—have courts that can overrule an act of parliament; we will look at this in more detail in Chapter 15.

In these and other ways, most parliamentary systems incorporate a few exceptions to the basic principles listed at the opening of this chapter. They are still "parliamentary systems," however.

PARLIAMENTS IN AUTOCRATIC SYSTEMS

Many states that are not parliamentary systems as described still have a parliamentary body. We saw in Chapter 11 that many nondemocratic systems have found it useful to hold elections for a variety of reasons; similarly, many of them find it useful to have a parliament. All a parliament is, after all, is a set of people who are designated to represent other groups of people, usually with some sort of geographic focus to the represented groups. It is not necessary that the parliament be able to operate independently or that it have discretion over laws. It can still sit and do a number of things.

The former Soviet Union's parliament, for instance, was the Supreme Soviet. In the Soviet system, almost all governmental decisions were taken elsewhere, within the Communist Party, and the parliament was set up so that it could not be a rival to the party. The parliament met only twice a year for a few days. It spent most of its time hearing long reports from the Central Committee of the party, reports that it ratified unanimously by a show of hands. A sizable number of the members were not members of the Communist Party, but few of them were repeaters from the preceding parliament. This made it unlikely that they would have the experience or confidence to act independently. Selection to the parliament was a token of honor for good citizenship in one's community, factory, or collective farm.

This parliament looks to have been a triviality, yet the Soviet Union made a great fuss about it. It was one of the chief bodies to result from the elections the Soviets conducted so enthusiastically, and they set great store by it. It must have been doing something, but what?

One thing it did was to serve as a symbol of a unified nation. As you recall, the Soviet Union sprawled over a vast area in which a number of different languages were spoken. The people of the Soviet Union ranged from nomadic deer herders in the north to Moslems in the south and European peoples on the Baltic coast. A parliament that drew individuals from all the regions of the country and was further drawn to give extensive play to such groups in the population as women, peasants, and blue-collar workers could

"TODAY THE PRIME MINISTER SIGNED TWO TREATIES, HELPED INCREASE OUR STEEL PRODUCTION, NARROWLY AVERTED WAR, AND SUGGESTED YOU BOTH SIGN UP AT SUNNYVALE RETIREMENT VILLAGE."

(© 2002 by Sidney Harris. Reprinted with permission.)

serve as a potent symbol of a unified population. This helps to explain the amount of fuss that was made over it as the Soviet authorities advertised this symbol of unity.

The Supreme Soviet also served other purposes. One need of the Soviet regime was to provide means for complaints and suggestions from the population at large to work their way into the decision-making process. We saw in Chapter 12 that the Communist Party served this need quite actively, but the members of the Supreme Soviet were also expected to be alert to problems of their constituents, and they could bring these to the attention of appropriate ministries in speeches, if they were able to get the floor, or through less formal means. The Supreme Soviet, like the Communist Party, served as a useful conduit for popular feeling in a governmental system that did not permit either a free press or the formation of organizations that might serve as rival foci of power.[4]

CONCLUSION

I have presented a form of government, parliamentary government, that is closely approximated in a majority of democracies. Its two central principles are that power is

---

[4]A good review is Stephen White, "The U.S.S.R. Supreme Soviet: A Developmental Perspective," *Legislative Studies Quarterly* 5 (May 1980): 247–74.

unified rather than divided and that it is lodged with a democratically elected parliament and a cabinet that is formed from and works within that parliament.

An irony of parliamentary government is that for members of the parliament who do not serve in its cabinet or in executive posts associated with the cabinet, this unity makes their job rather dull. Unlike a divided system like that of the United States, their main job is not to *decide* whether the cabinet should be doing what it is doing and writing the laws it is writing. That decision has been taken care of by the basic decision of the parties in the parliament to install this particular cabinet and not to bring it down. It follows that the cabinet's bills must almost always be passed in the end, or else the cabinet would fall. The task of ordinary members of the parliament, then, is to operate on the edges of bills as they come in, to discuss their merits, to suggest amendments that the cabinet may choose to accept, to question members of the cabinet on what they are doing, and—all the while—to groom themselves for eventual participation in cabinets of the future.

Example: Parliamentary Government in India

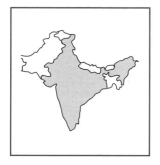

The general constitutional arrangement chosen for the new state of India in 1947 was largely drawn from the British parliamentary models, but a few devices were also borrowed from the United States. As is the case with any new state, including the United States in the early nineteenth century, India provides an interesting example of the evolution of governmental structure through custom and practice. It took the first four decades of politics in India to straighten out the relative power of the various parts of the government.

In the general outline of its constitution, India has a parliament consisting of two houses: The lower house is the Lok Sabha, or Council of the People, and the upper house is the Council of the States. A powerful prime minister and cabinet are responsible to the Lok Sabha, and a rather weak president oversees the whole structure. Thus far, India is a fairly standard parliamentary system, but it departs from common practice in two ways: (1) It is a federal system, with state governments that have a good deal of programmatic discretion, and (2) it has a powerful Supreme Court that can overturn actions of the rest of the government.

India is a state that faced grave problems on independence. Its people are among the poorest in the world, with an average annual income per person of $440. This places the country among the twenty most impoverished states of the world. At the same time, India's population of 1 billion people makes it the second largest state in the world and an important power on the international stage. India is deeply divided internally along lines of religion and language, with three major religions (Hindu, Sikh, and Moslem) and over fifteen major languages.

Until 1947, India was a colony of Great Britain. The pacifist leader Mohandas K. Gandhi and his Congress Party led a prolonged movement for independence, which succeeded in 1947. The Congress Party dominated early elections in the young democracy, and it was only in 1977 that an opposition coalition was able to break

Congress's hold on power. Until 1989, a somewhat changed Congress Party ruled under Prime Minister Rajiv Gandhi, but throughout the 1990s, the situation was fluid, with Congress sometimes controlling the government, sometimes not. The 1998 elections left no clear majority for any party or any stable coalition. The situation today is clearly one of competition, rather than a dominant-party system.

Against this background, let us look at the development of India's governmental institutions and particularly the Lok Sabha. One important issue that had to be worked out in practice over the early decades of independence was the power of the president, who is elected by an electoral college consisting of the members of both houses of Parliament plus the members of the state legislatures. Thus, it is conceivable that a president could be of a different party than the party that controlled the Lok Sabha and cabinet. The written constitution initially gave the president broad powers—among others, the power to rule by decree when Parliament was not in session, to declare a state of emergency and rule directly, and to dissolve Parliament or any state government and declare new elections. It might have happened that a strong, independent presidency would have evolved in India.

However, the dominance of the Congress Party ensured that this did not happen. Congress controlled both houses of Parliament and most state governments; therefore, a series of Congress Party presidents were selected by electoral colleges. The prime ministers, leaders of the Congress Party, made certain that weak and unaggressive people who would be willing to do what the prime minister told them to do were put into the presidency. Thus, the presidency developed into an office much like that of the queen in Great Britain. In a formal sense, all of the powers enumerated are the president's, but the president will exercise them only on the advice of the prime minister. This was formalized in an amendment to the Constitution in 1976, stating that the president "shall" act in accordance with the advice of the cabinet and prime minister. The practice was fixed even more firmly during a constitutional crisis the next year. In 1977, the Janata coalition won a majority of seats in the Lok Sabha, ousting the Congress Party after twenty years of dominance, and puts its own cabinet into place. This cabinet asked the president—B. D. Jatti, of the Congress Party—to dissolve the legislatures of the nine states that had Congress majorities and force new elections in those states. President Jatti hesitated for a day in doing what the cabinet requested, amid demonstrations and uproar, but finally gave in. Thus, the cabinet's supremacy over the president was established by something more dependable than words in a constitution; it was established by practice and precedent.

A second important question that had to be settled during this period was the relative power of Parliament and its cabinet vis-à-vis the Supreme Court. This question came to a point of crisis in 1967, when the Supreme Court ruled that an earlier amendment under which government land reforms were being administered was unconstitutional because it violated the fundamental rights guaranteed elsewhere in the Constitution.[5] (Among other things, the fundamental rights include a right against the

---

[5]Under the Indian Constitution, Parliament is responsible for initiating amendments to the Constitution. Many sorts of amendment can be passed by a simple majority in both houses, while certain sensitive areas require a two-thirds majority in both houses. Ratification by half the states is then necessary for the amendment to become law.

expropriation of property.) Therefore, the government could not constitutionally carry out land reform programs of the sort it wanted, and there was no way in which the Constitution could be amended that would allow it to do so. In effect, the court ruled that the fundamental rights constituted a special part of the Constitution that was above all parliamentary action.

As one might expect, this ruling caused considerable uproar. Over the next few years, the court held to its position that the fundamental rights occupied a special place in the Constitution and struck down various acts of Parliament in their name. A crisis was finally reached in 1971, when Prime Minister Indira Gandhi, frustrated at her inability to pass her reform programs, asked the president to dissolve the Lok Sabha and call for new elections. The single theme of this election was the question of parliamentary supremacy over the court. When her Congress Party swept to victory with 352 of the 518 seats in the Lok Sabha, the prime minister had a popular mandate to establish Parliament as supreme. Parliament amended the Constitution with this simple addition:

> Notwithstanding anything in this constitution, Parliament may, in exercise of its constituent power, amend by way of addition, variation or repeal, any provision of this Constitution in accordance with the procedure laid down in this Article.

The next year this amendment was challenged in the Supreme Court. After the longest series of arguments ever heard there, the court gave in and sustained Parliament's right to amend any part of the Constitution.

Between these two developments—the establishment of the supremacy of Parliament and its cabinet first over the president and then over the Supreme Court—a basically parliamentary framework similar to that of Britain's was ensured. A third crisis was required, however, to establish firmly the principle of democratic government. In 1975, Prime Minister Gandhi was found guilty in a state court of minor campaign irregularities. The opposition parties in Parliament, and some members of her own party, pressed her to resign as prime minister. To forestall such efforts, Gandhi struck first. She persuaded the president to declare a state of emergency so that she could rule dictatorially through him. She then had most of the leaders of the opposition arrested, banned a number of opposition organizations, and introduced a considerable degree of censorship for the press. In all, perhaps fifty thousand people were arrested for political reasons.[6]

This crisis for democracy was resolved in 1977, when Gandhi called for a new election to the Lok Sabha. Presumably, she thought that her party would win this election, but in a massive rejection of her seizure of power, the voters reduced the Congress Party to 153 out of the 543 seats in the Lok Sabha. Congress was out of power for the first time since 1945. Though Congress and Indira Gandhi returned to power in 1980 after the opposition parties proved incapable of governing effectively, the point had been made.[7] The 1977 election was a strong reaffirmation by the Indian people of their desire for democratic government.

---

[6] D. C. Gupta, *Indian Government and Politics,* 4th ed. (New Delhi: Vikas, 1978), p. 657.

[7] Indira Gandhi was assassinated in 1984 by her Sikh bodyguards, as a result of tensions with militant Sikhs. Her son Rajiv took her place as prime minister and leader of the Congress Party, but he was in turn assassinated in 1991 by Tamil separatists.

To focus more specifically on the Parliament of India and how it operates, let us first note that the upper house, the Council of States, has less power than the lower house. This is typical of parliamentary systems; another good example is the British House of Lords, whose mainly hereditary members have the power only to delay, not block, bills passed by the House of Commons. The members of the Council of States are not directly elected by voters, which would give them more prestige and legitimacy, but rather are chosen by the state legislatures and are sent to the Council of States to represent their states. Most bills require the Council of States' assent to become law, but there is an important limitation on this power. No money bills, including the annual budget and all tax laws, require the assent of the Council of States. The council discusses each money bill and may make suggestions to the Lok Sabha, but the Lok Sabha has sole authority to pass the bill. Finally, the most important of all limitations on the power of the Council of States is that the prime minister and cabinet are responsible only to the lower house. This is almost universally true of parliamentary systems. It means that the prime minister and cabinet require the support of a majority of the Lok Sabha to exercise their power (they can be ousted at any time by a majority vote on a motion of "no confidence"), but they cannot be ousted by the Council of States.

The Lok Sabha plays a role much like that of the House of Commons in Britain. It has full powers to pass or deny legislation, and the cabinet depends on it for its power. However, because of party discipline, the Lok Sabha is controlled by the cabinet and its members do not feel individually all that powerful. From 1991 to 1996, for instance, of 318 bills introduced by the cabinet, 284 were passed; of 406 bills introduced by individual members, not one was passed.[8]

Aside from the usual informal cabinet domination of Parliament via party discipline, the Indian Constitution also gives the cabinet some formal powers that allow it further to dominate the parliament. The most important of these is the power to rule by decree when Parliament is not sitting. This was originally intended to allow for small matters that might need immediate attention when Parliament was not in session, but cabinets have come to use it as a device for taking measures they are not sure they could get through Parliament. Such actions as wage freezes, excise taxes, and rules to control smuggling have become law in this way, sometimes just days before or after Parliament was in session.

Still, the Lok Sabha functions importantly as a place for debate and one where the opposition can regularly scrutinize what the cabinet is doing. "Question time" has been borrowed from the British and has taken on a vigorous life in India. During the first hour of each parliamentary day, members of the cabinet are questioned by members of the house and their answers debated. During the Tenth Lok Sabha (June 20, 1991, to May 10, 1996), 1,478 questions were debated in this way, out of 6,732 that had been submitted.[9] All in all, though the Lok Sabha has had the usual rocky road of an institution with a new constitution that is being "broken in," the parliamentary system of which it is a part seems to have established itself reasonably well in India.

---

[8]Lok Sabha Secretariat, *The Tenth Lok Sabha, 1991–1996: A Study* (New Delhi: Lok Sabha Secretariat, 1997), pp. 232–34.
[9]Ibid., p. 208.

Example: Parliamentary Government in Germany

Germany has a parliamentary system similar to the general model of parliamentary government presented in this chapter except that, in a number of important ways, the power of the parliament is limited so that the line of power and responsibility is not as clean as in a pure parliamentary system. The system was first set up in West Germany and has been extended, since German unification in 1990, to the eastern portion of the state as well. When the system was first set up in 1949, the disaster of Hitler's rule was still vivid in everyone's mind. The occupying forces from France, Britain, and the United States were anxious to prevent the rise of another dictator, as were the Germans who wrote the new Constitution with them. Accordingly, power was deliberately fragmented, so that it would be hard for any one person to seize it all. The resulting system of "checks and balances" may seem natural to American readers, but it blends awkwardly with parliamentary government and gives Germany a rather unusual form of parliamentarism.

Parliament is not wholly supreme in Germany, as it would be in a "pure" parliamentary system and as it nearly is in India. First, Germany, like India, is a federal system, so there are many areas of governmental activity that are not controlled by the national government. And compared with India, the national government has not devised as many ways of controlling what the state governments do. Furthermore, there is an active system of judicial review in Germany, with perhaps the most accessible Supreme Court in the world.[10] Among other things, the court has, for example, barred national administrations from outlawing the Communist Party and from establishing a national television network. Federalism and the system of judicial review were new constitutional devices for Germany in 1949, inserted into the Constitution to diffuse and limit the exercise of power.

Another limitation on the power of the lower house, the Bundestag, and its cabinet is that Germany's parliament has a powerful upper house that may bar the lower house from many actions. We have seen that the House of Lords in Britain and the Council of States in India have little power to block a bill. However, the upper house of the German parliament, the Bundesrat, does have the power to block bills of many kinds.

The Bundesrat was strengthened in the new Constitution to protect the powers of the newly established states. Its members are not directly elected but are appointed by the governments of the states. Under the Constitution, its consent is required for constitutional amendments and for any law that affects the administrative, tax, or territorial interests of the states. In practice, a series of Supreme Court decisions have established that about 60 percent of bills fall into these categories and require the support of a majority in the Bundesrat to become law. On all other bills, the lower house

---

[10] Any German citizen may bring a case directly to the Supreme Court by simple petition; this does not even require a lawyer.

may override a Bundesrat veto, but it requires more than a simple 50 percent majority in the lower house to do this.

As a result of these provisions, the lower house and its cabinet often do not have the free play to make policy that should theoretically be theirs in a parliamentary system. Whole areas of policy, such as education, are under the control of the states. The cabinet and lower house may find that what they wish to do is ruled unconstitutional by the Supreme Court. Finally, if the Bundesrat is controlled by a different party than the lower house, the cabinet may find that it continually has to compromise with the opposition to get its bills through. This was the case in the late 1970s, when a cabinet led by the Social Democratic Party was faced with a Bundesrat controlled by the Christian Democratic Party. It occurred again from 1991 to 1998, when the Social Democrats gained control of the Bundesrat, often blocking the cabinet—now led by the Christian Democrats. And finally, it happened again in the spring of 1999: the Social Democrats had won control of the Bundestag in 1998 and were the lead party in a coalition cabinet, but they lost control of the Bundesrat in 1999 when a *Land* that they had controlled came under Christian Democratic control, shifting the majority.

The system generally produces compromise, but it can sometimes produce gridlock. A good example was the government's failure in July 1997 to pass a major tax reform. The Christian Democratic-controlled cabinet passed in the Bundestag a program to reduce high-end income taxes. This was defeated in the Social Democratic-controlled Bundesrat. The Social Democrats then passed in the Bundesrat their own counterproposal, to reduce labor costs in return for increased taxes and social benefits; this plan in turn was defeated in the Bundestag. End result—no change.

The lower house is set up along the familiar lines of parliamentary government. The cabinet is responsible only to the lower house, as is standard parliamentary practice, and so the lower house controls who sits in the executive. In its turn, the cabinet uses its control of party organization to ensure strict party voting in support of its bills. From 1961 to 1980, there were only fifteen instances in which a member of a party broke ranks and voted against the party position in the Bundestag.[11]

Even within the lower house, however, there are more checks and balances than we find in a pure parliamentary system. While party leaders expect total support for their parties' positions, ordinary members have more influence over what those positions will be than is the case in Britain.

First, the parties meet regularly as caucuses to determine their positions on bills. Members actually spend more of their time in meetings of the party caucus than in full meetings of the house. Policies are debated extensively within the party caucus, and the parties have full committee structures within the caucus to give careful and skilled scrutiny to each proposed bill. Thus, the party position on bills is not dictated to ordinary members by the party leaders so strongly as it is in Britain.

---

[11]Tony Burkett, "Developments in the West German Bundestag in the 1970s," *Parliamentary Affairs* 34 (Summer 1981): 302.

Second, unlike the British House of Commons, there are about two dozen specialized standing committees with professional staffs, which scrutinize bills before they go to the full house. Parties are given strength on the committees proportional to their strength in the house, and each committee selects its own chair. Each bill must be considered twice by one of these committees before it comes before the full house for a vote, and it may be heavily amended by the committee.

The general tone of the Bundestag is businesslike and rather dull, with a strong overtone of interest-group neocorporatism. The members are highly skilled (about one-third hold doctorates) but tend not to be politically combative. In a survey in the late 1970s, 47 percent of the members were civil servants who had gone on leave to serve in the parliament, while a further 13 percent were officials of interest groups.[12] Full sessions of the house do not provide ringing rhetoric. For example, the Bundestag, like many parliaments, has a "question hour," but answers are often provided in writing by the minister rather than in person and are read to the Bundestag by an assistant.

The end result of all this is that German parliamentarism does not provide simple lines of responsibility. Even a defeat of the cabinet on a major bill in the lower house does not necessarily lead to the fall of the cabinet, because the Constitution provides for the ouster of a cabinet only under carefully specified conditions.[13]

The ruling parties cannot necessarily be held responsible by the electorate for the state of public policy, because the policy may actually not have been their choice. It may have been forced on them by the Bundesrat or the Supreme Court, or it might be policy of the "states" rather than of the central government. German parliamentarism, while it retains the general form and most of the flexibility of parliamentarism, lacks the usual advantage of a clean line of responsibility.

FURTHER READING

Abraham, Henry J. *The Judicial Process: An Introductory Analysis of the Courts of the United States, England and France.* New York: Oxford University Press, 1998.

Birch, Anthony H. *Representation.* New York: Praeger, 1971.

Bowler, Shaun; Farrell, David M.; and Katz, Richard S., eds. *Party Discipline and Parliamentary Government.* Columbus: Ohio State University Press, 1999.

Brand, Jack. *British Parliamentary Parties: Policy and Power.* New York: Oxford University Press, 1992.

Cain, Bruce; Ferejohn, John; and Fiorina, Morris. *The Personal Vote.* Cambridge: Harvard University Press, 1987.

---

[12]Ibid., p. 305. Interest-group officials generally take a special interest in their group's concerns, seeking positions on useful committees and in general binding the parliament and the interest-group system tightly together. This helps to produce a "neocorporatist" blending of interest groups and government.

[13]The only way a cabinet can be brought down is for the opposition to propose a motion of no confidence, including a statement of who the new chancellor would be; the motion requires a majority to pass. The cabinet is not required to resign if one of its major bills fails to pass.

Cox, Gary W. *The Efficient Secret.* New York: Cambridge University Press, 1987.

————, and McCubbins, Mathew D. *Legislative Leviathan: Party Government in the House.* Los Angeles: University of California Press, 1993.

Crossman, R. H. S. *The Myths of Cabinet Government.* Cambridge: Harvard University Press, 1972.

Doring, Herbert, ed. *Parliaments and Majority Rule in Western Europe.* New York: St. Martin's Press, 1995.

Fenno, Richard F., Jr. *Learning to Legislate: The Senate Education of Arlen Specter.* Washington, D.C.: Congressional Quarterly Press, 1991.

Jennings, Ivor. *Cabinet Government.* 3d ed. New York: Cambridge University Press, 1969.

Kommers, Donald P. *Judicial Politics in West Germany.* Beverly Hills, Calif.: Sage, 1976.

Kurian, George Thomas. *World Encyclopedia of Parliaments and Legislatures.* Washington, D.C.: Congressional Quarterly Books, 1997.

Laver, Michael, and Schofield, Norman. *Multiparty Government: The Politics of Coalition in Europe.* Oxford: Oxford University Press, 1990.

Miller, Warren E.; Pierce, Roy; Thomassen, Jacques; Herrera, Richard; Holmberg, Sören; Esaiasson, Peter; and Wessels, Bernhard. *Policy Representation in Western Democracies.* New York: Oxford University Press, 1999.

Olson, David M., and Mezey, Michael L., eds. *Legislatures in the Policy Process: The Dilemmas of Economic Policy.* New York: Cambridge University Press, 1991.

Pitkin, Hanna Fenichel. *The Concept of Representation.* Berkeley: University of California Press, 1967.

Przeworski, Adam; Stokes, Susan C.; and Manin, Bernard, eds. *Democracy, Accountability, and Representation.* New York: Cambridge University Press, 1999.

Rose, Richard. *The Problem of Party Government.* New York: Free Press, 1974.

Searing, Donald D. *Westminster's World: Understanding Political Roles.* Cambridge: Harvard University Press, 1994.

Strom, Kaare. *Minority Government and Majority Rule.* New York: Cambridge University Press, 1990.

————. "The Presthus Debacle: Intraparty Politics and Bargaining Failure in Norway." *American Political Science Review* 88 (March 1994): 112–27.

Parliamentary Affairs and *Legislative Studies Quarterly* are useful specialized journals relevant to this chapter.

WEBSITES OF INTEREST

Inter-Parliamentary Union, with links to the parliaments of many countries:
http://www.ipu.org/english/parlweb.htm

U.S. Senate:
http://www.senate.gov

U.S. House of Representatives:
http://www.house.gov

Roll Call, a daily newspaper covering the U.S. Congress:
http://www.rollcall.com

Project Vote Smart, a site with information about campaign finance and voting records of members of Congress:

http://www.vote-smart.org

British Parliament:

http://www.parliament.uk

Canadian government, with wide range of features on the Canadian Parliament, prime minister, and cabinet:

http://canada.gc.ca/main_e.html

15

NATIONAL
DECISION-MAKING
INSTITUTIONS:
PRESIDENTIAL
GOVERNMENT

Presidential government is a democratic system in which the legislature and the executive exist independently and are elected independently of each other. Both parts of the governmental apparatus are responsible for the making and carrying out of law; but they are independent, so it often happens that they compete and find themselves in conflict. The executive and the legislature are not forced into the kind of cooperation that tends to be ensured in a parliamentary system, where the two depend closely on one another.

Just as the political party provides a glue that allows the parliament and its cabinet to function in intimate cooperation, so, in a presidential system, the political party may operate to soften the natural competition between independent executives and legislatures. In the United States, for example, the president, as head of one of the two great parties, is always guaranteed a large number of friends in the Congress. The system does not force the sort of unity on the president and his party's members of Congress that we would see in a parliamentary system, but still the bond of party allows for a good deal of coordination and cooperation.

However, note two things about presidential-legislative cooperation via party ties:

1. Parties are often more loosely unified in presidential systems than in parliamentary systems. In parliamentary systems, the premier and cabinet hold over the heads of ordinary members of parliament the threat that they may not advance into executive office if they do not cooperate with the leadership. In a presidential system, the president has little control over the careers and advancement of members of the legislature and cannot force unity on them. Even when the president's party has a majority of the seats in the legislature, the president will usu-

ally not be able to control what happens in the legislature as closely as most cabinets can control their parliaments in parliamentary systems.

2.   There is no guarantee that the party that holds the presidency will also control the legislature. The two parts of the governmental apparatus are elected independently; therefore, it may well happen that one party will have prevailed in the presidential election and another in elections for the legislature. For instance, throughout the 1980s, the Republican Party held the U.S. presidency and at times controlled the Senate, but the Democratic Party controlled the House of Representatives. And the same situation held in reverse for much of the 1990s. When there is divided control such as this, cooperation between the two branches of government is even more fragile.

The most famous presidential system in the world, of course, is that of the United States. A number of Latin American states also use versions of the presidential system, as do several other states around the world, including France and Turkey. In some of these, unified parties provide for more coordination than is found in the United States. In Mexico, for instance, the huge Party of the Institutionalized Revolution held the presidency and controlled the Chamber of Deputies continually from 1929 to 1997, when it lost control of the Chamber. Mexico's Constitution also provides the president with a great deal of independent power; under these circumstances, at least until 1997, it did not prove difficult to provide coordinated policy making. As a rule, however, presidential systems exhibit a good deal less coordination between the executive and the legislature than we see in parliamentary systems.

The legislature is a coequal body to the executive in a presidential system, so how is the legislature organized and how does it function? In a parliamentary system, the cabinet organizes the business of the legislature, but in a presidential system, the legislature must organize itself. How is this done? The U.S. Congress provides a good example.

The U.S. Congress consists of two equal houses, the House of Representatives and the Senate. Each house is governed by leaders elected by the party that has a majority in the house and by strong, independent committees whose chairs are appointed from among members of the majority party. Seniority—the length of time one has served in the house— is the dominant factor in deciding who will chair committees. For instance, in 2001, the Republican Party had a majority in the House of Representatives, and the Democrats had a majority in the Senate. The majority leader of the Senate was Tom Daschle of South Dakota, and the speaker of the House was Dennis Hastert of Illinois. These two men exercised considerable influence over the business of their two houses, partly through their ability to persuade and partly through formal powers, such as the power to influence appointments to committees, to assign bills to committees, and to preside over debate.

However, the leaders cannot dominate their houses. Any bill must first be considered by a committee, and these committees operate independently and put their own considerable mark on bills that they bring to the full house. Power in each of the houses is so diffused—among leaders, committees, the minority party, and so on—that no one can be said to control what happens in either one.

The absence of control is heightened by the fact that voting in Congress is much less a party affair than it would be in a parliament. As we have seen, in a parliamentary system, regular failure by members to support their party's position would lead to collapse

(Copyright by Gene Basset. Reprinted with permission.)

of the cabinet; for this reason, among others, members usually vote tightly along party lines. In the Congress, this incentive for discipline is lacking, and so members of Congress choose their votes more individually. Through the 1980s and 1990s, fewer than half of all bills passed by the House of Representatives were "party votes" even in the modest sense that over half the Democrats voted on one side and over half the Republicans on the other.

PRESIDENTIAL AND PARLIAMENTARY SYSTEMS COMPARED

What difference does it make whether a state is a parliamentary or a presidential system? Some differences include the following (I will expand on each of these in the next several sections):

- Policy leadership is often more clearly lodged with a president than with a parliamentary cabinet.
- Responsibility for policy is more difficult to identify in a presidential system.
- Comprehensive policy is more difficult to accomplish in a presidential system than in a parliamentary system.
- Recruitment of executive leaders differs in the two systems.
- There are special problems for review and control of the executive in a presidential system.
- The symbolic and political aspects of the executive are unified in a presidential system but split in a parliamentary system.
- Constitutional review of some sort seems to be more necessary in a presidential system, as is true in general of divided systems of power.

Let us first consider the question of policy leadership. Presidents have a personal mandate from the voters; therefore, they are able to take more direct personal charge of policy than the cabinet can in a parliamentary system. A parliamentary cabinet owes its position to its parties' members in the parliament, and it must operate with them as a team. The president, on the other hand, is personally elected by the voters of the nation, and this is true of no other public official. This personal mandate focuses attention on the president, who is accordingly thrust into a position of policy leadership.

Unlike the cabinet in a parliamentary system, the presidential cabinet does not consist of party notables whose appointments are obligatory. Rather, presidents appoint a group of cabinet officials who will be beholden to them personally. Often, these officials come from positions in which they have had little political exposure: Over the last few decades, presidential cabinets in the United States have included college professors, lawyers, auto company executives, military officers, a president's brother, and other relatively nonpolitical figures. In general, prominent political figures are *not* included, and this helps to focus attention directly on the president and the president's staff.

In most presidential systems, the president is constitutionally designated as the commander in chief of the state's armed forces and is personally charged with the responsibility to direct the affairs of the state, dictatorially if necessary, in the event of war or emergency. The president is also given personal responsibility for the direction of foreign policy.

Finally, in the making of laws, the legislative branch in a presidential system habitually puts itself in a passive stance, waiting to respond to proposals that the president is expected to put forward.

A presidential system, then, provides for a coherent and unified policy leadership that may be lacking in a parliamentary cabinet, especially if that cabinet is formed of a coalition of parties and most especially if the state suffers from cabinet instability.

RESPONSIBILITY FOR POLICY

Though a presidential system provides a clear focus for *leadership,* ironically, it blurs the final *responsibility* for policies. In a presidential system, no one part of the governmental apparatus can be held responsible for any particular policy or any particular lack of policy. If the president proposes a new energy tax and the tax is defeated in Congress, who is responsible for the lack of tax reform? Is the Congress obstinate? Should the president have proposed a tax that would have been more apt to pass? Should the president have lobbied harder for the bill? It might also happen that the bill would pass, but with amendments that changed it substantially. Is it now the president's bill? Congress's? No one's?

Presidential systems do not present a clear picture of the responsibility for policies; therefore, they exhibit two important weaknesses. First, when voters cannot pin the responsibility for policies on any particular official, their electoral choices become less significant. Should a voter upset at inflation in the United States in 1948 have voted Republican? That would have been a vote against the party of President Harry Truman, who should perhaps have been held responsible for the inflation. What if the "do-nothing" Republican-controlled Congress was at fault, as Truman claimed? Faced with a choice like this, the poor bewildered voter must vote on less policy-related criteria, such as a candidate's personality or personal favors that an incumbent candidate has been able to do while in office. Eventually, elections come to function less as vehicles by which voters can affect the making of policy.[1]

A second weakness of presidential government caused by its blurring of responsibility is that when public officials do not have clear responsibility for a policy, they may literally begin to behave irresponsibly. If Congress is not directly held responsible for producing a balanced budget, it is easy for members of Congress to vote simultaneously to cut taxes (which will look good to their constituents) and to build highways (which will also look good). "Through the fault of no one in particular," the government may spend more than it takes in.

Campaign platforms of U.S. parties provide another example of the chronic irresponsibility of presidential systems. Because a party's president cannot be blamed for failing to enact into law the party's promises—after all, Congress might not cooperate—it becomes easy for the parties to promise in their campaign platforms whatever they think the voters would like to hear. With power as fragmented as it is in a presidential system, the parties will never lack for an alibi if the voters should take them to task for not delivering on their promises.

PRESIDENTIAL SYSTEMS AND COMPREHENSIVE POLICY

It is more difficult to make comprehensive policies in a presidential system than in a parliamentary one. Policies are more likely to be patched together of varied compromises or perhaps not put together at all. The United States is one of the few democracies that lacks a national energy policy, though this has not been for want of trying. Presidents have proposed energy policies to Congress but have never been able to get agreement on anything recognizable as a policy.

It is not enough that a mere majority of the people want something done, because a bill can be blocked at the many points in a fragmented system; considerably more than a majority is required if all the defensive positions provided by a fragmented system are to be overrun. Handgun control, prayer in the schools, and the equal rights amendment are examples of policies that a majority of the U.S. population want but that have been impossible to enact into law.

If you are suspicious of majorities, as many of the authors of the U.S. Constitution were, this may be seen as a good effect of the fragmentation of power. But there is no denying that it makes the government slow to respond to change.

RECRUITMENT OF EXECUTIVE LEADERS

There is a significant difference between the sorts of leaders who emerge in parliamentary and presidential systems. In a parliamentary system, all or almost all the leaders in the executive have emerged from careers in parliament; indeed, they continue to serve

---

[1] A large body of literature has long urged that the United States should try to accomplish "responsible party government" similar to that of Britain. The argument has been that U.S. parties should become more tightly disciplined, not that the constitutional division of power should be changed. A good example is E. E. Schattschneider, *Party Government* (New York: Holt, Rinehart and Winston, 1942).

in the parliament while they hold executive office. This means that they will have had fairly similar lives before they entered the executive. For a decade or two, their jobs will have consisted of crafting the wording of bills and serving the voters in their constituency. They will have had a long period of exposure to the wide range of issues facing the state in diplomacy, tax policy, education, defense, and so on.

The similarity of these executive officers is made greater by the fact that they are mostly selected from among the members of the parliament on the basis of a common set of criteria. Members who move up to executive office are those who do a good job of being a member of parliament: They debate well, they keep their noses to the grindstone, they do not make waves.

Recruitment in a parliamentary system has the virtue that officials are chosen *by those who know them and their work* (their fellow members of parliament) *during a career that has made them familiar with most of the issues they will have to face.* It has the disadvantage that *there is not much variety among the types of people chosen, they have had little experience in managing things* (legislators spend most of their time responding to initiatives of others), *and there are few "mavericks" or adventurers included.*

In a presidential system, recruitment into executive office is fairly independent of the legislative parts of government. While a president may have started off with a legislative career, this is by no means necessary. Consider the last ten presidents of the United States:

PRESIDENT	BACKGROUND
Dwight D. Eisenhower	Army general
John F. Kennedy	Senator
Lyndon B. Johnson	Senator
Richard M. Nixon	Senator; vice president
Gerald Ford	Member of Congress
Jimmy Carter	Farmer; governor of Georgia
Ronald Reagan	Film actor; governor of California
George Bush	Appointee to various foreign policy positions; vice president
William Clinton	Governor of Arkansas
George W. Bush	Governor of Texas

More than half of these men had established themselves with the public by something other than service in one of the houses of Congress.

Furthermore, the recruitment of other officials to staff the executive does not draw heavily on Congress in the United States or in most other presidential systems. Only a minority of the membership of recent U.S. presidents' cabinets have been drawn from careers in the Senate or House. Many of the most distinctive and interesting cabinet members have been drawn from careers that were far from Congress, careers that gave them interesting points of view of their own. Four examples are Robert McNamara, secretary of defense under Kennedy and Johnson, a Ford Motor Company executive; Henry Kissinger, secretary of state under Nixon and Ford, a university professor; Donna Shalala, secretary of health and human services under Clinton, chancellor of the University of Wisconsin; and Colin Powell, secretary of state under George W. Bush, Army general.

This sort of selection has the advantage that it brings varied talents and backgrounds to the task of executive so that through the introduction of new blood, problems may be seen in a new light. New points of view and the zeal of amateurs may be brought into policy making at a high level, as in Jimmy Carter's campaigns on behalf of human rights.

On the other hand, selection is often haphazard, because it is not done by those who have worked directly with the candidates; candidates may have little previous experience in important areas (Carter, Reagan, Clinton, and George W. Bush, for instance, had had no experience with foreign policy before they became president); and inappropriate choices are more likely than in a parliamentary system.[2]

In short, in a parliamentary system you know much more what you are getting than in a presidential system. For better or for worse, executive officials will not surprise you in a parliamentary system—but they will not disappoint you, either.

REVIEW AND CONTROL OF THE EXECUTIVE

Most organizations have some sort of plural board to which the executive leader is responsible and reports regularly. The president of a business corporation must report regularly to a board of directors, the president of a university reports to the board of trustees of the university, a superintendent of schools reports to a school board, and so on.

In a parliamentary system, the parliament serves this purpose. The prime minister and cabinet regularly report to the parliament on the conduct of their business, questions are asked, and so on. There is regular and frequent contact between the cabinet and the parliament regarding the conduct of government.[3]

In a presidential system, however, the members of the executive operate in relative isolation. The media looks over their shoulders constantly, of course, and there is occasionally contact between them and the legislature regarding a particular bill or investigation. However, there is no broader body to which the president or other members of the executive regularly report.

This isolation of the presidency often leads to an inward-looking presidential office, with "inside" staff persons accused by those on the outside of arrogance and insensitivity. More serious, the lack of some regular device for review and control of the president made the Watergate crisis a good deal more traumatic for the United States than it might otherwise have been. When President Nixon was implicated in petty crimes at the Watergate office complex and it became apparent that some airing of the question was needed, there was no regular stage available for this, and extraordinary procedures for impeachment were required. Had he been a prime minister, he would have been called to task in the parliament as a matter of ordinary business.

[2]An argument for the desirability of recruitment in the parliamentary mode is made in Harold W. Chase, Robert Holt, and John Turner, *American Government in Comparative Perspective* (New York: Franklin Watts, 1980), chap. 2.

[3]For further comparison along these lines, see William S. Livingston, "Britain and America: The Institutionalization of Accountability," *Journal of Politics* 38 (November 1976): 870–94.

(Cartoon by Dana Summers. Reprinted by permission of The *Orlando Sentinel*.)

THE SPLIT EXECUTIVE OF PARLIAMENTARY SYSTEMS

Oddly enough, given that parliamentary systems are based on the principle of unifying power, the executive is split in parliamentary systems into the prime minister and cabinet who are responsible for political and administrative leadership, and some other office that is responsible for the symbolic leadership of the state. In a presidential system, these functions are united in the president.

In Britain, the prime minister and cabinet are responsible for political and administrative leadership, but it is the queen who carries on the ceremonies and personifies the state. It is she who opens new hospitals and bridges; it is her health and that of her family that the media subjects to ghoulish scrutiny; it is she at whose death the nation will go into deep mourning. Like the president of the United States, she is greeted by a special song when she enters a room, and crowds press in on her wherever she goes. The prime minister remains a more mundane figure, one who goes about the daily business of governing but does not personally represent the state.

It is clear why the two kinds of executive function are united in one person in a presidential system. The executive is weakened in a presidential system by the fact that its legislature is not under its control; for strong leadership to be available to the state, almost everything that *can* be done to strengthen the president's hand *must* be done. One such thing, an important one, is to give presidents an aura of majesty that they can use to bolster their political power. More than one member of Congress has gone into the White House and walked out shaken, muttering, "When the president of the United States asks you to vote in the country's interest, what can you do?"

In a parliamentary system, there is no need to add to the power of the cabinet in this way, because the cabinet is capable of providing effective leadership without it. If it is not necessary to combine the two faces of the executive in a single office, as is done in presidential systems, there are some obvious advantages to separating them.

First, the symbolic representation of the state in a person appears to fill a deep need of a modern people. The devotion people feel for those who personify their state is real. Consider the following examples. At John F. Kennedy's assassination in 1963, many Americans felt what they later reported as an almost religious experience. In Britain, the most disturbing political event of the twentieth century, with the sole exception of the two world wars, occurred when Prince Edward VIII left the throne to marry a divorced American. Norwegians credit King Haakon VII with having almost singlehandedly kept the government from surrendering to Germany in 1941, taking his family into exile and making it possible for Norwegians to fight on in the Resistance. Finally, consider the heart-wrenching difficulty with which Americans faced what would have been a fairly simple task if they had not revered the presidency so much—the ouster of Richard M. Nixon in 1974 when he had been implicated in petty crimes.

If modern people need a person on whom to focus their reverence for the state, it is better if this is someone who has little involvement in day-to-day politics. The queen of Britain, the king of Sweden, the emperor of Japan, the "president" of Germany (not a president as the term is used in this chapter, but an almost purely ceremonial figure)—these people have almost no political power and are not involved in routine decision making. This allows them to serve as unblemished objects of national affection. Presidents of the United States, in contrast, must excite mixed feelings among the many people who find themselves in political disagreement with them. On the one hand, these people want to revere the president, but on the other hand, they find themselves faced with a political leader whose policies they may despise. Corporation executives and Republicans were in many ways deprived of an object for national reverence during the presidency of Franklin Delano Roosevelt, as were welfare recipients and Democrats during the presidency of Ronald Reagan, and conservative Republicans during the presidency of Bill Clinton.

Thus, one problem of blending the political executive and the symbolic executive in a single office is that the symbolic function cannot be performed as well when it is located in an office that is inevitably involved in controversy.

The flip side of this problem is that political leadership does not operate as cleanly when reverence for the state gets mixed up with it. A president of the United States gains unfair political advantage from serving as the symbol of the state. Franklin Roosevelt, Lyndon Johnson, Richard Nixon, and Ronald Reagan were quite adept at taking positions that had questionable public support, appearing on radio or television with the sober attention that a president can command, and selling that endangered program to the public. After all, this man is the president of the United States! Whom can we trust more than him?

We may welcome this as a way to cut through the confusion of the divided powers of a presidential system, but it is still unfortunate that, on any public issue at a given time, only one side is able to take advantage of this reverential response. In a parliamentary system, the cabinet and the opposition operate on more even terms in seeking public support for their political positions.[4]

WHY AREN'T ALL DEMOCRACIES PARLIAMENTARY SYSTEMS?

Let us review for a moment what we have looked at in this chapter. I first described how presidential government operates, and I noted the main difference between a parliamentary system and a presidential system: that the one unifies power and the other divides it. I then examined several aspects of presidential government that result from this difference:

- Concentration of policy leadership with the president
- Difficulty of locating responsibility for policies
- Difficulty of making comprehensive policy
- A different pattern of recruitment for executive leaders
- Special problems for review and control
- A merger of the symbolic and political aspects of the executive in a single office

While not every one of these differences showed the presidential system to disadvantage, most did. You have probably been left with the impression that parliamentary systems are better than presidential ones. The parliamentary system is a simpler, more direct, and usually more efficient way of making public choices. Why aren't all democracies parliamentary systems?

The main reason lies in the very faithfulness with which a parliamentary system transposes political divisions into the policy-making machinery. Policy is set and administered in a parliamentary system by a party or a cooperative coalition of parties that controls a majority of the votes in the parliament. This makes for straightforward policy making if a stable majority is possible in the parliament. If the country is divided into numerous parties that are intensely hostile to each other, however, it may be impossible to find a large enough number of members of parliament who can work together cooperatively as a governing coalition. It may be that no working majority is available.

Under these circumstances, a parliamentary system may limp along with an unstable government, as Italy has done since 1945, or the country may prefer to use some system that divides power but is more stable than what parliamentarism could provide.

France after World War II was plagued by parliamentary instability similar to that of Italy. The Communists could not cooperate with any of the other parties, Catholic parties had trouble cooperating with Socialists, and so on. In 1958, the regime collapsed through a revolt by French settlers in Algeria. The military terminated the fourth Republic and asked Charles de Gaulle to design a new system; his new constitution replaced parliamentary government with a version of presidential government.

In much of the South, too, democracies, whether or not they started out as parliamentary systems, have often found that they must provide a more stable base for executive

---

[4]Related arguments may be found in Edward Shils and Michael Young, "The Meaning of the Coronation," *Sociological Review* 1 (December 1953): 63–81; and in Lewis Lipsitz, "If, as Verba Says, the State Functions as a Religion, What Are We to Do Then to Save Our Souls?" *American Political Science Review* 52 (June 1968): 527–35.

Presidential Leadership

The presidency offers us a particularly good chance to study a vital aspect of politics that is much neglected in political science—leadership. Certainly, few things are more important to politics than the qualities that produce effective political leadership, but leadership is a difficult thing to pin down for analysis. Most political figures—members of Congress, prime ministers, cabinet officials—operate within such constraints of power that their main accomplishments come through bargaining and deal-making or through coalitions where their role is blended with that of others. It is often hard to pull out of a particular political outcome the contribution of any one person's leadership.

The American presidency, however, offers us an office whose leadership is available for examination every day in almost all political questions that face the country. Further, it is exceedingly well documented, with huge libraries of the papers of all postwar presidents. Various scholars have taken this opportunity to study leadership by studying the presidency—notably Richard E. Neustadt, who analyzed presidents' political strategies in *Presidential Power and the Modern Presidents* (New York: Free Press, 1991), and James David Barber, who analyzed presidents' emotional security and its effect on how productively they could provide leadership in *The Presidential Character* (Englewood Cliffs, N.J.: Prentice-Hall, 1977). But a superbly broad view of presidential leadership, based on decades of observation and reflection, is Fred I. Greenstein's *The Presidential Difference: Leadership Style from FDR to Clinton* (Princeton, N.J.: Princeton University Press, 2000).

Greenstein views leadership as a function of six qualities, which could probably never all be perfected in any one person; for him, each of our modern presidents has represented a mix of strengths and weaknesses on these six qualities:

- *proficiency as a public communicator*
- *organizational capacity*—the ability to choose good advisors and to use them in such a way that they did not just parrot back his desired opinion but helped him to work through policy choices in a thoughtful way
- *political skill*—the ability to get other people to do what he wanted
- *vision*—having an overarching goal and the ability to see how specific policies would help bring about that goal
- *cognitive style*—the ability to process the torrent of advice and information the president receives on every issue. In other words, the ability to understand the policies he was pushing for.
- *emotional intelligence*—"the ability to manage his emotions and turn them to constructive purposes, rather than being dominated by them and allowing them to diminish his leadership."[1]

Greenstein does not rank these six characteristics (and resists in his book playing the cheap and easy game of ranking the presidents), but it appears that for him, the most critical qualities are proficiency as a public communicator and emotional intelligence. Cognitive style appears to rank surprisingly low among the criteria for success. As Greenstein points out, the two presidents whom he regards as weakest in cognitive capacity—Truman, because he relied too much on oversimplified analogies drawn from his readings of popular history, and Reagan because he just didn't care about details—were two presidents who had a major impact on the country.

---

[1]Fred I. Greenstein, *The Presidential Difference: Leadership and Style from FDR to Clinton* (New York: Free Press, 2000), p. 6. Both Greenstein and I, by the way, use the exclusively male pronoun here to describe an office that until now has always been held by men. This almost certainly will not be the case for much longer.

leadership than is possible under parliamentarism, even at the cost of fragmenting and complicating public decision-making processes. Many Latin American democracies, under the influence of the United States, used presidential systems from the start; Mexico and Costa Rica are good examples. Many African and Asian democracies— faced with the political stresses of poverty, modernization, and ethnic diversity—have had to modify what started out as parliamentary systems. Nigeria, for example, abandoned parliamentarism when democratic government was reestablished in 1975 and set up a system with an independent presidency rather like that of the United States.[5] Turkey has established a presidential system similar to that of France. Russia has a strong presidency.

Perhaps the message of this chapter, in the end, is that a parliamentary system is the best form of democracy *if* a country is sufficiently unified to cooperate in parliamentary politics.

CONSTITUTIONAL REVIEW AND THE FRAGMENTATION OF POWER

Wherever power is fragmented, whether in a presidential system (which divides power between different parts of a national government) or a federal one (which divides power between a central government and regional governments), there is a need for some institution that can operate as a referee to adjudicate disputes among the various holders of power. If a president has part of the power and a legislature has another part, how do we resolve the kind of dispute that must inevitably occur when the legislature says to the president, "You've just done something that's supposed to be left up to us"—or vice versa? How do we resolve disputes over whether the central government or the regional governments have jurisdiction in a particular question? The solution is to have some third institution that is empowered to serve as a referee. In the United States, this is the Supreme Court.

Over the last two centuries, the U.S. Supreme Court has established that it has the right to annul acts of presidents and laws passed by Congress whenever it deems either body to have exceeded its proper powers. Although there is occasional grumbling about the Court and its power, it is striking how readily this essentially undemocratic arrangement is tolerated. Think of it! Nine people who are appointed by the president and the Senate and thereafter serve for the rest of their lives without ever being subject to popular election—these nine people wield huge power in our otherwise democratic system. The only explanation for Americans' ready toleration of this is their recognition that the fragmentation of power requires something like this to make their system work.

Constitutional review is found in almost all systems that fragment power and is rare in those that do not. There are two main ways by which a constitution may fragment power: by establishing a presidential system, as has been discussed here; or by establishing a federal system to divide power between a central government and regional governments.

[5]This, in turn, succumbed to a military coup in 1983, but an elected presidency was reestablished in 1999.

TABLE 15–1   CONSTITUTIONAL REVIEW, FEDERALISM, AND PRESIDENTIAL
GOVERNMENT: WESTERN EUROPE AND NORTH AMERICA

	Constitutional review	
States with a federal system and/or presidential government		
Austria	Yes	
Belgium		No
Canada	Yes	
France	Yes	
Germany	Yes	
Mexico	Yes	
Portugal	Yes	
Spain	Yes	
Switzerland		No
U.S.A.	Yes	
States with neither a federal system nor presidential government		
Denmark		No
Great Britain		No
Iceland		No
Ireland	Yes	
Italy	Yes	
Luxembourg		No
Netherlands		No
Norway		No
Sweden		No

(See Chapter 10.) In Table 15–1, the states of Western Europe and North America are
divided according to whether the governmental system is parliamentary or presidential
and according to whether power is unified geographically or fragmented federally; we
then note for each state whether it has a system of constitutional review. Belgium and
Switzerland are the only systems with fragmented power of either sort that do not provide for judicial review. While most unitary parliamentary systems do not provide for
constitutional review, Ireland and Italy do.

The main exception to this rule (that fragmented power is the reason for constitutional
review) is that constitutional review has also had some popularity since World War II as
a means of protecting individuals from the arbitrary use of state power. That is, constitutional review has been seen as a tool of "constitutionalism," in which a relatively nonpolitical court can help to place limits on the authority of the government.[6] This helps to

---

[6]See the discussion of constitutionalism in Chapter 10.

A president does many things—President George W. Bush shakes hands with Milwaukee Brewers' manager Davey Lopes, left, after throwing out the ceremonial first pitch before the start of the Brewers' home opener.

George Bush: © Morry Gash/AP/Wide World Photos.

explain the popularity of constitutional review in Germany after the Nazi dictatorship, although the federal system there probably would have required it in any case. More to the point, it also helps to explain the institution of constitutional review in Ireland and Italy, which have neither federal systems nor presidential governments.

A NOTE ON CONSTITUTIONS AND POWER

Having looked at formal governmental arrangements in this chapter and in Chapter 14, I should note an important principle of constitutions that is well illustrated by the development of some of the governmental institutions we have examined.

We saw in Chapter 10 that written constitutions are not static but change and develop as they are put to use. One predictable way in which constitutions change is this: *If power is given constitutionally to a body that lacks the resources to exercise it, informal mechanisms usually develop, leading to the de facto loss of that power* even though the formality of power remains.

One excellent example of this principle at work is the domination of parliaments by their cabinets. Parliaments are vested with supreme authority in the constitutions of parliamentary systems, but a parliament is too large and diverse a group to actually take charge of governmental policy by itself. Over the years, cabinets have developed ways to bully parliaments through the informal mechanism of the disciplined political party.

This has shifted actual power from the parliament to its cabinet, which allows policy to be made coherently; but the parliaments remain *formally* supreme. Political parties are rarely even mentioned in the constitutions of democracies, but they have become an important part of living constitutions.

A second example of this principle is the problem of "localism" in the French parliament before 1958. France long had a tradition of central governmental dominance over towns and regions. If a town wished to build a new school or pave a new set of streets, it needed to get the permission of the government in Paris to do so. These arrangements gave the central government great formal power, but its exercise involved such a huge number of minuscule decisions that it was impossible for any central operation to do a good job of making them. In self-defense, over the late nineteenth and early twentieth centuries, town governments devised ways in which they could get special treatment from the government in Paris. Parliament was a special target of these efforts because the members of the parliament were elected from local districts. Town governments tried, with a great deal of success, to convince the local members of parliament to take as one of their chief tasks in Paris the furthering of local causes. Members of parliament eventually spent much of their time and effort in making deals—trading votes with other members so that their towns could get the necessary permission and funds to build town halls or install streetlights. Party discipline declined, and many members' votes were heavily influenced by the deals they had cut with other members, so that the directions of party leaders were often ignored. This trend was a major cause of the increasing instability of the national government. (France had twenty-five different cabinets in the thirteen years from 1945 to 1958.) Therefore, the formal power over localities' decisions, supposed to *strengthen* the central government, helped to weaken it.

A third example is provided by the Bundesrat, the upper house of the German parliament, described in Chapter 14. The Bundesrat, you will recall, was established in the Constitution to protect the independence of the new "states" from the central government. If Germany was to be a federal system, it was reasoned, the states needed a lever in the central government to allow them a veto over actions that would take away their rights. Therefore, the Bundesrat was established. It consists of representatives from the state governments and must give its consent to any action affecting their tax, administrative, or territorial interests.

Ironically, setting up the Bundesrat and giving it these powers has made it, and the states that appoint its members, sufficiently important to national political leaders that they try to control what goes on in state politics and have undermined the independence of state leaders in important ways. Elections for state governments often turn on a national issue rather than on those of the state. Figures from the central government campaign hard in the state, not for local figures or for the local party but on national political questions. And once a state election is over, national leaders often put pressure on local leaders to form a particular sort of coalition in the state parliament solely because of the effect the nature of the local coalition will have on the state's votes in the Bundesrat.[7] The existence of the Bundesrat has arguably had an effect just the opposite of

---

[7]For an early example, see Arnold J. Heidenheimer, "Federalism and the Party System: The Case of West Germany," *American Political Science Review* 52 (September 1958): 809–28.

what was intended by the framers of Germany's Constitution. The states' prerogatives would have probably been protected adequately by the Supreme Court if the Bundesrat had never been set up, and local political leaders would have been free to operate more independently of national leaders.

In these examples, actual power relationships—the living constitution—have fit themselves to the power of groups in ways quite different from what was intended by those who designed the formal document. Such mismatches between reality and formal rules usually result from a failure to appreciate fully the "power" in "power and choice." If one thinks of politics primarily as a question of working out choices for the state, it will seem that an appropriate set of procedures should do that, and the choice making will follow from the procedures. This ignores the necessities of power and can lead to surprises for those who write rules.

Example: Presidential Government in France

After World War II, France set up a fairly standard parliamentary system. It was immobilized, however, by the hostility of various parties to each other and by weak discipline within many of them, which made it difficult for coalitions to form and hold together. The average life of a cabinet was about six months, and because ministers did not stay in place long enough to get full control of their offices, France was governed by its bureaucracy rather than by its elected leadership.[8] There was a sense of drift, and when in 1958 tensions associated with Algeria's war for independence were added to the mix, things fell apart. The military took over, and Charles de Gaulle, the hero of World War II, was brought in to set up a new system.

De Gaulle and his advisers designed a new type of democracy with elements of presidential and parliamentary government in which, however, the presidential elements have gradually come to dominate. As first designed, the system consisted of a cabinet responsible to the National Assembly (the lower house of parliament) and of a rather powerful but nonpolitical president. The president, indirectly elected by an assembly of parliament and of mayors, was, in turn, to designate the premier and to preside over the affairs of government, especially foreign affairs and defense policy. The president could bring issues before the French electorate in the form of a referendum and could, if necessary, declare a state of emergency and take over power for up to six months at a time. The president could not veto acts of parliament.

Although this was a powerful position, it did not provide much more than what is implicit in the powers of the queen of England or what was implicit in the powers of

---

[8]Ironically, the bureaucracy governed France rather well. During this period, France pioneered in establishing the European Economic Community, and its per capita income grew at a rate of 3.5 percent annually in real terms throughout the 1950s.

the French president from 1945 to 1958. The key question was whether the French president would act as a primarily symbolic figure, performing these functions only on the
advice of the cabinet, or would realize the full potential of the office's powers. De Gaulle
served as the first president under the new system from 1958 to 1969. He exercised his
potential power strongly and added to that power in three important ways:

- In 1962, he had the Constitution changed so that the president was directly
  elected. The president has since then carried great prestige as the only official
  elected by all the people of France.
- He set up an executive office with a structure that paralleled the ministries of the
  cabinet. Any bill that a ministry wished to submit to parliament had to be cleared
  by its counterpart bureau in the executive office. Eventually, many important
  policies began to be set in the executive office even without the knowledge of
  the minister involved.
- He established the principle that a president could dismiss a premier at will. The
  Constitution states that the president "designates" the premier but says nothing
  about dismissal. In 1962, de Gaulle asked his first premier, Michel Debre, to
  resign, and Debre did so. From that point on, another important element of presidential power had been established.

Today, as long as the same party simultaneously holds the presidency and controls
the parliament, the premier and cabinet function as agents of the president, conducting much of the day-to-day business of the state and representing the president in relations with the parliament.

The new Constitution included a large number of constraints on the independence
of the parliament, intended to prevent the immobility that had characterized French
government before 1958. An absolute majority of members is required to overthrow
a cabinet, so that abstentions or absent members count as votes in favor of the cabinet on a motion of confidence. When the cabinet submits a bill to the parliament, the
cabinet has the right to list the priority within which the bill will be debated and the
rules of debate; therefore, the cabinet is given considerable power in scheduling the
work of the parliament. (Among other rules, the cabinet can require that a bill be
voted on as a whole, rather than having a separate vote on any amendment; this frequently used device makes it difficult to amend a bill.) Members of the parliament
are constitutionally barred from offering amendments to a bill that would have the
effect of either adding to state expenditures or decreasing state revenues; an amendment requiring new expenditure, for instance, must include either a compensating cut
in some other expenditure or an increase in taxes. Finally, the independence and
power of parliamentary committees were decreased by the simple device of limiting
their number to six. This ensured that they would be large bodies (the average size of
committees is over a hundred members) covering broad areas of policy and that they
would never again be able to develop into tight-knit groups of specialists.

By laying down these rules, the new French Constitution brought about executive
supremacy of the sort that in most parliamentary systems is achieved informally
through the political party. Constitutional design was used to ensure executive
supremacy because parties had failed to establish the necessary discipline. One could

argue that the informal device is better because it is more flexible, but the constitutional devices appear to have worked well in France.

These rules established executive domination over the parliament, and—as things have developed in France—"executive" usually means the president. However, an oddity of the French hybrid of parliamentary and presidential systems is that, because the president governs through a cabinet that can be turned out of office at will by the National Assembly, it is crucial whether the same party controls the presidency and the National Assembly. If the president's party has a majority (or close to it) in the National Assembly, things work smoothly in the way I have described previously; the president names a cabinet, and the party's majority in the National Assembly supports it. This has been the situation for all but ten of the more than forty years since the establishment of the Fifth Republic.

However, if the president's party does not control the National Assembly, there is a possibility of deadlock. It is at least theoretically possible that the president could name cabinet upon cabinet that would be voted down by the National Assembly as quickly as they were named. The president could not rule under these circumstances.

Split control of the presidency and National Assembly has occurred three times. In 1985, conservatives won a majority in the National Assembly, and President François Mitterrand, a socialist, had to appoint Jacques Chirac, a Gaullist, to the premiership. No one knew how this would work; but it turned out that when the premier and the president are of different parties, more of the executive power rests with the premier than with the president, although both are then powerful. Mitterrand chose the ministers for defense and foreign affairs, while Chirac chose the rest; legislative initiatives lay wholly with Chirac and his cabinet, although Mitterrand limited Chirac's ability to promulgate decrees; and at international conferences both Mitterrand and Chirac represented France, dividing allotted speaking time between them (!).

This period of split control, dubbed "cohabitation" by the French, lasted only three years. In 1988, a newly reelected President Mitterrand took advantage of the enthusiasm over his victory and dissolved the National Assembly, calling for a new election of its members. The Socialists regained control, and the old constitutional system of presidential dominance was reestablished. Cohabitation emerged for a second time, however, when in 1993 the Socialists once again lost control of the National Assembly. This time it proceeded with less friction as the prickly Chirac decided not to serve under Mitterrand, and the new premier, Edouard Balladur, got along well with Mitterrand while still establishing clear dominance in the executive. In 1995, the system returned to "normal" when Chirac was elected president with a conservative majority in the National Assembly, but it reverted to "cohabitation" again when the Socialists won control of the National Assembly in the elections of 1997. Since 1997, Lionel Jospin has headed a Socialist-led cabinet and Chirac has receded into the role of president-as-head-of-state. Things have gone smoothly, and Jospin has proved a popular premier. By now, the French have worked out good precedents and traditions to handle cohabitation and indeed appear to like having the president and the cabinet be of different parties.

Nonetheless, this is still a constitutional oddity. In all sorts of ways, the constitution of France (constitution with a small *c*) changes abruptly when different parties come to control the National Assembly and the presidency. It is almost as if France has two constitutions, which switch on and off like lights.

Example: Presidential Government in Mexico

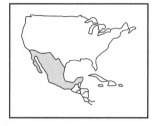

The presidency of Mexico offers a fascinating example of a political institution in transition. The Mexican presidential system arose out of a decade and a half of chaos, from 1910 to 1925. In a swirling tumult of banditry, revolutionary battles, and civil war, approximately a million Mexicans starved or were killed. The period of violence ended in the establishment of the dominant Party of the Institutionalized Revolution (PRI), which we examined in Chapter 12.[9] By the 1930s, the rule of the party had come to be centered on a strong presidency, and that regime has continued.

Under the system as it arose at that time and as it lasted until well into the 1990s, the president dominated Mexican politics. Although the Constitution provided for an independent Congress and Supreme Court much like those of the United States, neither of these bodies operated independently of the president. Until 1988, all but a handful of members of Congress were from the PRI, and even after 1988, the PRI always had clear majorities in both houses until 1997. The opposition was divided in the Congress, so that in the rare instances in which the president needed help(passing a constitutional amendment, for example, which requires a two-thirds majority), he was easily able to gain support from one of the other parties.

The Supreme Court has always been somewhat more insulated from the power of the president and has not infrequently ruled in favor of citizens who were suing the presidential office on minor technical matters. However, the court has always avoided confrontation with the president on important questions of policy. Like the U.S. Supreme Court, the Mexican court refuses to hear cases that it considers "political"; but unlike the U.S. Court, it has interpreted this stricture broadly to include almost any important area of presidential activity.

A president in office has had great power. What saved the system from an unbearable concentration of power was the firm tradition that presidents must step down after a single six-year term. For six years, a single person ruled, but then the party (influenced strongly by the incumbent president) chose another person to serve the next six years.[10] It was at this point that the system showed some flexibility over the years. The outgoing president based his decision on a combination of negotiations

---

[9]Actually, initially there was formed the Mexican Revolutionary Party; it restructured itself and changed its name to the PRI in 1946.

[10]Again, with increasing competition from opposition parties, the party's nomination will probably never again confer the office as automatically as it did through and including the 1988 election. In all elections since then, the outcome was open and competitive; the PRI candidate lost in the 2000 election.

among party leaders, consultations with the PRI's three "sectors," interest-group pressures, and consideration of the popular mood, or "temper of the times."[11] Therefore, when the mood was to the left, a president emerged from the left; corrupt presidents were often succeeded by reformers; and so on. Not only the holder of the presidential office changed, but so did most other executive officers, as the new president found jobs for the members of his faction. The holder of a job under one president in the past had only a 30 percent chance of holding a job under the next president.[12]

Such concentration of power, even if it was temporary, did encourage corruption and personal gain, which has been a chronic problem of Mexican politics. Mexico under the PRI appeared to go through alternate waves of corruption and reform. The administration of President Miguel Alemán from 1946 to 1952 was marked by large-scale corruption, as was that of López Portillo from 1976 to 1982. Various officials of the López Portillo administration are widely thought to have taken $3 billion or more from public funds; his successor, Miguel de la Madrid Hurtado, came to office pledged to a clean government and prosecuted some of the offenders of the previous regime. Although presidential corruption was obviously costly and broad, some speculated cynically that it had the hidden virtue of making possible the regular six-year transition in power. If it were not for the illicit wealth on which they could retire, so this reasoning went, some officials would have devised a way of subverting the six-year rule so that they could stay in office!

During the period of reform from 1982 to 2000, however, a series of three reform PRI presidents oversaw the gradual opening of the political and economic system that culminated in the PRI's final loss of power in the 2000 election. The last of the PRI presidents, Lopez Zedillo, was especially active in reform and in opening up the political system. In the congressional elections of 1997, the PRI lost control of the lower house of Congress, although it kept control of the Senate. This had enormous implications for the all-powerful Mexican presidency, since without control of the Congress, President Zedillo was unable to continue the one-man show that had always been the Mexican presidency. Fortunately, he was already oriented toward reform of the system. He had been trying to open up the party and take control away from the "dinosaurs"; for instance, he had encouraged his attorney general to fire all twenty-three hundred officers in the corrupt narcotics investigation agency, rehiring only six hundred who were judged reliable. With the PRI's loss of dominance in the Congress, Zedillo appeared almost to welcome his party's losses as a chance to establish more reasonable working relations with the Congress. He was patient with the inevitable growing pains of a new opposition who had never before held real power, and while he lost on several significant issues—elimination of his huge secret "President's discretionary fund"; establishment of a new fund that he opposed, which sent several hundred million dollars of federal money back to towns and cities with no strings

[11]Rubio F. Luis, "The Presidential Nomination Process," in George W. Grayson, ed., *Prospects for Democracy in Mexico* (New Brunswick, N.J.: Transaction Publishers, 1990), p. 76.
[12]Peter H. Smith, "Does Mexico Have a Power Elite?" in Jose L. Reyna and Richard S. Weinert, eds., *Authoritarianism in Mexico* (Philadelphia: Institute for the Study of Human Issues, 1977), p. 139.

attached; and a cut in the value-added tax—he was able to get his budget through the opposition-controlled Congress in essentially the form he had requested.

In 2000, the transformation was completed by the ousting of PRI from the presidency with Vicente Fox's election. Fox's experience in the presidency has shown that with openness and competition, it is also possible to have gridlock. While his PAN party is the largest party in the Congress, it does not have a majority. And Fox himself is also a good deal more centrist than most of his fairly conservative party. He has found that he must maneuver and bargain to get what he wants, and even though he started off with great personal popularity, he has had some defeats. A key measure to privatize the government-run oil monopoly has had very slow going, for instance.

The immense changes in the working of Mexican government over just twenty years illustrate how closely the formal governmental structures of politics interact with informal structures such as parties, interest groups, and the media. The written Constitution of Mexico did not change from the 1980s to 1997, but Mexico's governmental institutions changed immeasurably. They changed because the way in which parties structured political conflict changed. Just as we saw in Chapter 14 that parliamentary cabinet government depends crucially on parties that are internally disciplined, we see in the Mexican example that presidential government also depends crucially on the informal structures of politics to define how it works.

FURTHER READINGS

Abraham, Henry J. *The Judicial Process.* New York: Oxford University Press, 1998. Chapters on judicial review.

Bond, Jon R., and Fleisher, Richard. *The President in the Legislative Arena.* Chicago: University of Chicago Press, 1990.

Brichta, Avraham, and Zalmanovitch, Yair. "Proposals for Presidential Government in Israel." *Comparative Political Studies* 19 (October 1986): 57–68.

Edwards, George C., III, and Wayne, Stephen. *Presidential Leadership.* 5th ed. New York: Bedford St. Martins, 1999.

Edwards, George C., III; Kessel, John H.; and Rockman, Bert A., eds. *Researching the Presidency: Vital Questions, New Approaches.* Pittsburgh: University of Pittsburgh Press, 1993.

Fiorina, Morris P. *Congress: Keystone of the Washington Establishment.* 2d ed. New Haven: Yale University Press, 1989.

Greenstein, Fred I. *The Presidential Difference: Leadership Style from FDR to Clinton.* New York: Free Press, 2000.

Jacobs, Lawrence R., and Shapiro, Robert Y. *Politicians Don't Pander.* Chicago: University of Chicago Press, 2000.

Levy, Daniel C., and Bruhn, Kathleen. *Mexico: The Struggle for Democratic Development.* Berkeley: University of California Press, 2001.

Lijphart, Arend. *Patterns of Democracy: Government Forms and Performance in Thirty-Six Countries.* New Haven: Yale University Press, 1999.

Linz, Juan J., and Valenzuela, Arturo, eds. *The Failure of Presidential Democracy.* Baltimore: Johns Hopkins University Press, 1994.

Mainwaring, Scott. "Presidentialism, Multipartism, and Democracy: The Difficult Combination." *Comparative Political Studies* 26 (1993): 198–228.

————, and Shugart, Matthew Soberg, eds. *Presidentialism and Democracy in Latin America.* New York: Cambridge University Press, 1997.

Neustadt, Richard E. *Presidential Power and the Modern Presidents.* New York: Free Press, 1991.

Pfiffner, James P. *The Modern Presidency.* 3d ed. Boston: Bedford/St. Martin's, 2000.

"Presidential and Parliamentary Democracies: Which Works Best?" Special Conference Issue, *Political Science Quarterly* 109 (no. 3, 1994).

Rose, Richard. *The Postmodern President.* Chatham, N.J.: Chatham House, 1989.

————, and Suleiman, Ezra N., eds. *Presidents and Prime Ministers.* Washington, D.C.: American Enterprise Institute, 1980.

Schlesinger, Arthur M., Jr. *The Imperial Presidency.* Boston: Houghton Mifflin, 1973.

Shugart, Matthew Soberg, and Carey, John M. *Presidents and Assemblies: Constitutional Design and Electoral Dynamics.* New York: Cambridge University Press, 1992.

Skowronek, Stephen. *The Politics Presidents Make: Leadership from John Adams to George Bush.* Cambridge: Harvard University Press, 1993.

Wills, Gary. *Cincinnatus: George Washington and the Enlightenment.* Garden City, N.Y.: Doubleday, 1984.

WEBSITE OF INTEREST

White House:
http://www.whitehouse.gov

16

BUREAUCRACY
AND THE PUBLIC SECTOR

In the last few chapters, we reviewed the structure of governments. However, a great deal goes into policy making beyond what government leaders do. The government may establish by law that the speed limit on highways is fifty-five miles per hour, but what this means in detail is determined by thousands of traffic patrol officers across the country. It is they who decide whether this means that you are ticketed if you drive fifty-six miles per hour or whether there is a "zone of grace" so that you are ticketed only for speeds of sixty miles per hour or above. It is they who decide whether a woman with a bleeding wound in her arm is in bad enough shape that she is justified in speeding to the hospital at seventy-five miles per hour. It is they who decide whether to treat a well-dressed man in a dark-blue sedan differently from a young person in blue jeans who is driving a red sports car, warning the one and ticketing the other.

The local police officer, the public health inspector, the president of the state university, the teacher in a public school—these are as much a part of the policy-making machinery as the legislator, judge, or U.S. president. For most citizens, it is *these* people—and not the legislator, judge, or president—who embody the state and its policies. People receive the policies of the state from police officers, immigration officials, I.R.S. agents, schoolteachers, agricultural extension agents, and members of fire departments, not from the nation's president or members of Congress.

Any state, if its operations are at all complex, must have a large number of people like this—people who are not directly involved in politics in the sense that they share in making major decisions but who are involved in the construction and implementation of the policies that carry out those decisions. These are collectively called the *public administration* of the state. A modern state has a large number of people in its public administration. Figure 16–1 charts the growth of the public administration of the United States since 1950.

The number of public employees in the United States climbed from 6.4 million in 1950 to 20,264,000 in 1999, almost wholly from increases at the state and local levels. (Federal civilian employment increased over this period by about 1.2 million.) Public

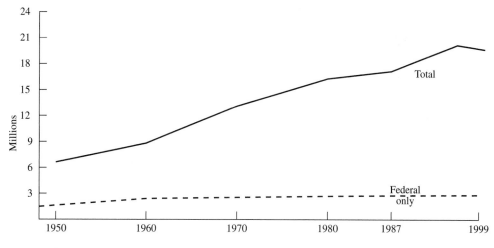

FIGURE 16–1
Total number of civilian public employees (combined local, state, and federal) in the United States, 1950–1999.

Source: U.S. Bureau of the Census, *Statistical Abstract of the United States.*

employment climbed not only in absolute numbers but also as a proportion of the total civilian labor force. In 1950, 11 percent of employed civilians were public employees; by 1999, this had risen to 15 percent. In other words, by 1999, better than one out of seven employed persons was a member of the U.S. public administration.

This actually understates the growth of government *operations* by a good deal. Federal operations grew by much more than the growth in federal employment shown in the chart. What happened is that the federal government has tended over the years to expand its operations by contracting jobs to private research firms and other organizations not directly in the government. The rapid growth of Washington, D.C., has been driven more by the growth of "beltway bandit" firms associated with the government than by direct growth of the government itself.

PUBLIC ADMINISTRATION AS A POLITICAL PROBLEM

That some part of policy making is done by such a large number of people poses something of a problem for the state. Public administrators as a group have significant governmental power, yet they are too numerous and individually too unimportant to be controlled effectively. Therefore, *a significant part of the governmental power of any state is necessarily not under close political control.*

Examples of the governmental discretion of administrators are numerous. American police officers have a good deal of discretion, for instance, in whom they stop to search for weapons or illegal substances; investigations of the New Jersey state police in 1999 revealed policies of "racial profiling"—identifying possible suspects based on certain physical characteristics—for stop-and-search actions that are probably widespread around the country. As another example, consider the agents of the I.R.S. in the United

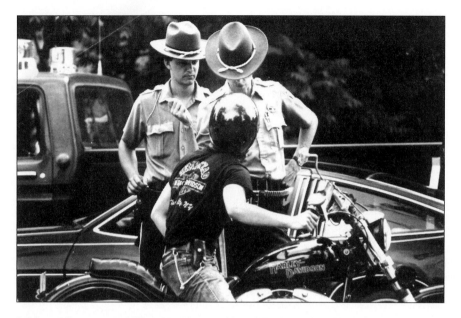

Public employees at work. The state meets a citizen, Woodstock, New York.
(Mark Antman/Stock, Boston)

States who audit taxpayers' returns. Inevitably, given the complexity of our tax laws, interpretation of the laws will vary from one agent to the next. As a result, the outcome of a tax audit depends at least to some extent on which agent handles it. Finally, consider that the teachers of America determine, by their individual actions, the grading system that has such important ultimate effects on students' careers.

These and other examples show that even rather minor administrators make a good deal of governmental policy. The politically responsive part of government (elected officials, party leaders, military juntas, courts, or whatever) must be concerned to make certain that, at least in broad outline, they control the policies implemented by administrators. This control is not easy to design, however. An early study in this area illustrates the problem. In 1948, the U.S. Supreme Court ruled that it was unconstitutional for school districts to schedule certain hours during the day in which religious groups would come to school and provide classes in religion for those students who desired it. (Students who did not wish to have religious instruction were sent to study hall.) The Court ruled that this practice violated the constitutional separation of church and state. Nearly ten years later, in a survey of Pennsylvania school superintendents, one-tenth of those responding stated that their school districts continued this practice, even though it was unconstitutional. The survey also ascertained that the superintendents understood the Court decision fully; they were acting not out of ignorance but deliberately.[1]

---

[1]Frank J. Sorauf, "Zorach v. Clausen: The Impact of a Supreme Court Decision," *American Political Review* 53 (September 1959): 777–91.

(© 2002 by Sidney Harris. Reprinted with permission.)

CHARACTERISTICS OF GOOD PUBLIC ADMINISTRATION

The way in which we organize our public administration should aim to help us maximize some desirable traits. Among these are the following:

1. *Honest, accurate translation of political leaders' decisions into more specifically designed policies:* This addresses the problem of making sure that political leaders control at least the broad outlines of policy.

2. *Flexibility in dealing with special cases at the point of delivery:* While administrators should be obedient to directions from above, they should not be slavishly obedient. If a police officer pulls a driver over for speeding and discovers that the driver is trying to get a child with a gaping wound to the hospital, we do not want the officer to write a ticket.

3. *But this flexibility should not be used arbitrarily:* "Arbitrary" action is action taken capriciously, without regard to the important circumstances of a case. Stopping and searching blacks because of their race is an arbitrary act, for example. Another example would be to allow some students to take a makeup examination but to deny the makeup opportunity to others who had had the same excuse.

4.   *Feedback of expert advice; active imagination and assertive inquiry on the part of administrators:* We hope that administrators, since they know more about their areas of work than anyone else, will not hang back from sharing their expertise with the public and their political leaders.

5.   *Efficiency:* We hope that all this can be done without costing too much.

All of these are desirable traits. However, some of them are to a certain extent mutually contradictory, so that all of them cannot be fully met simultaneously. For instance, there is some tension between item 1 (honest, accurate translation) and item 2 (expecting administrators to follow their own judgment). Item 3 is difficult because one person's capriciousness is another person's courageous judgment. Item 4 (feedback of expert advice) assumes an independent-minded set of administrators who may fit oddly the task of honest, accurate translation.

It follows that there is no one best way to organize public administration; various modes of organization will emphasize one or another of these good things. Therefore, under varying circumstances, varying modes may be preferred.

"BUREAUCRACY": A REFORM OF THE NINETEENTH CENTURY

Bureaucracy is one way to organize the public administration. The word *bureaucracy* is often used in common language to mean the public administration, usually with a connotation of distaste. However, social scientists have a precise meaning for it: a particular mode of administrative organization that was developed as a reform in the nineteenth century and spread widely to be the most generally used mode today.

Let us first set the stage of the eighteenth and early nineteenth centuries to show how bureaucracy developed as a reform of the systems then in place. At that time, in Europe and North America, positions in the public administration were treated as pieces of property, to be exchanged among people. In the United States, this took the form of the infamous "spoils system," in which administrative jobs were treated as commodities with which victorious candidates rewarded their party's workers. When the presidency changed hands, for instance, all post office managers in the country were fired and new people from the victorious party were put in their place. The same thing happened with state highway and surveyor jobs when one party replaced another in a state capital; so also with fire and police jobs when city hall changed hands.

In Europe, positions in the public administration were individually bought and sold more or less as investments. A wealthy family wishing to establish a son in a comfortable life would buy him a position in the customs service, an officer's commission in the army, or some similar position.

Such loose arrangements produced inefficient service, and there was little control over the quality of officials. In the United States, for example, some post office managers could not read. For most officials, getting the job in the first place was the only trick (what they did once they were there did not bear consequences for them), so controlling officials' actions was difficult.

In the nineteenth century, there arose a new method of organizing public administration, one that social scientists call "bureaucracy."[2] Under a system of bureaucracy:

1. Members of the public administration are appointed and promoted on the basis of their qualifications for the job they are to do.
2. Special requirements of training or experience are set for the position.
3. Administrative procedures are standardized, so that relatively little is left to individual officials' biases or passions.
4. Clear lines of command are established, in which an order from a high official goes to a lower official, who then passes the order on to the next level, and so on until it reaches the point of operation. This arrangement is called a *hierarchical command structure.*
5. Finally, public administrators are shielded from day-to-day political pressure, usually with a system of tenure.

This new, cleaner, and more efficient way of organizing the public administration was first used in appointments for procurement officers with the French and Prussian armies in the eighteenth and early nineteenth centuries. It demonstrated its usefulness in this area and spread rapidly. In the United States, the coming of the bureaucratic mode was embodied in the move for civil service reform at the turn of the century, which eventually took most administrative positions out of party control and based them on competitive civil service exams. By World War II, some form or another of bureaucracy was the usual method of organizing public administration throughout Europe and North America. As new states attained their independence, they also adopted some form of bureaucracy. It is today the usual mode of administrative organization throughout the world, although there are many variations on its themes.

BUREAUCRACY VERSUS FLEXIBILITY

As noted previously, there is no ideal way to organize administration. Of the various things that may be desirable in public administration, bureaucracy is particularly strong on the accurate translation of leaders' decisions and on preventing arbitrary behavior. Believe it or not, it is also rather efficient. (Bureaucracy has to some extent been identified in the public mind as wasteful because the public has high expectations for how cheaply one might expect administration to be done. Compared with private businesses, the administrative costs of public agencies are not that far out of line.)

However, the standardization and clarity of command that accomplish these good things mean that bureaucracy does not provide for local flexibility. Also, although the requirements for training and for decisions based on merit produce well-qualified officials, the system of standardization does not encourage independent-mindedness on their part, and so bureaucracy does not especially tend to produce helpful expert advice to political leaders. Administrators under most versions of bureaucracy tend to hold their advice until it is asked for.

[2]For the definitive statement, see Max Weber, "Bureaucracy," in H. H. Gerth and C. Wright Mills, *From Max Weber* (New York: Oxford University Press, 1958), pp. 196–244.

This means that the bureaucratic form of organization will fit some administrative needs better than others. Where standardization and obedience are especially important, bureaucratic organization fits well. Where independent and flexible judgment are especially important, it does not. Military service is one area in which standardization and obedience are important, because if a general is conducting a wheeling motion on a battlefield, everything could be lost if one battalion wheeled in the wrong direction. The bureaucratic model fits military operations well, and indeed the military—with its clean lines of command and its tendency to "do things by the book"—exemplifies the bureaucratic model. On the other hand, public enterprises in which obedience is less important than individuality are not as well served by bureaucratic organization. The university or college is such a place: The object is to put a gifted individual in the lab or in front of a class and let that person do creative things.

It follows that bureaucracy is a better form of organization for some areas of the public administration than for others, depending on the relative needs for smooth obedience and individualistic judgment. To a considerable extent, these differences are reflected in the organization of various agencies; almost universally the armed forces are the most bureaucratically organized agencies in any state's public administration, and universities tend to be rather decentralized.

However, there is often a tilt *toward* bureaucracy, with most operations being organized more bureaucratically than would really be necessary. Most public administrators appear to incline toward standardization and away from individual initiative, a natural result of the human desire for safety and security. An official working within standardized procedures, unlike one who is supposed to make independent choices, cannot be blamed for the results. Procedures shelter bureaucracies, so bureaucracies foster procedures. Impressionistic evidence for this, at least, is that there are apparently no armed forces in the world set up in anything but a straightforward bureaucratic mode; whereas universities, which would not require bureaucratic organization and would almost surely benefit by its absence, are nonetheless often hemmed in by tight rules.[3]

THE PROBLEM OF PROTECTED INCOMPETENCE

Another common problem of bureaucratic organization stems from a combination of two factors: (1) the difficulty in *public* administration, as compared with private business, of evaluating how well a person has performed a job, and (2) the requirement in a bureaucracy that administrators be shielded from direct political pressure, usually by a system of tenure.

In private business, a standard yardstick is available to evaluate how well a person has done in a job. If profits have gone up in that person's sector, if sales have been high, or whatever—if the person has made money for the company—then the job has been done well. You and your bosss know whether or not you have sold a million dollars of insurance this year. But how do we evaluate the performance of public administrators?

---

[3]For example, in some European universities, there are official limits on the number of pages that students may be required to read. In Norway in 1983, the limit for a fifteen-week political science course was six hundred pages.

There is no notion of "profit" in the operations of a public school, the army, or a state's highway department. A professor is supposed to teach well, but there is no dollar figure that can tell us *how* well the professor has taught. A highway superintendent is supposed to maintain the roads well, but there is no dollar figure that can tell us how well they have been maintained.

Combine this with the fact that political intervention against members of the bureaucracy is difficult and unlikely, and you have a situation in which incompetent administrators will rarely be removed from their positions. Few unambiguous standards of their performance are available, and—in the absence of clear-cut evidence—superiors will be reluctant to take action for fear that they will be accused of favoritism or political interference.

As a result, although bureaucracies do not particularly attract incompetent people—and although, by their entrance requirements, they have some success at selecting unusually competent people—those incompetents who do get in are less likely to be removed than they would be in private businesses.

ADJUSTMENTS TO BUREAUCRACY

Although bureaucracy is only one way to organize the public administration, it is the dominant mode of organization across the world, as we have seen. Indeed, it is so dominant that the word *bureaucracy* has become almost a synonym for public administration, in much the way that *Kleenex* has come to be synonymous with facial tissues or *Xerox* with photocopies.

As a term loosely signifying public administration, *bureaucracy* has a number of unpleasant connotations. Bureaucrats are thought to be lazy, arrogant, inflexible, shortsighted—and too numerous. Partly this derives from the fact that it is impossible to construct an ultimate, best form of organization for the public administration; as we have seen, the various characteristics we would wish to see in a good public administration are to some extent mutually contradictory. Partly it derives from real weaknesses of bureaucracy.

In various parts of the world, adjustments have evolved or have been invented that can soften bureaucracy when it is excessively "bureaucratic." Among these are the office of *ombudsman,* provisions for opening government files for inspection, informal interference in the bureaucracy by political leaders, and pressure from public opinion.

1. *The office of ombudsman* is a Swedish invention. An ombudsman is a government official whose primary duty is to seek out citizens' complaints of abuse by public administrators and to negotiate changes in the offending practices. The ombudsman idea has been copied in many other countries. In the United States, it has not been used at the national level; but Hawaii, Florida, and other states have established ombudsman offices. Many nongovernmental institutions have also found it an attractive idea. Universities have established ombudsman offices for their students or faculty, newspapers have set up a readers' ombudsman, and so on.

2. *Freedom of information laws* have been passed in many countries, and the United States has been a pioneer in this direction. Under such laws, individuals

are guaranteed the right to examine most kinds of "internal" governmental documents, including dossiers that may have been gathered on them personally. The intent of the laws is to allow citizens to find out what procedures administrators are following in processes that are of interest to them; more specifically, it allows citizens to check and correct any information the government has gathered about them.

3. ***"Interference" in administration by political leaders*** may act as a safety valve to help correct abuses. You will recall that in the bureaucratic mode of organization, administrators are shielded from much direct intervention by political leaders. This was intended to avoid the excesses of a spoils system.

    However, it does not compromise the bureaucratic model greatly if political leaders take advantage of their potential power over administrative budgets to seize bureaucrats' attention and get them to deal with a constituent's problem. In the United States, in particular, this has become a major part of the job of a member of Congress and has developed into an important correction of bureaucratic inflexibility. It is well understood that if you are having trouble getting a passport or your Social Security check has been held up, you should call your member of Congress for help. In 1998, for instance, the office of Representative Bruce Vento (Fourth Congressional District, Minnesota) assisted over six hundred constituents with a wide variety of concerns; the most common problems involved disputes with the Social Security Administration, Immigration and Naturalization Service, Medicare, and the Veterans Administration.[4]

4. ***Pressure from public opinion*** can help to correct bureaucratic sluggishness and abuse. Administrators are ultimately dependent on political processes for their offices' budgets, and so they must be attentive to public opinion. Also, because they are human, they want to be liked and admired for what they do. Public criticism hurts them and will usually lead to improvements where there have been problems. Agricultural agencies, welfare services, research agencies, the postal service—all are worried by stories in the media about shortcomings in their operations and keep in reasonably close touch with their "clients," the groups most affected by their policies.

    Perhaps the best evidence that public opinion serves as an important corrective to bureaucracy may be found by looking at an agency that is *not* under much direct pressure from public opinion. In democracies all over the world, immigration services are relatively free from pressures of public opinion because their "client group"—those who wish to enter the country as immigrants—cannot vote in elections and usually lack powerful friends. It is almost universally true that these offices are less responsive to their clients and more inclined to make arbitrary judgments than other government agencies.

- *Item:* The U.S. Immigration and Naturalization Service some years ago tried to save about $20 million by setting a rule that no visas could be renewed under any circumstances. It would have saved the money by eliminating the positions of clerks who at that time handled applications for renewal. This decision ignored sev-

---

[4]Personal communication.

eral important things: the hundreds of millions of dollars that would not have been spent in the United States by visitors who were unable to prolong their stay; the human hardship and ill will that would have resulted; and the fact that there would still have had to be some provision for emergency cases, such as heart attacks and appendectomies on the day of departure. The Immigration and Naturalization Service was eventually talked out of this silly idea.

- *Item:* A German visiting the United States on a valid visa was turned back at the Minneapolis airport and forced to return home because he had a pornographic homosexual magazine in his suitcase.
- *Item:* When the Norwegian government in 1980 decided to reduce the number of work permits it would grant to foreigners by 50 percent, the Norwegian Immigration Service also reduced the staff to deal with those requests by 50 percent. It forgot that although it was going to say yes only half as often, just as many people would be *asking.* It was not long before the office had such a backlog that applicants were required to wait nine months to a year for an answer.
- *Item:* In the late 1970s, until it was dissuaded by embarrassing publicity, the British Immigration Service required a virginity test of women who were applying for permission to immigrate to Britain.
- *Item:* In 1997, the U.S. Congress empowered Immigration and Naturalization Service border agents, after a brief examination and with no procedure for appeal, to turn back foreign citizens at the border and bar them from crossing the border for five years. In the first seven months of the new rule, twenty-three thousand people were barred, and in several incidents, it was clear that these were foreign citizens trying to visit family members in the United States, Canadians working for United States-based firms, and so on.[5]
- *Item:* In 2001, the Immigration and Naturalization Service, which was at that time taking more than two months to process applications for temporary work visas, offered a special expedited service that would take only fifteen days—for a fee of one thousand dollars!

SOCIAL REPRESENTATIVENESS OF PUBLIC ADMINISTRATION

Members of the public administration are not under direct political control, and adjustments such as those I have described can go only so far. Therefore, there has been recurrent concern over how socially representative top bureaucratic decision makers are; that is, there has been a concern that they should not be too different from the population as a whole in such things as class background, race, or gender. There has been some controversy over this. On the one hand, advocates of "representative bureaucracy" urge that if administrators are not politically responsible, we should at least do all we can to ensure that they will look at things in the same ways that the common people would. On the other hand, skeptics have responded that we should not want "common people" in positions of uncommon importance and that we should not expect top public administrators

---

[5]*New York Times,* 14 November 1997, p. 1.

TABLE 16–1   BACKGROUNDS OF EUROPEAN AND AMERICAN SENIOR CIVIL SERVANTS

	Britain	France	Germany	Italy	Netherlands	U.S.A.
Social class origin (percent)						
Management/professional	68%	96%	67%	82%	60%	69%
Middle	21%	3%	21%	16%	37%	18%
Working	13%	1%	12%	3%	4%	14%

Source: Calculated from Joel D. Aberbach, Robert D. Putnam, and Bert A. Rockman, *Bureaucrats and Politicians in Western Democracies* (Cambridge: Harvard University Press, 1981), table 3-3.

to be any more socially representative than the leaders of corporations, universities, or other large institutions.[6]

Whatever our feelings on this, certainly many governments have made efforts to ensure that top public administrators will be reasonably representative. Since the 1970s, the United States has tried by affirmative action programs to increase numbers of minority and women officials. Decades earlier, after World War II, many European countries (France, for example) attempted to increase the proportion of their officials who were from the working class. They did this by changing their entrance procedures and providing for internal promotions from less important administrative posts.

The effectiveness of such attempts is limited. As Table 16–1 shows, as of the 1970s, the class backgrounds of senior administrative officials were rather similar across a fairly varied set of countries, although France and Italy do stand out. In recent years, a similar concern in most countries has been to increase the representation of women and minorities in the bureaucracy. However, a study in 1987 showed that at that point, only 6 percent of department heads and 9 percent of deputy department heads were women across Western industrialized countries.[7]

CONCLUSION

The members of the public administration pose a dilemma for a state's political leaders. They are too numerous and individually too minor to control effectively, yet collectively they have a major impact on policies. We have reviewed in this chapter various ways by which the state may address its dilemma—establishment of the bureaucratic model, adjustments to the bureaucratic model, attempts to achieve "representative bureaucracy"—but none of these can be fully successful. This is a problem of politics in which "half a loaf" may be the best one can hope for.

[6]See discussions in Samuel Krislov, *Representative Bureaucracy* (Englewood Cliffs, N.J.: Prentice-Hall, 1974); Kenneth John Meier, "Representative Bureaucracy: An Empirical Analysis," *American Political Science Review* 69 (June 1975): 526–42; Sally Coleman Selden, *The Promise of Representative Bureaucracy* (London: M. E. Sharpe, 1997); and Kenneth J. Meier, Robert D. Winkle, and J. L. Polinard, "Representative Bureaucracy and Distributional Equity: Addressing the Hard Question," *Journal of Politics* 61 (November 1999): 1025–39.

[7]United Nations Office of Vienna, Centre for Social Development and Humanitarian Affairs, *Women in Politics and Decision-Making in the Late Twentieth Century* (Dordecht, Netherlands: Martinus Nijhof, 1992), p. 63.

Example: The French Bureaucracy

The "ordinary" bureaucracies of industrialized states do not vary greatly from one country to another. Mail carriers, teachers, agricultural extension agents, and so on, are organized and do their jobs in fairly similar ways around the industrialized world. Where there is considerable variation is in how the higher civil service—the managers, diplomats, specialists, and so on—are organized and work. In this realm, the French are quite distinctive; theirs is arguably the best civil service in the world.

In this section, we shall address almost solely the higher civil service. First, however, I should note one thing that *is* unusual about the "ordinary" French civil service: It is relatively large, perhaps due in part to the French state's high level of regulatory activity. There are approximately 6 million full-time local and national civil servants in France, including the military. They make up about 25 percent of the labor force, compared with 13 percent in Germany and Britain.[8]

The higher civil service of France consists of about four to six thousand highly trained persons. Most of these work within one of the ministries (defense, health, etc.), but at any given time, over a thousand of them are working in more independent ways, either as staff advisers to the premier or ministers or in relatively autonomous administrative bodies, which I shall describe. Furthermore, a certain number of them are at any time on loan to businesses, universities, or local government.

One of the things that distinguishes the French higher civil service is the training and ability of its members, which leads also to a high degree of self-confidence and pride. There are two main routes of entry into the higher civil service. If one wishes to be a specialist, such as a scientist or statistician, one usually receives a university education from one of the "great" technical schools, such as the Polytechnic or the School of Agronomy, followed by more specialized training at an institution such as the School of Mines or School of Statistics and Economic Administration. If one wishes to be a generalist, after university one enters the famous National School of Administration (the ENA). One of the most difficult schools in the world to enter, the ENA gives its graduates a general training in administration and in the social sciences. Whether from one of the "great schools" or the ENA, higher civil servants in France are noted for their verbal skill and for a tendency to abstraction and mathematical reasoning. They are pragmatic rather than ideological and usually emphasize economics over politics.

The second thing that sets French higher civil servants apart is the tradition of "detached service," whereby they may leave the national civil service for periods of time either on personal leave or on loan by the national government to work in business, local government, or the universities or to hold elective office. In the 1970s, for example, about one-fourth of the members of the parliament were civil servants on

[8]"France's Public Sector—They Love It," *The Economist,* 26 May 2001, p. 50.

leave from their administrative posts, and in 1984, there were twenty-five national civil servants on loan to the city of Paris.

Under these circumstances, the French have developed a more politicized civil service than that of most countries, one that lives on the frontier between "politics" and administration.[9] When François Mitterrand became president in 1981, for instance, about four hundred high administrators were replaced with others who would be more compatible with the new regime, although Mitterrand took pains to demonstrate that this was not done solely on the basis of party connections. Such politicization appears to have added vigor to the higher civil service and has allowed French civil servants to lead aggressively in the development of such new political thrusts as the campaign for a tunnel under the English Channel, the adoption of the value-added tax, and the formation of the Common Market.

It was stated previously that the French higher civil service is "arguably" the best in the world. The other side of the "argument" is raised by those who see the civil service as too insulated from the rest of the population, too haughty, and overly given to technical fixes:

Instead of a homogenous administration equally open to everyone, one sees established an aristocracy of a few thousand young men produced through privileged channels; the isolation of their education easily persuades them that they are destined to retain among themselves (and for themselves) the administration of the state, and above all its best jobs. Less and less are they touched by doubts; the assurance of their elders and their own success convinces them that it is enough to advance confidently under cover of their technique to make obstacles disappear. The sharing of a certain exoticism of language or of modern administrative techniques or of economics; the sense of making up a kind of network between the bosses and dauphins of the great public and private businesses; the exhilaration, still hardly acknowledged, of feeling in their hands such means of action, and such docile underlings; all these make up the psychology of a senior civil servant, young and ardent, certainly devoted to what he considers the public good, but more inclined to define it himself, or to let it be defined by the boss, than to listen on this subject to the aspiration of the country.[10]

Example: The Saudi Arabian Bureaucracy

A severe problem facing most states of the South is that their bureaucracies are newly established and often had to be assembled hurriedly as the state was formed. Technical expertise is scarce, and the bureaucracies have also not had time to build up an esprit de corps, with high expectations for performance, such as that seen in France. As a result, states of the South seem to be especially burdened with sluggish, cautious, inefficient administration.

---

[9]This also fits the more general culture of the French and other continental Europeans. English is the only European language that distinguishes between *politics* and *policy;* in French, both are called *politique.*

[10]"Le Regime des 'Jeunes Messieurs,' " *Courrier de la Republique,* November 1965, quoted in Anthony Sampson, *The New Europeans* (London: Hodder and Stoughton, 1968), p. 345.

TABLE 16–2   ATTITUDES OF SAUDI BUREAUCRATS

	Strongly agree (percent)	Agree (percent)	Disagree (percent)	Strongly disagree (percent)	Number answering question
It is best to change or cancel programs that cause social conflict.	25	59	14	2	(282)
Social change should not be instituted at the expense of traditional values.	37	53	8	2	(287)
It is best to consult with one's superior before making a decision.	26	57	15	1	(288)
In making decisions, no one should violate rules and regulations.	21	55	21	2	(286)

Source: From Saud Al Nimir and Monte Palmer, "Bureaucracy and Development in Saudi Arabia: A Behavioral Analysis," *Public Administration and Development*, 2 (April–June 1982) pp. 93–104. Copyright © 1982 John Wiley & Sons Limited. Reproduced with permission.

The bureaucracy of Saudi Arabia illustrates these problems. Saudi Arabia is not a poor country, and so it is spared the problems of poverty that many other states of the South endure. Like most of the states of the South, however, the Saudi government and public administration were established in their present form only in the last few decades; before that, the Saudis had had little experience in modern public administration.

A study of the values and attitudes of middle-range Saudi bureaucrats reveals a group of people who are cautious, wedded to routine, and not very ambitious.[11] Table 16–2 presents the bureaucrats' answers to several questions.

Answers to other questions were consistent with the four given in the table. For instance, 78 percent of the bureaucrats would prefer a low-paying job with few risks to a high-paying job with high risks. There is, of course, no "typical" state of the South. Saudi society is a conservative one, in which traditional values are strongly enforced. This may help to explain the bureaucrats' caution about social change, but it should not have much to do with their caution in dealings with their superiors, and in this the Saudi bureaucrats seem to be similar to those in most of the South. This caution may not be wholly a bad thing. It fits the standard bureaucratic model and should ensure the faithful transmission of orders. However, we saw earlier in this chapter that an emphasis on any one virtue in administration is purchased at the cost of other virtues. In this case, flexibility and innovation are lost—virtues that are important to states of the South that, like Saudi Arabia, are undergoing great social and economic change.

[11]Saud al Nimir and Monte Palmer, "Bureaucracy and Development in Saudi Arabia: A Behavioral Analysis," *Public Administration and Development* 2 (April–June 1982): 93–104.

Example: Battling the Bureaucracy in Brazil[12]

Wherever modern government structures are built on an already highly developed legal and administrative system, bureaucracies are bound to multiply. Brazil is no exception. What is exceptional is the degree to which Brazilians have managed to circumvent the more rigid and obstructive bureaucratic rules. In addition, the government has recently had some success in attacking the rules themselves.

Brazilians have described their federal administrative system as excessively centralized, formal, and distrustful of the public. This view dates back at least to the temporary transfer to Brazil of the Portuguese kingdom and its centralized administration in 1808, and perhaps even further, to 1549, when the first governor-general arrived with a framework of laws and regulations even before there were people to conform to them. The formalism embodied the prejudice that documents are more important than facts. The distrust showed in the controls that required endless lists of certificates, attestations, licenses, and other documents. Not many years ago, the case was reported of an export license that required 1,470 separate legal actions and involved thirteen government ministries and fifty agencies.

The *jeito* was employed to overcome such difficulties. This Portuguese term, corresponding roughly to "knack," "way," or "fix" in English, refers to the varied ways that Brazilians, like people in other countries, get around the maze of regulations and legal requirements. The jeito principle has been remarkably effective. It relies significantly on the *despachante* (roughly, an expeditor), who has counterparts in many countries but has been especially active in Brazil, where the lubrication of sticky administrative processes has been essential for social mobility and rapid economic development.

The despachante is an intermediary who, in return for a commission or fee, purchases and fills out the multiplicity of legal forms, delivers them to the proper persons, and extracts the needed permission or document. The system developed when the simplest transactions, such as obtaining a marriage license or identity card, could take ages or days or hours, depending on whether one used despachantes and how much they were paid. The despachantes are thriving, specialized professionals and have their own union and competitive examinations. Some specialize in police work, naturalizations, auto licenses, marriages, or "legalization of real estate." The despachantes who arrange imports and exports have long enjoyed a legal monopoly. Each typically has several employees, and almost all sizable businesses maintain their own despachantes.

[12]World Bank, *World Development Report 1987* (Oxford: Oxford University Press, 1987), p. 73; reprinted by permission.

Brazil's rapid economic growth and social evolution demonstrate that a complex bureaucracy need not be a barrier to development. The costs are nevertheless substantial. Moreover, such resourceful adaptations of the jeito may have been too effective and undermined attempts to reform public administration.

The most recent efforts to reform the system, rather than live with it, began in 1979. A national debureaucratization program was designed to simplify administrative procedures and, more broadly, to reverse what was seen as the relentless trend toward growth in government, excessive centralization, and abundant regulation.

The results in 1979–84 were impressive. On the basis of citizens' project (which surveyed all the points of contact of individuals, throughout their lives, with bureaucratic requirements), it was possible to eliminate or simplify a long list of documents and procedures ranging from notarization requirements and driver's licenses to passport extensions, university enrollment processes, and income tax returns. Evidence of residence, economic dependence, and so on, could be established with simply a written statement by the interested party rather than legal certificates and third-party attestation. Thus, a "presumption of truth" displaced the "rule of distrust." Other legal procedures were simplified. In all, more than 600 million documents a year were removed from circulation. The savings have been estimated at close to $3 billion a year, equivalent to about 1.5 percent of Brazil's GDP.

In the economic field, the main achievements were to simplify rural credit procedures, to change commercial registration procedures so that forming a company could take three days rather than three to six months, and to bring relief from bureaucracy to 1.5 million small enterprises. For the time being, however, the program has left many areas of regulation untouched, including some that are important to industrialization and trade.

It is significant that although a minister of debureaucratization was appointed, no new government department was formed. The program was implemented by an executive secretary and just twelve assistants. At the very least—and on a limited front—some progress has been made in simplifying the rules and changing the relationship between citizens and civil servants.

FURTHER READING

Aberbach, Joel D.; Putnam, Robert D.; and Rockman, Bert A. *Bureaucrats and Politicians in Western Democracies.* Cambridge: Harvard University Press, 1981.

Aberbach, Joel D., and Rockman, Bert A. *In the Web of Politics: Three Decades of the U.S. Federal Executive.* Washington, D.C.: Brookings Institution, 2000.

Allison, Graham T. *Essence of Decision: Explaining the Cuban Missile Crisis.* Boston: Little, Brown, 1971.

"Bureaucracy" in the *International Encyclopedia of the Social Sciences.*

Crozier, Michel. *The Bureaucratic Phenomenon.* Chicago: University of Chicago Press, 1987.

Glazer, Amihai, and Rothenberg, Lawrence S. *Why Government Succeeds and Why It Fails.* Cambridge: Harvard University Press, 2001.

Gruber, Judith E. *Controlling Bureaucracies.* Berkeley: University of California Press, 1987.

Kettl, Donald F.; Ingraham, Patricia W.; Sanders, Ronald P.; and Horner, Constance. *Civil Service Reform: Building a Government That Works.* Washington, D.C.: Brookings Institution, 1996.

Knott, Jack H., and Miller, Gary J. *Reforming Bureaucracy: The Politics of Institutional Choice.* Englewood Cliffs, N.J.: Prentice-Hall, 1987.

Naff, Katherine C. *To Look Like America.* Boulder, Colo.: Westview Press, 2001.

Page, Edward C., and Wright, Vincent. *Bureaucratic Elites in Western European States.* New York: Oxford University Press, 1999.

Selden, Sally Coleman. *The Promise of Representative Bureaucracy.* London: M. E. Sharpe, 1997.

Suleiman, Ezra N. *Politics, Power, and Bureaucracy in France.* Princeton, N.J.: Princeton University Press, 1974.

Wilson, James Q. *Bureaucracy: What Government Agencies Do and Why They Do It.* New York: Basic Books, 1989.

 WEBSITE OF INTEREST

U.S. Federal Government Agencies Directory, with links to all agencies that have websites:

http://www.lib.Lsu.edu/gov/fedgov.html

17

LAW AND THE COURTS

The *law* is a collection of rules laid down by the government, binding all members of the state, including members of the government itself. The law does two things: (1) It sets society's norms and rules for behavior; for instance, it may state that one may not steal others' property, that one may not expose oneself indecently, or that religious practice other than the state religion is illegal. (2) It sets the rules by which individuals in the state must relate to each other—rules governing divorce procedures, rules for the honoring of contracts, and so on.

The rules making up the "law" may reside in the state's constitution, may be statutes passed by the state's legislature, or may be decrees announced by the state's executive officers such as the president, military junta, dictator, or whatever. They may also, in some states, develop out of decisions of courts.

Courts are an odd part of the government in that they have the responsibility for interpreting all parts of the law and adjudicating—when various parts of the law are in conflict—which part takes precedence. Their oddity lies in that they are part of the government but must judge fairly among citizens of the state, including those in the government. Thus, while courts are part of the government, they must be to some extent independent of it. This independence has developed so far in some states that the courts are able to share independently in creating the law.

The tension implicit in being part of the government but at the same time independent of the government, and how this tension is resolved, are important aspects of the world's major legal systems, which we shall examine. *Legal systems* are general, organized sets of legal principles that form the basis of law and adjudication in states. They organize legal practice for states in a way somewhat parallel to the role ideologies play in organizing the thought processes of individuals.

ANGLO-SAXON CASE LAW

The legal system that is most familiar to Americans and Canadians is Anglo-Saxon case law. This is the system that developed in England during the late Middle Ages and early modern period and spread to such former British colonies as the United

States, Canada, India, and Nigeria. It is also often called "common law," though that term is more often applied to the specific body of English law that developed over centuries of case experience.

In the system of case law, courts are seen as largely independent of the state's government, so independent that in the cases they decide they share to some extent in the making of the law, because those cases serve as precedents for future decisions. This is why the system is called "case law."

The heart of the system is a belief that the law is something that exists partially independent of the government. From this there follow several important aspects of case law:

- The task of judges is to find proper law, and the law evolves over time with a certain degree of flexibility. Thus, the U.S. Supreme Court in its landmark *Brown* v. *Board of Education* decision took note of changing sociological evidence to decide that segregated schools (which had once been considered legal) were against the law.[1]
- Training of judges and lawyers proceeds in special schools, separate from the rest of the university; their training—largely by other lawyers—emphasizes clarity of thought and expression, and skills at searching out and applying precedents.
- The role of the judge is to be a neutral arbiter, ruling on behalf of the law after listening fairly passively to opposed arguments by the lawyers.
- Especially where the government brings charges against an individual (a criminal case), the law protects the individual against the disproportionate power of the government. The burden of proof lies with the government (the defendant is "considered innocent until proven guilty"), and a whole series of protections hold: An individual may not be held more than twenty-four hours without being charged (right of habeas corpus), spouses may not be forced to testify against each other, and so on.

I do not mean to suggest that in case law systems, the law is manufactured by judges. The courts base their decision not only on precedents but also on statutes passed by the government, including (in the case of the United States) the Constitution. If the government changes the law by statute, the courts follow its directions, and so the government is the *final* authority on the law. If the United States government were to amend the Constitution to make racially segregated schools constitutional, for instance, *Brown* v. *Board of Education* would be annulled. However, in the absence of government action, and by filling in the details of government statutes, the courts work with the government to make the law. For instance, when a tax code revision is passed in the United States, commentators will note that we need to wait for two or three years of court cases to know exactly what the new law means. In a case law system, then, courts operate largely independently of the rest of the government, although statutes and the constitution have the final word.

CONTINENTAL EUROPEAN CODE LAW

Case law developed in England out of local customs and was popular especially with the same emerging commercial elites who would help to develop the ideology of liberal-

[1]Brown v. Board of Education, 347 U.S. 484 (1954).

ism.[2] With its emphasis on the law as something existing at some remove from the government and on the law's capacity to restrain illegal governmental action, case law has a clear affinity with liberalism's desire for limited government.

On the continent of Europe, forces for limitations on governmental power were never as strong as in England, probably because the establishment and maintenance of the continental states were usually more difficult than the establishment of a secure state in England, protected as it was by the English Channel. The legal tradition on the continent has been to rely on variants of the Roman system of law, which involves a detailed code of law produced and interpreted by the government. The law, in this tradition, is an expression of governmental policy. Napoleon, when he was building his French Empire in the early nineteenth century, gave this tradition added life by encoding existing French law in the Code Napoleon; he later imposed similar codes in many of the European states he conquered. In one way or another, code law eventually dominated across the continent.

From the basic principle that the law is an instrument of the government rather than something that exists semi-independently of the government, there follow several notable characteristics of code law:

- It is not based nearly as much as case law on the accumulation of precedents. While code law judges try to keep in step with each other, lest the law degenerate into chaos, they rely more on the statute or code as an authority—not on previous judges' decisions. They do not "make the law" as case law judges do.
- The training of code law lawyers and judges, accordingly, is more general and not as specialized as what one finds in case law systems. Legal officials are seen primarily as just another kind of civil servant, so they are trained in the general university rather than in a separate school by special professors of law.
- The distinction between law as a tool of the state and law as something above the state is most marked in criminal cases, where the state itself (in the person of the prosecutor) is a party to the case. Under most code law systems, in a criminal case the judge is not a neutral arbiter of the arguments between the prosecution and defense; rather, as a servant of the state, the judge enters directly into argument, questioning witnesses and even, in some systems, directing the police investigation of the crime. The judge's role is not to pass judgment on the state's case but rather, as a servant of the state, to try actively on behalf of the state to learn the truth in the case. There is no presumption of innocence, as in case law; there is no presumption at all. The state, through the court, simply tries to find out what happened. Finally, in most code law systems, there do not exist the elaborate structures of protection for the accused that we see under case law—right of habeas corpus, right against self-incrimination, right against spouse's testimony, and so on. The task of the court is not to "prove guilt beyond any reasonable doubt"; rather, it is to decide what is most probably true in the case.

To an American raised on "innocent until proven guilty," this may seem strange.

The original code law systems were European. As new states were established in other parts of the world, unless they were former British colonies, they adopted some

---

[2]See Chapter 2.

form of code law. When a revolutionary government or a new state based on an independence movement has needed to make an abrupt break with the past, it has seemed more straightforward to design a code of law directly, rather than build one gradually through an accretion of judicial decisions.

In communist states, the spirit of law as servant of the state—or, in this case, servant of the revolution—was carried to an extreme form of code law. In criminal law, for instance, where in case law many barriers are raised to protect the accused from the state and in European code law there are no presumptions either way, in the communist variants of code law barriers were often raised against the accused, to make it certain that the state could convict a person if that was necessary. For instance, in the Soviet Union, a defendant was not told what the state's evidence was until the day before the trial, and this made it difficult to prepare a defense. A person charged with a crime did not personally choose a defense lawyer. Rather, a lawyer was assigned from the collective, and that lawyer was not supposed to put the client's interests ahead of the state. If the defense lawyer found evidence of guilt, it was the lawyer's duty to bring that evidence forward.

RELIGIOUS LAW: THE SHARIA

All states of the world have some version of case law or code law, often referred to as "Western law," introduced by the European powers or borrowed from them. A number of other legal systems survive partially, however. The most enduring are various forms of religious law; and of these, the most important is the Sharia—Islamic law—which makes up part of the legal system of such Islamic states as Morocco, Tunisia, Egypt, Syria, Iraq, Mauritania, Yemen, Iran, Afghanistan, and Pakistan.

No state is governed exclusively by the Sharia, and this is true of other traditional legal systems in use; rather, where it is used, it supplements and blends with Western law. For instance, the code systems of Egypt, Syria, and Iraq instruct judges to fill any gaps in the code according to principles of Islamic law.

Islamic law centers on obligations—to God and to other people—rather than on any sort of rights or entitlements. It is based on central Islamic principles of justice, good deeds, equality, and human brotherhood, as these were applied in the first few centuries after Muhammad to specific questions of behavior. The law was set by the tenth century A.D.; many elements that seem odd in modern society made sense for the medieval society in which they developed, but they have not changed since. For instance, polygamy apparently originated after the battle of Uhud in which many men were lost and their widows had to be provided for.[3] What seem to us unbearably harsh punishments, such as cutting off a hand for thievery, were common and perhaps enlightened in the tenth century; certainly, they did not differ from European practice of that time.

Unfortunately, because Islamic law is based on divine inspiration, it is not easily adapted by judges. It is not totally inflexible, however. New circumstances can be adjudicated by analogy to older cases, and complex evasions can be worked out that honor the letter, if not the spirit, of the old laws. For instance, the Sharia bars charging interest

---

[3]Noor Mohammed, "An Introduction to Islamic Law," in Kenneth Robert Redden, *Modern Legal Systems Cyclopedia* (Buffalo, N.Y.: Hein, 1990), p. 5a. 100.9.

Emile Durkheim's Theory of Law

Law is the set of rules that bind a society together, and so theorists of society have often looked to law as the critical point for analyzing society. Emile Durkheim, a great French sociologist of the nineteenth century, analyzed law in his work *The Division of Labor in Society* to address the question, "How do societies hold themselves together?" He saw law as functioning in varying ways at different stages of societal development to provide the mechanism for maintaining the society intact. In analyzing the role of law, he had a lot to say about why law develops as it does.

He first asked the question, "Why would people be moved to stay together as a society?" As an answer, he pointed to two bases for staying together: "mechanical solidarity," or the similarity among people of the same society that makes them feel akin to each other and comfortable with each other, and different from people not in that society; and "organic solidarity," the benefits of economic cooperation by which, for instance, a group of people with varying specialized skills are able by cooperating to build an automobile—something no one of them could possibly have done alone.

These two reasons for staying together as a society, however, operate under a natural tension. To build the kind of division of labor that yields large returns of organic solidarity, it is necessary for people to be *different* from each other. One person must be a designer, another a capable machinist, and so on. This must diminish the similarity that builds mechanical solidarity. Therefore, as society comes to rely more on organic solidarity, it must rely less on mechanical solidarity.

What does this imply for law? Durkheim points out that the two kinds of solidarity require different things of the law. Mechanical solidarity, based on people feeling similar to each other, requires law that makes people behave like each other and—when this similarity is broken—law that gives dramatic, public punishment. This reemphasizes the rules and reassures the public that the break has been compensated for. Laws will prescribe sexual practice, dietary practice, religion, dress, and so on; and punishment will be revengeful and memorable.

Organic solidarity, based on cooperation, needs law that ensures and regulates that cooperation—law enforcing the fulfillment of contracts, law regulating ownership of property, and so on. Where a law has been broken, what is needed is monetary compensation or enforcement of a contract, rather than societal retribution.

The development of law in modern societies—as improved technology makes the payoffs of cooperation ever greater, and we appear to rely more and more on "organic" rather than "mechanical" solidarity—does seem to bear Durkheim out. Punishments for crimes have become less dramatic and emphasize rehabilitation more than revenge. Public hangings were common in criminal cases in the United States in the nineteenth century, for instance, but are not used today. The vast body of contract law is a relatively "recent" addition of the last few centuries.

Durkheim is squarely on the "choice" side of "power and choice." He sees legal structures arising to suit the needs of individuals making up society, not because someone imposes them. The question Durkheim poses at the beginning is based on the idea that people choose to be in a society, that the existence of society is based not on the use of power but on an accumulation of individual choices.

on loans, because loans should be given out of a generous heart; but various evasions are used to get around this, such as giving a valuable gift in return for the "gift" of a loan. At its heart, however, a God-given law cannot be as flexible as human law.

It is perhaps the flexibility of Western systems that has led them to be so widely used. Modern commercial transactions, especially, require rules of a kind that most traditional legal systems never envisioned: enforcement of contracts, for instance. Where traditional law is used, it is always combined with many elements of Western law.

Trial in Kuwait of those who allegedly collaborated with Iraqi invaders in 1990.
(Gelin/Sipa Press)

THE BLENDING OF CASE LAW AND CODE LAW

I have probably exaggerated how sharp the distinction is between case law and code law. The differences between them are mostly differences of *degree*. For instance, case law is not "made by judges"; statute is also an important part of the law, and the state can always change "judge-made" law by passing a new law or amending the constitution. In code law, similarly, judges do not totally ignore precedent. They cannot decide a case by looking at the code and ignoring what other judges are doing, or things would become quite chaotic; nobody would know what the law was, because different judges might decide similar cases quite differently.

Therefore, the distinction between these two types is a matter of degree. Still, matters of degree can matter a great deal, as we have seen in comparing how criminal cases are handled in the two systems.

In recent years, we find that even these distinctions between the systems have been becoming less clear, as code law systems adopt some aspects of case law, and vice versa. For instance, in the general spirit of "constitutionalism," protections of individuals against abuse by the state have become popular even in many code law systems.[4] In 1959, France established for the first time the right of habeas corpus. In the mid–1990s, Italy changed its practice of putting judges in charge of the police investigation of a

[4]For a discussion of "constitutionalism," see Chapter 10.

crime. And, in 1999, the French parliament passed a bill to establish the presumption that an accused person is innocent until proven guilty.

Furthermore, most industrialized states with complex governmental structures have found it necessary to set up some sort of avenue for individuals to sue the state; if the state was supposed to pay you a pension through the social security system but did not, for example, you need some way to force it to honor its obligation. In standard code law systems, this was difficult because the law was a tool of the state and could not stand judge over it. Furthermore, faced with the complex governmental regulations of the twentieth century, government agencies often find themselves operating in quasi-judicial roles. An antitrust office, for instance, must rule on whether a proposed merger of companies will restrict trade unduly. Such decisions require "judicial" procedures within an administrative agency.

To handle questions like these, a wholly separate system of *administrative courts* has developed in many states, and these make law by precedent. In France, the administrative court system has a caseload larger than that of the regular courts, and its law is developed on a case basis.

Therefore, many code law systems are evolving to look more like case law systems. The opposite process has not been as marked, but some case law systems are becoming more like code law in certain ways. Legislatures and parliaments in some case law systems have begun to write codes in various areas to which judges are bound. For instance, many states in the United States have set up codes of uniform sentencing guidelines that set narrow ranges within which a judge may set the sentence of a person convicted of any particular crime. Also, in Great Britain—where case law started—after long debate, the European Convention on Human Rights was incorporated into English law in 2000, in effect inserting a code of human rights into the English legal system.

The historic differences in how legal systems originated in Europe may be receding far enough that the differences they produced are being overridden by the great *similarity* of conditions across modern industrialized states. These states need the strong coherence that code law can provide, but at the same time, their governmental operations are so large and complex that individuals feel a need for some protection against abuse by government. It may be that under these circumstances, a blend of code and case law is most appropriate.

COURTS

Courts are organized in sometimes rather complicated ways to take care of the variety of questions that come before them. The one common element to all courts is that, to the extent that a state has a tradition of constitutionalism, the courts are organized to be at some remove from other sources of political power. This is necessary if the courts are to be *independent* and able to give fair decisions no matter who is involved in a case.

Judges and other court officials in most of Europe are professional civil servants and are protected by the traditions of the bureaucratic model from political pressure.[5] In the United States, federal judges are appointed by the president with approval of the Senate, but the appointments are lifetime appointments so that no judge can be threatened with expulsion

---

[5]For a discussion of the "bureaucratic model," see Chapter 16.

for having made an unpopular decision. Judges for state and local courts are elected in many states, but those elections are usually set for long terms in office and are often formally non-partisan, to insulate the judges from the ordinary give-and-take of politics.

Where constitutionalism is less well established, however, the judiciary may have little independence. In Paraguay under Stroessner's military government, for example, the courts were subordinate to the military, and the president's office directed judicial decisions in all cases involving political prisoners.[6]

Courts are often organized separately to handle different kinds of law, especially:

- *Criminal law* involves a charge that a person has disobeyed a law prescribing proper conduct. In such cases, the state (through a prosecutor, district attorney, etc.) is the party that brings the case, and the person charged is the "defendant." The outcome of a criminal case is either acquittal of the defendant or punishment such as imprisonment or a fine.
- *Civil law* regulates relations between people. Civil cases may include disputes about the meaning of a contract, suits for damages in cases of injury, questions of mutual responsibility in marriage or divorce, and so on. The outcome of a civil case is some decision by the court as to mutual responsibilities—how much money is to be paid in child support, how a contract is to be met, or whatever. Civil cases usually involve private disputes rather than the breaking of a law that affects the broad public, so civil cases are usually conducted between individuals, without the state being involved as a party to the case.

  It is possible in civil law not only to get compensation for something that has happened in the past but to prevent a person from doing something in the future that will harm you or force them to do something that you wish. To do this, the court declares an "injunction" that the person should (or should not) do the thing required. An example would be an injunction against a neighbor draining a marsh that you share; the injunction might be necessary if the marsh, once drained, could never be the same again biologically, so that undoing the damage after the fact would not be possible.
- *Constitutional law* involves disputes about the nature of the political process and about whether laws are consistent with the constitution.

Aside from being organized by *substance,* courts may also be organized by *jurisdiction:*

- *Lower courts* handle disputes directly.
- *Appeals courts* handle disputes about whether lower courts have decided cases properly.
- *Juvenile courts* handle criminal cases involving defendants who are not yet adults. Using separate courts here allows for more flexible, private proceedings for defendants who are considered not yet fully responsible for their actions.
- *"State" courts* (federal systems only) handle cases under the separate "state" laws in a federal system.
- *Religious courts* are used in a state such as Iran, where religious law coexists with Western law.
- Many others.

[6]George Thomas Kurian, *Encyclopedia of the Third World* (New York: Facts on File, 1987), p. 1572.

"I WAS IN JAPAN FOR A WHILE. VERY BORING. NOBODY SUES ANYBODY THERE."

(© 2002 by Sidney Harris. Reprinted with permission.)

CONCLUSION

The "law" has a paradoxical character in that it is made by the government, but because it controls all parts of the state, it must control the government as well. Arrangements have been worked out to give varying degrees of independence to the law, but ultimately, the paradox remains.

Example: The Law in China

Chinese law is shaped by China's Confucian tradition and by the needs of the state's leaders. For thousands of years, until the end of the nineteenth century, China was dominated by Confucian thought. In the Confucian view of the world, society was meant to be in harmony. This harmony was thought to be maintained by leaders' continual demonstration of virtue, which instilled a sense of virtue into the rest of the people; and it was maintained also by complex networks of rites and mutual obligations based on the family and clan.

Problems were supposed to be worked out among disputants, perhaps with the help of a local person of superior rank, in a way that was conciliatory and that left everyone in agreement. No one was to lose; no one was to lose face. There were lawyers and law in China then, but they were to be appealed to as a last resort. The truth is, Confucian China *did not like law* and disapproved of it. Legal proceedings were made so unpleasant that most Chinese would go to any lengths to avoid them; and avoiding them was easier because the alternative of mediation and conciliation was urged on the disputants by their families and communities with a good deal of social pressure. Proceedings were deliberately made difficult and dangerous by Confucian rulers to discourage use of the law. The seventh-century Emperor K'ang Hsi is quoted as saying:

Lawsuits would tend to increase to a frightful amount, if people were not afraid of the tribunals, and if they felt confident of always finding in them ready and perfect justice. As man is apt to delude himself concerning his own interests, contests would then be interminable, and the half of the Empire would not suffice to settle the lawsuits of the other half. I desire, therefore, that those who have recourse to the tribunals should be treated without any pity, and in such a manner that they shall be disgusted with law, and tremble to appear before a magistrate.[7]

When the communists gained power in China after World War II, they continued the tradition of minimizing use of the law and legal procedures. From 1949 until 1976, the government passed little legislation, preferring to govern less formally through enunciation of doctrines by party leaders. Courts and the legal process were rarely used. In 1981, on the eve of Deng Xiaoping's opening of the system, there were only five thousand lawyers for a Chinese population of approximately 1 billion, compared with half a million lawyers for a U.S. population a quarter the size of China's.[8]

The Communist government changed the Confucian system markedly. The old aristocratic leadership and old networks of obligation and ancestral rites were replaced by factory committees, neighborhood committees, and party officials. However, the basic principle remained: disputes were resolved by conciliation and mediation processes with a great deal of social pressure on the disputants to reach a mutually acceptable consensus.

With the death of Mao Tse-tung in 1976, a power struggle developed between Mao's supporters, who had pushed society in a radical left direction during the Cultural Revolution of 1966–76, and more centrist leaders such as Deng Xiaoping, who had been victims of the Cultural Revolution. Deng and his supporters prevailed, and among the changes they introduced was a much greater reliance on law and legal proceedings than what had gone before. The body of statutes was expanded dramatically, with codes of law for many areas previously not ruled by law, including industrial safety, environmental protection, and patents; criminal law, marriage law, and many areas of civil law were expanded. The legal profession grew dramatically as well, with a tenfold increase by 1990. Especially in criminal law, changes were dramatic, with procedures set up rather along the lines of European code law.

---

[7]Cited in René David and John E. C. Brierly, *Major Legal Systems in the World Today,* 3d ed. (London: Steven, 1985), p. 520n.

[8]Xinhua General Overseas News Service, Item 1009065, 9 October 1990.

These changes were probably made for two reasons:

1.   *To establish a "rule of law":* The informal procedures of Confucian China, once the Confucian structure of society had been destroyed, left the way open for purely arbitrary power. Deng and his friends had suffered grievously from informal, arbitrary proceedings during the Cultural Revolution—Deng, for instance, was sentenced to hard labor, and his son was permanently crippled when his back was broken during interrogation—and they wanted to set up somewhat greater protections for the individual.

2.   *To handle the problem of economic disputes:* Deng wished to liberalize the Chinese economy, introducing large elements of market choice. Before 1976, there was little civil law in China. There was practically no individual property under communism, so there were few private disputes except for matters such as marriage that could be handled reasonably in conciliation by local bodies. With the development of a partial market economy, however, there would be long-distance disputes between suppliers and customers, partners, and so on, and these could not be handled locally. Also, economic exchanges required precise, dependable rules—not informal social processes for resolution. With the use of market mechanisms, civil law was necessary, and this could not easily be provided without building a more formal legal structure.

Economic development proved Deng right; by 1995, in the first eight months of the year, Chinese courts saw 697,000 cases involving disputes between businesses.[9]

Individuals have also begun to sue government agencies in increasing numbers. In 1990, there were thirteen thousand such suits, but in just five years, the number grew to 51,370. The outcomes are chancy. In one well-known case, three women who were forced to retire at age fifty-four by the China National Fisheries Group, even though Personnel Ministry regulations set the retirement age at sixty, sued and won in two different courts. But the courts have no power of enforcement, and the fisheries group simply ignored the judgments. On the other hand, in 1996, a restaurateur who had been jailed for fifteen days on charges that he had put opium in his hot pots successfully sued the police for false arrest. Overall, Professor Minxin Pei estimates that 39 percent of such suits have brought at least partial victory for the person bringing the suit.[10]

The legal system cannot change overnight, though. Even with a tenfold increase in the number of lawyers over the 1980s, there were only fifty thousand lawyers in China in 1990, and a number of them were part time and not fully trained. These are clearly insufficient to operate a full-scale legal system in a country of a billion people. Furthermore, old Confucian attitudes of disdain for the legal process die hard. In 1986, for instance, a woman who had been beaten by members of another clan petitioned the supreme court for compensation. When nothing came of the petition, she gave a copy of it to an editor of *People's Daily.* The editor sent it to the police, and she was sent to a concentration camp, beaten, and sent home. "The police said they

---

[9]"China's Litigation Boom," *Business Week,* 9 October 1995, p. 64.
[10]Elisabeth Rosenthal, "A Day in Court, and Sometimes Justices, for Chinese," *New York Times, 27* April 1998, p. A1.

would beat me to death for being a petitioner. Petitioners are all bad people, they said."[11] In January 2000, the *New York Times* quoted the official *China Youth Daily* saying that the use of confessions extracted by torture is still common: "It is commonplace for citizens to be arbitrarily summoned, forcibly seized, detained and even detained beyond legal time limits, and for citizens whose freedom has been restricted to be treated inhumanely."[12]

Example: The European Court of Justice

As you saw in the example at the end of Chapter 3, the European Union is an organization of fifteen Western European states attempting to merge their markets and economies. The Union has an elaborate governing structure, although the members remain independent, sovereign states.

One of the governing structures is a court, the European Court of Justice; observing this court provides us with a fascinating case of how a court may develop a body of law in "new ground"—fifteen independent states that are bound together to form a common market. The court consists of thirteen justices who are appointed by the unanimous consent of the fifteen member states. A justice serves a term of six years and is sworn to act on behalf of the Union.

The original basis of the European Union is the 1957 Treaty of Rome, which comes as close as anything to serving as the Union's constitution. The treaty was rather vague about the status and duties of the court. It stated that the court must ensure that "the law is observed" in applying the treaty (Article 164), and at various other points, it suggested that the court should apply general principles of law; but it did not spell out clearly the court's jurisdiction or powers.

Much like John Marshall's Supreme Court in the early days of the United States, the Court of Justice has made its place in the order of things through a series of decisions, in effect defining its powers by what it has been able to get away with. It has moved cautiously, but steadily, to make its law supreme within the European Union.

In an important early decision, the court ruled that the Rome Treaty set up a new order for the members, which was not governed by international law; in effect, the court established that the European Union would have an internal system of law. The key question was whether a member state could retaliate in kind if it was injured by another member violating the Rome Treaty. Under international law, this would be permitted; and so if the Rome Treaty were simply a treaty among sovereign states, a member could do this. The court ruled, however, that one member could not retaliate

[11]*The Economist,* 25 August 1990, p. 28.
[12]Elisabeth Rosenthal, "In China's Legal Evolution, the Lawyers Are Handcuffed," *New York Times,* 6 January 2000, p. A1.

against another but must instead seek relief through the Union's institutions. It thereby transformed the Treaty of Rome from a treaty into a constitution.

In a later decision, the Court of Justice expanded the right to bring cases from member states to include also individuals and corporations in those states. Therefore, citizens of states in the Union could bring cases against their own governments. Most cases in the court have involved trade regulations because the Union is, after all, primarily an organization to enforce free trade within its borders. Perhaps the most dramatic development of law by the Court of Justice, however, has been in the area of individual rights.

The Treaty of Rome did not specify many rights for individuals. It was a document intended to set up a free market, and most of the few rights that are mentioned in it are economic: the right to free movement of capital, the right to bargain collectively, the right of women to earn pay equal to that of men, and so on. The court, however, has gradually developed across several dozen cases a set of rights based on "the constitutional traditions common to the Member States" and on other treaties that member states may have signed, such as the European Convention on Human Rights—even though the court is nowhere directly empowered to enforce those treaties. Some of these cases have gone deeply into what would be considered the independent responsibilities of member states: British schools have been directed to stop using corporal punishment, the Dutch army has had to change its disciplinary procedures, German courts have had to provide access to lawyers before a suspect is charged with a crime. Among rights that the court has written into European Union law are freedom to practice religion; a right against *any* kind of discrimination based on gender, not only discrimination in pay; the right to education; and freedom from arbitrary governmental decision.

Because so little was written into the Treaty of Rome along these lines, the Court of Justice has proceeded by building a body of case law. As is usually true where case law develops, the court has been tolerated in this because it has been seen as a constructive force in the development of the Union and because the alternative—states retaliating against each other for trade violations, for instance—could bring chaos.

As is often the case with courts when expanding their powers, the European Court of Justice, in making the moves described above, appears to have followed a strategy of choosing relatively inconsequential cases in which neither side could easily protest the outcome. Since no serious ox is gored in such a case, it is less likely that anyone will cry foul, so an expansion of court powers can slip through in the absence of a more general protest against the actual outcome. A good example is *Costa* v. *ENEL* (1964), in which Flaminio Costa, a shareholder in an Italian utility company, sued when the Italian government nationalized the company. He argued that the nationalization violated E.E.C. rules (the European Union was at that time called the European Economic Community), but his claim was rejected by the Italian courts. The basic substance of the case was simple: E.E.C. rules clearly did not prohibit the nationalization, and the European Court of Justice ruled so. But the court took advantage of this case to insert into its decision another point that probably was not really required for its ruling: it first asked, Is E.E.C. law superior to national law, and does it confer a right on individuals to sue their national governments under the body of

E.E.C. law? The court ruled that E.E.C. law was superior in this way, thus expanding its jurisdiction. Neither side had a good basis from which to challenge the decision. A decision in which the court had upheld the actions of the Italian government gave the government no reason to protest the ruling—even though it was a decision that had the effect of taking power from the government. Costa might protest the outcome, but he had actually not been a major shareholder, so his interest was mainly symbolic; and in any case, the critical jurisdictional part of the court's decision was a part in which the court had ruled in his favor, saying that he did, indeed, have the right to sue the government in the European Court of Justice. He could hardly protest that part of the court's decision.[13]

Like courts everywhere, a basic problem for the Court of Justice is enforcing its decisions. Its authority could never have developed as it has if member states did not heed it when it ruled on a case. It has no power to force compliance and must rely on member states' governments to enforce its rulings, which could have posed grave problems except that there has been a remarkable record of compliance. There have been exceptions, though. An order to France to desist from restricting imports of mutton was defied for a couple of years. In general, states have followed the court's directions, and the more often this happens, the more solidly the court's power becomes rooted in habit and expectations.

FURTHER READING

Abraham, Henry J. *The Judicial Process.* New York: Oxford University Press, 1998.

Alter, Karen J. "The European Court's Political Power." *West European Politics* 19 (July 1996): 458–87.

Bartlett, Katherine T., and Kennedy, Rosanne, eds. *Feminist Legal Theory.* Boulder, Colo.: Westview, 1991.

Barton, John H.; Gibbs, James Lowell, Jr.; Hao Li, Victor; and Merryman, John Henry. *Law in Radically Different Cultures.* St. Paul, Minn.: West, 1983.

Baum, Lawrence. *The Puzzle of Judicial Behavior.* Ann Arbor: University of Michigan Press, 1997.

David, René, and Brierly, John E. C. *Major Legal Systems in the World Today.* 3d ed. London: Steven, 1985.

Epstein, Lee, ed. *Contemplating Courts.* Washington, D.C.: Congressional Quarterly Press, 1995.

Gibson, James L., and Caldeira, Gregory A. "The Legal Cultures of Europe." *Law and Society Review* 30 (1996): 55–85.

Gilman, Howard. *The Votes That Counted: How the Court Decided the 2000 Presidential Election.* Chicago: University of Chicago Press, 2001.

Glendon, Mary Ann; Gordon, Michael W.; and Osakwe, Christopher. *Comparative Legal Traditions.* St. Paul, Minn.: West, 1982.

Judicature 81 (May-June 1998), special issue, "Courts and Justice Abroad."

Redden, Kenneth Robert. *Modern Legal Systems Cyclopedia.* Buffalo, N.Y.: Hein, 1990.

---

[13]I am grateful to Gordon Silverstein for bringing this case to my attention.

WEBSITES OF INTEREST

United States federal judiciary:
http://www.uscourts.gov/links.html

Oyez,oyez,oyez: a database of major U.S. Supreme Court cases, including multimedia capacity to listen to the oral arguments of counsel:
http://oyez.nwu.edu/

Foreign and International Law Resources, Cornell Law Library:
http://www.law.cornell.edu/library/guides/forin/forin.html

FindLaw, for all aspects of law, including firms, laws, and legal news:
http://www.findlaw.com/12international/countries/

PART FIVE

INTERNATIONAL POLITICS

18

GLOBAL POLITICS: POLITICS AMONG STATES (AND OTHERS)

In the preceding chapters, we looked at the manner in which politics—the use of power to make collective choices for a group of people—is carried on within a state. However, states also carry on politics *among* themselves. For instance, they sign trade agreements setting up special arrangements for the exchange of goods between firms in two or more countries. Or a number of states may agree to coordinate their military activities, as in the NATO alliance. Regular exchanges of scientific information are set up among states. Agreements are drawn up in which groups of states commit themselves to such things as a promise not to test nuclear weapons in the open air. Treaties are drawn up to protect wildlife that migrates across state borders. Wars are fought and settled. Each of these events makes a collective choice for a group of two or more states, and so these are examples of politics—the use of power to make collective choices—*among* states rather than within one state. This is commonly called "international politics" or "global politics."

THE EVOLUTION OF THE INTERNATIONAL SYSTEM SINCE WORLD WAR II

Before analyzing international politics abstractly, it will be useful to review the development of the international system since World War II.

From the seventeenth century until the twentieth, most of the world's wealth and military power were concentrated in Europe, and various European states used that power to subjugate large populations around the world and form them into colonial empires. By the early twentieth century, European dominance was weakening, especially because of the increasing power of the United States and Japan. The Europeans then hastened their slide from power by squandering their wealth and slaughtering their youth in World Wars I and II. Although other powers such as the United States and Japan were eventually involved in these wars and they have been called "world wars," almost all of the fighting and destruction centered in Europe. The European states emerged from World War II in 1945 exhausted, with only enough strength left to reconstruct themselves internally.

Two major changes in international politics resulted from this exhaustion of Europe: (1) Two new superpowers—the Soviet Union and the United States—arose to fill the power vacuum, and (2) the European states' empires threw off European rule, because the Europeans no longer had the power to hold them in subjugation.

The rise of the Soviet Union and the United States to dominate world politics created quite a different kind of system than what had gone before. When Europe dominated world politics, a number of substantial powers were involved in the system because Europe was so fragmented. Britain, France, Germany, Italy, and to some extent the Soviet Union, Japan, and the United States could figure in alliances. Many varying combinations of states in alliance were possible, and patterns of alliance shifted as states jockeyed for position. In the world after 1945, however, and especially from 1945 to about 1960, the system of politics consisted of a bipolar rivalry between the United States and the Soviet Union.

The two superpowers had been allies in the war against Hitler and initially set out into their domination of the world with pledges to cooperate in building a new, peaceful political order. However, they differed deeply in political philosophy, and they had conflicting political and economic goals. The Soviet Union used its dominating military force in the region to bring most of Eastern Europe under its control for economic advantage and to insulate itself militarily and politically from Western European states such as Germany and France (which had frequently attacked it earlier in the century). By 1946, Winston Churchill had coined the phrase "Iron Curtain" in his famous speech at Westminster College, Missouri:

> From Stettin in the Baltic to Trieste in the Adriatic, an iron curtain has descended across the continent. Behind that line lie all the capitals of the ancient states of Central and Eastern Europe. Warsaw, Berlin, Prague, Vienna, Budapest, Belgrade, Bucharest and Sofia, all these famous cities and populations around them lie in what I must call the Soviet sphere, and all are subject in one form or another not only to Soviet influence but to a very high and, in many cases, increasing measure of control from Moscow.[1]

In 1947, President Harry S. Truman announced that the United States was sending economic aid to the embattled anticommunist government of Greece, and the Cold War was joined.

The period of rivalry between the Soviet Union and the United States from 1945 on into the 1960s (and periodically until 1989) is called the "Cold War" because while at times it involved intense animosity, it never developed into full-scale "hot" warfare. Various skirmishes were fought—the Soviet blockade of West Berlin in 1948, war between the United States and the Soviet client state of North Korea in 1950—but there was never direct fighting between the two superpowers. There is a clear reason for this. Not only was the international system turned into a bipolar system after 1945, but the

---

[1]Randolph S. Churchill, ed., *The Sinews of Peace: Post-War Speeches by Winston S. Churchill* (London: Cassell, 1948), p. 100.

two superpowers of that system were armed with a new kind of weapon that made a war between them essentially unwinnable. Nuclear weapons are so destructive that in an all-out nuclear war, either combatant would be able to ruin the other.[2] As a result, the bipolar system that followed World War II was marked by a frustrated rivalry in which the two superpowers chewed on their animosity toward each other but were not able to do much about it.

The other main result of Europe's exhaustion after World War II was the breakup of the old colonial empires. One hundred of today's 193 states were colonies of European states at the outbreak of World War II. In other words, there are more than twice as many states in the world now as there were in 1941. These new states receive sympathy and support from some of the older states—such as China, Egypt, and the states of Latin America—which, although they were independent before World War II, find that they share a common set of problems with the newer states. Together, these new and older states make up the South.

The growth in numbers and importance of the Southern states has changed the international system markedly. The South commands many of the world's natural resources and comprises about three-fourths of its population. However, it does not command anything close to a proportional share of wealth or military power. Most of the states of the South are individually weak, although some such as India, China, and Brazil have developed into moderately important powers. However, as a group they account for so much of the world that they cannot be ignored. Many Southern states, as they grow in wealth and military strength, appear to have a great potential as future powers. The United States, Japan, and the states of Western Europe court states of the South as important markets for the goods they buy and produce and as important powers for the future.

THE NEW WORLD ORDER

As of the early 1970s, then, the world could have been described as a fairly stable system of states dominated by two main conflicts—a military standoff in the Cold War animosity between the Soviet bloc and the bloc led by the United States, and an economic and political "north-south" tension between the South and the industrialized states of both blocs. Over the next three decades, however, five major developments changed this system into the more fluid, more complicated, but less tense one we face today:

1. *Steadily the set of actors involved in international politics expanded and became more varied.* At the beginning of this period, international politics were

---

[2]A revisionist literature has questioned whether nuclear weapons prevent war. This literature points out that in the 1920s, many people thought that the existence of poison gas, in combination with the development of modern air forces, had made all-out war unwinnable. Any power, even if it were going down in defeat, could launch such deathly attacks with gas canisters that the winner of the war would be destroyed. Therefore, it was agreed, no one would dare wage war against a power that had poison gas weapons. As it turned out, full-scale war was waged in World War II, but without gas. The participating powers had chemical weapons, but none used them for fear of retaliation in kind. The revisionist literature argues that all-out conventional warfare could similarly occur today without the use of nuclear weapons. See, for example, John Ellis van Courtland Moon, "Chemical Weapons and Deterrence: The World War II Experience," *International Security* 8 (Spring 1984): 3–35.

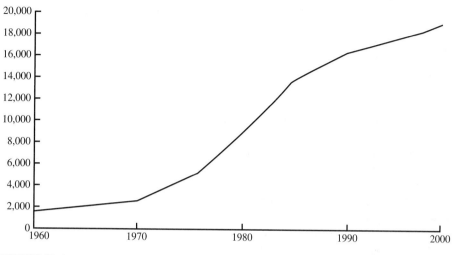

FIGURE 18–1
Growth of nongovernmental international organizations.
Source: Yearbook of International Organizations, various years.

conducted pretty much by the states of the world, plus the United Nations and its agencies. Starting in the early 1970s, however, the number of nongovernmental international organizations began to grow explosively—growth that continues, as we see in Figure 18–1.

Not all of these organizations are actively engaged in international politics. The International Political Science Association, for instance, exists mainly to promote communication among scholars, although it will occasionally act to promote or defend academic freedom in various parts of the world. Many others— Amnesty International, the International League for the Repatriation of Soviet Jews, the Pugwash Conferences on Science and World Affairs, the Union of National Radio and Television Organizations of Africa, the International Federation of Journalists, to name only a few—are politically active in all sorts of ways.

In addition to formal organizations, other kinds of new actors have joined the scene. We noted in Chapter 3 that many corporations are so large and their operations spread across so many states' boundaries that they bargain directly with the states almost as equals. Terrorist groups, too, have become significant actors in international politics. Throughout the 1980s, for instance, terrorist groups in Lebanon that were not directly associated with any government were an important international factor because of the leverage they gained by taking and holding hostages from Western states. More recently, the terrorist attack on the United States on September 11, 2001, reshaped the whole role of the United States in the world—a very different, also very important, example of how central nonstate actors have become in international politics. Another example of how important nonstate actors have become in international politics is provided in the box, "Banning Land Mines."

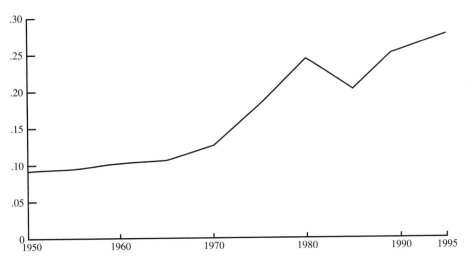

FIGURE 18–2
Trade in goods and services (exports plus imports) as a proportion of U.S. gross national product.
Source: U.S. Bureau of the Census. *Statistical Abstract of the United States,* various years.

Banning Land Mines

In September 1997, nearly one hundred states signed an international treaty in which they agreed not to use land mines and to destroy any they had already laid down. Land mines are a weapon that is especially dangerous for civilians. After a war is over, they usually remain hidden in the ground for years, so most of the victims they claim are farmers plowing fields or children at play.

The ban was not engineered by the states that signed it. Rather, it is a prime example of the growing influence of nonstate actors in international politics. In 1990, a coalition of the Vietnam Veterans of America (United States), Human Rights Watch (United States), Physicians for Human Rights (United States), Medico International (Germany), Handicap International (France), and the Mines Advisory Group (Britain) began to work for an international ban. They waged a vivid public relations campaign featuring the late Princess Diana of Britain comforting land mine victims in Bosnia and Angola. They garnered a key ally among the world's states in Canada, whose foreign minister took on the ban as a personal cause. In 1995, the International Red Cross joined in with a large ad campaign—the first time that this prestigious organization had ever joined a controversial cause. Canada called a special conference of states in 1996 to discuss a general ban, and from there, the process moved swiftly.

---

2.   ***The interdependence of the world's states grew enormously.*** One way this has shown up is in the dependence of states' economies on their trade with each other. For the United States, for instance, trade as a proportion of economic activity was fairly stable through the 1950s and 1960s, but it became an increasingly significant part of our economy in the 1970s. As seen in Figure 18–2, it doubled as a proportion of our gross national product between 1970 and 1980. Not only

did international trade play a larger role in states' economies, but because many of a state's largest corporations were spread across numerous countries, states' economies depended more on what was going on in other states than was the case in the first half of the twentieth century.

Environmental policy is another area in which interdependence has increased explosively. As the world becomes more industrialized, the environmental impact of what we do is less a matter of concern only for the polluting state and perhaps its nearest neighbors. The depletion of the ozone layer and the increase in carbon dioxide in the atmosphere that causes global warming affect all states' populations. These and other problems are the ultimate "externality"; as we saw earlier (p. 139), any externality forces a search for collective decisions. The Kyoto Accords to reduce global warming, signed by 178 states in 2001 (but not by the United States), are a good example of the environmental collective choice that externalities from the industrial economy increasingly require.

Finally, partly through the expansion of worldwide communications such as Cable News Network and partly because the people of the world are more literate and better educated than in the past, we seem more aware of what happens in other states than we used to be. What would once have been claimed as "internal affairs" of sovereign states—apartheid in South Africa, human rights abuses in many other states—are now part of international politics.

It is a cliché, but still a good one, that the world is becoming a smaller place.

3. *The bipolar system of rivalry between the Soviet Union and the United States disappeared.* This had already been happening, fairly slowly, for about twenty years as the U.S.S.R. and the U.S.A. gradually lost their monopolies of economic and military power to such upstarts (communist and noncommunist) as Japan, China, Germany, and France. The system of rivalry finally ended rather suddenly with the economic exhaustion of the Soviet Union about 1989 and its internal collapse after the failed coup of 1991.

The results of this shift are momentous. The way we defined the system of states—West, East, "Third World"—had been based on the old rivalry. Defense establishments suddenly found themselves searching for a new raison d'etre. Client states, such as Cuba and Pakistan, found themselves abandoned by their superpower partners.

4. *Starting roughly in the mid-1980s, a large number of states around the world shifted their economies more in the direction of open markets; as a result of this, the states of the world became somewhat more alike.* Partly this shift resulted from the collapse of formerly communist systems. Partly it resulted from the formation of new trade alliances and the necessity of meshing the economies of once heavily regulated states with the more open economies of their new partners; Mexico's economy moved to a more open condition after formation of the NAFTA partnership with the United States, for instance. Finally, a number of economies in Africa (early 1990s) and East Asia (after 1997) were forced to become more open following financial collapses bred by unwise governmental manipulation of their markets.

The states of the world therefore grew more similar to one another. There were fewer autocratic regimes at the end of the 1990s than there were twenty years before. Governments are more interested in open trade relations than they were when their economies were treated as fortresses. The technocrats who run most states' economic policies "speak the same language" and often were educated at the same American universities; therefore, negotiations for cooperative economic policy have become somewhat easier.

5. *In the late 1990s, a body of international law began to develop that might impose enforceable law on the leaders of states and thus on the states themselves.* A number of treaties had been in effect since the Second World War that brought the actions of states under international jurisdiction, but no one had tried seriously to enforce them. For instance, most of the states of the world had signed a convention against genocide in 1948. In the late 1990s, however, human rights organizations and their supporters in governmental posts successfully began to use these treaties to bring former heads of state to judgment for their actions. The first instance of this was the arrest of former President Augusto Pinochet of Chile, who had presided over a military dictatorship marked by the use of torture and kidnappings. After the return of democracy to Chile, Pinochet had lived in peaceful retirement as a result of the pacts by which democracy had been restored; but when he traveled to Britain in 1998, a Spanish judge asked for his extradition to Spain so that he could be tried for crimes against international law. Although heads of state traditionally had not been held personally liable for their actions as leaders of their state, the British Law Lords (the highest court in Britain) ruled in an important precedent that Pinochet was indeed liable as president for violations of the International Torture Convention, which Chile had signed. It is important to note that the International Torture Conventions treaty, under which Pinochet was tried, is one of the few international treaties that includes international jurisdiction—that is, it allows any country to punish violators of the treaty.

In a second important case, Serbia in 2001 surrendered its former president, Slobodan Milosevic, to NATO to be tried by the United Nations War Crimes Tribunal in the Netherlands for crimes associated with the deportation of hundreds of thousands of ethnic Albanians from the Serbian province of Kosovo. Unlike the trial of Pinochet, which was decided on very narrow grounds (the Law Lords ruled that Pinochet could be tried only for violations of the International Torture Conventions and then only for tortures committed after 1988, when Chile had signed the convention), the UN court worked with a broad case law based on the Nuremberg trials of Nazi war criminals and the general development of international law since those trials, including the Torture Convention and the International Convention on Genocide.

Finally, a move is underway to establish an International Criminal Court, based in the Netherlands, that would be able to try any individuals, including heads of state and other government officials, for a broad range of crimes, including genocide, "crimes against humanity," war crimes, and the crime of aggression. If and when a minimum of sixty states has ratified the treaty establishing the court, it will be established; as of late 2001, thirty-seven states had ratified the treaty.

We are still only beginning to work out the implications of these changes in the international system. There are many dangers inherent in some of the changes. There are likely to be more "small wars," for instance, as the superpowers no longer feel a need to keep a lid on boundary disputes around the world; and while these may be "small" wars, we have seen in Bosnia, Somalia, Kosovo, and other instances that they can be dirty and cruel. However, the new, fluid system also offers opportunities. It may be that with increased interdependence and the disappearance of bipolarity, the world will be able to search more cooperatively for collective decisions to address its collective problems.

In this regard we have seen both hopeful and unhopeful signs. The 1991 Gulf War was an indication of the possibilities of cooperation. In August 1990, Iraq blatantly invaded and seized its neighbor Kuwait. It is true that the separate existence of the two states was as usual the result of a colonial past (Iraq had long asserted a claim on Kuwait), and so the boundary issues were not altogether clear. However, the invasion *was* sudden, and the same sort of claims Iraq made could have justified hundreds of other invasions by other states in other parts of the world. Therefore, most of the world's states united in condemnation of Iraq's action.

Things might have stopped there, as they so often had in the past, with international condemnation. However, partly because of worldwide concern for supplies of oil ("interdependence" again) and partly because the U.S.S.R. and the U.S.A. did not veto each other's proposals in the United Nations (the end of bipolarity), the UN was able to function as its original designers had intended—to provide collective protection to small states threatened by larger ones. The protection was concrete: initially, a program of economic sanctions against Iraq, followed by military action.

On the other hand, one should not conclude that international relations in the post-Cold War era will necessarily be based on cooperation most—or even much—of the time. A cautionary example is provided by the tragic brutality that followed the breakup of Yugoslavia.

Yugoslavia was a state composed of quite disparate ethnic groups: Roman Catholic Slovenians and Croatians; Greek Orthodox Serbs, Montenegrens, and Macedonians; and Moslems who were mostly Bosnians but included Croatians and Serbs. Tensions were exacerbated by the fact that the Croatians had sided with the occupying German troops during World War II against guerrilla troops that were primarily Serbian. This multinational state had held together as a loose federation throughout the postwar period at least partly because of bipolarity, with the United States and the Soviet Union fearful of what would happen if the country were allowed to disintegrate.

In 1991, Slovenia and Croatia signaled their intention to declare independence. Serbia, the largest part of Yugoslavia, controlled most of the army and tried to block their secession. Slovenia established its independence after a few sharp battles; but in Croatia, a Serbian minority, supported by the Yugoslav army, tried to prevent Croatia from seceding or at least to isolate large areas of Croatia and add them to Serbia.

A prolonged civil war broke out in Croatia. In 1992, the situation turned from awful to horrible when Bosnia also declared its independence of Serbia and a complex four-party war ensued, with Croatians, Bosnian Moslems, Croatian and Bosnian Serb minorities, and Serbia fighting in varying combinations. At times, Croatia and the Serbs ganged up on the Moslems; at other times, Croatia shifted sides and attacked the Serbs. There

PEACE COMES TO BOSNIA

(Auth © 1995 The *Philadelphia Inquirer.* Reprinted with permission of Universal Press Syndicate. All rights reserved.)

were nauseating atrocities on all sides, and the prolonged siege and bombardment of the Moslem city of Sarajevo focused international attention on the events.

The rest of the world repeatedly declared their wish to help stop the fighting and return seized lands to the Bosnian Moslems, but they were ineffective in pursuing either goal. The United Nations declared an embargo on arms exports to any part of Yugoslavia, but this mostly hurt the Bosnian Moslems because Croatia and Serbia had ways to obtain arms despite the embargo. The European Union offered to mediate the conflict and discouraged American offers (admittedly halfhearted) to become involved. The Europeans appeared to believe Yugoslavia was in their sphere of interest and that they should take responsibility for it. While the E.U. formed a common policy toward the region and sent troops to dispense humanitarian aid under United Nations auspices, they were never able to take a tough stance toward any of the combatants that might have stopped the fighting.

Finally in 1995, after years of terrible bloodletting, the E.U. and the United States, under the auspices of their common NATO organization, decided to use massive air power to punish those who resisted peace accords. With this threat as a tool and with the offer of Russian, American, and Western European troops to help police any peace agreements, all participants were finally brought to serious negotiations. A peace treaty was signed in November 1995 in Dayton, Ohio. An uneasy peace holds in Bosnia, but keeping that peace requires the continuing presence of thousands of troops from the United States and other members of the United Nations.

The latest and possibly worst chapter of this tragedy took place in 1998 and 1999, when Serbian troops and militia devastated the largely Muslim province of Kosovo. Again NATO threatened massive air strikes if Serbia did not stop the atrocities, but this time, Serbia did not back down. A destructive air campaign against Serbia ensued, during which Serbia simply accelerated its ethnic cleansing of the province, at one point driving out almost the entire population. In the end, the air attacks were too much for Serbia, and it agreed to withdraw its forces from the province. But hundreds of thousands of Kosovars and many Serbs had died in what proved a rather hollow victory.

Even taking into account that this part of the world has been famously difficult to work with throughout history, the international system cannot be said to have worked well to prevent destruction and human suffering in this long, sad, and possibly preventable series of wars.

INTERNATIONAL POLITICS

The world has a full agenda of problems to address: the problem of environmental degradation; the peaceful transformation of the socialist societies in Eastern Europe and the former Soviet Union; help for the poorest states of the world (mostly in Africa), which are becoming poorer rather than better off; the population explosion, which again is occurring most rapidly in the poorest countries; the maintenance of international trade in the face of protectionist competition; the control of nuclear arms; and many more.

How are these to be addressed? I have argued that the changes of the last two decades may—*may*—provide new opportunities to find solutions to common problems. However, international politics has some special characteristics that make it unusually difficult to find common solutions, as compared with other types of politics. These enduring weaknesses may or may not stymie any hopes of a "new world order."

Let us look a bit more abstractly at international politics. We will first consider a few ways in which politics *among* states differs from politics *within* a state, the sort of politics with which we have been concerned so far in this book. It will be necessary, in doing this, to add one new concept, the "fiduciary political role." After we have looked at this question, we will conclude by examining the nature of power in international politics and the mechanisms of war and diplomacy by which international politics is carried on.

How is international politics like that which we have been looking at so far in this book, and how is it different? In its main outlines, politics among states is a good deal like politics within states. The same sorts of policy questions are addressed in both— regulation of potentially harmful behavior, aid programs for the weak, guarantees of standard weights and measures, and so on. Like politics within states, politics among states is marked by the use of force and by appeals to mutual self-interest, that is, by power and choice. Political decisions—decisions on behalf of groups of people—are reached in both types of politics. However, in important ways international politics differs from politics within a state. *The most important difference is that there is no single central authority to provide ultimate settlement of a dispute among states. Also, political*

figures are more likely to follow overtly selfish (selfish on behalf of their states' interests) *strategies in politics among states. Finally, political interchange does not proceed
as easily in politics among states as it does in politics within a state.* Let us look at each
of these points.

THE ABSENCE OF CENTRAL AUTHORITY

In politics as it is carried on within a state, the various antagonists are subject to a central authority that has enough power to settle a question firmly. If environmentalists
square off in conflict with a mining company, both sides know that ultimately their dispute will be resolved by some higher authority that has the power to make them accept
that decision, even if they do not agree with it. In the United States, that authority would
be Congress, the president, or perhaps the Supreme Court; in Britain, it would be the Parliament; in Saudi Arabia, it would be the king. Within any state, there is some central
authority, more powerful than any single political force, that can enforce decisions on
any question. The only exception to this would be a state involved in a civil war, which
is precisely a situation in which there is no clearly established central authority.

In politics conducted *among* states, however, there is no central position of authority.
Therefore, states that become involved in disputes must ultimately settle the disputes
themselves, whether by negotiations or through war. Other states may give helpful
advice and exert pressure on the disputants, but there is no body of any sort that can
impose a settlement.

The United Nations would be a potential body of authority. It is an organization of
189 states, most of the states of the world, that accepts responsibility for many of the
things a government would do within a state. That is, it is concerned to preserve law and
order by preventing violent solutions to disputes (i.e., wars); it promotes health programs, education, and research; it tries to see that poorer states are helped.

While the United Nations tries to do the *things* a government does, it cannot do them
the way a government would do them. It has no army or police force of its own to enforce
its decisions. Rather, it must depend on voluntary help from its member states. Few
states are going to send their soldiers voluntarily into a place where they are not
wanted—and risk war with the people on whom they are enforcing the United Nations'
decision; therefore, this has effectively meant that the UN can almost never send in a
police force unless the disputants agree voluntarily to accept it. (The Gulf War was the
first exception to this rule in decades.) The UN's attempt to pacify Somalia is a different question, because that involved bringing order to a region where the government had
broken down, rather than a case of interceding between warring parties. Even there,
though, the organization found it difficult to marshal the will to impose solutions.

Despite these limitations, the UN has frequently been able to play a helpful role when
the nations involved in a dispute want to bring in a neutral group to police their negotiated settlement. For instance, small United Nations forces supervised the initial disengagement of Egyptian and Israeli forces after their 1967 war. This is a far cry from the
real policing power that would give the United Nations the authority to force a decision
on the parties in dispute, but it has helped on occasion to reduce international violence.
The United Nations is discussed in more detail in an example at the end of this chapter.

Another potentially ultimate authority in the system of states is the International Court of Justice, headquartered in the Netherlands. The court is a branch of the United Nations, but the body of "international law" over which it decides goes back far beyond the United Nations, which was founded only in 1945. Since that time, about fifty cases have been tried in the court, but again, any solution laid down by the court sticks only if the parties of the dispute voluntarily abide by the court's ruling. In 1984, for instance, Nicaragua brought suit against the United States for mining its harbors. When the United States refused to admit that the court had jurisdiction, the court could do little. Most cases that come to the court are not of this sort but are cases in which those involved have agreed in advance to accept the court's decision, whatever it may be. In these circumstances, the court can serve as a useful tool for resolving disputes. Overall, however, it cannot play the role a government would play.

We noted above (p. 378) that developments in the late 1990s may produce new strands of international law in which heads of state (or at least former heads of state) may be punished for crimes committed by their states. The enforcing agents in these cases would be other states rather than an international authority. Even if this process continues, however, we will still be a long way from holding sitting rulers of powerful states accountable for their states' actions—in contrast to disgraced former rulers of weak states.

With no ultimate governmental authority in the world, politics among states is in many ways what we might expect politics within a state to be if that state had no government. States that are large and strong are able to bully smaller states, and they usually get what they want. Small states must attach themselves to stronger states, through alliances, for protection. In effect, gangs of states join together for mutual protection just as, in a governmentless state, people would form gangs.

FIDUCIARY POLITICAL ROLES AND INTERNATIONAL MORALITY

Before we consider the second special aspect of international politics, we must define a new concept—*the fiduciary role in politics.*[3] Someone acts in a fiduciary role if that person operates as an agent on behalf of another person's interest. A real estate agent acts in a fiduciary role on behalf of a person who wishes to sell a house, or a lawyer acts in a fiduciary role for a client.

The important thing about fiduciary roles for our purposes is that a person acting in a fiduciary role stands in a peculiar moral position. Let us assume that the fiduciary agent is personally upright and moral and that among the agent's "upright" traits is a strong sense of duty toward the person whose interests are being represented. Now let us suppose that the agent is caught in circumstances in which doing the thing that is personally moral will hurt the interests of the person who is represented. Consider the lawyer, for instance, who may need to browbeat a timid witness to defend a client. What is the right thing to do? We hope such a lawyer would never browbeat a timid person on her own behalf, but is it right for her to impose her personal scruples on the client's case and thereby injure the client's interests?

---

[3]William H. Riker presents the concept of fiduciary role in much the way it is used here in *A Theory of Political Coalitions* (New Haven: Yale University Press, 1962), pp. 24–27.

This sort of situation arises frequently in modern life because we have given more and more of our activities over to agents. A corporation president might be generous personally and wish to pay the company's workers more than the going rate, but it is the stockholders who will pay if the company does this, not the president. Is it right for the president to be generous with their money? A real estate agent might not remain silent about that tiny leak in the north gable in trying to sell his own house, but is he right to impose his openness on his client? We recognize that a different moral situation exists when people do something on behalf of others than when they do it to help themselves. We feel differently about a woman who shoplifts caviar than we do about a mother, in dire straits, who steals food for her children.

How does all this relate to international politics? It is important to international politics because here, more than in the politics within a state, almost all decisions are made by those who see themselves as acting in fiduciary roles, on behalf of the people in the state they represent. In politics as it occurs *within* a state, political figures act to some extent as fiduciary agents (members of Congress, for instance, represent their constituents); but they are largely personal decision makers who represent no clear single interest. Leaders of states (and the diplomats and others who help them to construct the state's position in international politics), however, work on behalf of a single clear "client," the people of that state. It is well understood that a state's leader owes first duty in international politics to the state and its interests, and that anything or anyone else in the world for whom the leader feels affection must run a distant second. We expect George W. Bush to serve the interests of the United States, Jacques Chirac to serve the interests of France, and Hosni Mubarak to serve the interests of Egypt.

This gives a different and colder moral tone to international politics than we find in politics within states. We expect leaders of states to be more cold-blooded in international politics than they would be domestically. What is regarded as personal virtue in domestic affairs may be seen as perverse and harmful in international politics.

Leaders of states have often been forgiven for official acts that, if done for personal gain, would have blackened their names forever. Harry Truman, for instance, killed thousands of Japanese civilians when he ordered atomic bombs dropped on Hiroshima and Nagasaki, and Winston Churchill launched devastating firebomb attacks on German cities. However, they were judged at least partly in light of their official positions. That leaders of states see themselves as filling fiduciary roles is reinforced by *nationalism,* which sees other peoples as being less human, less deserving of justice and mercy, than our own. This makes the leaders and populations of states more comfortable than they might otherwise be with their states' amoral behavior.

This case should not be overstated, however, because the political actions of states are not *solely* based on calculations of cold rationality. Emotions play a role, and some of these may be generous. For instance, U.S. support for Great Britain in World War II was based on more than rational considerations, although there were elements of rationality involved. U.S. support of Israel over the last few decades has involved something beyond rationality. In its broad outlines, however, international politics is distinguished from politics within states by its relatively greater tone of calculation.

IMPEDIMENTS TO INTERNATIONAL COMMUNICATION

A third major difference between international politics and politics within states is that communication between leaders is more cumbersome and more vulnerable to misunderstanding than communication within any one state. Within a state, the various political leaders speak the same language. More important, they "speak the same language" in that they know each other fairly well, have a common fund of experiences and stories, and share the same culture.

In international politics, the people involved must often use interpreters to converse, which makes the proceedings more formal and slow, and leaves a good deal of room for misunderstanding. The problem of interpretation can lead to amusing moments, as when President Jimmy Carter's statement that he was happy to be in Poland was translated as "I lust for Poland." The formalization of interchanges can produce more important glitches than that.

More serious yet is the frequent lack of shared assumptions and motivations, which may lead to a failure of communication between states. After World War I, U.S. diplomacy was deeply flawed by President Woodrow Wilson's inability to understand the motives of the United States' allies, Britain, France, and Italy. The leaders of Britain and France in the 1930s responded to Hitler in what was probably an inappropriately gentle way because they did not understand what he wanted to do. In the postwar period, U.S. and Soviet leaders had continual trouble dealing with one another appropriately because they approached their mutual interchanges with such different historical and political assumptions.

POWER AND INTERNATIONAL POLITICS

Under these circumstances—with most decisions made by reciprocal bargaining or through conflict, with a relatively naked rationality operating and with severe difficulties of communication—international politics is a rough game. More simply and directly than in politics within a state, the raw power of the participants determines the outcomes.

On what is this power based? First and foremost, a state's *military power* determines its overall power in international politics. Military power is hard to assess. Different states emphasize different types of arms. Israel does not have much of a navy, but it has an excellent small army and air force. How do we compare it with Great Britain, which has an excellent small navy? How does nuclear capacity figure in our calculations? Beyond this problem of comparing apples and oranges, there are imponderable questions such as toughness, morale, and battle readiness that must be considered. Israel's armed forces are stronger than their small size would suggest, because of their spirit and their level of training and because they have had frequent combat experience; they are "tried and true." Finally, any armed force will fight better when defending its home soil. A smaller and weaker army may be able to defend itself successfully against a stronger army under some circumstances.

A good example of this is the tough resistance that Argentina was able to maintain in 1982 against the more imposing and experienced British armed forces in the Falkland Islands war, although Argentina eventually lost. An even better example is the defeat dealt to the large and powerful U.S. forces by North Vietnam in the early 1970s.

TABLE 18–1   TEN MAJOR MILITARY POWERS

	Persons in uniform	Of these, air force	Defense budget (billions of dollars, 2000)	Nuclear weapons?
China	2,470,000	420,000	14.5	Yes
France	294,430	60,500	27.0	Yes
Germany	321,000	73,300	23.3	No
Great Britain	212,450	54,730	34.5	Yes
India	1,100,000	150,000	15.9	Yes
Israel	172,500	36,000	7.0	Rumored
Italy	250,600	59,600	16.0	No
Japan	236,700	44,200	45.6	No
Russia	1,004,100	184,600	29.0	Yes
U.S.A.	1,365,800	353,600	293.3	Yes

Source: International Institute for Strategic Studies, *The Military Balance, 2000–2001* (London: International Institute for Strategic Studies, 2000).

Table 18–1 displays a few aspects of the military strength of the ten states that are probably the strongest military powers in the world.

Population

A state with a large number of people—such as India, Indonesia, or Nigeria—gains power from the mass of its population. Nigeria is a leading state of sub-Saharan Africa primarily because it has the largest population of the region. This large population gives it sufficient "critical mass" so that it is the natural center for cultural and economic activity in the region; it therefore becomes a hub of communication.

Another reason population per se serves as a basis of power is that in wartime, even if a state does not have a particularly good army, it may be difficult to defeat if it has a large population. Hitler discovered this when he invaded the Soviet Union in 1941. The Soviet army was initially no match for the Germans and retreated rapidly. However, the Germans kept going and going and going, and were still only part of the way into Russia. Their lines of communication stretched over a thousand miles, they were sitting in the midst of a hostile population, winter came on, and still there was a large population left in regions they had not yet occupied. From the remnant of Russia, Stalin was able to build a powerful army that eventually defeated the Germans.

Population alone will not make a state strong. In the nineteenth century, China, the largest state in the world, was dominated easily by the smaller European powers. Today, the two largest states in the world, India and China, are still only intermediate powers.

Economic Power

Even if it is not militarily powerful, a state may figure importantly in international politics if it controls something of economic importance. Saudi Arabia has only a small military force, for instance, but it has often been able to get other states to do what it wishes because they depend on it for their oil imports. Germany's army is large and effective, but it is constitutionally limited to defense and so cannot realistically be used as a threat to make other states do what it wishes. Greater leverage for Germany comes from the fact that until its economic problems caused by reunification in 1990, it had the strongest, most stable economy in Europe. Its central bank so dominated the European economies that Germany, in effect, set economic policy for many of them until the establishment in 1998 of the European Central Bank—designed to Germany's specifications—for most members of the European Union.

Economic position may also *fail* to provide a political tool, however, as is illustrated by the various attempts of the United States in the 1970s to use threats of economic punishment to get the Soviet Union to do what it wanted. The United States could not credibly threaten the Soviet Union militarily (a war between the two superpowers would be so destructive that no one would dare to start it); therefore, the United States at various times tried to use its economic muscle to influence the Soviets. When the Soviet Union invaded Afghanistan, the United States canceled its exports of grain to the Soviets, promising to start them up again if the Soviets changed their policy. Similarly, in the 1970s, the United States tried through economic sanctions to get Soviet and Polish leaders to liberalize the regime in Poland. These efforts did not work because the United States was not important enough economically to the Soviet bloc countries, whose economies were rather self-contained, to force them to back down on policies that were important to them. Economic sanctions as a tool of international politics are discussed in more detail in the "The Process of International Politics" section.

Geography

Many states are protected by natural formations that render them more secure militarily than their armed power alone would suggest they should be. Great Britain has always benefited from the fact that it is an island, separated from the rest of Europe by the English Channel. It was this that prevented Hitler from invading England during World War II. Similarly, Switzerland has always been rather secure in its rough mountains. Until the coming of air transportation, the United States was sufficiently isolated from Europe that it could get by with a small army. Germany has suffered over the centuries because it sits in the middle of a wide plain stretching from northern France into Russia, a plain along which armies can move easily.

Leadership

Finally, skilled leadership may make a difference in the weight a state carries in international politics. Charles de Gaulle, by skillful diplomacy and a flair for public relations, was able to make France the leading state of Western Europe in the late 1960s and 1970s. Woodrow Wilson's leadership probably diminished the influence of the United States at the end of World War I. Hitler and Mussolini led their states into disastrous, overreaching wars of conquest.

THE PROCESS OF INTERNATIONAL POLITICS

If power is the basic tool of international politics, how exactly does it work? What do the leaders of states, of international organizations, and of nongovernmental organizations do as they make collective choices in international politics?

Diplomacy and Other Nonmilitary Measures

Though ultimately the military power of states remains in the background of most major international decisions, the vast majority of things that happen in international politics do not directly invoke military power. Thousands of small decisions are made every day—small-scale trade decisions, issuing of amnesty to refugees, visits of scholarly delegations—and these do not involve the full power of a state. Also, many large and important actions take place without any military involvement: the formation and expansion of the European Union, for instance, or the international agreement to ban the use of land mines (see box, p. 376).

The process of reaching international decisions in such ways is called *diplomacy*. States maintain a formal diplomatic apparatus for conducting politics with other states. The United States, for instance, employs over two thousand foreign service officers to conduct its diplomacy; in addition, a number of ambassadors and high-ranking officials in the State Department are directly appointed by the president from outside the professional ranks of foreign service officers.

Small-scale transactions, such as handling visitors' problems or promoting local business deals, are dealt with through a system of *consulates*. These are local offices to represent a state in major cities of another state. Germany, for instance, operates ten consulates in major cities in the United States. Consuls, who are in charge of the consulates, do not represent their governments in major international negotiations; their job is to maintain a ceremonial presence locally for the state (U.S. consuls host a Thanksgiving dinner each year for local notables in their city, for instance) and to take care of the myriad of small problems and decisions that come up from day to day.

Ambassadors are the officials charged by their state to conduct high-level politics with the state to which they are posted. A state appoints only a single ambassador to another state, and that person will be based in the capital city. Ambassadors, or even higher officials from the foreign ministry, will represent the state in negotiations over major agreements.

Another major function of ambassadors and the rest of the diplomatic corps is to gather information about the state to which they are posted—commercial information, political information, and military information. They do this openly, by reading the press and talking to the state's leaders and citizens. But these efforts are often supplemented by spying operations (the United States' Central Intelligence Agency, for instance) that mix open and clandestine information gathering.

It is in diplomacy, rather than military action, that most activity by international organizations and nongovernmental international actors take place. The box on p. 376 describes one such set of activities by nongovernmental actors; another example would be the active lobbying of the European Community governing structures by international interest groups such as the Cereal Producers' Association. Another example would be

A meeting of the G8 leaders in 1998. The leaders of the seven largest economies of the world plus Russia meet periodically to discuss common economic problems.

(Witt/Hadj/Chamussy/Sipa Press)

the initiatives of Amnesty International to obtain better treatment of political prisoners in numerous states by publicizing the cases and bringing international public opinion to bear on those states. The one exception to the "nonmilitary" nature of nongovernmental actors is international terrorism, in which groups seek to meet their international goals by independent violent action such as bombings or kidnappings.

That diplomacy does not directly involve military action does not mean that it is purely cooperative. The use of power in diplomacy, like the use of power in any other sort of politics, may run the full range from persuasion to coercion. In persuasion, diplomats will try to convince another state that it is in that state's interest to do what the first state wants. A good example might be trade negotiations, in which one state might try to convince another that open trade in a certain commodity would benefit both. Relations between states such as Canada and the United States consist almost wholly of persuasion.

Further along the coercion continuum, diplomats of a state might argue with leaders of another state that if the state does not open its markets, the first state might have to shift its trade elsewhere.

Furthest along the continuum, short of military action, would be a threat by diplomats of the possibility of military action. United States diplomats have often cautioned various Mideast states that if they did not do what the United States was asking, the United States might attack them. This is still diplomacy, not military activity; but it certainly is not warm and fuzzy.

Economic Sanctions   A form of nonmilitary coercion that is often used by the United States, even in dealing with our friends, is the imposition of *economic sanctions*. Imposition of an economic sanction consists of a state or group of states deliberately withholding normal economic relations to punish another state. For instance, the United Nations has asked for members to withhold most trade from Iraq since 1990 to force it to destroy its weapons of mass destruction.

This is certainly direct coercion, though it involves no military activity. It is the analogue, in international relations, of a strike or consumer boycott in domestic politics. In a few important instances, economic sanctions have been successful. The United Nations' boycott of trade with Iraq kept Iraq involved for several years in a grudging process of disarmament and inspections, even if it did not succeed in ridding Iraq of its major weaponry. The most successful use of economic sanctions was an international boycott of investment in South Africa that led to the fall of that country's undemocratic, white-dominated government.

The key to success in economic sanctions is that one must be able to close the spigot completely. In the Iraq and South Africa cases, nearly all states of the world cooperated in the boycotts, so Iraq and South Africa had no alternative sources of supply.

The United States has often been tempted to pursue unilateral economic boycotts of other states because all by itself it is such a large economic force in the world. These have almost never been successful, yet we keep trying. At various times, we have withheld trade from Cuba, Iran, the Soviet Union, Vietnam, China, and numerous other countries. At the same time, "states" and cities of the United States, pursuing their own miniforeign policies, have enforced economic sanctions on such states as Pakistan, Switzerland, and Indonesia. Inevitably, the target country has bought from Germany, France, or some other supplier the things we were unwilling to sell it. We can inflict pain and inconvenience on a target, but rarely can we inflict enough to make it buckle. Economic sanctions hurt the sanctioner as well. It is estimated that in 1995, the United States lost $20 billion of exports, at a cost of 250,000 jobs, to enforce its trade sanctions.[4] We have also not added to the world's love for us.

It is easy to understand why a state, especially a genuinely major economic force such as the United States, might turn to economic sanctions. No one wants to use military force if it can be avoided. Economic sanctions do give us the feeling of doing something, whether or not they have any effect; but they rarely succeed, unless they are universally enforced.

War

The vast majority of international transactions are conducted peacefully, through diplomacy. However, war is a real part of international politics as well. Many important international political outcomes, such as the freeing of Kuwait after its invasion by Iraq in 1990, the unification of South Vietnam and North Vietnam in 1975, and the occupation of Kosovo by the United States and its allies in 1999, have resulted directly from military action. Even when diplomats negotiate peaceably, their states' power—that is, their capacity to wage war or their capacity to manipulate economic outcomes—always underlies the negotiations.

[4]Cited by Paul Magnusson, *Business Week,* 17 November 1997, p. 115.

War is also not a sometime thing in international politics. Even though most international politics does not involve war directly, there is almost always some warfare going on, somewhere. Since 1939, there has not been a single day that war was not being waged somewhere in the world.

Because war is so damaging to so many people, political scientists have long wrestled with the question of why wars occur. The causes of war appear to be complex:

- *Nationalism* probably is not a major determinant of whether war occurs, because wars were already a common tool of political leaders long before the modern era in which nationalism blossomed. If nationalism is not a cause of war, however, it certainly has added to the brutality of war, along with its companion, racism (the other great popular emotion of the modern era). Atrocities come naturally if you think of your enemy as less human than yourself.

- *Transitions* seem to breed war. Change breeds uncertainty in which leaders may imagine either great threats or great opportunities for conquest and expansion. Change also may create unstable state boundaries. One example of change that bred numerous wars was the establishment of new states throughout the South after World War II, as former colonies attained national independence. As noted (p. 47), many of these new states had arbitrary boundaries, which might throw together historically hostile peoples. Numerous civil wars followed the establishment of these new states.

   Another period of danger is the breakup of empires, when a former hegemon that has kept order in a region loses its capacity to hold things together. The breakup of the Turkish Empire after World War I is an example. The breakup of the Soviet Union and its system of satellite states in Eastern Europe since 1989 has involved dangers of this sort as well.

- *Misperceptions by leaders,* either of their risks or of their opportunities, may spark wars (which might suggest that we should applaud effective spying rather than look askance at it!). *All* of the states that joined initially in the bloody combat of World War I thought they and their allies were so strong that they would win the war in a matter of weeks. They could not have been more wrong. Similarly, Saddam Hussein of Iraq badly miscalculated when he invaded Iran in 1980. He thought the new Islamic government of Iran would be weak and that he could seize territory by invading the country. Due to his miscalculation, Iraq became bogged down in an eight-year war that killed over a million young men.

- *Rich, powerful states* do not seem to make war with each other very often. They have too much to lose in war, and each has too much capacity to damage the other. Similarly, desperately poor states tend not to engage in war at all, because they do not have the capacity to win a war. Most wars involve in-between states that are poor but not destitute; or they may involve a conflict between a powerful state and an in-between state.

- *The most fascinating regularity* that political scientists have explored is the almost universal observation that democracies do not wage war with other democracies. There has never been a case in which two well-established democracies have gone to war, although there have been "gray area" cases in which a democracy warred with a marginally democratic state.

Political scientists debate whether this regularity is due to mere coincidence or really means something, but those who argue that it does mean something note that it could be caused by popular aversion to warfare. In this interpretation, it is ordinary people who bear the costs of war, not leaders. In a democracy, unlike an autocratic system, the people can hold leaders accountable for an unpopular policy, so leaders will try to avoid involvement in war. Therefore, if two state leaders involved in a conflict are democratically accountable to their people, they will probably try to resolve the conflict by some means other than war.

The causes of war are multiple and complex. (I have not even gone into the further complication that wars seem to cycle over time with some periods having large numbers of wars and other periods being relatively peaceful.) However, the costs of war are so terrible that working through the complexities to our best understanding of war is one of the most important projects of political science.

POWER AND CHOICE IN INTERNATIONAL POLITICS

It is easy to see the "power" side of international politics, but with no central authority to define common goals for the international system, it is not so easy to see that international politics may also involve "choice." Some theorists think that the international system may work toward certain common goals, however, even in the absence of a coordinating authority. Two examples are balance-of-power theory and regime theory.

Hans Morgenthau developed in the 1950s an elegant analysis of international politics based on the concept of the "balance of power," which assumes that the international system has a natural tendency to prevent any one state from dominating the system.[5]

This tendency, a characteristic of the system as a whole, is supposed to result if the states within it individually try to maintain their own power. If any one state begins to grow too large, other states become alarmed and combine against it, thus keeping power balanced. In this way, the system operates with a "hidden hand" to maintain itself as a multiple set of competitive states. Historic examples of the balance of power at work include the fairly evenly matched alliance structure in Europe on the eve of World War I; the combination of numerous European states to balk an ambitious Napoleon; and the role of Britain over four centuries, throwing its support first to one, then to another European power, always on the weaker side, to prevent any one power from dominating the continent of Europe. The Cold War between the Soviet Union and the United States, with their rather evenly matched alliances, may be interpreted as a natural working out of the balance of power. Morgenthau credits the balance of power with a number of good things: the maintenance of a varied system of states; in particular, the protection of small states; and, under some circumstances, a decrease in warfare.

[5]Hans Morgenthau, *Politics Among Nations*, 5th rev. ed. (New York: Knopf, 1978), chaps. 11–14.

Regime theory is quite a different kettle of fish, but it, too, sees international politics as transcending the power relationships of states. A "regime" is:

> (a set of) principles, norms, rules, and decision-making procedures around which actors' expectations converge in a given issue-area.[6]

In other words, above and beyond the power relationships of states and other international actors, there may emerge a set of values and principles in the international community that modifies the behavior of the members of the community. States may be moved by a shared vision of the common good, not just by narrow interpretations of their individual interests. Since the Second World War, for instance, a basic assumption of the international order, embodied in institutions such as the International Monetary Fund, has been that trade should expand so that all economies may operate more efficiently. This "regime" has not been uncontested; leaders of the South have argued that the regime should instead emphasize redistribution of wealth, rather than taking the disparities between North and South as a given and striving only for maximal exchange and overall efficiency of the world economy. The point is, though, that there may be a set of values that has had a power of its own and has affected how states act above and beyond the power relationships of those involved.

Proponents of regime theory see it as a way to address common problems in a more hopeful way than my bleak description of the "fiduciary role" might lead us to expect. Critics argue that regimes are froth on the international system, that they are no more than expressions of the power relationships of those involved—that the international regime on trade, for instance, has been what it was because that suited Western and especially United States' interests.

At this point, balance-of-power analysis and regime theory are important for us because they suggest that even in the anarchy of international politics, politics may be interpreted as more than the exercise of power. As I have tried to show throughout this book, a proper understanding of politics always requires that we remain simultaneously aware of its two sides. With some of the changes described in this chapter, the bleak picture of traditional international politics may have acquired some cooperative highlights. The growth of interdependence and the entry of more nonstate actors (which softens somewhat the starkness of the fiduciary role) may make international politics in the future a more balanced mix of "power" and "choice."

CONCLUSION

The unpredictability and danger of international politics can be awesome, especially in the nuclear age. Politics on this level can be analyzed in the same ways that we analyze other kinds of politics, but the high stakes involved put a greater edge on that analysis than we feel in the study of politics within states. In a general text such as this, we have been able to touch only briefly on international politics, but I hope that you will have developed a taste for more. We urgently need to build a better understanding of international politics.

---

[6]Stephen D. Krasner, ed., *International Regimes* (Ithaca, N.Y.: Cornell University Press, 1983), p. 1.

Example: A Failure of the New World Order: Ethnic Conflict in Rwanda

Rwanda is a small, landlocked state in central Africa, about the size of Massachusetts. It is an agricultural country with significant exports of coffee and tea, and with milk production and grain for local consumption. The country is one of the most densely populated in Africa, with over seven hundred people per square mile—a population density slightly greater than that of Massachusetts.

Before Rwanda came into contact with Europeans at the end of the nineteenth century, it was already a fairly well-developed state ruled by a king. The population was ethnically divided between two tribes. The Tutsis were a tribe of cattle herders and warriors. They controlled politics (the king and most warriors were Tutsi), even though they were numerically a distinct minority. The much larger Hutu tribe were land-based farmers, raising crops rather than grazing cattle on the open range. As of the 1956 census, 16 percent of Rwandans were Tutsi, and 83 percent Hutu.

The "tribal" distinction was to some extent physical, with Tutsis taller and longer-faced, but there had been a good deal of intermarriage over the years, and this had blended such physical differences significantly. The operating distinction was in part also an economic one between haves and have-nots. A Hutu could become a Tutsi if he acquired large numbers of cattle, and a Tutsi could become so impoverished that he sank to being a Hutu.

When Rwanda was colonized, first by the Germans and then by the Belgians, the colonizers found a state in which a Tutsi king ruled, but with a good deal of autonomy for localities, many of which were led by Hutus. In setting up a rationalized bureaucracy for tax collection and road-building, the Belgians relied exclusively on the Tutsis to control the population and rewarded them with weapons and power. In so doing, they greatly sharpened the distinction between Tutsi and Hutu and the hierarchical organization of the state. At the same time, by introducing Western ideas of justice and equality, they helped to develop a sense of grievance among the Hutus. When they granted the country independence in 1962, the Belgians left behind a powder keg of ethnic power relationships and resentments.

Even before independence, a brief, bloody civil war in 1959 had led to the overthrow of the monarchy and had given effective political power to the Hutus. Thousands of Tutsis had fled Rwanda at that time. After independence, there were periodic outbursts of ethnic violence. In 1964, approximately twenty thousand Tutsis were killed in massacres by the Hutus. In 1972, the military (dominated by Tutsis) led a massacre of over one hundred thousand Hutus; they concentrated on the better educated, seen as the greatest threat.

Throughout the 1980s, about 250,000 mainly Tutsi refugees lived outside Rwanda in neighboring countries. In the early 1990s, a Tutsi-led rebel force known as the Front Patriotique Rwandais (FPR), based in these refugee groups, began to have significant success against the Hutu-led government, and by 1993, they occupied much of the northern part of the country. The government and the rebels reached a peace accord that called for democratic, multiparty elections, but it was a fragile peace. It was especially ominous that the (now predominantly Hutu) army refused to honor some of the peace directives from the government, even though the government was nominally in charge of the army.

On April 6, 1994, newly elected President Juvénal Habyarimana, who had been actively promoting reconciliation, was assassinated when the plane in which he and the president of neighboring Burundi were passengers was shot down over Rwanda's capital. Immediately, a well-organized campaign of assassinations and massacres began in which Habyarimana's allies (including the prime minister and the president of the Constitutional Court) were murdered, along with other Hutus who favored reconciliation, educated Tutsis, and a number of United Nations personnel. Over the following several weeks, an organized campaign to kill all Tutsis was carried out, in which an estimated five hundred thousand Tutsis—half the total population and including many children—died. The killings were brutal. Some of the tall Tutsis had their feet chopped off "to bring them down to our size."

Meanwhile, the rebel Tutsi force continued to gain ground on the government, although it was too late to save many Tutsis from murder. By July, they effectively controlled the country. Millions of Hutus fled the country to live as refugees in neighboring Zaire. They were kept there by rumors their leaders spread of Tutsi vengeance, even though there was remarkably little evidence of any revenge by the new Tutsi-led government.

A chilling history! Yet the United States and other Western countries did not pay much attention to it, except for brief expressions of horror at moments when the violence periodically erupted at its worst. Rwanda is not of great economic importance, lacks natural resources such as oil, and is not strategically located with regard to shipping lanes or to international conflicts. In the words of Neville Chamberlain at the time that France and Britain acquiesced in Hitler's dismemberment of Czechoslovakia, Rwanda's suffering was "a quarrel in a far-away country between people of whom we know nothing."

The lack of Western attention to the continuing problems of Rwanda is exemplified by the fact that until the horrendous genocide of 1994, the media in the United States consistently showed more concern for the mountain gorillas of Rwanda (which had been filmed in the popular movie *Gorillas in the Mist*) than for the people of that unfortunate country. A keyword search in June 1994 found 1,123 articles combining the keywords *gorilla* and *Rwanda,* but only 138 combining *guerrilla* and *Rwanda.*[7] However, 1993 was a year in which hundreds of Rwandan civilians were killed by both sides, and hundreds of thousands were made homeless. The major coverage of Rwanda that year consisted of stories in the *New York Times, Newsweek, Houston Chronicle,* and Reuters News Service warning that Dian Fossey's camp (featured in the movie) was threatened by the war:

[The *Houston Chronicle* article] mentioned the war's human toll only in writing that "the hunger and desperation of a million war refugees" had made Rwanda a less "enticing place for

---

[7]Ken Silverstein, "Guerrillas in the Mist," *Washington Monthly,* September 1994, p. 21.

visiting scientists to work." Just as tragically, the war had "ruined the eco-tourism trade that made gorilla sightseeing . . . one of Rwanda's leading sources of overseas income."[8]

The Western response even to the 1994 genocide was half-hearted. The French, who had had a continuing relationship with the Hutu government, consistently had the largest Western military presence in the area. Though at times they intervened to protect the Tutsis, it was usually late and sporadic. As late as May, after several hundred thousand had been killed, the French continued to ship arms to the Hutu militias carrying out the organized murders. The strongest French effort eventually came in protecting the Hutu government as it fled the victorious rebels in July.

Britain offered fifty unarmored trucks to aid in helping prevent the slaughter.

The United States was not bathed in glory, either. American diplomats as a matter of stated policy denied the term *genocide* in reference to Rwanda until late in the killings, by which time over a third of Tutsis had been killed. America offered only slow-arriving logistical support to help move troops from other African countries to restore order. In the end, little was done, and order settled on the deathly country without much help from anyone.

After the victory of the Tutsi rebels, a massive exodus of Hutus began. For the next two years, about one-fourth of the population of Rwanda lived in squalid refugee camps on its border, mainly in neighboring Zaire. They were Hutus, afraid to return home because they believed they would be attacked by Tutsi hard-liners in the army. In the meantime, they were often terrorized by the Zairean army—which wanted to force them back to Rwanda to ease the burden of caring for them—and by their own defeated Hutu army, which was trying to prepare a new invasion of Rwanda. The United Nations tried

[8]Ibid., p. 23.

Bodies float at the bottom of a waterfall after a massacre of Hutu refugees in Rwanda.
(AP/Wide World Photos)

to be helpful by offering humanitarian aid, building camp shelters, and sending observers to check on conditions in Rwanda's prisons. There was little more the United Nations could do. The situation was in the end "resolved" by the descent of Zaire into a chaotic civil war in which thousands of the Hutus, innocent bystanders in Zaire's internal conflict, were killed. The remaining Hutus fled back to Rwanda. They were initially repatriated with relatively little violence. However, the basic ethnic conflict between Tutsis and Hutus remains unresolved, and as of 2001, the cycle of Hutu-Tutsi killing was once again escalating, with outright civil war in the northwest region of Rwanda.

I titled this "A Failure of the New World Order," but this may have been unfair. Perhaps there was little the rest of the world could do about the ethnic poison in Rwanda. However, much of the poison was created by the rest of the world during the colonial period. It does not feel right to throw up our hands at a problem like this.

Example: The United Nations

The United Nations was established by the victorious Allies at the end of World War II as an organization to help maintain world peace. It was to do this partly by imposing sanctions against those who broke the peace and partly through programs to remove what were thought to be the causes of war—poverty, suffering, and ignorance. Today, the United Nations has 189 members, nearly all of the world's states.

The decision-making structure of the United Nations was set up by the victorious powers to make them the core of the organization and the guardians of peace. The members of the United Nations are represented in a General Assembly, each with one vote. This is democratic, although it does give undue voting power to tiny countries. However, the victorious Allies added to this General Assembly another body, the Security Council. This body must also agree to any significant action of the United Nations, and each of the World War II victors (the United States, France, Britain, Russia, and China) was made a permanent member of the Security Council. Ten other states rotate on and off the council for terms of two years each. Not only were the victors made permanent members of the Security Council, but each was given an individual veto over its decisions. That is, each of the five permanent members was given the right to veto significant actions of the UN.

The executive leader of the United Nations is the secretary-general, an individual elected by the General Assembly for a term of five years. The present secretary-general is Kofi Annan of Ghana, who was elected in 1997. The secretary-general manages the operations of the UN but works most effectively when persuading rather than pushing. Some secretaries-general have been effective world diplomats; others have been primarily managers of the organization.

This structure might have worked well if the victorious powers had remained united and had operated cooperatively as guardians of world peace. That is what the structure was designed for. Shortly after the establishment of the United Nations, however, the Cold War descended on the world. From then on, either the Soviet Union or the United States was likely to veto any important action of the organization. About one-third of resolutions of the Security Council have been vetoed by one or another of its permanent members.

Despite this problem, however, the United Nations has developed an important role of peacekeeper in local disputes where the superpowers agreed they wanted to lessen the likelihood of conflict. This is now likely to happen more often, since with the end of the Cold War, the likelihood has increased that the five permanent members of the Security Council will find themselves in agreement on issues.

When acting as a peacekeeper, the United Nations organizes a corps of soldiers from states not involved in a conflict who go to the site of the conflict and separate the antagonists. Often this involves establishment of a demilitarized buffer zone between two territories, which the antagonists agree to keep free of their own troops and which the United Nations peacekeeping force patrols. Over the years, the United Nations has mounted about fifty peacekeeping operations in conflicts such as those between Israel and Egypt, India and Pakistan, and to enforce the peace agreement in Bosnia. As of 2001, the UN was operating fourteen separate peacekeeping operations around the world.

Beyond its important peacekeeping function, the United Nations operates a wide range of agencies that work to improve the condition of humanity in everything from helping refugees to encouraging trade and development. The scope of this work is large. The United Nations buys half of the world's vaccines for children, protects 22 million refugees, and is the world's largest customer for condoms.[9] The UN's Main agencies and their focuses are:

UNICEF	children
ERC	emergency relief
UNHRC	refugees
WFP	food
UNDP	development
UNCTAD	trade
UNESCO	education and science

With the end of the Cold War, the prospects for the United Nations to function effectively have improved a great deal. First, though, it must solve several problems that threaten to hold it back. The system of permanent membership does not respond well to changes in relative positions in the world. Britain and France are now less weighty members of the world community than Japan, for instance, and it should be appropriate to suggest changes in the membership of the Security Council. This is sensitive. A second problem is that of ingrown bureaucracy; someone needs to clean house. Finally, the organization has severe financial problems, primarily because the United States had refused to pay its dues for several years.

Despite these problems, the outlook for the organization is good. Against all odds, it managed to operate with some success even during the Cold War. Now in the post-Cold War era, the problems the organization must deal with look as though they should be solvable.

---

[9]"Pope Kofi's Unruly Flock," *The Economist,* 8 August 1998, p. 19.

A PERSONAL NOTE

Let me close this book with a personal note. We tend, when analyzing politics, to think of it in the abstract and rather dispassionately. We analyze people's actions according to the resources available to them and according to a rational application of those resources to their goals. By and large, this analysis works well. We can usually tell which of two countries will be able to impose its will upon another, what sort of people will turn out to vote in greater numbers at election time, how a change in party finance will affect candidates' strategies, and so on. Sometimes, however, passionate belief can cut through all this. Ideas and ideology can take on a power of their own, which transcends analysis. No political scientists in the early 1960s predicted the tumultuous events of the civil rights movement. Who would have thought that little Vietnam would be able to best the United States in a war? That primitive Afghanistan would be able to defy the Soviet Union for years on end? That the democratic opposition would eventually triumph over the Communist Party in Eastern Europe and the Soviet Union?

As a small dog, if it is on its home ground, may be able to send a larger one running away with its tail down, so may the weaker side—even a very weak side—prevail in politics if its supporters believe strongly enough that they are right.

This book has emphasized the analysis of politics, and surely this is important. I hope you will also remember the importance of passion and belief, though. As Marshall McLuhan put it, "Nothing is inevitable as long as one person is aware that it is happening."

FURTHER READING

Deibert, Ronald. *Virtual Resources: International Relations Research on the Internet.* Institute of International Relations, University of British Columbia, Working Paper No. 13, April 1997.

Gilpin, Robert. *Global Political Economy: Understanding the International Economic Order.* Princeton, N.J.: Princeton University Press, 2001.

Goldman, Kjell. "International Relations: An Overview." In *A New Handbook of Political Science,* edited by Robert E. Goodin and Hans-Dieter Klingemann. New York: Oxford University Press, pp. 401–27.

Goldstein, Judith, and Keohane, Robert O., eds. *Ideas and Foreign Policy: Beliefs, Institutions, and Political Change.* Ithaca, N.Y.: Cornell University Press, 1993.

Keck, Margaret E., and Sikkink, Kathryn. *Activists Beyond Borders: Advocacy Networks in International Politics.* Ithaca, N.Y.: Cornell University Press, 1998.

Kennedy, Paul. *The Rise and Fall of the Great Powers.* New York: Random House, 1987.

Keohane, Robert. *After Hegemony: Cooperation and Discord in the World Political Economy.* Princeton, N.J.: Princeton University Press, 1984.

———, ed. *Neorealism and Its Critics.* New York: Columbia University Press, 1986.

———, and Nye, Joseph S. *Power and Interdependence.* 2d ed. Glenview, Ill.: Scott, Foresman, 1989.

Krasner, Stephen D., ed. *International Regimes.* Ithaca, N.Y.: Cornell University Press, 1983.

Ku, Charlotte, and Diehl, Paul F., eds. *International Law: An Anthology.* Boulder, Colo.: Lynne Rienner Publishers, 1997.

Mearshimer, John J. *The Tragedy of Great Power Politics.* New York: W. W. Norton, 2001.

Pirages, Dennis. *Global Technopolitics: The International Politics of Technology and Resources.* Pacific Grove, Calif.: Brooks/Cole, 1989.

Porter, Gareth, and Brown, Janet Welsh. *Global Environmental Politics.* Boulder, Colo.: Westview, 1991.

Ray, James Lee. *Democracy and International Conflict.* Columbia: University of South Carolina Press, 1995.

Rosecrance, Richard. *Rise of the Trading State.* New York: Basic Books, 1986.

Rosenau, James N. *Turbulence in World Politics.* Beverly Hills, Calif.: Sage, 1990.

Siverson, Randolph M. "A Glass Half-Full? No, But Perhaps a Glass Filling: The Contributions of International Politics Research to Policy." *PS* 33 (March 2000): 59–64.

Snyder, Jack. *Myths of Empire: Domestic Politics and International Ambition.* Ithaca, N.Y.: Cornell University Press, 1991.

Stoessinger, John G. *Why Nations Go To War.* 7th ed. New York: St. Martin's Press, 1998.

Urquhart, Brian. *Decolonization and World Peace.* Austin: University of Texas Press, 1989.

Vasquez, John. *The War Puzzle.* New York: Cambridge University Press, 1993.

Vernon, Raymond. *In the Hurricane's Eye: The Troubled Prospects of Multinational Enterprises.* Cambridge: Harvard University Press, 1998.

Waltz, Kenneth. *Theory of International Politics.* Reading, Mass.: Addison-Wesley, 1979.

Weart, Spencer R. *Never at War: Why Democracies Will Not Fight One Another.* New Haven: Yale University Press, 1998.

Young, Oran R. *International Cooperation: Building Regimes for Natural Resources and the Environment.* Ithaca, N.Y.: Cornell University Press, 1989.

 WEBSITES OF INTEREST

United Nations:
http://www.un.org

European Union delegation to the United States:
http://www.eurunion.org

Foreign Affairs guide to international affairs:
http://www.foreignaffairs.org/

International Institute for Strategic Studies:
http://www.iiss.org/

Stockholm International Peace Research Institute:
http://www.sipri.se/

United Nations Environmental Programme page of updates on negotiations in progress for international environmental agreements:
http://www.unep.ch/

Union of International Associations:
http://www.uia.org

APPENDIX

PRINCIPLES OF
POLITICAL ANALYSIS

There are a number of basic principles of argument and logic that students should learn in an introductory political science course. In part, these should have shown up implicitly in much of the material you have already read and discussed in this course, but it is also helpful to look at them more directly. They are included here not as a tag end or afterthought but because this seems to be the best way to handle them. Some instructors may prefer to use this section at the beginning of a course, some at the end, others at some other point. Locating this discussion in an appendix leaves to the instructor the decision of how to handle it.

FALSIFIABILITY

The most basic principle of political argument is that to be useful, any statement about politics must be *falsifiable*. That is, it must be at least potentially possible that the statement is not true and could therefore be falsified. For example, the statement "two-party systems tend to produce less redistribution of income than multiparty systems" would be falsified if we compared the two-party and multiparty systems of the world and found that there was little difference between the two in the degree of income redistribution they produced. The statement "Ted Kennedy has shown little sympathy for blacks" would be falsified if one produced a long list of statements and actions in which Ted Kennedy demonstrated sympathy for blacks.

On the other hand, some statements about politics are true by definition. "Robert Dole lost the 1996 presidential election because most of the voters chose Bill Clinton" is one example. "The poor countries of the world are more backward economically than rich countries" is another. Think about it: How would you go about falsifying either of these statements? They are true by definition.

These statements could not possibly be demonstrated to be false; therefore, they are automatically true. Such a statement does not tell anything about the world that we did not already know before we read the statement. Literally, a statement that is not falsifiable says nothing about the world. Such statements are called *tautologies.*

The two examples given are fairly obvious, and so you might wonder why the importance of falsifiability is emphasized here. Surely, mustn't it be obvious when a statement says nothing new? If so, it wouldn't seem to be much of a problem. As it happens, though, it is not always immediately clear that a statement is a tautology. Consider the following: "A country with a large agricultural sector and a large industrial sector to its economy will tend to have a small service sector." Such a country will not "tend" to have a small service sector; it will *always* have a small one, because this statement is true by definition. To have a large agricultural sector means that a large percentage of the labor force is employed in agriculture; if the country also has a large industrial sector, then another large percentage of the labor force is employed in industry. What's left is the service sector. The percentages employed in different sectors must always sum to 100 percent, so if the first two percentages are large, there cannot be much left for the service sector. Its percentage must by definition be small, and so the statement is a tautology—although to most people it would not be obvious, at first glance, that such was the case.

As you become involved in the analysis of politics, you will be surprised by how often statements about politics turn out, on closer examination, to be true by definition.

We have now cleared the underbrush a bit and know that we are to deal only with statements that are at least potentially falsifiable. Clearly, however, some of these statements will be more interesting than others, and we don't want to waste our time with the uninteresting ones. This leads us to the following question:

WHAT MAKES A STATEMENT INTERESTING?

There are three kinds of statements about politics:

- *Statements of fact:* These state what *is,* they *describe* reality. Examples: "The American president is elected for a four-year term." "There are two major political parties in West Germany." "Chile and Argentina have been engaged in a dispute over boundaries for decades."
- *Statements of value:* These state *how good* something is; they *evaluate* reality. Examples: "The U.S. Constitution provides the best governmental system in the world." "Sales taxes are not as good as income taxes because they are regressive." "A planned economy provides a better life for people than a free-market economy."
- *Explanatory statements:* These state *why* something is as it is; they *analyze* reality. Examples: "Bill Clinton defeated Robert Dole in the 1996 presidential election because most voters were satisfied with the economy." "People whose parents were interested in politics tend to be especially interested in politics themselves." "The sending of unclear diplomatic signals increases the likelihood that war will break out."

All three types of statement are appropriate areas for political investigation and argument. Whatever sort of statement you make, however, you want it to be interesting. A statement will be relatively interesting to the extent that it offers your readers something that (1) is of concern to them and (2) would have been difficult for them to accomplish for themselves. That the statement must be of concern to your readers is obvious and requires no further comment. (Most American readers, for instance, would not be much concerned about the precise arrangements for choosing a king in Sweden, and statements about it would not be especially interesting to them.) However, note the further condition for interest—that the statement should offer your readers something that would have been difficult for them to accomplish for themselves. This is not so obvious.

Consider two descriptive statements about Congress: "Congress has 535 members," and "Three-fourths of the members of Congress have cast a vote at one time or another on direct instructions from a lobbyist." (The second of these is imaginary and, one hopes, false!) These two statements would be of equal *concern* to students of Congress, but the second statement would be more interesting to them because it is something that would have been difficult for them to learn for themselves. They could have learned how many members there are in Congress by a quick glance in any encyclopedia, but it would take a clever investigator, working for a long time, to ascertain the truth of the second statement.

Similarly, "justice is good" is not an interesting statement of value. Presumably, everyone would be able to agree with it without much thought, and so it does not provide us with much that is new. However, the statement "discrimination is good" is a challenging statement, one that goes against the grain. It would not automatically occur to most of your readers and would require a good deal of argument to be rendered plausible for them. Arguing for this statement requires a lot of thought, which you must provide for your readers, and will thus be proportionately more interesting to them.

As a final example, the explanatory statement "Rich countries will tend to have bigger armies than poor countries" is not an interesting explanation of the size of armies, because it is so obvious that coming up with it did not require much thought. "Countries with high unemployment, and therefore cheap labor, will tend to have large armies" is a more interesting explanation of the same thing. A thoroughly obvious, hence uninteresting, explanation is called a *trivial explanation.*

As a general rule, statements of value and explanatory statements require more thought on the part of the writer than descriptive statements, and they are therefore more likely to be interesting statements. Students writing papers are often tempted to write descriptive papers, laying out a set of descriptive statements, because this is easier than justifying statements of value or explanation. You should remember that unless you choose a *challenging* descriptive problem, your work will not be a particularly interesting one. Often you will be given a particular descriptive investigation as an exercise; you might, for instance, be asked to trace the progress of a bill through the legislative process. If so, describe away! If you are asked to "write a term paper about some aspect of the legislative process," however, you will be able to write a more interesting paper if you choose a question of value or of explanation.

CAUSATION AND EXPLANATION

Let us look a bit more closely at explanation. An explanatory statement necessarily involves the notion of causation. We *explain* a certain thing by saying that another thing *causes* it. For example, we might explain that the U.S. government has difficulty making broad, systematic policy in areas such as energy by blaming it on the separation of powers in the American system. That is, we *explain* the existence of the difficulty by saying that the difficulty is *caused* by the separation of powers. (Presumably this would be because there are many points at which the political power of opponents can be decisive—the presidency, either house of Congress, or the courts. As a result, "difficult" programs are hard to pass.)

In the example, we cannot conceive of any way to explain the American difficulty except to assert one or another possible cause of the difficulty. So to explain is to analyze causes.

What is causation? What does it mean to say that one thing causes another? In general, we think that to cause something is to *bring it about,* to bring it forth, to produce it. Turning a key causes my car to start. Russia's opposition to a proposal causes the defeat of the proposal in the United Nations. The increasing electoral advantages of incumbents in U.S. congressional elections have caused an increase in the average seniority of members of Congress. And so on.

We think of causation as working only forward in time. For one thing to produce another thing, the "producer" has to precede the "product" temporally. So it doesn't make sense to think of Ronald Reagan's electoral victory in 1984 as having caused Walter Mondale to argue for tax increases during the 1984 campaign; but it does make sense to think of Mondale's position as one of the causes of Reagan's electoral victory.

However, temporal precedence is not enough to establish one thing as a cause of another. We do not think of winter as causing spring, for instance, even though we know that "when winter comes, spring can't be far behind." Although the seasons unfold together, we do not think of one season as bringing the other about. Similarly, it is probably true that brunettes tend to be Democrats, since for historical reasons a number of ethnic groups with dark hair—blacks, Native Americans, Chicanos, southern Europeans—have gravitated to the Democratic Party. Although people acquire their hair color long before they give a thought to which party they will support, we do not think of hair color as causing people's party preferences. It is only a coincidence that the two tend to vary together.

Political scientists put a great deal of effort into trying to sort out what things cause the things in which we are interested. Why does the United States have only two major parties? Why are states of the South less likely than Western states to be well-established democracies? Why do communist economies not grow more quickly than they do? If we could experiment with politics in a laboratory, as chemists or physicists do in their specialties, we could hold all other possible factors constant; we could allow only the one we wished to examine to vary and then see whether, when it varied, the thing we were trying to explain also varied. For instance, a physicist may place two identical weights on identical wheelchairs on slopes of different angles and measure the effect of the angle of slope on the speed of descent; since nothing else varies, it is clear that only differing angles of slope can be causing differing speeds of descent. If we could manipulate things in this way, we would feel confident in stating that the one thing was causing the other to vary. However, with rare exceptions, we cannot experiment with the things we are examining in political science. We cannot change the electoral system of the United States to see what effect this would have on the number of parties or change states of the South to industrial states to see whether their political regimes would change or change command economies to market economies to see whether they would become more productive.

What we *can* do is observe variations and changes as they occur around us and try to figure out which variations or changes actually cause other things to happen. For instance, many states of the South, especially in East Asia, are becoming industrialized, so we can watch to see how this changes their politics. The challenge in basing analysis on such changes is that no one thing ever changes in isolation from everything else, in the way a physicist can arrange it in the laboratory. Everything is always changing at once, and we must use our creative sense to try to sort out *which* changes have caused *which* others.

For example, in 1961, France changed its electoral system to one based on a presidency, which should, in principle, tend to bring about a two-party system. Over the years since then, France has indeed seen a coalescence of its party system into five parties, organized in two well-defined blocs. Did the new electoral system bring about the coalescence? At the same time that France was adjusting to its new electoral arrangements, it was also experiencing unprecedented prosperity, which might perhaps have made people less likely to support small radical parties. Also, it was at this time that the popular Charles de Gaulle served as president. He drew a large political party about himself— something he could probably have done no matter what the electoral system was—and that knocked out several smaller parties. What, then, was the effect of the change in electoral arrangements on the number of parties?

Under such circumstances, we cannot be certain of the effects of one thing on another. We can and do use our common sense, asking, for example, what the effects of electoral systems *should* be. And we can look at overall patterns across many cases, asking what has happened after changes of electoral system in other countries. The result is not a firm, indisputable finding but rather something on which to form conclusions and something that can be disputed. There is nothing wrong with this.

HISTORICAL EXPLANATION

A natural affinity between the field of history and what we have been discussing should be apparent to you. Historians follow a series of events as they move forward in time, linking them to one another. This is much like the analysis of causation that political scientists frequently engage in.

There is a difference in emphasis between the two fields, however. Historians are more often concerned to present a single train of events—a biography of Lincoln, a history of negotiations at the Council of Europe, a military history of World War II, and so on—with causal analysis left somewhat implicit. Political scientists, on the other hand, are more likely to be looking for overall patterns (embodied in theories) and less concerned with tracing carefully through any single case or train of events.

This is only a difference of degree. Political historians and political scientists are engaged in the same task—to make sense out of the myriad political events occurring around us—and both historians and political scientists do this by *explaining* certain things, showing that they are caused by other things.

Remember from our earlier discussion that it is not enough to show that one thing happened before another. If we are to treat the earlier event as causing the later one, we must also establish some basis for treating it as having brought the other about or having produced it. *This necessity holds as much for the historian as for the political scientist.*

This is an important point for students in political science courses, because as you are assigned research papers to write, a deceptively simple route may appear to be a paper that traces the history of something: a history of the arms race between the Soviet Union and the United States, a biography of Senator Jesse Helms, a history of the diplomacy leading up to the Bosnia peace accords, a description of how the National Security Council developed, a tracing of changes in French fiscal policy after the socialists came to power, and so on. Any of these could make an excellent topic for a paper, but if you do it right, it will be neither easier nor more difficult than any other topic would be. To do the job right is to try to establish causal relationships among the events as they transpire. If, in attempting to write a paper of this sort, you lay out the events—first X happened, then Y, then Z—you will have merely described things. As noted, you will not have an interesting paper. However, if you operate as good historians do—that is, if you try to explain why the train of events occurred as it did—you will have an interesting and not necessarily easily written paper.

A FEW COMMON PITFALLS IN ANALYSIS

As you analyze politics, you must think straight. For the most part, common sense will carry you well; and practice and criticism from your readers will help to sharpen your abilities. As an introductory help, you may find it useful to consider three common flaws in analysis that you should watch out for in your own writing and the work of others.

1 *Begging the Question.*   Frequently writers answer a question with an answer that restates the question. It looks as though it has answered the question, but it has not. It has turned the question into another form and does not produce much progress. This is called "begging the question."

For example, a person analyzing the victory of North Vietnam in the Vietnam War might state that North Vietnam won because it was more powerful than South Vietnam. This does not really answer the question we want to see addressed; rather, it changes it slightly into the question: Why was North Vietnam more powerful than South Vietnam? Similarly, an analysis of American voting behavior concluding that people vote for candidates they prefer would not seem to have brought us forward. It would leave us with the further question: Why do people prefer certain candidates over others? Questions of value can also be begged. For instance, a paper arguing that socialism is a better system than capitalism because it is more just—unless it expanded on this to show what was meant by "justice"—would leave us with the question: What makes socialism more just than capitalism?

These examples may have seemed rather simple, and you may have wondered why you would need to be cautioned to watch out for a flaw that is so easily avoided. However, begging a question is actually easy to do. Not all instances of it are as obvious as the examples used here. For instance, people often argue about policy on the basis of "natural rights," rights so basic to the nature of humanity that they take priority over all else. The Declaration of Independence appeals to "certain inalienable rights, [among which are] life, liberty, and the pursuit of happiness" and argues that because the king of England had violated these rights, his rule was outlaw; hence, it was proper to rise in revolution against him. At a later period, administrators in Hitler's Germany were charged with the crime of having obeyed and enforced Hitler's laws. This was a crime because the laws themselves were in violation of natural rights. Basic privacy, the right of a woman to control her own body, and the fetus's right to life are other things that have been defended at one time or another as natural rights.

This sort of argument comes readily to us, and we slip easily into it. It is a useful rhetorical device. We should realize, however, when we assert the existence of natural rights, that unless we accompany this assertion with an analysis of human nature, we are begging the question in the following way: "X should be defended because it is a natural right." What makes it a natural right? That it is basic to the nature of a human being. But how do we know what is basic to the nature of a human being?

2 Circular Argument.   A circular argument is one in which a person proves A from B, but we know that B is true only because of A. In other words, B implies A, but we believe B only if we first believe A. The argument goes in a circle and does not offer any new reason to believe either A or B.

Suppose, for example, we argued that political influence of the military is a major cause of the size of defense budgets, but we measured "military influence" by the size of the armed forces. In this case, we would be asserting that military influence is what causes defense budgets to be large, but because our measure of "military influence" is something that is a direct result of the size of defense budgets, finding that the two things tend to rise and fall together would give us no new reason to believe the original statement.

Dilbert: By Scott Adams

(DILBERT reprinted by permission of United Feature Syndicate, Inc.)

3 Post Hoc Explanation.   A post hoc explanation is the "Monday-morning quarterback" of explanation. It consists of taking a set of things that have already happened, showing that one of them plausibly could have resulted from the others and, on the basis of this, asserting that those others are a cause of the thing in question.

For example, many commentators have looked at the sequence of events leading up to World War II and have asserted that it was the appeasement of Britain and France that led Hitler on and resulted in his frantic war of conquest. This is certainly plausible, but it is post hoc.

The danger in post hoc explanations is that for *any* event, there will be some set of things that happened at more or less the same time and that may look like a plausible explanation for it. If those same things happen again in the future, they may or may not produce that same result. It is not that a post hoc explanation is *wrong* but that it leaves us with a greater feeling of certainty than we should have. We confuse the set of events that first suggested an idea to us with verification of the idea. What has suggested that appeasement encourages aggressors? The events leading to World War II. How do we know that it's true? Look at Hitler!

The three problems of argument noted are by no means the only ones you will learn to watch for, but they are three common problems. In the end, these three, and the rest, boil down to a matter of common sense. If you are endowed with some of that, you won't go wrong.

GLOSSARY

Following most terms, the first page on which the term is introduced substantively appears in parentheses. A few items have no such reference; these are terms such as *welfare state* that are not explicitly introduced in this book but belong in a glossary for readers of the book.

ambassador (p. 388) An official charged by his or her state to conduct high-level politics with another state to which he or she is posted.

American conservatism (p. 20) The rather loose ideology known in the United States as "conservatism." It is really a variant of the more general ideology of liberalism and has relatively little to do with the more general ideology of conservatism; therefore, it has been distinguished in this book by the name *American conservatism.* American conservatism is particularly suspicious of governmental intervention to make people more equal but is often willing to entrust government with power to maintain morality.

American liberalism (p. 20) The rather loose ideology known in the United States as "liberalism." It is only a variant of the more general ideology of liberalism; therefore, it has been distinguished in this book by the name *American liberalism.* American liberalism is particularly concerned to make people equal, and it is relatively willing to entrust government with power to bring this about; it is also particularly concerned to maintain freedom of expression.

arbitrary action (p. 128) Action that is taken capriciously. The people affected do not know what to expect before the action and do not learn afterward the grounds on which the action was chosen.

authority (p. 146) Power based on a general agreement that the holder of the power has the right to issue certain commands and that those commands should be obeyed.

autonomous state (p. 52) A state in which the government and bureaucracy are relatively insulated from political pressures of groups in the society.

balance of power (p. 392)   The idea that the international system works in a natural way to keep the power of states balanced so that no one state can achieve domination of the entire system.

begging a question (p. 406)   "Answering" a question (failing to answer it) by offering a rephrasing of it as an answer. Example: "Why did Britain win the Falkland Islands war?" "Because Britain was more successful militarily than Argentina." (This leaves us with the question "Why was Britain more successful militarily than Argentina?", which restates the original.)

"behavioralist" political science (p. 14)   Political science that emphasizes statistical analysis and abstract theories seeking out basic, essential regularities across a set of events.

bureaucracy (p. 342)   A way of organizing the public administration that emphasizes professionalism, recruitment, and promotion on the basis of merit, standardization of procedures, and the smooth flow of commands.

cabinet (in parliamentary system) (p. 296)   The executive portion of a parliamentary government. It consists of ministers, most of whom are usually members of the parliament. Each minister is responsible for the administration of some part of the government's services, such as health or defense. The cabinet leads the parliament, proposing legislation, conducting the country's foreign policy, and so on. It serves at the pleasure of the parliament and can be ousted by a majority vote of no confidence.

case law (p. 355)   A legal system emphasizing the independence of the judiciary from the rest of the government. Under case law, the ongoing stream of prior decisions (precedents) becomes an important part of current law. Predominant in Britain and its former colonies.

causation (p. 403)   An interpretation of relations between events in which one event "brings about" or produces another event. Example: "Independence of their central banks is a major cause of low inflation for states."

central bank (p. 108)   A bank set up by a government to help handle its transactions, to coordinate the policies of private banks, and, above all, to manage interest rates in the economy.

circular argument (p. 407)   An argument in which one proves A from B but in which A provides our only evidence that B is true.

coalition (p. 298)   A tactical combination of varied groups, constructed so that the groups will in combination be large enough to command power that they can then share among themselves. Frequently applied to parliamentary government, in which 50 percent of the votes in parliament are required to form a cabinet but in which it may be necessary to combine two or more parties to amass 50 percent of the votes.

code law (p. 356)   A legal system emphasizing a relative subordination of the judiciary to the rest of the government. Legal interpretation consists primarily of reading and applying codes of legal statute passed by the parliament, rather than looking to the precedent of prior court decisions. Used in various forms in most parts of the world except Britain and its former colonies.

codetermination (p. 116)   German system by which corporations are legally required to include workers' representatives on their boards of directors.

collective good (p. 138) Something that benefits all members of the collectivity and that no one can be prevented from using. It is usually chosen by governmental authority because it is difficult to get individuals voluntarily to pay part of the cost of the good.

committees (legislative) (p. 303) Small group of legislators whose task (usually) is to review carefully a proposed piece of legislation and recommend to the full legislature what action should be taken on it. In many legislatures, bills may be amended by the committee or killed in entirety. Committees may also perform other tasks, such as investigating an area of possible legislation.

communism (p. 31) The more militant branch of socialism. Communists argue that the only way to build a socialist state is by revolution. Therefore, they are sometimes less interested in electoral activity than the democratic socialists. After the 1920s, communists acknowledged the leadership of the Soviet Union in the formulation of their goals and strategies. See also *socialism; democratic socialism.*

conservatism (p. 24) An ideology positing that the most important goal of politics is to create stable communities based on a hierarchy of power in which leaders and followers have reciprocal responsibilities and obligations. Unlike liberalism, conservatism is not suspicious of power and does not seek to limit the power of the state. Rather, the point of conservatism is that power should be in the hands of a traditional class of rulers. See also *American conservatism.*

constitution (p. 204) A set of rules by which power is distributed in a political group, such as the state. This usually consists in part of a formal set of rules, but it always contains various informal mechanisms, traditions, and understandings by which power is assigned to people.

constitutionalism (p. 215) The doctrine that states' constitutions should be designed fairly, not to give undue advantage to any particular group, and that the government should then be faithful to that constitution. In this way, individuals are protected against arbitrary governmental action.

constitutional review (p. 326) A system under which a judicial or quasi-judicial part of the government can annul acts of other parts of the government if, in its judgment, those acts violate the constitution of the state.

consulates (p. 388; *contrast* ambassador) Offices maintained by a state in major cities of another state to deal with individuals' problem regarding trade, immigration, travel, and so forth.

corruption (p. 111) Improperly performing one's public tasks to receive personal benefits (bribes, etc.).

coup (p. 188) The forceful deposition of a government by all or a portion of the armed forces and installation of a new military government.

court politics (p. 194) The political process in a state where great power is vested in a single person, as in traditional monarchy or in a personal dictatorship.

courts (pp. 355 and 361) Governmental institutions charged with interpreting the law.

crisis transitions (p. 177) Transitions from an autocratic to a democratic system that take place in the context of an economic crisis.

democracy (p. 169) A state in which qualified citizens vote at regular intervals to choose, among alternative candidates, the people who will be in charge of setting the state's policies.

democratic socialism (p. 31)   The branch of socialism that supports electoral democracy and holds that the proper way for workers to control society is to win elections. Democratic socialists are also more moderate than communists in the goals they set, being more willing to settle for piecemeal progress rather than holding out for a complete remaking of society. See also *socialism; communism.*

dictatorship   A governmental arrangement in which those who hold power did not gain power by any regular constitutional process and are not responsible in their exercise of power to any formal set of rules.

diplomacy (p. 388)   The conduct of relations between states and other global actors other than by war.

dominant-party system (p. 257; *contrast* one-party system)   A political party system in which various parties are allowed to function openly and with reasonable effectiveness but in which a single party nonetheless holds power all the time.

due process (p. 128)   An expectation that certain procedures must always be followed in making a policy and that if they were not, the policy should be void.

economic sanctions (p. 389)   A form of nonmilitary coercion in which a state or group of states deliberately withholds normal economic relations with another state to punish it.

efficient policies (p. 131)   Policies that produce the greatest good at the least cost.

electoral system (p. 227)   A set of rules by which the outcomes of an election (a set of officers elected or whatever) is determined from the distribution of votes cast by the electorate.

empirical theory (p. 14)   A theory describing how things work in the world we observe.

established church   A church or other organized religion that is established by law as the official church or religion of a state and that has political and legal ties to the government of the state. Examples are the Anglican church, established in Great Britain; the Roman Catholic church, established in Italy and many other countries; and Judaism, established in Israel.

European Union (p. 64)   An organization of fifteen Western European states that have set up a rather weak common government and have coordinated many of their economic policies.

externality (p. 139)   A situation in which there are social costs or benefits beyond the individual costs and benefits involved in a transaction.

fascism (p. 31)   A political movement that appeared in many countries in the 1920s and 1930s. Fascism stressed militaristic pageantry and a strident nationalism as ways of binding the people to a single dramatic dictator. Franco, Mussolini, and Hitler were fascist dictators.

federal state (p. 211)   A state in which the constitution grants to regional governments a legal monopoly over certain political decisions, such as educational policy. Therefore, two different governments will control the same group of people, but with regard to different political questions.

fiduciary role (p. 383)   A role in which one acts as an agent on behalf of someone else's interests. This role often places the agent in problematic positions.

***glasnost* (p. 262)**   Mikhail Gorbachev's campaign in the late 1980s to make politics in the Soviet Union more open and competitive, ending tight control of politics by the Communist Party.

global politics (p. 372; *contrast* international politics)   Politics conducted above the level of a state. It is essentially the same thing as international politics but includes the connotation that not only states but also international organizations and non-governmental organizations are actors in the process.

government (p. 51)   The group of people within the state who have the ultimate authority to act on behalf of the state.

gross domestic product, or GDP (p. 96)   The total value of all goods and services exchanged in a society; that is, the sum of such things as the value of all food sold, the value of all mechanics' work on automobiles, the value of all educational activity, and so on. The higher the GDP, the greater the total amount of economic activity in the society. Per capita GDP divides GDP by the population to measure how economically well-off the average person is.

habeas corpus (p. 356)   The right not to be held indefinitely by the police without being formally charged with a crime.

higher civil service (p. 349)   Specialized and executive members of the public administration, corresponding to professionals and managers in the private sector.

ideology (p. 18)   A set of ideas that are related and that modify one another; that is, an organized set of ideas about something.

implicit power (p. 6)   Power in which A does what B desires not because of anything B says or does but because (1) A senses that B wants something done and (2) for any of a variety of reasons, A wishes to do what B wants done.

import-substitution industrialization (p. 99)   A policy especially followed by many states of the South in the 1960s and 1970s whereby the states erected high tariff barriers against imports, hoping to build their domestic industries.

incentive compatibility (p. 208)   A situation in which those who make decisions on behalf of society benefit personally when their decisions benefit society. When incentive compatibility is present, society does not need to depend on nobility of character in its officials; it can depend on a more reliable force—their concern for their own self-interest.

incrementalism (p. 134)   A policy of making decisions cautiously and implementing them through small staged changes rather than in bold sweeps.

inflation (p. 103)   A situation in which most prices are rising at the same time and the value of the currency is therefore declining in real terms.

institutional interest group (p. 276)   A group that is primarily set up for some purpose other than political activity but becomes politically active to defend its interests in the policy decisions of the state.

interest group (p. 268)   An organized group of citizens that has as one of its goals ensuring that the state follows certain policies.

International Court of Justice (p. 383)   The court that hears cases at law between states. It has no power to enforce its ruling.

international politics (pp. 372 and 381)   Politics conducted among states rather than within a single state.

interpretive political science (p. 14)   Political science that emphasizes historical, anthropological, and (sometimes) legal methods, and the complex whole that is being studied.

justice (p. 125)   A situation in which people are treated as they deserve. See *procedural justice* and *substantive justice.*

legal systems (p. 355)   General, organized sets of legal principles.

legitimacy (p. 148)   A belief on the part of large numbers of people in a state that the existing governmental structure and/or the particular persons in office should appropriately wield authority.

liberalism (p. 21)   An ideology positing that the most important goal of politics is to help individuals develop their capacities to the fullest. To this end, people should be regulated and aided by governments as little as possible, so that they will learn from the experience of being responsible for their own decisions. Liberalism may be summarized by the slogan, "That government is best which governs least." See also *American liberalism.*

manifest power (p. 6)   Power based on an observable action by A that causes B to do what A wants.

market mechanism (p. 135)   A mechanism whereby social choice results from choices of all members of the collectivity rather than from a decision made by the central governing unit.

mobilization (p. 246)   The systematic stimulation of concerted effort by large numbers of people, as in elections or demonstrations. This term is used especially in reference to such stimulation conducted on its own behalf by the government.

multinational corporations   Corporations such as Exxon or ITT that have become so large and conduct their operations in so many different states that we can no longer realistically think of them as belonging to any particular state.

multiparty system (p. 259)   A democratic system in which there are more than two major parties.

nation (p. 46)   A large group of people who are bound together and recognize a similarity among themselves because of a common culture; in particular, a common language seems important in creating nationhood. Nations often but not always coincide with the political boundaries of states. The Kurdish language and culture is spread across parts of Turkey, Iraq, and Iran; Irish nationalists and British nationalists are mixed together in Northern Ireland, where they are at each other's throats. There are many similar examples of mismatches between national "boundaries" and the boundaries of states. Such mismatches are a potent source of political turmoil.

nationalism (p. 50)   Passionate identification with a state on the part of its citizens.

nationalization of industry (p. 76)   The acquisition of an industrial operation by the government, which then operates it directly as part of the governmental administration.

nation-state (p. 51)   A term often used to signify today's states; it takes cognizance of the fact that states in the modern era try to develop a sense of nation to coincide with the boundaries of the state, so that emotions of nationalism will lodge on the state as well.

neocorporatism (p. 286)   A system of government and interest groups in which all interests are organized but—instead of responding to groups' pressures—the government actively involves the groups themselves in the job of governing. This active governmental role distinguishes neocorporatism from pluralism.

normative theory (p. 14)   A theory that involves making a judgment about the world, not describing how it works.

ombudsman (p. 345)   A government official whose primary duty is to seek out citizens' complaints of abuse by public administrators and to negotiate changes in the offending practices.

one-party state (p. 192)   A state in which the government is based on, and in turn supports, a single political party. No other party is allowed to function in other than a token way.

one-party system (p. 255; *contrast* **dominant-party system)**   A political system in which only a single political party is allowed to be active.

pacts (p. 174)   In general, agreements; specifically, with regard to democratization, agreements between the leaders of the new democracy and supporters of the older authoritarian system that soften the change for the latter and help them to accept the democracy.

paradox of participation (p. 234)   The paradox that no one should vote if their only reason for voting is that they wish to help their favored candidate win. The odds that the rest of the voters will produce a tie are incredibly small, and that is the only circumstance in which the person's vote will make any difference to the candidate.

parliamentary government (p. 296)   A democracy in which the executive and legislative functions are merged in one institution, the parliament. The parliament is the state's supreme legislature, but it also appoints a committee (the cabinet) to serve as the political executive for the state.

party identification (p. 249)   A personal identification with a political party; not just agreement with its policies or candidates of the moment but an enduring identification with the party itself.

pluralism (p. 285)   A system of government and interest groups in which all interests organize and compete freely, with no one group dominating, and in which the government is open to pressure from the groups so that policy is largely the outcome of groups' competing pressures.

political culture (p. 158)   The attitudes and beliefs held communally by a people, forming the basis for their political behavior.

political economy (p. 95)   A subfield of political science that focuses on ways the state and the economy interact. Political economy is concerned with how the economy affects the state (for example, effects of the economy on elections) and how the state affects the economy (for example, whether independent central banks reduce inflation).

political party (p. 244)   A group of officials or would-be officials who are linked with a sizable group of citizens into an organization; a chief object of this organization is to ensure that its officials attain power or are maintained in power.

political psychology (p. 96)   A subfield of political science that focuses on how individuals, both among political elites and ordinary citizens, make their choices in political decisions. Political psychology draws heavily on the field of psychology for insights and theory.

political science (p. 13)   The academic field that takes as its sole and general task the analysis of politics, especially the politics of the state.

political socialization (p. 160)   The process of learning the facts, assumptions, and attitudes we use in responding to politics. Political socialization occurs most rapidly in childhood and youth but continues throughout life.

politics (p. 3)   The making of common decisions for a group of people through the exercise of power by some members of the group over other members.

post hoc explanation (p. 407)   An explanation tailored to the particular set of events to be explained. (*Post hoc* means "after this.") A danger in this is that mere coincidences may be treated as general relationships in the explanation.

power (p. 5)   The ability of one person to cause another to do what the first wishes, by whatever means. See also *implicit power* and *manifest power.*

presidential government (p. 316)   A democratic system in which the legislature and executive exist independently and are elected independently of each other. The president takes a leading role in forming policy but must have the consent of the legislature if that policy is to be enacted. A presidential system divides power, whereas a parliamentary system unifies it.

privatization   Selling to the public or by some other means transforming to private ownership economic enterprises that were previously owned and managed by the state.

procedural justice (p. 128)   A concept of justice less concerned with fairness of distribution to people than with the procedures by which decisions are reached about them.

progressive taxation (p. 107)   A system of taxes that takes a greater proportion of a person's income if the income is high than if the income is low.

promotional interest group (p. 277)   The "typical" interest group—an organized group of citizens, one of whose primary purposes is to affect the policies of the state.

proportional representation electoral system, or PR (p. 228)   An electoral system in which parties receive a number of seats in the legislature roughly proportional to the number of votes that were cast for them among the electorate.

public administration (p. 338)   The set of people who are not involved directly in the making of major political decisions but who construct and implement the policies that carry out those decisions. Examples are police officers, public health nurses, I.R.S. agents, and public university presidents.

question time (p. 301)   A device, originating in the British House of Commons and since imitated in many parliaments, by which cabinet members appear regularly in the parliament to answer questions from members about the administration of their offices. These questions and answers often spark hot debate.

radicalism (p. 134)   Making decisions in bold sweeps and changing policies rapidly, so as not to miss opportunities that might disappear if one moved slowly.

rational choice models of politics (p. 95)   Models of politics that are based on a core assumption that all who are involved act "rationally"; that is, they make their decisions in order to further certain specific goals. A rational choice model posits what those goals are and then proceeds by deductive logic to demonstrate what political choices a person should make if those are her or his goals.

referendum (pp. 227 and 232)   An election in which voters choose directly whether a particular proposal will become law; this contrasts with other kinds of elections in which voters choose among various candidates for a political office.

regime theory (p. 393)   A theory of international relations emphasizing the importance of "regimes," or sets of principles and values that transcend state boundaries and regulate in an informal way areas of policy such as trade, development of the polar regions, and so on.

regional integration (p. 58)   A partial merging of the political and economic structures of several states in the same region of the world. The most successful attempt at regional integration to date has been the formation of the European Union.

regressive taxation (p. 107)   A system of taxes that takes a greater proportion of a person's income if the income is low than if the income is high.

regulation (p. 75)   Direct laying down of rules by the government as to how people may conduct their affairs. This is distinguished from *indirect* governmental direction of choices, as when a government taxes liquor heavily to discourage its use but does not actually make its use illegal. The latter would constitute regulation.

rent (p. 98)   *Not* the charge you pay to live in an apartment. In its specialized usage in political economy, *rents* are transfers of money that do not relate to production. Though rents can be good and useful (Social Security is a rent, for instance), they are troubling because: (a) many rents are not good and useful (pork barrel projects, for instance); and (b) rents tend to pull money away from investment.

representative bureaucracy (p. 347)   The idea that members of the public administration should be similar to the groups they serve in such characteristics as class, race, and gender, so that they will be able to serve them better.

sectoral interest group (p. 276)   A group representing a section of the economy. Examples are trade unions, professional associations, corporations, and trade associations.

selective incentive (p. 274)   Benefits that an organization offers its members in addition to the central purposes of the organization. A trade union, for example, may offer its members such added benefits as low-cost package vacations.

Sharia (p. 358)   Islamic law, based on a set of rules for moral conduct developed over the first few centuries after the death of Muhammad.

single-member-district plurality electoral system, or SMDP (p. 228)   An electoral system in which the state is divided into geographic subdivisions, each subdivision is represented by a single member in the legislature, and the candidate who attains a plurality of votes in that subdivision is the one who fills the seat.

social capital (p. 157)   The interwoven network of associational activities (clubs, churches, civic associations, neighborhoods, etc.) through which people are involved in their communities and build a reservoir of trust and positive expectations about collective action.

social movement (p. 283)   A loosely organized group of people who ordinarily have little power but challenge the state power—usually through disruption and sometimes violently. The object of a social movement is usually an emotional issue, which may range from a very local question such as the location of a new highway all the way up to the constitution or identity of the state.

socialism (p. 27)   An ideology positing that society consists of classes (groups of people similarly placed economically) constantly in conflict. To create a just society in which people are equal, the working class should take over the state and direct all industries.

sovereignty (p. 46)   The legal capacity of a geographic unit to maintain ultimate responsibility for the conduct of its own affairs.

state (pp. 12 and 40)   The basic unit by which people are organized politically; often casually called "country" or "nation." States are militarily independent of each other and are guided by governments that typically regulate the economy, set the laws of the state, and so on. States in the twentieth century tended to be relatively large territories with stable boundaries whose populations are bound together by intimate political ties. In marginal cases such as the European Union, it can be a bit tricky to say exactly whether a unit is or is not a "state." In the United States, *state* also has a second meaning, referring to one of the fifty regional divisions (California, Alaska, Florida, Minnesota, etc.) into which the United States is divided.

substantive justice (p. 128)   A concept of justice that emphasizes people receiving what they need and deserve, whether on the basis of the contributions they make to common efforts, of their need for the reward, or of at least approximate equality of treatment.

tautology (p. 402)   A statement that is logically true and thus cannot be shown false by an examination of evidence. Example: "All brunettes have dark hair."

theory (p. 14)   A statement linking specific instances to broader principles.

trivial explanation (p. 403)   An explanation that is obvious to the audience and therefore not interesting to them. Example: "Why does John eat so much?" "Because he's hungry."

two-party system (p. 258)   A democratic system in which two parties regularly receive 90 percent or more of votes cast but in which it is rare for either of them to receive more than 55 or 60 percent of the votes. These two parties will replace each other in office fairly frequently.

unitary state (p. 211)   A state in which no other governmental body but the central government has any areas of policy that are exclusively under its control. In a unitary state, local and regional governments may potentially be overruled by the central government in any political decision they make.

United Nations (pp. 59 and 397)   An organization of almost all the world's states. The UN provides a forum at which complaints can be aired; it has often helped to cool off conflicts between states; and its specialized committees seek to improve world standards of health, education, and so on.

welfare state   A state in which the government seeks, by a complex set of policies, to ensure that its citizens will not suffer great economic insecurity or grievous want. Such policies may include guaranteed pensions, public provision of health care, public attempts to prevent unemployment, public help in the care of children, and so on. Most industrialized states have established welfare states since World War II.

BIBLIOGRAPHY

Aberbach, Joel D.; Putnam, Robert D.; and Rockman, Bert A. *Bureaucrats and Politicians in Western Democracies.* Cambridge: Harvard University Press, 1981.

Aberbach, Joel D., and Rockman, Bert A. *In the Web of Politics: Three Decades of the U.S. Federal Executive.* Washington, D.C.: Brookings Institution, 2000.

Abraham, Henry J. *The Judicial Process: An Introductory Analysis of the Courts of the United States, England, and France.* New York: Oxford University Press, 1998.

Adams, John Clarke, and Barile, Paolo. *The Government of Republican Italy.* 3d ed. Boston: Houghton Mifflin, 1972.

Alba, Victor. *Politics and the Labor Movement in Latin America.* Stanford, Calif.: Stanford University Press, 1968.

Aldrich, John. *Why Parties? The Origin and Transformation of Party Politics in America.* Chicago: University of Chicago Press, 1995.

Alesina, Alberto. "Elections, Party Structure and the Economy." In *Modern Political Economy,* edited by Jeffrey Banks and Eric Hanushek. New York: Cambridge University Press, 1995.

Alexander, Herbert, and Shiratori, Rei. *Comparative Political Finance Among the Democracies.* Boulder, Colo.: Westview Press, 1994.

Alford, Robert R. *Health Care Politics.* Chicago: University of Chicago Press, 1975.

Allison, Graham T. *Essence of Decision: Explaining the Cuban Missile Crisis.* Boston: Little, Brown, 1971.

Almond, Gabriel A. *A Discipline Divided: Schools and Sects in Political Science.* Newbury Park, Calif.: Sage, 1990.

———, and Verba, Sidney. *The Civic Culture.* Boston: Little, Brown, 1965.

———, eds. *The Civic Culture Revisited.* Boston: Little, Brown, 1980.

Alt, James, and Alesina, Alberto. "Political Economy: An Overview." In *A New Handbook of Political Science,* edited by Robert E. Goodin and Hans-Dieter Klingemann. New York: Oxford University Press, 1997.

Alter, Karen J. "The European Court's Political Power." *West European Politics* 19 (July 1996): 458–87.

Alvarez, Sonia. *Engendering Democracy: Women's Movements in Transition Politics*. Princeton, N.J.: Princeton University Press, 1990.

Anderson, Benedict. *Imagined Communities: Reflections on the Origin and Spread of Nationalism,* rev. ed. New York: Verso, 1991.

Anderson, Charles. *Statecraft*. New York: Wiley, 1977.

Anglin, Douglas. "Southern African Responses to Eastern European Developments." *Journal of Modern African Studies* 28 (no. 3, 1990): 431–56.

Anheier, Helmut K.; Salamon, Lester M.; and Archambault, Edith. "Participating Citizens: U.S.-Europe Comparisons in Volunteer Action." *Public Perspective* 5 (no. 3, March/April 1994): 16–34.

Arendt, Hannah. *The Origins of Totalitarianism*. New York: Harcourt Brace, 1951.

Arian, Alan, and Barnes, Samuel. "The Dominant Party System: A Neglected Model of Democratic Stability." *Journal of Politics* 36 (August 1974): 592–614.

Bachrach, Peter, and Baratz, Morton S. "The Two Faces of Power." *American Political Science Review* 56 (December 1962): 947–53.

Baker, Kendall; Dalton, Russell; and Hildebrandt, Kai. *Germany Transformed*. Cambridge: Harvard University Press, 1981.

Baker, Pauline H. "Nigeria: Lurching Toward Unity." *Wilson Quarterly* 4 (Winter 1980): 70–80.

Bakvis, Herman, and Chandler, William M. *Federalism and the Role of the State*. Toronto: University of Toronto Press, 1987.

Ball, A., and Millard, F. *Pressure Politics in Industrial Societies*. Atlantic Highlands, N.J.: Humanities Press International, 1987.

Barber, Benjamin. *Strong Democracy*. Berkeley: University of California Press, 1984.

Barber, James David. *The Presidential Character*. 2d ed. Englewood Cliffs, N.J.: Prentice-Hall, 1977.

Barnes, Samuel H.; Kaase, Max; and Allerbeck, Klause. *Political Action: Mass Participation in Five Western Democracies*. Beverly Hills, Calif.: Sage, 1979.

Bartlett, Katherine T., and Kennedy, Rosanne, eds. *Feminist Legal Theory*. Boulder, Colo.: Westview, 1991.

Barton, John H.; Gibbs, James Lowell, Jr.; Li, Victor Hao; and Merryman, John Henry. *Law in Radically Different Cultures*. St. Paul, Minn.: West, 1983.

Batalla, Javier Ortiz. *Essays on the Early History of Latin American Central Banking*. Ph.D. dissertation in economics, University of California–Los Angeles, 1993.

Bates, Robert H. *Markets and States in Tropical Africa*. Berkeley: University of California Press, 1981.

Bauer, Raymond A.; Pool, Ithiel de Sola; and Dexter, Lewis Anthony. *American Business and Public Policy*. New York: Atherton, 1963.

Baum, Lawrence. *The Puzzle of Judicial Behavior*. Ann Arbor: University of Michigan Press, 1997.

Baumgartner, Frank, and Leech, Beth. *Basic Interests: The Importance of Groups in Politics and Political Science*. Princeton, N.J.: Princeton University Press, 1998.

Beck, Paul A. *Party Politics in America*. 8th ed. Reading, Mass.: Addison-Wesley, 1997.

Beer, Samuel. *British Politics in the Collectivist Age*. New York: Knopf, 1965.

Bermeo, Nancy. "Myths of Moderation: Confrontation and Conflict During Democratic Transitions." *Comparative Politics* 29 (April 1997): 305–22.

Berry, Jeffrey M. *The Interest Group Society*. 3d ed. New York: Longmann, 1997.

Berry, William D. "The Confusing Case of Budgetary Incrementalism: Too Many Meanings for a Single Concept." *Journal of Politics* 52 (February 1990): 167–96.

Bienen, Henry. "Military Rule and the Political Process: Nigerian Examples." *Comparative Politics* 10 (January 1978): 205–25.

———, with Fitton, Martin. "Soldiers, Politicians and Civil Servants." In *Soldiers and Oil*, edited by K. Panter-Brick. London: Frank Cass, 1978.

Billig, Michael; Condor, Susan; Edwards, Derek; Gane, Mike; Middleton, David; and Radley, Alan. *Ideological Dilemmas: A Social Psychology of Everyday Thinking.* Beverly Hills, Calif.: Sage, 1998.

Birch, Anthony H. *Representation.* New York: Praeger, 1971.

Bond, Jon R., and Fleisher, Richard. *The President in the Legislative Arena.* Chicago: University of Chicago Press, 1990.

Bowler, Shaun; Farrell, David M.; and Katz, Richard S., eds. *Party Discipline and Parliamentary Government.* Columbus: Ohio State University Press, 1999.

———; Todd, Donovan; and Tolbert, Caroline J., eds. *Citizens as Legislators: Direct Democracy in the United States.* Columbus: Ohio State University Press, 1998.

Brand, Jack. *British Parliamentary Parties: Policy and Power.* New York: Oxford University Press, 1992.

Bratton, Michael, and van de Walle, Nicholas. "Neopatrimonial Regimes and Political Transitions in Africa." *World Politics* 46 (1994): 453–89.

Brichta, Avraham, and Zalmanovitch, Yair. "Proposals for Presidential Government in Israel." *Comparative Political Studies* 19 (October 1986): 57–68.

Burkett, Tony. "Developments in the West German Bundestag in the 1970s." *Parliamentary Affairs* 34 (Summer 1981): 291–307.

Burnham, Walter Dean. *Critical Elections and the Mainsprings of American Politics.* New York: Norton, 1970.

Cain, Bruce; Ferejohn, John; and Fiorina, Morris. *The Personal Vote.* Cambridge: Harvard University Press, 1987.

Cameron, David. "The Expansion of the Public Economy: A Comparative Analysis." *American Political Science Review* 72 (December 1978): 1243–61.

Campbell, Angus; Converse, Philip; Miller, Warren E.; and Stokes, Donald. *The American Voter.* New York: Wiley, 1960.

Casper, Gretchen. *Fragile Democracies: The Legacies of Authoritarian Rule.* Pittsburgh: University of Pittsburgh Press, 1995.

Cassels, Alan. *Fascism.* Arlington Heights, Ill.: Harlan Davidson, 1985.

Cederman, Lars-Erik. *Emergent Actors in World Politics: How States and Nations Develop and Dissolve.* Princeton, N.J.: Princeton University Press, 1997.

Centeno, Miguel. *Democracy Within Reason: Technocratic Revolution in Mexico.* University Park: Penn State University Press, 1994.

Chase, Harold W.; Holt, Robert; and Turner, John. *American Government in Comparative Perspective.* New York: Franklin Watts, 1980.

Chrines, S. B. *English Constitutional History.* London: Oxford University Press, 1947.

Christiansen, Peter Mark, and Rommetvedt, Hilmar. "From Composition to Lobbyism? Parliaments, Executives, and Organized Interests in Denmark and Norway." *Scandinavian Political Studies* 22 (1999): 195–220.

Chubb, John E., and Moe, Terry M. *Politics, Markets, and America's Schools.* Washington, D.C.: Brookings Institution, 1990.

Churchill, Randolph S., ed. *The Sinews of Peace: Post-War Speeches by Winston S. Churchill.* London: Cassell, 1948.

Claude, Inis. *States and the Global System.* New York: St. Martin's Press, 1988.

Collier, David, ed. *The New Authoritarianism in Latin America.* Princeton, N.J.: Princeton University Press, 1979.

Conover, Pamela Johnston, and Feldman, Stanley. "Belief System Organization in the American Electorate: An Alternate Approach." In *The Electorate Reconsidered,* edited by John Pierce and John L. Sullivan. Beverly Hills, Calif.: Sage, 1980.

Conradt, David. *The German Polity.* 5th ed. New York: Longmann, 1993.

Coulter, Philip B. *Measuring Inequality.* Boulder, Colo.: Westview Press, 1989.

Cox, Gary W. *The Efficient Secret.* New York: Cambridge University Press, 1987.

————. *Making Votes Count: Strategic Coordination in the World's Electoral Systems.* New York: Cambridge University Press, 1997.

————, and McCubbins, Mathew D. *Legislative Leviathan: Party Government in the House.* Los Angeles: University of California Press, 1993.

Crossman, R. H. S. *The Myths of Cabinet Government.* Cambridge: Harvard University Press, 1972.

Crozier, Michel. *The Bureaucratic Phenomenon.* Chicago: University of Chicago Press, 1963.

Dahl, Robert. *Who Governs?* New Haven: Yale University Press, 1961.

————. *Modern Political Analysis.* 4th ed. New York: Prentice-Hall, 1984.

————. *On Democracy.* New Haven: Yale University Press, 1998.

Dalton, Russell J. *Citizen Politics in Western Democracies.* 2d ed. Chatham, N.J.: Chatham House, 1997.

————. "Communists and Democrats: Democratic Attitudes in the Two Germanies." *British Journal of Political Science* 24 (1994): 469–93.

————, et al., eds. *Electoral Change in Advanced Industrial Democracies: Realignment or Dealignment?* Princeton, N.J.: Princeton University Press, 1984.

————, and Kuechler, Manfred, eds. *Challenging the Political Order: New Social Movements in Western Democracies.* New York: Oxford University Press, 1990.

————, and Wattenberg, Martin P., eds. *Parties Without Partisans: Political Change in Advanced Industrial Democracies.* New York: Oxford University Press, 2000.

Das, Dilip K. *Korean Economic Dynamism.* New York: St. Martin's Press, 1992.

David, René, and Brierly, John E. C. *Major Legal Systems in the World Today.* 3d ed. London: Steven, 1985.

Davis, Otto; Dempster, M. A. H.; and Wildavsky, Aaron. "A Theory of the Budgetary Process." *American Political Science Review* 60 (September 1966): 529–47.

Deibert, Ronald. *Virtual Resources: International Relations Research on the Internet.* Institute of International Relations, University of British Columbia, Working Paper No. 13, April 1997.

Delli Carpini, Michael X., and Keeter, Scott. *What Americans Know About Politics and Why It Matters.* New Haven: Yale University Press, 1995.

Deutsch, Karl. *Nationalism and Social Communication.* Cambridge: MIT Press, 1953.

Diamond, Larry; Kirk-Greene, Anthony; and Oyediran, Oyeleye, eds. *Transition Without End: Nigerian Politics and Civil Society Under Babangida.* Boulder, Colo.: Lynne Rienner Publishers, 1997.

Diamond, Larry; Plattner, Marc F.; Chu, Yun-han; and Tien, Hung-mao, eds. *Consolidating the Third Wave Democracies.* Baltimore: Johns Hopkins University Press, 1997.

Digeser, Peter. "The Fourth Face of Power." *Journal of Politics* 54 (November 1992): 977–1007.

Dinan, Desmond. *Ever Closer Union: An Introduction to European Integration.* Boulder, Colo.: Lynn Rienner Publishers, 1999.

di Palma, Guiseppi. *To Craft Democracies: An Essay on Democratic Transitions.* Berkeley: University of California Press, 1990.

Dodd, Lawrence C., and Oppenheimer, Bruce I. *Congress Reconsidered.* 2d ed. Washington, D.C.: Congressional Quarterly Press, 1981.

Dogan, Mattei, ed. *Comparing Nations: Concepts, Strategies and Substance.* Cambridge, Mass.: Blackwell, 1994.

Doring, Herbert, ed. *Parliaments and Majority Rule in Western Europe.* New York: St. Martin's Press, 1995.

Downing, Brian. *The Military Revolution and Political Change.* Princeton, N.J.: Princeton University Press, 1992.

Downs, Anthony. *An Economic Theory of Democracy.* New York: Harper & Row, 1957.

Drake, Paul, and McCubbins, Matthew, eds. *The Origins of Liberty: Political and Economic Liberalization in the Modern World.* Princeton, N.J.: Princeton University Press, 1998.

Duchacek, Ivo D. *The Territorial Dimensions of Politics Within, Among and Across Nations.* Boulder, Colo.: Westview Press, 1986.

Duverger, Maurice. *Political Parties.* New York: Wiley, 1954.

Easton, David; Gunnell, John G.; and Graziano, Luigi, eds. *The Development of Political Science: A Comparative Survey.* New York: Routledge, 1991.

Ebenstein, Alan; Ebenstein, William; and Fogelman, Edwin. *Today's Isms: Communism, Fascism, Capitalism, Socialism.* 11th ed. Englewood Cliffs, N.J.: Prentice-Hall, 2001.

Eckstein, Harry, and Gurr, Ted Robert. *Patterns of Authority.* New York: Wiley, 1975.

Edwards, George C., III, and Wayne, Stephen. *Presidential Leadership.* 5th ed. New York: Bedford St. Martin's, 1999.

Edwards, George C., III; Kessel, John H.; and Rockman, Bert A., eds. *Researching the Presidency: Vital Questions, New Approaches.* Pittsburgh: University of Pittsburgh Press, 1993.

Ehrmann, Henry. *Politics in France.* 4th ed. Boston: Little, Brown, 1983.

Epstein, Lee, ed. *Contemplating Courts.* Washington, D.C.: Congressional Quarterly Press, 1995.

Ertman, Thomas. *Birth of the Leviathan.* New York: Cambridge University Press, 1997.

Evans, Peter B. *Embedded Autonomy: States and Industrial Transformation.* Princeton, N.J.: Princeton University Press, 1995.

———; Rueschmayer, D.; and Skocpol, Theda, eds. *Bringing the State Back In.* Cambridge, England: Cambridge University Press, 1985.

Fenno, Richard F. *Home Style: House Members in Their Districts.* Boston: Little, Brown, 1978.

———. *Learning to Legislate: The Senate Education of Arlen Specter.* Washington, D.C.: Congressional Quarterly Press, 1991.

Fiorina, Morris P. *Congress: Keystone of the Washington Establishment.* 2d ed. New Haven: Yale University Press, 1989.

Flanigan, William H., and Zingale, Nancy. *Political Behavior of the American Electorate.* 8th ed. Washington, D.C.: Congressional Quarterly Press, 1994.

Freeman, John R. *Politics and Markets: The Politics of Mixed Economies.* Ithaca, N.Y.: Cornell University Press, 1989.

Frieden, Jeffrey A. *Debt, Development and Democracy.* Princeton, N.J.: Princeton University Press, 1991.

———. "Invested Interests: The Politics of National Economic Policies in a World of Global Finance." *International Organization* 45 (1991): 425–51.

Friedrich, Carl. *Limited Government: A Comparison.* Englewood Cliffs, N.J.: Prentice-Hall, 1974.

Fukuyama, Francis. "The End of History?" *National Interest* 16 (Summer 1989): 3–19.

Gaines, Brian. "Duverger's Law and the Meaning of Canadian Exceptionalism." *Comparative Political Studies* 32 (1999): 835–61.

Gellner, Ernest. *Culture, Identity and Politics.* New York: Cambridge University Press, 1987.

———. *Nations and Nationalism.* Ithaca, N.Y.: Cornell University Press, 1983.

Gerber, Elisabeth R. *The Populist Paradox: Interest Group Influence and the Promise of Direct Legislation.* Princeton, N.J.: Princeton University Press, 1999.

Gerth, H. H., and Mills, C. Wright. *From Max Weber.* New York: Oxford University Press, 1958.

Gibson, James L., and Caldeira, Gregory A. "The Legal Cultures of Europe." *Law and Society Review* 30 (1996): 55–85.

Gibson, James L., and Duch, Raymond M. "Emerging Democratic Values in Soviet Political Culture." In *Public Opinion and Regime Change,* edited by Arthur H. Miller, William M. Reisinger, and Vicki L. Hesli. Boulder, Colo.: Westview Press, 1993.

Gillman, Howard. *The Vote That Counted: How the Court Decided the 2000 Presidential Election.* Chicago: University of Chicago Press, 2001.

Gilpin, Robert. *Global Political Economy: Understanding the International Economic Order.* Princeton, N.J.: Princeton University Press, 2001.

Ginsberg, Benjamin. *The Consequences of Consent: Elections, Citizen Control, and Popular Traditions.* Reading, Mass.: Addison-Wesley, 1982.

Glazer, Amihai, and Rothenberg, Lawrence S. *Why Government Succeeds and Why It Fails.* Cambridge: Harvard University Press, 2001.

Glendon, Mary Ann; Gordon, Michael W.; and Osakwe, Christopher. *Comparative Legal Traditions.* St. Paul, Minn.: West, 1982.

Glouchevitch, Philip. *Juggernaut: The German Way of Business.* New York: Simon & Schuster, 1992.

Goldman, Kjell. "International Relations: An Overview." In *A New Handbook of Political Science,* edited by Robert E. Goodin and Hans-Dieter Klingemann, pp. 401–27. New York: Oxford University Press, 1997.

Goldstein, Judith, and Keohane, Robert O., eds. *Ideas and Foreign Policy: Beliefs, Institutions, and Political Change.* Ithaca, N.Y.: Cornell University Press, 1993.

Goldwin, Robert A.; Kaufman, Art; and Schambra, William A., eds. *Forging Unity out of Diversity: The Approaches of Eight Nations.* Washington, D.C.: American Enterprise Institute, 1989.

Goodin, Robert E., and Klingemann, Hans-Dieter, eds. *A New Handbook of Political Science*. New York: Oxford University Press, 1997.

Gourevitch, Peter. *Politics in Hard Times: Comparative Responses to International Economic Crises*. Ithaca, N.Y.: Cornell University Press, 1986.

Graber, Doris. *Mass Media and American Politics*. Washington, D.C.: Congressional Quarterly Press, 1980.

Gramsci, Antonio. *Letters from Prison*. New York: Columbia University Press, 1994.

Grayson, George W., ed. *Prospects for Democracy in Mexico*. New Brunswick, N.J.: Transaction, 1990.

Greenstein, Fred I. *The Presidential Difference*. New York: Free Press, 2000.

Gruber, Judith E. *Controlling Bureaucracies*. Berkeley: University of California Press, 1987.

Gupta, D. C. *Indian Government and Politics*. 4th ed. New Delhi: Vikas, 1978.

Haber, Paul Lawrence. "Identity and Political Process: Recent Trends in the Study of Latin American Social Movements." *Latin American Research Review* 31 (1996): 171–88.

Haggard, Stephen. *Pathways from the Periphery: The Politics of Growth in the Newly Industrializing Countries*. Ithaca, N.Y.: Cornell University Press, 1990.

———, and Kaufman, Robert. *The Political Economy of Democratic Transitions*. Princeton, N.J.: Princeton University Press, 1995.

Hall, Peter. *Governing the Economy: The Politics of State Intervention in Britain and France*. New York: Oxford University Press, 1986.

———. "The Political Economy of Europe in an Era of Interdependence." In *Continuity and Change in Contemporary Capitalism*, edited by Herbert Kitschelt, Peter Lange, Gary Marks, and John D. Stephens. New York: Cambridge University Press, 1999.

Hardin, Garret. "The Tragedy of the Commons." *Science* 162 (13 December 1968): 1243–48.

Hartz, Louis. *The Liberal Tradition in America*. New York: Harcourt Brace, 1955.

Harvey, Jack, and Bather, L. *The British Constitution*. 3d ed. London: Macmillan, 1972.

Heidenheimer, Arnold J. "Federalism and the Party System: The Case of West Germany." *American Political Science Review* 52 (September 1958): 809–28.

———; Heclo, Hugh; and Adams, Carolyn. *Comparative Public Policy*. 2d ed. New York: St. Martin's Press, 1983.

Heisler, Martin O., ed. *Politics in Europe*. New York: David McKay, 1974.

Helm, Jutta. "Codetermination in West Germany: What Difference Has It Made?" *West European Politics* 9 (1986): 637–58.

Hendel, Samuel. *The Soviet Crucible*. Boston: Duxbury, 1980.

Herz, John H. *The Nation-State and the Crisis of World Politics*. New York: David McKay, 1976.

Hirschman, Albert O. "On Democracy in Latin America." *New York Review of Books* 10 (April 1990).

Hobsbawm, E. J. *Nations and Nationalism Since 1780: Programme, Myth, Reality*. Cambridge, England: Cambridge University Press, 1990.

Hochschild, Jennifer. *What's Fair?: American Beliefs About Distributive Justice*. Cambridge: Harvard University Press, 1981.

Horowitz, Donald L. *A Democratic South Africa? Constitutional Engineering in a Divided Society*. Berkeley: University of California Press, 1991.

———. *Ethnic Groups in Conflict*. Berkeley: University of California Press, 1985.

Human Rights Watch World Report 1996. New Haven: Yale University Press, 1995.

Hunter, Floyd. *Community Power Structure.* Chapel Hill: University of North Carolina Press, 1953.

Huntington, Samuel P. *The Clash of Civilizations and the Remaking of World Order.* New York: Simon & Schuster, 1996.

———. *The Third Wave: Democratization in the Late Twentieth Century.* Norman: Oklahoma University Press, 1991.

Ichilov, Orit. *Political Socialization, Citizenship Education, and Democracy.* New York: Teachers College Press, 1990.

Inglehart, Ronald. *Culture Shift in Advanced Industrial Society.* Princeton, N.J.: Princeton University Press, 1990.

Iyengar, Shanto, and Kinder, Donald R. *News That Matters: Television and American Opinion.* Chicago: University of Chicago Press, 1987.

———. *Power Without Force: The Political Capacity of Nation-States.* Ann Arbor: University of Michigan Press, 1993.

Jacobs, Eric, and Worcester, Robert. *We British: Britain Under the MORIscope.* London: Weidenfeld and Nicolson, 1990.

Jacobs, Lawrence R. *The Health of Nations: Public Opinion and the Making of American and British Health Policy.* Ithaca, N.Y.: Cornell University Press, 1993.

———, and Shapiro, Robert Y. *Politicians Don't Pander.* Chicago: University of Chicago Press, 2000.

Jacobson, Harold K. *Networks of Interdependence: International Organizations and the Global Political System.* 2d ed. New York: Knopf, 1984.

Janda, Kenneth. *A Conceptual Framework for the Comparative Analysis of Political Parties.* Beverly Hills, Calif.: Sage, 1970.

———. *Political Parties: A Cross-National Survey.* New York: Free Press, 1980.

Jaros, Dean. *Socialization to Politics.* New York: Praeger, 1973.

Jennings, Ivor. *Cabinet Government.* 3d ed. New York: Cambridge University Press, 1969.

Jennings, W. Ivor. *The British Constitution.* 3d ed. Cambridge, England: Cambridge University Press, 1950.

Jones, Mark. *Electoral Laws and the Survival of Presidential Democracies.* Notre Dame, Ind.: University of Notre Dame Press, 1995.

Joseph, Richard. *State, Conflict, and Democracy in Africa.* Boulder, Colo: Lynne Rienner Publishers, 1998.

Judicature 81 (no. 6, May–June 1998). Special issue, "Courts and Justice Abroad."

Katz, Richard S., and Mair, Peter. *How Parties Organize: Change and Adaptation in Party Organizations in Western Democracies.* Thousand Oaks, Calif.: Sage, 1995.

———. *Party Organizations: A Data Handbook.* Thousand Oaks, Calif.: Sage, 1992.

Keck, Margaret E., and Sikkink, Kathryn. *Activists Beyond Borders: Advocacy Networks in International Politics.* Ithaca, N.Y.: Cornell University Press, 1998.

Keeler, John T. S. "Agricultural Power in the European Community." *Comparative Politics* 28 (1996): 127–49.

Kennedy, Paul. *The Rise and Fall of the Great Powers.* New York: Random House, 1987.

Keohane, Robert. *After Hegemony: Cooperation and Discord in the World Political Economy.* Princeton, N.J.: Princeton University Press, 1984.

———, ed. *Neorealism and Its Critics.* New York: Columbia University Press, 1986.

————, and Nye, Joseph S. *Power and Interdependence.* 2d ed. Glenview, Ill.: Scott, Foresman, 1989.

Kettl, Donald F.; Ingraham, Patricia W.; Sanders, Ronald P.; and Horner, Constance. *Civil Service Reform: Building a Government That Works.* Washington, D.C.: Brookings Institution, 1996.

King, Gary; Keohane, Robert; and Verba, Sidney. *Designing Social Inquiry: Scientific Inference in Qualitative Research.* Princeton, N.J.: Princeton University Press, 1994.

Kitschelt, Herbert. *The Transformation of European Social Democracy.* New York; Cambridge University Press, 1994.

Klitgaard, Robert. *Controlling Corruption.* Berkeley: University of California Press, 1988.

Knott, Jack H., and Miller, Gary J. *Reforming Bureaucracy: The Politics of Institutional Choice.* Englewood Cliffs, N.J.: Prentice-Hall, 1987.

Krasner, Stephen D. "Approaches to the State: Alternative Conceptions and Historical Dynamics." *Comparative Politics* 17 (1984): 223–46.

————, ed. *International Regimes.* Ithaca, N.Y.: Cornell University Press, 1983.

Krislov, Samuel. *Representative Bureaucracy.* Englewood Cliffs, N.J.: Prentice-Hall, 1974.

Ku, Charlotte, and Diehl, Paul F., eds. *International Law: An Anthology.* Boulder, Colo.: Lynne Rienner Publishers, 1997.

Kurian, George Thomas. *Encyclopedia of the Third World.* New York: Facts on File, 1987.

————. *World Encyclopedia of Parliaments and Legislatures.* Washington, D.C.: Congressional Quarterly Books, 1997.

Laitin, David. *Hegemony and Culture.* Chicago: University of Chicago Press, 1986.

Landes, David S. *The Wealth and Poverty of Nations: Why Some Are So Rich and Some So Poor.* New York: W. W. Norton, 1999.

Lane, Robert E. *Political Ideology: Why the American Common Man Believes What He Does.* New York: Free Press, 1962.

Lange, P., and Garrett, G. "The Politics of Growth: Strategic Interaction and Economic Performance in the Advanced Industrial Democracies, 1974–1980." *Journal of Politics* 47 (August 1985): 792–827.

LaPalombara, Joseph. *Interest Groups in Italian Politics.* Princeton, N.J.: Princeton University Press, 1964.

Laqueur, Walter, ed. *Fascism: A Reader's Guide.* Berkeley: University of California Press, 1976.

Lasswell, Harold R., and Kaplan, Abraham. *Power and Society.* Yale Law School Studies, vol. 2. New Haven: Yale University Press, 1950.

Lave, Charles A., and March, James G. *An Introduction to Models in the Social Sciences.* New York: Harper & Row, 1975.

Laver, Michael, and Schofield, Norman. *Multiparty Government: The Politics of Coalition in Europe.* Oxford: Oxford University Press, 1990.

Leduc, Lawrence; Niemi, Richard G.; and Norris, Pippa, eds. *Comparing Democracies: Elections and Voting in Global Perspective.* Beverly Hills, Calif.: Sage, 1996.

Lehmbruch, Gerhard, and Schmitter, Philippe C., eds. *Patterns of Corporatist Policy-Making.* Beverly Hills, Calif.: Sage, 1982.

Lenin, V. I. "State and Revolution." In *Sources in Twentieth-Century Political Thought,* edited by Harry Kariel. New York: Free Press, 1964.

Levi, Margaret. *Of Rule and Revenue.* Berkeley: University of California Press, 1988.

Levite, Ariel, and Tarrow, Sidney. "Legitimation of Excluded Parties in Dominant Party Systems: A Comparison of Israel and Italy." *Comparative Politics* 15 (April 1983): 295–327.

Levy, Daniel C., and Bruhn, Kathleen. *Mexico: The Struggle for Democratic Development.* Berkeley: University of California Press, 2001.

Lewis-Beck, Michael S. *Economics and Elections.* Ann Arbor: University of Michigan Press, 1988.

Li, Richard P. Y., and Thompson, William R. "The 'Coup Contagion' Hypothesis." *Journal of Conflict Resolution* 19 (March 1975): 63–88.

Lichbach, Mark Irving, and Zuckerman, Alan S., eds. *Comparative Politics: Rationality, Culture, and Structure.* New York: Cambridge University Press, 1997.

Liddle, William. "Indonesia." In *Comparative Governance,* edited by W. Phillips Shively. New York: McGraw-Hill (Primis Div.), 1998.

Lijphart, Arend. *Electoral Systems and Party Systems.* New York: Oxford University Press, 1994.

———. *Patterns of Democracy: Government Forms and Performance in Thirty-Six Countries.* New Haven: Yale University Press, 1999.

Lindblom, Charles. *The Intelligence of Democracy.* New York: Free Press, 1965.

———. *Politics and Markets.* New York: Basic Books, 1977.

Linz, Juan J. "Transitions to Democracy." *Washington Quarterly* (Summer 1990): 143–64.

———, and Stepan, Alfred. *The Breakdown of Democratic Regimes.* Baltimore: Johns Hopkins University Press, 1978.

———, and Stepan, Alfred. *Problems of Democratic Transition and Consolidation.* Baltimore: Johns Hopkins University Press, 1996.

———, and Valenzuela, Arturo, eds. *The Failure of Presidential Democracy.* Baltimore: Johns Hopkins University Press, 1994.

Lipset, Seymour Martin, and Rokkan, Stein. *Party Systems and Voter Alignments.* New York: Free Press, 1967.

Lipset, Seymour Martin; Trow, Martin A.; and Coleman, James S. *Union Democracy.* Garden City, N.Y.: Doubleday, 1962.

Lipsitz, Lewis. "If, as Verba Says, the State Functions as a Religion, What Are We to Do Then to Save Our Souls?" *American Political Science Review* 52 (June 1968): 527–35.

Little, Richard D. "Mass Political Participation in the U.S. and the U.S.S.R." *Comparative Political Studies* 8 (January 1976): 437–60.

Livingston, William S. "Britain and America: The Institutionalization of Accountability." *Journal of Politics* 38 (November 1976): 870–94.

Loewenberg, Gerhard. *Parliament in the German Political System.* Ithaca, N.Y.: Cornell University Press, 1967.

———. "The Remaking of the German Party System." *Polity* 1 (Fall 1968): 86–113.

———, and Patterson, Samuel C. *Comparing Legislatures.* Boston: Little, Brown, 1979.

Lok Sabha Secretariat. *The Tenth Lok Sabha, 1991–1996: A Study.* New Delhi: Lok Sabha Secretariat, 1992.

Loomis, Burdett A., and Cigler, Allan J., eds. *Interest Group Politics.* Washington, D.C.: Congressional Quarterly Press, 1983.

Luis, Rubio F. "The Presidential Nomination Process." In *Prospects for Democracy in Mexico,* edited by George W. Grayson. New Brunswick, N.J.: Transaction, 1990.

Lukes, Steven. *Power: A Radical View.* London: Macmillan, 1974.

Lutz, Donald S. "The Iroquois Confederation Constitution: An Analysis." *Publius* 28 (1998): 99–127.

MacIver, R. M. *The Web of Government.* New York: Macmillan, 1947.

Maier, Charles S., ed. *Changing Boundaries of the Political.* Cambridge, England: Cambridge University Press, 1987.

Mainwaring, Scott. "Party Systems in the Third Wave." *Journal of Democracy* 9 (1998): 67–71.

———. "Presidentialism, Multipartism, and Democracy: The Difficult Combination." *Comparative Political Studies* 26 (1993): 198–228.

———, and Scully, Timothy, eds. *Building Democratic Institutions: Party Systems in Latin America.* Stanford, Calif.: Stanford University Press, 1995.

———, and Shugart, Matthew Soberg, eds. *Presidentialism and Democracy in Latin America.* New York: Cambridge University Press, 1997.

Maisel, L. Sandy, ed. *The Parties Respond: Changes in the American Party System.* 2d ed. Boulder, Colo.: Westview, 1994.

Mandel, Ernest. *Late Capitalism.* London: NLB, 1975.

Mansbridge, Jane J. *Why We Lost the ERA.* Chicago: University of Chicago Press, 1986.

Maravall, José Maria. "The Myth of the Authoritarian Advantage." *Journal of Democracy* 5 (1994): 17–31.

Marcus, George E.; Sullivan, John L.; Theiss-Morse, Elizabeth; and Wood, Sandra L. *With Malice Towards Some: How People Make Civil Liberties Judgments.* New York: Cambridge University Press, 1995.

Marks, Gary, and McAdam, Doug. "Social Movements and the Changing Structure of Political Opportunity in the European Union." *West European Politics* 19 (1996): 249–79.

Massey, Douglas S., and Espinosa, Kristin E. "What's Driving Mexico-U.S. Migration? A Theoretical, Empirical, and Policy Analysis." *American Journal of Sociology* 102 (January 1997): 939–99.

McCloskey, Herbert. "Consensus and Ideology in American Politics." *American Political Science Review* 58 (June 1964): 361–82.

McCormick, Richard L., ed. *Political Parties and the Modern State.* New Brunswick, N.J.: Rutgers University Press, 1984.

Mearshimer, John J. *The Tragedy of Great Power Politics.* New York: W. W. Norton, 2001.

Medish, Vadim. *The Soviet Union.* 2d ed. Englewood Cliffs, N.J.: Prentice-Hall, 1984.

Meier, Kenneth John. "Representative Bureaucracy: An Empirical Analysis." *American Political Science Review* 69 (June 1975): 526–42.

———; Winkle, Robert D.; and Polinard, J. L. "Representative Bureaucracy and Distributional Equity: Addressing the Hard Question." *Journal of Politics* 61 (November 1999): 1025–39.

Meyer, David S., and Tarrow, Sidney, eds. *The Social Movement Society: Contentious Politics for a New Century.* Lanham, England: Rowman & Littlefield, 1998.

Michels, Robert. *Political Parties.* New York: Free Press, 1962.

Migdal, Joel. *Strong Societies and Weak States.* Princeton, N.J.: Princeton University Press, 1988.

———. "Studying the State." In *Comparative Politics: Rationality, Culture, and Structure,* edited by Mark Lichbach and Alan Zuckerman. New York: Cambridge University Press, 1997.

Miller, Arthur H., and Borrelli, Stephen A. "Confidence in the Government During the 1980s." *American Politics Quarterly* 19 (1991): 147–73.

Miller, Warren E.; Pierce, Roy; Thomassen, Jacques; Herrera, Richard; Holmberg, Sören; Esaiasson, Peter; and Wessels, Bernhard. *Policy Representation in Western Democracies.* New York: Oxford University Press, 1999.

Millet, Kate. *Sexual Politics.* Garden City, N.Y.: Doubleday, 1970.

Moe, Terry. *The Organization of Interests.* Chicago: University of Chicago Press, 1980.

Moon, John Ellis van Courtland. "Chemical Weapons and Deterrence: The World War II Experience." *International Security* 8 (Spring 1984): 3–25.

Moore, Stanley W., et al. *The Child's Political World: A Longitudinal Perspective.* New York: Praeger, 1985.

Morgenthau, Hans. *Politics Among Nations.* 5th rev. ed. New York: Knopf, 1978.

Motyl, Alexander J., ed. *Encyclopedia of Nationalism.* San Diego: Academic Press, 2000.

Myers, David J., and O'Connor, Robert E. "Support for Coups in Democratic Political Culture: A Venezuela Exploration." *Comparative Politics* 30 (January 1998): 193–212.

Naff, Katherine C. *To Look Like America.* Boulder, Colo.: Westview Press, 2001.

Nagel, Jack H. *The Descriptive Analysis of Power.* New Haven: Yale University Press, 1975.

Needler, Martin C. "Political Development and Military Intervention in Latin America." *American Political Science Review* 60 (September 1966): 616–26.

———. *Mexican Politics.* 2d ed. New York: Praeger, 1990.

———. "The Logic of Conspiracy: The Latin American Military Coup as a Problem in the Social Sciences." *Studies in Comparative International Development* 13 (Fall 1978): 28–40.

Nelson, Barbara, and Chowdhury, Najma, eds. *Women and Politics Worldwide.* New Haven: Yale University Press, 1994.

Nettl, J. P. "The State as a Conceptual Variable." *World Politics* 20 (July 1968): 559–92.

Neumann, Franz. *Behemoth: The Structure and Practice of National Socialism, 1933–1944.* New York: Oxford University Press, 1944.

Neustadt, Richard E. *Presidential Power and the Modern Presidents.* New York: Free Press, 1991.

Niemi, Richard G., and Junn, Jane. *Civic Education: What Makes Students Learn.* New Haven: Yale University Press, 1998.

al Nimir, Saud, and Palmer, Monte. "Bureaucracy and Development in Saudi Arabia: A Behavioral Analysis." *Public Administrations and Development* 2 (1982): 93–104.

Norris, Pippa. *Critical Citizens.* New York: Oxford University Press, 1999.

North, Douglas. *Institutions, Institutional Change and Economic Performance.* New York: Cambridge University Press, 1990.

Nye, Joseph S. *Bound to Lead: The Changing Nature of American Power.* New York: Basic Books, 1990.

———; Zelikow, Philip D.; and King, David C. *Why People Don't Trust Government.* Cambridge: Harvard University Press, 1997.

O'Donnell, Guillermo. *Modernization and Bureaucratic Authoritarianism: Studies in South American Politics.* Berkeley: Institute of International Studies, University of California Press, 1973.

————; Schmitter, Philippe; and Whitehead, Laurence. *Transitions from Authoritarian Rule: Prospects for Democracy.* Baltimore: Johns Hopkins University Press, 1986.

Oliver, James. "Citizen Demands in the Soviet System." *American Political Science Review* 63 (June 1969): 465–75.

Olsen, David M., and Mezey, Michael L., eds. *Legislatures in the Policy Process: The Dilemmas of Economic Policy.* New York: Cambridge University Press, 1991.

Olson, Mancur. *The Logic of Collective Action.* Cambridge: Harvard University Press, 1965.

————. *The Rise and Decline of Nations: Economic Growth, Stagflation and Social Rigidities.* New Haven: Yale University Press, 1982.

Olson, Susan M. *Clients and Lawyers, Securing the Rights of Disabled Persons.* Westport, Conn.: Greenwood, 1984.

Opp, Karl Dieter; Voss, Peter; and Gern, Christiana. *A Spontaneous Revolution: East Germany 1989.* Ann Arbor: University of Michigan Press, 1995.

Ostrogorski, M. *Democracy and the Organization of Political Parties.* Garden City, N.Y.: Doubleday, 1964.

Ostrom, Elinor. *Governing the Commons: The Evolution of Institutions for Collective Action.* Cambridge, England: Cambridge University Press, 1991.

Padgett, L. Vincent. *The Mexican Political System.* 2d ed. Boston: Houghton Mifflin, 1976.

Page, Benjamin I. *Who Gets What from Government.* Berkeley: University of California Press, 1983.

Page, Edward C., and Wright, Vincent. *Bureaucratic Elites in Western European States.* New York: Oxford University Press, 1999.

Paltiel, Khayam. "Campaign Finance: Contrasting Patterns and Reforms." In *Democracy at the Polls,* edited by David Butler. Washington, D.C.: American Enterprise Institute, 1981.

Panebianco, Angelo. *Political Parties: Organization and Power.* New York: Cambridge University Press, 1988.

Pastor, Robert A. "Post-Revolutionary Mexico: The Salinas Opening." *Journal of Interamerican Studies and World Affairs* 32 (Fall 1990): 10.

Pateman, Carole. *Participation and Democratic Theory.* Cambridge, England: Cambridge University Press, 1970.

Patterson, Thomas E. *The Mass Media Election.* New York: Praeger, 1980.

————. *Out of Order: How the Decline of Political Parties and the Growing Power of the News Media Undermine the American Way of Electing Presidents.* New York: Knopf, 1994.

Peterson, Paul. *City Limits.* Chicago: University of Chicago Press, 1981.

Pfiffner, James P. *The Modern Presidency.* 3d ed. Boston: Bedford/St. Martin's, 2000.

Pharr, Susan J., and Putnam, Robert D. *Disaffected Democracies: What's Troubling the Trilateral Countries?* Princeton, N.J.: Princeton University Press, 2000.

Philip, Alan Bult, ed. *Directory of Pressure Groups in the European Community.* London: Longmann, 1991.

Phillips, Kevin R. *The Politics of Rich and Poor: Wealth and the American Electorate in the Reagan Aftermath.* New York: Random House, 1990.

Pirages, Dennis. *Global Technopolitics: The International Politics of Technology and Resources.* Pacific Grove, Calif.: Brooks/Cole, 1989.

Pitkin, Hanna Fenichel. *The Concept of Representation.* Berkeley: University of California Press, 1967.

Piven, Frances Fox, and Cloward, Richard A. *Regulating the Poor.* New York: Pantheon, 1971.

Popkin, Samuel L. *The Reasoning Voter.* Chicago: University of Chicago Press, 1991.

Porter, Gareth, and Brown, Janet Welsh. *Global Environmental Politics.* Boulder, Colo.: Westview, 1991.

Powell, G. Bingham, Jr. "American Voter Turnout in Comparative Perspective." *American Political Science Review* 80 (March 1986): 17–44.

———. *Elections as Instruments of Democracy.* New Haven: Yale University Press, 2000.

Pridham, Geoffrey, and Vanhanen, Tatu, eds. *Democratization in Eastern Europe.* London: Routledge, 1994.

Przeworski, Adam. "Some Problems in the Study of the Transition to Democracy." In *Transitions from Authoritarian Rule: Comparative Perspectives,* edited by Guillermo O'Donnell, Philippe C. Schmitter, and Laurence Whitehead. Baltimore: Johns Hopkins University Press, 1986, pp. 47–63.

———. *Democracy and the Market.* Cambridge, England: Cambridge University Press, 1991.

———; Alavarez, Mike; Cheibub, José Antonio; and Limongi, Fernando. *Democracy and Development: Political Institutions and Material Well-being in the World, 1950–1990.* New York: Cambridge University Press, 2000.

———, and Sprague, John. *Paper Stones: A History of Electoral Socialism.* Chicago: University of Chicago Press, 1986.

———; Stokes, Susan C.; and Manin, Bernard, eds. *Democracy, Accountability, and Representation.* New York: Cambridge University Press, 1999.

Putnam, Robert. "Bowling Alone: America's Declining Social Capital." *Journal of Democracy* 6 (no. 1, January 1995): 65–78.

———. *Making Democracy Work: Civic Traditions in Modern Italy.* Princeton, N.J.: Princeton University Press, 1994.

———. "The Strange Disappearance of Civic America." *American Prospect* (Winter 1996): 34–48.

———; Pharr, Susan; and Dalton, Russell J. *What Is Troubling the Trilateral Democracies?* Princeton, N.J.: Princeton University Press, 2000.

Quinton, Anthony, ed. *Political Philosophy.* New York: Oxford University Press, 1967.

Ramseyer, J. Mark, and Rosenbluth, Frances. *Japan's Political Marketplace.* Cambridge: Harvard University Press, 1993.

Rawls, John. *Political Liberalism.* New York: Columbia University Press, 1993.

———. *A Theory of Justice.* Cambridge, Mass.: Belknap, 1971.

Ray, James Lee. *Democracy and International Conflict.* Columbia: University of South Carolina Press, 1995.

Redden, Kenneth Robert. *Modern Legal Systems Cyclopedia.* Buffalo, N.Y.: Hein, 1990.

Reischauer, Robert D., and Aaron, Henry J., eds. *Setting National Priorities: 1999.* Washington, D.C.: Brookings Institution, 1999.

Reno, William. *Warlord Politics and African States.* Boulder, Colo.: Lynne Rienner Publishers, 1998.

Reshetar, John S., Jr. *The Soviet Polity.* 3d ed. New York: Harper & Row, 1989.

Reyna, Jose L., and Weinert, Richard S., eds. *Authoritarianism in Mexico.* Philadelphia: Institute for the Study of Human Issues, 1977.

Rigby, Thomas H. *Communist Party Membership in the U.S.S.R., 1917–1967.* Princeton, N.J.: Princeton University Press, 1968.

Riker, William. *A Theory of Political Coalitions.* New Haven: Yale University Press, 1962.

———. *Federalism: Origin, Operation, Significance.* Boston: Little, Brown, 1964.

———, and Ordeshook, Peter C. *An Introduction to Positive Political Theory.* Englewood Cliffs, N.J.: Prentice-Hall, 1973.

Roeder, Philip G. *Red Sunset: The Failure of Soviet Politics.* Princeton, N.J.: Princeton University Press, 1993.

Rogowski, Ronald. *Commerce and Coalitions: How Trade Affects Domestic Political Coalitions.* Princeton, N.J.: Princeton University Press, 1989.

Rokeach, Milton. *The Open and Closed Mind: Investigations into the Nature of Belief Systems and Personality Systems.* New York: Basic Books, 1960.

Roper, Burns. "Democracy in America: How Are We Doing?" *Public Perspective* 5 (March/April 1996): 3–5.

Rose, Richard. *Do Parties Make a Difference?* Chatham, N.J.: Chatham House, 1980.

———. "Still the Era of Party Government." *Parliamentary Affairs* 36 (Summer 1983): 282–99.

———. *The Postmodern President.* Chatham, N.J.: Chatham House, 1989.

———, and Suleiman, Ezra N., eds. *Presidents and Prime Ministers.* Washington, D.C.: American Enterprise Institute, 1980.

———. *The Problem of Party Government.* New York: Free Press, 1974.

Rose-Ackerman, Susan. *Corruption and Government: Causes, Consequences, and Reform.* New York: Cambridge University Press, 1999.

Rosecrance, Richard. *Rise of the Trading State.* New York: Basic Books, 1986.

Rosenau, James N. *Turbulence in World Politics.* Beverly Hills, Calif.: Sage, 1990.

Rosenstone, Steven J., and Hansen, John Mark. *Mobilization, Participation and Democracy in America.* New York: Macmillan, 1993.

Rouiquie, Alain. *The Military and the State in Latin America.* Berkeley: University of California Press, 1987.

Rudolph, James D. *Peru: The Evolution of a Crisis.* Westport, Conn.: Praeger, 1992.

Saalfeld, Thomas. "Germany: From Dictatorship to Parliamentary Democracy." *Parliamentary Affairs* 50 (July 1997): 380–95.

Sampson, Anthony. *The New Europeans.* London: Hodder and Stoughton, 1968.

Sartori, Giovanni. *Parties and Party Systems.* Cambridge, England: Cambridge University Press, 1976.

Schapiro, Leonard. *The Communist Party of the Soviet Union.* New York: Random House, 1960.

Schares, Gail E. "Experts in Overalls." *Business Week,* 23 October 1992, p. 90.

Schattschneider, E. E. *Party Government.* New York: Holt, Rinehart and Winston, 1942.

———. *The Semisovereign People.* New York: Holt, Rinehart and Winston, 1960.

Schlesinger, Arthur M., Jr. *The Imperial Presidency.* Boston: Houghton Mifflin, 1973.

Schlesinger, Joseph. *Ambition and Politics: Political Careers in the United States.* Chicago: Rand McNally, 1966.

————. *Political Parties and the Winning of Office*. Ann Arbor: University of Michigan Press, 1991.

Schlozman, Kay Lehman, and Tierney, John T. *Organized Interests and American Democracy*. New York: Harper & Row, 1986.

Schmidt, Vivien A. *Democratizing France: The Political and Administrative History of Decentralization*. Cambridge, England: Cambridge University Press, 1991.

Schmitter, Philippe, and Karl, Terry. "What Democracy Is . . . and Is Not." *Journal of Democracy* 2 (1991): 75–88.

Schmitter, Philippe, and Lehmbruch, Gerhard, eds. *Trends Toward Corporatist Intermediation*. Beverly Hills, Calif.: Sage, 1979.

Schulman, Paul R. "Nonincremental Policy Making: Notes Toward an Alternative Paradigm." *American Political Science Review* 69 (December 1975): 1354–70.

Schwartz, Barry. *George Washington: The Making of an American Myth*. New York: Free Press, 1987.

Scott, James C. *The Moral Economy of the Peasant*. New Haven: Yale University Press, 1976.

————. *Seeing Like a State: How Certain Schemes to Improve the Human Condition Have Failed*. New Haven: Yale University Press, 1998.

————. *Weapons of the Weak: Everyday Forms of Peasant Resistance*. New Haven: Yale University Press, 1985.

Searing, Donald D. *Westminster's World: Understanding Political Roles*. Cambridge: Harvard University Press, 1994.

Sebaldt, Martin. *Organisierter Pluralismus*. Opladen, Germany: Westdeutscher Verlag GmbH, 1997.

Selden, Sally Coleman. *The Promise of Representative Bureaucracy*. London: M. E. Sharpe, 1997.

Sen, Amartya. *Development as Freedom*. New York: Knopf, 1999.

Shamir, Michal, and Sullivan, John. "The Political Context of Tolerance: The United States and Israel." *American Political Science Review* 77 (December 1983): 911–28.

Shils, Edward, and Young, Michael. "The Meaning of the Coronation." *Sociological Review* 1 (December 1953): 63–81.

Shirk, Susan. *The Political Logic of Reform in China*. Berkeley: University of California Press, 1993.

Shively, W. Phillips. "From Differential Abstention to Conversion." *American Journal of Political Science* 36 (May 1992): 309–30.

————. "The Nature of Party Identification." In *The Electorate Reconsidered*, edited by John C. Pierce and John L. Sullivan. Beverly Hills, Calif.: Sage, 1980.

Shugart, Matthew Soberg, and Carey, John M. *Presidents and Assemblies: Constitutional Design and Electoral Dynamics*. New York: Cambridge University Press, 1992.

Siaroff, Alan. "Corporatism in 24 Industrial Democracies: Meaning and Measurement." *European Journal of Political Research* 36 (1999): 175–205.

Sigel, Roberta S. *Political Learning in Adulthood*. Chicago: University of Chicago Press, 1989.

Silverstein, Ken. "Guerillas in the Mist." *Washington Monthly,* September 1994, p. 21.

Sisk, Timothy. *Democratization in South Africa: The Elusive Social Contract*. Princeton, N.J.: Princeton University Press, 1995.

Siverson, Randolph M. "A Glass Half-Full? No, But Perhaps a Glass Filling: The Contributions of International Politics Research to Policy." *PS* 33 (March 2000): 59–64.

Skidmore, Thomas E. *The Politics of Military Rule in Brazil, 1964–1985.* Oxford: Oxford University Press, 1988.

Skilling, H. Gordon, and Griffiths, Franklyn, eds. *Interest Groups in Soviet Politics.* Princeton, N.J.: Princeton University Press, 1971.

Skinner, B. F. *Walden Two.* New York: Macmillan, 1948.

Skocpol, Theda. *States and Social Revolutions.* Cambridge, England: Cambridge University Press, 1979.

Skowronek, Stephen. *Building a New American State: The Expansion of National Administrative Capacities, 1877–1920.* Cambridge, England: Cambridge University Press, 1982.

———. *The Politics Presidents Make: Leadership from John Adams to George Bush.* Cambridge: Harvard University Press, 1993.

Sniderman, Paul. *Personality and Democratic Politics.* Berkeley: University of California Press, 1975.

Snyder, Jack. *Myths of Empire: Domestic Politics and International Ambition.* Ithaca, N.Y.: Cornell University Press, 1991.

Solomon, Robert C., and Murphy, Mark C., eds. *What Is Justice? Classic and Contemporary Readings.* Oxford: Oxford University Press, 1990.

Solzhenitsyn, Alexander. *The Gulag Archipelago, 1918–1956.* New York: Harper & Row, 1974.

Sorauf, Frank J. *Inside Campaign Finance.* New Haven: Yale University Press, 1992.

———. "Zorach vs. Clausen: The Impact of a Supreme Court Decision." *American Political Science Review* 53 (September 1959): 777–91.

Speer, Albert. *Inside the Third Reich.* New York: Macmillan, 1970.

Steinmo, Sven. "Political Institutions and Tax Policy in the United States, Sweden, and Britain." *World Politics* 61 (1989): 500–35.

———. *Taxation and Democracy.* New Haven: Yale University Press, 1993.

Stepan, Alfred. *Rethinking Military Politics: Brazil and the Southern Cone.* Princeton, N.J.: Princeton University Press, 1988.

Stoessinger, John G. *Why Nations Go to War.* New York: St. Martin's Press, 1998.

Stokes, Susan C. *Cultures in Conflict: Social Movements and the State in Peru.* Berkeley: University of California Press, 1995.

———. "Political Parties and Democracy." *Annual Review of Political Science* 2 (1999): 243–67.

Strøm, Kaare, and Svåsand, Lars, eds. *Challenges to Political Parties: The Case of Norway.* Ann Arbor: University of Michigan Press, 1996.

———. *Minority Government and Majority Rule.* New York: Cambridge University Press, 1990.

———. "The Presthus Debacle: Intraparty Politics and Bargaining Failure in Norway." *American Political Science Review* 88 (March 1994): 112–27.

Suleiman, Ezra N. *Politics, Power, and Bureaucracy in France.* Princeton, N.J.: Princeton University Press, 1974.

Sullivan, John L.; Piereson, James; and Marcus, George E. "An Alternative Conceptualization of Political Tolerance." *American Political Science Review* 73 (September 1979): 781–94.

Sullivan, John L.; Walsh, Pat; Shamir, Michal; Barnum, David G.; and Gibson, James L. "Why Politicians Are More Tolerant: Selective Recruitment and Socialization Among Political Elites in Britain, Israel, New Zealand, and the United States." *British Journal of Political Science* 23 (January 1993): 60.

Sullivan, John L.; Shamir, Michal; Walsh, Patrick; and Roberts, Nigel S. *Political Tolerance in Context: Support for Civil Liberties in the United States, Israel, and New Zealand.* Boulder, Colo.: Westview Press, 1985.

Taagepera, Rein, and Shugart, Matthew S. *Seats and Votes: The Effects and Determinants of Electoral Systems.* New Haven: Yale University Press, 1989.

Tarrow, Sidney. *Power in Movement: Social Movements and Contentious Politics.* 2d ed. New York: Cambridge University Press, 1998.

Teague, Paul. "Lean Production and the German Model." *German Politics* 6 (1997): 76–94.

Teixeira, Roy A. *The Disappearing American Voter.* Washington: Brookings Institution, 1992.

Thomas, Clive S. *First World Interest Groups: A Comparative Perspective.* Westport, Conn.: Greenwood Press, 1993.

Tilly, Charles. *Coercion, Capital, and European States, A.D. 990–1992.* Cambridge, Mass.: Blackwell, 1992.

Tinker, Irene, ed. *Persistent Inequalities: Women and World Development.* Oxford: Oxford University Press, 1990.

Titmuss, Richard M. *The Gift Relationship: From Human Blood to Social Policy.* New York: Pantheon Books, 1971.

Tribe, Lawrence H., and Dorf, Michael C. *On Reading the Constitution.* Cambridge: Harvard University Press, 1991.

Truman, David B. *The Governmental Process.* 2d ed. New York: Knopf, 1951.

Tuchman, Barbara W. *A Distant Mirror: The Calamitous Fourteenth Century.* New York: Knopf, 1978.

Tufte, Edward R. *Political Control of the Economy.* Princeton, N.J.: Princeton University Press, 1978.

United Nations Development Programme. *Human Development Report, 1998.* New York: Oxford University Press, 1998.

United Nations Office of Vienna, Centre for Social Development and Humanitarian Affairs. *Women in Politics and Decision-Making in the Late Twentieth Century.* Dordrecht, Netherlands: Martinus Nijhof, 1992.

Urquhart, Brian. *Decolonization and World Peace.* Austin: University of Texas Press, 1989.

Valenzuela, Arturo. "The Military in Power: The Consolidation of One-Man Rule." In *The Struggle for Democracy in Chile, 1982–1990,* edited by Paul Drake and Ivan Jaksic. Lincoln: University of Nebraska Press, 1991.

Valenzuela, J. Samuel, and Valenzuela, Arturo. "Modernization and Dependency." *Comparative Politics* 10 (1978): 535–57.

Van Creveld, Martin. *The Rise and Decline of the State.* New York: Cambridge University Press, 1999.

Van Dijk, Teun A. *Ideology: A Multi-Disciplinary Approach.* Thousand Oaks, Calif.: Sage, 1998.

Vasquez, John. *The War Puzzle.* New York: Cambridge University Press, 1993.

Verba, Sidney, and Nie, Norman H. *Participation in America.* New York: Harper & Row, 1972.

Verba, Sidney; Schlozman, Kay Lehman; and Brady, Henry. *Voice and Equality: Civic Voluntarism in American Politics.* Cambridge: Harvard University Press, 1995.

Vernon, Raymond. *In the Hurricane's Eye: The Troubled Prospects of Multinational Enterprises.* Cambridge: Harvard University Press, 1998.

Voegelin, Eric. *Order and History.* Baton Rouge: Louisiana State University Press, 1956.

Vogel, Steven. *Freer Markets, More Rules: Regulatory Reform in Advanced Industrial Countries.* Ithaca, N.Y.: Cornell University Press, 1996.

Wahlke, John C. "Liberal Learning and the Political Science Major." *PS* 24 (March 1991): 48–60.

Walker, Jack L., Jr. *Mobilizing Interest Groups in America.* Ann Arbor: University of Michigan Press, 1991.

Wallerstein, Immanuel. *The Capitalist World Economy.* Cambridge, England: Cambridge University Press, 1979.

Waltz, Kenneth. *Theory of International Politics.* Reading, Mass.: Addison-Wesley, 1979.

Weart, Spencer R. *Never at War: Why Democracies Will Not Fight One Another.* New Haven: Yale University Press, 1998.

Weiler, J. H. H. *The Constitution of Europe.* New York: Cambridge University Press, 1999.

Weissberg, Robert. *Public Opinion and Popular Government.* Englewood Cliffs, N.J.: Prentice-Hall, 1976.

Wesson, Robert, ed. *Democracy: A Worldwide Survey.* New York: Praeger, 1987.

Wheare, K. D. *Federal Government.* 4th ed. London: Oxford University Press, 1963.

White, Stephen. "The U.S.S.R. Supreme Soviet: A Developmental Perspective." *Legislative Studies Quarterly* 5 (May 1980): 247–74.

Whitehead, Laurence. "Comparative Politics: Democratization Studies." In *A New Handbook of Political Science,* edited by Robert E. Goodin and Hans-Dieter Klingemann, pp. 353–71. New York: Oxford University Press, 1997.

Wiarda, Howard, ed. *New Directions in Comparative Politics,* rev. ed. Boulder, Colo.: Westview Press, 1991.

———. "Mexico: The Unravelling of a Corporatist Regime?" *Journal of Interamerican Studies and World Affairs* 30 (Winter 1988–89): 7.

Wildavsky, Aaron B. *Speaking Truth to Power.* New Brunswick, N.J.: Transaction Books, 1987.

Williamson, John, ed. *Latin American Adjustment: How Much Has Happened?* Washington, D.C.: Institute for International Economics, 1990.

Wills, Gary. *Cincinnatus: George Washington and the Enlightenment.* Garden City, N.Y.: Doubleday, 1984.

Wilson, Frank L. "French Interest Groups: Pluralist or Neocorporatist?" *American Political Science Review* 77 (December 1983): 895–910.

Wilson, James Q. *Bureaucracy: What Government Agencies Do and Why They Do It.* New York: Basic Books, 1989.

———. *Political Organizations.* New York: Basic Books, 1973.

World Bank. *World Development Report.* New York: Oxford University Press, 2000.

Wright, John R. *Interest Groups and Washington Representatives.* Boston: Allyn and Bacon, 1996.

Young, Oran R. *International Cooperation: Building Regimes for National Resources and the Environment.* Ithaca, N.Y.: Cornell University Press, 1989.

Zaller, John R. *The Nature and Origins of Mass Opinion.* New York: Cambridge University Press, 1992.

INDEX